Communications in Computer and Information Science 449

More information about this series at http://www.springer.com/series/7899

Joaquim Filipe · Ana Fred (Eds.)

Agents and Artificial Intelligence

5th International Conference, ICAART 2013 Barcelona, Spain, February 15–18, 2013 Revised Selected Papers

Editors
Joaquim Filipe
INSTICC/Polytechnic Institute of Setúbal
Setúbal
Portugal

Ana Fred
Instituto de Telecomunicações
Lisbon
Portugal

ISSN 1865-0929 ISSN 1865-0937 (electronic)
ISBN 978-3-662-44439-9 ISBN 978-3-662-44440-5 (eBook)
DOI 10.1007/978-3-662-44440-5

Library of Congress Control Number: 2014953272

Springer Heidelberg New York Dordrecht London

Printed on acid-free paper

Springer is part of Springer Science+Business Media (www.springer.com)

Preface

The present book includes extended and revised versions of a set of selected papers from the Fifth International Conference on Agents and Artificial Intelligence (ICAART 2013), held in Barcelona, Spain, from February 15 to 18, 2013, which was organized by the Institute for Systems and Technologies of Information, Control and Communication (INSTICC) and held in cooperation with the Association for the Advancement of Artificial Intelligence (AAAI).

The purpose of the International Conference on Agents and Artificial Intelligence (ICAART) is to bring together researchers, engineers, and practitioners interested in the theory and applications in these areas. The conference was organized in two simultaneous tracks: artificial intelligence and agents, covering both applications and current research work within the area of agents, multi-agent systems and software platforms, distributed problem solving and distributed AI in general, including Web applications, on one hand, and within the area of non-distributed AI, including the more traditional areas such as knowledge representation, planning, learning, scheduling, perception and also not so traditional areas such as reactive AI systems, evolutionary computing and other aspects of computational intelligence and many other areas related to intelligent systems, on the other hand.

ICAART 2013 received 269 paper submissions from 50 countries, in all continents. To evaluate each submission, a double-blind paper review was performed by the Program Committee, whose members are highly qualified researchers in ICAART topic areas. Based on the classifications provided, only 97 papers were selected for oral presentation (37 full papers and 60 short papers) and 59 papers were selected for poster presentation. The full paper acceptance ratio was about 14 %, and the total oral acceptance ratio (including full papers and short papers) 36 %. These strict acceptance ratios show the intention to preserve a high quality forum which we expect to develop further next year.

We would like to highlight that ICAART 2013 included also three plenary keynote lectures, given by internationally distinguished researchers, namely—Elias M. Awad (University of Virginia, USA), Jaap van den Herik (Tilburg University, The Netherlands), and Wiebe van der Hoek (University of Liverpool, UK).

We would like to express our appreciation to all of them and in particular to those who took the time to contribute with a paper to this book.

We must thank the authors, whose research and development efforts are recorded here. We also thank the keynote speakers for their invaluable contribution and for taking the time to synthesize and prepare their talks. Finally, special thanks to all the members of the INSTICC team, whose collaboration was fundamental for the success of this conference.

December 2013

Joaquim Filipe
Ana Fred

Organization

Conference Chair

Ana Fred	Instituto de Telecomunicações, Instituto Superior Técnico, Technical University of Lisbon, Portugal

Program Chair

Joaquim Filipe	Polytechnic Institute of Setúbal/INSTICC, Portugal

Organizing Committee

Marina Carvalho	INSTICC, Portugal
Helder Coelhas	INSTICC, Portugal
Vera Coelho	INSTICC, Portugal
Andreia Costa	INSTICC, Portugal
Bruno Encarnação	INSTICC, Portugal
Ana Guerreiro	INSTICC, Portugal
André Lista	INSTICC, Portugal
Carla Mota	INSTICC, Portugal
Raquel Pedrosa	INSTICC, Portugal
Vitor Pedrosa	INSTICC,Portugal
Cláudia Pinto	INSTICC, Portugal
Cátia Pires	INSTICC, Portugal
Susana Ribeiro	INSTICC, Portugal
Sara Santiago	INSTICC, Portugal
Margarida Sorribas	INSTICC, Portugal
José Varela	INSTICC, Portugal
Pedro Varela	INSTICC, Portugal

Program Committee

Thomas Ågotnes	University of Bergen, Norway
Jose Aguilar	Universidad de Los Andes, Venezuela
H. Levent Akin	Bogazici University, Turkey
Klaus-Dieter Althoff	German Research Center for Artificial Intelligence/University of Hildesheim, Germany
Francisco Martínez Álvarez	Pablo de Olavide University of Seville, Spain
Frédéric Amblard	IRIT - Université Toulouse 1 Capitole, France

Cesar Analide	University of Minho, Portugal
Andreas S. Andreou	Cyprus University of Technology, Cyprus
Plamen Angelov	Lancaster University, UK
Tsz-Chiu Au	Ulsan National Institute of Science and Technology, Korea, Republic of
Senén Barro	University of Santiago de Compostela, Spain
Roman Barták	Charles University in Prague, Faculty of Mathematics and Physics, Czech Republic
Teresa M.A. Basile	Università degli Studi di Bari, Italy
Bernhard Bauer	University of Augsburg, Germany
Jacob Beal	BBN Technologies, USA
Nabil Belacel	National Research Council Canada, Canada
Orlando Belo	University of Minho, Portugal
Jamal Bentahar	University of Minho, Portugal
Christoph Benzmüller	Freie Universität Berlin, Germany
Greet Vanden Berghe	KAHO St.-Lieven, Belgium
Carole Bernon	University of Paul Sabatier - Toulouse III, France
Daniel Berrar	Tokyo Institute of Technology, Japan
Juan A. Botía Blaya	University of Murcia, Spain
Andre Pinz Borges	Pontifical Catholic University of Paraná, Brazil
Djamel Bouchaffra	Oakland University, Algeria
Bruno Bouchard	LIARA Laboratory, Université du Québec à Chicoutimi, Canada
Danielle Boulanger	IAE- Université Jean Moulin Lyon 3, France
Jean-Louis Boulanger	CERTIFER, France
Ivan Bratko	Faculty of Computer and Information Science, University of Ljubljana, Slovenia
Paolo Bresciani	Fondazione Bruno Kessler, Italy
Joost Broekens	MMI, Delft University of Technology, Netherlands
Giacomo Cabri	Università di Modena e Reggio Emilia, Italy
Silvia Calegari	Universita' Degli Studi Di Milano Bicocca, Italy
Rui Camacho	Faculdade de Engenharia da Universidade do Porto, Portugal
Valérie Camps	IRIT - Université Paul Sabatier, France
Jose Jesus Castro-schez	Escuela Superior de Informática, Universidad de Castilla-La Mancha, Spain
Patrick De Causmaecker	Katholieke Universiteit Leuven, Belgium
Luigi Ceccaroni	Barcelona Digital Technology Centre, Spain
Georgios Chalkiadakis	Technical University of Crete, Greece
François Charpillet	Loria - Inria Lorraine, France
Ke Chen	The University of Manchester, UK
Xiaoping Chen	University of Science and Technology of China, China
Marco Chiarandini	University of Southern Denmark, Denmark
Anders Lyhne Christensen	Instituto Superior das Ciências do Trabalho e da Empresa, Portugal

Paolo Ciancarini	University of Bologna, Italy
Silvano Cincotti	University of Genoa, Italy
Davide Ciucci	Universita' Degli Studi Di Milano Bicocca, Italy
Diane Cook	Washington State University, USA
Daniel Corkill	University of Massachusetts Amherst, USA
Gabriella Cortellessa	ISTC-CNR, Italy
Paulo Cortez	University of Minho, Portugal
Massimo Cossentino	National Research Council, Italy
Anna Helena Reali Costa	Universidade de São Paulo, Brazil
Fabiano Dalpiaz	University of Toronto, Canada
Rajarshi Das	IBM T.J. Watson Research Center, USA
Mehdi Dastani	Utrecht University, Netherlands
Darryl N. Davis	University of Hull, UK
Scott A. DeLoach	Kansas State University, USA
Andreas Dengel	German Research Center for Artificial Intelligence (DFKI GmbH), Germany
Enrico Denti	Alma Mater Studiorum - Università di Bologna, Italy
Julie Dugdale	Laboratoire d'Informatique de Grenoble, France
Edmund Durfee	University of Michigan, USA
Stefan Edelkamp	Universität Bremen, Germany
Thomas Eiter	Technische Universität Wien, Austria
Fabrício Enembreck	Pontifical Catholic University of Paraná, Brazil
Floriana Esposito	Università degli Studi di Bari, Italy
Alessandro Farinelli	University of Verona, Italy
Maria Fasli	University of Essex, UK
Stefano Ferilli	University of Bari, Italy
Alberto Fernández	University Rey Juan Carlos, Spain
Antonio Fernández-Caballero	Universidad de Castilla-la Mancha, Spain
Edilson Ferneda	Catholic University of Brasília, Brazil
Klaus Fischer	German Research Center for Artificial Intelligence DFKI GmbH, Germany
Adina M. Florea	University "Politehnica" of Bucharest, Romania
Roberto Flores	Christopher Newport University, USA
Claude Frasson	University of Montreal, Canada
Naoki Fukuta	Shizuoka University, Japan
Wai-Keung Fung	Robert Gordon University, UK
Enrico H. Gerding	University of Southampton, UK
Hamada Ghenniwa	Western University, Canada
Joseph Giampapa	Carnegie Mellon University, USA
Maria Gini	University of Minnesota, USA
Paolo Giorgini	University of Trento, Italy
Herman Gomes	Federal University of Campina Grande, Brazil
Madhu Goyal	University of Technology, Sydney, Australia
Dominic Greenwood	Whitestein Technologies AG, Switzerland
Eric Gregoire	Universite d Artois, France

Sven Groppe	University of Lübeck, Germany
Renata Guizzardi	Federal University of Espirito Santo (UFES), Brazil
Kasper Hallenborg	University of Southern Denmark, Denmark
Minghua He	Aston University, UK
Pedro Rangel Henriques	University of Minho, Portugal
Andreas Herzig	University of Toulouse, CNRS, France
Henry Hexmoor	Southern Illinois University at Carbondale, USA
Wiebe van der Hoek	UK
Wladyslaw Homenda	Warsaw University of Technology, Poland
Wei-Chiang Hong	Hangzhou Dianzi University, Taiwan
Mark Hoogendoorn	Vrije Universiteit Amsterdam, The Netherlands
Ales Horak	Masaryk University, Czech Republic
Enda Howley	National University of Ireland Galway, Ireland
Marc-Philippe Huget	University of Savoie, France
Luke Hunsberger	Vassar College, USA
Carlos Iglesias	Universidad Politécnica de Madrid, Spain
Luis Iribarne	University of Almería, Spain
Fuyuki Ishikawa	National Institute of Informatics, Japan
Takayuki Ito	Nagoya Institute of Technology, Japan
François Jacquenet	University of Saint-Étienne, France
Yanguo Jing	London Metropolitan University, UK
Eugene Santos Jr.	Dartmouth College, USA
Geylani Kardas	Ege University International Computer Institute, Turkey
Oleksiy Khriyenko	University of Jyväskylä, Finland
Matthias Klusch	Deutsches Forschungszentrum für Künstliche Intelligenz, Germany
Fernando Koch	IBM Research Brazil, Brazil
Martin Kollingbaum	University of Aberdeen, UK
Sébastien Konieczny	CNRS - CRIL, France
Igor Kotenko	St. Petersburg Institute for Informatics and Automation of the Russian Academy of Sciences (SPIIRAS), Russian Federation
Ryszard Kowalczyk	Swinburne University of Technology, Australia
Tsvi Kuflik	The University of Haifa, Israel
James Lam	The University of Hong Kong, Hong Kong
Anna T. Lawniczak	University of Guelph, Canada
Ho-fung Leung	The Chinese University of Hong Kong, Hong Kong
Jingpeng Li	University of Stirling, UK
Luis Jiménez Linares	University of de Castilla-La Mancha, Spain
Chao-Lin Liu	National Chengchi University, Taiwan
Honghai Liu	University of Portsmouth, UK
Juan Liu	School of Computer, Wuhan University, China
Shih-Hsi Liu	California State University, Fresno, USA

Stanley Loh	ULBRA, Brazil
Stephane Loiseau	LERIA, University of Angers, France
Gabriel Pereira Lopes	FCT/UNL, Portugal
Noel Lopes	IPG, Portugal
Adolfo Lozano-Tello	Universidad de Extremadura, Spain
Hongen Lu	La Trobe University, Australia
Bernd Ludwig	University of Regensburg, Germany
Xudong Luo	Sun Yat-Sen University, China
José Machado	University of Minho, Portugal
Nadia Magnenat-Thalmann	University of Geneva, Switzerland
Prabhat K. Mahanti	University of New Brunswick, Canada
Jan Maluszynski	Linkoeping University, Sweden
Jerusa Marchi	Universidade Federal de Santa Catarina, Brazil
Elisa Marengo	Free University of Bozen-Bolzano, Italy
Goreti Marreiros	Polytechnic Institute of Porto, Portugal
Nicola Di Mauro	Università di Bari, Italy
Amnon Meisels	Ben-Gurion University, Israel
Benito Mendoza	CUNY - New York City College of Technology, USA
Daniel Merkle	University of Southern Denmark, Denmark
Marjan Mernik	University of Maribor, Slovenia
Bernd Meyer	Monash University, Australia
Ali Minai	University of Cincinnati, USA
Masoud Mohammadian	University of Canberra, Australia
Ambra Molesini	Alma Mater Studiorum - Università di Bologna, Italy
José Moreira	Universidade de Aveiro, Portugal
Haralambos Mouratidis	University of East London, UK
Christian Müller-Schloer	Leibniz Universität Hannover, Germany
Nysret Musliu	Vienna University of Technology, Austria
Radhakrishnan Nagarajan	University of Kentucky, USA
Kai Nagel	School V - Mechanical Engineering and Transport Systems, Germany
Tomoharu Nakashima	Osaka Prefecture University, Japan
José Neves	University of Minho, Portugal
Jens Nimis	Hochschule Karlsruhe - Technik und Wirtschaft, Germany
Paulo Novais	Universidade do Minho, Portugal
Luis Nunes	Instituto Universitário de Lisboa (ISCTE-IUL) and Instituto de Telecomunicações (IT), Portugal
Andreas Oberweis	Karlsruhe Institute of Technology (KIT), Germany
Michel Occello	Université Pierre-Mendès-France, France
John O'Donoghue	Imperial College London, UK
Sancho Oliveira	Instituto Universitário de Lisboa (ISCTE-IUL), Portugal

Andrea Omicini	Alma Mater Studiorum - Università di Bologna, Italy
Flavio Oquendo	European University of Brittany - IRISA-UBS, France
Charlie L. Ortiz	SRI International, USA
Stanislaw Osowski	Warsaw University of Technology, Poland
Djamila Ouelhadj	LMMG (Logistics and Mathematics Management Group), UK
Nandan Parameswaran	University of New South Wales, Australia
Andrew Parkes	University of Nottingham, UK
Oscar Pastor	Universidad Politécnica de Valencia, Spain
Krzysztof Patan	University of Zielona Gora, Poland
Catherine Pelachaud	CNRS - Télécom ParisTech, France
Wojciech Penczek	Institute of Computer Science, Poland
Loris Penserini	MIUR - Italian Ministry of Research and Education, Italy
Célia da Costa Pereira	Université de Nice Sophia Antipolis, France
Laurent Perrussel	IRIT - University of Toulouse 1 Capitole, France
Paolo Petta	Österreichische Studiengesellschaft für Kybernetik, Austria
Gabriella Pigozzi	Université Paris Dauphine, France
Eric Platon	National Institute of Informatics, Japan
Agostino Poggi	University of Parma, Italy
David Powers	Flinders University, Australia
Marco Prandini	University of Bologna, Italy
Mariachiara Puviani	Università di Modena e Reggio Emilia, Italy
Daowen Qiu	Sun Yat-sen University, China
Rong Qu	University of Nottingham, UK
Franco Raimondi	Middlesex University, UK
Zbigniew W. Ras	University of North Carolina at Charlotte, USA
Marek Reformat	University of Alberta, Canada
Luís Paulo Reis	University of Minho, Portugal
Alessandro Ricci	Alma Mater Studiorum - Università di Bologna, Italy
Miguel Rocha	University of Minho, Portugal
Fátima Rodrigues	Instituto Superior de Engenharia do Porto (ISEP/IPP), Portugal
Daniel Rodriguez	University of Alcalá, Spain
Pilar Rodriguez	Universidad Autónoma de Madrid, Spain
Juha Röning	University of Oulu, Finland
Rosaldo Rossetti	Laboratório de Inteligência Artificial e Ciência de Computadores, LIACC/FEUP, Portugal
Ruben Ruiz	Universidad Politécnica de Valencia, Spain
Fariba Sadri	Imperial College London, UK
Manuel Filipe Santos	University of Minho, Portugal
Jorge Gomez Sanz	Universidad Complutense de Madrid, Spain

Fabio Sartori	Università degli Studi di Milano Bicocca, Italy
Jurek Sasiadek	Carleton University, Canada
Ichiro Satoh	National Institute of Informatics, Japan
Edson Scalabrin	Pontificia Universidade Católica do Paraná, Brazil
Andrea Schaerf	Università di Udine, Italy
Christoph Schommer	University of Luxembourg, Campus Kirchberg, Luxembourg
Michael Schumacher	University of Applied Sciences Western Switzerland, Switzerland
Frank Schweitzer	ETH Zurich, Switzerland
Murat Sensoy	Ozyegin University, Turkey
Peer Olaf Siebers	Nottingham University, UK
Flavio S. Correa Da Silva	University of Sao Paulo, Brazil
Viviane Silva	Universidade Federal Fluminense, Brazil
Ricardo Silveira	Universidade Federal de Santa Catarina, Brazil
Olivier Simonin	INRIA - LORIA, France
David Sislak	Czech Technical University in Prague - Agent Technology Center, Czech Republic
Adam Slowik	Koszalin University of Technology, Poland
Alexander Smirnov	SPIIRAS, Russian Academy of Sciences, Russian Federation
Marina V. Sokolova	Instituto de Investigación en Informática de Albacete, Spain
Armando J. Sousa	Faculdade de Engenharia da Universidade do Porto, Portugal
Antoine Spicher	LACL - Université Paris-Est Créteil, France
Mark Steedman	University of Edinburgh, UK
Bruno Di Stefano	Nuptek Systems Ltd., Canada
Sebastian Stein	University of Southampton, UK
Kathleen Steinhofel	King's College London, UK
Roy Sterritt	University of Ulster, UK
Adrian Stoica	NASA-JPL, USA
Thomas Stützle	Université Libre de Bruxelles, Belgium
Kaile Su	Peking University, China
Toshiharu Sugawara	Waseda University, Japan
Shiliang Sun	East China Normal University, China
Zhaohao Sun	PNG University of Technology (1); Federation University Australia (2), Australia
Boontawee Suntisrivaraporn	Sirindhorn International Institute of Technology, Thailand
Pavel Surynek	Charles University in Prague, Czech Republic
Ryszard Tadeusiewicz	AGH University of Science and Technology, Poland
Nick Taylor	Heriot-Watt University, UK
Patrícia Tedesco	Universidade Federal de Pernambuco/FADE, Brazil

Michael Thielscher	The University of New South Wales, Australia
Paola Turci	University of Parma, Italy
Anni-Yasmin Turhan	Technische Universität Dresden, Germany
Franco Turini	KDD Lab, University of Pisa, Italy
Paulo Urbano	Faculdade de Ciências da Universidade de Lisboa, Portugal
Visara Urovi	University of Applied Sciences Western Switzerland, Sierre (HES-SO), Switzerland
David Uthus	Google, USA
Eloisa Vargiu	Barcelona Digital Technology Center, Spain
Matteo Vasirani	University Rey Juan Carlos, Spain
K. Brent Venable	University of Padova, Italy
Laurent Vercouter	LITIS, France
Srdjan Vesic	CNRS, France
Jose Vidal	University of South Carolina, USA
Serena Villata	INRIA Sophia Antipolis, France
Mirko Viroli	University of Bologna, Italy
Giuseppe Vizzari	University of Milano-Bicocca, Italy
Dirk Walther	Universidad Politécnica de Madrid, Spain
Yves Wautelet	KU Leuven, Belgium
Rosina Weber	iSchool at Drexel, USA
Mary-Anne Williams	University of Technology, Sydney, Australia
Cees Witteveen	Delft University of Technology, Netherlands
Stefan Woltran	Technische Universität Wien, Austria
T.N. Wong	The University of Hong Kong, Hong Kong
Franz Wotawa	Graz University of Technology, Austria
Bozena Wozna-Szczesniak	Jan Dlugosz University, Poland
Feiyu Xu	Deutsches Forschungszentrum für Künstliche Intelligenz (DFKI), Germany
Seiji Yamada	National Institute of Informatics, Japan
Xin-She Yang	National Physical Lab, UK
Li-Yan Yuan	University of Alberta, Canada
Laura Zavala	Megar Evers College of the City University of New York, USA
John Zeleznikow	Victoria University, Australia
Xiaoqin Zhang	University of Massachusetts Dartmouth, USA
Hong Zhu	Oxford Brookes University, UK

Auxiliary Reviewers

João Emílio Almeida, Portugal
Annalisa Appice, Italy
Francisco de Assis Pereira Vasconcelos de Arruda, Brazil
Maria Martinez Ballesteros, Spain
Berardina Nadja De Carolis, Italy
Claudio Cavancanti, Brazil
Yaser Chaaban, Germany

Guoqing Chao, China
Angelos Chliaoutakis, Greece
Sviatlana Danilava, Luxembourg
Luke Day, UK
Richard Dobson, UK
Sidath Gunawardena, USA
Agnieszka Jastrzebska, Poland
Ryo Kanamori, Japan
Heiko Maus, Germany
Radu-Casian Mihailescu, Spain
Mihail Minev, Luxembourg
Jorge Antonio Reyes Molina, Chile
Fabricio Narcizo, Brazil
Sebastian Niemann, Germany
Emmanuil Orfanoudakis, Greece
Takanobu Otsuka, Japan
Mathias Pacher, Germany
Ji Ruan, Australia
Luca Sabatucci, Italy
Patrik Schneider, Austria
Honglei Shi, China
Valdinei Silva, Brazil
Songzheng Song, Singapore
Ouala Abdelhadi Ep Souki, UK
Jing Zhao, China

Invited Speakers

Elias M. Awad	University of Virginia, USA
Jaap van den Herik	Tilburg University, The Netherlands
Wiebe van der Hoek	University of Liverpool, UK

Contents

Invited Paper

Agents

Artificial Intelligence

Invited Paper

Investigations with Monte Carlo Tree Search for Finding Better Multivariate Horner Schemes

H. Jaap van den Herik[1(✉)], Jan Kuipers[2], Jos A.M. Vermaseren[2], and Aske Plaat[1]

[1] Tilburg Center for Cognition and Communication, Tilburg University, Warandelaan 2, 5037 AB Tilburg, The Netherlands
jaapvandenherik@gmail.com

[2] Nikhef Theory Group, Science Park 105, 1098 XG Amsterdam, The Netherlands

Abstract. After a computer chess program had defeated the human World Champion in 1997, many researchers turned their attention to the oriental game of Go. It turned out that the minimax approach, so successful in chess, did not work in Go. Instead, after some ten years of intensive research, a new method was developed: MCTS (Monte Carlo Tree Search), with promising results. MCTS works by averaging the results of random play-outs. At first glance it is quite surprising that MCTS works so well. However, deeper analysis revealed the reasons.

The success of MCTS in Go caused researchers to apply the method to other domains. In this article we report on experiments with MCTS for finding improved orderings for multivariate Horner schemes, a basic method for evaluating polynomials. We report on initial results, and continue with an investigation into two parameters that guide the MCTS search. Horner's rule turns out to be a fruitful testbed for MCTS, allowing easy experimentation with its parameters. The results reported here provide insight into how and why MCTS works. It will be interesting to see if these insights can be transferred to other domains, for example, back to Go.

Keywords: Artificial intelligence · High energy physics · Horners rule · Monte Carlo Tree Search · Go · Chess

1 Introduction

In 1965, the Soviet mathematician Aleksandr Kronrod called chess the Drosophila Melanogaster of Artificial Intelligence [29]. At that time, chess was a convenient domain that was well suited for experimentation. Moreover, dedicated research programs all over the world created quick progress. In half a century the dream of

Parts of this work have appeared in a keynote speech by the first author at the International Conference on Agents and Artifical Intelligence ICAART 2013 in Barcelona under the title "Connecting Sciences." These parts are reprinted with permission by the publisher.

J. Filipe and A. Fred (Eds.): ICAART 2013, CCIS 449, pp. 3–20, 2014.
DOI: 10.1007/978-3-662-44440-5_1

Fig. 1. Example of a Go board.

beating the human world champion was realized. On May 11, 1997 Garry Kasparov, the then highest rated human chess player ever, was defeated by the computer program DEEP BLUE, in a highly publicized six game match in New York.

So, according to some, the AI community lost their Drosophila in 1997, and started looking for a new one. The natural candidate was an even harder game: the oriental game of Go. Go is played on a 19×19 board, see Fig. 1. Its state space is much larger than the chess state space. The number of legal positions reachable from the starting position in Go (the empty board) is estimated to be $\mathcal{O}(10^{171})$ [1], whereas for chess this number is "just" $\mathcal{O}(10^{46})$ [15]. If chess is a game of tactics, then Go is a game of strategy. The standard minimax approach that worked so well for chess (and for other games such as checkers, Awari, and Othello) did not work well for Go, and so Go became the new Drosophila. For decades, computer Go programs played at the level of weak amateur. After 1997, the research effort for computer Go intensified. Initially, progress was slow, but in 2006, a breakthrough happened. The breakthrough and some of its consequences, are the topic of this article.

The remainder of the contribution is structured as follows. First, the techniques that worked so well in chess will be discussed briefly. Second, the new search method that caused the breakthrough in playing strength in Go will be described. Then, a successful MCTS application to Horner's rule of multivariate polynomials will be shown. It turns out that Horner's rule yields a convenient test domain for experimentation with MCTS. We complete the article by an in-depth investigation of the search parameters of MCTS.

A note on terminology. The rule published by William Horner almost two centuries ago is called Horner's *rule*. It is a technique to reduce the work required for the computation of a polynomial in a single variable at a particular value. Finding better variable orderings of multivariate polynomials, in order to then apply Horner's rule repeatedly, is called finding better Horner *schemes*.

2 The Chess Approach

The heart of a chess program consists of two parts: (1) a heuristic evaluation function, and (2) the minimax search function. The purpose of the heuristic evaluation function is to provide an estimate of how good a position looks, and sometimes of its chances of winning the game [17]. In chess this includes items such as the material balance (capturing a pawn is good, capturing a queen is usually very good), mobility, and king safety. The purpose of the search function is to look ahead: if I play this move, then my opponent would do this, and then I would do that, and ..., etc. By searching more deeply than the opponent the computer can find moves that the heuristic evaluation function of the opponent mis-evaluates, and thus the computer can find the better move.

Why does this approach fail in Go? Originally, the main reason given was that the search tree is so large (which is true). In chess, the opening position has 20 legal moves (the average number of moves is 38 [18,22]). In Go, this number is 361 (and thereafter it decreases with one per move). However, soon it turned out that an even larger problem was posed by the construction of a good heuristic evaluation function. In chess, material balance, the most important term in the evaluation function, can be calculated efficiently and happens to be a good first heuristic. In Go, so far no good heuristics have been found. The influence of stones and the life and death of groups are generally considered to be important, but calculating these terms is time consuming, and the quality of the resulting evaluation is a mediocre estimator for the chances of winning a game.

Alternatives. Lacking a good evaluation function and facing the infeasibility of a full-width look-ahead search, most early Go programs used as a first approach the knowledge-based approach: (1) generate a limited number of likely candidate moves, such as corner moves, attack/defend groups, connecting moves, and ladders, and (2) search for the best move in this reduced state space [34]. The Go heuristics used for choosing the candidate moves can be generalized in move patterns, which can be learned from game databases [44,45]. A second approach was to use neural networks, also with limited success [19]. This approach yielded programs that could play a full game that looked passable, but never reached more than weak amateur level.

3 Monte Carlo

In 1993, the mathematician and physicist Bernd Brügmann was intrigued by the use of simulated annealing for solving the traveling salesman problem. If such a basic procedure as randomized local search (also known as Monte Carlo) could find shortest tours, then perhaps it could find good moves in Go? He wrote a 9×9 Go program based on simulated annealing [7]. Crucially, the program did not have a heuristic evaluation function. Instead it played a series of random moves all the way until the end of the game was reached. Then the final position was trivially scored as either a win or a loss. This procedure of randomized play-outs was repeated many times. The result was averaged and taken to be an estimate of the "heuristic" value of each move. So instead of searching a tree, Brügmann's program searched paths, and instead of using the minimax function to compute the scores, the program took the average of the final scores. The program had no domain knowledge, except not to fill its own territory. Could this program be expected to play anything but meaningless random moves?

Surprisingly, it did. Although it certainly did not play great or even good moves, the moves looked better than random. Brügmann concluded that by just following the rules of the game the average of many thousands of plays yielded better-than-random moves.

At that time, the attempt to connect the sciences of physics and artificial intelligence appeared to be a curiosity. Indeed, the hand-crafted knowledge-based programs still performed significantly better. For the next ten years not much happened with Monte Carlo Go.

Monte Carlo Tree Search. Then, in 2003, Bouzy and Helmstetter reported on further experiments with Monte Carlo playouts, again stressing the advantage of having a program that can play Go moves without the need for a heuristic evaluation function [2,5]. They tried adding a small 2-level minimax tree on top of the random playouts, but this did not improve the performance. In their conclusion they refer to other works that explored statistical search as an alternative to minimax [24,38] and concluded: "Moreover, the results of our Monte Carlo programs against knowledge-based programs on 9×9 boards and the ever-increasing power of computers lead us to think that Monte Carlo approaches are worth considering for computer Go in the future."

They were correct.

Three years later a breakthrough took place by the repeated introduction of MCTS and UCT. Coulom [16] described Monte Carlo evaluations for tree-based search, specifying rules for node selection, expansion, playout, and backup. Chaslot et al. coined the term Monte Carlo Tree Search or MCTS, in a contribution that received the ICGA best publication award in 2008 [10,12]. In 2006 Kocsis and Szepesvari [25] laid the theoretical foundation for a selection rule that balances exploration and exploitation and that is guaranteed to converge to the minimax value. This selection rule is termed UCT, short for **U**pper **C**onfidence bounds for multi-armed bandits [4] applied to **T**rees (see Eq. (4)). Gelly et al. [21] used UCT in a Go program called MoGo, short for Monte Carlo Go, which was instantly successful. MoGo received the ICGA award in 2009. Chaslot et al. [11] also described the application of MCTS in Go, reporting that it outperformed minimax, and mentioned applications beyond Go.

Since 2006 the playing strength of programs improved rapidly to the level of strong amateur/weak master (2-3 dan). The MCTS breakthrough was confirmed when, for the first time, a professional Go player was beaten in a single game. In August 2008 at the 24th Annual Go Congress in Portland, Oregon, MoGo-Titan, running on 800 cores of the Huygens supercomputer in Amsterdam, beat 8P dan professional Kim MyungWan with a 9-stone handicap [14]. Further refinements have increased the playing strength. At the Human versus

Computer Go Competition that was held as part of the IEEE World Congress on Computational Intelligence in June 2012 in Brisbane, Australia, the program ZEN defeated the 9P dan professional Go player Takemiya Masaki with a four-stone handicap (≈5P dan) on the 19×19 board.

The main phases of MCTS are shown in Fig. 2. They are explained briefly below.

After the introduction om MCTS, there has been a large research interest in MCTS. Browne et al. [8] provides an extensive survey, referencing 240 publications.

MCTS Basics. MCTS consists of four main steps: selection, expansion, simulation (playout), and back-propagation (see Fig. 2). The main steps are repeated as long as there is time left. For each step the activities are as follows.

(1) In the selection step the tree is traversed from the root node until we reach a node, where a child is selected that is not part of the tree yet.
(2) Next, in the expansion step the child is added to the tree.
(3) Subsequently, during the simulation step moves are played in self-play until the end of the game is reached. The result R of this—simulated—game is $+1$ in case of a win for Black (the first player in Go), 0 in case of a draw, and -1 in case of a win for White.
(4) In the back-propagation step, R is propagated backwards, through the previously traversed nodes. Finally, the move played by the program is the child of the root with the best win/visit count, depending on UCT probability calculations (to be discussed briefly below).

Crucially, the selection rule of MCTS allows balancing of (a) exploitation of parts of the tree that are known to be good (i.e., high win rate) with (b) exploration of parts of the tree that have not yet been explored (i.e., low visit count).

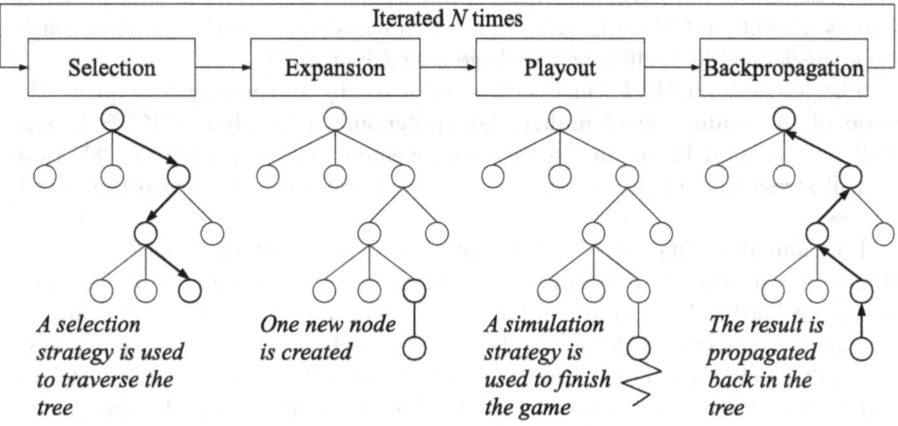

Fig. 2. The basic Monte Carlo Tree Search scheme.

Originally MCTS used moves in the playout phase that were strictly random. However, soon better results were obtained by playing moves that use small (fast) amounts of domain knowledge. Nowadays, many programs use pattern databases for this purpose [21]. The high levels of performance that are currenlty achieved with MCTS depend to a large extent on enhancements of the expansion strategy, simulation phase, and the parallelization techniques. (So, after all, small amounts of domain knowledge are needed, albeit not in the form of a heuristic evaluation function. No expensive influence or life-and-death calculations are used, but fast pattern lookups.)

Applications Beyond Go. The striking performance of MCTS in Go has led researchers to apply the algorithm to other domains. Traditionally, best-first algorithms rely on domain knowledge to try the "best" moves first. This domain knowledge is often hard to codify correctly and is expensive to compute. Many researchers have looked for best-first algorithms that could somehow do without domain knowledge [35–37,42]. The ability of MCTS to magically home in on clusters of "bright spots" in the state space without relying on domain knowledge has resulted in a long list of other applications, for example, for proof-number search [40]. In addition, MCTS has been proposed as a new framework for game-AI for video games [13], for the game Settlers of Catan [43], for the game Einstein würfelt nicht [32], for the Voronoi game [6], for Havannah [31], for Amazons [28], and for various single player applications [39,41].

4 Horner's Rule for Multivariate Polynomials

We will now turn our attention to one such application domain: that of finding better variable orderings for applying Horner's rule to evaluate multivariate polynomials efficiently.

One area where finding solutions is important, and where good heuristics are hard to find, is equation solving for high energy physics (HEP). In this field large equations (often very large) are needed to be solved quickly. Standard packages such as Maple and Mathematica are often too slow, and scientists frequently use a specialized high-efficiency package called Form [27].

The research on MCTS in Form was started by attempting to improve the speed of the evaluation of multivariate polynomials. Applying MCTS to this challenge resulted in an unexpected improvement, first reported in [26]. Here we will stress further investigations into parameters that influence the search process.

Polynomial evaluation is a frequently occurring part of equation solving. Minimizing its cost is important. Finding more efficient algorithms for polynomial evaluation is a classic problem in computer science. For single variable polynomials, the classic Horner's rule provides a scheme for producing a computationally efficient form. It is conventionally named after William George Horner (1819) [20], although references to the method go back to works by the mathematicians Qin Jiushao (1247) and Liu Hui (3rd century A.D.). For multivariate polynomials Horner's rule is easily generalized but the order of the variables is unspecified. Traditionally greedy approaches such as using (one of) the most-occurring variable(s) first are used. This straightforward approach has given remarkably efficient results and finding better approaches has proven difficult [9].

For polynomials in one variable, Horner's rule provides a computationally efficient evaluation form:

$$a(x) = \sum_{i=0}^{n} a_i x^i = a_0 + x(a_1 + x(a_2 + x(\cdots + x \cdot a_n))). \tag{1}$$

The rule makes use of the repeated factorization of the terms of the n-th degree polynomial in x. With this representation a dense polynomial of degree n can be evaluated with n multiplications and n additions, giving an evaluation cost of $2n$, assuming equal cost for multiplication and addition.

For multivariate polynomials Horner's rule must be generalized. To do so one chooses a variable and applies Eq. (1), treating the other variables as constants. Next, another variable is chosen and the same process is applied to the terms within the parentheses. This is repeated until all variables are processed. As a case in point, for the polynomial $a = y - 6x + 8xz + 2x^2yz - 6x^2y^2z + 8x^2y^2z^2$ and the order $x < y < z$ this results in the following expression

$$a = y + x(-6 + 8z + x(y(2z + y(z(-6 + 8z))))). \tag{2}$$

The original expression uses 5 additions and 18 multiplications, while the Horner form uses 5 additions but only 8 multiplications. In general, applying Horner's rule keeps the number of additions constant, but reduces the number of multiplications.

After transforming a polynomial with Horner's rule, the code can be further improved by performing a common subexpression elimination (CSE). In Eq. (2), the subexpression $-6+8z$ appears twice. Eliminating the common subexpression results in the code

$$\begin{aligned} T &= -6 + 8z \\ a &= y + x(T + x(y(2z + y(zT)))), \end{aligned} \tag{3}$$

which uses only 4 additions and 7 multiplications.

Horner's rule reduces the number of multiplications, CSE also reduces the number of additions.

Finding the optimal order of variables for applying Horner's rule is an open problem for all but the smallest polynomials. Different orders impact the cost evaluating the resulting code. Straightforward variants of local search have been proposed in the literature, such as most-occurring variable first, which results in the highest decrease of the cost at that particular step.

MCTS is used to determine an order of the variables that gives efficient Horner schemes in the following way. The root of the search tree represents the situation where no variables are chosen yet. This root node has n children. Each of these children represents a choice for variables in the trailing part of the order, and so on. Therefore, n equals the depth of the node in the search tree. A node at depth d has $n - d$ children: the remaining unchosen variables.

In the simulation step the incomplete order is completed with the remaining variables added randomly. This complete order is then used for applying Horner's rule followed by CSE. The number of operators in this optimized expression is counted. The selection step uses the UCT criterion with as score the number of operators in the original expression divided by the number of operators in the optimized one. This number increases with better orders.

In MCTS the search tree is built in an incremental and asymmetric way; see Fig. 3 for the visualization of a snap shot of an example tree built during an MCTS run. During the search the traversed part of the search tree is kept in memory. For each node MCTS keeps track of the number of times it has been visited and the estimated result of that node. At each step one node is added to the search tree according to a criterion that tells where most likely better results can be found. From that node an outcome is sampled and the results of the node and its parents are updated. This process is illustrated in Fig. 2. We will now again discuss the four steps of MCTS, as we use them for finding Horner orderings.

Selection. During the selection step the node which most urgently needs expansion is selected. Several criteria are proposed, but the easiest and most-used criterion is the UCT criterion [25]:

$$UCT_i = \langle x_i \rangle + 2C_p \sqrt{\frac{2 \log n}{n_i}}. \tag{4}$$

Here $\langle x_i \rangle$ is the average score of child i, n_i is the number of times child i has been visited, and n is the number of times the node itself has been visited. C_p is a problem-dependent constant that should be determined empirically. Starting at the root of the search tree, the most-promising child according to this criterion is selected and this selection process is repeated recursively until a node is reached with unvisited children. The first term of Eq. (4) biases nodes with previous high rewards (exploitation), while the second term selects nodes that have not been visited much (exploration). Balancing exploitation versus exploration is essential for the good performance of MCTS.

Expansion. The selection step finishes in a node with unvisited children. In the expansion step one of these children is added to the tree.

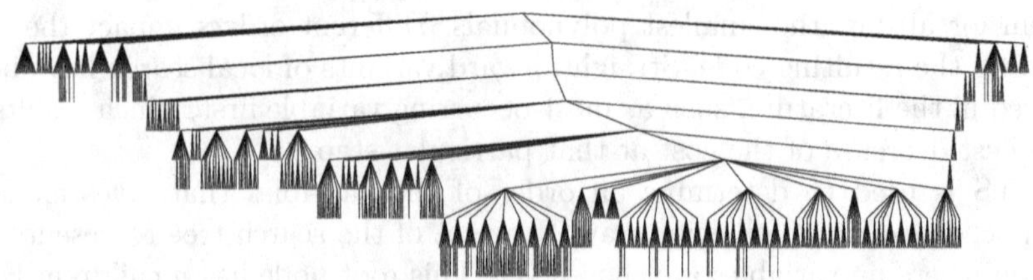

Fig. 3. Example of how an MCTS search expands the tree asymmetrically. Taken from a search for a Horner scheme.

Simulation. In the simulation step a single possible outcome is simulated starting from the node that has just been added to the tree. The simulation can consist of generating a fully random path starting from this node to a terminal outcome. In most applications more advanced programs add some known heuristics to the simulation, reducing the randomness. The latter typically works better if specific knowledge of the problem is available. In our MCTS implementation a fully random simulation is used. (We use domain-specific enhancements, such as CSE, but these are not search heuristics that influence the way MCTS traverses the search space.)

Backpropagation. In the backpropagation step the results of the simulation are added to the tree, specifically to the path of nodes from the newly added node to the root. Their average results and visit count are updated.

The MCTS cycle is repeated a fixed number of times or until the computational resources are exhausted. After that the best result found is returned.

Sensitivity to C_p and N. The performance of MCTS-Horner followed by CSE has been tested by implementing it in FORM [26,27]. MCTS-Horner was tested on a variety of different multivariate polynomials, against the currently best algorithms. For each test-polynomial MCTS found better variable orders, typically with half the number of operators than the expressions generated by previous algorithms. The results are reported in detail in [26].

The experiments showed that the effectiveness of MCTS depends heavily on the choice for the exploitation/exploration constant C_p of Eq. (4) and on the number of tree expansions (N). In the remainder of this section we will investigate the sensitivity of the performance of MCTS-Horner to these two parameters.

When C_p is small, MCTS favors parts of the tree that have been visited before because the average score was good ("exploitation"). When C_p is large, MCTS favors parts of the tree that have not been visited before ("exploration").

Finding better variable orderings for Horner's rule is an application domain that allows relatively quick experimentation. To gain insight into the sensitivity of the performance in relation to C_p and to the number of expansions a series of scatter plots have been created.

The results of MCTS followed by CSE, with different numbers for tree expansions N as a function of C_p are given in Fig. 4 for a large polynomial from high energy physics, called HEP(σ). This polynomial has 5717 terms and 15 variables. The formula is typical for formulas that are automatically produced in particle reactions calculations; these formulas need to be processed further by a Monte Carlo integration program.

The number of operations of the resulting expression is plotted on the y-axis of each graph. The lower this value, the better the algorithm performs. The lowest value found for this polynomial by MCTS+CSE is an expression with slightly more than 4000 multiplication and addition operations. This minimum is achieved in the case of $N = 3000$ tree expansions for a value of C_p with $0.7 \lesssim C_p \lesssim 1.2$. Dots above this minimum represent a sub-optimal search result.

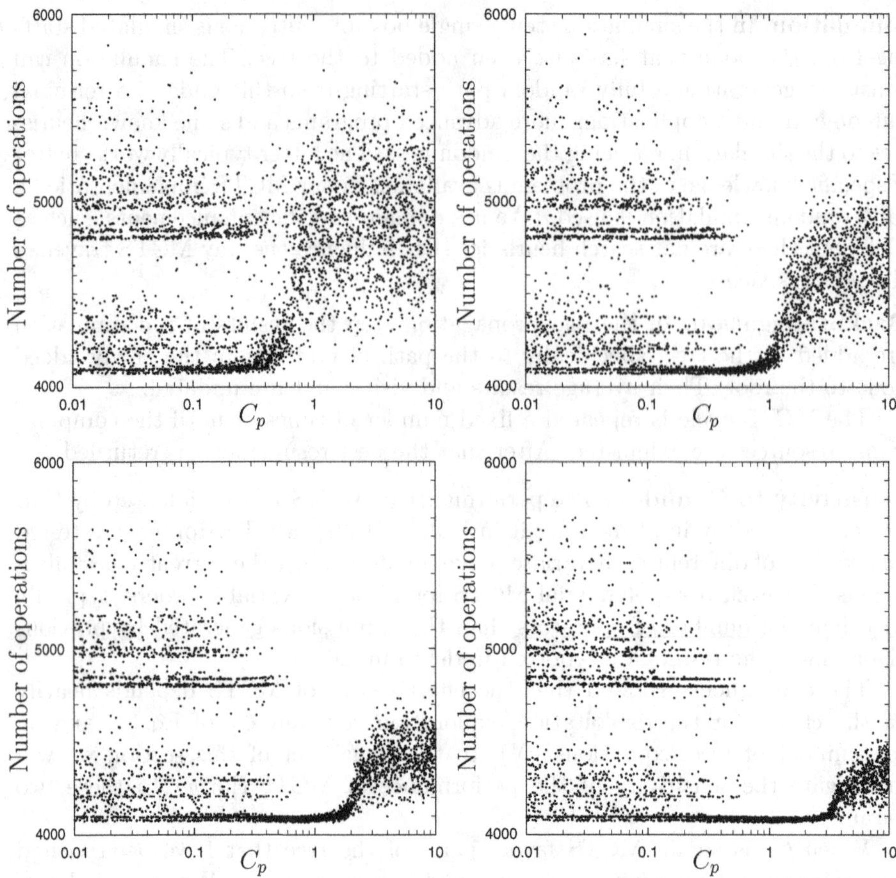

Fig. 4. Four scatter plots for $N = 300$, 1000, 3000, 10000 points per MCTS run. Each plot represents the average of 4000 randomized runs, for the HEP(σ) polynomial (see text).

For small values of the numbers of tree expansions MCTS cannot find a good answer. With $N = 100$ expansions the graph looks almost random (graph not shown). Then, as we move to 300 tree expansions per data point (left upper panel of Fig. 4), some clearer structure starts to emerge, with a minimum emerging at $C_p \approx 0.6$. With more tree expansions (see the other three panels of Fig. 4) the picture becomes clearer, and the value for C_p for which the best answers are found becomes higher, the picture appears to shift to the right. For really low numbers of tree expansions (see again upper left panel of Fig. 4) there is no discernible advantage of setting the exploitation/exploration parameter at a certain value. For slightly larger numbers of tree expansion, but still low (see upper right panel) MCTS needs to exploit each good result that it obtains. As the number of tree expansions grows larger (the two lower panels of Fig. 4) MCTS achieves better results when its selection policy is more explorative. It can afford to look beyond the narrow tunnel of exploitation, to try a few explorations beyond the path that is known to be good, and to try to get out of local optima. For the graphs with tree expansions of 3000 and 10000 the range of good results for C_p becomes wider, indicating that the choice between exploitation/exploration becomes less critical.

For small values of C_p, such that MCTS behaves exploitatively, the method gets trapped in one of the local minima as can be seen from scattered dots that form "lines" in the left-hand sides of the four panels in Fig. 4. For large values of C_p, such that MCTS behaves exploratively, many of the searches do not lead to the global minimum found as can be seen from the cloud of points on the right-hand side of the four panels. For intermediate values of $C_p \approx 1$ MCTS balances well between exploitation and exploration and finds almost always an ordering for applying Horner's rule that is very close to the best one known to us.

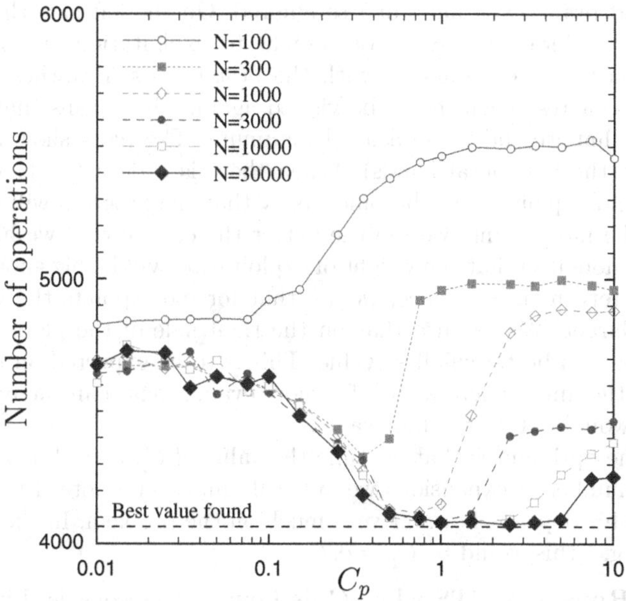

Fig. 5. Results for MCTS Horner orders as function of the exploitation/exploration constant C_p and of the number of tree expansions N. For $N = 3000$ (green line/solid bullets) the optimum for C_p is $C_p \approx 1$.

Results. The results of the test with HEP(σ) for different numbers of tree expansions are shown in Fig. 5, reproduced from [26]. For small numbers of tree expansions low values for the constant C_p should be chosen (less than 0.5). The search is then mainly in exploitation mode. MCTS quickly searches deep in the tree, most probably around a local minimum. This local minimum is explored quite well, but the global minimum is likely to be missed. With higher numbers of tree expansions a value for C_p in the range $[0.5, 2]$ seems suitable. This range gives a good balance between exploring the whole search tree and exploiting the promising nodes. Very high values of C_p appear to be a bad choice in general, nodes that appeared to be good previously are not exploited anymore so frequently.

Here we note that these values hold for HEP(σ), and that different polynomials give different optimal values for C_p and N. Below we report on investigations with other polynomials.

Varying the Number of Tree Expansions. Returning to Fig. 4, let us now look closer at what happens when we vary the number of tree expansions N. In Fig. 4 we see scatter plots for 4 different values of N: 300, 1000, 3000, and 10000 expansions.

On the right side (larger values of C_p) of each plot we see a rather diffuse distribution. When C_p is large, exploration is dominant, which means that at each time we try a random (new) branch, knowledge about the quality of previously visited branches is more or less ignored. On the left side there is quite some structure. Here we give a large weight to exploitation: we prefer to go to the previously visited branches with the best results. Branches that previously had a poor result will never be visited again. This means that there is a large chance that we end up in a local minimum. The plots show indeed several of those (the horizontal bands). When there is a decent balance between exploration and exploitation it becomes likely that the program will find a good minimum. The more points we use the better the chance that we hit a branch that is good enough so that the weight of exploitation will be big enough to have the program return there. Hence, we see that for more points the value of C_p can become larger. We see also that on the right side of the plots using more evaluations gives a better smallest value. This is to be expected on the basis of statistics. In the limit, where we ask for more evaluations than there are leafs in the tree, we would obtain the best value.

Clearly the optimum is that we tune the value of C_p in such a way that for a minimum number of expansions we are still almost guaranteed to obtain the best result. This depends however very much on the problem. In the case of the formula of Fig. 4 this would be $C_p = 0.7$.

Repeating Runs of MCTS when C_p is Low. If we reconsider Fig. 4, i.e., we take a layman's look, we notice that at the left sides of the panels the distributions are nearly identical, independent of the number of tree expansions N. What does it mean? How can we influence the observed result? A new approach reads as follows. If, instead of 3000 expansions in a single run, we take, say, 3 times 1000 expansions and take the best result of those, the left side of the graphs is expected to become more favorable. The idea of repeated runs has been implemented in FORM and the result is illustrated in Fig. 6. N is the number of tree expansions in a single MCTS run. R is the number of MCTS runs. The idea is best formulated by taking $N \times R$ as constant. In the experiments, we noticed a number of curious issues. We mention three of them explicitly. (1) When each

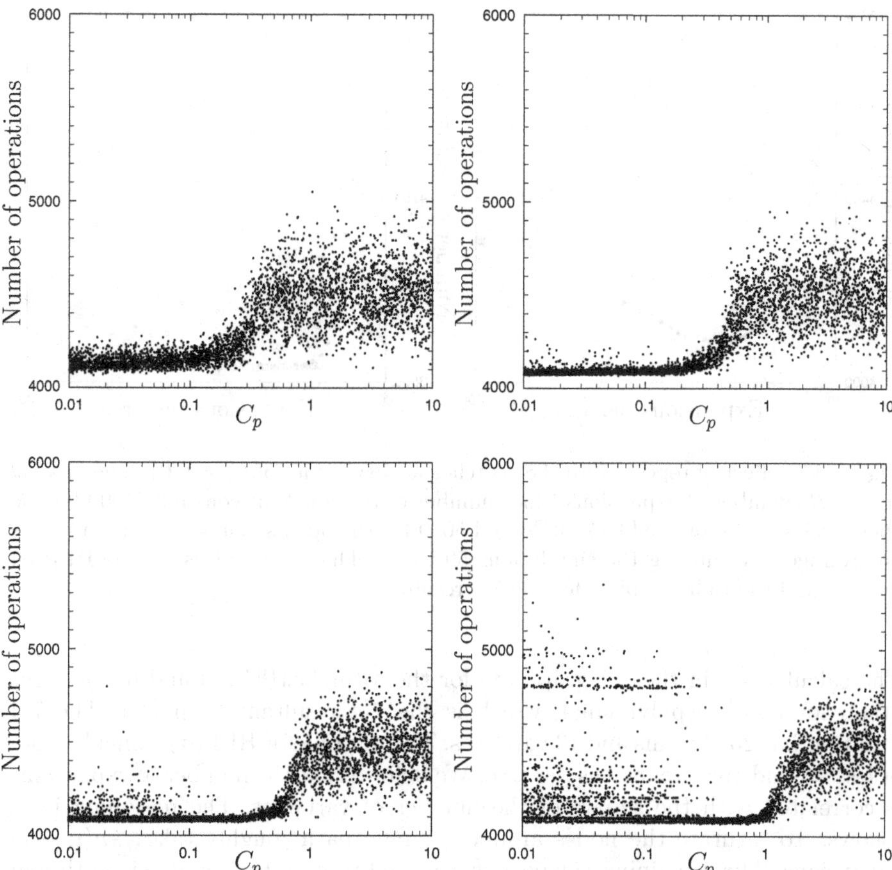

Fig. 6. Experiment for $N \times R$ constant. The polynomial HEP(σ) with 30 runs of 100 expansions, 18 runs of 167 expansions, 10 runs of 300 expansions, and 3 runs of 1000 expansions respectively. For comparison, the graph with a single run of $N = 3000$ can be found in Fig. 4, left bottom.

run has too few points, we do not find a suitable local minimum. (2) When a run has too few points the results revert to that of the almost random branches for large values of C_p. (3) The multiple runs cause us to lose the sharp minimum near $C_p = 0.7$, because we do not have anymore a correlated search of the tree. However, if we have no idea what would be a good value for C_p (i.e., we do not know where to start) it seems appropriate to select a value that is small and make multiple runs provided that the number of expansions N is sufficiently large for finding a reasonable local minimum in a branch of the tree.

Our next question then is: "What is a good value for the number of tree expansions per run?" Below we investigate and answer this question with the help of Fig. 7. We select a small value for C_p (0.01) and make runs for several values of the total number of tree expansions (with $N \times R = 1000, 3000, 5000$).

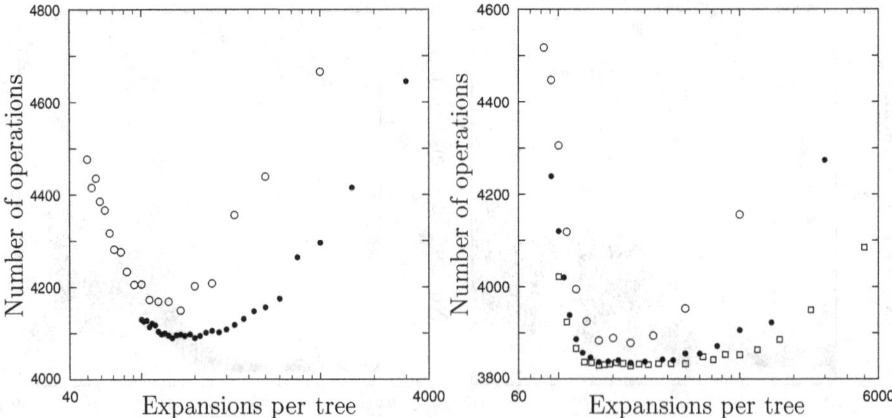

Fig. 7. The effect of repeated MCTS searches for low values of $C_p = 0.01$. The *product* of $N \times R$ (number of expansions times number of runs) is kept constant (1000 for the open circles, 3000 for the black circlesand 5000 for the open squares). The data points are averaged by running the simulations 50 times. The left graph is for the HEP(σ) formula and the right graph is for the 7-4 resultant.

The calculations in the left graph are for the formula HEP(σ) and in the right graph for another polynomial, which is the 7-4 resultant from [30]. The 7-4 resultant has 2562 terms and 13 variables. The minima for HEP(σ) coincide more or less around 165 expansions per tree. We believe that the number of expansions is correlated with the square of the number of variables. The reasoning is as follows. To saturate the nodes around a single path roughly takes $\frac{1}{2}n(n+1)$ expansions. The remaining expansions are used to search around this path and are apparently sufficient to find a local minimum. Returning to the right top panel of Fig. 6, it was selected with 18 runs of 167 expansions per tree (with the minimum of 165 expansions per tree in mind). For the formula involved this seems to be the optimum if one does not know about the value $C_p = 0.7$ or if one cannot run with a sufficient number of expansions to make use of its properties.

We have also made a few runs for the 7-5 and 7-6 resultants (also taken from [30]) and find minima around 250 and 300 respectively.[1] The results suggest that if the number of variables is in the range of 13 to 15 an appropriate value for the number of expansions is 200–250. This number will then be multiplied by the number of runs of MCTS to obtain an indication for the total number of tree expansions.

For reasons of comparison, we remark that similar studies of other physics formulas with more variables ($\mathcal{O}(30)$) show larger optimal values for the number of expansions per run and less pronounced local minima. Yet, also here, many

[1] The 7-5 resultant has 11380 terms and 14 variables, the 7-6 resultant has 43166 terms and 15 variables.

smaller runs may produce better results than a single large run, provided that the runs have more than a given minimum of tree expansions.

Future Work. This investigation into the sensitivity of (1) the number of tree expansions N, (2) the exploration/exploitation parameter C_P, and (3) the number of reruns of MCTS R has yielded interesting insights into the relationships between these parameters and the effect on the efficiency of MCTS in finding better variable orderings for multivariate polynomials to apply Horner's rule. We have used a limited number of polynomials for our experiments. In future work we will address the effect of different polynomials. In addition, it will be interesting to see if similar results can be obtained for other application domains, in particular for the game of Go.

5 Discussion

From the beginning of AI in 1950, chess has been called the Drosophila of AI. It was the testbed of choice. Many of the findings from decades of computer chess research have found their way to other fields, such as protein sequencing, natural language processing, machine learning, and high performance search [23]. After DEEP BLUE had defeated Garry Kasparov, research attention shifted to Go.

For Go, no good heuristic evaluation function seems to exist. Therefore, a different search paradigm was invented: MCTS. The two most prevailing characteristics are: no more minimax, and no need for a heuristic evaluation function. Instead, MCTS uses (1) the average of random playouts to guide the search, and (2) by balancing between exploration and exploitation, it appears to be able to detect by itself which areas of the search tree contain the green leaves, and which branches are dead wood. Having a "self-guided" (best-first) search, without the need for a domain-dependent heuristic, can be highly useful. For many other application domains the construction of a heuristic evaluation function is an obstacle, too. Therefore we expect that there are many other domains that could benefit from the MCTS technology, and, indeed, many other applications have already been found how to adapt MCTS to fit their characteristics (see, for example, [6,13,28,31,32,40,41,43]). In this paper one such adaptation has been discussed, viz. with Horner schemes. Finding better variable orders for applying the classic Horner's rule algorithm is an exciting first result [26], allowing easy investigation of two search parameters. It will be interesting to find out whether similar results can be found in MCTS as applied in Go programs, and other application domains.

References

1. Allis, V.: Searching for Solutions in Games and Artificial Intelligence. (Ph.D. thesis), University of Limburg, Maastricht, The Netherlands (1994)
2. Althöfer, I.: The origin of dynamic komi. ICGA J. **35**(1), 31–34 (2012)

3. Aoyama, T., Hayakawa, M., Kinoshita, T., Nio, M.: Tenth-Order QED Lepton Anomalous Magnetic Moment – Eighth-Order Vertices Containing a Second-Order Vacuum Polarization. e-Print: arXiv:1110.2826 [hep-ph] (2011)
4. Auer, P., Cesa-Bianchi, N., Fischer, P.: Finite-time analysis of the multiarmed bandit problem. Mach. Learn. **47**(2), 235–256 (2002)
5. Bouzy, B., Helmstetter, B.: Monte-Carlo Go developments. In: van den Herik, H.J., Iida, H., Heinz, E.A. (eds.) ACG-10. IFIP, vol. 135, pp. 159–174. Springer, Boston (2003)
6. Bouzy, B., Métivier, M., Pellier, D.: MCTS experiments on the voronoi game. In: van den Herik, H.J., Plaat, A. (eds.) ACG 2011. LNCS, vol. 7168, pp. 96–107. Springer, Heidelberg (2012)
7. Brügmann, B.: Monte-Carlo Go. In: AAAI Fall symposium on Games: Playing, Planning, and Learning (1993). http://www.cgl.ucsf.edu/go/Programs/Gobble.html
8. Browne, C.B., Powley, E., Whitehouse, D., Lucas, S.M., Cowling, P.I., Rohlfshagen, P., Tavener, S., Perez, D., Samothrakis, S., Colton, S.: A survey of Monte Carlo Tree Search Methods. IEEE Trans. Comput. Intell. AI Games **4**(1), 1–43 (2012)
9. Ceberio, M., Kreinovich, V.: Greedy algorithms for optimizing multivariate Horner schemes. ACM SIGSAM Bull. **38**, 8–15 (2004)
10. Chaslot, G., Saito, J.-T., Bouzy, B., Uiterwijk, J.W.H.M., van den Herik, H.J.: Monte-Carlo strategies for computer Go. In: Proceedings of the 18th BeNeLux Conference on Articial Intelligence, pp. 83–90 (2006)
11. Chaslot, G.M.J.-B., de Jong, S., Saito, J.-T., Uiterwijk, J.W.H.M.: Monte-Carlo tree search in production management problems. In: Proceedings of the BeNeLux Conference on Artificial Intelligence, Namur, Belgium, pp. 91–98 (2006)
12. Chaslot, G.M.J-B., Winands, M.H.M., Uiterwijk, J.W.H.M., van den Herik, H.J., Bouzy, B.: Progressive strategies for Monte-Carlo tree search. In: Wang, P., et al. (eds.) Proceedings of the 10th Joint Conference on Information Sciences (JCIS 2007), pp. 655–661. World Scientific Publishing Co., Pte. Ltd. (2007); New Mathematics and Natural Computation, vol. 4(3), pp. 343–357 (2008)
13. Chaslot, G.M.J-B., Bakkes, S., Szita, I., Spronck, P.: Monte-Carlo tree search: a new framework for game AI. In: Mateas, M., Darken, C. (eds.) Proceedings of the 4th Artificial Intelligence and Interactive Digital Entertainment Conference. AAAI Press, Menlo Park (2008)
14. Chaslot, G.M.J.-B., Hoock, J.-B., Rimmel, A., Teytaud, O., Lee, C.-S., Wang, M.-H., Tsai, S.-R., Hsu, S.-C.: Human-computer go revolution 2008. ICGA J. **31**(3), 179–185 (2008)
15. Chinchalkar, S.: An upper bound for the number of reachable positions. ICCA J. **19**(3), 181–182 (1996)
16. Coulom, R.: Efficient selectivity and backup operators in Monte-Carlo tree search. In: van den Herik, H.J., Ciancarini, P., Donkers, H.H.L.M.J. (eds.) CG 2006. LNCS, vol. 4630, pp. 72–83. Springer, Heidelberg (2007)
17. Donkers, J.H.L.M., van den Herik, H.J., Uiterwijk, J.W.H.M.: Selecting evaluation functions in opponent model search. Theoret. Comput. Sci. (TCS) **349**(2), 245–267 (2005)
18. de Groot, A.D.: Het denken van den schaker, Ph. D. thesis in dutch (1946); translated in 1965 as "Thought and Choice in chess", Mouton Publishers, The Hague (2nd edn. 1978). Freely available as e-book from Google (1946)
19. Enzenberger, M.: Evaluation in go by a neural network using soft segmentation. In: van den Herik, H.J., Iida, H., Heinz, E.A. (eds.) Advances in Computer Games. IFIP, vol. 135, pp. 97–108. Springer, Boston (2003)

20. Horner, W.G.: A new method of solving numerical equations of all orders, by continuous approximation. Philos. Trans. (R. Soc. Lond.) 109, 308–335 (1819); Reprinted with appraisal in Smith, D.E.: A Source Book in Mathematics, McGraw-Hill (1929); Dover reprint, vol. 2 (1959)
21. Gelly, S., Wang, Y., Munos, R., Teytaud, O.: Modification of UCT with patterns in monte-carlo go. Inst. Nat. Rech. Inform. Auto. (INRIA), Paris, Technical report (2006)
22. Hartmann, D.: How to extract relevant knowledge from grandmaster games. Part 1: Grandmaster have insights–the problem is what to incorporate into practical problems. ICCA J. **10**(1), 14–36 (1987)
23. van den Herik, H.J.: Informatica en het Menselijk Blikveld. Inaugural address Rijksuniversiteit Limburg, Maastricht, The Netherlands (1988)
24. Junghanns, A.: Are there practical alternatives to alpha-beta? ICCA J. **21**(1), 14–32 (1998)
25. Kocsis, L., Szepesvàri, C.: Bandit based monte-carlo planning. In: European Conference on Machine Learning, pp. 282–293. Springer, Berlin, Germany (2006)
26. Kuipers, J., Vermaseren, J.A.M., Plaat, A., van den Herik, H.J.: Improving multivariate Horner schemes with Monte Carlo tree search, July 2012. arXiv 1207.7079
27. Kuipers, J., Ueda, T., Vermaseren, J.A.M., Vollinga, J.: FORM version 4.0 (2012) (preprint). arXiv:1203.6543
28. Kloetzer, J.: Monte-Carlo opening books for amazons. In: van den Herik, H.J., Iida, H., Plaat, A. (eds.) CG 2010. LNCS, vol. 6515, pp. 124–135. Springer, Heidelberg (2011)
29. Landis, E.M., Yaglom, I.M.: About aleksandr semenovich kronrod. Russ. Math. Surv. **56**, 993–1007 (2001)
30. Leiserson, C.E., Li, L., Maza, M.M., Xie, Y.: Efficient evaluation of large polynomials. In: Fukuda, K., Hoeven, J., Joswig, M., Takayama, N. (eds.) ICMS 2010. LNCS, vol. 6327, pp. 342–353. Springer, Heidelberg (2010)
31. Lorentz, R.: Experiments with monte carlo tree search in the game of havannah. ICGA J. **34**(3), 140–149 (2011)
32. Lorentz, R.J.: An MCTS program to play einstein würfelt nicht!. In: van den Herik, H.J., Plaat, A. (eds.) ACG 2011. LNCS, vol. 7168, pp. 52–59. Springer, Heidelberg (2012)
33. Moch, S.-O., Vermaseren, J.A.M., Vogt, A.: Nucl. Phys. B688, B691, 101–134, 129–181 (2004); B724, 3–182 (2005)
34. Müller, M.: Computer Go. Artif. Intell. **134**(1–2), 145–179 (2002)
35. Pearl, J.: Asymptotical properties of minimax trees and game searching procedures. Artif. Intell. **14**(2), 113–138 (1980)
36. Pearl, J.: Heuristics Intelligent Search Strategies for Computer Problem Solving. Addison-WesleyPublishing Co, Reading (1984)
37. Plaat, A., Schaeffer, J., Pijls, W., de Bruin, A.: Best-First Fixed-Depth Minimax Algorithms. Artificial Intelligence **87**(1–2), 255–293 (1996)
38. Rivest, R.: Game-tree searching by min-max approximation. Artif. Intell. **34**(1), 77–96 (1988)
39. Rosin, C.D.: Nested rollout policy adaptation for monte carlo tree search. In: Proceedings of the Twenty-Second International Joint Conference on Artificial Intelligence, IJCAI-2011, pp. 649–654 (2011)
40. Saito, J.-T., Chaslot, G.M.J.-B., Uiterwijk, J.W.H.M., van den Herik, H.J.: Monte-carlo proof-number search for computer go. In: van den Herik, H.J., Ciancarini, P., Donkers, H.H.L.M.J. (eds.) CG 2006. LNCS, vol. 4630, pp. 50–61. Springer, Heidelberg (2007)

41. Schadd, M.P.D., Winands, M.H.M., van den Herik, H.J., Chaslot, G.M.J.-B., Uiterwijk, J.W.H.M.: Single-player monte-carlo tree search. In: van den Herik, H.J., Xu, X., Ma, Z., Winands, M.H.M. (eds.) CG 2008. LNCS, vol. 5131, pp. 1–12. Springer, Heidelberg (2008)
42. Stockman, G.C.: A minimax algorithm better than alpha-beta? Artif. Intell. **12**(2), 179–196 (1979)
43. Szita, I., Chaslot, G., Spronck, P.: Monte-Carlo tree search in settlers of catan. In: van den Herik, H.J., Spronck, P. (eds.) ACG 2009. LNCS, vol. 6048, pp. 21–32. Springer, Heidelberg (2010)
44. van der Werf, E.C.D., van den Herik, H.J., Uiterwijk, J.W.H.M.: Learning to score final positions in the game of Go. Theoret. Comput. Sci. **349**(2), 168–183 (2005)
45. van der Werf, E.C.D., Winands, M.H.M., van den Herik, H.J., Uiterwijk, J.W.H.M.: Learning to predict Life and Death from Go game records. Inf. Sci. **175**(4), 258–272 (2005)

Agents

COHDA: A Combinatorial Optimization Heuristic for Distributed Agents

Christian Hinrichs[1](✉), Sebastian Lehnhoff[2], and Michael Sonnenschein[1]

[1] University of Oldenburg, Oldenburg, Germany
christian.hinrichs@uni-oldenburg.de,
sonnenschein@informatik.uni-oldenburg.de

[2] OFFIS Institute for Information Technology, Oldenburg, Germany
sebastian.lehnhoff@offis.de

Abstract. Solving Distributed Constraint Optimization Problems has a large significance in today's interconnected world. Complete as well as approximate algorithms have been discussed in the relevant literature. However, these are unfeasible if high-arity constraints are present (i.e., a fully connected constraint graph). This is the case in distributed combinatorial problems, for example in the provisioning of active power in the domain of electrical energy generation. The aim of this paper is to give a detailed formalization and evaluation of the COHDA heuristic for solving these types of problems. The heuristic uses self-organizing mechanisms to optimize a common global objective in a fully decentralized manner. We show that COHDA is a very efficient decentralized heuristic that is able to tackle a distributed combinatorial problem, without being dependent on centrally gathered knowledge.

Keywords: Self-organization · Cooperation · Smart grid

1 Introduction

In decentralized systems, where the search space of a given optimization problem is distributed into disjoint subspaces, centralized optimization approaches often cannot be applied. For example, the global collection of data might violate privacy considerations or bandwidth restrictions. The gathering of such data might even be impossible, as it is the case if local search spaces are partially unknown or cannot be enumerated (i.e. due to infiniteness). Another limitation is that distributed search spaces are often not independent. Such interdependencies require to evaluate search spaces with relation to each other. Thus, a parallel search for optimal solutions would require a large communication overhead.

For instance, this type of problem is present in the transition of today's electricity grid to a decentralized smart grid. Here, we have to cope with an increasing number of distributed energy resources (DER). Usually, the operation of these DER is individually configured, according to the constraints given at the

J. Filipe and A. Fred (Eds.): ICAART 2013, CCIS 449, pp. 23–39, 2014.
DOI: 10.1007/978-3-662-44440-5_2

place of installation. For example, a combined heat and power plant (CHP) primarily has to satisfy the (varying) thermal energy needs of a building. Electrical energy is produced only as a side-product, so that e.g. the provisioning of active power by this unit is difficult to request directly. Because of this rather dynamical behavior of such DER, an adaptive, decentralized control scheme is crucial for a reliable operation of the system (see [17,22] for more details regarding ongoing work in this domain).

In the contribution at hand, we focus on day-ahead planning of the provisioning of active power, which can be expressed as a distributed combinatorial problem: Given a set of DER and a global target power profile, each unit has to select its own mode of operation for the planning horizon in such a way, that the resulting individual power profiles of all units jointly match the global target profile as close as possible. For this purpose, the distributed heuristic COHDA is developed which makes use of self-organization strategies. In hitherto existing population-based heuristics, each individual represents a complete solution to the given problem within a common search space. In our approach, however, an individual incorporates a local, dependent search space, and thus defines a *partial* solution that can only be evaluated with respect to all other individuals. The task of each individual is to find a partial local solution that, if combined with the local solutions of the other individuals, yields the optimal global solution.

The problem stated in this contribution is formulated as an instance of a *distributed constraint optimization problem* (DCOP). In [4], a thorough examination of heuristic approaches from the DCOP domain as well as from the context of game theory is presented, and [12] puts DCOPs into perspective of cooperative problem solving in multi-agent systems. All mentioned approaches therein rely on communication between individuals which are directly connected in the constraint graph of the problem to solve. However, the problem considered in the present contribution induces a fully connected constraint graph, which renders these approaches unfeasible due to communication complexity. The consequence would be a broadcasting of messages, which has been realized in the COBB approach [18]. Technically, broadcasting can be done in two ways: by sending messages directly to all other existing individuals, or by using a central black board where the relevant information is posted publicly. The former method would lead to an explosion of the number of transferred messages. The latter method, as used in [14], is able to avoid this (if a suitable *adjustment schedule* is used, c.f. [4]), but introduces the problem of a centralized information repository with the drawbacks mentioned earlier. In contrast, the EPOS approach, as introduced in [19,20], uses a *tree overlay* organization structure and thus is based on a partial representation of the constraint graph. Following, EPOS does fulfill the demand for an algorithm that can handle fully connected constraint graphs in the context of distributed constraint optimization problems. The tree overlay, however, imposes hierarchical relations on the agents. Hence, there are still centralized components present in the architecture of this approach. Furthermore, the optimization process is carried out in an iterative bottom-up fashion, which leads to a rather synchronous execution paradigm. We believe that a more convenient approach with regard to decentralized settings is possible. Therefore, we introduced the COHDA heuristic in [6].

In order to compensate for the condensed presentation in [6], the aim of this paper is to evaluate the COHDA heuristic in more detail. Hence, we will give a detailed formalization of the heuristic and a thorough description of the approach first. In addition, we extend COHDA to the multi-objective case. Subsequently, we evaluate the heuristic with respect to different parameters: message delay, network density, planning horizon, search space complexity and population size. Note that the first two are user-defined parameters, while the last three are problem-specific. From the results, the properties adaptivity, robustness, scalability, and anytime behavior are derived.

The contribution at hand is a revised version of [8].

2 Method

Constraint optimization problems (COP) can be formulated with an integer programming model, if we assume that each search space is discrete by nature, and that the elements within are known and may be enumerated. Let $c \in \mathbb{R}^q$ be the *target* that should be matched, where q is the number of dimensions (i.e. in the context of power provisioning, q denotes the planning horizon). We now assume that there are m disjoint search spaces (i.e. electrical generators). Now let the ith search space contain n_i elements. The jth element in such a search space describes a partial solution to the problem, denoted with $w_{ij} \in \mathbb{R}^q$ (i.e. a feasible power profile). The goal is to *select* an element w_{ij} from each search space i, such that the sum of these selected values approaches c as close as possible (c.f. [6]):

$$\min \left\| c - \sum_{i=1}^{m} \sum_{j=1}^{n_i} (w_{ij} \cdot x_{ij}) \right\|_1 \tag{1}$$

$$\text{subject to} \quad \sum_{j=1}^{n_i} x_{ij} = 1, \; i = 1 \ldots m,$$

$$x_{ij} \in \{0, 1\}, \; i = 1 \ldots m, \; j = 1 \ldots n_i,$$

Here, each search space has an associated selection variable x_{ij}, which defines whether an element has been chosen ($x_{ij} = 1$) or not ($x_{ij} = 0$). This model is a generalization of the well-known subset-sum problem, where solutions exceeding the target are not allowed (whereas our model approximates c from any side).

2.1 Mapping to a Distributed System

So far, the above formulation is only suitable from a central perspective. In the aimed setting however, each search space is represented by an autonomous decision maker, which we call *agents*. The task of each agent a_i is to select one of its elements w_{ij} with respect to the common global target c. More formally, an agent a_i has to find an assignment of *its own* selection variables x_{ij}, such that the objective function in (1) is minimized globally.

Definition 1. *A selection of an agent a_i is a tuple $\gamma_i = \langle i, j \rangle$ where i is the identifier of a_i, and j identifies the selected element w_{ij} such that $x_{ij} = 1$ and $\sum_{j=1}^{n_i} x_{ij} = 1$.*

Agents are autonomous, so they may change their selection at any time. Therefore, we need to define the *state* of an agent.

Definition 2. *The state of an agent a_i is given by $\sigma_i = \langle \gamma_i, \lambda_i \rangle$, where γ_i is a selection containing an assignment of a_i's decision variables x_{ij}, and λ_i is a unique number within the history of a_i's states. Each time an agent a_i changes its current selection γ_i to $\acute{\gamma_i}$, the agent enters a new state $\acute{\sigma_i} = \langle \acute{\gamma_i}, \lambda_i' \rangle$ where $\lambda_i' = \lambda_i + 1$. This imposes a strict total order on a_i's selections, hence λ_i reflects the "age" of a selection.*

In order to decide which of its local elements w_{ij} to select optimally, an agent has to take the current selections (i.e. states) of the other agents in the system into account.

Definition 3. *A configuration $\Sigma = \{\sigma_i, \sigma_k, \ldots\}$ is a set of states. A state belonging to an agent a_i can appear in a configuration no more than once:*

$$\sigma_i \in \Sigma \wedge \sigma_k \in \Sigma \Rightarrow i \neq k$$

Note that this definition allows a configuration to be incomplete with regard to the population of agents in the system. A configuration that contains states for all existing agents is called *global.*

Definition 4. *A global configuration regarding the whole system is denoted by $\Sigma_{global} = \{\sigma_i \mid i = 1 \ldots m\}$.*

On the other hand, Definition 3 enables us to model a local view that an agent a_i has on the system. This is quite similar to the definition of *context* in [16]. We call such a local view a *perceived configuration.*

Definition 5. *A perceived configuration of an agent a_i is a configuration $\Sigma_i = \{\sigma_k \mid a_i \text{ is aware of } a_k\}$.*

Following, if we assume that an agent a_i is able to somehow perceive a configuration Σ_i containing information about other agents that a_i is aware of (we will address this later), it may now select one of its own elements w_{ij} with respect to the currently chosen elements of other agents in Σ_i and the optimization goal c.

2.2 Introducing Local Constraints

Furthermore, we introduce local constraints, which impose a penalty value p_{ij} to each element w_{ij} within the search space of an agent a_i.

Definition 6. *The penalty function $\Pi_i : \mathbb{R}^q \mapsto \mathbb{R}$ of an agent a_i maps an element w_{ij} to a penalty value p_{ij}.*

These local constraints are known to the corresponding agent only, as described in the introductory example (i.e. for a CHP unit, heating preferences defined by residents). Thus, each agent has two objectives: minimizing the common objective function as given in (1), and minimizing its local penalties that are induced by contributing a certain element w_{ij}. This compound optimization goal at agent level may be expressed with a utility function:

$$z_i = \alpha_i \cdot z_i^1 + (1 - \alpha_i) \cdot z_i^2 \tag{2}$$

Here, z_i^1 represents the common global objective function and z_i^2 incorporates the local constraints. The parameter α_i allows an agent a_i to autonomously adjust its preference for optimizing the global goal versus optimizing its local constraints. Note that the domains of z_i^1 and z_i^2 must be carefully defined in this model (i.e. normalized to [0.0, 1.0]), so that α_i gains the desired effect.

From a global point of view, this yields the *distributed-objective multiple-choice combinatorial optimization problem* (DO-MC-COP):

$$\begin{aligned}
\min \quad & \sum_{i=1}^{m} z_i && (3)\\
\text{where} \quad & z_i = \alpha_i \cdot z_i^1 + (1 - \alpha_i) \cdot z_i^2 \ ,\\
& z_i^1 = \left\| c - \left(\sum_{j=1}^{n_i} (w_{ij} \cdot x_{ij}) + \sum_{w \in \phi(\Sigma_i)} w \right) \right\|_1 \ ,\\
& z_i^2 = \sum_{j=1}^{n_i} \Pi_i\,(w_{ij}) \cdot x_{ij} \ ,\\
& \phi\,(\Sigma) = \{ w_{ij} \mid \langle \langle i,j \rangle, \lambda \rangle \in \Sigma \} \ ,\\
\text{subject to} \quad & \sum_{j=1}^{n_i} x_{ij} = 1, \ i = 1 \ldots m \ ,\\
& x_{ij} \in \{0,1\}, \ i = 1 \ldots m, \ j = 1 \ldots n_i \ ,\\
& \alpha_i \in \mathbb{R}, \ 0 \leq \alpha_i \leq 1, \ i = 1 \ldots m \ .
\end{aligned}$$

Summarizing, in this model there are m decision makers (agents) a_i, that pursue a common goal by each contributing one solution element w_{ij} from their associated local search space, while at the same time minimizing the resulting local penalty $\Pi_i\,(w_{ij})$.

Obviously, if an agent a_i changes its state σ_i, this should have an effect on the decision making of the other agents in the system. Thus, the definition of how an arbitrary agent a_k perceives a configuration Σ_k, and how this relates to Σ_{global}, is crucial for solving the DO-MC-COP in a distributed way. The following section addresses these questions and describes a self-organizing approach to this distributed-objective problem.

2.3 COHDA

In nature, we find many examples of highly efficient systems, which perform tasks in a completely decentralized manner: swarming behavior of schooling fish or flocking birds [23], foraging of ants [9] and nest thermoregulation of bees [10]. Even processes within single organisms show such astonishing behavior, for instance the neurological development of the fruit fly [13] or the foraging of *Physarum polycephalum*, a single-celled slime mold [26], which both exhibit rules for adaptive network design. One of the core concepts in these examples is self-organization. From the perspective of multi-agent systems, this term can be defined as *"the mechanism or the process enabling a system to change its organization without explicit external command during its execution time"* [24]. From the perspective of complex systems theory, this is related to emergence, which can be defined as *"properties of a system that are not present at the lower level [...], but are a product of the interactions of elements"* [5]. Such systems usually exhibit a number of desirable properties like adaptivity, robustness, scalability, and anytime behavior [2,21].

The COHDA heuristic, as originally proposed in [6], applies these concepts to create a self-organizing heuristic for solving distributed combinatorial problems. The key concept in COHDA is a partial representation of the (usually fully connected) constraint graph of the problem to solve, in order to reduce coordination complexity. Note that this graph induces the communication network of the system. But unlike other approaches mentioned in the introduction, a specific graph topology is not required. Instead, the heuristic adapts to whatever topology is given by real-world requirements (i.e. physical communication lines in power grids), or is defined by the system operator. This is combined with an information spreading strategy that, despite the partial constraint graph, allows the heuristic to converge rapidly to a global solution.

As described above, the heuristic has to cope with an arbitrary communication topology. This can be expressed with a graph $\mathcal{G} = (\mathcal{V}, \mathcal{E})$, where each agent is represented by a vertex $a_i \in \mathcal{V}$. Edges $e = (a_i, a_k) \in \mathcal{E}$ depict communication links. Thus, we can define the *neighborhood* of an agent:

Definition 7. *Given a set of edges $\mathcal{E}$, the neighborhood of an agent a_i is defined as $\mathcal{N}_i = \{a_k \mid (a_i, a_k) \in \mathcal{E}\}$.*

An agent may not communicate with any other agent outside of its neighborhood. Just like flocking birds, the agents now observe their local environment and react to changes within their perception range. For that purpose, each agent a_i maintains a configuration Σ_i, which reflects the knowledge of a_i about the system.

This configuration is initially empty, but is updated during the iterative process through information exchange with other agents (hence, Σ_i is called the *perceived configuration* of a_i, see Definition 5). Now, whenever an agent a_i enters a new state σ_i by changing the assignment of its decision variables x_{ij}, its neighboring agents $a_k \in \mathcal{N}_i$ perceive this event. These agents now each update their current local view Σ_k on the system, and react to this event by re-evaluating their search spaces and subsequently adapting their own decision variables.

However, usually $\Sigma_k \neq \Sigma_{global}$, hence an agent has to deal with incomplete, local knowledge. Thus, for improving the local search at agent level, the COHDA heuristic uses an information spreading strategy besides this reactive adaptation. Whenever a local change is published to the neighborhood, the publishing agent a_i not only includes information about its updated state σ_i, but publishes its whole currently known perceived configuration Σ_i as well. A receiving agent a_k now updates its existing knowledge base Σ_k with this two-fold information $(\Sigma_i \cup \{\sigma_i\})$. In this update procedure, an element $\sigma_y = \langle \gamma_y, \lambda_y \rangle \in \Sigma_i$ of the sending agent a_i is added to Σ_k of the receiving agent a_k if and only if any of the following conditions hold:

1. Σ_k does not already contain a state from a_y, such that $\forall \sigma_z \in \Sigma_i : z \neq y$.
2. Σ_k already contains a state σ_z with $z = y$, but σ_z has a lower value λ_z, such that $\exists \sigma_z = \langle \gamma_z, \lambda_z \rangle \in \Sigma_i : z = y \wedge \lambda_z < \lambda_y$. This means, σ_z is outdated (see Definition 2), and hence σ_y replaces σ_z in Σ_k.

Using this information spreading strategy, agents build a complete representation Σ_{global} of the whole system over time, and take this information into account in their decision making as well. However, due to possibly rather long communication paths between any two agents, these global views on the system are likely to be outdated as soon as they are built and represent *beliefs* about the systems rather than facts. Nevertheless, they provide a valuable guide in the search for optimal local decisions.

In order to ensure convergence and termination, a third information flow is established on top of that. In addition to the perceived configuration Σ_i (which reflects the currently known system configuration including the agent's own current state σ_i), each agent keeps track of the *best known configuration* Σ_i^* it has seen during the whole process so far.

Definition 8. *A configuration* $\Sigma_i^* = \{\sigma_i^*, \sigma_k^*, \dots\}$ *is an arbitrary snapshot of the system taken by an agent* a_i.

Definition 9. *The best* Σ_i^* *over all agents in the population is denoted by* Σ^*.

Whenever an agent updates its Σ_i by means of received information, it compares this new configuration Σ_i to Σ_i^*. If Σ_i yields a better solution quality than Σ_i^* according to DO-MC-COP (3), Σ_i is stored as new best known configuration Σ_i^*. In addition to σ_i and Σ_i, an agent a_i also exchanges its Σ_i^* with its neighbors, everytime it changes. Thus, when an agent a_k receives a Σ_i^* from a neighbor a_i, the agent replaces its currently stored Σ_k^* by Σ_i^*, if the latter yields a better solution quality than the former.

The whole process can be summarized in the following three steps:

1. (`update`) An agent a_i receives information from one of its neighbors and imports it into its own knowledge base. That is, its beliefs Σ_i about the current configuration of the system is updated, as well as the best known configuration Σ_i^*.
2. (`choose`) The agent now adapts its own decision variables x_{ij} according to the newly received information, while taking its own local objectives into account as well. If it is not able to improve the believed current system configuration Σ_i, the state σ_i^* stored in the currently best known configuration Σ_i^* will be taken. The latter causes a_i to revert its current state σ_i to a previous state σ_i^*, that once yielded a better believed global solution.
3. (`publish`) Finally, the agent publishes its belief about the current system configuration Σ_i (including its own new state $\acute{\sigma}_i$), as well as the best known configuration Σ_i^* to its neighbors. Local objectives are not published to other agents, thus maintaining privacy.

Accordingly, an agent a_i has two behavioral options after receiving data from a neighbor. First, a_i will try to improve the currently believed system configuration Σ_i by choosing an appropriate w_{ij}, and subsequently adding its new state $\acute{\sigma}_i$ to Σ_i. Yet, this only happens if the resulting Σ_i would yield a better solution quality than Σ_i^*. In that case, Σ_i replaces Σ_i^*, so that they are identical afterwards. If the agent cannot improve Σ_i over Σ_i^*, however, the agent reverts its state to the one stored in Σ_i^*. This state, σ_i^*, is then added to Σ_i afterwards. Thus, Σ_i always reflects the current view of a_i on the system, while Σ_i^* always represents the currently pursued goal of a_i, since it is the best configuration the agent knows. In either case, Σ_i and Σ_i^* both contain a_i's current state after Step 2.

As can be seen from the above description, the COHDA heuristic is inherently *adaptive*: the agents permanently adapt to changes in their environment; for more details on this see [7]. Also, since an overall best configuration Σ^* (Definition 9) can be identified at any point in time, which is replaced only when an even better configuration is found, the heuristic exhibits the *anytime behavior* [2]. In order to reveal the properties *scalability* and *robustness*, we performed a simulation-based evaluation. This evaluation will be discussed in the following sections.

2.4 Implementation

We implemented the proposed heuristic COHDA in a multi-agent system (MAS). In our simulation environment, agents communicate asynchronously, using a network layer as communication backend. This backend may be a physical one, so as to be able to distribute the MAS over arbitrary machines. In our evaluation however, we used a simulated network layer, in order to have full control over message travelling times, and to permit deterministic repetitions of simulation runs. For this, we used predefined seeds for the random number generators. This allows us to simulate unsteady communication layers with varying message delays. Technically, our simulation is event-driven, i.e., agents react to events (messages from other agents) in the continuous time domain, which is induced by the above mentioned varying message delays. For the ease of evaluation, however, the simulation status is reported to the experimenter exactly every integer-valued time step. Following, from the user perspective, a discrete-time simulation is performed. Our implementation ensured that we were able to monitor (and count) all exchanged messages.

In the conducted experiments, each agent represents a simulated combined heat and power (CHP) device with an $800\,l$ thermal buffer store. We used the simulation model of an EcoPower CHP as described in [3]. For each of those devices, the thermal demand for a four-family house during winter was simulated according to [11]. The devices were operated in heat driven operation and thus primarily had to compensate the simulated thermal demand. Additionally, after shutting down, a device would have to stay off for at least two hours. However, due to their thermal buffer store and the ability to modulate the electrical power output within the range of $[1.3\,\text{kW},\ 4.7\,\text{kW}]$, the devices had still some degrees of freedom left.

For each conducted experiment, and for each agent, the simulation model has been instantiated with a random initial temperature level of the thermal buffer store and a randomly generated thermal demand. Subsequently, a number of feasible power profiles were generated from each of these simulation models. The resulting sets of power profiles are then used as local search spaces by the agents. The global goal c of the optimization problem was generated as a random electrical power profile, which was scaled to be feasible for the given population of CHP devices. However, we cannot guarantee that an optimal solution actually lies within in the set of randomly enumerated search spaces. The task of the agents now was to select one element out of their given sets of power profiles each, so that the sum of all selected power profiles approximates the target profile c as exactly as possible.

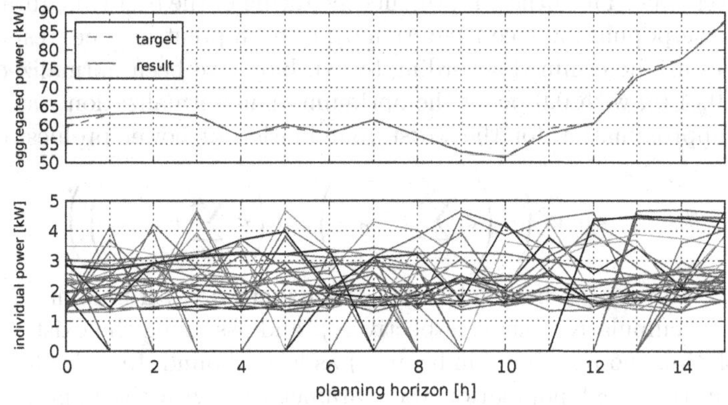

Fig. 1. Optimization result of a single simulation run with 30 CHP (and local search spaces comprising 2000 feasible power profiles each), for a planning horizon of four hours in 15-min. intervals.

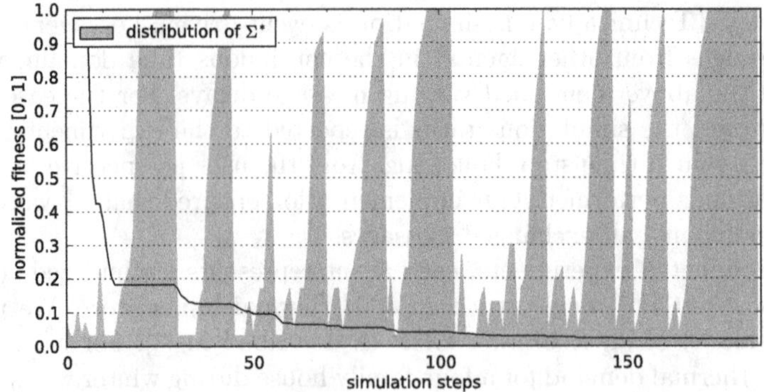

Fig. 2. Detailed illustration of the COHDA heuristic during a simulation.

3 Results

As a first step, we examined the general behavior of the heuristic without penalties. In Fig. 1, the results of a single simulation run ($m = 30$ devices with $n = 2000$ possible power profiles each) are visualized. The planning horizon was set to four hours in 15-min. intervals. The upper chart shows the target profile (dashed line) and the resulting aggregated power output (solid line). The individual power output profiles of the devices are depicted in the lower chart. The latter is quite chaotic, which is due to the limited sets of available power output profiles per device. Nevertheless, the heuristic was able to select 30 profiles (one for each device), whose sum approximates the target profile with a remaining imbalance of less than 2.5 kW per time step in the planning horizon.

In Fig. 2, the process of the heuristic for this simulation run is shown in detail. This data is visible to the simulation observer only, the individual agents still act upon local knowledge. The solid line depicts the global fitness value of the heuristic over time. This fitness represents the rating of the best configuration Σ^* existing in the population (see Definition 9), at each point in time, respectively. These values are determined according to (3), but have been normalized to the interval [0.0, 1.0], with 0.0 being the optimum. The normalization was done by taking an approximation for the worst combination of power profiles as upper bound:

$$d_{worst} = \max\left(d\left(c, \sum_{i=1}^{m} w_{i,min}\right), d\left(c, \sum_{i=1}^{m} w_{i,max}\right)\right)$$

(with $w_{i,min}$ and $w_{i,max}$ being elements of an agent a_i with minimal and maximal absolute cumulative value, respectively), and assuming the existence of an optimal solution (no remaining imbalance) as lower bound. In order to examine convergence, the agent population was parametrized with the upper bound as initial solution.

In general, the fitness value decreases over time (lower is better, so this means an improvement of the fitness) until it converges to a near-optimal solution. However, it is not strictly decreasing, since there are non-decreasing intervals. This is due to the information spreading strategy in COHDA, and can be explained with the distribution ratio of Σ^*. The latter is visualized by the shaded area (the higher, the more agents are aware of the current Σ^*). Recall that an agent a_i inherits a received Σ_k^* from a neighbor a_k if Σ_k^* yields a better rating than the currently stored Σ_i^* of the agent a_i. Thus, a configuration with very good rating prevails and spreads in the network, until a better rated configuration is found somewhere. As an example, consider the situation at simulation step 12. Some agent, say a_i, has found a configuration Σ_i^* with a normalized fitness rating of ≈0.18. This configuration is, at that time, the best configuration found in the whole population, therefore $\Sigma^* = \Sigma_i^*$. The agent publishes Σ_i^* to its neighbors, who accept it as a new best configuration, and re-publish it again to their respective neighbors. Hence, the distribution of Σ^* (shaded area) rises in the following time steps, but the fitness value (solid line) remains constant. In simulation step 30, however, some agent a_k finds an even better configuration Σ_k^*. Thus the fitness value improves and, from this point in time, $\Sigma^* = \Sigma_k^*$. At the same time, the distribution of the (new) Σ^* drops dramatically, since this configuration is known to a_k only and has yet to be spread in the network. The heuristic terminates after 185 simulation steps, where a certain Σ^* has been distributed to all agents, and no better configuration can be found. The final fitness value is 0.02, which amounts to a total remaining imbalance of 7.09 kW (0.007 % of the targeted 1004.13 kW in total over the planning horizon).

Figure 3 shows the aggregated behavior of the COHDA heuristic for 100 simulation runs. For each simulation run, the same CHP devices and thus the same local search spaces were used, but the communication network was initialized with different seeds for the random number generator. This yielded a different communication graph in each run, as well as different generated message delays.

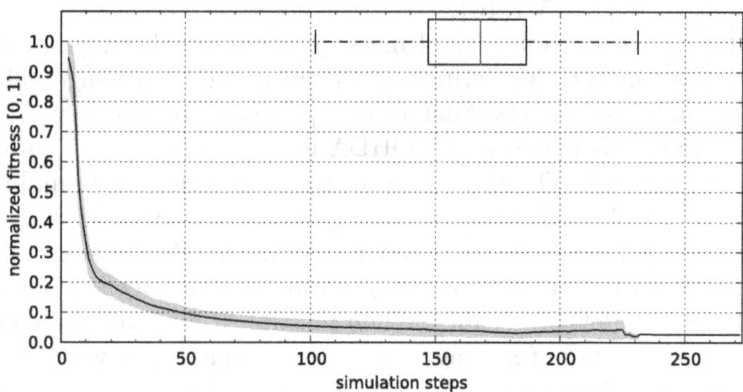

Fig. 3. Aggregated behavior of COHDA for 100 simulation runs with 30 CHP (and local search spaces comprising 2000 feasible power profiles each), for a planning horizon of four hours in 15-min. intervals.

The solid line represents the mean fitness over time, while the shaded area around this line depicts the standard deviation. Obviously, in this example the COHDA heuristic is able to converge to near optimal solutions independently from the underlying communication backend. On average over all 100 simulation runs, each agent sent 1.5 ± 0.04 messages per simulation step. The boxplot visualizes simulation lengths, with 169.69 ± 28.38 simulation steps being the mean.

3.1 Performance Criteria

Besides the inspection of the general behavior, simulation performance can be measured in terms of (a) the resulting fitness after termination, (b) the simulation length, or (c) the average number of exchanged messages per agent per simulation step during the process. In our experiments, the influence of different input parameters on each of these numbers (a–c) has been analyzed. From the resulting interactions, properties like robustness and scalability may be derived. If not stated otherwise, the experiments were conducted using a message delay $msg_{max} = 2$ (see Sect. 3.2), a small world network topology with $\phi = 2.0$ (see Sect. 3.3), a target comprising $q = 16$ dimensions (see Sect. 2.3), a population size of $m = 30$ agents, and no penalties (such that $\alpha_i = 1.0$ in (2)). Each examined scenario was simulated 100 times. Figure 4 shows a summary of our results. We will discuss each part in the following sections.

3.2 Message Delay

An important property of the simulated communication backend is its ability for delayed messages. In order to evaluate the robustness of the heuristic against a non-deterministic communication layer, we tested the approach with different amounts of message delays. To accomplish that, we defined an interval $[1, msg_{max}]$, from which a random number is generated for each sent message. The message is then delayed for the according number of simulation steps. We evaluated $msg_{max} \in \{1, 2, 5, 7, 10\}$.

Figure 4(a) shows the influence of message delays on the simulation performance, as defined in Sect. 3.1 (criteria a–c). Fortunately, message delays have absolutely no influence on the final fitness produced by the heuristic (criterion a, top chart). This means that COHDA is very stable against an unsteady communication network. The time until termination (criterion b, middle chart) consequentially rises linearly with increasing message delay. With regard to the amount of exchanged messages (criterion c, bottom chart), a strongly decreasing trend towards less than one sent message on average per agent per simulation step with increasing delay is visible. When multiplied with the number of simulation steps, the number of messages per agent throughout a whole simulation run can be determined (chart not shown here). We find a minimum of exchanged messages per simulation run with $msg_{max} = 2$. Following, COHDA does not only cope with, but even benefits from a slight variation at agent level introduced by message delays (for details on inter-agent variation see [1]).

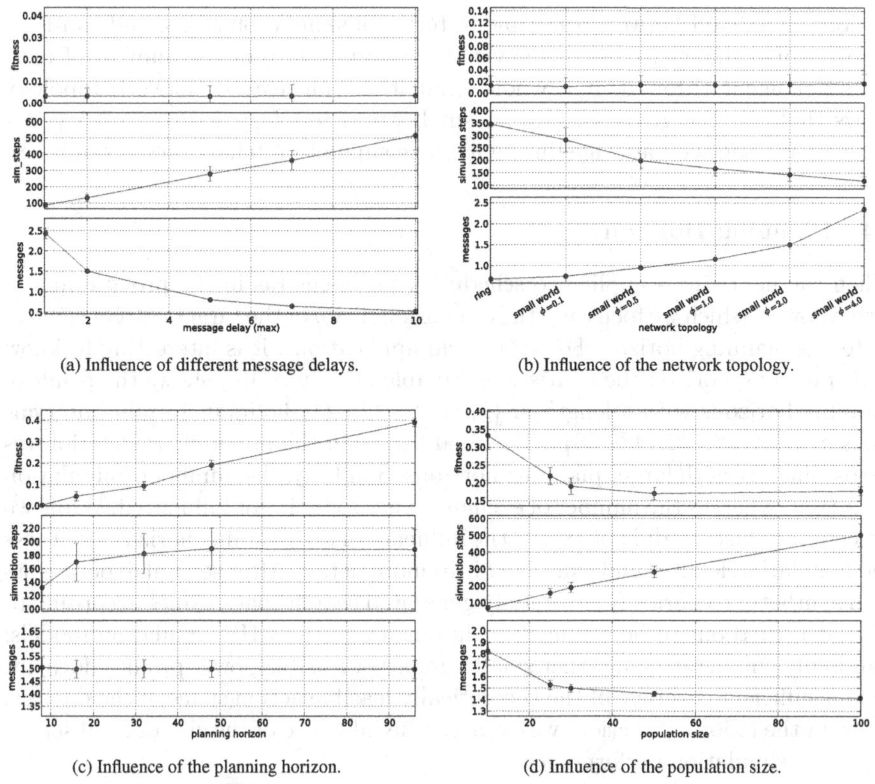

(a) Influence of different message delays.

(b) Influence of the network topology.

(c) Influence of the planning horizon.

(d) Influence of the population size.

Fig. 4. Performance analysis of COHDA regarding different input parameters.

3.3 Network Density

The composition of an agents' neighborhood is directly coupled to the underlying communication graph $\mathcal{G} = (\mathcal{E}, \mathcal{V})$. Preliminary experiments showed a beneficial impact of random graphs with a low diameter. Thus, we evaluated the following topologies:

- *Ring*: The agents are inserted into a ring-shaped list. Each agent is then connected to its predecessor and successor.
- *Small World*: This network comprises an ordered ring with $|\mathcal{V}| \cdot \phi$ additional connections between randomly selected agents, cf. [25]. We examined $\phi \in \{0.1,\ 0.5,\ 1.0,\ 2.0,\ 4.0\}$.

In Fig. 4(b), the results of these experiments are visualized. We ordered the plotted data according to the approximated average neighborhood size, which defines the overall density of the communication graph. Similar to the previous section, there is no influence of the network density on solution quality. Expectedly, the message complexity increases with larger neighborhoods. Similarly, simulation length decreases with more connections. As in the previous section, a trade-off between run-time in terms of simulation steps, and run-time in terms of exchanged messages is visible. A comparison of the number of messages per agent throughout a whole simulation run against network topology shows that, for the given scenario, a small world topology with $\phi = 0.5$ yields the least messages on average during a whole simulation (chart not shown here).

3.4 Planning Horizon

When the heuristic is applied to scheduling problems (as in the provisioning of active power, which we focus at), the dimensionality q of the target $c \in \mathbb{R}^q$ is interpreted as planning horizon. For real-world applications, it is interesting to know what planning horizon the heuristic is capable of. Figure 4(c) shows the result of planning horizons with a length of $\{2,\ 4,\ 8,\ 12,\ 24\}$ hours in 15-min. intervals (thus $q \in \{8,\ 16,\ 32,\ 48,\ 96\}$). The final fitness in the upper chart deteriorates almost linearly with larger planning horizons. Similarly, the number of simulation steps rises, whereas the number of exchanged messages is not influenced. While we expected the last, we did not expect the influence of the planning horizon on fitness and simulation length, and examined it in more detail. After several experiments with synthetic scenarios (i.e. carefully generated search space values according to [15]), it turned out to be a side effect in our use of the CHP simulation models: Randomly enumerating a rather small number of feasible power profiles does not yield a sufficient coverage of the theoretically feasible action space of the devices. Thus, in the following section, we examine the influence of the size of local search spaces on simulation performance.

3.5 Search Space Complexity

We analyzed scenarios with $\{20,\ 200,\ 2000,\ 20000\}$ pre-generated feasible power profiles per device. This yielded fitness values of 0.12 ± 0.06, 0.02 ± 0.02, 0.003 ± 0.004 and 0.001 ± 0.002, respectively. Since the coverage of the theoretically feasible action space of the simulated devices increases with larger enumerated local search spaces (c.f. Sect. 3.4), simulation fitness improves significantly. The number of simulation steps and the number of exchanged messages per agent per simulation step were constant (132 ± 21 and 1.5 ± 0.04, respectively).

3.6 Population Size

Another interesting property regarding real-world applications is the influence of population size on the heuristic. In Fig. 4(d), a linear increase in simulation steps until termination can be seen. This is consequently due to the increased coordination complexity in larger networks. Yet, since the increase is linear at most, this shows that COHDA is quite robust against the number of participating individuals. Interestingly, the final fitness as well as the number of exchanged messages per time step significantly improve with larger population sizes. The former may be related to the increased diversity, which could already be observed

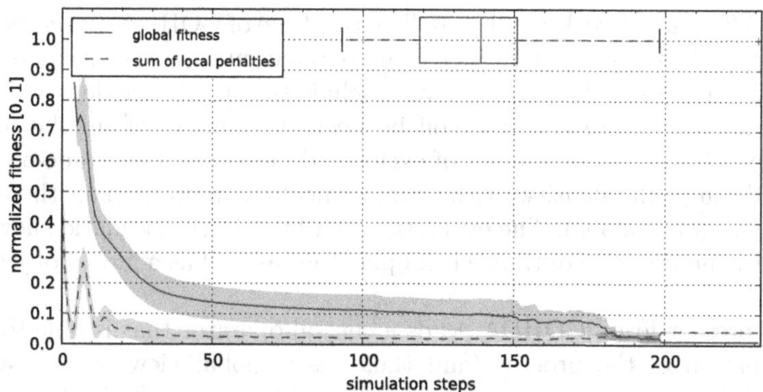

Fig. 5. Aggregated performance of COHDA over 100 simulation runs with distributed local objective functions ($\forall i: \ \alpha_i = 0.5$).

to be beneficial in the analysis of the sizes of local search spaces in the previous section. The latter can be attributed to an increased diameter of the communication graph with larger population sizes. Here, information spreads more slowly, and it takes a longer time for the system to converge.

3.7 Bi-Objective Behavior

As described in Sect. 2.2, we introduced local objective functions at agent level for the COHDA heuristic. As a proof of concept, we conducted an experiment (100 simulation runs) with randomly generated penalty values $p_{ij} \in [0, \max(c)]$. The preference adjustment parameter, as defined in (2), was set to $\alpha_i = 0.5$ for all agents, so that the local objectives were considered equally important to the global objective. Figure 5 shows the aggregated results of 100 simulation runs. The heuristic was able to minimize local penalties to a normalized value of 0.02 ± 0.01. At the same time, the global objective fitness could be optimized to a normalized value of 0.15 ± 0.07, which amounts to a remaining imbalance of 33.12 kW $\pm$ 17.02 in total over the planning horizon (0.06 % $\pm$ 0.03 of the targeted 544.26 kW).

4 Conclusions

In the contribution at hand, we presented COHDA, which is a self-organizing heuristic for solving distributed combinatorial problems. It was shown that COHDA is inherently adaptive, and exhibits anytime behavior. We applied the heuristic to a problem from the smart grid domain, and performed a thorough evaluation under varying conditions. For this, we implemented an asynchronous multi-agent system with full control over the communication backend. Regarding our example application, it could be shown that the heuristic exhibits convergence and termination, and is robust against unsteady communication networks as well as different network topologies. The run-time of COHDA, in terms of simulation steps, rises linearly with increasing population sizes. Yet it is unaffected by the size of local search spaces, so we conclude that the heuristic is sufficiently scalable. However, there is a trade-off between the number of simulation steps until termination, and the number of exchanged messages. This trade-off can be adjusted through the density of the communication network (i.e., the average size of the neighborhoods). The evaluation of a bi-objective scenario showed the ability of the heuristic to optimize local penalties as well as a global objective in parallel.

In the present form, COHDA needs a central operator that is able to detect the termination of the process (and thus has a global view on the system). But the actual optimization process is still performed in a truly decentralized manner! A fully decentralized variant of COHDA, however, could be realized by including a distributed termination detection algorithm.

Acknowledgments. Due to the vast amounts of simulations needed, all experiments have been conducted on HERO, a multi-purpose cluster installed at the University of Oldenburg, Germany. We would like to thank the maintenance team from HERO for their valuable service. We also thank Ontje Lünsdorf for providing the asynchronous message passing framework used in our simulation environment, and Jörg Bremer for providing the CHP simulation model.

References

1. Anders, G., Hinrichs, C., Siefert, F., Behrmann, P., Reif, W., Sonnenschein, M.: On the influence of inter-agent variation on multi-agent algorithms solving a dynamic task allocation problem under uncertainty. In: Sixth IEEE International Conference on Self-Adaptive and Self-Organizing Systems (SASO 2012), pp. 29–38. IEEE Computer Society, Lyon (2012)
2. Bernon, C., Chevrier, V., Hilaire, V., Marrow, P.: Applications of self-organising multi-agent systems: an initial framework for comparison. Informatica **30**(1), 73–82 (2006)
3. Bremer, J., Sonnenschein, M.: A Distributed greedy algorithm for constraint-based scheduling of energy resources. In: SEN-MAS'2012 Workshop, Proceedingsof the Federated Conference on Computer Science and Information Systems, pp. 1285–1292, Wrocław, Poland (2012)
4. Chapman, A.C., Rogers, A., Jennings, N.R., Leslie, D.S.: A unifying framework for iterative approximate best-response algorithms for distributed constraint optimization problems. Knowl. Eng. Rev. **26**(04), 411–444 (2011)
5. Gershenson, C.: Design and Control of Self-organizing Systems. Ph.D. Thesis, Vrije Universiteit Brussel (2007)
6. Hinrichs, C., Lehnhoff, S., Sonnenschein, M.: A decentralized heuristic for multiple-choice combinatorial optimization problems. In: Helber, S., et al. (eds.) Operations Research Proceedings 2012, pp. 297–302. Springer, Heidelberg (2014)
7. Hinrichs, C., Lehnhoff, S., Sonnenschein, M.: Paving the Royal road for complex systems: on the influence of memory on adaptivity. In: Pelster, A., Wunner, G. (eds.) International Symposium Selforganization in Complex Systems: The Past, Present, and Future of Synergetics. Springer (2013) (in press)

8. Hinrichs, C., Sonnenschein, M., Lehnhoff, S.: Evaluation of a self-organizing heuristic for interdependent distributed search spaces. In: Filipe, J., Fred, A.L.N. (eds.) International Conference on Agents and Artificial Intelligence (ICAART 2013), vol. 1 - Agents, pp. 25–34. SciTePress (2013)
9. Hölldobler, B., Wilson, E.O.: The Ants. Belknap Press of Harvard University Press, Cambridge (1990)
10. Jones, J.C., Myerscough, M.R., Graham, S., Oldroyd, B.P.: Honey Bee Nest Thermoregulation: Diversity Promotes Stability. Science (New York, N.Y.) **305**(5682), 402–404 (2004)
11. Jordan, U., Vajen, K.: Influence of the DHW load profile on the fractional energy savings: A case study of a solar combi-system with TRNSYS simulations. Solar Energy **69**, 197–208 (2001)
12. Kaddoum, E.: Optimization under Constraints of Distributed Complex Problems using Cooperative Self-Organization. Ph.D. Thesis, Université de Toulouse (2011)
13. Kroeker, K.L.: Biology-inspired networking. Commun. ACM **54**(6), 11 (2011)
14. Li, J., Poulton, G., James, G.: Coordination of distributed energy resource agents. Appl. Artif. Intell. **24**(5), 351–380 (2010)
15. Lust, T., Teghem, J.: The multiobjective multidimensional knapsack problem: a survey and a new approach. Int. Trans. Oper. Res. **19**(4), 495–520 (2012)
16. Modi, P., Shen, W., Tambe, M., Yokoo, M.: ADOPT: Asynchronous distributed constraint optimization with quality guarantees. Artif. Intell. **161**(1–2), 149–180 (2005)
17. Nieße, A., Lehnhoff, S., Tröschel, M., Uslar, M., Wissing, C., Appelrath, H.J., Sonnenschein, M.: Market-based self-organized provision of active power and ancillary services: An agent-based approach for smart distribution grids. Complex. Eng. (COMPENG) **2012**, 1–5 (2012)
18. Penya, Y.: Optimal allocation and scheduling of demand in deregulated energy markets. Ph.D. Thesis, Vienna University of Technology (2006)
19. Pournaras, E.: Multi-level Reconfigurable Self-organization in Overlay Services. Ph.D. Thesis, Technische Universiteit Delft (2013)
20. Pournaras, E., Warnier, M., Brazier, F.M.: Local agent-based self-stabilisation in global resource utilisation. Int. J. Autonomic Comput. **1**(4), 350 (2010)
21. Prehofer, C., Bettstetter, C.: Self-organization in communication networks: principles and design paradigms. IEEE Commun. Mag. **43**(7), 78–85 (2005). http://ieeexplore.ieee.org/lpdocs/epic03/wrapper.htm?arnumber=1470824
22. Ramchurn, S.D., Vytelingum, P., Rogers, A., Jennings, N.R.: Putting the"Smarts" into the smart grid: A grand challenge for artificial intelligence. Commun. ACM **55**(4), 86 (2012)
23. Reynolds, C.W.: Flocks, herds and schools: A distributed behavioral model. SIGGRAPH Comput. Graph. **21**(4), 25–34 (1987)
24. Serugendo, G., Gleizes, M.P., Karageorgos, A.: Self-organisation in multi-agent systems. Knowl. Eng. Rev. **20**(2), 65–189 (2005)
25. Strogatz, S.H.: Exploring complex networks. Nature **410**(March), 268–276 (2001)
26. Tero, A., Takagi, S., Saigusa, T., Ito, K., Bebber, D.P., Fricker, M.D., Yumiki, K., Kobayashi, R., Nakagaki, T.: Rules for biologically inspired adaptive network design. Science (New York, N.Y.) **327**(5964), 439–442 (2010)

Rough Terrain Motion Planning for Actuated, Tracked Robots

Michael Brunner(✉), Bernd Brüggemann, and Dirk Schulz

Fraunhofer Institute for Communication,
Information Processing and Ergonomics FKIE, Wachtberg, Germany
{michael.brunner,bernd.brueggemann,dirk.schulz}@fkie.fraunhofer.de

Abstract. Traversing challenging structures like boulders, rubble, stairs and steps, mobile robots need a special level of mobility. Robots with reconfigurable chassis are able to alter their configuration to overcome such structures.

This paper presents a two-stage motion planning scheme for reconfigurable robots in rough terrain. First, we consider the robot's operating limits rather than the complete states to quickly find an initial path in a low dimensional space. Second, we identify path segments which lead through rough areas of the environment and refine those segments using the entire robot state including the actuator configurations. We present a roadmap and a RRT* method to perform the path refinement.

Our algorithm does not rely on any detailed structure/terrain categorization or on any predefined motion sequences. Hence, our planner can be applied to urban structures, like stairs, as well as rough unstructured environments.

Keywords: Mobile robot · Motion planning · Obstacle · Rough terrain · Reconfigurable chassis · Sampling-based · RRT*

1 Introduction

Many structures which are regularly encountered in robotic tasks are perceived as obstacles for fixed-chassis robots. Steps and stairs are usually untraversable obstacles in urban environments; debris, rubble, rocks or steep inclinations in unstructured outdoor environments are often impossible to traverse with normal fixed-chassis systems. Therefore, these structures and objects have to be circumvented if possible.

Using articulated actuators robots with reconfigurable chassis can change their configuration to improve traction and stability or to lift themselves over edges. This provides those systems with an increased mobility compared to fixed-chassis robots and enables them to overcome a wide variety of environments. Fixed-chassis robots are most often unable to traverse the same kind of environments because their ability to negotiate obstacles is limited due to their construction. The challenges they can overcome are restricted by the diameter

J. Filipe and A. Fred (Eds.): ICAART 2013, CCIS 449, pp. 40–61, 2014.
DOI: 10.1007/978-3-662-44440-5_3

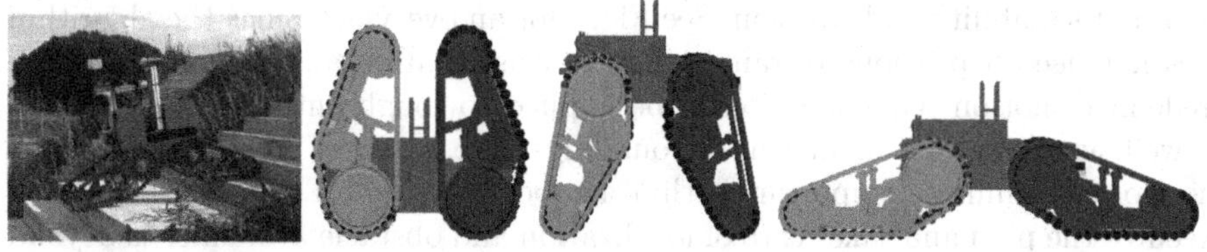

Fig. 1. The Telerob Telemax is 65 cm long, 40 cm wide and weighs about 70 kg. It has 4 tracks which can be rotated. Extended, the robot's length is about 120 cm. The robot is skid-steered and drives up to 1.2 m/s. Configurations are: (left) folded (actuators at −90°), (middle) extended (actuators at 80°) and (right) maximal ground contact (actuators at 21°).

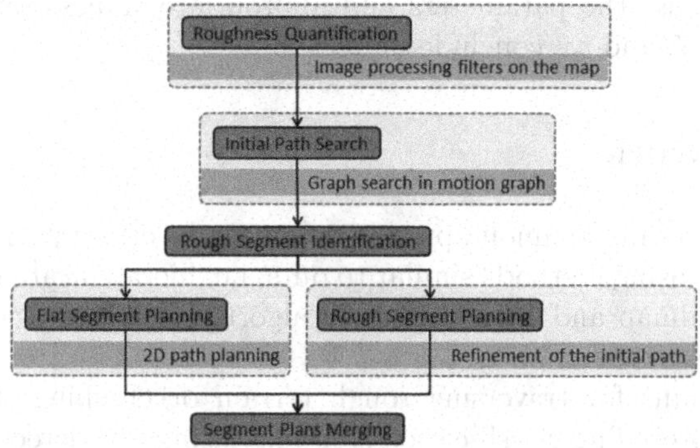

Fig. 2. Method overview: Using filters from image processing we perform a roughness quantification of the map. The initial path is found within a regular grid performing a graph search. Afterwards the rough segments are identified. For flat segments we apply a 2D planning scheme; rough segments are refined by a second planning step using an A*-search or a RRT*-search. Finally the segment plans are merged to provide the final path.

of their wheels or their track heights and to some extend to their centers of mass. The mobility of actuated systems is dominated by the number, length and agility of their actuators.

Controlling a mobile robot in rough terrain and steering it through difficult situations is a challenging task even for a trained operator. The operator must consider many different aspects to guarantee the safety of the system in such environments. Among those aspects are the robot's stability as tipping over becomes increasingly more likely, the inertia and momentum must be kept in mind when operating a system close to its limits, and finally, the system may react differently to the same commands because the contacts with the ground can change often in rough terrain.

In this paper, we present a hierarchical approach to motion planning for reconfigurable robots like the Packbot or the Telemax (Fig. 1). First, we generate an approximate solution and refine it in a subsequent phase. The refinement concentrates on path segments in rough areas and accounts for the actuators and the robot's stability and traction. See Fig. 2 for an overview. Since the algorithm does not need a previous terrain/structure classification and does not use any predefined motion sequences, it can be applied to rough outdoor environments as well as structures in urban surroundings. We consider our method to be the global planning component within a robotic system. The controller which executes the plan and takes care of localization and obstacle avoidance is beyond the scope of this work.

The remainder of this paper is organized as follows: Sect. 2 names related work in this area of research. Section 3 gives a short overview of our method and names key differences to related works. In Sect. 4 we introduce the roughness quantification. Section 5 describes the hierarchical planning scheme including the roadmap planner (A*) and the sampling-based planner (RRT*) (Sect. 5.3). In Sect. 6 we discuss the parameters and appropriate values. Experiments are provided in Sect. 7, and we conclude in Sect. 8.

2 Related Work

This section focuses on common approaches to rough terrain path planning and on previous work using methods similar to ours, i.e. hierarchical methods, methods applying roadmap and sampling-based algorithms to rough terrain motion planning for tracked robots.

Many algorithms for traversing rough terrain or climbing structures, like stairs, involve a preceding classification step (e.g. using line detection to identify stairs). This information is used to steer the system during climbing, fixing its heading to the gradient of the staircase [1,2]. In [3] a two dimensional A*-search on behavior maps is used to find paths in rough environments for a tracked robot, similar to our model. The path represents a sequence of predefined skills encoded in the behavior maps. Fuzzy rules and Markov random fields are used to classify the environment and facilitate skill selection. A comprehensive approach to traverse rough outdoor terrain as well as stairs is presented in [4]. The framework includes a mapping component, a terrain classification and a two-phase planning algorithm. A high-level planner samples a transition graph across different terrain types and provides an initial path. In the second phase specialized terrain sub-planners refine the path and return gait primitives for a RHex robot (e.g. stair-climbing gait primitives). The approaches above are limited to the set of terrain types or structures which are imposed by their classification scheme or to the set of motion sequences. On the contrary, our algorithm does not rely on such a terrain/structure classification or on a set of motion sequences. Hence, it can be applied to a broader range of different environments.

We utilize a two-phase planning method which produces an initial approximate solution followed by a refinement of the initial result. As in [4], other works also use a similar approach. Kalakrishnan and colleagues introduced a controller for fast quadruped locomotion over rough terrain [5]. The controller decomposes the controlling task into several sub-tasks; first, they generate a terrain reward map using a learned foothold ranking function and then produce an approximate path. In subsequent steps this first solution is improved to ensure kinematic reachability and a smooth and collision-free trajectory. Like our method, this is a multi-phase algorithm which requires a map and implements a terrain analysis. However, our terrain analysis relies on a roughness quantification similar to [6] instead of a ranking function of the actuator contacts. On the contrary, the authors of [5] propose a reactive controller to traverse rough terrain rather than a planning algorithm. Also the terrain interaction of tracked robots is quite distinct compared to the interaction of their legged robot.

Further, path refinement can also be achieved by path optimizing methods. CHOMP [7] is an optimization method for continuous trajectories using covariant gradient descent. It can optimize a path over a variety of criteria. Since it is applicable to unfeasible paths, it can be used as a standalone motion planner. STOMP [8] is a stochastic path optimizer using a path integral approach which does not require any gradient information like CHOMP. Therefore, it can overcome local minima and more general costs are applicable. The major drawback of both methods is the limitation to trajectories of a predefined fixed length. This makes them inapplicable for the path refinement within a certain proximity of the initial path.

In this work we present a roadmap algorithm for rough terrain path planning. Roadmap methods are commonly applied to this problem in the literature. An Anytime A*-search is used to find paths in a multi-resolution 4D state lattice for indoor environments [9]. The resolution of the lattice is adjusted with respect to terrain or task characteristics (e.g. narrow passages and goal proximity). The online navigation utilizes a precomputation step which determines paths for constrained areas. In [10] the Fast Marching Method (FMM), a breadth-first search algorithm, is used on a 3D lattice to plan stable paths for actively reconfigurable robots. The system's stability guides the search on a triangular mesh of the environment. The actuators of the Packbot robot used in this research are actively controlled like the actuators of our Telemax platform.

The authors of [11] present an approach to motion planning on rough terrain for a wheeled robot with passive suspension using an A*-search on a discretized configuration space with heuristics to limit the search space. The algorithm considers the robot's stability, mechanical limits, collisions with the ground, and uncertainties on the terrain model and the robot position. While in [11] they also use a graph-search and measure the robot's stability, their algorithm does not have to account for actuators due to the robot's passive suspension. In contrast, we must include the actively controlled actuators during planning.

Magid et al. developed a rough terrain planning algorithm for a tracked robot with four actively controlled crawlers [12]. They use a graph-search to find motion sequences in a discretizied state space, which also allows for motions of controlled balance-losing (e.g. insignificant falls from small edges). However, rather than autonomous navigation their application is to reduce the burden on operators of search and rescue missions by proposing paths through rough terrain. Unlike us, they categorize the states to distinguish between different transition types and consider controlled balance-losing states. However, they also plan on a discrete state space and use a robot with actively controlled crawlers, similar to our model.

Sampling-based methods have also been used to find paths through rough environments. Reference [13] presents a RRT-based algorithm which finds routes of low mechanical work following valleys and saddle points in continuous cost spaces. Their method also includes a mechanism based on stochastic optimization to filter irrelevant configurations and to control the exploration behavior. In [14] a RRT variant is employed for kinematic path planning for a LittleDog robot. The authors bias the search in the task space and use motion primitives to speed up planning. Reference [15] uses different terrain parameters to guide the RRT expansions and iteratively increases its roughness tolerance if no solution is found.

3 Overview and Discriminators

We start with a short overview of our algorithm. We employ a hierarchical algorithm for motion planning of actively reconfigurable robots in rough environments. Although we developed our algorithm for a tracked robot model, with minor changes it is usable for other articulated robot models with similar locomotion (e.g. wheeled platforms). Given a map we compute the roughness and slopes of the environment (Sect. 4). In the preliminary planning phase we build a motion graph according to the robot's operating limits and perform a graph-search to find an initial path (Sect. 5.1). During the detailed motion planning step we refine the initial path in rough areas only. To this end, we first identify the path segments leading through rough terrain. In flat areas we do not perform a detailed planning and apply default configurations instead. On one side, the roadmap planner constructs a state graph considering the actuators for a tube-like area around each rough path segment. Using a graph-search we find sequences of robot states including the actuators. On the other side, the sampling-based planner uses a focused sampling procedure and searches in a continuous state space for an optimal solution (Sect. 5.3). Consult Fig. 2 for a scheme of our algorithm.

Our algorithm applies to tracked reconfigurable robots like ours (see Fig. 1), but not to systems with legged locomotion since the robot-terrain interactions are very distinct. However, parts may be used across different locomotion models, e.g. the roughness quantification and some of the metrics. Further, looking at a complete robot system, we consider our method to be the global planning component which provides a plan. It must be followed by a feedback controller which takes care of the plan execution using sensor data for localization and obstacle avoidance in potentially dynamic environments. Such a controller is beyond the scope of this paper.

In the following we state how our approach differs from other approaches. First, we distinguish between flat and rough regions, but do not rely on a previous detailed structure/terrain classification or on motion sequences a priori designed to overcome specific challenges. Therefore, we are not limited to a previously defined set of terrain classes, a set of structures reliably identifiable with the robot's sensors or a set of motion sequences. However, we approximate the terrain through a least-squares plane (similar to [16]), which works reasonably well on generally continuous surfaces, but not on discontinuous environments. Nevertheless, our algorithm can be applied to traverse rough outdoor environments as well as to overcome challenging structures in urban surroundings.

Second, rather than taking the entire preliminary path to guide the second detailed motion planning, we solely consider path segments which lead through rough areas. Since a detailed motion planning is not necessary for path segments on flat regions, planning can be significantly simplified. Thus, we are able to reduce planning time.

Further, we use simpler robot and terrain models compared to planetary rover path planning approaches. They often utilize detailed dynamic and mechanic models to capture the robot-terrain interaction in depth [17]. Such models are not always obtained easily and, thus, not necessarily available for a specific robot model.

4 Map and Terrain Roughness

Whether a given structure is traversable or not cannot be determined easily. In 2D navigation this is usually addressed with a simple threshold on the height differences; everything above this threshold is untraversable. For rough terrain and challenging structures this question becomes very hard to answer. While for 2D navigation a 2D laser range finder is sufficient to gather the necessary information about the surroundings, even a 3D sensor is often not enough to navigate through rough environments due to the still limited sensor coverage.

There are several reasons why it seems it is often extremely difficult to reliably decide on the traversability of challenging structures or rough terrain based on local sensor information solely. First, the dimensions of rough areas or challenging structures usually exceed the sensor range; second, some sections of the environment are often occluded; third, the limiting narrow view of sensors mounted on a mobile robot makes it difficult to get a sufficient overview; finally, while traversing rough terrain, the robot's state often orients the sensors such that they are unable to cover the environment. For example, consider a flight of stairs; the very narrow view makes it hard to recognize the stairs especially all the way to the top. While on the stairs and close to the top the sensors cover very little of the ground.

Additionally, the robotic system is exposed to unnecessary risk if it starts to traverse an area which turns out to be ultimately untraversable. A map allows to decide whether an area is likely to be traversable and to assess the risk of a path and whether driving through a hazardous area is worth the risk or circumventing the region is more reasonable.

On the other side, the validity of the planning is closely related to the level of detail of the map. Large detailed maps are rarely available. This may be solved by a coarse map with detailed patches for rough regions or variable resolution maps Araujo2002. For our research, we use a map of the environment to avoid

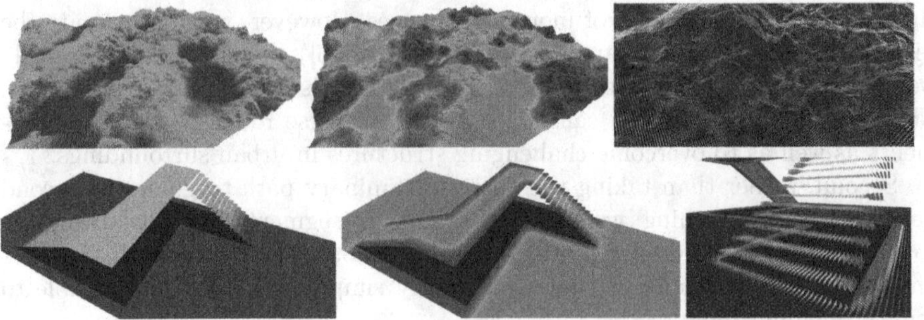

Fig. 3. Two maps (left), the roughness (middle) and the slopes (right). The risk value associated with a region is based on the height differences in this area. The gradients represent the direction and magnitude of the environmental slopes. The colors indicate the degree of roughness/inclination, ranging from green for flat regions/low inclinations over yellow to red, very rough areas/high inclinations (Color figure online).

the complex perceptual task of 3D navigation in rough terrain. This simplifies the perceptual component and allows us to focus on the motion planning aspect of this problem [5].

4.1 Roughness

In our approach we use a heightmap to represent the environment because it is simple to use and sufficient for our application. In order to assess the difficulty of a position within the map, we use techniques from image processing to compute the roughness of the terrain. First, we apply a maximum filter with a window $w_{x,y}$ of size $x \times y$ to the direct height differences of neighboring cells. A distortion of the range of values can be prevented by a threshold h_{max} which conveniently can be set to the robot's maximal traversable height. The threshold is also used to scale the values to $[0, 1]$. Subsequently, we apply a two dimensional Gaussian blur to smooth the transitions. The maximum filter prevents isolated peaks to be smoothed by the Gaussian filter. Figure 3 shows an example of the roughness quantification.

4.2 Gradients

As the roughness considers the local height differences between neighboring cells, it cannot account for the inclination of a greater area. An area cannot be traversed if a cliff is too high or if the inclination is too steep. Therefore, the inclination serves as a second criterion to determine the overall roughness of an area. To compute the gradients at a position within the map, we use the Sobel operator with a large base of the same size as the previous filters, i.e. $x \times y$. The values are also normalized to $[0, 1]$ using the maximal traversable slope of the given robot model.

Using an appropriate kernel size allows us to virtually inflate hazardous areas. This is commonly done in 2D navigation to keep the robot away from obstacles.

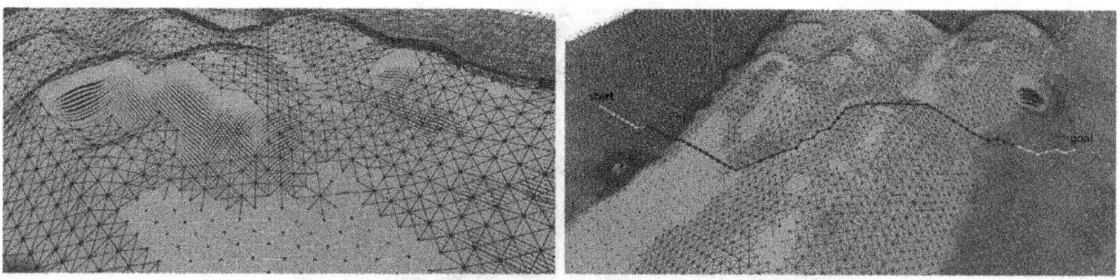

Fig. 4. Left: The motion graph encodes the traversability of the terrain. Flatter areas are white and rougher areas are grey. Right: The initial path split into segments. Path segments through flat regions are yellow; segments through rough regions are purple (Color figure online).

In contrast, very rough areas are avoided by the robot, but if required, will not prohibit traversal. Another benefit is the simple and highly parallelizable computation.

The overall roughness quantification consists of the roughness r inferred from the height difference and the slope s.

$$R = \frac{r + s}{2}. \tag{1}$$

The value of the roughness quantification is used in both the initial path search and the detailed motion planning to adjust the planning according to the difficulty of the environment.

5 Motion Planning Algorithm

Driving with actively reconfigurable robots on rough terrain introduces a large planning space. Additionally, aspects of the robot state, like the stability, are not naturally satisfied and must be tested. The robot's actuators must be incorporated into the planning process, and the quality of the path must be judged not only by its length but also by the robot's stability and traction as well as the time required for translation, rotation and for actuator movements. First, we employ a initial path search to quickly find an environment-driven path to the goal. Subsequently, the path is used to focus the search of the detailed planning. This phase determines the final path consisting of the robot configurations including the actuators.

5.1 Initial Path Search

The initial path search utilizes the previously discussed roughness quantification to force the robot to avoid hazardous areas and to prefer less risky routes. In flat regions the consideration of the complete state is not necessary, whereas it is essential in rough regions to increase the robot's safety and ensure successful traversal. At the beginning we do not know through which parts of the

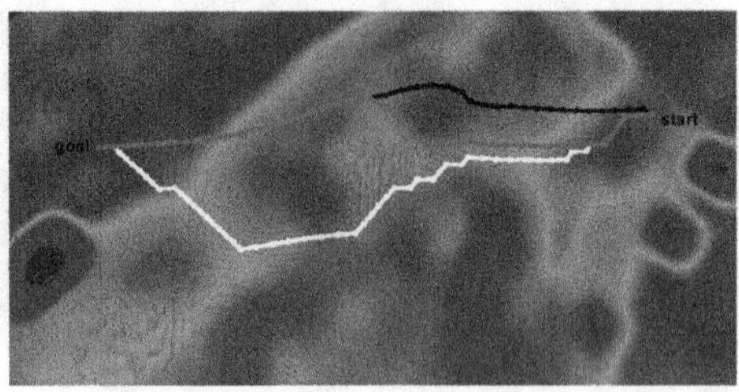

Fig. 5. Influence of the safety weight on the initial path search. The image shows three paths with different safety weights w_1. The black path is obtained with $w_1 = 0.0$, the blue path with $w_1 = 0.75$ and the white path with $w_1 = 1.0$. The map is colored according to the risk values (Color figure online).

environment the path will lead and if considering the complete state is really necessary. Therefore, we use the utmost operating limits of the mobile system setting the actuators aside. The maximal traversable height and slope of the robot constitute the operating limits. This way we obtain the least restrictive limit.

We build a motion graph (Fig. 4) which represents the ability of the mobile robot to traverse the environment. The motion graph is based on the operating limits of the robot as discussed before. The transition costs are given by the time t required to traverse a graph edge e. Hereby, we reduce the permissible velocity according to the terrain roughness:

$$t = \frac{d}{\max\left(v_{\min}, (1 - w_1 \cdot R) \cdot v_{\max}\right)}, \tag{2}$$

where d is the length of edge e and R the maximal value of the roughness quantification of the vertices of e. $v_{\min}$ and $v_{\max}$ are the minimal velocity the robot should drive in very rough areas and the robot's maximal velocity, respectively. A safety weight w_1 allows the adjustment of the importance of safety. Low safety weights diminish the influence of the risk, hence lead to possibly shorter but riskier paths. On the contrary, high values increasingly force the robot to take low risk paths. With those edge weights we find a path performing a usual Dijkstra-search. We start the search at the goal point to facilitate fast replanning in case of deviation from the plan (see Fig. 4).

The safety weight of the initial path search determines the major direction of the path as subsequent route corrections are limited to the focus on the rough path segments. We performed several planning queries with different safety weights keeping start and goal location the same (Fig. 5). We show three paths determined with different weights w_1. Disregarding safety completely ($w_1 = 0.0$) leads to a straight path within the motion graph. Increasing the value to 0.75 changes the beginning of the path to avoid riskier areas and climb the hill directly with the inclination. This reduces the time spend in those regions and increases the safety by reducing the system's roll angle. The weight $w_1 = 1.0$ forces the path to follow the dig in the middle of the hill and to circumvent the high risk areas. Which weight to choose best for a given planning query cannot be answered generally for all environments; it depends on the environment, its roughness and its composition of rough areas.

5.2 Identification of Rough Path Segments

The planning problem can be considerably simplified in flat areas. Then it basically becomes a 2D navigation problem as the actuators are not required to aid the systems' stability. Therefore, the planning time can be reduced by avoiding unnecessary planning in a high-dimensional space for easily accessible parts of the environment. On the other hand, rough areas require a detailed planning of the robot's configurations including the actuators and the validation of the robot's safety to ensure successful traversal.

While constructing the motion graph, we distinguish between areas of moderate roughness and steepness, and regions of higher roughness and challenging steepness. See the left image of Fig. 4 for an example. We use this distinction in the second planning phase to split up the initial path into easy and hard segments and to determine whether a detailed planning of the robot motions is necessary. This allows us to handle larger planning queries as we focus on a subset of the state space. Also, this significantly reduces the planning time.

The size of the state graph in the second planning phase depends on the chosen discretization, the path focus and the length of the rough segments. If we plan without focusing the second search on the initial path, the graph size depends on the roughness and the distance to the goal. Depending on these factors, our roadmap method (Sect. 5.3) will run out of memory before returning a valid path. The path bias towards the rough segments of the initial path, used by the sampling-based method (Sect. 5.3), allows us to find better solutions within fewer iterations.

5.3 Detailed Motion Planning

Rough terrain is more challenging and exposes the mobile robot to a greater risk than flat environments. Therefore, we have to refine the initial path in rough areas using the complete robot states. The state of a reconfigurable robot may look like

$$(x, y, z, \theta, \psi, \phi, a_1, \ldots, a_n),$$

where the first part describes the 6D pose of the robot. a_i are the control values of n actuators. Reducing the state to the controllable part leads to

$$(x, y, \theta, a_1, \ldots, a_n).$$

The controllable parts still result in a large intractable search space. Therefore, we use the initial path to focus the search of the second planning phase. First, we split the path into segments leading through flat areas with low inclinations and segments through rough regions with higher slopes (see the right image of Fig. 4). For flat segments the stability of the robot system can be safely assumed as done in 2D navigation. Further, any robot configuration may be applied with little or no risk. This way, we avoid unnecessary planning in a high dimensional space for easily accessible parts of the environment and reduce planning time. However, rough regions require an additional planning of the robot's actuators to ensure safety and task completion.

The detailed motion planning accounts for the environmental risk, the system's stability and its traction, and for the time consumed by translation, rotation and actuator movements. Since the robot's speed is very low when traversing hazardous areas, we put forces and dynamic stability aside. To quantify the stability and the traction we approximate the robot's footprint by the best fitting plane [16]. This limits the current approach to mainly continuous environments (e.g. hills, stairs, ramps).

Cost Function. The hierarchical approach allows us to use two different cost functions for the two planning phases. The cost function of the detailed planning step is more comprehensive compared to the cost function of the initial path search. It considers the robot's safety c_{safety} and an execution time c_{time}.

$$c = w_2 \cdot c_{\text{safety}} + (1 - w_2) \cdot \xi \cdot c_{\text{time}} \tag{3}$$

The normalization factor ξ brings the safety cost and the time cost to the same range of values. The safety weight w_2 allows to control the trade-off between safety and time. More safety is gained by adjusting the actuators to the environment; however, this requires more time to move the actuators. This cost function is only applied in rough regions and may not be applicable in flat areas. In flat areas actuator movements are generally unnecessary and solely introduce costs, and thus should not be favored.

System Safety. The safety of the system is measured by several factors. The roughness quantification, the robot's stability and an estimate of the traction contribute to the safety value. The safety cost c_{safety} for moving from state x_i to state x_j is given by

$$c_{\text{safety}}(i,j) = \frac{R_{ij} + \frac{1}{2}(S_{ij} + T_{ij})}{2}, \tag{4}$$

where $R_{ij} = \max\{R_i, R_j\}$ is the maximal value of the roughness quantification, $S_{ij} = \max\{S_i, S_j\}$ the maximal stability cost and $T_{ij} = \max\{T_i, T_j\}$ the maximal traction cost of the involved states.

Stability. The Normalized Energy Stability Margin (NESM) [19] is used to assess the stability of the robotic system. In contrast to the commonly used projection of the center of mass onto the supporting polygon, the NESM considers the actual position of the center of mass and directly provides a notion of quality. The NESM basically indicates the amount of energy required to tip the robot over the "weakest" edge of the supporting polygon. To provide an accurate estimate of the center of mass and to account for the varying weight distributions of different configurations, we compute the distributed center of mass.

We touch the basics of the Normalized Energy Stability Margin just very briefly; a more detailed discussion is given in [19]. Let V be the vector from the border to the center of mass. Θ depicts the angle between V and the vertical plane, and ψ the inclination of the rotation axis, i.e. the edge of the supporting polygon. Then the energy stability level for an edge of the supporting polygon is given by

$$h = |V|(1 - cos(\Theta)) \cdot cos(\psi). \tag{5}$$

The NESM is defined as the minimum over the energy levels h_i of all edges, $s = min_i(h_i)$. The stability cost of a robot state x is then given through

$$S = 1 - \xi_s \cdot s(x), \tag{6}$$

where $\xi_s = \frac{1}{s_{max}}$ is a normalization term to scale the cost to $[0, 1]$. ξ_s is given by the most stable configuration on flat ground.

Traction Estimate. A sufficient traction is necessary to traverse rough terrain and challenging structures. However, we do not want to rely on any terrain properties because such information is usually unavailable and hard to estimate with sufficient accuracy. Therefore, we use the actuators' ground contact as an indicator of the traction since the friction between to objects generally increases with the size of the contact area between them. The traction cost T of a state x is given by the average over the actuators' angles to the surface.

$$T = \xi_t \cdot \frac{1}{n} \sum_{k=1}^{n} \psi(a_k), \tag{7}$$

where $\psi(a_k)$ provides the angle to the surface for actuator a_k. $\xi_t = \frac{1}{\pi/2}$ normalizes the cost to $[0, 1]$. The smaller the angle, the greater the estimated traction and the safer the state x in terms of traction.

Execution Time. The time cost includes the time required for translation t_v, rotation t_ω and for actuator movements t_a. We use a triangle inequality to favor simultaneous execution.

$$c_{\text{time}} = \frac{t_v^2 + t_\omega^2 + t_a^2}{t_v + t_\omega + t_a} \tag{8}$$

Translation. To measure the time required for translation, we use the same function as for the initial path search.

$$t_v = t_v(i, j) = \frac{d_{ij}}{\max\left(v_{min}, (1 - w_2 \cdot R_{i,j}) \cdot v_{max}\right)}, \tag{9}$$

where d_{ij} is the distance between x_i and x_j, and v_{min} and v_{max} are the minimal and maximal forward velocity, respectively.

Rotation. The physically possible rotational velocity is influenced by the robot's ground contact. If the actuators are all flat on the ground, the friction will be quite high and the engines must overpower these forces before the robot starts to rotate. We approximated a function $\omega(\cdot)$ which provides the maximal rotational velocity given the actuator configuration. Using this information the time required for turning from state x_i to state x_j is given by

$$t_\omega = t_\omega(i,j) = \frac{|\theta_i - \theta_j|}{\frac{1}{2}(\omega(a_i) + \omega(a_j))}, \tag{10}$$

where θ_i and θ_j are the orientations of the two states and a_i and a_j are the actuator configurations.

Actuators. The cost to move the actuators from one configuration to another is defined through the time required to do so.

$$t_a = t_a(i,j) = \max_k \left(\frac{|a_{i,k} - a_{j,k}|}{v_k} \right), \tag{11}$$

where $a_{i,k}$ and $a_{j,k}$ are the values of the kth actuator of the two states. v_k is the velocity of the kth actuator.

The safety weight of the second planning phase mainly influences the choice of actuator configurations; higher values will result in safer states at each path position. To achieve a common basis for the comparison, we selected an initial path, held it constant for all second phase planning queries and shrunk the focus of the second planning phase to solely include the initial path (Fig. 6 top-left). Hence, we prevented impacts of different initial paths and of later route corrections during the second planning phase. This also fixes the number of translations and rotations leaving only the actuator configurations to be determined.

The top-right image of Fig. 6 shows the number of actuator changes within a plan for different safety weights. In this setting the actuators are the only means to increase the safety of the system. With increasing safety weights the number of actuator changes also increases. Decreasing values in between are explained by longer sequences of the same configurations.

The safety cost of the paths is depicted in the bottom-left image of Fig. 6. Raising the safety weight leads to more actuator adjustments in order to reach better suited robot states in every position. Ultimately, this increases the total safety (reduced costs) of the final path.

Similar, the bottom-right image of Fig. 6 displays the execution time of the paths using different safety weights. The higher number of state corrections through actuator adjustments results in a higher execution time comprising the time required for the adjustments. The execution time almost triples from about 20 s at $w = 0.0$ to roughly 55 s at $w = 1.0$. The execution time still grows even though the actuator changes decrease in between. This is caused by lower rotational velocities of more stable configurations with higher traction. The rotational velocity of reconfigurable robots depends on its actuator configuration. For example, consider the Telemax robot. If the flippers are completely stretched, the robot will be 120 cm long with maximal ground contact. In this configuration rotation takes considerably longer than with all flippers folded.

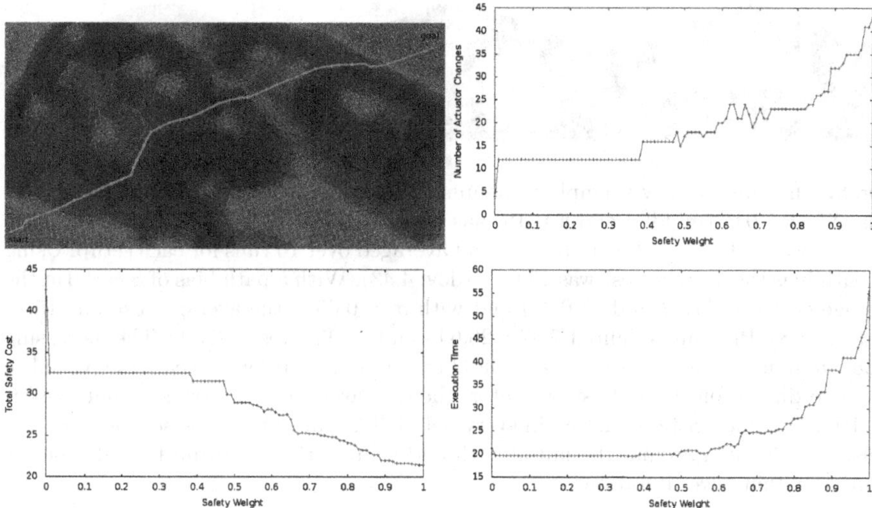

Fig. 6. Influence of the safety weight on the detailed motion planning: The path used for evaluation is shown in the top-left corner. We fixed the initial path and reduced the further path corrections to exactly the initial path, leaving only the actuator configurations mutable. The curves show the safety costs and the execution time (seconds) of the final state space paths for different weights. As only the actuator configurations are mutable, we displayed the number of configuration changes in the top-right image. The decrease in actuator changes in between is due to sequences of the same actuator configuration. The increasing execution time for those values of w_2 are caused by higher rotation times in stable and high traction configurations.

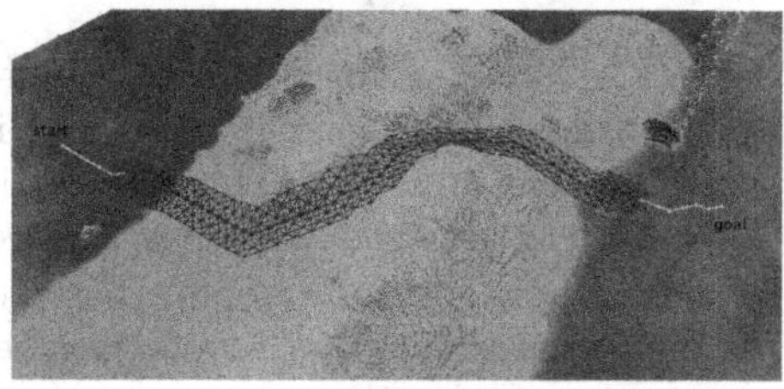

Fig. 7. A tube around a rough path segment (blue). The tube is used to focus the search of the second planning step (Color figure online).

Ultimately, the planning of the actuator positions is essential to increase the safety of the robotic system during rough terrain traversal. This leads to a significant increase of the path's execution time due to the time needed for the actuator adjustments and the increased duration of rotational maneuvers.

Roadmap Planner. The roadmap planner uses an A*-search on a graph of the discretized state space X_s. We focus the state space on tube-like areas around rough path segments (Fig. 7) and perform the refinement within these boundaries. This concentrates the search on the promising region and makes it feasible.

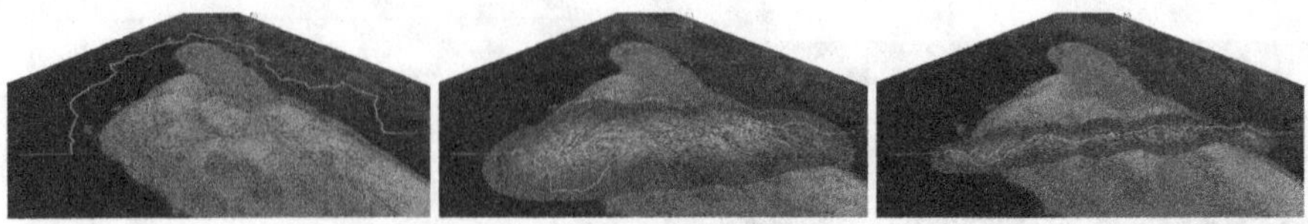

Fig. 8. The images show exemplary planning queries using no path bias (left), a path bias of $\sigma = 2.0\,\mathrm{m}$ (middle) and a path bias of $\sigma = 0.65\,\mathrm{m}$ (right). The final path costs were determined after 10 000 iterations and averaged over 10 runs for each setup. Using no path bias the average cost was 29.69 (stdev: 4.43). With a path bias of $\sigma = 2.0\,\mathrm{m}$ the average cost was 17.02 (stdev: 0.36) and with $\sigma = 0.65\,\mathrm{m}$ the average cost was 15.78 (stdev: 0.28). Planning required 7.87 s, 26.64 s and 65.95 s, respectively. The increasing time requirements are due to a greater number of rewiring options. Because we visualize only two dimensions of a 7D state vector, the displayed planning trees do not exhibit the RRT* characteristic structure in every detail. The path bias increases the sampling density in the area around the initial path and enables the algorithm to find a better solution within fewer iterations.

The state graph $G_s(V_s, E_s)$ models a discrete configuration space X_s including the actuators. The edge weights are defined by the cost function which is described above. To find a path with respect to the entire robot state including the actuators, we perform an A*-search. The heuristic is the time required for the straight-line to the goal with maximal velocity. The A*-search allows us to construct the state graph G_s on demand during the search. The refined path considers the difficulty of the environment, the stability and traction of the system as well as the time required to execute the plan. If several rough path segments exist, the path planning can be parallelized.

RRT*-Planner. The RRT*-planner is an alternative approach to refine the initial path in rough areas of the environment. It uses a modified version of the asymptotically optimal RRT* algorithm [20]. This planner is able to search a continuous state space, hence, can consider more different configurations than the roadmap planner. We describe a position sampling based on the initial path, a sampling heuristic for the actuator values of robots with several independent actuators and the state rejection mechanism.

Path Bias. The initial path search provides an approximate solution. We use this solution to initialize the RRT*-search and to focus the expansion of the algorithm. We sample a position from a normal distribution centered at the initial path. We first determine a position p on the initial path uniformly at random and then sample from a two dimensional normal distribution around p. The standard deviation of the normal distribution determines the level of focus. In our setup we use $\sigma = 0.65\,\mathrm{m}$, i.e. the robot length. Focusing the RRT*-search on the area of the initial path is based on a similar approach in [21]. It reduces the number of iterations required to achieve better solutions compared to a non-biased search. See Fig. 8 for an analysis.

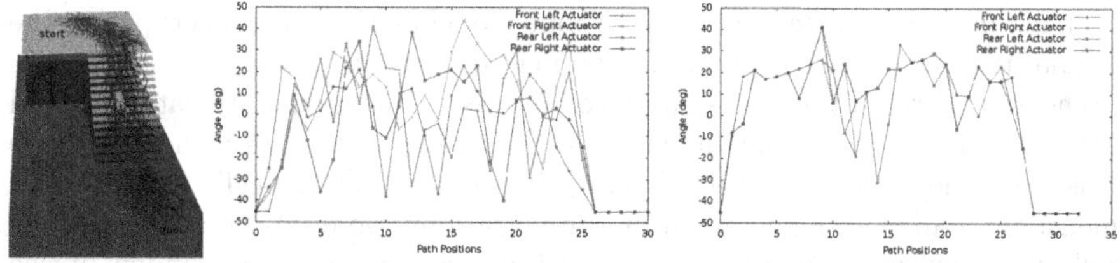

Fig. 9. The left image shows the map with the planning query and an exemplary solution. The plots show the actuator values of a sample solution using no heuristic (middle) and using the two-fold actuator sampling (right). We used the following category probabilities: all actuators equal ($p = 0.20$), front as well as rear actuators equal ($p = 0.65$), left as well as right actuators equal ($p = 0.10$), and all actuators different ($p = 0.05$). We performed 10 queries for each setting. The average cost for the two-fold sampling was 8.13 with a standard deviation of 0.13. The average cost for the non-guided sampling was 9.06 with a standard deviation of 0.17. Planning took about 22.35 s on average for 5000 iterations. The two-fold actuator sampling generates smoother motions and decreases path costs.

Actuator Sampling. When operators control robots with several actuators which can be adjusted independently (for instance the Telemax robot, Fig. 1), they often prefer less complex configurations. For many situations it is not required to treat the actuators differently. Sometimes the front and rear actuators are adjusted differently. In only few situations different controls for the left and right actuators are needed. Configurations which position all actuators in a different way are very rare. To introduce this information into the planning process and to prefer less erratic actuator movements, we bias the sampling through a two-step procedure. We determined a set of categories of actuator configurations and sample a category according to its utility.

The categories for the Telemax robot are: all actuators equal, front as well as rear actuators equal, left as well as right actuators equal, and all actuators different. Each category requires a different number of actuator values: one for the first, two for the second and third, and four values for the last category. We sample the corresponding number of actuator values and construct the final configuration. The two-fold sampling smooths actuator motions and decreases path costs (Fig. 9).

State Rejection. If a new state involves more costs than the current best path, it cannot be part of the final solution. Thus, we reject these states which are guaranteed not to contribute to the optimal solution [21]. This prevents the planning tree from becoming cluttered with obstructive states. It increases efficiency as those states are not considered in neighborhood queries and rewiring steps.

6 Parameter Settings

The purpose of this section is to name the parameters of our method and to give guidelines for appropriate values. First of all, many of the quantities used in our method are determined by the robot model or the general setup, e.g. the maximal traversable height/slope or the maximal velocity.

The kernel size of the filters employed in the roughness quantification should be the diagonal of the robot dimensions. So a cell's roughness value and slope is based on the area of the robot's footprint centered at the cell. As the robot dimensions change with the actuator configurations, we used the average of the smallest and largest configuration, i.e. for the Telemax a squared window of size 100 cm.

We consistently set the resolution of the maps to 5 cm. The resolution of the motion graph should be set such that the diagonal edges are shorter than the robot length. Using half the robot size (Telemax: 30 cm), we do not need any validity tests between robot positions (i.e. vertices) as the tests at the robot positions cover the transition edges between them. To distinguish between flat areas and rough areas we specify the maximal height and maximal slope which can be traversed using a 2D navigation scheme without utilizing the actuators. We set the value to 9 cm and 15° considering the capabilities of the Telemax with default actuator configuration.

The minimal velocity v_{min} used in the cost terms for the translation time specifies the velocity the robot should drive in the very rough areas. We set the value to 0.12 m/s, i.e. 10 % of the robot's maximal velocity of 1.2 m/s. The normalization factors ξ_s and ξ_t are determined through the most stable configuration on flat ground and $\frac{1}{\pi/2}$, the maximal angle to the surface, respectively. ξ normalizes the time cost with respect to the safety cost and is set to 0.5.

The two safety weights w_1 for the initial path search and w_2 for the detailed motion planning allow to adjust the importance of the safety for the planning queries. The former will influence the major direction of the path as it determines the initial path. The latter influences the robot configurations and the actuators. Appropriate values depend on the application and the robot model. However, we used values of $w_1 = 0.75$ and $w_2 = 0.5$ in our experiments.

6.1 Roadmap Planner

The size of the tube around rough segments determines the state space expansion for the detailed motion planning. We required all positions to be less than 75 cm away from the path. Hence, we include all positions (vertices) which need at most two edges to reach the path provided a graph resolution of 30 cm (half the Telemax length). We found including two positions to either side of the path in the tube as a reasonable trade-off between the state space expansion and planning time.

6.2 RRT*-Planner

We use the adaptive ball formulation [20] with the RRT*. The ball determines the neighborhood of some node; hence, the radius depicts the size of this neighborhood. A large radius means many, potentially too many, neighbors will be

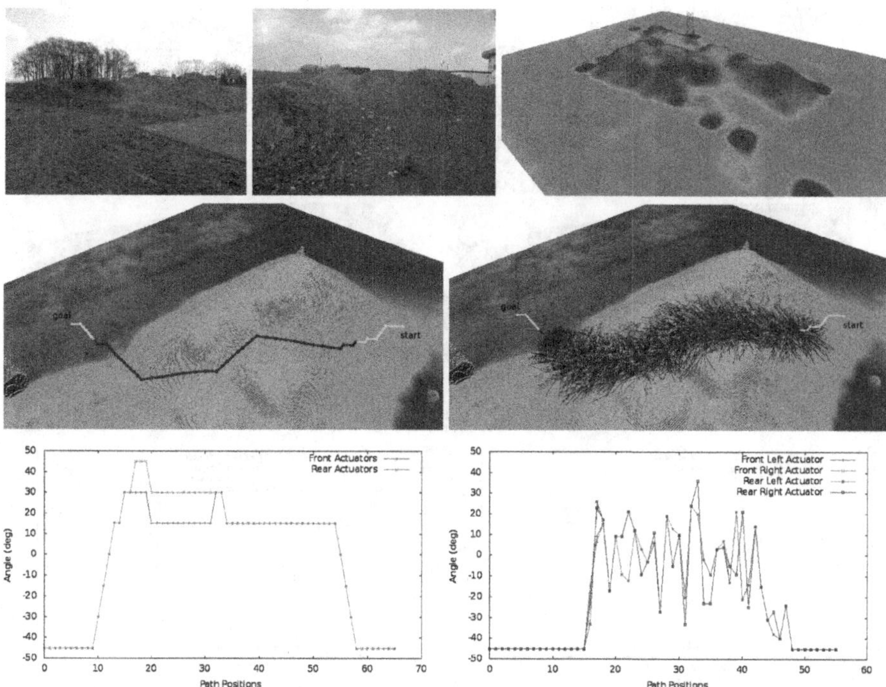

Fig. 10. First row: Two pictures of a hill of rubble and the map of size 36.4 × 30.45 m captured with a laser range finder. Second row: The plans produced by the roadmap planner and by the sampling-based planner. Third row: The actuator joint values of the path produced by the roadmap planner and the sampling-based planner. Values below zero indicate folded configurations and values greater zero correspond to expanded configurations. The safety weights are $w_1 = 1.0$ and $w_2 = 0.5$ and the sampling-based planner ran for 10 000 iterations.

included and tested for optimal solutions and the runtime increases. If too few neighbors are considered, the optimal solution may not be found. In our setup, we started with an radius of $r = 0.65$ m (the length of the Telemax) and decreased over time.

The path focus helps to find better solutions in less time. However, if the focus is too loose, the space to be searched becomes too large and the benefit decreases. If it is too strict, the space may be to small for a reasonable refinement of the initial path. We set $\sigma = 0.65$ m (the length of the Telemax) for the normal distribution for all experiments.

The actuator sampling uses a special configuration distribution when used for robots with several independent actuators. The probabilities are based on observations of operators, which prefer certain groups of configurations. We found the following values to work well for the Telemax robot: $p = 0.20$ for all actuators equal, $p = 0.65$ for both front and both rear actuators equal, $p = 0.10$ for the left and the right actuators equal and $p = 0.05$ for all actuators different.

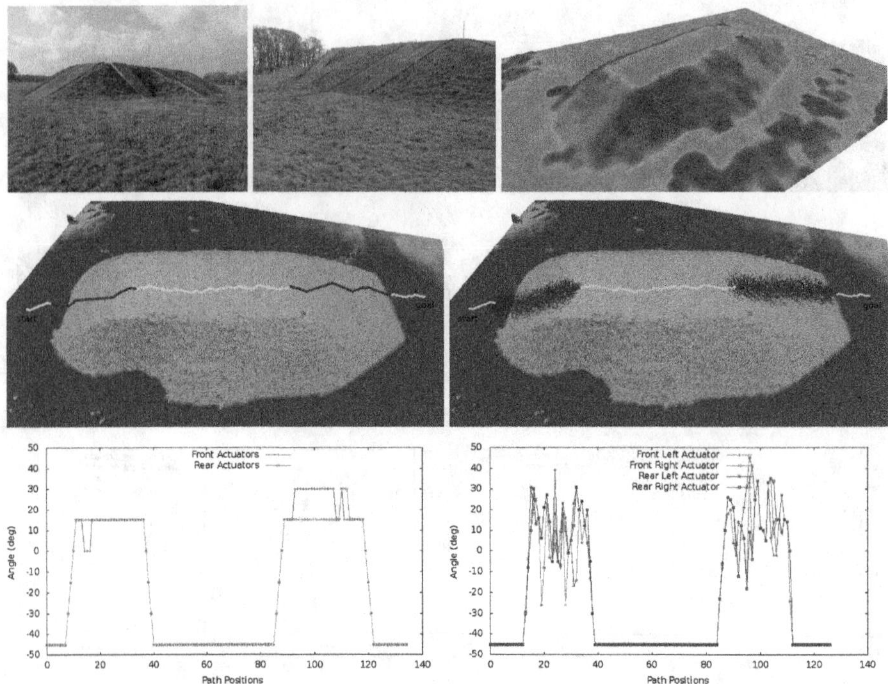

Fig. 11. First row: Two pictures of a testing hill and the map of size 43.95 × 32.95 m captured with a laser range finder. Second row: The plan provided by the roadmap planner and the sampling-based planner. Third row: The actuator joint values of the path by the roadmap planner and the sampling-based planner. Values below zero indicate folded configurations and values greater zero correspond to expanded configurations. The safety weights were set to $w_1 = 0.5$ and $w_2 = 0.75$. The sampling-based planner ran for 10 000 iterations.

The appropriate number of iterations depends on the size of the rough path segment. If the segment is short and the number of iterations is high, the neighbor queries will return large numbers of configurations, hence the planning time increases. On the other hand, if the number of iterations is too low for a lengthy segment, only a few rewiring options are tested and better solution may be missed. However, for most queries 10 000 iterations work reasonably well.

7 Experimental Results

We performed tests with the Telemax robot in maps recorded with a laser range finder. The environments are shown in Figs. 10 and 11. Their sizes are 36.4 × 30.45 m and 43.95 × 32.95 m, respectively. These are quite large environments compared to related works, which usually focus on smaller patches of purely rough terrain.

We used the following values for the roadmap planner: The resolution of the maps was 0.05 m and 0.3 m (half the robot length) for the motion graphs. We considered eight orientations in each position (45° steps). The actuator values were bound to $[-45°, 45°]$ in steps of 15°. Further, both front, respectively both rear actuators were required to be the same. We chose a folded configuration with all actuator values equal to $-45°$ as default configuration. The default configuration was applied in flat areas. The maximal ground contact is reached with all actuators at 21° (see Fig. 1 right).

To setup the RRT*-planner we used the same map resolution, the same range of actuator values and the same safety weight. The additional parameters for the RRT* algorithm were set to $r = 0.65$ m as initial radius size of the adaptive ball formulation.

As the roadmap planner is a deterministic planner, we performed a single query. To measure the performance of the sampling-based RRT*-planner, we performed 10 times the same query and measured the average. The simulation was performed on a 3.33 GHz Intel Xeon CPU and 12 GB memory. If a path contained several rough segments, we parallelize the planning queries for the rough segments. We compared the actuator values, the planning time and the cost of the final path.

We tested the algorithms on two different maps. In the first scenario, the robot had to cross a hill of rubble through the low risk areas, avoiding high elevations (Fig. 10). In the second scenario, the robot climbed a steep ramp, crossed the top of a hill and descended over a ramp on the other side (Fig. 11).

The roadmap planner provided a solution in less time than the RRT*-planner. Both planners found a stable and valid path. The cost of the plan produced by the RRT*-planner is slightly higher. The roadmap planner needed 45.85 s to return a path of cost 18.06. In comparison, the RRT*-planner required about 65.32 s on average to provide a plan with an average cost of 19.03 and a standard deviation of 0.26. For the second scenario, the roadmap planner took about 41.23 s to find a solution of cost 45.61. The RRT*-planner required about 76.88 s to generate a plan. The average cost is 48.47 with a standard deviation of 0.3.

The differences in path quality between the roadmap planner and the RRT*-planner are tolerable considering the following advantages of the sampling-based approach. To be tractable the roadmap algorithm must plan on a considerable smaller and discretized state space. The RRT*-planner, in contrast, considers a continuous state space, which does not limit a solution to grid positions. This is beneficial especially if the environment involves inclinations and structures that are not aligned with the grid. The continuous state space allows more configurations to be used. Thus, the approach has the potential to overcome more challenging obstacles. Finally, the sampling-based approach scales better to larger configuration spaces.

8 Conclusions and Future Work

In this paper we presented a motion planning algorithm for robots with actively reconfigurable chassis to find safe paths through rough terrain. We introduced a hierarchical planner which quickly determines an initial path considering only the robot's operating limits rather than the complete states. The initial path is used to focus the search in the high dimensional state space of the second detailed motion planning phase. We plan the robot's motions in detail only in rough areas where it is really necessary. We described a roadmap method and a RRT* approach to refine the initial path during the second planning phase. Our algorithm does not rely on predefined motion sequences or on a terrain classification. Hence, it can be applied to urban structures, like stairs, as well as to rough unstructured environments.

Future work will focus on overcoming more challenging obstacles, like boxes or high steps. This will require a more accurate modeling of the robots footprint and the contact points with the environment. Also, we will investigate methods which reuse previous planning results to answer replanning queries to the same goal if the robot deviates from the previous plan. The current controller is solely based on differential GPS; we are planning to improve the path execution through a more sophisticated controller.

References

1. Mourikis, A.I., Trawny, N., Roumeliotis, S.I., Helmick, D.M., Matthies, L.: Autonomous stair climbing for tracked vehicles. Int. J. Robot. Res. **26**, 737–758 (2007)
2. Mihankhah, E., Kalantari, A., Aboosaeedan, E., Taghirad, H., Moosavian, S.A.A.: Autonomous staircase detection and stair climbing for a tracked mobile robot using fuzzy controller. In: IEEE International Conference on Robotics and Biomimetics (2009)
3. Dornhege, C., Kleiner, A.: Behavior maps for online planning of obstacle negotiation and climbing on rough terrain. In: IEEE/RSJ International Conference on Intelligent Robots and Systems (2007)
4. Rusu, R.B., Sundaresan, A., Morisset, B., Hauser, K., Agrawal, M., Latombe, J.C., Beetz, M.: Leaving flatland: efficient real-time three-dimensional perception and motion planning. J. Field Robot. **26**, 841–862 (2009)
5. Kalakrishnan, M., Buchli, J., Pastor, P., Mistry, M., Schaal, S.: Learning, planning, and control for quadruped locomotion over challenging terrain. Int. J. Robot. Res. **30**, 236–258 (2010)
6. Molino, V., Madhavan, R., Messina, E., Downs, A., Balakirsky, S., Jacoff, A.: Traversability metrics for rough terrain applied to repeatable test methods. In: IEEE/RSJ International Conference on Intelligent Robots and Systems (2007)
7. Ratliff, N., Zucker, M., Bagnell, J. A., Srinivasa, S.: CHOMP: Gradient optimization techniques for efficient motion planning. In: IEEE International Conference on Robotics and Automation (2009)
8. Kalakrishnan, M., Chitta, S., Theodorou, E., Pastor, P., Schaal, S.: STOMP: Stochastic trajectory optimization for motion planning. In: International Conference on Robotics and Automation (2011)
9. Rufli, M., Ferguson, D., Siegwart, R.: Smooth path planning in constrained environments. In: IEEE International Conference on Robotics and Automation (2009)
10. Miro, J., Dumonteil, G., Beck, C., Dissanayake, G.: A kyno-dynamic metric to plan stable paths over uneven terrain. In: IEEE/RSJ International Conference on Intelligent Robots and Systems (2010)

11. Hait, A., Simeon, T., Taix, M.: Algorithms for rough terrain trajectory planning. Adv. Robot. **16**, 673–699 (2002)
12. Magid, E., Tusubouchi, T., Koyanagi, E., Yoshida, T., Tadokoro, S.: Controlled balance losing in random step environment for path planning of a teleoperated crawler-type vehicle. J. Field Robot. **28**, 932–949 (2011)
13. Jaillet, L., Cortes, J., Simeon, T.: Sampling-based path planning on configuration-space costmaps. IEEE Trans. Robot. **26**, 35–646 (2010)
14. Shkolnik, A., Levashov, M., Manchester, I.R., Tedrake, R.: Bounding on rough terrain with the LittleDog robot. Int. J. Robot. Res. **30**, 192–215 (2011)
15. Ettlin, A., Bleuler, H.: Rough-terrain robot motion planning based on obstacleness. In: 9th International Conference on Control, Automation, Robotics and Vision (2006)
16. Magid, E., Ozawa, K., Tsubouchi, T., Koyanagi, E., Yoshida, T.: Rescue robot navigation: static stability estimation in random step environment. In: Carpin, S., Noda, I., Pagello, E., Reggiani, M., von Stryk, O. (eds.) SIMPAR 2008. LNCS (LNAI), vol. 5325, pp. 305–316. Springer, Heidelberg (2008)
17. Howard, T.M., Kelly, A.: Optimal rough terrain trajectory generation for wheeled mobile robots. Int. J. Robot. Res. **26**, 141–166 (2007)
18. Araujo, R., Gouveia, G., De Almeida, A.: Learning variable-resolution maps for navigation in dynamic worlds. In: IEEE Industrial Electronics Society 28th Annual Conference, vol. 3, pp. 2403–2408 (2002)
19. Hirose, S., Tsukagoshi, H., Yoneda, K.: Normalized energy stability margin and its contour of walking vehicles on rough terrain. In: IEEE International Conference on Robotics and Automation (ICRA) (2001)
20. Karaman, S., Frazzoli, E.: Sampling-based algorithms for optimal motion planning. Int. J. Robot. Res. **30**, 846–894 (2011)
21. Akgun, B., Stilman, M.: Sampling heuristics for optimal motion planning in high dimensions. In: IEEE/RSJ International Conference on Intelligent Robots and Systems, pp. 2640–2645 (2011)

A Framework Covering the Influence of FFM/NEO PI-R Traits over the Dialogical Process of Rational Agents

Jean-Paul Sansonnet[1] and François Bouchet[2](✉)

[1] LIMSI-CNRS, BP 133, 91403 Orsay Cedex, France
[2] SMART Laboratory, McGill University, 3700 McTavish Street, Montreal, Canada
fbouchet@gmail.com

Abstract. In this article we address coverage and comprehensiveness issues raised by the integration of a large class of psychological phenomena into rational dialogical agents. These two issues are handled through the definition of a generic framework based on the notion of personality engine, which makes it possible to reify in separate modules in one hand the application-dependent parts and on the other hand the resources involved in the representation of the psychological phenomena. We introduce an enriched taxonomy of personality traits, based on the well-used FFM/NEO PI-R taxonomy and we show how it can be applied on an example of agents, taken from the literature. Then we introduce the necessary concepts for modeling a personality engine. A case study, using a simplified world of dialogical agents, shows how those agents can be provided with a personality engine affecting the way they communicate with each other, and demonstrates how it can be used to implement the example. Finally, we compare our approach to other attempts at implementing personality features in rational agents.

Keywords: Cognitive agent modeling · Personality traits · Dialogical agents

1 Introduction

Designing virtual humans or agents to be used as long-term companions require them to display a believable behavior which remains consistent over time. In psychology, the concept of personality trait [6,15] is defined as an habitual pattern of behavior or emotion, and therefore provides an appropriate theoretical foundation to build upon to reach the aforementioned goal. Once personality traits have been identified (or designed, in the case of an artificial agent), it is possible to anticipate (or define) their influence, in order to know extent how one will usually react in a particular situation: not only from an emotional perspective, with works from [28] often used to implement psychological phenomena into artificial agents, but also from a rational point of view [8], as studied for artificial agents by Rousseau and Hayes-Roth [32,33].

J. Filipe and A. Fred (Eds.): ICAART 2013, CCIS 449, pp. 62–79, 2014.
DOI: 10.1007/978-3-662-44440-5_4

However, most research works on the computational implementation of psychological phenomena (*cf.* discussion in Sect. 4) usually fail to take into account two key notions: *coverage*, as they often focus only on a small subset of psychological phenomena (*e.g.* considering few traits), and *comprehensiveness*, because they resort to procedural implementations (*e.g.* hard-coded rules) therefore excluding experts (*i.e.* psychologists) from the agent's behavior design process. The work presented in this paper aims at addressing those two restrictions.

Coverage Issues. A key question regarding the principle of influence lies in the actual *extent* of the psychological influence over the reasoning. Typically, artificial agents focus on distinct subsets of domain-dependent psychological notions (*e.g.* a poker player [13]). However, the growing interest in conversational agents [5] opens new perspectives where psychological notions become first class citizens (*e.g.* a different approach to poker player [23]), thus leading to a need not only for larger psychological domains, but also for a more generic way to handle them.

Research works in psychology offer several personality traits taxonomies, but because such taxonomies try to cover a large set of aspects of the personality of a person, they are in turn too general from a computational viewpoint: Catell's 16 personality factors [6], only 5 large classes in a single level for the Five Factor Model (FFM) [16], and 30 bipolar classes in the two-level Revised NEO Personality Inventory (FFM/NEO PI-R), which extends FFM. It is therefore difficult to define a precise interpretation of their classes in terms of operators over the rational process of agents, even for FFM/NEO PI-R, the most fine-grained of the commonly used taxonomies. For example, this led us [34] to propose an extended version of FFM/NEO PI-R with a third level of so-called *behavioral schemes* that increases the precision in terms of classes (69 bipolar schemes) and lexical semantics (each scheme being defined by a set of actual behaviors).

Comprehensiveness Issues. Assuming that a well-grounded and precise taxonomy of personality is available, a second question follows: what kind of influence operators over the agent's process can be elicited from and associated with the taxonomy classes? Some works have proposed models describing how influences operators can be associated with taxonomy classes (*cf.* examples in Sect. 4), proving the feasibility of such an approach on case studies, but they are usually based on small subsets of arbitrarily chosen psychological behaviors (an agent is 'lazy' etc. [35]). Therefore there is a need for a more comprehensive approach to the systematic implementation of *complete* personality traits domains (*e.g.* covering FFM) onto the rational process of artificial agents[1], with two main requirements:

- *Computational implementation*: no complete, orthogonal, and approved set of operators that would apply to main agent frameworks (from different fields such as artificial intelligence, multi-agents systems or intelligent virtual agents) currently exists. A *modular* and flexible approach is needed, to allow subsets of operators to be implemented in distinct frameworks.

[1] Complete coverage has been attempted for emotions, as in OCC [28].

– *Psychological relevance*: we need a model of relationships between classes and operators approved by psychologists. It would require a *declarative* approach, where distinct models of relationships could be shared by psychologists for experimentation and discussion, thus excluding procedural encoding.

Managing Influences with Personality Engines. We propose an approach in which resources are both application-dependent and designer-dependent representations, and where the *personality engines* combine those resources to implement actual scenarios. This concept of personality engine allows to easily implement and test various psychological hypotheses through resource combination, but also to apply them to a wide variety of application domains for experimentation and evaluation purposes.

This article is organized as follows: in Sect. 2, we introduce the enriched taxonomy of personality we have chosen to use in this study, show how it can be used on an example from the literature and introduce the concepts necessary to define a personality engine. Section 3 presents a case study using a simplified world of dialogical agents, shows how those agents can be provided with a personality engine affecting the way they communicate with each other, and demonstrates how it can be used to implement the example from Sect. 2. Section 4 compares our approach to other attempts at implementing personality features in agents.

2 The Personality Engine

2.1 An Enriched Personality Domain

The Traditional FFM/NEO PI-R Taxonomy. Several theoretical approach to study human personality have been developed over years: Freudian psychoanalysis, types and traits, Maslow and Rogers' humanistic psychology, Bandura's social-cognitive theory, etc. Among them, personality traits have been widely used as a ground for studies in affective computing [31] and cognitive agents [18]. We will therefore rely on them and focus on the FFM/NEO PI-R taxonomy [17], which is the most prominent one in the context of computational studies (*cf.* [21]). The FFM/NEO PI-R taxonomy is made of five classes of psychological behaviors, also called O.C.E.A.N. traits. namely **O**penness, **C**onscientiousness, **E**xtraversion, **A**greeableness, **N**euroticism. Each FFM trait is divided into six sub-classes (called *facets*) resulting in 30 bipolar[2] positions [7], listed in Table 1. The semantics of each facet is intuitively defined by a unique gloss[3], *e.g.* facet Fantasy is defined by "receptivity to the inner world of imagination" and Aesthetics by "appreciation of art and beauty".

[2] Each facet has a positive (*resp.* negative) pole noted + (*resp.* −) associated with the concept (*resp.* the antonym of the concept). Facets are referred to using the name of their + pole.

[3] A gloss is a short natural language phrase defining intuitively a lexical semantics sense, as found in dictionaries or in WordNet synsets [12].

Table 1. Two-level FFM/NEO PI-R taxonomy.

FFM Traits	FFM/NEO PI-R facets (each symbol includes a + and a – (antonym) pole)
Openness	Fantasy, Aesthetics, Feelings, Actions, Ideas, Values
Conscientious-ness	Competence, Orderliness, Dutifulness, Achievement-striving, Self-discipline, Deliberation
Extraversion	Warmth, Gregariousness, Assertiveness, Activity, Excitement-seeking, Positive-emotions
Agreeableness	Trust, Straightforwardness, Altruism, Compliance, Modesty, Tender-mindedness
Neuroticism	Anxiety, Angry-Hostility, Depression, Self-consciousness, Impulsiveness, Vulnerability

The Enriched FFM/NEO PI-R/BS Taxonomy. The FFM/NEO PI-R grounded on state of the art research in psychology, which allows us to safely consider that it covers a large part of the domain of a person's personality traits. However, when one is interested in the computational expression of psychological phenomena such as personality traits, the facet definitions (based on a unique gloss per facet as in the aforementioned examples) are too general from two complementary points of view:

(1) They can cover a large set of psychological behaviors so that scripting the psychology of a character can be imprecise. A third level, breaking down facets into smaller subsets would facilitate an association with more specific behaviors.
(2) Definitions are so general that defining a precise functional relation between facets and influence operators can be difficult, which also encourages to go towards breaking down facets into more specific psychological behaviors.

These considerations led us to rely on an enriched three-level taxonomy of FFM/NEO PI-R, called FFM/NEO PI-R/BS [2] and available on the Web[4], in which each facet of FFM/NEO PI-R, is decomposed in so-called behavioral schemes (or *schemes* in short). It extends FFM/NEO PI-R by associating glosses to the senses of a large set of 1 055 personality adjectives, using the WordNet database [12], completed and aligned with 300 Goldberg's questionnaire so-called *q-items*[5], and for each FFM/NEO PI-R position, glosses and items have been clustered into sets[6] of congruent operational behaviors: the schemes. Quantitatively, FFM/NEO PI-R/BS taxonomy features: $N_{\text{facet}} = 30$, $N_{\text{gloss}} = 766$, $N_{\text{scheme}} = 69$, $\overline{N}_{\text{glosses/facet}} = 26$ and $\overline{N}_{\text{schemes/facet}} = 2.3$.

Example: Defining a Personality Profile into the FFM/NEO PI-R/BS Taxonomy. We propose to consider an example taken from CyberCafe in Rousseau

[4] http://perso.limsi.fr/jps/research/rnb/toolkit/taxo-glosses/taxo.htm
[5] http://ipip.ori.org/newNEOKey.htm
[6] Like facets, schemes are bipolar and are often referred to by their +pole.

and Hayes-Roth (1996), in which several characters who endorse the same interactional role of a *waiter* (w_i) have distinct psychological profiles P(w_i), entailing distinct psychological behaviors B(w_i) such as:

P(w_1)	realistic, insecure, introverted, passive, secretive
B(w_1)	Such a waiter does and says as little as he can
P(w_2)	imaginative, dominant, extroverted, active, open
B(w_2)	This waiter takes initiative, comes to the customer without being asked for, talks much
$w_{3,4}$	etc.

Considering the psychological profile P(w_1) of waiter w_1, it can easily be transposed onto the FFM/NEO PI-R/BS taxonomy in terms of scheme activations (formal definition is given in Sect. 2.2):

P' (w_1) = {
realistic ⇒ **O-fantasy-PRACTICAL;**
insecure ⇒ **C-competence-INSECURE;**
introverted ⇒ **E* (-COLD, -NONGOSSIPMONGER, -SOLITARY, -UNCOMMUNICATIVE, -UNCHARISMATIC,**
-DISCRET, -SUBMISSIVE, -PLEADING, -LANGUID, -APATHETIC, -ASCETIC, -BLASE) ;
passive ⇒ **E-activity-APATHETIC;**
secretive ⇒ **A-trust-SECRETIVE**
}

where elements of P(w_1) are transposed in order, separated by ';' in P'(w_1). We can notice that this profile mainly activates negative poles and that a FFM/NEO PI-R/BS scheme can easily be found to correspond to each P trait (which means that P traits are more schemes than actual FFM traits or FFM/NEO PI-R facets). The only exception is *introverted*, which is associated to the whole FFM trait -Extraversion, thus entailing 12 schemes, which adds precision. The same remarks apply to P(w_2) but for the activation of positive poles; it is actually likely that P(w_1) and P(w_2) were hand-built.

P'(w_1) offers a more systematic positioning in FFM/NEO PI-R and a more precise behavioral definition because the definition B(w_1) is replaced with the glosses associated with the activated schemes in FFM/NEO PI-R/BS. For example, -PRACTICAL is defined by the WordNet glosses (N_i) and Goldberg's q-items (Q_i) associated to it:

N618	guided by practical experience and observation rather than theory
N626	aware or expressing awareness of things as they really are
N788	freed from illusion
N1232	concerned with the world or worldly matters
N795	sensible and practical
Q6	Spend time reflecting on things
Q7	Seldom daydream
Q8	Do not have a good imagination
Q9	Seldom get lost in thought

and so on for -INSECURE, - COLD etc.

In summary, FFM/NEO PI-R/BS offers a personality description: not only it covers the eight classes proposed in Cybercafe [32], but it also enables a more precise and practical behavioral description, which justifies our decision to use it in the following sections.

2.2 Architecture of a Personality Engine

Personality Engine Structure. We define a personality engine PE as a 5-tuple such as $\mathtt{PE} = \langle \mathtt{O}, \mathtt{W}, \mathtt{T}, \Omega_{\mathtt{W}}, \mathtt{M}\rangle$ where:

- O is a *personality ontology* that enables precise descriptions of personalities. We will use in this paper the set Σ of bipolar schemes from FFM/NEO PI-R/BS (described in Sect. 2.1), thus $|\Sigma| = 69$. The subset of positive (*resp.* negative) positions is denoted $+\Sigma$ (*resp.* $-\Sigma$), and their union is $\pm\Sigma$ such as $\pm\Sigma = +\Sigma \cup -\Sigma$ and $|\pm\Sigma| = 138$;
- W is an agent *world* model that includes: their internal structure $\mathtt{W}_s$; their external communication protocols $\mathtt{W}_c$; their rational decision making process $\mathtt{W}_r$. For example, a BDI-based model [30] or a more specific one, such as the one defined in Sect. 3.1;
- T is an *application topic* enabling the instantiation of W in a particular case;
- $\Omega_{\mathtt{W}}$ is a set of *influence operators* over $\mathtt{W}_r \cup \mathtt{W}_c = \mathtt{W}_{rc}$;
- M is an *activation matrix*, establishing a relation over $\pm\Sigma \times \Omega_{\mathtt{W}}$.

O, W and T are considered as given resources, whereas $\Omega_{\mathtt{W}}$ and M must be elicited from the resources, as explained in Sects. Influence Operators Elicitation and Activation Matrix Elicitation.

Influence Operators Elicitation. Given an agent model W, influence operators are meta rules $\omega \in \Omega_{\mathtt{W}}$ controlling or altering the non structural parts of W, *i.e.* $\mathtt{W}_{rc}$.

Example. Let us consider some plan in $\mathtt{W}_r$ containing the expression $e = \text{PAR}[a_1, a_2, a_3]$, which is a set of three actions to be executed in no particular order (like operator PAR of CSP). One can define the rule $\omega_1 = \text{PAR} \rightarrow \text{SEQ}$ which, applied to e, can intuitively stand for an indication to an agent to execute its actions routinely (and correctly). On the contrary, a rule $\omega_2 = \text{SEQ} \rightarrow \text{PAR}$

could stand for a disorderly agent (and sometimes lead to incorrect executions of the plan).

This simple example shows that whenever, formally, any rule over $\mathtt{W}_{rc}$ is an influence operator, only those that could be interpreted in terms of psychological behaviors are actually relevant. Consequently, one has to consider operator elicitation as an operation from $\mathtt{W}_{rc} \times \mathtt{O} \longmapsto \Omega_{\mathtt{W}}$ rather than $\mathtt{W}_{rc} \longmapsto \Omega_{\mathtt{W}}$.

The definition of an algorithm that takes a couple of resources W and O and automatically produces the[7] set $\Omega_{\mathtt{W}}$ is still an open question. For the time being, we have to restrict to hand-built operators sets, which are de facto designer(s)-dependent. The notion of personality engine makes it possible to handle the management of this diversity (*e.g.* distinct propositions $\mathtt{PE}_i$, based over the same W and/or O, can be tested and systematically compared). An example of operator elicitation is detailed in Sect. 3.2.

Operators Intensity and Direction. Operators like PAR and SEQ, are activated straightforwardly: they are applied or not. However, various operators can be activated in more complex manners through argument passing. We will consider two frequent cases:

- An intensity is given, *cf.* activation levels in Table 3;
- Operators also working in reverse or antonym mode can be given a direction (*e.g.* operator ω_{-safe} in Sect. 2.3).

Activation Matrix Elicitation. Once given the set schemes $\sigma \in \pm\Sigma$ and a set of influence operators $\omega \in \Omega_{\mathtt{W}}$, the designer(s) of a particular processing engine must elicit how $\pm\sigma_i$ are linked to ω_i, that is which schemes activate which operators. This relation, which is again designer-dependent, is established by a multi-valued matrix M of so-called *activation levels* $\lambda_{i,j}$ such that $\mathtt{M} = \pm\Sigma \times \Omega_{\mathtt{W}}$. Elements $\lambda_{i,j}$ of M have the following values and conventions:

2 activate operator with strong force
1 activate operator with moderate force
0 the operator is deactivated
-1 activate antonym operator (if it exists) with moderate force
-2 activate antonym operator (if it exists) with strong force

2.3 Instantiating Personality Engines

Once given a particular personality engine $\mathtt{PE}_0$, one has a symbolic structure that can be instantiated into actual situations varying from two main points of view: application topics and personality profiles.

[7] Using 'the' raises issues of existence (no possible influences found) and unicity (several distinct sets found thus prompting an order relation).

Application Topics. Let $\mathtt{T}_0$ be a particular topic providing a set of available actions $\alpha_i \in \mathtt{A}(\mathtt{T}_0)$. The topic also provides influence operators of $\mathtt{PE}_0$ with application-dependent information about α_i. For example, let ω_{+safe} be an operator that sorts a set of actions from the safest to the least safe: $\omega_{+safe} \doteq Sort(\{\alpha_i\}, \prec_{danger})$. To be operational, operator ω_{+safe} requires topic $\mathtt{T}_0$ to provide a measure function $\mu_{danger} : \mathtt{A}(\mathtt{T}_0) \longmapsto [0,1]$. Operator ω_{+safe} has an antonym, ω_{-safe}, that sorts actions in reverse order.

Personality Profiles. Intuitively, personality profiles are often defined as sets of adjectives/adverbs describing the behavior of a person. For instance, in the Cybercafe example (*cf.* Sect. 2.1), personality profile $\mathrm{P}(\mathrm{w}_1)$ was first defined with a set of common *words*: {realistic, insecure, introverted, passive, secretive}. The research about personality trait taxonomies enables more precise definitions that use a mapping in terms of sets of well-grounded *concepts*, like $\mathrm{P}'(\mathrm{w}_1)$. Using FFM/NEO PI-R/BS prompts the following definition:

Given an individual x, its personality profile $\mathrm{P}(x)$ can be defined as a set of $|\Sigma|$ functions $\mathrm{p}(\sigma_i) : \Sigma \longrightarrow \{+, \asymp, -\}$ where:

- $\asymp$ means that with regard to scheme σ_i, person x's behavior is not significantly deviant from an average behavior;
- $+$ means x's behavior is deviant from average according to +pole;
- $-$ means x's behavior is deviant from average according to -pole.

Notation. When one considers the 69 schemes of Σ, people tend to exhibit an average behavior for most of them. Consequently $\mathrm{P}(x)$ is often a scarce vector with most elements valued with $\asymp$, so $\mathrm{P}(x)$ is preferably given as a set of non $\asymp$ schemes. For example, Paul's personality will be denoted in short: $\mathrm{P}(Paul)$ = {-HARDWORKER, -ATTENTIVE, HARMLESS, EMPATHIC, -SHOWY}, ignoring the 64 other schemes for which his behavior doesn't stand out.

3 Case Study

In this section we present a case study showing how personality engines can be defined, then instantiated in actual situations. To support the eliciting process of influence operators, one must chose an application model, to focus on agents' communication, well-used KQML [14], ACL-FIPA [27] or BDI models with logics (KGP [22], 2APL [9], Golog-based etc.).

3.1 TALKINGS: A Typical World of Dialogical Agents

We consider here a simplified model, called (a simple world of agents interacting through message passing), that allows a comprehensive presentation of our approach. For this example, we have chosen to focus on conversational agents, a fast growing application domain. Consequently, we will consider traits and operators associated with social and dialogical aspects of the agents, which cover about 55% of the FFM/NEO PI-R/BS schemes [34]. The process described here is complementary to non-dialogical aspects of the agents studied in [3]).

Table 2. Intuitive semantics of the levels of activation of the message operators.

levels 1	levels 2	Operators: CODE	*Label*	Definition	Activation levels λ: -2	-1	0	1	2	Range
Proaction	Explicit	A	*Ask*	probability for the agent to tend to use *Ask* or *Propose*	-	-	none	ask if needed	ask even if not needed	$[\![0, 2]\!]$
		P	*Propose*		-	-	none	propose if needed	propose even if not needed	
		D	*Dominance*	probability for the agent to use the force or its antonym	inferior	supporter	none	equal	superior	$[\![-2, 2]\!]$
		F	*Feeling*		aggressive	cold	none	polite	warm	
		M	*Motivation*		show false motive	hide motive	none	motive if needed	motive even if not needed	
		I	*Incentive*		menace		none		promise	
	Implicit	G	*Guess*	capacity of the agent to perceive other agents in terms of their rational processes, their mental states, etc.	perceive false	do not perceive	none	perceive if explicit	perceive even if not explicit	
		C	*Conflict*	attitude of the agent about risking to provoke conflicts	like conflicts	accept conflicts	none	dislike conflicts	avoid any conflict	
		S	*Sincerity*	sincerity of the agent about all parts of a sent message	tell false facts	actively hide facts	none	frank	very/too frank	
Reaction	Explicit	A+ / A- / P+ / P-	*Reaction*	typical reaction to an *Ask* or *Propose* depending on the global evaluation by *b* of the Forces expressed	always no	yes but with protest	none	yes but can be conditional	always yes	$[\![-2, 2]\!]$
	Implicit	B	*Bond*	reaction to results of G (*e.g.* perceiving *a* is sad, *b* will: +) feel sad; 0) not care; -) feel happy)	bond to reverse	do not bond	none	bond if needed	bond even if not needed	
		N	*Negotiate*	reaction in the management of conflicts existing and explicit	increase	sustain	none	settle	always yield	

Note: level 2 (*resp.*-2) includes level 1 (*resp.*-1), *i.e.* it can exhibit behaviors of level 1 (*resp.*-1)

Agent Model. Let TALKINGS be an actual world composed of physical or abstract entities, which is accessed through a representation of its entities into a symbolic model $\mathcal{M}$. An entity $e_i \in \mathcal{M}$ is defined in $\mathcal{L}_M$, its associated language of description, as a set of rule-based definitions of the general form $\text{D}_i = leftpart \mapsto rightpart$ such that $\forall e_i \in \mathcal{L}_M;\ e_i = \{\text{D}_i\}$.

Agents. $a_i \in \mathcal{A}$ represent dialogical entities of $\mathcal{M}$ that can perform practical reasoning. An agent $a_i \in \mathcal{A}$ is defined as a 5-tuple $\langle id, K, S, \Phi, \Psi \rangle$ where:

- id is a string providing a unique identifier for the agent;
- Knowledge base $K = k_i \in \mathcal{L}_k$ is a set of propositions over $\mathcal{M}$;
- Social base S is the set of roles endorsed by the agent (over TALKINGS, or relatively to another agent of TALKINGS);
- Feature base Φ is the set of physical attributes of the agent (to simplify, Φ will not be considered further);
- Psychological base $\Psi = \Psi_T \cup \Psi_M$ is a set of static traits Ψ_T and dynamic moods Ψ_M (dynamic moods are out of scope here since we focus on personality associated with static traits).

Message Structure. Collectives $c_i \in \mathcal{C}$ of TALKINGS agents can support the operation: SEND$[t, a, \{b_i\}, m]$ that enables the transfer of a message m at turn t between the sender agent a and one or more receiver agents $\{b_i\}$. In the following, we restrict this definition to interactions between the couple of agents $a \Leftrightarrow b$ (in the following, a denotes the so-called *speaker* and b its *interlocutor*) hence considering operations of the form SEND$[t, a, b, m]$. A message m into such SEND operations contains four expressions, explicitly stated by speaker agent a towards interlocutor agent b:

$$m = \langle \text{Reaction}, \text{Proaction}, \text{Forces}, \text{Content} \rangle$$

Reaction is the attitude that a adopts, and expresses explicitly, in reaction to its own evaluation of the previous message from b at turn $t-1$. Reactions are organized on a -/+ scale, ranging from total disagreement (noted No) to total agreement (noted Yes). The first message of the first turn of a session has an empty reaction (noted –).

Proaction is the main attitude stated by a towards b. Two main proactive attitudes are considered, according to the direction of the intention of a:

- *Ask*, represented as $a \xleftarrow{A\ Content} b$, where agent a sends a query to b about Content;
- *Propose*, represented as $a \xrightarrow{P\ Content} b$, where agent a sends a proposition to b about Content.

Forces are optional modalities of proaction operators (A|P), explicitly expressed by a, in order to contribute to the expected success of the message. A message from a is considered successful when in reply from b, the reaction of b is positive and the proaction of b is relevant to a. We consider four distinct forces ; each one is organized as a bipolar $-/+$ scale:

- *Dominance* ranges from force -submissive to +dominant, which can modalize operators A|P, *e.g.* A -submissive can be viewed as begging and A +dominant as requesting.
- *Feelings* ranges from force -aggressive to +affective, when used with operators A|P.
- *Motivation* ranges from force -hide to +open. An agent using open force explains clearly and frankly the rational motive(s) of the sending. Conversely, the agent can try to hide its rational motives or even to express untrue motives.
- *Incentive* ranges from force -menace to +promising. An agent a using +promise force attempts at facilitating the success of its message by providing rational positive reasons for b to react positively to it, or by addressing direct rewards. Conversely, a can try to obtain agreement from b through -menace (*e.g.* by stating rational negative outcomes for b if it disagrees) or by addressing direct threats.

Content is the body of the message, that is the object of the proaction. Five main classes of objects are considered:

- *Knowledge* is a fact $k_i \in \mathcal{L}_k$;
- *Action* is an operation upon the world. For example, $A\ a(x)$ means a asks b to execute $a(x)$, while $P\ a(x)$ means a intends to execute $a(x)$;
- *Resource* is an entity in the world that can be possessed and transferred;

- *Norm* describes rights or duties of agents in a given collective c_i;
- *Emotion* describes a personal mental state (*e.g.* mood) or an interpersonal affective relationship.

With these definitions, the structure of a message m can be represented as:

$$-|Yes|No \ \times \ A|P \ \times \ [D][F][M][I] \ \times \ k|a|r|n|e$$

where | separates alternatives, [] embraces optional forces, k, a, r, n, e are the five types of content and $\times$ is the Cartesian product, thus defining the message domain. A turn t is a couple $\langle \text{SEND}[t, a, b, m], \ \text{SEND}[t, b, a, m'] \rangle$ where m' is the reply to m. A simple interactional session is a sequence of turns; more complex sessions can include sub-sessions (called threads) *e.g.* in case of conditional reactions.

Table 3. Excerpt from Activation matrix $\mathtt{M}_{\text{TALKINGS}}$. When $\lambda_{i,j} = \emptyset$ then $\lambda_{i,j} =$ GenericAgent$_j$.

			Proaction									Reaction							
		Operator code	A	P	D	F	M	I	G	C	S	A+	A-	P+	P-	B	N		
		Value range	02	02	2-2	2-2	2-2	2-2	2-2	2-2	2-2					2-2	2-2		
		Generic agent	1	1	1	1	1	1	1	1	1	1	-1	1	-1	1	1	Waiters	
T	Facet	Scheme																w_1	w_2
O	fantasy	-PRACTICAL																*	
O	fantasy	+IDEALISTIC		2		2	2	2		-1	2	2		2			0		*
O	fantasy	+CREATIVE		2			2				-2								*
C	competence	-INSECURE	2	0	-2		2	0		2			1		1		2	*	
E	warmth	+FRIENDLY			-1	2			2			2		2		2			*
E	warmth	-COLD				-1			-1	-1	-1					-1		*	
E	assertiv.	+DOMINEER.	2		2	-1	0	-1		-1	-1		-2		-2		-1		*
E	activity	+ACTIVE		2						-1		2		2			-1		*
E	activity	-APATHETIC	0	0	-2	0	0	0					1		1	-1	2	*	
A	trust	-SECRETIVE				0	-1	0				-1	-2			0		*	

-PRACTICAL is the antonym pole of scheme +IDEALISTIC *resp.* +FRIENDLY/-COLD, +ACTIVE/-APATHETIC.

3.2 Building a Personality Engine in TALKINGS

Eliciting Influence Operators. Considering the previous agent's model (*i.e.* $\mathtt{W} =$ TALKINGS), it is possible to associate with the model a set of influence operators Ω_{TALKINGS} that define meta control over the rational decision making process of the agents $\mathtt{W}_r$ and over the message passing process $\mathtt{W}_c$. We will focus here on the operation of building and sending messages, *i.e.* on $\mathtt{W}_c$. Browsing the model, described in Sect. 3.1, we can define 15 operators organized in a 2×2 ontology, mirroring the model structure: at the first level of the ontology, influence operators on message passing can be divided into two main classes, *proaction* and *reaction*, and at the second level, we can distinguish for each class *implicit* and *explicit* operators. We therefore distinguish:

- *Explicit proaction* operators, which are expressed into messages.
- *Implicit proaction* operators, which are not explicitly expressed in messages but can influence the way messages are built and are related to the social capacities of the agent.
- *Explicit reaction* operators, which are expressed into messages, in terms of Yes/No reactions.
- *Implicit reaction* operators, which mirrors implicit proaction.

Table 2 gives a list of exhibited message operators together with an abridgment of their semantics associated with their activation levels λ, ranging on scales with discrete positions defined in Sect. 2.2.

While we have used a simplified communicating agent model, together with the description of the FFM/NEO PI-R/BS schemes, it was possible to exhibit 12 operators, defined and organized as in Table 2. In comparison, the eight "types of behaviors" similar to our operators (Perceiving, Reasoning, Learning, Deciding, Acting, Interacting, Revealing, Feeling) given in Cybercafe [33] remain rather general, although some can be directly mapped onto TALKINGS operators such as Perceiving and Guess, Learning and Ask, Revealing and Motivation. Feeling would not be handled here since we consider interactions only and not internal emotions.

Establishing an Activation Matrix. Given the set $\pm\Sigma$ and the set Ω_{TALKINGS} of elicited operators in the case study TALKINGS, it is possible to define an activation matrix $\mathtt{M}_{\text{TALKINGS}}$, which establishes the relationships between the schemes and the operators. Table 3 shows an excerpt of a proposition for $\mathtt{M}_{\text{TALKINGS}}$ (from the 138 schemes of $\pm\Sigma$, we display only the 10 schemes used in the example of Sect. 3.2). Not to overload Table 3, activation values $\lambda_{i,j}$ that are associated with an average behavior are factorized in headline "Generic agent" and represented as empty cells.

Example of Personality Scripting. As an example of instantiation of the personality engine defined for TALKINGS, we consider P'(w_1) from the Cybercafe example (*cf.* Sect. 2.1). For simplification purposes, the 12 schemes associated with adjective 'introverted' are coerced into a single one **E**warmth-COLD (first arbitrarily chosen) thus prompting a new profile:

P"(w_1) = {
  Ofantasy-PRACTICAL;
  Ccompetence-INSECURE;
  Ewarmth-COLD;
  Eactivity-APATHETIC;
  Atrust-SECRETIVE
}

Respectively for waiter w_2 we have:

P”(w_2) = {
Ofantasy+CREATIVE;
Eassertiveness+DOMINEERING;
Ewarmth+FRIENDLY[10];

[10] First scheme chosen with same rule in P”(w_1).
Eactivity+ACTIVE;
Efantasy+IDEALISTIC[11]
}.

Values of activation levels associated with P”(w_1) and P”(w_2) in $\mathrm{M}_{\mathrm{TALKINGS}}$ are given in Table 3. For example, crossing Tables 2 and 3, it is possible to identify the influences of one of the schemes of P”(w_1) *e.g.* **A**trust-SECRETIVE (last line of Table 3):

A/0	don't ask explicitly (while average behavior would be 1: ask if needed by the rational process)
P/0	don't propose explicitly (idem)
F/0	no sensibility to inner feelings activated (idem)
M/-1	hide one's own motives
I/0	usage of positive or negative incentives over others deactivated
A-/-2	react explicitly always by a rejection when asked with a force considered negative
A+/-1	react explicitly positively but with protest, when asked with a force considered positive
B/0	no bond positive or negative is activated (while the average behavior would be 1: bond if needed by the rational process *e.g.* in social condolences)

Operators A, P, F, I, B are controlled via deactivation ($\lambda = 0$). Actually average behavior often uses ($\lambda = 1$)

One can make the following remarks:

R1: Over the set of 12 operators in Table 3, scheme +PRACTICAL is not distinct from Generic agent. This is consistent with the fact that Bratman's agents implement an implicit personality close to scheme +PRACTICAL and be viewed as a particular case.

R2: All lines of Table 3 are distinct, entailing that all schemes are distinct concepts with distinct sets of influences.

R3: It happens that profiles of the Cybercafe waiters, P”(w_1) and P”(w_2) activate exclusive schemes (*). Their definition is not always consistent, meaning that some schemes are activated by contradictory levels *e.g.* 1 and -2. In theory, when a personality is scripted, nothing prevents from defining conflicting activations of the same operator: our approach makes it easier to automatically check for such cases and to handle them manually or automatically, according to an order relation possibly provided by psychologists.

3.3 Discussion

Relevance and Completeness of the Operators. The process of operator elicitation ensures that all operators defined in trait Conscientiousness are relevant. For example, in the case study above, because they are synthesized from scheme glosses, they are activated in a non trivial manner at least once[8] (*i.e.* $\forall\sigma \in \mathsf{M}_{\text{TALKINGS}}, \exists j$ such that $\lambda_{i,j} \neq$ generic-agent (i)).

Conversely, the elicitation process does not ensure that all possible operators are found; from a psychological point of view this is not yet attainable. Actually this issue is in support of our approach that is based on the state of the art of the coverage of the domain of the psychology of a person, that is to say trait taxonomies, in particular FFM/NEO PI-R. Moreover, the refined version FFM/NEO PI-R/BS, grounded on large ascertained lexical resources (*e.g.* WordNet), covers according to the state of current literature, the effective behaviors that are associated with personality traits, hence restricting the risk of silence.

Validation of Activation Matrix Values. Weights $\lambda_{i,j} \in \mathsf{M}_{\text{TALKINGS}}$ are set by annotators. This results in (1) inter annotator quantitative differences that can be partly controlled with statistic tools acting over the annotating group; (2) qualitative controversies between computer science experts and psychologists. The proposed approach has the virtue of putting into light the essential issue of those qualitative controversies, usually embedded in the programming process of the procedural approaches, listed in Sect. 4. In our case, the use of a declarative method, through a matrix of activation levels instead of procedural rules, increases the comprehensiveness and the tracking of the traits/behaviors association. Moreover, the declarative approach clarifies the discussions with psychologists, who *in fine* must validate the decisions.

Evaluation of the Model. In this paper we propose an approach for handling the phenomena, stated in the literature, of personality traits influence over plans and actions. Our purpose is not the direct evaluation of a particular model (composed of: a specific rational model, a specific set of influence operators and a specific set of activation levels) through an experimentation. Here we pursue a double objective:

1. present a proof of concept of the principle of influence: 'points of influence' actually exist in the rational decision making process;
2. propose a method that is (a) generic *i.e.* not designed for a small set of specific traits but covering a large domain of the personality of a person; and (b) declarative *i.e.* using explicit levels instead of embedded rules.

For example, a consequence is that Tables 2 and 3 must be viewed as instances of our approach. As such, they need to be evaluated through proper experiments, but which are beyond the scope of this paper.

[8] Except for first line of Table 3 (O fantasy -practical), which is similar to a line generic-agent as this trait can be viewed as Bratman's notion of practical reason (1987).

4 Related Works

Since works of Rousseau and Hayes-Roth (1996), extensive research has been undertaken, especially recently, involving both psychological phenomena and artificial agents in at least four communities: rational agents, multi-agents systems, conversational agents and affective computing.

Gratch and Marsella (2004) have implemented a psychological model, mainly dedicated to emotions, based on traditional SOAR architecture, but most authors have proposed improvements of BDI architectures exhibiting both rational reasoning modules and psychological reasoning modules [24]. For example, the eBDI model [20] implements emotions in a BDI framework, in which they give a good introduction about the necessity to implement emotions into rational agents. Indeed, BDI architectures offer an open and flexible engine (the deliberation cycle), for example using tools like 2APL [9], which is why we rely on it for the support of the framework that underlies this study.

However our approach is distinct from most studies using BDI engines, mainly because in those studies the psychology of the agent is based on *dynamic* mental states (like moods and affects, as in Sect. 3.1), which influence the bodily (facial and gestural) expression of *emotions*, but they have no or little impact upon the decision making process of the agent, especially for controlling conversational strategies. Instead, in our approach the *static* features of the personality of an agent are expressed through its influences upon operational behaviors.

Using the BDI platform JACK [19], CoJACK [11] provides an additional layers which intends to simulate physiological human constraints like the duration taken for cognition, working memory limitations (*e.g.* "loosing a belief" if the activation is low or "forgetting the next step" of a procedure), fuzzy retrieval of beliefs, limited attention or the use of moderators to alter cognition. A similar approach is taken for conversational agents in PMFserv [36].

However, in these studies, authors focus on the influence of *physical* or *cognitive* capacities over the deliberation cycle but not on actual psychological phenomena like moods or traits.

Closer to our work, Malatesta et al. (2007) use traits to create different expressions of emotions, especially by influencing the appraisal part of the OCC theory [28]. They focus on how agents evaluate the results of their actions and of external events, whereas we focus on the way they perform a task. In the same way, Rizzo et al. (1997) have shown that goals and plans can be used to represent a character's personality in an efficient way, by attributing specific behaviors to the pursuit of each goal. Personality traits are used to choose between the multiple goals of a BDI agent (*i.e.* traits influence Desires). Once chosen, goals are planned and executed directly.

However, in our case, traits operate on already planned goals (*i.e.* traits influence Intentions). This remark also applies to [26], based on the architecture of conversational agent GRETA [29], which involves models of personality for the expression of emotions (face, gesture, etc.) and to the FATIMA architecture [10] stemming from [29], which implements personality traits.

Finally, all these studies share the same approach to psychology, each of them focusing on particular capacities or particular traits. They do not attempt to cover a whole domain, hence they are not concerned with managing and comprehensiveness issues.

5 Conclusions

The principle that personality traits influence the mental state and the rational decision process of people has been widely applied to implement psychological phenomena into artificial agents. However we are far from the situation where a generic model can be approved because significant parts are still author-dependent (*e.g.* OCC [28] for emotions) or designer-dependent (as in Sect. 4).

We have shown in this article an approach based on personality engines which provides three main advantages: Firstly, it reduces and reifies author/designer-dependent parts in only three main kinds of resources: trait ontologies, sets of influence operators and activation matrices. Secondly, it defines a process for designing the resources and for implementing, in a declarative way (activation matrix), personality influences in dialogical agents. Thirdly, it offers an architecture where these resources can be flexibly combined (*cf.* Sect. 3.2) and easily observed (*cf.* Sect. 3.2). Moreover, although our approach could be extended to other psychological taxonomies, it relies on the well-grounded FFM/NEO PI-R, enriched with behavioral schemes that make it easier to design the resources.

We intend to extend this work in two main directions: first, by eliciting operators over outstanding BDI (*e.g.* 2APL) agent frameworks in order to demonstrate its independence with regard to the model of rational agents that is chosen, and second, by experimenting the whole architecture through actual scenarios, supervised by psychologists. For example, the perception of the implemented agent's personality by human users could be evaluated after an interactive session with questionnaires such as the Agent Persona Instrument [1].

References

1. Baylor, A., Ryu, J.: The api (agent persona instrument) for assessing pedagogical agent persona. In: World Conference on Educational Multimedia, Hypermedia and Telecommunications, vol. 2003, pp. 448–451 (2003)
2. Bouchet, F., Sansonnet, J.P.: Classification of wordnet personality adjectives in the NEO PI-R taxonomy. In: Fourth Workshop on Animated Conversational Agents, WACA 2010, Lille, France, pp. 83–90 (2010)
3. Bouchet, F., Sansonnet, J.P.: Influence of personality traits on the rational process of cognitive agents. In: The 2011 IEEE/WIC /ACM International Conferences on Web Intelligence and Intelligent Agent Technology, Lyon, France (2011)
4. Bratman, M.E.: Intentions, Plans, and Practical Reason. Harvard University Press, Cambridge (1987)
5. Cassell, J., Sullivan, J., Prevost, S., Churchill, E. (eds.): Embodied Conversational Agents. MIT Press, Cambridge (2000)

6. Cattell, R.B., Eber, H.W., Tatsuoka, M.M.: Handbook for the Sixteen Personality Factor Questionnaire (16 PF). Institute for Personality and Ability Testing, Champain (1970)
7. Costa, P.T., McCrae, R.R.: The NEO PI-R Professional Manual. Psychological Assessment Resources, Odessa (1992)
8. Damasio, A.R.: Descartes Error: Emotion, Reason and the Human Brain. G.P. Putnam's Sons, New York (1994)
9. Dastani, M.: 2APL: a practical agent programming language.In: AAMAS '08:The Seventh International Joint Conference on Autonomous Agents and Multiagent Systems, vol. 16, pp. 214–248. Springer-Verlag, Estoril (2008)
10. Doce, T., Dias, J., Prada, R., Paiva, A.: Creating individual agents through personality traits. In: Safonova, A. (ed.) IVA 2010. LNCS, vol. 6356, pp. 257–264. Springer, Heidelberg (2010)
11. Evertsz, R., Ritter, F.E., Busetta, P., Pedrotti, M.: Realistic behaviour variation in a BDI-based cognitive architecture. In: Procedings of SimTecT'08, Melbourne, Australia (2008)
12. Fellbaum, C.: WordNet: An Electronic Lexical Database. MIT Press, Cambridge (1998)
13. Findler, N.V.: Studies in machine cognition using the game of poker. Commun. ACM **20**(4), 230–245 (1977)
14. Finin, T., Fritzson, R., McKay, D., McEntire, R.: KQML as an agent communication language. In: Proceedings of the Third International Conference on Information and Knowledge Management, pp. 456–463. ACM, Gaithersburg (1994)
15. Goldberg, L.R.: An alternative description of personality: the big-five factor structure. J. Pers. So. Psychol. **59**, 1216–1229 (1990)
16. Goldberg, L.R.: The development of markers for the big-five factor structure. Psychol. Assess. **4**, 26–42 (1992)
17. Goldberg, L.R.: Language and individual differences: The search for universal in personality lexicons. Rev. Pers. Soc. Psychol. **2**, 141–165 (1981)
18. Gratch, J., Marsella, S.: A domain-independent framework for modeling emotion. J. Cogn. Syst. Res. **5**(4), 269–306 (2004)
19. Howden, N., Rannquist, R., Hodgson, A., Lucas, A.: Intelligent agents - summary of an agent infrastructure. In: Proceedings of the 5th International Conference on Autonomous Agents, Montreal (2001)
20. Jiang, H., Vidal, J.M., Huhns, M.N.: eBDI: an architecture for emotional agents. In: AAMAS '07: Proceedings of the 6th International Joint Conference on Autonomous Agents and Multiagent Systems, pp. 1–3. ACM, New York (2007)
21. John, O.P., Robins, R.W., Pervin, L.A. (eds.): Handbook of Personality: Theory and Research, 3rd edn. The Guilford Press, New York (2008)
22. Kakas, A., Mancarella, P., Sadri, F., Stathis, K., Toni, F.: The KGP model of agency. In: ECAI, pp. 33–37. IOS Press, Valencia (2004)
23. Koda, T., Maes, P.: Agents with faces: the effect of personification, pp. 189–194 (1996)
24. Lim, M.Y., Dias, J., Aylett, R.S., Paiva, A.C.R.: Improving adaptiveness in autonomous characters. In: Prendinger, H., Lester, J.C., Ishizuka, M. (eds.) IVA 2008. LNCS (LNAI), vol. 5208, pp. 348–355. Springer, Heidelberg (2008)
25. Malatesta, L., Caridakis, G., Raouzaiou, A., Karpouzis, K.: Agent personality traits in virtual environments based on appraisal theory predictions. In: Artificial and Ambient Intelligence, Language, Speech and Gesture for Expressive Characters, achie AISB'07, Newcastle, UK (2007)

26. McRorie, M., Sneddon, I., de Sevin, E., Bevacqua, E., Pelachaud, C.: A model of personality and emotional traits. In: Ruttkay, Z., Kipp, M., Nijholt, A., Vilhjálmsson, H.H. (eds.) IVA 2009. LNCS, vol. 5773, pp. 27–33. Springer, Heidelberg (2009)
27. O'Brien, P.D., Nicol, R.C.: FIPA towards a standard for software agents. BT Technol. J. **16**(3), 51–59 (1998)
28. Ortony, A., Clore, G.L., Collins, A.: The Cognitive Structure of Emotions. Cambridge University Press edition, Cambridge (1988)
29. Pelachaud, C.: Some considerations about embodied agents. In: International Conference on Autonomous Agents, Barcelona (2000)
30. Rao, A.S., Georgeff, M.P.: BDI agents: from theory to practice. In: Proceedings First International Conference on Multi-agent Systems (ICMAS-95), pp. 312–319 (1995)
31. Rizzo, P., Veloso, M.V., Miceli, M., Cesta, A.: Personality-driven social behaviors in believable agents. In: AAAI Symposium on Socially Intelligent Agents, pp. 109–114 (1997)
32. Rousseau, D.: Personality in computer characters. AAAI Technical report WS-96-03, pp. 38–43 (1996)
33. Rousseau, D., Hayes-Roth, B.: Personality in synthetic characters. Technical report, KSL 96–21. Knowledge Systems Laboratory, Stanford University (1996)
34. Sansonnet, J.P., Bouchet, F.: Extraction of agent psychological behaviors from glosses of wordnet personality adjectives. In: Proceedings of the 8th European Workshop on Multi-Agent Systems (EUMAS'10), Paris, France (2010)
35. Sansonnet, J.P., Bouchet, F.: Integrating psychological behaviors in the rational process of conversational assistant agents. In: Murray, R.C., McCarthy, P.M. (eds.) Proceedings of the 24th International FLAIRS Conference (FLAIRS-24), Palm Beach, Florida, pp. 440–445 (2011)
36. Silverman, B.G., Cornwell, M., O'Brien, K.: Human behavior models for agents in simulators and games. PRESENCE **15**, 139–162 (2006)

Instrumentalization of Norm-regulated Transition System Situations

Magnus Hjelmblom[1,2(✉)]

[1] Faculty of Engineering and Sustainable Development, University of Gävle, Gävle, Sweden
mbm@hig.se
[2] Department of Computer and Systems Sciences, Stockholm University, Stockholm, Sweden

Abstract. An approach to normative systems in the context of multi-agent systems (MAS) modeled as transition systems, in which actions are associated with transitions between different system states, is presented. The approach is based on relating the permission or prohibition of actions to the permission or prohibition of different types of state transitions with respect to some condition d on a number of agents $x_1, ..., x_\nu$ in a state. It introduces the notion of a norm-regulated transition system situation, which is intended to represent a single step in the run of a (norm-regulated) transition system. The normative framework uses an algebraic representation of conditional norms and is based on a systematic exploration of the possible types of state transitions with respect to $d(x_1, ..., x_\nu)$. A general-level Java/Prolog framework for norm-regulated transition system situations has been developed, and this implementation together with a simple example system is presented and discussed.

Keywords: Transition system · Multi-agent system · Norm-regulated · Norm-governed · Normative system

1 Introduction

Many dynamic systems, including multi-agent systems (MAS), may be modeled as transition systems, in which the actions of an agent are associated with transitions between different states of the system. There is a number of different approaches to normative systems in this context. The permission or prohibition of a specific action in a transition system is naturally connected to permissible or prohibited transitions between states of the system, and norms (sometimes referred to as 'social laws') may then be formulated as restrictions on states and state transitions.

This paper will introduce the notion of a *norm-regulated transition system situation*, which is intended to represent a single step in the run of a (norm-regulated) transition system. The permission or prohibition of actions in this framework is related to the permission or prohibition of different types of state

J. Filipe and A. Fred (Eds.): ICAART 2013, CCIS 449, pp. 80–94, 2014.
DOI: 10.1007/978-3-662-44440-5_5

transitions with respect to some condition d on a number of agents $x_1, ..., x_\nu$ in a state. The framework uses an algebraic representation of conditional norms, based on the representation used in the norm-regulated DALMAS architecture (see Previous Work, Sect. 1.2). The novel feature presented here is primarily an extension to the DALMAS's normative framework, based on a systematic exploration of the possible types of state transitions with respect to $d(x_1, ..., x_\nu)$. A norm-regulated transition system situation is easily instrumentalized into a general-level Prolog module that can be used to implement a wide range of specific norm-regulated dynamic systems.

Important norm-related issues such as enforcement of norms, norm change and consistency of normative systems are beyond the scope of this paper; however, the approach presented here is general in nature, and may be combined with many different approaches to, e.g., norm enforcement. The term 'agent' will be frequently used for some sort of 'acting entity' within a dynamic system, but no special assumptions are made about for example autonomy, reasoning capability, architecture, and so on.

1.1 Transition System Situations

A labelled transition system (LTS) is usually defined (see for example [4, p. 174]) as an ordered 3-tuple $\langle S, E, R\rangle$ where S is a non-empty set of *states*; E is a set of transition *labels*, often called *events*; and $R \subseteq S \times E \times S$ is a non-empty set of labelled *transitions*. If (s, ε, s') is a transition, s is the initial state and s' is the resulting state of ε. An event ε is *executable* in a state s if there is a transition $(s, \varepsilon, s') \in R$, and *non-deterministic* if there are transitions $(s, \varepsilon, s') \in R$ and $(s, \varepsilon, s^*) \in R$ with $s' \neq s^*$. A *path* (or *run*) of length m ($m \geq 0$) of a labelled transition system is a sequence $s_0\varepsilon_0 s_1 \cdots s_{m-1}\varepsilon_{m-1}s_m$ such that, for $i \in \{1, .., m\}$, $(s_{i-1}, \varepsilon_{i-1}, s_i) \in R$.

In the following, we restrict our attention to transition systems in which all events are deterministic. This means that, for each state s, the labels associated with the outgoing transitions from s are distinct. Furthermore, we assume that a ν-ary condition d is true or false on ν agents $x_1, ..., x_\nu \in \Omega$ in s, where Ω is a set of agents associated with s; this will be written $d(x_1, ..., x_\nu; s)$. In the special case when the sequence of agents is empty, i.e. $\nu = 0$, d represents a proposition which is true or false in s. Let us now focus on an arbitrary state in a deterministic LTS, with the added requirement that each event ε represents an action a performed by a single agent x. This is written $\varepsilon = x{:}a$, referring to both to the moving agent x and an action a. The term *transition system situation* will be used for an ordered 5-tuple $\mathbf{S} = \langle x, s, A, \Omega, S\rangle$ characterized by a set of states S, a state s, an agent-set $\Omega = \{x_1, ..., x_n\}$, the acting ('moving') agent x, and an action-set $A = \{a_1, ..., a_m\}$. In this setting, a may be regarded as a function such that $a(x, s) = s^+$ means that s^+ is the resulting state when x performs act a in state s.[1] In the following, the abbreviation s^+ will be used for $a(x, s)$ when there is no need for an explicit reference to the action a and the acting agent x.

[1] Note that no special assumptions are made regarding whether or not s_0 is an element of S, i.e. whether or not the action a may lead back to s_0.

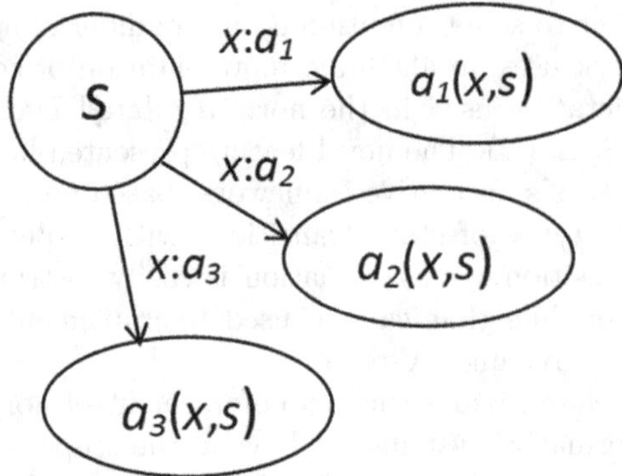

Fig. 1. A state diagram for a transition system situation with three events.

As indicated by Fig. 1, a transition system situation is intended to represent, for example, a 'snapshot' of a labelled transition system in which each transition is deterministic and represents the action of a single agent. In this case, s represents an arbitrarily chosen state in the LTS, and S is the set of states reachable from s by all transitions $x{:}a$, $a \in A$. At the same time, a transition system situation is designed to be general enough to also represent a step in a run of other kinds of dynamic systems, including systems modeled by finite automata (see for example [11]) or Petri nets, and deterministic DALMASes.

1.2 Related Work

This section will give a brief overview of different approaches to the design of normative systems and the formulation of norms. A common feature of many approaches is the idea to partition states and (possibly) transitions into two categories, for example 'permitted' and 'non-permitted'. This may be accomplished with the use of if-then-else rules or constraints on the states and/or the transitions between states. The Ballroom system in [5] and the anticipatory system for plot development guidance in [11] both serve as examples of this approach. Some approaches are purely algebraic or based on modal logics, for example temporal or deontic logic. The DALMAS architecture (see Previous Work below) for norm-regulated MAS is based on an algebraic approach to the representation of normative systems. Dynamic deontic logic [20] and Dynamic logic of permission [19] are two well-known examples of the modal logic approach. Other examples are the combination of temporalised agency and temporalised normative positions [6], in the setting of Defeasible Logic, and Input/Output Logic by Makinson and van der Torre (see for example [18]). Vázquez-Salceda et al. use a language consisting of deontic concepts which can be conditional and can include temporal operators. They characterize norms by whether they refer to states (i.e., norms concerning that an agent sees to it that some condition holds) or actions (i.e., norms concerning an agent performing a specific action), whether they are conditional, whether they include a deadline, or whether they are norms concerning other norms. Reference [26] $n\mathcal{C}+$, an extension of the action language $\mathcal{C}+$, is employed within the context of 'coloured agent-stranded transition systems' [4] to formulate two kinds of norms: *state permission laws* and *action permission laws.* A state permission law states that certain (types of) states are permissible or prohibited, while an action permission law states that specific (types of) transitions are permissible or prohibited in certain states. By picking out the component ('strand') corresponding to an individual agent's contribution to an event, different categories of non-compliant behaviour ('sub-standard' resp. 'unavoidably non-compliant' behaviour) can be distinguished. Cliffe et al. use Answer Set Programming (ASP) for representing institutional norms, as part of the representation and analysis of specifications of agent-based institutions [1,2]. In Deontic Petri nets, and variants thereof such as Organizational Petri nets, varying degrees of 'ideal' or 'sub-ideal' (more or less 'allowed' or 'preferred') behaviour is modeled by preference orderings on executions of Petri nets; see for example [3,23].

Previous Work: The DALMAS Architecture. DALMAS [22] is an abstract architecture for a class of (norm-regulated) multi-agent systems. A deterministic DALMAS is a simple multi-agent system in which the actions of an agent are connected to transitions between system states. In a deterministic DALMAS the agents take turns to act; only one agent at a time may perform an action. Therefore, each individual step in a run of the system may be represented by a transition system situation.

A DALMAS is formally described by an ordered 9-tuple, where the arguments are various sets, operators and functions which give the specific DALMAS its unique features. Of particular interest is the deontic structure-operator, which for each situation of the system determines an agent's *deontic structure* (i.e., the set of permissible acts) on the feasible acts in the current situation, and the preference structure-operator, which for each situation determines the *preference structure* on the permissible acts. In a *norm-regulated simple deterministic* DALMAS, the deontic structure consists of all acts that are not explicitly prohibited by a normative system; thereby employing what is often referred to as 'negative permission'. The preference structure consists of the most preferable (according to the agent's *utility function*) of the acts in the deontic structure. In other words, a DALMAS agent's behaviour is regulated by the combination of a normative system and a utility function. The normative system consists of conditional norms using the Kanger-Lindahl theory of normative positions, expressed in an algebraic notation for norms. See for example [12,14,21] for an introduction. A general-level Java/Prolog implementation of the DALMAS architecture has been developed, to facilitate the implementation of specific systems. The **Colour &Form** system, the **Waste-collector** system and the **Forest Cleaner** system are three specific systems that have been implemented using this framework. The reader is referred to [7,8,10,22] for a description of these systems and their implementations.

2 Normative Systems and Types of State Transitions

In this section, which is a slight reformulation of Sect. 2 in [9], we consider the transition from a state s to a following state s^+, and focus on the condition $d(x_1, ..., x_\nu)$. To facilitate reading, X_ν will be used as an abbreviation for the argument sequence $x_1, ..., x_\nu$. With regard to $d(X_\nu)$, there are four possible alternatives for the transition from s to s^+, since in s as well as in s^+, $d(X_\nu)$ or $(d^\neg)(X_\nu)$ could hold[2]:

I. $d(X_\nu; s)$ and $d(X_\nu; s^+)$
II. $\neg d(X_\nu; s)$ and $d(X_\nu; s^+)$
III. $d(X_\nu; s)$ and $\neg d(X_\nu; s^+)$
IV. $\neg d(X_\nu; s)$ and $\neg d(X_\nu; s^+)$

Each alternative represents a basic type of transition with regard to the state of affairs $d(X_\nu)$; we say that $\{\text{I}, \text{II}, \text{III}, \text{IV}\}$ is the set of *basic transition types* with regard to $d(X_\nu)$. In the vein of [24], I could be written $0{:}d(X_\nu) \wedge 1{:}d(X_\nu)$, II could be written $0{:}\neg d(X_\nu) \wedge 1{:}d(X_\nu)$, and similarly for III and IV.

Let the *situation* $\langle x, s\rangle$ be characterized by the moving agent x and the state s in a transition system situation **S**. We now wish to be able to determine the transition type for the transition represented by action a performed by agent $x_{\nu+1}$ in $\langle x, s\rangle$. (The point of the separation between $x_{\nu+1}$ and the moving agent x is to allow for systems in which normative conditions may apply to other agents than the 'moving' agent, e.g. agents wishing to perform some sort of 'reaction' or 'punishment' act. In most simple systems, however, $x_{\nu+1}$ will be identified with x.) Therefore, we define a 'basic transition type operator' B_j^a, $j \in \{\text{I}, \text{II}, \text{III}, \text{IV}\}$, such that the $\nu + 1$-ary 'transition type condition' $B_j^a d(X_\nu, x_{\nu+1}; x, s)$ indicates whether or not, in the situation $\langle x, s\rangle$, the event $x_{\nu+1}{:}a$ (representing a being performed by $x_{\nu+1}$) has basic transition type j with regard to $d(X_\nu)$: For all ν-ary conditions d and for all agents $X_\nu, x_{\nu+1}$, all acts a and all situations $\langle x, s\rangle$,

1. $B_{\text{I}}^a d(X_\nu, x_{\nu+1}; x, s)$ iff $[d(X_\nu; s) \wedge d(X_\nu; a(x_{\nu+1}, s)]$
2. $B_{\text{II}}^a d(X_\nu, x_{\nu+1}; x, s)$ iff $[\neg d(X_\nu; s) \wedge d(X_\nu; a(x_{\nu+1}, s))]$
3. $B_{\text{III}}^a d(X_\nu, x_{\nu+1}; x, s)$ iff $[d(X_\nu; s) \wedge \neg d(X_\nu; a(x_{\nu+1}, s))]$
4. $B_{\text{IV}}^a d(X_\nu, x_{\nu+1}; x, s)$ iff $[\neg d(X_\nu; s) \wedge \neg d(X_\nu; a(x_{\nu+1}, s))]$

We note in passing the following symmetries:

- $B_{\text{I}}^a d(X_\nu, x_{\nu+1}; x, s)$ iff $B_{\text{IV}}^a (d^\neg)(X_\nu, x_{\nu+1}; x, s)$
- $B_{\text{II}}^a d(X_\nu, x_{\nu+1}; x, s)$ iff $B_{\text{III}}^a (d^\neg)(X_\nu, x_{\nu+1}; x, s)$.

[2] We can form negations $(d^\neg)$ of conditions in the following way: $(d^\neg)(X_\nu)$ iff $\neg d(X_\nu)$. In the following, the latter notation will be used to facilitate the presentation. Note that conjunctions $(c \wedge d)$ and disjunctions $(c \vee d)$ may be formed in a similar way; hence, it is possible to construct Boolean algebras of conditions.

2.1 Prohibition of State Transition Types

$\{\mathrm{I}, \mathrm{II}, \mathrm{III}, \mathrm{IV}\}$ is the set of atoms of the boolean algebra generated by $d(X_\nu; s)$ and $d(X_\nu; s^+)$. This algebra has 16 elements, as shown in Table 1, where 'X' denotes that a basic transition type is one of the disjuncts of the element, while '-' denotes that it is not. I.e., each subset of $\{\mathrm{I}, \mathrm{II}, \mathrm{III}, \mathrm{IV}\}$ represents a combination (by disjunction) of basic transition types with regard to $d(X_\nu)$. For each element (i.e., for each row in the table) we obtain conditions on state transitions. E.g., row 5 represents the condition $\neg d(X_\nu; s) \wedge d(X_\nu; s^+)$, and row 8 represents the condition

$$(\neg d(X_\nu; s) \wedge d(X_\nu; s^+)) \vee (d(X_\nu; s) \wedge \neg d(X_\nu; s^+)) \vee (\neg d(X_\nu; s) \wedge \neg d(X_\nu; s^+))$$

which may be simplified to $\neg d(X_\nu; s) \vee \neg d(X_\nu; s^+)$.

Table 1. Possible combinations of basic transition types.

	(I)	(II)	(III)	(IV)	
1	-	-	-	-	-
2	-	-	-	X	$\neg d(X_\nu; s) \wedge \neg d(X_\nu; s^+)$
3	-	-	X	-	$d(X_\nu; s) \wedge \neg d(X_\nu; s^+)$
4	-	-	X	X	$\neg d(X_\nu; s^+)$
5	-	X	-	-	$\neg d(X_\nu; s) \wedge d(X_\nu; s^+)$
6	-	X	-	X	$\neg d(X_\nu; s)$
7	-	X	X	-	$\neg(d(X_\nu; s) \leftrightarrow d(X_\nu; s^+))$
8	-	X	X	X	$\neg d(X_\nu; s) \vee \neg d(X_\nu; a(x, s))$
9	X	-	-	-	$d(X_\nu; s) \wedge d(X_\nu; s^+)$
10	X	-	-	X	$d(X_\nu; s) \leftrightarrow d(X_\nu; s^+)$
11	X	-	X	-	$d(X_\nu; s)$
12	X	-	X	X	$d(X_\nu; s) \vee \neg d(X_\nu; s^+)$
13	X	X	-	-	$d(X_\nu; s^+)$
14	X	X	-	X	$\neg d(X_\nu; s) \vee d(X_\nu; s^+)$
15	X	X	X	-	$d(X_\nu; s) \vee d(X_\nu; s^+)$
16	X	X	X	X	$\top$

The idea now is to formulate (conditional) norms whose normative consequents prohibit one or more basic transition types. A specific act a is taken to be prohibited for $x_{\nu+1}$ if, in a certain state s, the normative system contains a norm which prohibits the type of transition represented by $x_{\nu+1}{:}a$. For each transition type condition, i.e. for each row in Table 1, we may now stipulate that if the transition type condition holds of the transition $(s, x_{\nu+1}{:}a, a(x_{\nu+1}, s))$ then it is not permissible for $x_{\nu+1}$ to perform a in the situation $\langle x, s\rangle$. E.g., for row 5

Table 2. Meaningful combinations of prohibited state transition types.

(I)	(II)	(III)	(IV)	$C_j^a d(X_\nu, x_{\nu+1}; x, s)$
-	-	-	-	-
-	-	X	-	$d(X_\nu; s) \wedge \neg d(X_\nu; a(x_{\nu+1}, s))$
-	-	-	X	$\neg d(X_\nu; s) \wedge \neg d(X_\nu; a(x_{\nu+1}, s))$
-	X	-	-	$\neg d(X_\nu; s) \wedge d(X_\nu; a(x_{\nu+1}, s))$
X	-	-	-	$d(X_\nu; s) \wedge d(X_\nu; a(x_{\nu+1}, s))$
-	-	X	X	$\neg d(X_\nu; a(x_{\nu+1}, s))$
-	X	X	-	$\neg(d(X_\nu; s) \leftrightarrow d(X_\nu; a(x_{\nu+1}, s)))$
X	-	-	X	$d(X_\nu; s) \leftrightarrow d(X_\nu; a(x_{\nu+1}, s))$
X	X	-	-	$d(X_\nu; a(x_{\nu+1}, s))$

we may stipulate that if $\neg d(X_\nu; s)$ and $d(X_\nu; a(x_{\nu+1}, s))$, then act a is not permissible for $x_{\nu+1}$ in $\langle x, s\rangle$, by defining a normative operator P_{II} such that for all ν-ary conditions d, all agents $X_\nu, x_{\nu+1} \in \Omega$, all actions $a \in A$, and all situations $\langle x, s\rangle$,

$$P_{\text{II}} d(X_\nu, x_{\nu+1}; x, s) \text{ iff}$$
$$[\text{if } B_{\text{II}}^a d(X_\nu, x_{\nu+1}; x, s), \text{then } a \text{ is prohibited for } x_{\nu+1}].$$

Similarly, for row 8 we may define $P_{\text{II,III,IV}}$ such that for all ν-ary conditions d, all agents $X_\nu, x_{\nu+1} \in \Omega$, all actions $a \in A$, and all situations $\langle x, s\rangle$,

$$P_{\text{II,III,IV}} d(X_\nu, x_{\nu+1}; x, s) \text{ iff}$$
$$[\text{if } B_{\text{II}}^a d(X_\nu, x_{\nu+1}; x, s) \text{ or } B_{\text{III}}^a d(X_\nu, x_{\nu+1}; x, s) \text{ or } B_{\text{IV}}^a d(X_\nu, x_{\nu+1}; x, s),$$
$$\text{then } a \text{ is prohibited for } x_{\nu+1}].$$

A closer look at Table 1 reveals, however, that not all disjunctions of basic transition types can be meaningfully linked with a prohibition. As discussed in [9], norms based on the prohibition of elements containing I $\vee$ III or II $\vee$ IV are not meaningful. Table 2 contains the rows (slightly reordered) that represent meaningful normative conditions. It is convenient to define a 'transition type operator' C_j^a, $j \in \{2, 2', 4, 4', 5, 6, 6', 7\}$, for each of the rows in Table 2 (except the first, which expresses no restrictions at all)[3]:

For all ν-ary conditions d and for all agents $X_\nu, x_{\nu+1}$, all acts a and all situations $\langle x, s\rangle$,

1. $C_2^a d(X_\nu, x_{\nu+1}; x, s)$ iff $B_{\text{III}}^a d(X_\nu, x_{\nu+1}; x, s)$ iff $[d(X_\nu; s) \wedge \neg d(X_\nu; a(x_{\nu+1}, s)]$
2. $C_{2'}^a d(X_\nu, x_{\nu+1}; x, s)$ iff $B_{\text{IV}}^a d(X_\nu, x_{\nu+1}; x, s)$ iff $[\neg d(X_\nu; s) \wedge \neg d(X_\nu; a(x_{\nu+1}, s))]$
3. $C_4^a d(X_\nu, x_{\nu+1}; x, s)$ iff $B_{\text{II}}^a d(X_\nu, x_{\nu+1}; x, s)$ iff $[\neg d(X_\nu; s) \wedge d(X_\nu; a(x_{\nu+1}, s))]$
4. $C_{4'}^a d(X_\nu, x_{\nu+1}; x, s)$ iff $B_{\text{I}}^a d(X_\nu, x_{\nu+1}; x, s)$ iff $[d(X_\nu; s) \wedge d(X_\nu; a(x_{\nu+1}, s))]$
5. $C_5^a d(X_\nu, x_{\nu+1}; x, s)$ iff $[B_{\text{III}}^a d(X_\nu, x_{\nu+1}; x, s)$ or $B_{\text{IV}}^a d(X_\nu, x_{\nu+1}; x, s)]$ iff $\neg d(X_\nu; a(x_{\nu+1}, s))$

[3] The numbering is based on the numbering used in [8].

6. $C_6^a d(X_\nu, x_{\nu+1}; x, s)$ iff $[B_{\rm II}^a d(X_\nu, x_{\nu+1}; x, s)$ or $B_{\rm III}^a d(X_\nu, x_{\nu+1}; x, s)]$ iff $[\neg d(X_\nu; s) \wedge d(X_\nu; a(x_{\nu+1}, s))] \vee [d(X_\nu; s) \wedge \neg d(X_\nu; a(x_{\nu+1}, s))]$
7. $C_{6'}^a d(X_\nu, x_{\nu+1}; x, s)$ iff $[B_{\rm I}^a d(X_\nu, x_{\nu+1}; x, s)$ or $B_{\rm IV}^a d(X_\nu, x_{\nu+1}; x, s)]$ iff $[d(X_\nu; s) \wedge d(X_\nu; a(x_{\nu+1}, s))] \vee [\neg d(X_\nu; s) \wedge \neg d(X_\nu; a(x_{\nu+1}, s))]$
8. $C_7^a d(X_\nu, x_{\nu+1}; x, s)$ iff $[B_{\rm I}^a d(X_\nu, x_{\nu+1}; x, s)$ or $B_{\rm II}^a d(X_\nu, x_{\nu+1}; x, s)]$ iff $d(X_\nu; a(x_{\nu+1}, s))$

The 'transition type condition' $C_j^a d(X_\nu, x_{\nu+1}; x, s)$ indicates whether or not, in situation $\langle x, s\rangle$, the event $x_{\nu+1}{:}a$ has any of the corresponding basic transition types with regard to $d(X_\nu)$. The following symmetries hold (cf. the observation in [22, p. 148]):

- $C_2^a d(X_\nu, x_{\nu+1}; x, s)$ iff $C_4^a (d^\neg)(X_\nu, x_{\nu+1}; x, s)$
- $C_{2'}^a d(X_\nu, x_{\nu+1}; x, s)$ iff $C_{4'}^a (d^\neg)(X_\nu, x_{\nu+1}; x, s)$
- $C_5^a d(X_\nu, x_{\nu+1}; x, s)$ iff $C_7^a (d^\neg)(X_\nu, x_{\nu+1}; x, s)$
- $C_6^a d(X_\nu, x_{\nu+1}; x, s)$ iff $C_6^a (d^\neg)(X_\nu, x_{\nu+1}; x, s)$
- $C_{6'}^a d(X_\nu, x_{\nu+1}; x, s)$ iff $C_{6'}^a (d^\neg)(X_\nu, x_{\nu+1}; x, s)$

Next, we define a normative 'transition type prohibition operator' P_1 such that it imposes no restriction on the actions performed by $x_{\nu+1}$, and, for each C_j^a, a transition type prohibition operator P_j, $j \in \{2, 2', 4, 4', 5, 6, 6', 7\}$, such that for all ν-ary conditions d, all agents $X_\nu, x_{\nu+1} \in \Omega$, all actions $a \in A$, and all situations $\langle x, s\rangle$,

$$P_j d(X_\nu, x_{\nu+1}; x, s) \text{ iff [if } C_j^a d(X_\nu, x_{\nu+1}; x, s), \text{then } a \text{ is prohibited for } x_{\nu+1}].$$

Note for example that $P_5 d(X_\nu, x_{\nu+1}; x, s)$ iff $P_{\rm I,IV} d(X_\nu, x_{\nu+1}; x, s)$. From the symmetry principles above it follows that

- $P_1 d(X_\nu, x_{\nu+1}; s)$ iff $P_1 (d^\neg)(X_\nu, x_{\nu+1}; x, s)$
- $P_2 d(X_\nu, x_{\nu+1}; s)$ iff $P_4 (d^\neg)(X_\nu, x_{\nu+1}; x, s)$
- $P_{2'} d(X_\nu, x_{\nu+1}; s)$ iff $P_{4'} (d^\neg)(X_\nu, x_{\nu+1}; x, s)$
- $P_5 d(X_\nu, x_{\nu+1}; s)$ iff $P_7 (d^\neg)(X_\nu, x_{\nu+1}; x, s)$
- $P_6 d(X_\nu, x_{\nu+1}; s)$ iff $P_6 (d^\neg)(X_\nu, x_{\nu+1}; x, s)$
- $P_{6'} d(X_\nu, x_{\nu+1}; s)$ iff $P_{6'} (d^\neg)(X_\nu, x_{\nu+1}; x, s)$

Now suppose that $P_j d(X_\nu, x_{\nu+1}; x, s)$ holds (is 'in effect') in situation $\langle x, s\rangle$, and that the corresponding transition type condition $C_j^a d(X_\nu, x_{\nu+1}; x, s)$ also holds for some action a and some agent $x_{\nu+1}$. Then a is prohibited for $x_{\nu+1}$: For all actions $a \in A$ and all agents $x_{\nu+1} \in \Omega$,

$$\begin{gathered} \textit{Prohibited}_{x,s}(x_{\nu+1}, a) \text{ if there exists a condition } d, \\ \text{a sequence of agents } x_1, ..., x_\nu, \text{ and a } j \in \{2, 2', 4, 4', 5, 6, 6', 7\}, \text{ such that} \\ P_j d(x_1, ..., x_\nu, x_{\nu+1}; x, s) \ \&\ C_j^a d(x_1, ..., x_\nu, x_{\nu+1}; x, s). \end{gathered}$$

2.2 Norm-regulated Transition System Situations

A *norm-regulated transition system situation* is represented by an ordered pair $\langle \mathbf{S}, \mathcal{N} \rangle$ where $\mathbf{S} = \langle x, s, A, \Omega, S \rangle$ is a transition system situation and $\mathcal{N}$ is a normative system. We assume that (1) an event ε is of the form $x_{\nu+1}{:}a$ (i.e., represents an action a performed by an agent $x_{\nu+1}$; see Sect. 1.1) and (2) that norms apply to an individual agent $x_{\nu+1}$ in a state s. A norm in $\mathcal{N}$ is represented by an ordered pair $\langle G, C \rangle$, where the condition G on a situation $\langle x, s \rangle$ is the *ground* of the norm and the (normative) condition C on $\langle x, s \rangle$ is its *consequence.* (See, e.g., [22]) For example, $\langle g, P_j c \rangle$ represents the sentence

$$\forall x_1, x_2, ..., x_\nu, x_{\nu+1} \in \Omega : g(x_1, x_2, ..., x_p, x_{\nu+1}; x, s) \rightarrow \\ P_j c(x_1, x_2, ..., x_q, x_{\nu+1}; x, s)$$

where Ω is the set of agents, $x_{\nu+1}$ is the agent to which the norm applies, x is the 'moving' agent in the situation $\langle x, s \rangle$, and $\nu = \max(p, q)$. If the condition specified by the ground of a norm is true in some situation, then the (normative) consequence of the norm is in effect in that situation. To ensure that the agent $x_{\nu+1}$ to which the norm applies is the same as the moving agent x, we apply the 'move operator' M_i. This operator transforms a condition d on p agents in a state s to a condition $M_i d$ on $p+1$ agents in the situation $\langle x, s \rangle$, while at the same time identifying $x_{\nu+1}$ with x. (See [7,22] for an explanation of the operator M_i.) If the normative system contains a norm whose ground holds in the situation $\langle x, s \rangle$ and whose consequence prohibits the type of transition represented by the event $x_{\nu+1}{:}a$, then action a is prohibited for $x_{\nu+1}$ in $\langle x, s \rangle$:

$$\begin{gathered} \textit{Prohibited}_{x,s}(x_{\nu+1}, a) \text{ according to } \mathcal{N} \\ \text{if there exists a condition } d \text{ and a condition } c \text{ and a } j \in \{2, 2', 4, 4', 5, 6, 6', 7\} \\ \text{such that } \langle M_i d, P_j c \rangle \text{ is a norm in } \mathcal{N}, \text{ and there exist } x_1, ..., x_\nu \text{ such that} \\ M_i d(x_1, ..., x_p, x_{\nu+1}; x, s) \;\&\; C_j^a c(x_1, ..., x_q, x_{\nu+1}; x, s), \text{ where } \nu = \max(p, q). \end{gathered}$$

Since each situation for a DALMAS can be viewed as a transition system situation, it is straightforward to develop the DALMAS architecture (see Sect. 1.2) into an architecture for norm-regulated transition system situations. This means extending the set of seven type-operators T_i with corresponding E_i^a operators into a set of nine type-operators P_i with corresponding C_i^a operators, which calls for the definition of a structure similar to an *np-cis*[4]. The details are left for future work. The existing general-level Java/Prolog DALMAS implementation is easily adapted into a general-level implementation of norm-regulated transition system situations. In this framework, a norm is represented by a Prolog term `n/3` of the form `n(Id/N,OpG*G,OpC*C)`, where `Id` is an identifier of a norm-system and `N` is an identifier of an individual norm. `OpG*G` is a compound term representing an operator `OpG` applied to (the functor of) a state condition predicate `G`, forming the norm's ground. Similarly, `OpC*C` represents the norm's consequence.

[4] Normative-position condition-implication structure; see, e.g., [14,22].

2.3 Applications

The existing implementation of the **Colour&Form** DALMAS (see Sect. 1.2) has been adapted to serve as a demonstration of the use of norm-regulated transition system situations. The **Waste-collector** DALMAS and the **Forest Cleaner** DALMAS implementations may be adapted in a similar manner. However, the use of norm-regulated transition system situations is not limited to the DALMAS context. Many kinds of dynamic systems (including different types of transition systems and multi-agent systems) in which state transitions are connected to the actions of a single 'moving' agent, could be modelled and implemented by (iterated) use of a norm-regulated transition system situation. One example is the **Rooms** system, an implementation of (a variant of) the *Rooms* example by Craven and Sergot in [4, p. 178ff]. The example consists of a world in which agents of two categories ('male' and 'female') move around in a world of rooms that can contain any number of agents. Some rooms are connected by doorways (each connecting two rooms) through which the agents can pass[5], but only one agent at a time. The behaviour of the agents is regulated by a normative system stating that a female agent may not be alone in a room with a male agent. The restriction that only one agent at a time may move through a doorway is represented by the restriction that an event ε represents an action performed by a single agent x. To add some dynamics to the system, the behaviour of the agents is further governed by a simple utility function such that $left \succ_f stay \succ_f right$ and $right \succ_m stay \succ_m left$, where $\succ$ is the relation 'better than' and f and m stands for 'female' and 'male', respectively. Figure 2 shows both a text-based and a graphical view of the initial state of the system, and the set of permissible acts for the acting agent f_1. The normative system contains the single norm $\langle M_0 opposite\_sex, P_7 alone\rangle$, which states that an agent may not act so that a pair of agents $\langle x_i, x_j\rangle$ such that x_i and x_j have opposite sex, end up alone in the same room. This includes moving to a room containing a single agent of the opposite sex as well as leaving two other agents of opposite sex alone in the same room. We see that of the two feasible acts $stay$ and $left$ in the current situation, only $stay$ is permissible according to the normative system, since if f_1 moves left she ends up alone with m_2.

The source code for the **Colour and Form** system and the **Rooms** system, as well as for the general-level Java/Prolog implementation of norm-regulated transition system situations is available for download[6] and is publicly and freely disseminated. The example systems are quite simple, but nicely illustrate some features of iterated use of norm-regulated transition system situations, e.g. the ability to investigate the interplay between a normative system that determines the scope of permissible actions for agents and utility functions that represent the preferences of the agents. They demonstrate that the general-level Java/Prolog

[5] More precisely, the agents may choose between three acts: $left$, $stay$ or $right$, but $left$ and $right$ are only feasible if there is a doorway in the corresponding direction. Note that the specific example in [4, p. 178ff] has one female and two male agents and two rooms, while the **Rooms** system has three rooms.

[6] http://drp.name/norms/nrtssit

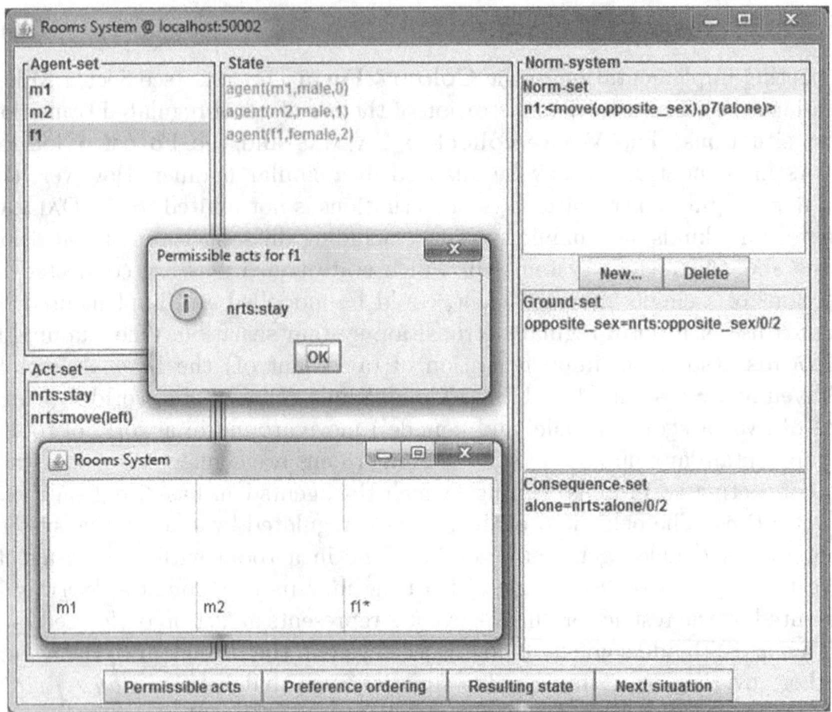

Fig. 2. Screenshot: Initial situation of a **Rooms** system execution.

implementation can be used as a tool for the implementation of such systems. The framework includes a Prolog logic server as a backend and (if desired) a Java user interface as frontend, functioning as a lookup-service that answers questions such as 'is act a permissible for x in state s, according to normative system $\mathcal{N}$' or 'which acts are permissible for x in state s, according to $\mathcal{N}$'. At the system level, it could be used to maintain a normative system for some society, in combination with some norm enforcement strategy. At the agent level, it could be used as a common normative framework that is shared by individual agents that take norms into account in their reasoning cycle, or as part of an agent's internal architecture, either to represent a model of society's normative system or to represent an agent's 'internal' normative system ('ethics'). Naturally, the use of both Java and Prolog as implementation languages has both advantages and disadvantages. The primary advantage is that this approach combines the strengths of two different programming paradigms and languages. On the other hand, it demands skills in both object-oriented and logic programming of the developer wishing to use the framework to develop a specific system.

Remark 1. Regarding computational complexity, it can be noted that the framework works well for the simple systems discussed here, but certainly has room for various performance optimizations. Still, even with such optimizations made, scaleability will remain a challenge for this framework as well as for most other frameworks for norm-regulated multi-agent systems (see, e.g., [24, p. 52]), since the time to test each norm is in the worst case roughly proportional to n^ν, where n is the size of the agent set Ω, $\nu = \max(p, q)$ and p and q is the arity of the ground (resp. consequence) of the norm.[7] One way to, at least partially, address these issues is to explore the possibility to express a normative system in an economic way by its set of 'minimal norms' (see for example [17,22]).

3 Conclusions and Future Work

This paper has introduced the notion of a transition system situation, which is intended to represent a single step in the run of many kinds of transition systems. In a norm-regulated transition system situation, the permission or prohibition of actions is related to the permission or prohibition of different types of state transitions with respect to some condition d on a number of agents $x_1, \ldots, x_\nu$ in a state. The framework uses a representation of conditional norms based on the algebraic approach[8] to normative systems used in [22] and a systematic exploration of the possible types of state transitions with respect to $d(x_1, \ldots, x_\nu)$.

By adaption of the existing implementation of the DALMAS architecture, a general-level Java/Prolog framework for norm-regulated transition system situations (together with some simple example systems) has been developed. The set of eight transition type conditions C_i^a is an extension of the set of six E_i^a conditions in [22]. These conditions were intended as an interpretation in the DALMAS context of Lindahl's set of one-agent types of normative positions. The (potential) connection between the combination of P_i and C_i^a and the Kanger-Lindahl theory of normative positions is interesting. It has been partly investigated in [8], but deserves to be further explored.

Lindahl and Odelstad argue that a normative system should express "... general rules where no individual names occur. If the task is to represent a normative system this feature of generality has to be taken into account." [17, p. 5] An advantage of their algebraic approach to normative systems, besides for example efficient automation and mechanization (see, e.g., [25, p. 197] with references), is in fact the expressive power it yields. The algebraic normative framework presented in this paper allows the construction of norms based on conditions on an arbitrary number of agents, in contrast to for example Dynamic deontic logic [20] and Dynamic logic of permission [19] which both have their roots in Propositional Dynamic Logic (PDL). Unlike in the agent-stranded coloured transition systems [4,24], the framework presented in this paper does not explicitly distinguish between state permission laws and action permission laws. It allows, however, a state permission law to be represented implicitly as a special case, by a norm which prohibits all transitions that lead to an undesired state. Our

[7] As noted in [21, p. 31], the computational complexity of any specific implementation may be more formally analysed through algorithmic analysis, e.g. average-case analysis.

[8] This approach was originally developed in a series of papers; see for example [13,15–17].

framework treats all norms as action permission laws, in the sense that actions are prohibited in different states as a consequence of certain transition types being prohibited by the normative system. It allows the creation of norms that forbid specific named actions in certain situations, by choosing a normative consequence that forbids the agent to act so that it ends up in a state where the last action performed was the prohibited action. This requires some sort of history of actions to be part of the state of the system.

The idea to base norms on permissible and prohibited types of state transitions has, to the author's knowledge, not been systematically explored before. It appears that the language for action permission laws used by Craven and Sergot also allows the formulation of norms that prohibit certain types of transitions, but an example of this feature is not given in [4]. In Dynamic deontic logic it is only the state resulting from a transition that determines if the transition is classified as 'permitted/non-permitted', while in Dynamic logic of permission, it is executions of actions that are classified as 'permitted/non-permitted'. van der Meyden's treatment of permission uses the process semantics for actions, in which the denotation of an action expressions is a set of sequences of states. This allows for the description of the states of affairs during the execution of an action; the permission of an action is not dependent only on the state resulting from the execution of the action, but also on the intermediate states.

The systematic treatment of the different types of transitions ensures that the set of transition type operators C_j^a and the corresponding prohibition operators P_j exhaust the space of meaningful transition type prohibitions. Therefore, norm-regulated transition system situations could be used in a given problem domain to systematically search for the 'best' normative system for (a class of) dynamic systems, according to some criteria for evaluation of the system's performance. For example, as suggested in [8], a genetic algorithm or some other mechanism from machine learning could be employed to seek the optimal normative system for a particular task. This requires some mechanism for *norm change*. In the current architecture, norms may be changed 'from the outside', but not 'from the inside' as a consequence of an action by an agent in a state s, since the normative system $\mathcal{N}$ is not itself considered a part of s. An interesting line of future work is to explore the possibility to let the normative system be a part of the state, thereby letting agents choose actions that modify the normative system. Norm change is another area in which the notion of 'minimal norms' may be of special significance, as suggested in [17, Sect. 2.1.2 and 4.3].

The requirement that each event ε in a norm-regulated transition system situation represents an action performed by a single agent deserves further attention. It corresponds roughly to the restriction in the *Rooms* example (Sect. 2.3) that only one agent at a time can move through a doorway. This raises a number of questions regarding the relationship between norm-regulated transition system situations and transition systems in which a single transition may correspond to the simultaneous action of several agents, possibly including 'actions' by the environment itself. These issues deserve a deeper discussion, which is left for future papers.

Another interesting issue is *consistency*. An inconsistent normative system may lead to a situation in which the deontic structure is empty, i.e. all actions are prohibited. How the system should behave in such a situation is heavily dependent on the nature of the specific application at hand; this is not specified by the general-level framework.

Acknowledgements. The author wishes to thank Jan Odelstad and Magnus Boman for valuable ideas and suggestions, participants of ICAART 2013 for discussions in relation to this paper and the organizers of the conference for the opportunity to expand my conference paper.

References

1. Cliffe, O., De Vos, M., Padget, J.: Specifying and analysing agent-based social institutions using answer set programming. In: Boissier, O., Padget, J., Dignum, V., Lindemann, G., Matson, E., Ossowski, S., Sichman, J.S., Vázquez-Salceda, J. (eds.) ANIREM 2005 and OOOP 2005. LNCS (LNAI), vol. 3913, pp. 99–113. Springer, Heidelberg (2006)
2. Cliffe, O., De Vos, M., Padget, J.: Answer set programming for representing and reasoning about virtual institutions. In: Inoue, K., Satoh, K., Toni, F. (eds.) CLIMA VII. LNCS (LNAI), vol. 4371, pp. 60–79. Springer, Heidelberg (2007)
3. Combettes, S., Hanachi, C., Sibertin-Blanc, C.: Organizational petri nets for protocol design and enactment. In: Proceedings of the Fifth International Joint Conference on Autonomous Agents and Multiagent Systems, AAMAS '06, pp. 1384–1386. ACM, New York (2006). doi:10.1145/1160633.1160892
4. Craven, R., Sergot, M.: Agent strands in the action language nC+. J. Appl. Log. **6**(2), 172–191 (2008). doi:10.1016/j.jal.2007.06.007. selected papers from the 8th International Workshop on Deontic Logic in Computer Science, 8th International Workshop on Deontic Logic in Computer Science
5. Gaertner, D., Clark, K., Sergot, M.J.: *Ballroom etiquette*: a case study for norm-governed multi-agent systems. In: Noriega, P., Vázquez-Salceda, J., Boella, G., Boissier, O., Dignum, V., Fornara, N., Matson, E. (eds.) COIN 2006. LNCS (LNAI), vol. 4386, pp. 212–226. Springer, Heidelberg (2007)
6. Governatori, G., Rotolo, A., Sartor, G.: Temporalised normative positions in defeasible logic. In: Proceedings of the 10th International Conference on Artificial Intelligence and Law, ICAIL '05, pp. 25–34. ACM, New York (2005). doi:10.1145/1165485.1165490
7. Hjelmblom, M.: Deontic action-logic multi-agent systems in Prolog. Technical report 30, University of Gävle, Division of Computer Science (2008). http://urn.kb.se/resolve?urn=urn:nbn:se:hig:diva-1475
8. Hjelmblom, M.: State transitions and normative positions within normative systems. Technical report 37, University of Gävle, Department of Industrial Development, IT and Land Management (2011). http://urn.kb.se/resolve?urn=urn:nbn:se:hig:diva-10595
9. Hjelmblom, M.: Norm-regulated transition system situations. In: Filipe, J., Fred, A. (eds.) Proceedings of the 5th International Conference on Agents and Artificial Intelligence, ICAART 2013, pp. 109–117. SciTePress, Portugal (2013)
10. Hjelmblom, M., Odelstad, J.: jDALMAS: a Java/Prolog framework for deontic action-logic multi-agent systems. In: Håkansson, A., Nguyen, N.T., Hartung, R.L., Howlett, R.J., Jain, L.C. (eds.) KES-AMSTA 2009. LNCS (LNAI), vol. 5559, pp. 110–119. Springer, Heidelberg (2009)

11. Laaksolahti, J., Boman, M.: Anticipatory guidance of plot. CoRRcs.AI/0206041 (2002). doi:10.1007/978-3-540-45002-3_14
12. Lindahl, L.: Position and change: a study in law and logic. Synthese library, D. Reidel Pub. Co. (1977). http://www.google.com/books?id=_QwWhOK8aY0C
13. Lindahl, L., Odelstad, J.: Normative systems and their revision: an algebraic approach. Artif. Intell. Law **11**, 81–104 (2003). doi:10.1023/B:ARTI.0000046005.10529.47
14. Lindahl, L., Odelstad, J.: Normative positions within an algebraic roach to normative systems. J. Appl. Log. **2**(1), 63–91 (2004). doi:10.1016/j.jal.2004.01.004. the Sixth International Workshop on Deontic Logic in Computer Science
15. Lindahl, L., Odelstad, J.: Intermediaries and intervenients in normative systems. J. Appl. Log. **6**(2), 229–250 (2008). doi:10.1016/j.jal.2007.06.010. selected papers from the 8th International Workshop on Deontic Logic in Computer Science
16. Lindahl, L., Odelstad, J.: Stratification of normative systems with intermediaries. J. Appl. Log. **9**(2), 113–136 (2011). doi:10.1016/j.jal.2010.01.002. special Issue: Selected and revised papers from the Ninth International Conference on Deontic Logic in Computer Science (DEON 2008)
17. Lindahl, L., Odelstad, J.: The theory of joining-systems. In: Gabbay, D., Horthy, J., Parent, X., van der Meyden, R., van der Torre, L. (eds.) Handbook of Deontic Logic and Normative Systems, vol. 1, pp. 545–634. College Publications, London (2013)
18. Makinson, D., van der Torre, L.: What is input/output logic? input/output logic, constraints, permissions. In: Boella, G., van der Torre, L., Verhagen, H. (eds.) Normative Multi-agent Systems. No. 07122 in Dagstuhl Seminar Proceedings, Internationales Begegnungs- und Forschungszentrum für Informatik (IBFI), Schloss Dagstuhl, Germany, Dagstuhl, Germany (2007). http://drops.dagstuhl.de/opus/volltexte/2007/928
19. van der Meyden, R.: The dynamic logic of permission. J. Log. Comput. **6**(3), 465–479 (1996)
20. Meyer, J.J.C.: A different approach to deontic logic: deontic logic viewed as a variant of dynamic logic. Notre Dame Journal of Formal Logic **29**(1), 109–136 (1987). doi:10.1305/ndjfl/1093637776
21. Odelstad, J.: Many-sorted implicative conceptual systems. Ph.D. thesis, Royal Institute of Technology, Computer and Systems Sciences, DSV (2008), qC 20100901
22. Odelstad, J., Boman, M.: Algebras for agent norm-regulation. Ann. Math. Artif. Intell. **42**, 141–166 (2004). doi:10.1023/B:AMAI.0000034525.49481.4a
23. Raskin, J.F., van der Torre, L.W., Tan, Y.H.: How to model normative behavior in petri nets. In: Proceedings of the 2nd Modelage Workshop on Formal Models of Agents, pp. 223–241 (1996). http://hdl.handle.net/2013/ULB-DIPOT:oai:dipot.ulb.ac.be:2013/70564
24. Sergot, M.J.: Action and agency in norm-governed multi-agent systems. In: Artikis, A., O'Hare, G.M.P., Stathis, K., Vouros, G.A. (eds.) ESAW 2007. LNCS (LNAI), vol. 4995, pp. 1–54. Springer, Heidelberg (2008)
25. Solin, K.: Modal semirings with operators for knowledge representation. In: Filipe, J., Fred, A. (eds.) Proceedings of the 5th International Conference on Agents and Artificial Intelligence, ICAART 2013, pp. 197–202. SciTePress, Portugal (2013)
26. Vázquez-Salceda, J., Aldewereld, H., Dignum, F.P.M.: Implementing norms in multiagent systems. In: Lindemann, G., Denzinger, J., Timm, I.J., Unland, R. (eds.) MATES 2004. LNCS (LNAI), vol. 3187, pp. 313–327. Springer, Heidelberg (2004)

Path Planning for Tentacle Robots Using Soft Constraints

Jing Yang(✉), Patrick Dymond, and Michael Jenkin

Department of Electrical Engineering and Computer Science, York University, Keele Street, Toronto 4700, Canada
{jyang,dymond,jenkin}@cse.yorku.ca
http://www.cse.yorku.ca

Abstract. Tentacle robots – robots with many degrees of freedom with one fixed end – offer advantages over traditional robots in many scenarios due to their enhanced flexibility and reachability. Planning practical paths for these devices is challenging due to their high number of degrees of freedom (DOFs). Sampling-based path planners are a common approach to the high DOF planning problem associated with tentacle robots but the solutions found using such planners are often not practical in that they do not take into account soft application-specific constraints. This paper describes a general sample adjustment method for tentacle robots which adjusts the nodes and edges generated by the sampling-based planners within their local neighborhood to satisfy soft constraints associated with the problem. Experiments with real and simulated tentacle robots demonstrate that our approach is an effective enhancement to the basic probabilistic planner to find practical paths.

Keywords: Probabilistic motion planning · Soft constraints · Tentacle robots

1 Introduction

Tentacle robots, also known as snake or serpentine robots, are manipulator robots with many degrees of freedom (DOFs) (see Fig. 1). Such devices have received considerable attention from the robotics community due to their applicability in a wide range of different domains (see [28,30] for recent surveys). Tentacle robots are often an attractive alternative to traditional robotic systems for difficult terrains and challenging grasping scenarios, including search and rescue missions in complex urban environments, planetary surface exploration, minimally invasive surgery, and inspection of piping and nuclear systems [4,6,8]. Unlike traditional manipulator robots which tend to have small numbers of

This is an extended version of "Planning Practical Paths for Tentacle Robots" which appeared in the 5th International Conference on Agents and Artificial Intelligence (ICAART), Barcelona, Spain, 2013.

J. Filipe and A. Fred (Eds.): ICAART 2013, CCIS 449, pp. 95–111, 2014.
DOI: 10.1007/978-3-662-44440-5_6

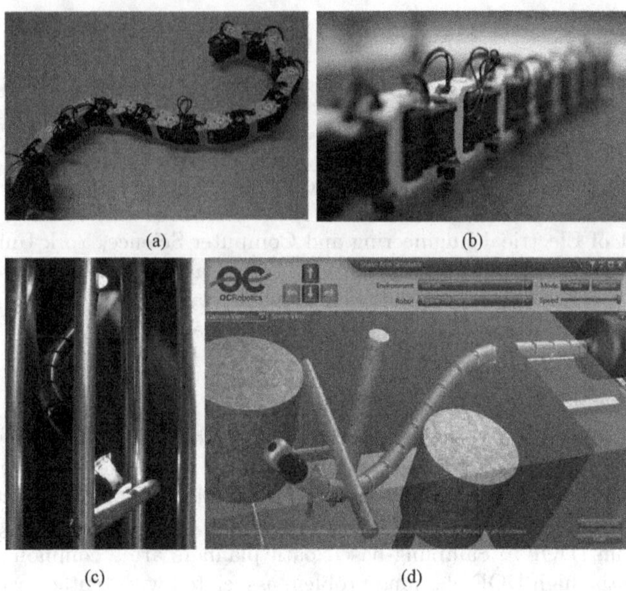

Fig. 1. Tentacle robots. (a) and (b) are images of a planar tentacle robot created from ten Dynamixel AX-12 servos. (c) and (d) are real and simulated images of OC Robotics 3D tentacle robot. The pictures (c) and (d) are © OC Robotics and are used with permission.

DOFs, tentacle robots utilize redundant DOFs in order to enhance their ability to deal with complex environments and tasks.

Since it can be difficult to plan a path for robots with many DOFs, early methods for high DOF robots aimed at finding any solution to the planning problem within a reasonable time. With the development of sampling-based algorithms and their application in practice, the focus has shifted to considering the quality of the path obtained as well [1,7,9,15,19,27,29,31]. A shortcoming of basic sampling-based planning approaches is that they can obtain highly 'non-optimal' solutions since they rely upon randomization to explore the search space. Although basic sampling-based planning algorithms may find a valid solution, that solution may not be practical in that it does not meet soft constraints that exist within the problem domain. Furthermore, it has been proven that the standard Probabilistic Roadmap Method (PRM) and Rapidly-exploring Random Tree (RRT) are not asymptotically optimal, i.e. the cost of the solution returned by the algorithm is not guaranteed to converge to the optimal cost as the number of samples increases [15]. Optimality cannot be generated by simply sampling more densely.

The need to properly represent and use soft constraints is particularly important for redundant DOF robots such as tentacle devices. For these devices the high number of DOFs provide the opportunity to deal with complex environments and to produce solutions that are not only correct (e.g., they grasp the object through free space, for grasping tasks) but also optimize other requirements of the problem space. The high number of DOF's coupled with the random nature of the planning algorithm often leads to motion paths that involve the robot "flailing about" as it gets from the start to the goal state. One way of reducing these unwanted motions and taking soft constraints is to use an appropriate controller that takes the path identified by the path planner as input and only integrates the soft constraints while executing the path [3,20]. There are many issues with this approach. Perhaps most critically the paths produced may be infeasible for a real robot. For example, following the path produced may require that the robot move extremely slowly in order to minimize the influence of dynamics and other physical constraints. These controllers are also system specific, and it can be very hard to develop a good 'general' controllers or to know which controller to use for a given task.

Rather than incorporating soft constraints as a secondary "refining" process a more general approach is to augment sampling-based path planning with mechanisms that generate paths that are both correct and also optimize the soft constraints. Such augmentation can take place at different points in the path planning process, including as a path refining task. This paper concentrates on optimizations performed during the sampling phase of the algorithm. Perturbing each randomly generated sample within its local neighborhood to enhance compliance with the soft constraints often leads to more practical paths for the robot. The framework described here is intended to be robot independent, but the approach is described and tuned here towards tentacle robots such as those shown in Fig. 1.

This paper is structured as follows: Sect. 2 reviews existing sampling-based planning algorithms that address the path quality problem and the current methods used to plan paths for tentacle robots. Section 3 formulates the practicality of paths in terms of soft constraints and describes constraints particularly critical for tentacle robots. In Sects. 4 and 5, path planning strategies are developed to find paths of user-preferred qualities based on this formalism. Section 6 compares paths obtained with a practicality-aware planning approach and a basic PRM to different test environments using both real and simulated tentacle robots. Finally Sect. 7 summarizes the work and provides possible directions for future research.

2 Related Work

2.1 Sampling-Based Path Planning

Instead of computing an exact representation of the planning space, sampling-based planners generate a number of discrete sample points in configuration space and test motions between these points and the start and goal states. Such planners usually represent motions as a graph as in the PRM [16,17], or as a tree as in the RRT [23]. These methods are probabilistically complete. It is not guaranteed that these planners will find a path even though one exists, but if they do find a path the path will take the device from the initial configuration to the goal. Randomized path planning algorithms that address the problem of path quality can be divided into three broad categories based on where these issues are integrated within the algorithm: pre-processing, post-processing, and customized learning.

Pre-processing Approaches. Pre-processing approaches consider the specific preferences of desired paths in the pre-processing phase, i.e. during the roadmap construction phase before a query is made. Because of its probabilistic nature, the PRM roadmap often contains nodes and edges that lack practical usage or are redundant. Aiming at finding shorter paths with higher clearance, Nieuwenhuisen and Overmars [26] proposed to add nodes and edges to create "useful" cycles, which provide short paths and alternative paths in different homotopy classes. Based on this work, another PRM variant by Geraerts [9] attempts to retract nodes and edges to the medial axis to generate high clearance paths.

Post-processing Approaches. Given a path found by the sampling-based path planner, post-processing approaches modify the path in accordance with the required practicality preference by adding new nodes, smoothing the path, eliminating unnecessary loops or detours, etc. Path pruning and shortcut heuristics are common post-processing techniques for creating shorter and smoother paths [9,14]. Retraction algorithms add clearance to a given path [10]. Post-processing algorithms may take multiple paths as input rather than just a single one. For example, the path merging algorithm described in [27] computes a path with improved quality by hybridizing high-quality sub-paths. The algorithm considers the generalized formulation of path quality measures rather than specific requirements. Path refining approaches, mentioned earlier, fall into the post-processing category.

Customized Learning. Although post-processing algorithms have shown some success in improving the path quality and can be used by all the path planners, the final path depends on the original paths, i.e. they cannot find alternative routes that deviate considerably from the original ones. To avoid this problem, customized learning algorithms integrate the requirement for path quality in the learning phase. For example, Kim et al. [19] use an augmented version of Dijkstra's algorithm to extract a path from a roadmap on criteria other than path length.

The approach of initially finding an approximate solution is utilized by the Fuzzy PRM [25], Lazy PRM [2], IRC (Iterative Relaxation of Constraints) [1] and C-PRM (Customizable PRM) [29] algorithms where the roadmap nodes and edges are not validated, or are only partially validated, during roadmap construction. During the learning phase, the path is searched by strengthening the constraints (obstacle collision, path length or other specified preferences) iteratively. These methods are designed to decrease the roadmap construction costs, while only increasing the query costs slightly.

2.2 Path Planning for Tentacle Robots

There has been relatively little work devoted explicitly to tentacle robot path planning. One approach is based on the definition of *tunnels* in the workspace [5]. Methods from differential geometry are then used to guarantee that the tentacle is confined to the tunnels, and therefore avoids any obstacles. Later work proposed to use the results of the Generalized Voronoi Graph (GVG) approach to construct the tunnels themselves [6]. Motion planning is then achieved via a nose-following approach which allows the end-effector to move along the GVG followed by the rest of body.

Sampling-based planning algorithms such as PRMs and RRTs are popular because of their success in a wide range of applications and in high-dimensional configuration spaces. This makes them an appealing choice for tentacle robot path planning, but they suffer from the problem of generating less than optimal paths for the robot. A physics-based sampling strategy for finding *realistic* paths for a highly articulated chain robot is presented in [8]. This method exploits the coherence between joint angles via an "adaptive forward dynamics" framework in order to determine which joints have the greatest impact on the overall motion. Then, only the most important joints are considered. The samples are then biased by using constraint forces designed to avoid collisions while moving toward the goal (similar to a potential field approach).

3 Problem Statement

Formally, given a robot $\mathcal{A}$, a static workspace $\mathcal{W}$ containing a set of obstacles, an initial configuration θ_{init} and a goal configuration θ_{goal}, the objective of path planning is to determine a feasible path $\mathcal{P}$ between θ_{init} and θ_{goal} [21]. In its most basic form, a feasible solution to the basic path planning problem only considers geometric constraints that arise from collision with obstacles and is often inadequate to describe realistic path planning problems.

Soft constraints can be added to the basic path planning problem in a number of different ways. Following the PDDL3.0 approach [12], the syntax for soft constraints can be broken down into two components: (i) the identification of the soft constraints; and (ii) the description of how the satisfaction of these constraints affects the quality of the path. Similar to the descriptions of hard constraints, soft constraints can be described using predicates of the planning problem. Each binary soft constraint is associated with a violation penalty weight such that paths, or portions of paths can be compared. Let $\mathcal{S}$ be the set of soft constraints. The following typical soft constraints for tentacle robots are described in terms of inequalities between the value computed from the robot's configuration and a corresponding threshold λ:

Safe Clearance from Obstacles (SCO). A soft constraint for keeping a safe clearance from the obstacles [32] is given by

$$\left(\sum_{i=1}^{N} \frac{1}{D_i} \right) \leq \lambda_{SCO} \tag{1}$$

where D_i is the minimum distance between the i-th link of the manipulator and obstacles, and λ_{SCO} is a pre-defined upper bound (similar to λ_{JLA} and λ_{PEE} below);

Joint Limit Avoidance (JLA). A soft constraint for joint limit avoidance [32] is given by

$$\left(\sum_{i=1}^{N} \frac{\theta_{i,Max} - \theta_{i,Min}}{(\theta_{i,Max} - \theta_i)(\theta_i - \theta_{i,Min})} \right) \leq \lambda_{JLA} \tag{2}$$

where $\theta_{i,Max}$ and $\theta_{i,Min}$ are the maximum and minimum permissible joint angles and θ_i is the current joint angle for the i-the joint.

Precision of End-Effector (PEE). It is often required to ensure the precision with which a tentacle robot approaches a point or follows a path defined by the pose of the end-effector (EEF) [13]. Let $x \in \mathbb{R}^m$ represent the output position vector of the EEF and $\theta \in \mathbb{R}^n$ the vector of joint angles of the robot. An infinitesimal error in the EEF position can be mapped from the joint errors through:

$$\Delta x = J \Delta c \tag{3}$$

where the $m \times n$ matrix J, called the Jacobian, is a geometrically dependent structure relating the joint errors to the output errors [18,24]. The Euclidean norm of the EEF error is therefore bounded above by

$$\frac{||\Delta x||}{||\Delta c||} \leq \sigma_{max} \tag{4}$$

where σ_{max} is the Jacobian's maximum singular values. A soft constraint for the generalized EEF precision can be defined by bounding σ_{max}:

$$\sigma_{max} \leq \lambda_{PEE} \tag{5}$$

Note that we do not attempt to distinguish degrees of satisfaction of a soft constraint – we are only concerned with whether or not the constraint is satisfied. However, a soft constraint may be counted multiple times depending on the number of the violation occurrences exhibited while executing the path. Let $\mathbb{P}$ denote the set of all feasible paths. Here we define a cost function that describes the overall practicality of a path and then define the path planning with soft constraints using the cost function.

Cost Function. Consider a feasible configuration $\theta \in \mathcal{C}_{free}$, where $\mathcal{C}_{free}$ is the free configuration space, i.e. θ meets all the hard constraints such as not colliding with the surrounding obstacles and staying within the joint limits. Given a soft constraint s, the cost function of the configuration $cost_s : \mathcal{C}_{free} \rightarrow [0,1]$, i.e. a $cost_s(\theta) \in [0,1]$ can be computed for each $\theta \in \mathcal{C}_{free}$. This cost function can be continuous or discrete. In its simplest version, the cost function $cost_s$ is binary, i.e. 0 when the soft constraint is satisfied by θ, and 1 when violated. Given a set of soft constraints $\mathcal{S}$ with associated violation penalty weights, $\forall s \in \mathcal{S}, w(s) > 0$, the cost of a feasible configuration is the summation of the penalty weights of all the costs of soft constraints that are violated by θ, defined as

$$cost : \mathcal{C}_{free} \to \mathbb{R}_{\geq 0}, \; cost(\theta) = \sum_{s \in \mathcal{S}} w(s) \cdot cost_s(\theta) \tag{6}$$

A path $\mathcal{P}$ of length l is represented by a unit-speed parametric function $\tau : [0, l] \to \mathcal{C}_{free}$ with $\tau(t) = \theta_t, \; \theta_t \in \mathcal{P}$. Then the parametric cost function is defined as:

$$v : [0, l] \to \mathbb{R}_{\geq 0} v(t) = cost \circ \tau(t) = cost(\theta_t) \tag{7}$$

Given a feasible path $\mathcal{P}$, its cost is the integral of the cost of all the configurations along the path, defined as

$$cost : \; \mathbb{P} \to \mathbb{R}_{\geq 0}, \; cost(\mathcal{P}) = \int_0^l v(t)dt \tag{8}$$

A discrete approximation of the integral leads to

$$cost : \; \mathbb{P} \to \mathbb{R}_{\geq 0}, \; cost(\mathcal{P}) \sim \frac{1}{n} \sum_{k=0}^{n-1} v((\frac{k}{n-1})l) \tag{9}$$

This provides a cost function that penalizes paths with sections that violate the soft constraints provided.

Path Planning with Soft Constraints. Given a path planning problem $(\mathcal{A}, \mathcal{W}, \theta_{init}, \theta_{goal})$, a set of soft constraints $\mathcal{S}$ with corresponding penalty weights and a cost function *cost*, generate a feasible path $\mathcal{P}$ such that $cost(\mathcal{P})$ is minimized. The algorithm here generates a roadmap within the environment. The roadmap must be connected to θ_{init} and θ_{goal} and a path must exist within the roadmap for a path to be found.

4 Sampling with Soft Constraints

Following [16], the PRM roadmap with soft constraints generation algorithm is outlined in Algorithm 1. During node generation, instead of choosing completely random configurations as in the basic PRM, a sampling method with soft constraints (i.e. *SamplingSC* and *SamplingHCSC*) is used (line 4) and the new configuration that satisfies some or all the soft constraints is added to the set of vertices V. Connections are then attempted between vertices within a distance r using a simple straight-line local planner.

It is observed that for a collision-free node to be useful for path planning it must be part of a connected free region. Within any region we can expect some locations to be more practical than others. Ensuring that more practical

Algorithm 1. Roadmap Generation with Soft Constraints.

$V \leftarrow \emptyset$
$E \leftarrow \emptyset$
for $i = 1, ..., n$ **do**
  $\theta_{rand} \leftarrow$ sampling with soft constraints
  $X \leftarrow Near(G = (V, E), \theta_{rand}, r)$
  $V \leftarrow V \cup \{\theta_{rand}\}$
  for all $x \in X$, in order of increasing $||x - \theta_{rand}||$ **do**
    if θ_{rand} and x are not in the same connected component of $G = (V, E)$ **then**
      if $(v, x) \models \mathcal{H}$ **then**
        $E \leftarrow E \cup \{(v, x), (x, v)\}$
      end if
    end if
  end for
end for
return $G = (V, E)$

nodes are chosen during the roadmap seeding process while still sampling the space sufficiently densely to construct paths is likely to improve overall path practicality, at least as measured by node-based soft constraints. Given a feasible node we can search within a local region of this node to enhance the practicality of this node. In order to take advantage of this, the planner adjusts a node within its free space to states with fewer soft constraint violations before adding them to the roadmap. We present two node adjustment strategies *SamplingSC* and *SamplingHCSC* as outlined in Algorithms 2 and 3 to accomplish this task.

Algorithm 2. SamplingSC (random sampling with soft constraints).

repeat
  $\theta_{rand} \leftarrow$ a randomly chosen configuration in $\mathcal{C}$
until $\theta_{rand} \models \mathcal{H}$
$\theta_{new} \leftarrow \theta_{rand}$
for $i \leftarrow 1, ..., k$ **do**
  $d \leftarrow \mathcal{N}(0, r^*)$
  $\theta_i \leftarrow$ a random configuration at distance d from θ_{rand}
  if $\theta_i \models \mathcal{H}$ and $cost(\theta_i) < cost(\theta_{new})$ **then**
    $\theta_{new} \leftarrow \theta_i$
  end if
end for
return θ_{new}

In *SamplingSC*, for each randomly generated feasible node θ_{new}, k attempts are made to adjust θ_{new} to reduce the soft constraint cost associated with the node. New samples are generated in θ_{new}'s neighborhood according to the normal distribution $\mathcal{N}(0, r^*)$, where the scale r^* is chosen based on the assumed local complexity of the configuration space. Each of these new samples is first tested for

Algorithm 3. SamplingHCSC (random sampling with hill-climbing soft constraint satisfaction).

```
repeat
    θ_rand ← a randomly chosen configuration in C
until θ_rand ⊨ H
θ_new ← θ_rand
u ← a random direction
for i ← 1, ..., k do
    θ_i ← move θ_new in the direction of u by step size d_step
    if θ_i ⊨ H and cost(θ_i) < cost(θ_new) then
        θ_new ← θ_i
    else
        return θ_new
    end if
end for
return θ_new
```

compliance with the hard constraints. If the test passes then the soft constraints are applied. The valid node with minimum soft constraint cost from this sample is then added in the roadmap.

Choosing k and r^* are application-specific issues. Note that during the node adjustment step k nodes are not added to the roadmap. Rather, each node is augmented up to k times while retaining fixed the total number of nodes. On the one hand, k should not be too small, because we want to give our planner a good chance to make an improvement. On the other hand, making k too large increases the running time unnecessarily. In essence we assume that within some radius (defined by r^*) of a node, there exists a more practical common homotopic path. In this work we assume a single r^* but clearly it would be possible to set $r^* = f(\theta)$ for complex non-homogeneous environments or to set $r^* = g(n)$ according to the density of the sampling.

SamplingHCSC is a greedy strategy that can be considered as an alternative to *SamplingSC*. Instead of attempting to reduce the cost of a sample once, the *SamplingHCSC* iterates the maximum of k steps toward a random direction u until a hard constraint is violated or the soft constraint cost stops decreasing. The random direction u incorporates all of the degrees of freedom of the robot.

Once the roadmap $\mathcal{R}$ is constructed, finding a path between θ_{init} and θ_{goal} involves connecting these points to $\mathcal{R}$. If θ_{init} and θ_{goal} do not belong to the same connected component, then more nodes need to be generated for $\mathcal{R}$ to connect the components to which θ_{init} and θ_{goal} belong. If this cannot be accomplished after a maximal number of trials then failure is reported. Otherwise, the algorithm proceeds to the next phase: extracting an optimal path from $\mathcal{R}$. Given the nature of the **cost** function of paths, it is possible to use Dijkstra's algorithm [19] to find the minimum cost path in $\mathcal{R}$ from θ_{init} to θ_{goal}.

5 Postprocessing with Soft Constraints

Path pruning "shortcut heuristics" are smoothing techniques for creating shorter and smoother paths. The shortcut method tries to iteratively improve the path obtained using PRM by replacing one part of the path with a shorter local path. In each iteration two nodes in the path are considered as the endpoints of a potential shortcut. Let a and b denote the two nodes. If the local path $LP(a, b)$ is collision-free then the local path $LP(a, b)$ replaces the path between a and b that stays within the graph/tree structure. Due to their simplicity, shortcut algorithms have been widely used to improve the quality of paths computed by randomized planners [11].

Algorithm 4. Shortcut with Soft Constraints (discrete path $\mathcal{P} = \theta_0, \theta_1, ...\theta_{m-1}$).

loop
    $a, b \leftarrow$ two random indices in $[0, m)$ and $(a < b)$
    $\mathcal{P}_1 \leftarrow \theta_0, ...\theta_{a-1}$
    $\mathcal{P}_2 \leftarrow \theta_a, ...\theta_b$
    $\mathcal{P}_3 \leftarrow \theta_{b+1}, ...\theta_{m-1}$
    if $LP(\theta_a, \theta_b) \models \mathcal{H}$ and $cost(LP(\theta_a, \theta_b)) < cost(\mathcal{P}_2)$ **then**
        $\mathcal{P} \leftarrow \mathcal{P}_1 \cup LP(\theta_a, \theta_b) \cup \mathcal{P}_3$
    end if
end loop

The goal of the traditional shortcutting methods is to find a shorter path that is in the same homotopy class of an existing path. However, this can bring the robot close to an obstacle or violate other soft constraints. We augment the shortcut algorithm with soft constraints (shown in Algorithm 4) which compares the soft constraint cost of the new local path and the original part of the path before replacement. We expect that this method will be slower than the original heuristic as the cost comparison takes extra computational time. However, we expect that the resultant path will be more practical.

6 Experimental Validation

This section describes experiments of the algorithm using two tentacle robot models. The first tentacle robot is a planar robot built from ten Robotis Dynamixel AX-12 servos (Fig. 1(a-b)). The robot is approximately 67 cm long when it lies straight. One end of the robot is fixed and rollers have been installed to reduce friction between the robot and the table top. The planar robot has 10 DOFs. The other robot is a simulated tentacle robot moving in 3-dimensional space. This simulation is based on a commercially available tentacle robot developed by OC Robotics Inc. developed for operation in complex environments such as nuclear power plants (Fig. 1(c-d)). This 3D robot has a mobile base that can translate in one dimension and 7 joints, each of which consists of two DOFs – roll and pitch, so

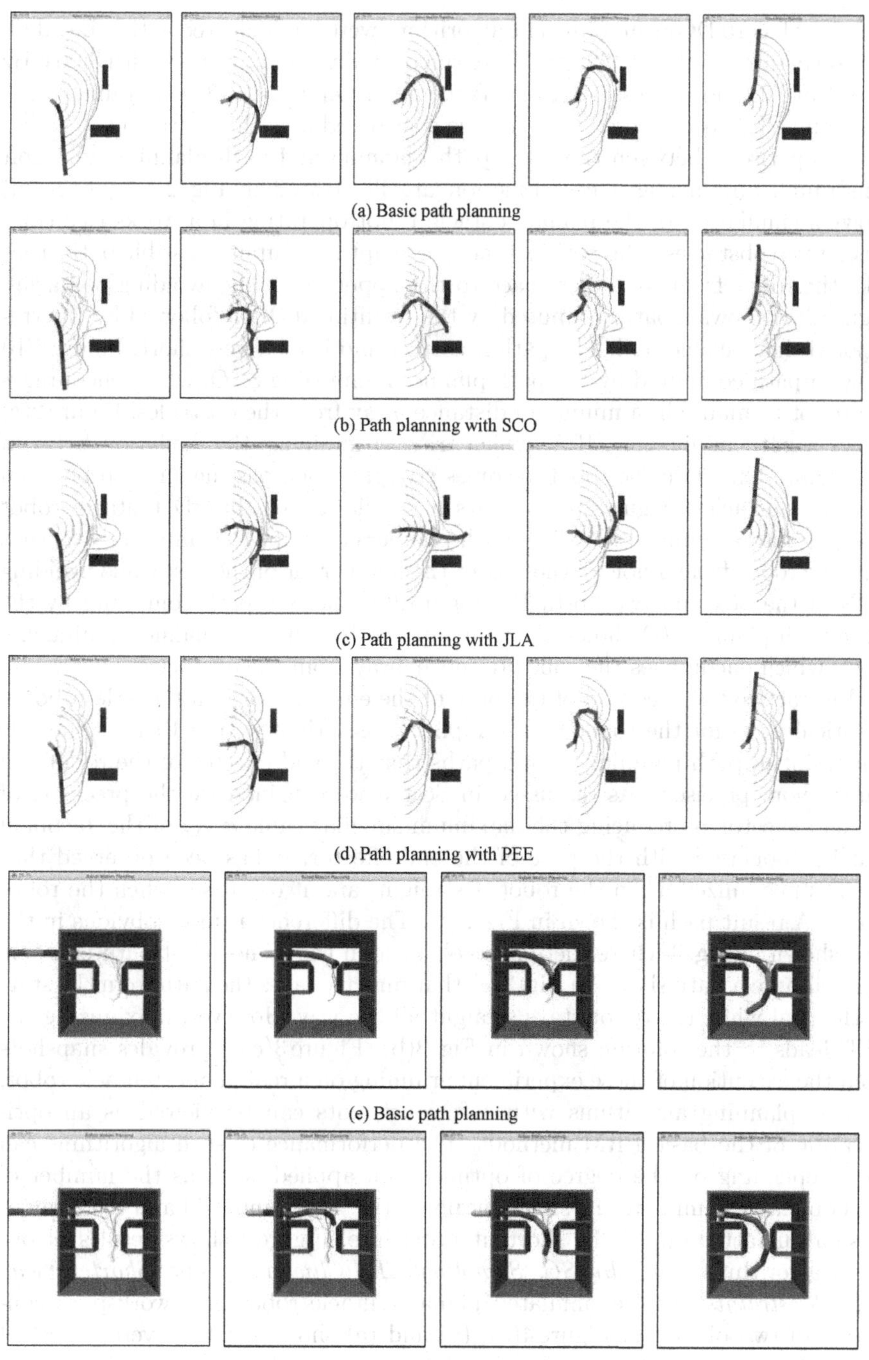

(a) Basic path planning

(b) Path planning with SCO

(c) Path planning with JLA

(d) Path planning with PEE

(e) Basic path planning

(f) Path planning with SCO

Fig. 2. (a-d) Path planning for a planar tentacle robot in a workspace with two rectangular obstacles. (e-f) Path planning for a 3D tentacle robot in a confined workspace.

the robot has 15 DOFs in total. The algorithms were implemented within Lavalle's Motion Strategy Library [22], and were run on a Mac running OS X with 3.06 GHz Intel Core 2 Duo processor and 2 GB memory. Only one soft constraint (SCO, JLA, and PEE as discussed in Sect. 3) is considered in each experiment.

Comparisons between the basic path planning and path planning with soft constraints minimizing a cost function are illustrated in Fig. 2. Figure 2(a-d) shows a simulation of the planar tentacle robot operating in a workspace comprising two obstacles. The path planners attempt to compute possible paths that take the robot from the lower space to the upper one while avoiding obstacles. Figure 2(a) shows a path computed by the traditional PRM followed by the traditional shortcut method. The path is correct and is relatively short. Figure 2(b) shows a path computed by our path planner minimizing SCO, which encourages the robot to maintain a minimum distance away from the obstacles. Figure 2(c) shows a path minimizing JLA, which tries to minimize the deviation between each joint. Therefore the robot becomes straight when passing the gap between the two obstacles. Figure 2(e-f) shows a simulation of the 3D tentacle robot reaching into a confined box. The path planners attempt to compute paths that take the robot from a hole of the box to the lower front of the box while avoiding walls of the box and two obstacles. Figure 2(e) shows a path computed by the basic path planner; (f) shows a path computed by our path planner minimizing SCO, which encourages the robot to move away from the obstacles.

In practice the precision of the pose of the end effector of a tentacle robot is a critical issue for the robot to accomplish tasks. Here we use PEE as the soft constraint in path planning to find paths that the end effector of the robot can follow more precisely. As discussed in Sect. 3 we can increase the precision of the end-effector by reducing the maximum singular value σ_{max} of the Jacobian matrix associated with the pose of the end effector. It has been observed that σ_{max} is maximized when the robot is straight, and it decreases when the robot bends. A result path is shown in Fig. 2(c). The difference is more obvious in the case shown in Fig. 3 where there is no obstacle in the scene. Most path planners will compute a path shown in Fig. 3(a) that directly takes the path from the start to the goal while the robot stays straight all the way. However, maximizing the PEE leads to the solution shown in Fig. 3(b). Figure 3(c-d) provides snapshots from the execution of these experiments running on a real planar tentacle robot.

Our planning algorithms with soft constraints can be viewed as an optimization of the basic PRM methods. The performance of such algorithms can vary depending on the degree of optimization applied, such as the number of adjustments attempts in the sampling phase (i.e. the number k) and the number of shortcut attempts of the shortcut procedure. Figure 4 shows results of our three algorithms (*SamplingSC*, *SamplingSCHillClimbming*, and *Shortcut with Soft Constraints*) on the simulated planar tentacle robot in a workspace consisting of two obstacles. Figure 4(a), (c) and (e) show that the average cost of the path as measured in terms of violations from soft constraints is reduced when the degree of optimization increases, i.e. more node adjustment or shortcut attempts are made. The optimization methods reduce the path cost quickly

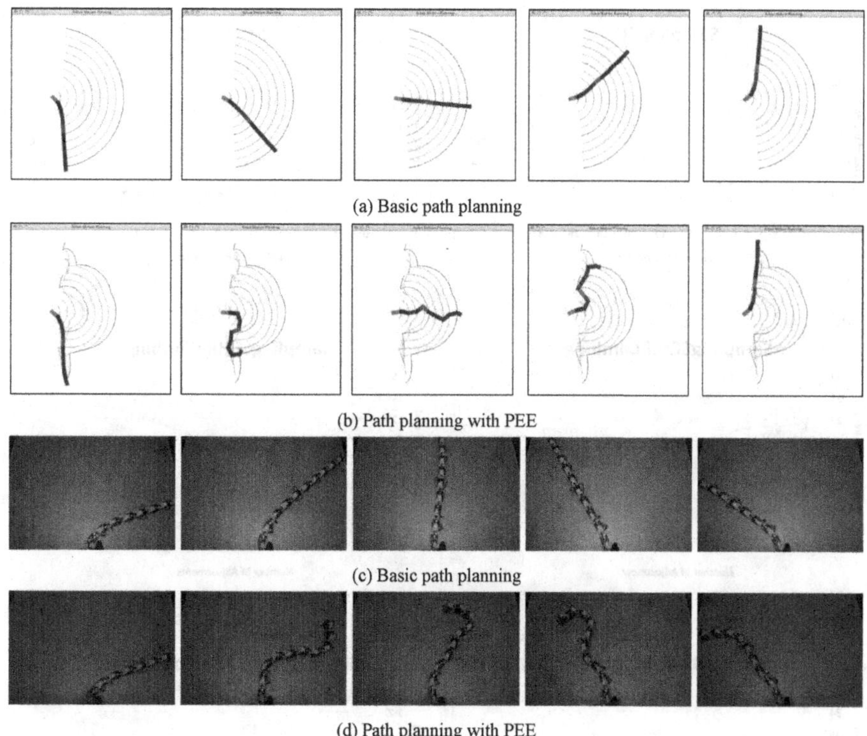

(a) Basic path planning
(b) Path planning with PEE
(c) Basic path planning
(d) Path planning with PEE

Fig. 3. Path planning in the absence of obstacles in simulations (a-b) and on a real robot (c-d).

at first, while further optimization efforts have a reduced rate of return. Clearly the shortcut method outperforms the two sampling methods in reducing path cost. This is because the shortcut method takes a given path as an input so its task is more focused than sampling methods which try to optimize the nodes of the entire roadmap. Therefore, the sampling methods aim at generating a "better" roadmap, which can be beneficial for multiple queries of paths.

Figure 4(b), (d) and (f) show the running time of the three optimization methods. Clearly the time increases with the degree of optimization because of the computation required by the optimization, and the amount of additional time depends on the computation of the soft constraints. In this example, computing SCO is expensive as it requires the distance to be computed between each robot link and the obstacles, and computing JLA and PEE are relatively less expensive as they do not require examining geometry of the workspace. PEE involves matrix computation, so it is more expensive to compute than JLA. If a robotic system is implemented in a sequential fashion such that optimizations must be completed before beginning execution of the path, it is unclear when to stop the optimization to achieve an ideal balance between computation and path quality.

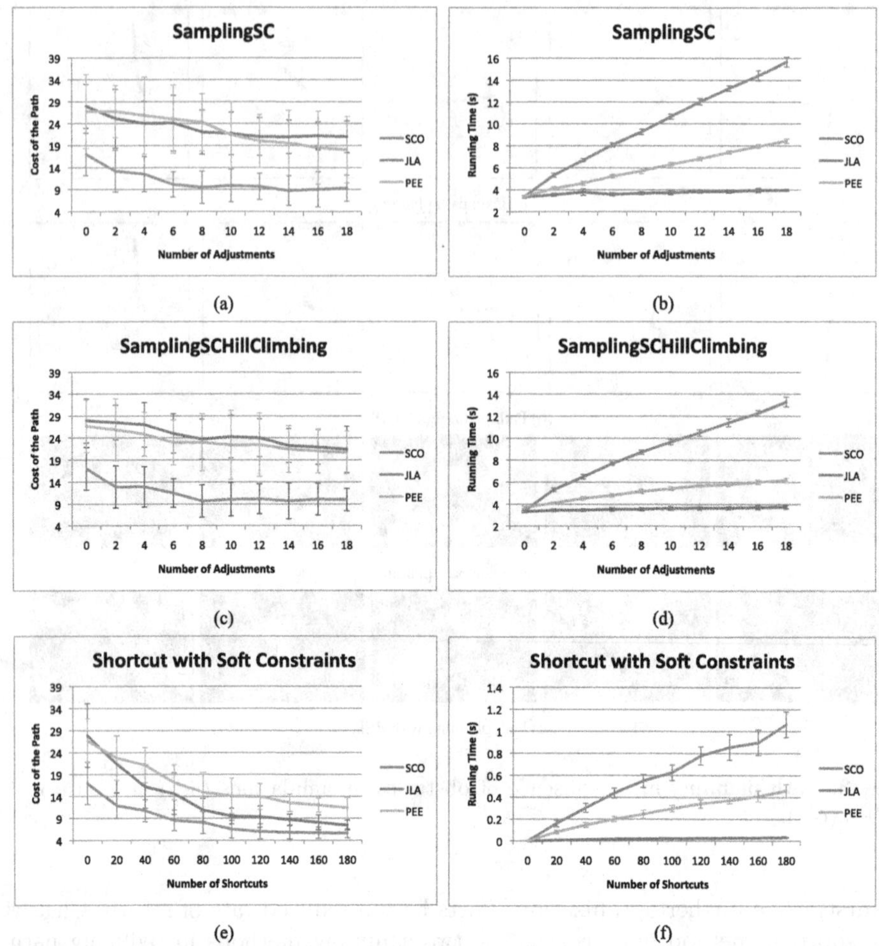

Fig. 4. Cost of the paths found by and running time of (a-b) *SamplingSC*; (c-d) *SamplingSCHillClimbming*; and (e-f) *Shortcut with Soft Constraints*. Results are averaged for 20 independent runs for each case. Standard deviations are shown (SCO - safe clearance from obstacles, JLA - joint limit avoidance, PEE - precision of the end effector).

7 Summary and Future Work

Path planning is an important but difficult problem in robot planning with high numbers of DOFs. Sampling-based path planning algorithms are successful in solving high-dimensional problems. However, their ability to find paths that meet certain soft constraints is still limited. This paper describes an approach to the problem of planning practical paths for tentacle robots in terms of soft constraints and develops sample adjustment strategies for sampling-based path planners to take into account these soft constraints.

We have shown the effectiveness of our approach using both a simulated and real tentacle robot. Three soft constraints are used separately in the test model. Although the resultant path is not optimal due to the randomness of the planner, it shows consistent improvement over the path computed by the basic PRM as the degree of optimization increases.

Currently we only considered single soft constraint and single optimization methods with fixed level of optimization. It is possible to run multiple optimizations to address multiple soft constraint problems. Ideally, resources will be redistributed amongst these optimization methods in a way that an optimal (or good enough) solution can be found efficiently and effectively. Ongoing work includes the development of an auction-based system to coordinate multiple optimization methods.

Acknowledgments. The financial support of NSERC Canada and NCFRN are gratefully acknowledged. The authors would like to thank Robert Codd-Downey and Junquan Xu for their help with the robot infrustructure.

References

1. Bayazit, O.B.: Solving motion planning problems by iterative relaxation of constraints. Ph.D. thesis, Texas A&M University (2003)
2. Bohlin, R., Kavraki, L.E.: Path planning using lazy PRM. In: Proceedings of IEEE International Conference on Robotics & Automation (ICRA), San Francisco, vol. 1, pp. 521–528 (2000)
3. Bruce, J., Veloso, M.: Real-time multi-robot motion planning with safe dynamics. In: Multi-Robot Systems: From Swarms to Intelligent Automata, Proceedings from the 2005 International Workshop on Multi-Robot Systems, Washington, D.C., vol. 3, pp. 159–170 (2005)
4. Buckinham, R., Graham, A.: SAFIRE - a robotic inspection system for CANDU feeders. In: Proceedings of International Conference on CANDU Maintenance, Toronto (2011)
5. Chirikjian, G.S., Burdick, J.W.: An obstacle avoidance algorithm for hyper-redundant manipulators. In: Proceedings of IEEE International Conference on Robotics & Automation (ICRA), Tsukuba, Japan, vol. 1, pp. 625–631 (1990)
6. Choset, H., Henning, W.: A follow-the-leader approach to serpentine robot motion planning. ASCE J. Aerosp. Eng. **12**, 65–73 (1999)
7. Garber, M., Lin, M.C.: Constraint-based motion planning using voronoi diagrams. In: Proceedings of Fifth International Workshop on Algorithmic Foundations of Robotics (WAFR), Nice, France (2002)
8. Gayle, R., Redon, S., Sud, A., Lin, M., Manocha, D.: Efficient motion planning of highly articulated chains using physics-based sampling. In: Proceedings of IEEE International Conference on Robotics & Automation (ICRA), Rome, pp. 3319–3326 (2007)
9. Geraerts, R.: Sampling-based motion planning: analysis and path quality. Ph.D. thesis, Utrecht University (2006)
10. Geraerts, R., Overmars, M.: On improving the clearance for robots in high-dimensional configuration spaces. In: Proceedings of IEEE/RSJ International Conference on Intelligent Robots and Systems (IROS), Edmonton, pp. 679–684 (2005)

11. Geraerts, R., Overmars, M.H.: Creating high-quality paths for motion planning. Int. J. Robot. Res. **26**, 845–863 (2007)
12. Gerevini, A., Long, D.: Plan constraints and preferences in PDDL3 - the language of the fifth international planning competition. University of Brescia, Technical report (2005)
13. Hill, B., Tesar, D.: Design of mechanical properties for serial manipulators. Ph.D. thesis, University of Texas at Austin (1997)
14. Hsu, D.: Randomized single-query motion planning in expansive spaces. Ph.D. thesis, Stanford University (2000)
15. Karaman, S., Frazzoli, E.: Sampling-based algorithms for optimal motion planning. Int. J. Robot. Res. **30**, 846–894 (2011)
16. Kavraki, L.E., Latombe, J.-C., Motwani, R., Raghavan, P.: Randomized query processing in robot path planning. J. Comput. Syst. Sci. **57**, 50–60 (1998)
17. Kavraki, L.E., Svestka, P., Latombe, J.-C., Overmars, M.: Probabilistic roadmaps for path planning in high dimensional configuration spaces. IEEE Trans. Robot. Autom. **12**, 566–580 (1996)
18. Khalil, W., Dombre, E.: Modeling, Identification and Control of Robots. Hermes Penton Ltd, London (2002)
19. Kim, J., Pearce, R.A., and Amato, N.M.: Extracting optimal paths from roadmaps for motion planning. In: Proceedings of IEEE International Conference on Robotics & Automation (ICRA), Taipei, vol. 2, pp. 2424–2429 (2003)
20. Kobilarov, M., Sukhatme, G.S.: Near time-optimal constrained trajectory planning on outdoor terrain. In: Proceedings of IEEE International Conference on Robotics & Automation (ICRA), Barcelona, pp. 1833–1840 (2005)
21. Latombe, J.-C.: Robot Motion Planning. Kluwer, Boston (1991)
22. LaValle, S.M.: Planning Algorithms. Cambridge University Press, Cambridge (2006)
23. LaValle, S.M., Kuffner, J.J.: Rapidly-exploring random trees: progress and prospects. In: Proceedings of International Workshop on Algorithmic Foundations of Robotics (WAFR), Hanover, NH (2000)
24. Manseur, R.: Robot Modeling and Kinematics. Da Vinci Engineering Press, Boston (2006)
25. Nielsen, C., Kavraki, L.E.: A two-level fuzzy PRM for manipulation planning. In: Proceedings of IEEE/RSJ International Conference on Intelligent Robots and Systems (IROS), Takamatsu, Japan, vol. 3, pp. 1716–1722 (2000)
26. Nieuwenhuisen, D., Overmars, M.H.: Useful cycles in probabilistic roadmap graphs. In: Proceedings of IEEE International Conference on Robotics & Automation (ICRA), New Orleans, vol. 1, pp. 446–452 (2004)
27. Raveh, B., Enosh, A., Halperin, D.: A little more, a lot better: Improving path quality by a path merging algorithm. IEEE Trans. Robot. **27**, 365–371 (2011)
28. Rollinson, D., Choset, H.: Virtual chassis for snake robots. In: Proceedings of IEEE International Conference of Intelligent Robot and Systems (IROS), San Francisco, pp. 221–226 (2011)
29. Song, G., Miller, S., Amato, N.M.: Customizing PRM roadmaps at query time. In: Proceedings of IEEE International Conference on Robotics & Automation (ICRA), Seoul, Korea, pp. 1500–1505 (2001)
30. Transeth, A.A., Pettersen, K.Y., Liljebäck, P.: A survey on snake robot modeling and locomotion. Robotica **27**, 999–1015 (2009)

31. Wein, R., van den Berg, J.P., Halperin, D.: The visibility-voronoi complex and its applications. In: Proceedings of Annual Symposium on Computational Geometry (SCG), New York, pp. 63–72 (2005)
32. Zghal, H., Dubey, R.V., Euler, J.A.: Collision avoidance of a multiple degree of freedom redundant manipulator operating through a window. In: Proceedings of IEEE American Control Conference, San Diego, pp. 2306–2312 (1990)

Artificial Intelligence

Enhancing Products by Embedding Agents: Adding an Agent to a Robot for Monitoring, Maintenance and Disaster Prevention

Leo van Moergestel[1](✉), Erik Puik[1], Daniël Telgen[1], Hendrik Folmer[1], Matthijs Grünbauer[1], Robbert Proost[1], Hielke Veringa[1], and John-Jules Meyer[2]

[1] HU Utrecht University of Applied Sciences, Utrecht, The Netherlands
leo.vanmoergestel@hu.nl
http://www.hu.nl

[2] Utrecht University, Utrecht, The Netherlands

Abstract. Monitoring of computer networks, complex technical systems like aeroplanes is common practice. In this article the use of a monitoring agent in an arbitrary product is discussed. The product itself could be any product with sufficient hardware capabilities. The focus is on the product enhancement by adding an embedded agent. This so-called product agent can represent the product in the internet of things and it can also be a member of a multiagent system. In this way exchange of parts and subsystems is possible. The possibilities and advantages of this concept are discussed as well as a more elaborate example of the implementation in an experimental discovery robot.

Keywords: Agents · Monitoring agent · Product life cycle

1 Introduction

Agent technology for agile manufacturing was the starting point of this research. In this research the concept of a product agent was introduced. Every product to be made starts as a software entity or agent that is programmed to meet its goal: the production of a single product. To be able to reach its goal this agent knows what should be done to create the product. This entity is called a product agent and it guides the product along the production cells to be used for manufacturing and it will collect all kinds of important manufacturing data during the production process. When the product is finished, this agent has all the manufacturing details and this agent is still available for further use containing valuable information about the product. The next step in this approach is to investigate and study the roles of this product agent in the other phases of the life cycle of the product.

In this paper we study the implementation of a product agent that has not been used to create the product itself, but this agent is created for a specific phase in the life cycle of the product. First the use and roles of agents in all phases of

J. Filipe and A. Fred (Eds.): ICAART 2013, CCIS 449, pp. 115–130, 2014.
DOI: 10.1007/978-3-662-44440-5_7

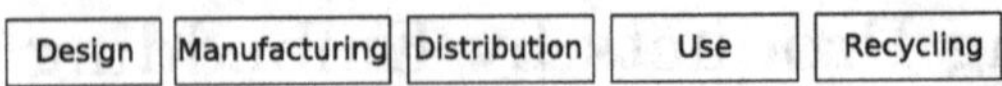

Fig. 1. Life cycle of a product.

the life cycle are discussed as well as how agents could be implemented for these different phases. Next we focus on the use phase. The case study for our product agent in the use phase is based on a discovery robot. This robot is also introduced and globally described. After this description of the product, the embedding of the product agent is discussed and some results of the implementation of the product agent in this complex system are shown.

2 Role of Agents in the Lifecycle of a Product

In Fig. 1 the life cycle of an arbitrary product is shown. After the design, the product is manufactured in the production phase, next the product is distributed. A very important phase is the use of the product and finally the product should be recycled. In all these phases, the product agent can play a role that will be globally described in the next sections

2.1 Design and Production

In our view the design of a product will be greatly influenced by the individual end-user requirements. This means that cost-effective small scale manufacturing will become more and more important. In [1,2] a manufacturing system based on a grid of cheap and versatile production units called equiplets is described. This grid is capable of agile multiparallel production. In this model every single product is guided through the production environment by the already introduced product agent. This agent is responsible for the manufacturing of the product as well as for collecting relevant production information of this product. This is normally a function of the so-called Manufacturing Execution System (MES) [3]. The result is that every product has its own production journal in contrast to batch production using a MES that generates one journal for a whole batch of products. In Fig. 2 the agent based manufacturing is depicted. In this figure the product agent is hopping from equiplet to equiplet to guide the product along the production machines or equiplets and monitor success or failure of the production steps [4]. To make a smooth transition from design to production possible, the product agent is designed as a co-design for the product. Because of the fact that the same equiplets that are used in the production phase are also used in the product design phase, a short time-to-market can be realised. Though this is all based on our own special production environment, we expect this approach to be useful in other production environments as well.

The concept of using agents for production is not new. Among others a multiagent-based production system is also developed by Jennings and Bussmann [5]. This system focuses on reliability and minimizing downtime in a production line. This approach is used in the production of cylinder-heads in car manufacturing. The roles of the agents in this production system differ from our approach.

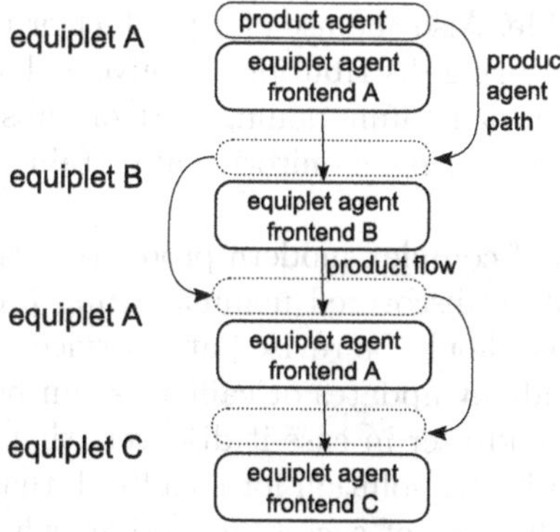

Fig. 2. Product agent and equiplet agents during production.

2.2 Distribution

Product agents can negotiate with logistic systems to reach their final destination. Logistic applications based on multi agents systems already exist [6]. Information of product handling and external conditions, like temperature, shocks etcetera can be measured by cheap wireless sensors and collected by the guidance agent during the transport or after arrival at the destination. The handling and external conditions during transport can be important during product use, especially for product quality, maintenance and repair.

2.3 Use

The role of the product agent during the use of the product could focus on several topics. The first question one should ask is: who will benefit from these agents, i.e. who are the stakeholders. In a win situation both the end-user as well as the manufacturer could benefit from the information. If a product is a potential hazard (in case of misuse) for the environment, the environment could also be a winner if the agent is capable of minimizing the effects of misuse or even prevent it.

Collecting Information. A product agent can log information about the use of the product as well as the use of the subsystems of the product. Testing the health of the product and its subsystems can also be done by the agent. These actions should be transparent for the end-user. If a product needs resources like fuel or electric power, the agent can advise about this. An agent can suggest a product to wait for operation until the cost of electric power is low i.e. during the night.

Maintenance and Repair. Based on the logging information about the product use and the use of the subsystems, an agent can suggest maintenance and repair or replacement of parts. Repairing a product is easier if information about its construction is available. Also the use of a product or the information about transport circumstances during distribution can give a clue for repair. An agent can also identify a broken or malfunctioning part or subsystem. This could be achieved by continuous monitoring, monitoring at certain intervals or a power-on self test (POST).

An important aspect of complex modern products is the issue of updates or callbacks in case of a lately discovered manufacturing problem or flaw. In the worst situation, a product should be revised at a service center or the manufacturing site. Information about updates or callbacks can be send to the product agent that can alert the end-user in case it discovers that it fits the callback or update criteria. This is a better solution for a callback than globally advertising the problem and alert all users of a certain product when only a subgroup is involved.

Miscellaneous. Use of product agents could result in transparency of the status of a product after maintenance by a third party. The agent can report to the end-user what happened during repair so there is a possibility to check claimed repairs. Of course the agent should be isolated from the system during repair to prevent tampering with it. Recovery, tracking and tracing in case of theft or loss are also possible by using this technique. When the end-user wants to replace a certain device by a new one, the product agent can give advice about the properties the replacing device should have, based on what the product agent has learned during the use phase.

2.4 Recycling

Complex products will have a lot of working subsystems at the moment the end-user decides it has come to the end of its life cycle. This is normally the case when a certain part or subsystem is broken. The other remaining parts or subsystems of the product are still functional, because in a lot of complex products the mean times between failure (MTBF) of the subsystems are quite different. The product agent is aware of these subsystems or components and depending on the economical value and the remaining expected lifetime these components can be reused. This could be an important aspect of 'green manufacturing'. An important issue here is that designers should also take in account the phase of destruction or recycling. Disassembly and reuse of subsystems should be a feature of a product for this approach to be successful.

The product agent can reveal where rare or expensive material is situated in the product so this material can be recovered and recycled. This way the product agent can contribute to the concept of zero waste. *Zero waste is just what it sounds like - producing, consuming, and recycling products without throwing anything away* [7].

3 Product Types

This approach of having an agent for a product could be used on different kind of products, but one should investigate if the final product has intelligence and hardware to communicate with the agent. Some products have this by nature (computers, cell-phones); for other products (cars, machinery, domestic appliances) it should be a small investment. An important aspect will be the possibility to connect to certain subsystems for monitoring important events. If temperature is an important item for the product agent, connection to a temperature sensor or at least a place where this temperature data is available is a must. If this connection is not available, a temperature measurement system should be added to the agent.

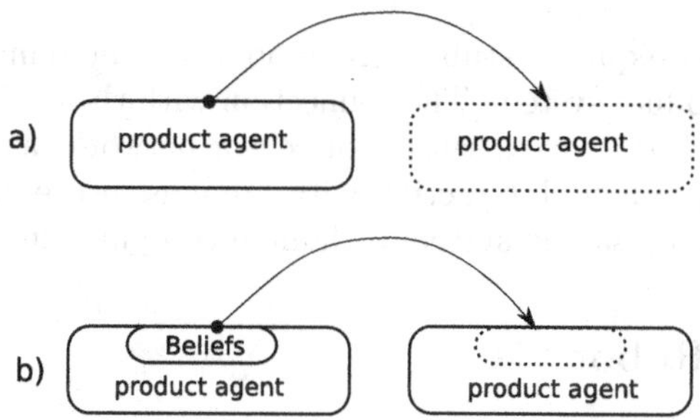

Fig. 3. Mobile agent versus moving data.

3.1 Where Do These Agents Reside?

A product agent should stay alive or at least the information the agent has collected and the knowledge the agent has learned should be available under all circumstances. To accomplish this, two solutions are available. The agent can be a mobile agent moving from platform x to platform y as depicted in Fig. 3a. The other solution requires moving data (beliefs of the agent) from one agent to a newly created agent as shown in Fig. 3b. In our case both agents should be product agents.

The second solution is much easier to implement because of the fact that only transport of data is required, while in the case of moving agents, the whole executable should be adapted to the new situation. Another advantage of the second approach is that a product agent can be added in any phase of the life cycle. This is also what has been done for this specific research. A product agent was added to a system in the use phase. The biggest challenge for implementing the approach of a product agent or guidance agent will be in the use phase. This is where the product is under control of the end-user and not as during the production under control of the manufacturer. In the latter case an agent-based infrastructure can be implemented for the production system or production line. The same is true for transport and even disassembly of the product. In case of the use phase, the agents should reside in a system that is connected to the product, but should be available at the moment the product itself is broken. This is comparable to the case of the so-called black box in aeroplanes. There are several possibilities, depending on the type of product:

- The agent runs on its own separate hardware that is closely tied to the product;
- The agent runs on the hardware of the product but stores information on a special place on the product itself. This information can be recovered after breakdown;
- The agent runs on the hardware of the product but stores information on a remote system;
- The agent runs on a remote system that has a continuous connection;
- The agent runs remote on a system using a 'connect when necessary' approach.

The last two options require a stub or entry point for the remote agent to make contact with the product system. The connection with the environment could be established by wired or wireless sensors or sensor networks as well as computer subsystems in the product. Interaction with humans in the environment could be established by a messaging system or human computer interface (HCI).

4 Discovery Robot

This section gives details of the a discovery robot that was built by our research group. To investigate the implementation of the product agent during the use phase, the product agent was embedded in this complex technical system. To understand the details of the product agent implementation, it is important to have a global understanding of the construction and working of the discovery robot. In this section we present a short overview of the robot capabilities, the architecture, the software and an example of a result produced by the robot system.

4.1 Robot Capabilities

The robot that will be used as a platform for the product agent is capable of mapping a room with objects by using a laser scanner. The robot can move by itself using the map that has been created by the laser-scan. It is possible to direct the robot to a certain point in its map. The robot is also capable to avoid newly introduced obstacles and other moving objects. This robot is used as a system that will be enhanced by a product agent.

4.2 Architecture

Figure 4 shows a picture of the hardware of the robot. Two motors are connected to two wheels. Two swivelling wheels are added to keep the platform in balance. Attached to the platform is the laser scanner, printed circuit boards, a WiFi transceiver, a camera and a set of ultrasonic sensors placed in a circle at the edges of the platform. These ultrasonic sensors are not yet used at this stage. A block diagram of the robot is depicted in Fig. 5. An important aspect is shown in this figure. An external computer is part of the system. This computer is used to do the heavy calculation to generate the map information, to display the map in real-time and to plan the path the robot has to follow. A wireless Ethernet connection (WiFi) connects the robot with this external system.

4.3 Software

The software for this robot is based on ROS. ROS is an acronym for Robot Operating System [8]. ROS is not really an operating system but it is middle-ware specially designed for robot control and it runs on Linux. In ROS a process is called a node. These nodes can communicate by a publish and subscribe mechanism. In ROS this communication mechanism is called a topic. Figure 6 shows the relation between two nodes and one topic.

A node that produces data can publish this in one or more topics. Other nodes interested in these data can subscribe to one or more topics. TCP/IP is used to actually carry out the communication. This platform has been chosen for the following reasons:

Fig. 4. Discovery robot.

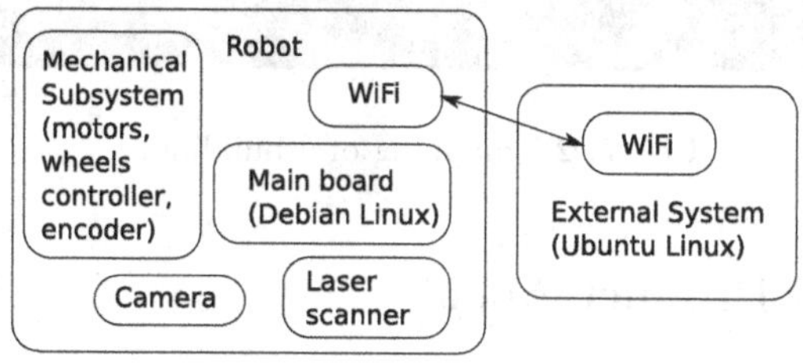

Fig. 5. Block diagram of the robot.

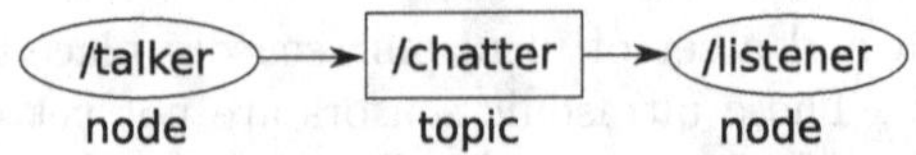

Fig. 6. Two nodes connected by a topic.

- open source, so easy to adapt, compliant with a lot of open source tools;
- wide support by an active community;
- huge amount of modules already available;
- nodes that are parts of ROS can live on several different platforms, assumed that a TCP/IP connection is available.

The mapping is done using SLAM. SLAM stands for Simultaneous Localisation And Mapping [9]. This module was already available in ROS and fitted well to the on board laser scanner.

4.4 Results

The results of a mapping in progress are displayed in Fig. 7. Here the robot mapped the corridors in a rather big building with three wings. The corridors are plotted as a light grey shape. The length of the longest corridor in this map is about 50 m. In this stage, the robot is not yet autonomous, but is controlled by a human operator that uses the external system and the on-board camera to guide the robot during the mapping. When the map is completed, the robot is capable to navigate autonomously to a given point in the map, even if new or moving obstacles are introduced in the mapped environment.

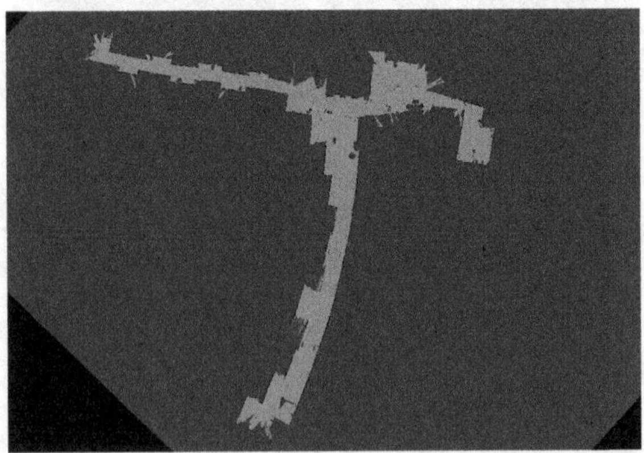

Fig. 7. 2D mapping of a building.

5 Embedded Product Agent

This section describes the product agent and also shows some results of its functioning.

5.1 Functional Requirements

The product agent that is added to the robot has the following requirements:

- monitoring status of the system or subsystems;
- monitoring health of the system or subsystems. The difference between health and status will be explained in the next subsection;
- react only in case of emergency;
- the robot should operate without the agent;
- making useful data available to the outside world, like construction details, materials used and its localisation in the robot.

5.2 Implementation

The first step in implementing this robot is to make an overview of information available in the system. Different types of information are considered:

1. status: is data available and of interest to the product agent and/or the end-user;
2. health: has to do with the condition of components that have mechanical parts or deteriorate during use;
3. alarm: an internal condition that could result in a troublesome situation or disaster;
4. additional information: this is the information that was conceived in earlier phases of the life-cycle.

Because the ROS environment is already available, it seems a natural choice to use this environment to implement the agent. The agent consists of ROS-nodes, ROS topics and some other subsystems. In Fig. 8 the internal modules of the agent are shown. All parts surrounded by an ellipse are ROS nodes. The rectangles represent topics. For human interfacing a small web server is included. This server is capable to serve static pages, containing technical data about the robot as well as dynamic pages containing data collected during use. Figure 8 shows the internal parts of the product agent and Fig. 9 shows the product agent

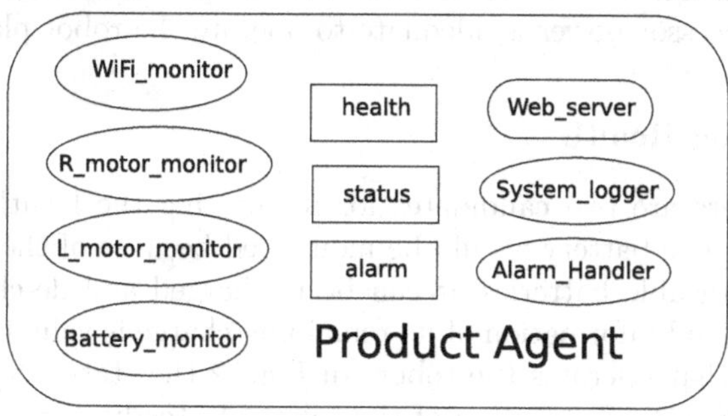

Fig. 8. Architecture of the product agent.

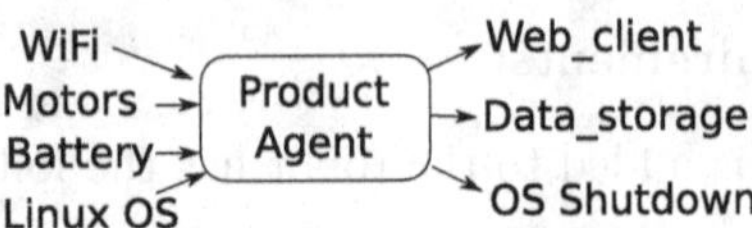

Fig. 9. The product agent and its environment.

in its the environment. The product agent interacts with its environment. The agent gets its information from the robot and its operating system. The agent will log this information and can also display information on a web browser (web client) by using the aforementioned webserver. A shutdown can be performed in case of a certain alarm condition.

5.3 Monitoring Status

The monitoring function is an important aspect of the product agent. In our prototype a selection of possibilities was made. A node will monitor the use of the motors and this will be available to subscribers of the health topic. The status topic is comparable to the health topic, but here information is made available that is not a result of the wear and tear of for example mechanical parts or of the de-charging of the battery, but is a result of measurements of interesting data like the strength of the WiFi signal. There is one topic that can trigger a node that will issue a system shut-down. This topic is called the alarm topic. Apart from these nodes, the agent can also retrieve its information directly from the Linux environment. Commands are available to get the CPU-load and memory usage. The pseudo filesystem `/proc` offers also a wealth of technical information that can be useful for the product agent. Examples of what can be retrieved from the product agent are plots displayed in the following two figures. Figure 10 shows a picture of the strength of the WiFi signal. The robot first moved away from the wifi access point and then returned towards the wifi access point again. The plotted data show a global decreasing and again an increasing trend but there are also strong fluctuations. These fluctuations are normal and due to all kinds of reflections and interference that occur in an indoor environment. In Fig. 11 the load of the processor is plotted. This curve is quite smooth and shows that the available processor power is adequate to operate the robot platform.

5.4 Monitoring Health

In the robot there are two candidates for monitoring the health. The motors and the battery. The battery should be monitored because of the fact that, like almost all rechargeable batteries, it can be re-charged and de-charged a finite amount of times and information of its remaining charge is valuable information to the end-user that operates the robot. In Fig. 12 the status of the battery is plotted during 90 min of operation of the robot. A steady decrease is shown as might be expected.

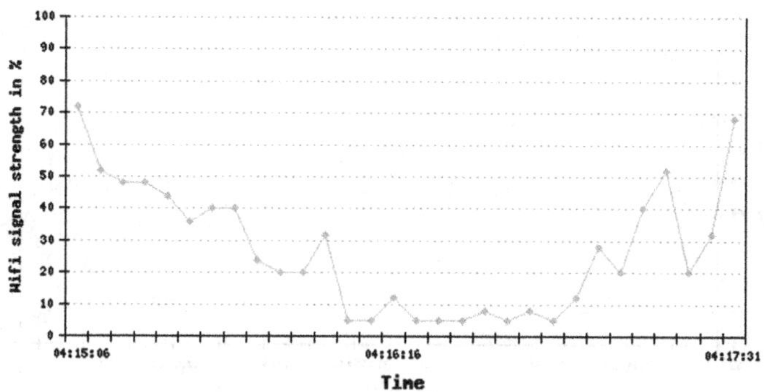

Fig. 10. Strength of the WiFi signal.

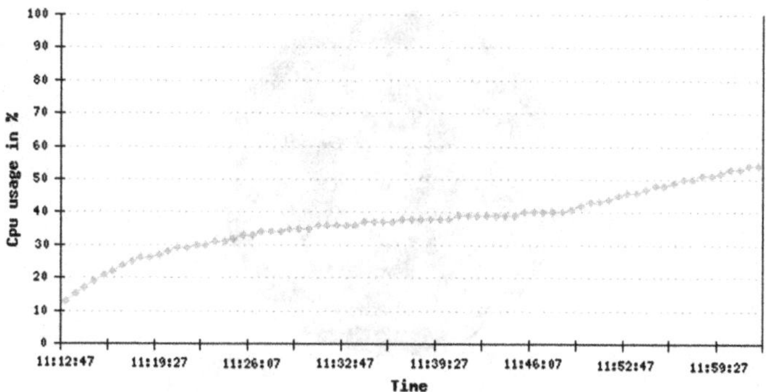

Fig. 11. CPU load.

5.5 Alarm Conditions

In this section an alarm condition will be described. The fact that the type of battery that is used in the robot should never be completely discharged gives rise to such an alarm condition. When the charge capacity drops below 10 % a system shut-down action should be triggered. By shutting down the system, the discharge of the battery will stop, thus preventing the loss of a rather expensive component. To implement this feature an Analog to Digital Converter (ADC) should be available to check the status of the battery.

5.6 Extra Functionality

The extra functionality that is offered by our implementation is embedded documentation and a mapping of materials and components that are of interest during the recycle phase. The information is offered using the same web-interface as was used in the monitor section previously discussed. The documentation is comparable to printed documentation that could be bundled with any device.

Fig. 12. Charge status of the battery.

Fig. 13. Discovery robot subsystems.

This includes a user manual, a technical manual and a maintenance manual including a trouble shooting section.

In Fig. 13 a webpage is displayed showing the subsystems of the robot. This allows the user to select a subsystem to get more detailed information about that specific subsystem. Important information for the recycle phase is also offered using the web interface. Two different approaches are implemented. Using the web interface from Fig. 13, one could point at any part of the robot and receive information about the 'ingredients'. An example is given in Fig. 14. This is the result of selecting the wheels of the web page shown in Fig. 13. As a response the information about the material available in these parts is displayed. The materials as well as other relevant information is shown in Fig. 14.

Another approach is presented in Fig. 15. A list of interesting materials is presented and by clicking on an item, the subsystems containing this material are highlighted as shown in Fig. 15, where the subsystems containing gold are shown. These examples only show the interface designed for human users. The information is also available in a machine readable form using XML.

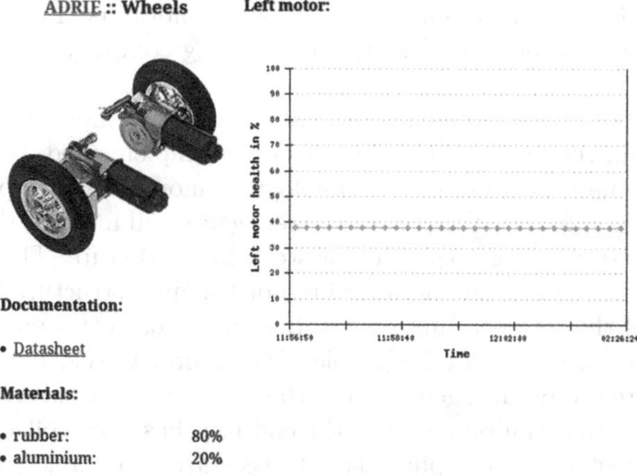

Fig. 14. Motor and wheel subsystem.

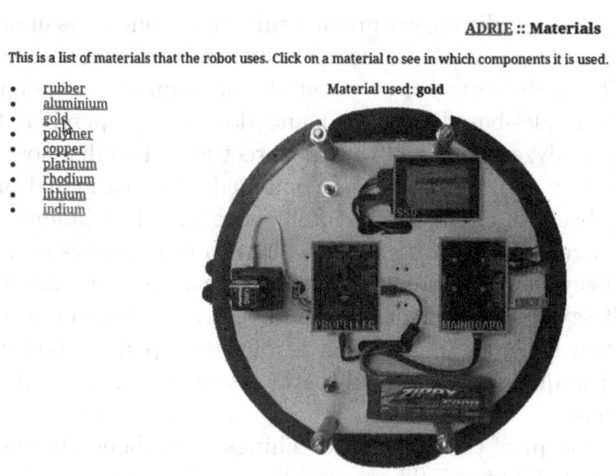

Fig. 15. Where is the gold hidden?

6 Related Work

The work on ROS played a very important role in this research. By using ROS we had a stable and well developed platform for our robot. The use of proven modules prevented reinventing solutions to already solved problems. The work on discovery robots is huge, [10,11] show some developments focussing on multiagent and swarm solutions. Agents for distribution, logistic applications and product manufacturing already exist [12]. In most situations agents represent human operators or negotiators. Jennings and Bussmann introduce the concept of a product agent, in their terms workpiece agents, during the production. These agents do not however perform individual product logging. The use of a product is also studied by observing and/or interviewing end-users [13,14]. Some software applications do connect with their originating company to report the use by end-users.

Several proposals and implementations of including monitoring and documentation within the product itself are made and implemented. Burgess [15,16] describes Cfengine that uses agent technology in monitoring computer systems and ICT network infrastructure. In Cfengine, agents will monitor the status and health of software parts of a complex network infrastructure. These agents are developed and introduced in the use phase of this infrastructure and focus on the condition of the software subsystems. In our approach this monitoring function for hardware and software is the role of the product agent but that role has been played already by an agent during the manufacturing phase where valuable information that can be useful to the end-user has been collected. Actually this product agent in the use phase is not necessarily the same software entity that played the role of product agent during production, but the belief base of the product agent is kept intact and handed over to a new incarnation of the product agent.

In [17] an integrated diagnostic architecture for autonomous underwater vehicles is described. In this work the focus is on an intelligent system for system diagnostics. The architecture uses a variety of domain dependent diagnostic tools (rulebase, model-based methods) and domain independent tools (correlator, topology analyzer, watcher) to first detect and then diagnose the location of faults. This work could be used and combined with the model present in the current paper, because the artificial intelligence based techniques can applied in the product agent. Our work expands the idea of diagnosis and related data to the whole lifecycle of a product. By using this same agent again in the final phase of the life-cycle, component reuse and smart disassembly is a very important aspect when it comes to recycling of rare or expensive building material. The status of the quality of used sub-parts is available from and presented by the product agent.

In [18] the concept of the 'Internet of Things' is explained by the first user of the term 'Internet of Things'. The main idea of this concept is that the content of Internet is not only built and used by humans and therefore largely depending on humans, but the content will also be built by things connected to the Internet that are programmed to do so. The work presented in the current paper shows a possible technique to implement this concept of the 'Internet of Things'.

7 Discussion

In this paper the focus was on implementing a product agent in a complex product. This product was a discovery robot but could have been any other technical system. For every system the requirements for a product agent should be specified. However some global specifications are applicable for every system. The choices for monitoring subsystems made in this research were limited only to a few due to the fact that a proof of concept was the goal of this research.

The actions the agent can perform are in this case displaying and storing system status and system health status as well as system design and technical data. The agent is not influencing the robot itself however one alarm condition is implemented resulting in a system shut-down. It is not a difficult task to expand the capabilities of the agent. The robot itself will be further developed. For the product agent a wide variety of future enhancements is possible, especially when product agents of a certain type of product are united in a multiagent system:

- A model that builds a failure overview of subsystems. This way an accurate insight in the reliability of subsystems and components can be obtained. This model only works if a huge amount of product agent are participating.
- On behalf of the end-user, a product agent can report component failure and suggest or order replacement parts.
- An interesting model to implement the previous feature could be a marketplace in cyberspace where product agents can negotiate with other product agents about exchanging parts.

In all these enhancements special attention should be paid to security and the protection of privacy of the end-users of product agent enhanced systems. An important aspect is the fact that the agent should store its information at a safe place in case the robot hardware will fail. In our case this is the remote system where the agent has the possibility to store important data.

8 Conclusions

Product agents can play an important role in every part of the life cycle of a product. An important property of these agents is that they should have no direct impact on the product or system they are living in. However useful information should be collected and in case of disaster, these agents should keep a log of the events leading to the disaster.

Product agents can be a virtual digital equivalent of a product and this concept will be an enabling technology in implementing the internet of things.

The concept presented here is a natural evolution of the concept of using agents during production. However in case of products made by production technology not based on agent technology, a product agent can be added afterwards, as described in our case study. The information that could have been collected during design and production is added afterwards and will play a role in the recycle phase or maintenance during use phase.

The ROS platform proved to a very good platform to implement the product agent. This is because of the fact that the data-communication infrastructure between nodes is already implemented in a way that helps a lot in both the design and the implementation of the product agent.

References

1. Puik, E., van Moergestel, L.: Agile multi-parallel micro manufacturing using a grid of equiplets. In: Ratchev, S. (ed.) IPAS 2010. IFIP AICT, vol. 315, pp. 271–282. Springer, Heidelberg (2010)

2. van Moergestel, L., Meyer, J., Puik, E., Telgen, D.: Simulation of multiagent-based agile manufacturing. In: CMD 2010 Proceedings, pp. 23–27 (2010)
3. Kletti, J.: Manufacturing Execution System - MES. Springer, Heidelberg (2007)
4. van Moergestel, L., Meyer, J., Puik, E., Telgen, D.: Decentralized autonomous-agent-based infrastructure for agile multiparallel manufacturing. In: ISADS 2011 Proceedings, pp. 281–288 (2011)
5. Bussmann, S., Jennings, N., Wooldridge, M.: Multiagent Systems for Manufacturing Control. Springer, Heidelberg (2004)
6. Burmeister, B., Haddadi, A., Matylis, G.: Application of multi-agent systems in traffic and transportation. IEEE Proc. Softw. Eng. **144**(1), 51–60 (1997)
7. Gunther, M.: The end of garbage. Fortune **155**, 158–166 (2007)
8. Quigley, M., Gerkey, B., Conley, K., Faust, J., Foote, T., Leibs, J., Berger, E., Eheeler, R., Ng, A.: Ros: an open source robot operating system. In: Open-Source Software Workshop of the International Conference on Robotics and Automation (ICRA) (2009)
9. Durrant-Whyte, H., Bailey, T.: Simultaneous localization and mapping (slam): part i the essential algorithms. Robot. Autom. Mag. **13**(2), 99–110 (2006)
10. Wnuk, K., Fulkerson, B., Sudol, J.: A scalable architecture for multi agent vision based robot scavenging. In: American Association for Artificial Intelligence (2006)
11. Blazovics, L., Varga, C., Csorba, K., Fehér, M., Forstner, B., Charaf, H.: Vision based area discovery with swarm robots. In: Second Eastern European Regional Conference on the Engineering of Computer Based Systems, ecbs-eerc, pp. 149–150 (2011)
12. Paolucci, M., Sacile, R.: Agent-Based Manufacturing and Control Systems: New Agile Manufacturing Solutions for Achieving Peak Performance. CRC Press, Boca Raton (2005)
13. Nielsen, J., Levy, J.: Measuring usability: preference vs. performance. Commun. ACM **37**, 66–75 (1994)
14. Nielsen, J., Mack, R.: Usability Inspection Methods. Wiley, New York (1994)
15. Burgess, M.: Cfengine as a component of computer immune-systems. In: Proceedings of the Norwegian Informatics Conference (1998)
16. Burgess, M., Hagerud, H., Straumnes, S., Reitan, T.: Measuring system normality. ACM Trans. Comput. Syst. (TOCS) **20**(2), 125–160 (2002)
17. Hamilton, K., Lane, D., Brown, K., Taylor, J.: An integrated diagnostic architecture for autonomous underwater vehicles. J. Field Robot. **24**, 497–526 (2007)
18. Ashton, K.: That 'the internet of things' thing. RFID J. (2009)

Epistemic and Probabilistic ATL with Quantification and Explicit Strategies

Henning Schnoor(✉)

Institut für Informatik, Christian-Albrechts-Universität zu Kiel, 24098 Kiel, Germany
henning.schnoor@email.uni-kiel.de

Abstract. We introduce QAPI (quantified ATL with probabilism and incomplete information), which extends epistemic and probabilistic ATL with quantification of strategies and a flexible mechanism to reason about strategies in the object language. This allows QAPI to express complex strategic properties such as equilibria and to treat the behavior of the "counter-coalition" in a very flexible way. We provide bisimulation relations, model checking results, and study the issues arising from the interplay between quantifiers and both epistemic and temporal operators.

Keywords: ATL · Multi-agent systems · Epistemic logic

1 Introduction

ATL (Alternating-time temporal logic) [2] is a logic to reason about strategic properties of games. Its strategy operator $\langle\langle A\rangle\rangle\,\varphi$ expresses "there is a strategy for coalition A to achieve φ." We introduce QAPI (quantified ATL with probabilism and incomplete information), a powerful epistemic and probabilistic extension of ATL with quantification of and explicit reasoning about strategies. QAPI's key features are:

- *Strategy variables* allow explicit reasoning about strategies in the object language,
- A *generalized strategy operator* flexibly binds the behavior of some coalitions to strategies, while the remaining players exhibit standard ATL "worst-case" behavior,
- *Quantification* of strategy variables expresses dependence between strategies.

Existential quantification of strategies already appears as part of the $\langle\langle.\rangle\rangle$-operator of ATL, however QAPI makes this explicit and allows separating the *quantification* of a strategy and the *reasoning* about it in the formulas. To this end, the logic can reason directly about the effect of a coalition following a strategy and express statements as "if coalition A follows strategy s, then φ is true."

QAPI generalizes e.g., ATL*, strategy logic [5], ATLES [16], (M)IATL [1], ATEL-R* and ATOL [11]. QAPI can reason about equilibria and express that

J. Filipe and A. Fred (Eds.): ICAART 2013, CCIS 449, pp. 131–148, 2014.
DOI: 10.1007/978-3-662-44440-5_8

a coalition *knows* a strategy to be successful. This requirement is often useful, and is e.g., hard-coded into the strategy definition in [13]. In addition, QAPI features probabilistic reasoning.

We illustrate QAPI's advantages with an important example. When evaluating $\langle\langle A\rangle\rangle\,\varphi$ in ATL, the behavior of players not in A (we denote this "counter-coalition" with $\overline{A}$) is universally quantified: A must succeed for every possible behavior of $\overline{A}$. Hence A has a strategy for φ only if such a strategy works even in the worst-case setting where

- $\overline{A}$'s only goal is to stop A from reaching the goal,
- the players in $\overline{A}$ know A's goal,
- $\overline{A}$'s actions may depend on unknown information.

These issues are particularly relevant when players have incomplete information about the game. Variants of ATL for this case were suggested in e.g., [9–11,13,14]. These logics restrict agents to strategies that can be implemented with the available information, but still require them to be successful for every possible behavior of the counter-coalition. Hence the above limitations still apply—for example, "A can achieve φ against every strategy of $\overline{A}$ that uses only information available to $\overline{A}$" cannot be expressed.

QAPI's direct reasoning about strategies provides a flexible way to specify the behavior of all players, and in particular addresses the above-mentioned shortcomings with a fine-grained specification of the behavior of the "counter-coalition" $\overline{A}$. For example, the following behaviors of $\overline{A}$ can be specified:

- $\overline{A}$ continues a strategy for their own goal—i.e., $\overline{A}$ is unaware of (or not interested in) what A does,
- $\overline{A}$ follows a strategy tailor-made to counteract the goal φ, but that can be implemented with information available to $\overline{A}$—here $\overline{A}$ reacts to A with "realistic" capabilities, i.e., strategies based on information actually available to $\overline{A}$,
- $\overline{A}$ plays an arbitrary sequence of actions, which does not have to correspond to an implementable strategy—this is the pessimistic view of the logics mentioned above: A must be successful against every possible behavior of the players in $\overline{A}$.

As we will demonstrate, detailed reasoning about the counter-coalition is only one advantage of QAPI. Our results are as follows:

1. We prove that QAPI has a natural notion of bisimulation which is more widely applicable than the one in [14], even though QAPI is considerably more expressive. In particular, our new definition can establish strategic and epistemic equivalence between finite and infinite structures.
2. We discuss the effects of combining quantification, epistemic, and temporal operators in detail. The combination of these operators can lead to unnatural situations, which motivate the restriction of QAPI to prefix quantification.

3. We prove complexity and decidability results for model checking QAPI. In the memoryless case, QAPI's added expressiveness compared to ATL* comes without significant cost: The complexity ranges from PSPACE to 3EXPTIME for games that are deterministic or probabilistic. Hence the deterministic case matches the known PSPACE-completeness for ATL* with memoryless strategies [13]. As expected, the problem is undecidable in the perfect-recall case.

Related Work. We only mention the most closely related work (in addition to the papers mentioned above) from the very rich literature. QAPI is an extension of the ATL*-semantics introduced in [14], and utilizes the notion of a strategy choice introduced there. In this paper, we extend the semantics and the results of [14] by the use of strategy variables, quantification, and explicit strategy assignment, which leads to a much richer language. QAPI's approach of allowing first-order like quantification of strategies is very similar to the treatment of strategies in strategy logic [5]. However, the combination of epistemic aspects and quantification reveals some surprising subtleties, which we discuss in Sect. 4, and to the best of our knowledge, there are no results on bisimulations for strategy logic.

Relaxations of ATL's universal quantification over the counter-coalition's behavior were studied in [1,16] for the complete-information case. In [15], QAPI is used to specify strategic and epistemic properties of cryptographic protocols, the bisimulation and model checking results from the present paper are used to obtain a protocol verification algorithm.

2 Syntax and Semantics of QAPI

2.1 Concurrent Game Structures

We use the definition of concurrent game structures from [14], which is based on the ones from [2,7,11]):

Definition 1. *A* concurrent game structure (CGS) *is a tuple* $\mathcal{C} = (\Sigma, Q, \mathbb{P}, \pi, \Delta, \delta, \mathsf{eq})$, *where*

- Σ *and* $\mathbb{P}$ *are finite sets of* players *and* propositional variables, Q *is a (finite or infinite) set of* states,
- $\pi \colon \mathbb{P} \rightarrow 2^Q$ *is a* propositional assignment,
- Δ *is a* move function *such that* $\Delta(q, a)$ *is the set of* moves *available at state* $q \in Q$ *to player* $a \in \Sigma$. *For* $A \subseteq \Sigma$ *and* $q \in Q$, *an* (A, q)-move *is a function* c *such that* $c(a) \in \Delta(q, a)$ *for all* $a \in A$.
- δ *is a* probabilistic transition function *which for each state* q *and* (Σ, q)*-move* c, *returns a discrete*[1] *probability distribution* $\delta(q, c)$ *on* Q *(the state obtained when in* q*, all players perform their move as specified by* c*),*

[1] A probability distribution Pr on Q is discrete, if there is a countable set $Q' \subseteq Q$ such that $\sum_{q \in Q'} \Pr(q) = 1$.

– eq *is a function* eq: $\{1,\ldots,n\} \times \Sigma \to \mathcal{P}(Q \times Q)$, *where* $n \in \mathbb{N}$ *and for each* $i \in \{1,\ldots,n\}$ *and* $a \in \Sigma$, eq(i,a) *is an equivalence relation on* Q. *We also call each* $i \in \{1,\ldots,n\}$ *a* degree of information.

Moves are merely "names for actions" and only have meaning in combination with the transition function δ. A subset $A \subseteq \Sigma$ is a *coalition of* $\mathcal{C}$. We omit "of $\mathcal{C}$" when $\mathcal{C}$ is clear from the context, omit set brackets for singletons, etc. The coalition $\Sigma \setminus A$ is denoted with $\overline{A}$. We write $\Pr(\delta(q,c) = q')$ for $(\delta(q,c))(q')$, i.e., consider $\delta(q,c)$ as a random variable on Q. The function eq expresses incomplete information: It specifies pairs of states that a player cannot distinguish. By specifying several relations eq$(1,a),\ldots,$ eq(n,a) for each player, we can specify how much information a player may use to reach a certain goal. This is useful e.g., in security definitions [6,15].

$\mathcal{C}$ is *deterministic* if all distributions $\delta(q,c)$ assign 1 to one state and 0 to all others, $\mathcal{C}$ has *complete information* if eq(i,a) is always the equality relation.

2.2 QAPI Syntax: Strategies, Strategy Choices, and Formulas

The core operator of QAPI is the *strategy operator*: $\langle\langle A : \mathrm{S}_1, B : \mathrm{S}_2\rangle\rangle_i^{\geq\alpha} \varphi$ expresses "if coalition A follows S_1 and B follows S_2, where both coalitions base their decisions only on information available to them in information degree i, the run of the game satisfies φ with probability $\geq \alpha$, no matter what players from $\overline{A \cup B}$ do." Here, S_1 and S_2 are variables for *strategy choices* which generalize strategies (see below). While similar to the ATL-operator $\langle\langle . \rangle\rangle$, the strategy operator is much more powerful: It allows to flexibly bind a strategy to a coalition. This allows, for example, to model that a coalition *commits* to a strategy (in ATL*, a strategy is revoked when the $\langle\langle . \rangle\rangle$-operator is nested) and much more (see examples below).

Definition 2. *Let* $\mathcal{C}$ *be a CGS with* n *degrees of information. Then* strategy formulas for $\mathcal{C}$ *are the ones generated by the following grammar:*

$$\varphi_s = p \mid \varphi_s \wedge \varphi_s \mid \neg\varphi_s \mid \langle\langle A_1 : \mathrm{S}_1, \ldots, A_m : \mathrm{S}_m\rangle\rangle_i^{\blacktriangleleft\alpha} \varphi_p \mid \mathcal{K}^k_{A,i}\varphi_s$$
$$\varphi_p = \varphi_s \mid \varphi_p \wedge \varphi_p \mid \neg\varphi_p \mid \mathsf{X}\varphi_p \mid \mathsf{P}\varphi_p \mid \mathsf{X}^{-1}\varphi_p \mid \varphi_p \mathsf{U} \varphi_p$$

where p *is a propositional variable,* A, A_1, $\ldots$, A_m *are coalitions,* $1 \leq i \leq n$, $0 \leq \alpha \leq 1$, *and* $\blacktriangleleft$ *is one of* $\leq, <, >, \geq$, *and* ψ *is a path formula, and* S_i *is an* A_i*-strategy choice variable for each* i, *and* $k \in \{D, E, C\}$.

Formulas of the form φ_s (φ_p) are called *state formulas* (*path formulas*). The values D, E, and C indicate different standard notions of knowledge, namely *distributed knowledge*, *shared knowledge* ("everybody knows"), and *common knowledge.* We use standard abbreviations like $\varphi \vee \psi = \neg(\neg\varphi \wedge \neg\psi)$, $\Diamond\varphi = \mathsf{true}\mathsf{U}\varphi$, and $\Box\varphi = \neg\Diamond\neg\varphi$. A $\langle\langle . \rangle\rangle$-formula is one whose outmost operator is the strategy operator. In a CGS with only one degree of information, we omit the i subscript of the strategy operator; in a deterministic CGS we omit the probability bound $\blacktriangleleft \alpha$ (and understand it to be read as ≥ 1). Quantified strategy formulas are strategy formulas in which the appearing strategy choice variables are quantified:

Definition 3. *Let $\mathcal{C}$ be a CGS, let φ be a strategy formula for $\mathcal{C}$ such that every strategy choice variable appearing in φ is one of* $\mathrm{S}_1, \ldots, \mathrm{S}_n$. *Then*

$$\forall \mathrm{S}_1 \exists \mathrm{S}_2 \forall \mathrm{S}_3 \ldots \exists \mathrm{S}_n \varphi$$

is a quantified strategy formula *for $\mathcal{C}$.*

Requiring a strict $\forall\exists\ldots$-alternation is without loss of generality and can be obtained via dummy variables. On the other hand, allowing quantification only in the prefix is a deliberate restriction of QAPI, the reasons for which we discuss in detail in Sect. 4.

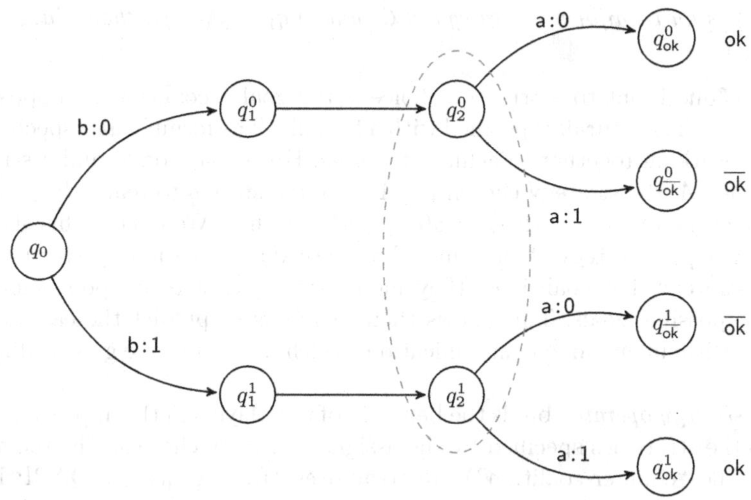

Fig. 1. Strategy choices.

Definition 4. *For a player* a, *an* a-strategy *in a CGS* $\mathcal{C} = (\Sigma, Q, \mathbb{P}, \pi, \Delta, \delta, \mathsf{eq})$ *is a function* s_a *with* $s_a(q) \in \Delta(q, a)$ *for each* $q \in Q$. *For an information degree* i, s_a *is* i-uniform *if* $q_1 \sim_{\mathsf{eq}_i(a)} q_2$ *implies* $s_a(q_1) = s_a(q_2)$. *For* $A \subseteq \Sigma$, *an* A-strategy *is a family* $(s_a)_{a \in A}$, *where each* s_a *is an* a*-strategy.*

Our strategies are *memoryless*: A move only depends on the current state, not on the history of the game. With incomplete information, the question how players can *identify* suitable strategies is relevant. Consider the CGS in Fig. 1. The players are a and b, the game starts in q_0. The first move by b controls whether the next state is q^0_1 or q^1_1. For $x \in \{0,1\}$, q^x_1 is always followed by q^x_2. In q^x_2, the move 0 leads to a state satisfying ok iff $x = 0$; move 1 is successful iff $x = 1$. Player a cannot distinguish q^0_2 and q^1_2. We ask whether he has a strategy leading to ok that is successful started in both q^0_1 and q^1_1. If a can only use strategies, he must play the same move in q^0_2 and in q^1_2, and thus fails in one of them. However, if a can *decide* on a strategy and remember this decision, a can choose in q^0_1 (q^1_1) a strategy playing 0 (1) in every state, and be successful.

Strategy choices [14] formalize how a player chooses a strategy, and distinguish between states where a strategy is *identified* and where it is *executed*: In state q_1^0 or q_1^1, player a uses his information to choose the strategy that he follows from then on. When using only strategies, the knowledge has to be present at the time of *performing* a move. Hence strategy choices give players additional capabilities over the pure memoryless setting, by allowing to remember *decisions*. In contrast to the *perfect recall* case, where players remember the entire run of a game, there is no significant computational price, whereas perfect recall makes the model checking problem undecidable (cp. Sect. 6).

Definition 5. *A* strategy choice *for a coalition A in a CGS $\mathcal{C} = (\Sigma, Q, \mathbb{P}, \pi, \Delta, \delta, \mathsf{eq})$ is a function S such that for each $a \in A$, $q \in Q$, each $\langle\langle . \rangle\rangle_i$-formula φ, $\mathsf{S}(a, q, \varphi)$ is an i-uniform a-strategy in $\mathcal{C}$, and if $q_1 \sim_{\mathsf{eq}_i(a)} q_2$, then $\mathsf{S}(a, q_1, \varphi) = \mathsf{S}(a, q_2, \varphi)$.*

Note that one input to a strategy choice is the goal a coalition is supposed to achieve, which is naturally specified with a formula. The formula also specifies the coalition working together to achieve the goal. For a coalition A and a strategy choice S for A, the strategy chosen for A by S in a state q to reach the goal φ is the A-strategy $(s_a)_{a \in A}$ with $s_a = \mathsf{S}(a, q, \varphi)$ for each a. We denote this strategy with $\mathsf{S}(A, q, \varphi)$. Strategy choices model the *decision* of a single player to use a certain strategy. For coalitions, they model strategies agreed upon before the game for possible goals. This allows their members to predict the each other's behavior without in-game communication, which is helpful in e.g., coordination games.

The *strategy operator* binds the behavior of the players in the appearing coalitions to the strategies specified by the assigned strategy choices. The remaining players (the "counter-coalition") are treated as "free agents" in QAPI: Every possible behavior of these players is taken into account. Such a behavior may not even follow any strategy, for example they may perform different moves when encountering the same state twice during the game. This is formalized as a *response* (see. [14]) to a coalition A, which is a function r such that $r(t, q)$ is a $(\overline{A}, q)$-move for each $t \in \mathbb{N}$ and each $q \in Q$. This models an arbitrary reaction to the outcomes of an A-strategy: In the i-th step of a game, $\overline{A}$ performs the move $r(i, q)$, if the current state is q. Essentially, a response is an arbitrary sequence of actions where we additionally ensure that only actions applicable in the relevant states are chosen.

When a coalition A follows the strategy s_A, and the behavior of $\overline{A}$ is defined by the response r, the moves of all players are fixed; the game is a Markov process. A *path* in a CGS $\mathcal{C}$ is a sequence $\lambda = \lambda[0]\lambda[1] \dots$ of states of $\mathcal{C}$.

Definition 6. *Let $\mathcal{C}$ be a CGS, let s_A be an A-strategy, let r be a response to A. For a set M of paths over $\mathcal{C}$, and a state $q \in Q$, $Pr(q \to M \mid s_A + r)$ is the probability that in the Markov process resulting from $\mathcal{C}$, s_A, and r with initial state q, the resulting path is in M.*

A key feature of QAPI is the flexible binding of strategies to coalitions, which is done using the strategy operator. As a technical tool to resolve possible ambiguities, we introduce a "join" operation on strategy choices: If the coalitions $A_1, \ldots, A_n$ follow strategy choices $\mathsf{S}_1, \ldots, \mathsf{S}_n$, the resulting "joint strategy choice" for $A_1 \cup \cdots \cup A_n$ is $\mathsf{S}_1 \circ \cdots \circ \mathsf{S}_n$. This is a "union" of the S_i with a tie-breaking rule for players appearing in several of the coalitions: These always follow the "left-most" applicable strategy choice. We define the (associative) operator $\circ$ as follows:

$$\mathsf{S}_1 \circ \mathsf{S}_2(a, q, \varphi) = \begin{cases} \mathsf{S}_1(a, q, \varphi), & \text{if } a \in A_1, \\ \mathsf{S}_2(a, q, \varphi), & \text{if } a \in A_2 \setminus A_1. \end{cases}$$

This definition ensures that if a coalition $A_1 \cup \cdots \cup A_n$ is instructed to follow the strategy choice $\mathsf{S}_1 \circ \cdots \circ \mathsf{S}_n$, then even if $A_i \cap A_j \neq \emptyset$, for each agent the strategy choice to follow is well-defined.

2.3 QAPI Semantics: Evaluating Formulas

We define QAPI's semantics in two stages: We first handle strategy formulas, where instantiations for the appearing strategy choice variables are given. This naturally leads to the semantics definition for quantified formulas. Our semantics is natural: Propositional variables and operators are handled as usual, temporal operators behave as in LTL, and $\langle\langle A_1 : \mathsf{S}_1, \ldots, A_n : \mathsf{S}_n\rangle\rangle_i^{\geq\alpha} \psi$ expresses that when coalitions $A_1, \ldots, A_n$ follow the strategies chosen for the goal ψ by the strategy choices $\mathsf{S}_1, \ldots, \mathsf{S}_n$ with information degree i available, the formula ψ is satisfied with probability $\geq \alpha$. $\mathcal{K}$ expresses group knowledge.

Definition 7. *Let $\mathcal{C} = (\Sigma, Q, \mathbb{P}, \pi, \Delta, \delta, \mathsf{eq})$ be a CGS, let $\overrightarrow{\mathsf{S}} = (\mathsf{S}_1, \ldots, \mathsf{S}_n)$ be a sequence of strategy choices instantiating*[2] *the strategy choice variables $\mathsf{S}_1, \ldots, \mathsf{S}_n$. Let φ be a state formula, let ψ_1, ψ_2 be path formulas, let λ be a path over Q, let $t \in \mathbb{N}$. We define*

- $\mathcal{C}, \overrightarrow{\mathsf{S}}, q \models p$ *iff* $q \in \pi(p)$ *for* $p \in \mathbb{P}$,
- *conjunction and negation are handled as usual,*
- $(\lambda, t), \overrightarrow{\mathsf{S}} \models \varphi$ *iff* $\mathcal{C}, \overrightarrow{\mathsf{S}}, \lambda[t] \models \varphi$,
- $(\lambda, t), \overrightarrow{\mathsf{S}} \models \mathsf{X}\psi_1$ *iff* $(\lambda, t+1), \overrightarrow{\mathsf{S}} \models \psi_1$,
- $(\lambda, t), \overrightarrow{\mathsf{S}} \models \mathsf{P}\psi_1$ *iff there is some* $t' \leq t$ *and* $(\lambda, t'), \overrightarrow{\mathsf{S}} \models \psi_1$,
- $(\lambda, t), \overrightarrow{\mathsf{S}} \models \mathsf{X}^{-1}\psi_1$ *iff* $t \geq 1$ *and* $(\lambda, t-1), \overrightarrow{\mathsf{S}} \models \psi_1$,
- $(\lambda, t), \overrightarrow{\mathsf{S}} \models \psi_1 \mathsf{U} \psi_2$ *iff there is some* $i \geq t$ *such that* $(\lambda, i), \overrightarrow{\mathsf{S}} \models \psi_2$ *and* $(\lambda, j), \overrightarrow{\mathsf{S}} \models \psi_1$ *for all* $t \leq j < i$,
- *If* $k \in \{D, E, C\}$, *then* $\mathcal{C}, \overrightarrow{\mathsf{S}}, q \models \mathcal{K}^k_{A,i}\varphi$ *iff* $\mathcal{C}, \overrightarrow{\mathsf{S}}, q' \models \varphi$ *for all* $q' \in Q$ *with* $q \sim^k_{A,i} q'$ *(see below),*

[2] I.e., if S_i is an A-strategy choice variable for some coalition A, then S_i is a strategy choice for A.

- $\mathcal{C}, \vec{\mathsf{S}}, q \models \overbrace{\langle\langle A_{i_1} : \mathsf{S}_{i_1}, \ldots, A_{i_m} : \mathsf{S}_{i_m} \rangle\rangle_i^{\blacktriangleleft\alpha}\, \psi_1}^{=:\varphi_1}$ *iff for every response r to the coalition* $A_{i_1} \cup \cdots \cup A_{i_m}$, *we have*
$Pr\left(q \to \left\{\lambda \,|\, (\lambda, 0), \vec{\mathsf{S}} \models \psi_1\right\} \,|\, \mathsf{S}_{i_1} \circ \cdots \circ \mathsf{S}_{i_m}(A_{i_1} \cup \cdots \cup A_{i_m}, q, \varphi_1) + r\right) \blacktriangleleft \alpha.$

The relations $\sim^D_{A,i}$, $\sim^E_{A,i}$, and $\sim^C_{A,i}$ referenced in Definition 7 represent different possibilities to model group knowledge. For a coalition A and an information degree i, they are defined as follows:

- $\sim^D_{A,i} = \bigcap_{a \in A} \mathsf{eq}(i, a)$ expresses *distributed knowledge*: $\mathcal{K}^D_{A,i}\varphi$ is true if φ can be deduced from the combined knowledge of every member of A (with respect to information degree i),
- $\sim^E_{A,i} = \bigcup_{a \in A} \mathsf{eq}(i, a)$ models *shared knowledge* ("everybody knows"): $\mathcal{K}^E_{A,i}\varphi$ is true if every agent in A on his own has enough information to deduce that φ holds (with respect to information degree i),
- $\sim^C_{A,i}$ is the reflexive, transitive closure of $\sim^E_{A,i}$. This models *common knowledge*: $\mathcal{K}^C_{A,i}\varphi$ expresses that (in A, with information degree i), everybody knows that φ is true, and everybody knows that everybody knows that φ is true, ..., etc.

These concepts have proven useful to express the knowledge of a group. See [8] for detailed discussion. The semantics for the quantified case are defined in the natural way:

Definition 8. *Let $\mathcal{C}$ be a CGS, let $\psi = \forall \mathsf{S}_1 \exists \mathsf{S}_2 \forall \mathsf{S}_3 \ldots \exists \mathsf{S}_n \varphi$ be a quantified strategy formula for $\mathcal{C}$, let q be a state of $\mathcal{C}$. Then ψ is* satisfied in $\mathcal{C}$ at q, *written $\mathcal{C}, q \models \psi$, if for each $i \in \{2, 4, \ldots n\}$, there is a function s_i such that for all strategy choices S_1, S_3, ..., S_{n-1}, if S_i is defined as $s_i(\mathsf{S}_1, \ldots, \mathsf{S}_{i-1})$ for even i, then $\mathcal{C}, (\mathsf{S}_1, \ldots, \mathsf{S}_n), q \models \varphi$.*

Constant strategy choices (which only depend on the player, not on the state or the formula) are essentially strategies. We introduce quantifiers $\exists_c$ and $\forall_c$ quantifying over constant strategy choices.

3 Examples

3.1 Restricted Adversaries

The following expresses "A can achieve φ against every uniform strategy of $\overline{A}$:"

$$\exists \mathsf{S}_1 \forall \mathsf{S}_2 \left\langle\left\langle A : \mathsf{S}_1, \overline{A} : \mathsf{S}_2 \right\rangle\right\rangle_1 \varphi.$$

This is weaker than $\exists \mathsf{S}_1 \langle\langle A : \mathsf{S}_1 \rangle\rangle_1 \varphi$: In the latter, $\overline{A}$ is not restricted to any strategy at all, while in the former, $\overline{A}$ has to follow a uniform strategy.

3.2 Sub-coalitions Changing Strategy

Often, when a coalition $A' \subsetneq A$ changes the strategy, they rely on $A \setminus A'$ to continue the current one. Assume that A works together to reach a state where $A' \subsetneq A$ has strategies for φ_1 and φ_2, *if players in* $A \setminus A'$ *continue their earlier strategy.* We express this as

$$\exists_c \mathrm{S}_A \exists \mathrm{S}_{A'} \langle\langle A : \mathrm{S}_A\rangle\rangle_1 \Diamond (\langle\langle A' : \mathrm{S}_{A'}, A : \mathrm{S}_A\rangle\rangle_1 \Diamond\varphi_1 \wedge \langle\langle A' : \mathrm{S}_{A'}, A : \mathrm{S}_A\rangle\rangle_1 \Diamond\varphi_2) .$$

This expresses that A uses a *fixed strategy* and does not change behavior depending on whether A' attempts to achieve φ_1 or φ_2. In particular, $A \setminus A'$ does not need to know which of these goals A' attempts to achieve. We use the same strategy choice for φ_1 and φ_2 to require A' to identify the correct strategy with the available information.

3.3 Knowing whether a Strategy is Successful

The following expresses "there is an A-strategy such that there is no B-strategy such that the coalition C can know that its application successfully achieves φ:"

$$\exists_c \mathrm{S}_A \forall_c \mathrm{S}_B \neg\mathcal{K}^C \langle\langle A : \mathrm{S}_A, B : \mathrm{S}_B\rangle\rangle_1 \varphi.$$

This is very different from expressing that A has a strategy preventing φ, i.e., $\exists \mathrm{S}_A \langle\langle A : \mathrm{S}_A\rangle\rangle_1 \neg\varphi$, since (i) There may be a successful strategy for B, but not enough information for C to determine that it is successful, (ii) the goal φ may still be reachable if B does not follow a (uniform) strategy.

3.4 Winning Secure Equilibria (WSE)

If player a (b) has goal φ_a (φ_b), a WSE [4] is a pair of strategies (s_a, s_b) such that both goals are achieved when a and b play s_a and s_b, and if b plays such that φ_a is not reached anymore, but a still follows s_a, then b's goal φ_b is also not satisfied anymore (same for player a). QAPI can express this as follows: Both goals are reached if (s_a, s_b) is played, and neither player can reach his goal without reaching that of the other player as well, if the latter follows the WSE strategy.

$$\begin{aligned} &\exists_c \mathrm{S}_a \exists_c \mathrm{S}_b \langle\langle a : \mathrm{S}_A, b : \mathrm{S}_B\rangle\rangle_1 (\varphi_a \wedge \varphi_b) \\ &\wedge \langle\langle a : \mathrm{S}_A\rangle\rangle_1 (\varphi_b \rightarrow \varphi_a) \\ &\wedge \langle\langle b : \mathrm{S}_B\rangle\rangle_1 (\varphi_a \rightarrow \varphi_b) . \end{aligned}$$

3.5 Expressing ATEL-R* and ATOL

ATOL [11] requires *identifying* strategies with the agent's knowledge. ATOL's key operator is defined as follows (right-hand side in our notation)—in the following, A is the coalition *playing*, and Γ the one *identifying* the strategy:

$\mathcal{C}, q \models \langle\langle A \rangle\rangle_{\mathcal{K}(\Gamma)} \varphi$ iff there is a constant strategy choice S_A such that for all $q' \in \mathcal{C}$ with $q' \sim_\Gamma q$, we have that $\mathcal{C}, q' \models \langle\langle A : \mathsf{S}_A \rangle\rangle_1 \varphi$.

The above can be translated into QAPI by writing

$$\mathcal{C}, q' \models \mathcal{K}^\Gamma \langle\langle A : \mathrm{S}_A \rangle\rangle_1 \varphi,$$

where S_A's quantification depends on the parity of negation and is restricted to constant strategy choices.[3] In [11], it is stated that requiring "Γ knows that A has a strategy to achieve φ" is insufficient to express $\langle\langle A \rangle\rangle_{\mathcal{K}(\Gamma)} \varphi$. It suffices in QAPI since we quantify S_A *before* the $\mathcal{K}$-operator, hence Γ knows that the *fixed* A-strategy is successful. ATEL-R* would quantify the strategy *after* the $\mathcal{K}$-operator in a formula like $\mathcal{K}_\Gamma \langle\langle A \rangle\rangle \varphi$: A could choose a *different* strategy in each state. ATEL-R* (ATOL with recall) can be expressed in MQAPI analogously. The above highlights the usefulness of QAPI's ability to directly reason about strategy choices. Strategy logic [5], ATLES [16], and (M)IATL [1] can be expressed similarly.

4 Quantification and Epistemic/Temporal Operators

We now study the interplay between quantifiers and temporal or epistemic operators: Applying quantifiers in the scope of epistemic or temporal operators often leads to highly counter-intuitive behavior. This behavior is the reason why QAPI only allows quantification in a quantifier block prefixing the formula. The issues we demonstrate here are not specific to QAPI or the concept of strategy choices, but arise in any formalism combining the operators we discuss here with some mechanism of requiring agents to "know" which strategy to apply. The core issue is that an unrestricted $\exists$-quantifier adds a high degree of non-uniformity to the agent's choices, which is incompatible with the epistemic setting.

To demonstrate these issues, in this section, we consider QAPI^{infix}, which is QAPI with arbitrary nesting of quantifiers and other operators. The semantics is defined by applying quantification in every state in the obvious way. Clearly, quantification can be pulled outside of the scope of propositional, X, and $\Diamond$-operators. The remaining temporal and epistemic operators cannot be handled so easily.

4.1 Quantification in the Scope of Temporal Operators

Consider the QAPI^{infix}-formula $\mathbb{A}\Box\exists \mathrm{S}_A \langle\langle A : \mathrm{S}_A \rangle\rangle_1^{\geq 1} \psi$: The quantifier $\mathbb{A}$ abbreviates $\exists \mathrm{S}_\emptyset \langle\langle \emptyset : \mathrm{S}_\emptyset \rangle\rangle_1^{\geq 1}$ and expresses quantification over all reachable paths

[3] It is not sufficient to rely on the uniformity of strategy choices (the same strategy must be chosen in A-indistinguishable states), since there must be a single strategy that is successful in all Γ-indistinguishable states, and Γ might have less information than A.

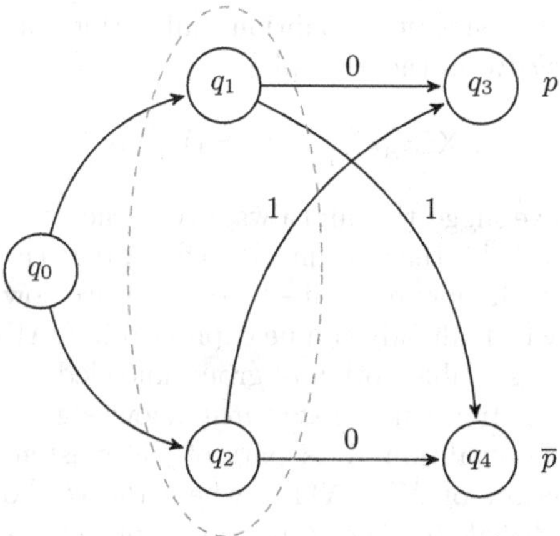

Fig. 2. Infix quantification example.

(essentially $\mathbb{A}$ is CTL's **A**-operator). The formula expresses that in all reachable states, there is a strategy choice for A that accomplishes ψ. There are no uniformity or epistemic constraints on the $\exists$-quantifier: Even in states that look identical for all members of A, completely different strategy choices can be applied. This is problematic in an epistemic setting: Consider the CGS with two players a and b in Fig. 2. We only indicate the moves of player a. The game is turn-based, where it is b's turn in the state q_0 and a's turn in the remaining states. The first action of b chooses whether the next state is q_1 or q_2, these two states are indistinguishable for a. In q_1, player a must play 0 to reach a state where p holds, in state q_2, a must play 1 to achieve this. Now consider the following formula (we consider the coalition $A = \{a\}$):

$$\mathbb{A}\mathrm{X}\exists \mathrm{S}_A \, \langle\langle A : \mathrm{S}_A \rangle\rangle_1^{\geq 1} \, p.$$

This formula is true in q_0: In both possible follow-up states, there is a strategy choice that allows player a to enforce that p is true in the next state: In q_1 (q_2), we choose a strategy choice S_1 that for every possible goal and in every state always plays the move 0 (1). *Individually*, these strategy choices satisfy every imaginable uniformity condition, since they fix one move forever. However, intuitively in q_1, player a cannot achieve $\mathsf{X}p$, since a cannot identify the correct strategy choice to apply. This shows that having an existential quantifier in the scope of a temporal operator yields counter-intuitive results.

A natural way to address this problem is to restrict quantification to be "uniform" and demand that the quantifier chooses the same strategy choice in the states indistinguishable for A. We can express this in QAPI^{infix} by requiring that the strategy choice "returned" by the quantifier is successful in all indistinguishable states—in other words, requiring A to know that the strategy choice is successful. In this case, the same strategy choice can be used in all indistinguishable states as intended. In the above example, we therefore would consider the following formula (for singleton-coalitions, all notions of knowledge coincide, we use *common knowledge* in the example):

$$\mathbb{A}\mathrm{X}\exists \mathrm{S}_A \mathcal{K}^C_{A,1} \langle\langle A : \mathrm{S}_A \rangle\rangle^{\geq 1}_{1}\, p.$$

If we follow the above suggestion and always combine existential quantification with requiring the knowledge that the introduced strategy choice accomplishes its goal, the behavior is much more natural—however, as we now demonstrate, these are exactly the cases which already can be expressed in QAPI.

We now discuss the suitable notion of group knowledge to apply in formulas of the above structure. If we use *distributed* knowledge, we essentially allow coordination inside the coalition A as part of the existential quantifier. This is similar to the behavior of ATL/ATL*, where the $\langle\langle . \rangle\rangle$-operator also allows coordination. Hence *distributed knowledge* does not achieve the desired effect. However, *shared knowledge* ("everyone knows") and *common knowledge* do not suffer from these issues: In both cases, each agent on his own can determine whether the current strategy "works." We now support this intuition by formal arguments: In the case of *shared knowledge* or *common knowledge*, the existential quantifier can indeed be exchanged with the $\Box$ operator, the same does not hold for *distributed knowledge.*

Proposition 1. *Let φ be a formula in which the variable S_A does not appear, and which does not use past-time operators, and let $k \in \{E, C\}$. Then*

$$\Box\exists \mathrm{S}_A \mathcal{K}^k_{A,i} \langle\langle A : \mathrm{S}_A \rangle\rangle^{\geq\alpha}_{i}\, \varphi \equiv \exists \mathrm{S}_A \Box \mathcal{K}^k_{A,i} \langle\langle A : \mathrm{S}_A \rangle\rangle^{\geq\alpha}_{i}\, \varphi.$$

We require that φ does not contain S_A, since the idea of the above discussion is the direct coupling of the existential quantification of S_A and the group knowledge about the effects of its application. Requiring that φ does not have past-time operators is clearly crucial for memoryless strategies: If φ, e.g., requires to play a specific move if and only if that move has been played previously, then the strategy choice clearly must depend on the history and the above equivalence does not hold. Proposition 1 does not hold for distributed knowledge instead:

Example 1. Consider a CGS $\mathcal{C}$ with players a and b and two Boolean variables x and y, where player a (b) only sees the value of variable x (y) and the values of the variables change randomly in every transition. Each player always has the moves 0 and 1 available. Consider the coalition $A = \{\mathsf{a}, \mathsf{b}\}$ and the formula φ expressing "a moves according to y and b moves according to x"[4] Since the distributed knowledge of A allows to identify the values of both x and y, in each state there is a strategy choice achieving φ, however clearly there is no single strategy choice which works in all states. Hence, the formula $\Box\exists \mathrm{S}_A \mathcal{K}^D_{A,1} \langle\langle A : \mathrm{S}_A \rangle\rangle^{\geq 1}_{1}\, \varphi$ is always true in $\mathcal{C}$, while $\exists \mathrm{S}_A \Box \mathcal{K}^D_{A,1} \langle\langle A : \mathrm{S}_A \rangle\rangle^{\geq 1}_{1}\, \varphi$ is always false.

[4] To express this as a variable, the CGS needs to record the last move of each player in the state in the obvious way.

Proposition 1 can be generalized in several directions. For ease of presentation we only present the above simple form of Proposition 1 which supports the main argument of this section: "Intuitively sensible" applications of quantifications inside $\Box$-operators can be eliminated.

4.2 Quantification in the Scope of Epistemic Operators

We now show that quantification in the scope of epistemic operators leads to similar issues as the case of temporal operators considered above. We again consider the CGS in Fig. 2. In q_0, the formula

$$\mathbb{A}\mathsf{X}\mathcal{K}^{d}_{A,1}\exists \mathrm{S}_A \langle\langle A : \mathrm{S}_A\rangle\rangle^{\geq 1}_{1} \mathsf{X}p$$

is true: Agent a (who alone forms the coalition A) knows that there is a successful strategy choice, since there is one in both q_1 and in q_2. However, as seen above, he does not know this strategy choice.

We now present a similar result to Proposition 1, for quantification in the scope of epistemic operators, and identify cases in which these operators commute. For this, we exhibit a "maximal" class of formulas for which knowledge and quantification can always be exchanged. When discussing whether quantification of a variable S_i commutes with an operator (epistemic or otherwise), clearly we are only interested in formulas in which the variable S_i actually plays a non-trivial role. To formalize this, we extend the concept of a "relevant" variable which is well-known in propositional logic, to the class of strategy variables:

Definition 9. *Let φ be a formula with free strategy variables among $\{\mathrm{S}_1, \ldots, \mathrm{S}_n\}$. We say that the variable S_i is* relevant *for φ if there exists a CGS $\mathcal{C}$, a state q of $\mathcal{C}$, and strategy choices $\mathsf{S}_1, \ldots, \mathsf{S}_n, \mathsf{S}'_i$ such that $\mathcal{C}, (\mathsf{S}_1, \ldots, \mathsf{S}_n), q \models \varphi$ and $\mathcal{C}, (\mathsf{S}_1, \ldots, \mathsf{S}_{i-1}, \mathsf{S}'_i, \mathsf{S}_{i+1}, \ldots, \mathsf{S}_n), q \not\models \varphi$.*

This means that there exists a situation where it matters which strategy choice is used to instantiate the variable S_i. Examples for an irrelevant variable S_A are $\langle\langle A : \mathrm{S}_A\rangle\rangle^{\geq 1}_{i} (\Diamond x \vee \Box\neg x)$ or $\langle\langle A : \mathrm{S}_A\rangle\rangle^{\geq 0}_{i} \Diamond x$.

Definition 10. *For a coalition A and a degree of information i, $k \in \{D, E, C\}$, a formula φ is k-i-*simple *in S_A, if one of the following conditions is true:*

- *S_A is an irrelevant variable of φ, or*
- *φ is equivalent to a formula of the form $\mathcal{K}^{k}_{A,i}\psi$.*

Formulas that are k-i-simple give a "natural" semantics when prefixed with an existential quantifier, since in the same way as there, the non-uniformity of the existential quantifier is reduced using the epistemic operator. We now show that in these cases, infix quantification again is not necessary, as here, the existential and the epistemic operators commute:

Lemma 1. *If φ is k-i-simple and has a single free strategy variable, then for all CGS $\mathcal{C}$ and states q,*

$$\mathcal{C}, q \models \mathcal{K}^{k}_{A,i}\exists s_A\varphi \textit{ if and only if } \mathcal{C}, q \models \exists s_A\mathcal{K}^{k}_{A,i}\varphi.$$

This class of formulas is maximal—as soon as we have a formula that depends on the variables S_A and of which A's knowledge does not suffice to determine the truth, we cannot swap the above operators.

Proposition 2. *Let φ be a formula such that φ is not k-i-simple in S_A and the coalition A is bound to S_A in the entire formula, then $\exists \mathrm{S}_A \mathcal{K}^k_{A,i}\varphi \not\equiv \mathcal{K}^k_{A,i}\exists \mathrm{S}_A\varphi$.*

The prerequisite that A is bound to S_A in the entire formula is necessary to e.g., preclude cases where S_A is only used in a non-meaningful way. It is not a strong requirement, as (with infix quantification) usually the subformula directly succeeding the existential quantifier will be the one "talking about" the quantified strategy choice. It is possible to strengthen Proposition 2, however again the simple form here suffices to show that in the cases where quantification in the scope of an epistemic operator gives a satisfactory semantics, the quantifier can be moved out of scope of that operator, and hence QAPI suffices.

4.3 Discussion

Nesting of quantification and epistemic or temporal operators leads to counter-intuitive behavior, since quantification introduces a degree of non-uniformity, whereas a core issue in the epistemic setting is to enforce sufficient uniformity to ensure that agents have enough knowledge to decide on the "correct" move to play in every situation. Although we did not give a complete characterization of the cases in which temporal/epistemic operators and quantifiers commute and it is notoriously difficult to give a good definition of a "natural" semantics, our results give strong evidence for our claim: In the cases where infix quantification leads to a natural semantics, the quantifiers can be swapped with the temporal/epistemic operators, hence infix quantification is unneeded.

Another reason why QAPI only allows quantifiers in the prefix of a formula is that in the presence of strategy choices, infix quantification does not seem to be particularly useful: Quantification of *strategies* that may be different in any state should be handled by strategy choices in a way that is compatible with the epistemic setting, since strategy choices may return different strategies in states that are distinguishable for an agent. On the other hand, infix quantification of *strategy choices* is very unnatural: Strategy choices express "global behavior" of coalitions allowing prior agreement, but during the game only rely on communication that is part of the game itself. Quantification inside formulas would express "prior agreement" *during the game*, which defeats its purpose.

There may be interesting properties that can only be expressed using $\mathrm{QAPI}^{\mathit{infix}}$, but usually, QAPI is sufficient and avoids the above problems.

5 Simulations

Bisimulations relate structures in a truth-preserving way. They allow to obtain decidability results for game structures with infinite state spaces (if a bisimilar finite structure exists), or can reduce the state space of a finite system. In [15],

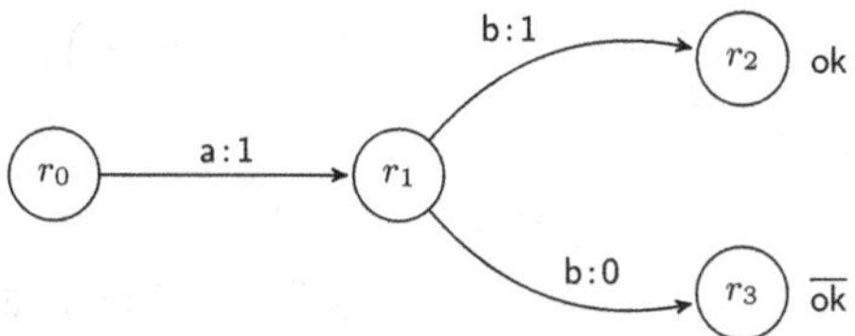

Fig. 3. Game structure $\mathcal{C}_1$.

our bisimulation results are used to obtain a model-checking algorithm on an infinite structure by utilizing a bisimulation between this structure and a finite one. We give the following definition, which is significantly less strict than the one in [14]: For example, our definition can establish bisimulations between structures with different numbers of states (see example below). This is not possible in the definition from [14], since there a bisimulation is essentially a relation Z which is a simulation in *both directions simultaneously*. Since a simulation in the sense of [14] is a function between state spaces, this implies that Z must contain, for every state in one CGS, *exactly* one related state in the other. Hence such a Z induces a bijection between state spaces, and is essentially an isomorphism. The following definition is somewhat simplified to increase readability, it only treats game structures that have a single degree of information, which is therefore omitted here.

Definition 11. *Let $\mathcal{C}_1$ and $\mathcal{C}_2$ be CGSs with state sets Q_1 and Q_2, the same set of players, and the same set of propositional variables. A* probabilistic bisimulation *between $\mathcal{C}_1$ and $\mathcal{C}_2$ is a pair of functions (Z_1, Z_2) where $Z_1 \colon Q_1 \to Q_2$ and $Z_2 \colon Q_2 \to Q_1$ such that there are* move transfer functions *Δ_1 and Δ_2 such that for $\{i, \bar{\imath}\} = \{1, 2\}$ and all $q_i \in Q_i$, $q_{\bar{\imath}} = Z_i(q_i)$, and all coalitions A:*

- *q_i and $q_{\bar{\imath}}$ satisfy the same propositional variables,*
- *if c_i is a (A, q_i) move, the $(A, q_{\bar{\imath}})$-move $c_{\bar{\imath}}(a) = \Delta_i(a, q_i, c_i(a))$ for all $a \in A$ satisfies that for $\{j, \bar{\jmath}\} = \{1, 2\}$ and all $(\overline{A}, q_j)$-moves $c_j^{\overline{A}}$, there is a $(\overline{A}, q_{\bar{\jmath}})$-move $c_{\bar{\jmath}}^{\overline{A}}$ such that for all $q_i' \in Q_i$, $Pr\Big(Z_{\bar{\imath}}(\delta(q_{\bar{\imath}}, c_{\bar{\imath}} \cup c_{\bar{\imath}}^{\overline{A'}})) = q_i'\Big) = Pr\Big(\delta(q_i, c_i \cup c_i^{\overline{A}}) = q_i'\Big)$.*
- *if $q_i \sim_a q_i'$, then $\Delta_i(a, q_i, c) = \Delta_i(a, q_i', c)$ for all c*
- *if $q_i \sim_a q_i'$, then $Z_i(q_i) \sim_a Z_i(q_i')$*
- *if $q_{\bar{\imath}} \sim_A q_{\bar{\imath}}'$, there is q_i' with $Z_i(q_i') = q_{\bar{\imath}}'$ and $q_i \sim_A q_i'$.*
- *$Z_1 \circ Z_2$ and $Z_2 \circ Z_1$ are idempotent.*

Theorem 1. *Let $\mathcal{C}_1$ and $\mathcal{C}_2$ be concurrent game structures, let (Z_1, Z_2) be a probabilistic bisimulation between $\mathcal{C}_1$ and $\mathcal{C}_2$, let q_1 and q_2 be states of $\mathcal{C}_1$ and $\mathcal{C}_2$ with $Z_1(q_2) = q_1$ and $Z_2(q_1) = q_2$. Let φ be a quantified strategy state formula. Then $\mathcal{C}_1, q_1 \models \varphi$ if and only if $\mathcal{C}_2, q_2 \models \varphi$.*

Consider the games $\mathcal{C}_1$ and $\mathcal{C}_2$ in Figs. 3 and 4. In both, player a starts, he has a single choice in $\mathcal{C}_1$ and 4 choices in $\mathcal{C}_2$. The move by b then determines whether ok holds in the final state. In states r_1 of $\mathcal{C}_1$ and q_1, q_2, and q_3 of $\mathcal{C}_2$, a must

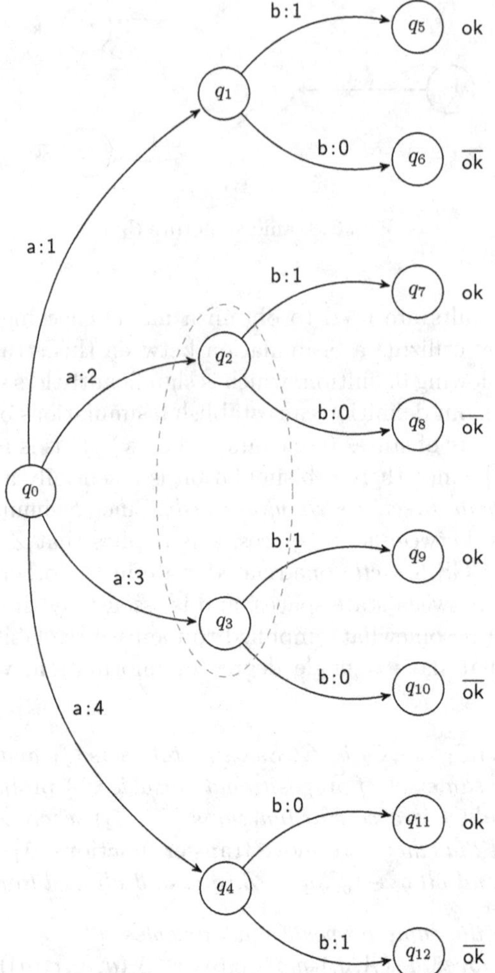

Fig. 4. Game structure $\mathcal{C}_2$.

play 1 to make ok true, in state q_4 of $\mathcal{C}_2$, he must play 0. States q_2 and q_3 are indistinguishable for a in $\mathcal{C}_2$. CGSs $\mathcal{C}_1$ and $\mathcal{C}_2$ with state sets Q_1 and Q_2 are bisimilar via (Z_1, Z_2), where $Z_2 \colon Q_2 \to Q_1$ is defined as follows:

- $Z_2(q_0) = r_0$,
- $Z_2(q_1) = Z_2(q_2) = Z_2(q_3) = Z_2(q_4) = r_1$,
- $Z_2(q_5) = Z_2(q_7) = Z_2(q_9) = Z_2(q_{11}) = r_2$,
- $Z_2(q_6) = Z_2(q_8) = Z_2(q_{10}) = Z_2(q_{12}) = r_3$.

The move transfer function swaps moves 0 and 1 when transferring from r_1 to q_4. $Z_1 \colon Q_1 \to Q_2$ maps r_0 to q_0, r_1 to q_1, r_2 to q_5 and r_3 to q_6, the move transfer functions map all of a's possible moves in q_0 to the move 1, the moves of b are mapped to themselves (note that q_4 is not used in this direction). It is easy to check that (Z_1, Z_2) is a bisimulation.

Theorem 1 states that state related via both Z_2 and Z_1 satisfy the same formulas. This applies to (r_0, q_0), (r_1, q_1), (r_2, q_5), and (r_3, q_6). The example shows a bisimulation between structures with complete and incomplete information, and with different cardinalities.

6 Model Checking Complexity

Model checking is the problem to determine, for a CGS $\mathcal{C}$, a quantified strategy formula φ, and a state q, whether $\mathcal{C}, q \models \varphi$. We state the following results for completeness, the proofs are straight-forward using results and techniques from the literature [2,3,5,14]. We note that the model-checking problem for a version of QAPI with perfect recall strategies can easily seen to be undecidable.

Theorem 2. *The QAPI model-checking problem is*

1. PSPACE-*complete for deterministic CGSs,*
2. *solvable in* 3EXPTIME *and* 2EXPTIME-*hard for probabilistic structures.*

References

1. Ågotnes, T., Goranko, V., Jamroga, W.: Alternating-time temporal logics with irrevocable strategies. In: Samet [12], pp. 15–24
2. Alur, R., Henzinger, T.A., Kupferman, O.: Alternating-time temporal logic. J. ACM **49**(5), 672–713 (2002)
3. Brázdil, T., Brozek, V., Forejt, V., Kucera, A.: Stochastic games with branching-time winning objectives. In: LICS, pp. 349–358. IEEE Computer Society (2006)
4. Chatterjee, K., Henzinger, T.A., Jurdzinski, M.: Games with secure equilibria. Theor. Comput. Sci. **365**(1–2), 67–82 (2006)
5. Chatterjee, K., Henzinger, T.A., Piterman, N.: Strategy logic. In: Caires, L., Vasconcelos, V.T. (eds.) CONCUR 2007. LNCS, vol. 4703, pp. 59–73. Springer, Heidelberg (2007)
6. Cortier, V., Küsters, R., Warinschi, B.: A cryptographic model for branching time security properties – the case of contract signing protocols. In: Biskup, J., López, J. (eds.) ESORICS 2007. LNCS, vol. 4734, pp. 422–437. Springer, Heidelberg (2007)
7. Chen, T., Lu, J.: Probabilistic alternating-time temporal logic and model checking algorithm. In: Lei, J. (ed.) FSKD (2), pp. 35–39. IEEE Computer Society (2007)
8. Halpern, J.Y., Moses, Y.: Knowledge and common knowledge in a distributed environment. J. ACM **37**, 549–587 (1990)
9. Herzig, A., Troquard, N.: Knowing how to play: uniform choices in logics of agency. In: Nakashima, H., Wellman, M.P., Weiss, G., Stone, P. (eds) AAMAS, pp. 209–216. ACM (2006)
10. Jamroga, W.: Some remarks on alternating temporal epistemic logic. In: Proceedings of Formal Approaches to Multi-Agent Systems (FAMAS 2003), pp. 133–140 (2004)
11. Jamroga, W., van der Hoek, W.: Agents that know how to play. Fundamenta Informaticae **63**(2–3), 185–219 (2004)

12. Samet, D. (ed.): Proceedings of the 11th Conference on Theoretical Aspects of Rationality and Knowledge (TARK-2007), Brussels, Belgium, 25–27 June (2007)
13. Schobbens, P.-Y.: Alternating-time logic with imperfect recall. Electron. Notes Theoret. Comput. Sci. **85**(2), 82–93 (2004)
14. Schnoor, H.: Strategic planning for probabilistic games with incomplete information. In: van der Hoek, W., Kaminka, G.A., Lespérance, Y., Luck, M., Sen, S. (eds) AAMAS, pp. 1057–1064. IFAAMAS (2010)
15. Schnoor, H.: Deciding epistemic and strategic properties of cryptographic protocols. In: Foresti, S., Yung, M., Martinelli, F. (eds.) ESORICS 2012. LNCS, vol. 7459, pp. 91–108. Springer, Heidelberg (2012)
16. Walther, D., van der Hoek, W., Wooldridge, M.: Alternating-time temporal logic with explicit strategies. In: Samet [12], pp. 269–278

Emergent Image Segmentation by Means of Evolved Connectionist Models and Using a Topological Active Net Model

Jorge Novo(✉), Cristina V. Sierra, José Santos, and Manuel G. Penedo

Computer Science Department, University of A Coruña, A Coruña, Spain
{jnovo,cristina.delavega,santos,mgpenedo}@udc.es

Abstract. We developed a novel method for image segmentation using deformable models. The deformable model adjustment is controlled by an Artificial Neural Network (ANN), which defines the deformations of the segmentation model through time. As deformable model we used Topological Active Nets, model which integrates features of region-based and boundary-based segmentation techniques. The evolved Artificial Neural Network learns to move each node of the segmentation model based on its energy surrounding. The ANN is applied to each of the nodes and in different temporal steps until the final segmentation is obtained. The ANN training is automatically obtained by simulated evolution, using differential evolution. This way, segmentation is an emergent process, result of the small deformations in the active model elements and through time. The new proposal was tested in different artificial and real images, showing the capabilities of the methodology.

Keywords: Topological Active Nets · Differential evolution · Artificial Neural Networks · Medical imaging

1 Introduction and Previous Work

The active nets model for image segmentation was proposed [1] as a variant of the deformable models [2] that integrates features of region–based and boundary–based segmentation techniques. To this end, active nets distinguish two kinds of nodes: internal nodes, related to the region–based information, and external nodes, related to the boundary–based information. The former model the inner topology of the objects whereas the latter fit the edges of the objects. The Topological Active Net (TAN) [3] model was developed as an extension of the original active net model. It solves some intrinsic problems to the deformable models such as the initialization problem. It also has a dynamic behavior that allows topological local changes in order to perform accurate adjustments and find all the objects of interest in the scene. The model deformation is controlled by energy functions in such a way that the mesh energy has a minimum when

J. Filipe and A. Fred (Eds.): ICAART 2013, CCIS 449, pp. 149–161, 2014.
DOI: 10.1007/978-3-662-44440-5_9

the model is over the objects of the scene. This way, the segmentation process turns into a minimization task.

The energy minimization of a given deformable model has been faced with different minimization techniques. One of the simplest methods is the greedy strategy [4]. The main idea implies the local modification of the model in a way the energy of the model is progressively reduced. The segmentation finishes when no further modification implies a reduction in terms of energy. As the main advantages, this method is fast and direct, providing the final segmentations with low computation requirements. However, as a local minimization method, it is also sensitive to possible noise or complications in the images. This method was used as a first approximation to the energy minimization of the Topological Active Nets [3].

As the local greedy strategy presented relevant drawbacks, especially regarding the segmentation with complex and noisy images, different global search methods based on evolutionary computation were proposed. Thus, a global search method using genetic algorithms [5] was designed. As a global search technique, this method provided better results working under different complications in the image, like noise or fuzzy and complex boundaries, situations quite common working under real conditions. However, this approach presented an important drawback, that is the complexity. The segmentation process needed large times and computation requirements to reach the desired results. As an improvement of the genetic algorithm approach, another evolutionary optimization technique was proposed [6]. This new approach, based in differential evolution, allowed a simplification of the previous method and also speed up the segmentation process, obtaining the final results in less generations (implying less time).

There is very little work regarding emerging systems and deformable models for image segmentation. "Deformable organisms" were used for an automatic segmentation in medical images [7]. Their artificial organisms possessed deformable bodies with distributed sensors, while their behaviors consisted of movements and alterations of predefined body shapes (defined in accordance with the image object to segment). The authors demonstrated the method with several prototype deformable organisms based on a multiscale axisymmetric body morphology, including a "corpus callosum worm" to segment and label the corpus callosum in 2D mid-sagittal MR brain images.

In this paper, we used Differential Evolution (DE) [8,9] to train an Artificial Neural Network (ANN) that works as a "segmentation operator" that knows how to move each TAN node in order to reach the final segmentations. Section 2 details the main characteristics of the method. It includes the basis of the Topological Active Nets, deformable model used to achieve the segmentations (Sub-sect. 2.1), the details of the ANN designed (Sub-sect. 2.2) and the optimization of the ANN parameters using the DE method (Sub-sect. 2.3). In Sect. 3 different artificial and real images are used to show the results and capabilities of the approach. Finally, Sect. 4 expounds the conclusions of the work.

2 Methods

2.1 Topological Active Nets

A Topological Active Net (TAN) is a discrete implementation of an elastic n-dimensional mesh with interrelated nodes [3]. The model has two kinds of nodes: internal and external. Each kind of node represents different features of the objects: the external nodes fit their edges whereas the internal nodes model their internal topology.

As other deformable models, its state is governed by an energy function, with the distinction between the internal and external energy. The internal energy controls the shape and the structure of the net whereas the external energy represents the external forces which govern the adjustment process. These energies are composed of several terms and in all the cases the aim is their minimization.

Internal Energy Terms. The internal energy depends on first and second order derivatives which control contraction and bending, respectively. The internal energy term is defined through the following equation for each node:

$$E_{int}(v(r,s)) = \alpha \left(|v_r(r,s)|^2 + |v_s(r,s)|^2\right) + \\ \beta \left(|v_{rr}(r,s)|^2 + |v_{rs}(r,s)|^2 + |v_{ss}(r,s)|^2\right) \tag{1}$$

where the subscripts represent partial derivatives, and α and β are coefficients that control the first and second order smoothness of the net. The first and second derivatives are estimated using the finite differences technique.

External Energy Terms. The external energy represents the features of the scene that guide the adjustment process:

$$E_{ext}(v(r,s)) = \omega\ f[I(v(r,s))] + \frac{\rho}{|\aleph(r,s)|} \sum_{p \in \aleph(r,s)} \frac{1}{\|v(r,s) - v(p)\|} f[I(v(p))] \tag{2}$$

where ω and ρ are weights, $I(v(r,s))$ is the intensity of the original image in the position $v(r,s)$, $\aleph(r,s)$ is the neighborhood of the node (r,s) and f is a function, which is different for both types of nodes since the external nodes must fit the edges whereas the internal nodes model the inner features of the objects.

If the objects to detect are bright and the background is dark, the energy of an internal node will be minimum when it is on a point with a high grey level. Also, the energy of an external node will be minimum when it is on a discontinuity and on a dark point outside the object. Given these circumstances, the function f is defined as:

$$f[I(v(r,s))] = \begin{cases} IO_i(v(r,s)) + \tau IOD_i(v(r,s)) & \text{for internal nodes} \\ IO_e(v(r,s)) + \tau IOD_e(v(r,s)) + \\ \xi(G_{max} - G(v(r,s))) + \delta GD(v(r,s)) & \text{for external nodes} \end{cases} \tag{3}$$

where τ, ξ and δ are weighting terms, G_{max} and $G(v(r,s))$ are the maximum gradient and the gradient of the input image in node position $v(r,s)$, $I(v(r,s))$ is the intensity of the input image in node position $v(r,s)$, IO is a term called "In-Out" and IOD a term called "distance In-Out", and $GD(v(r,s))$ is a gradient distance term. The IO term minimizes the energy of individuals with the external nodes in background intensity values and the internal nodes in object intensity values meanwhile the terms IOD act as a gradient: for the internal nodes (IOD_i) its value minimizes towards brighter values of the image, whereas for the external nodes its value (IOD_e) is minimized towards low values (background).

The adjustment process consists of minimizing these energy functions, considering a global energy as the sum of the different energy terms, weighted with the different exposed parameters, as used in the optimizations with a greedy algorithm [3] or with an evolutionary approach [5,6].

2.2 Artificial Neural Networks for the Image Segmentation

A new segmentation technique that uses Artificial Neural Networks (ANNs) to perform the optimization of the Topological Active Nets is proposed in this work. In particular, we used a classical multilayer perceptron model that is trained to know how the TAN nodes have to be moved and reach the desired segmentations.

The main purpose of the ANNs consist of providing, for a given TAN node, the most suitable movement that implies an energy minimization of the whole TAN structure. This is not the same as the greedy algorithm, which determines the minimization for each node movement. All the characteristics of the network were designed to obtain this behavior, and are the following:

Input. The ANN is applied iteratively to each of the TAN nodes. For each TAN node, the four hypothetical energy values that would take the mesh if the given node was moved in the four cardinal directions are calculated. The ANN receives as inputs the four increments (positive or negative) in energy in these new positions with respect to the current position. Moreover, these energy increments are normalized with respect to the energy in the present position, given the high values that the energy normally takes, following the formula:

$$\Delta E'_i = (E_i - E_c)/E_c \tag{4}$$

where E_i is the given hypothetical energy to be normalized and E_c is the energy with the TAN node in the present location.

Hidden Layers. One single hidden layer composed by a different number of nodes. The sigmoid transfer function was used for all the nodes.

Output. The network provides the movement that has to be done in each axis for the given TAN node. So, it has two output nodes that specify the shift in both directions of the current position.

These characteristics can be seen in Fig. 1. In this case, we obtain the values of the hypothetical energies that would be taken if we move the central node in the x and y axes, represented by the E_{x-}, E_{x+}, E_{y-} and E_{y+} values. The corresponding energy increments are introduced as the input values in the corresponding ANN, that produces, in this example, a horizontal displacement for the

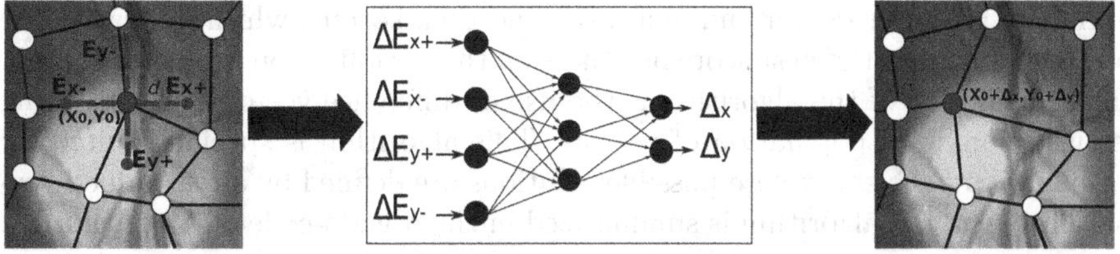

Fig. 1. Diagram of the shift production for a given TAN node using the ANN.

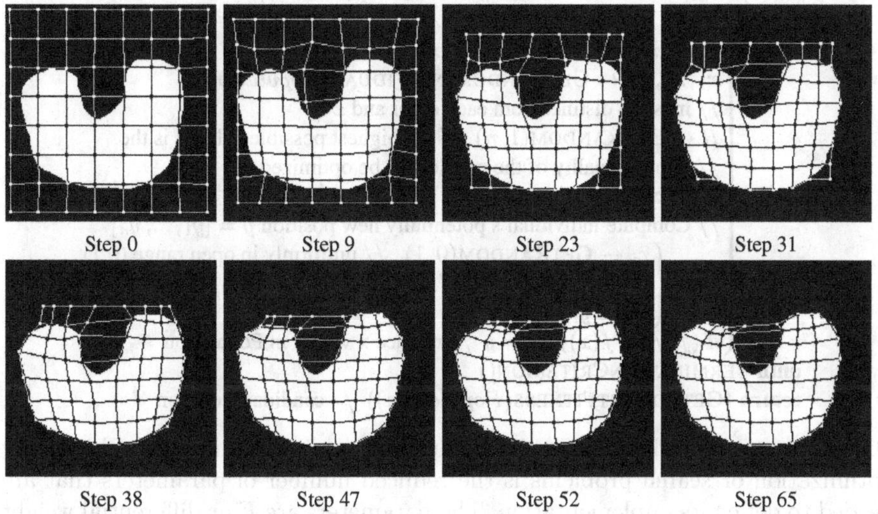

Fig. 2. Emergent segmentation provided by the ANN in different steps.

given TAN node. This movement, provided by the network outputs, is restricted in a small interval of pixels around the current position, typically between 1 and 5 pixels in both axes and directions.

Once we have the ANN correctly trained (with the evolutionary algorithm), we can use it as a "segmentation operator" that progressively moves the entire set of TAN nodes until, after a given number of steps, the TAN reaches the desired segmentation. In this process, the ANN is applied to each of the nodes sequentially. Such a temporal "step" is the application of the ANN to all the nodes of the TAN. An example of segmentation is shown in Fig. 2, where the TAN was established initially in the limits of the image and all the nodes were moved until a correct segmentation was reached.

2.3 Differential Evolution for the Optimization of the Artificial Neural Network

Differential Evolution (DE) [8,9] is a population-based search method. DE creates new candidate solutions by combining existing ones according to a simple formula of vector crossover and mutation, and then keeping whichever candidate solution which has the best score or fitness on the optimization problem at hand. The central idea of the algorithm is the use of difference vectors for generating perturbations in a population of vectors. This algorithm is specially suited for optimization problems where possible solutions are defined by a real-valued vector. The basic DE algorithm is summarized in the pseudo-code of Algorithm 2.1.

Algorithm 2.1. DIFFERENTIAL EVOLUTION(*Population*)

```
for each Individual ∈ Population
  do {Individual ← INITIALIZERANDOMPOSITIONS()
repeat
  for each Individual x ∈ Population
       ⎧ x1, x2, x3 ← GETRANDOMINDIVIDUAL(Population)
       ⎪ // must be distinct from each other and x
       ⎪ R ← GETRANDOM(1, n) // the highest possible value n is the
       ⎪ // dimensionality of the problem to be optimized
       ⎪ for each i ∈ 1 : n
    do ⎨ // Compute individual's potentially new position y = [y1, ..., yn]
       ⎪          ⎧ ri ← GETRANDOM(0, 1) // uniformly in open range (0,1)
       ⎪       do ⎨ if ((i = R) || (ri < CR))  yi = x1i + F(x2i − x3i)
       ⎪          ⎩   else yi = xi
       ⎩ if (f(y) < f(x))  x = y // replace x with y in Population
until TERMINATIONCRITERION()
return (GETLOWESTFITNESS(Population)) // candidate solution
```

One of the reasons why Differential Evolution is an interesting method in many optimization or search problems is the reduced number of parameters that are needed to define its implementation. The parameters are F or differential weight and CR or crossover probability. The weight factor F (usually in $[0, 2]$) is applied over the vector resulting from the difference between pairs of vectors (x_2 and x_3). CR is the probability of crossing over a given vector (individual) of the population (x_1) and a vector created from the weighted difference of two vectors ($F(x_2 - x_3)$), to generate the candidate solution or individual's potentially new position y. Finally, the index R guarantees that at least one of the parameters (genes) will be changed in such generation of the candidate solution.

When compared with the classical evolutionary algorithms such as a Genetic Algorithm (GA), DE has a clear advantage. The main problem of the GA methodology is the need of tuning of a series of parameters: probabilities of different genetic operators such as crossover or mutation, decision of the selection operator (tournament, roulette,), tournament size. Hence, in a standard GA it is difficult to control the balance between exploration and exploitation. On the contrary, DE reduces the parameters tuning and provides an automatic balance in the search. As it was indicated [10], the fundamental idea of the algorithm is to adapt the step length ($F(x_2 - x_3)$) intrinsically along the evolutionary process. At the beginning of generations the step length is large, because individuals are far away from each other. As the evolution goes on, the population converges and the step length becomes smaller and smaller.

In our application, a single ANN was used to learn the movements that have to be done by the internal and the external nodes. In the evolutionary population, each individual encodes the ANN. The genotypes code all the weights of the connections between the different nodes of the ANN. The weights were encoded in the genotypes in the range $[-1, 1]$, and decoded to be restricted in an interval [-MAX_VALUE, MAX_VALUE]. In the current ANN used, the interval $[-1, 1]$ was enough to determine output values in the whole range of the transfer functions of the nodes.

We initialized the TAN nodes in the borders of the images and applied a fixed number of steps. Each step consists of the modification produced by the ANN for each of the nodes of the TAN. Finally, the fitness associated to each individual or encoded ANN is the energy that has the final configuration of the TAN which must be minimized. So, the fitness is defined only by the final emergent segmentation provided by an encoded ANN.

Moreover, the usual implementation of DE chooses the base vector x_1 randomly or as the individual with the best fitness found up to the moment (x_{best}). To avoid the high selective pressure of the latter, the usual strategy is to interchange the two possibilities across generations. Instead of this, we used a tournament to pick the vector x_1, which allows us to easily establish the selective pressure by means of the tournament size.

3 Results

Different representative artificial and real CT images were selected to show the capabilities and advantages of the proposed method. Regarding the evolutionary DE optimization, all the processes used a population of 1000 individuals and the tournament size to select the base individual x_1 in the DE runs was 5 % of the population. We used a fixed value for the CR parameter (0.9) and for the F parameter (0.9). These values provided the best results in all the images. In the calculation of the fitness of the individual, we applied a number of steps between 50 and 400, depending on the complexity and the resolution of the image.

Table 1 includes the energy TAN parameters used in the segmentation examples. Those were experimentally set as the ones in which the corresponding ANN gave the best results for each training.

Table 1. TAN parameter sets used in the segmentation processes of the examples.

Figures	Size	α	β	ω	ρ	ξ	δ	τ
3,4,5	8×8	1.0	1.0	10.0	4.0	0.0	6.0	30.0
6	12×12	0.0	2.0	20.0	3.0	0.0	5.0	0.0
7	8×8	4.5	0.8	10.0	2.0	7.0	20.0	40.0
8	8×8	4.5	0.8	10.0	2.0	7.0	20.0	40.0

3.1 Segmentation of Artificial Images

Firstly, we tested the methodology with artificial images with different characteristics. In this case, we used a training set of 4 artificial images, each one with different characteristics (different shapes, inclusion of concavities, holes, etc.). The fitness is defined as the sum of the individual fitnesses provided by the same ANN (individual) in all the training images.

Figure 3 shows the final segmentations obtained with the training set. Moreover, we tested the trained ANNs with a different set of images. Once we have the ANNs trained, the segmentation is fast and direct, applying the modifications to the TAN nodes a given number of steps until we reach the final segmentation. Note that two of the images have great difficulties for a perfect segmentation, with a big hole and a deep concavity, so some nodes can incorrectly fall in the hole or the concavity. For testing the trained ANN, we scaled and rotated a couple of difficult images of the training dataset, to verify the independence of the training regarding modifications in the used objects. Figures 4 and 5 show the final results with the test set of images. As the Figures show, the ANNs are able to reach correct results, which demonstrates that the ANN has learned to move correctly the nodes, independently of the training image or images used, to provide a final correct segmentation.

3.2 Comparison of the Proposed Method and the Greedy Algorithm

We compared the proposed method with respect to the greedy approach previously defined. We selected a domain with real difficult images, as we segmented

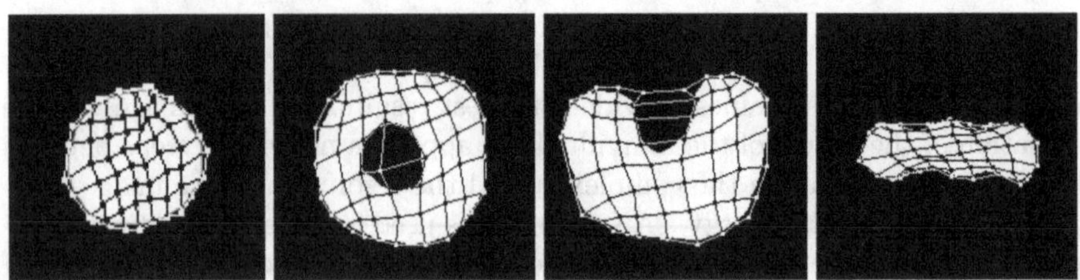

Fig. 3. Results obtained with the best ANN for the segmentation of the training images.

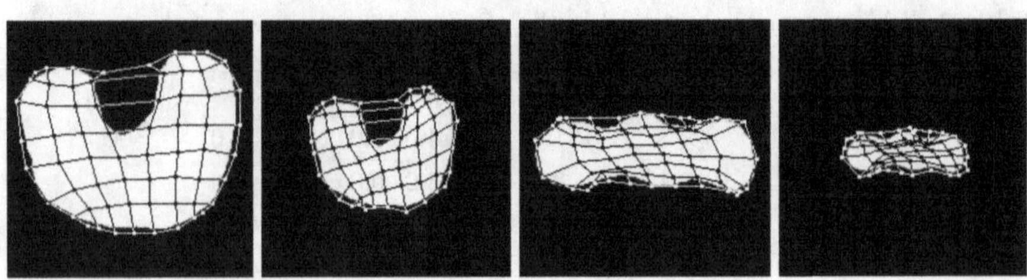

Fig. 4. Results obtained when the best ANN is tested with scaled artificial objects.

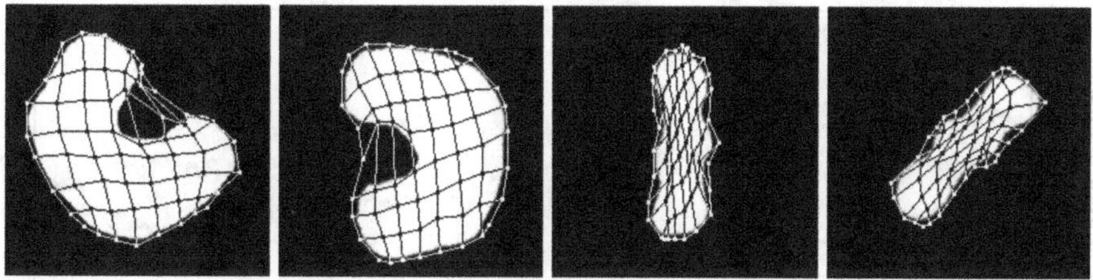

Fig. 5. Results obtained when the best ANN is tested with rotated artificial objects.

the optic disc in eye fundus images, as detailed in [11]. The objective is the segmentation of the optic disc (oval bright area in the image) which also provides the localization of the center of the optic disc. As Fig. 6 shows, the greedy local search falls in local minima quite fast, being impossible to reach the optic disc boundary (Fig. 6(a)). On the contrary, the ANN learned how to move all the nodes and was capable to reach an acceptable result (Fig. 6(b)–(d)). Note the capability of the evolved ANN to overcome the high level of noise, that prevents the correct segmentations by the greedy methodology.

In this case, additionally to the TAN energy parameters depicted in Table 1, we also used the ad-hoc energy terms designed for this specific task, as detailed in [11]. These energy terms are "circularity", that potentiates a circular shape of the TAN, and "contrast of intensities", that tries to put the external nodes in

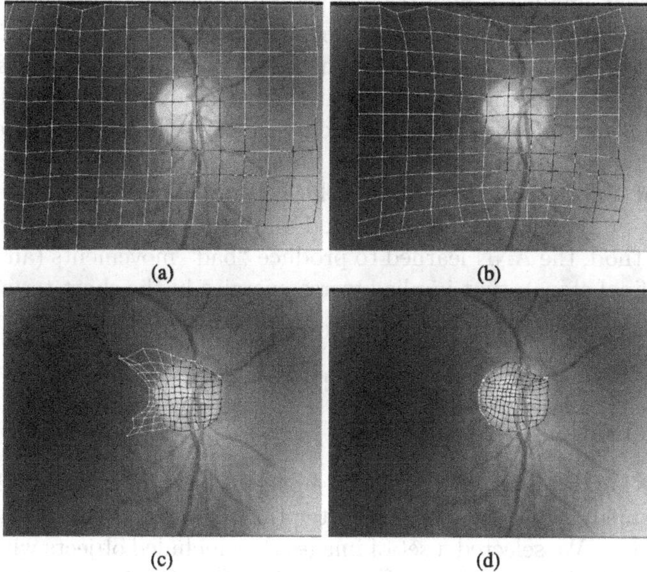

Fig. 6. Comparison between the greedy algorithm and the proposed method. (a) Final result with the greedy approach. (b)–(d) Segmentation provided by the ANN in different temporal steps: 30, 171 and 399.

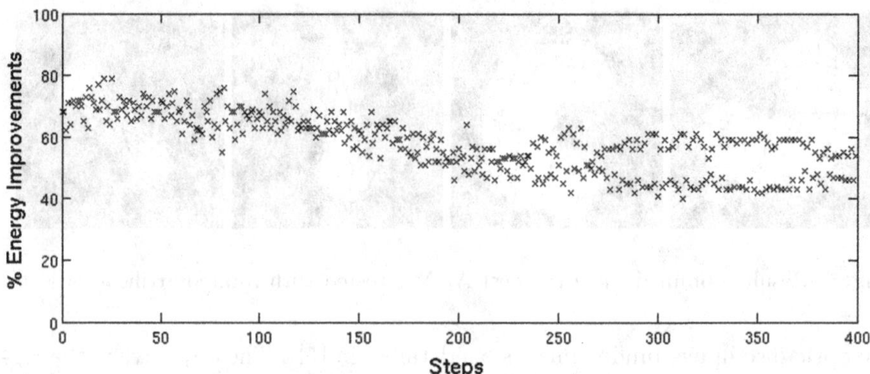

Fig. 7. Percentage of TAN node movements with an energy maintenance or improvement, over the temporal steps, and using the trained ANN in the segmentation of Fig. 6.

locations with bright intensities in the inside and dark intensities outside. This term was designed to avoid the falling of the external nodes in the inner blood vessels. In this segmentation, the corresponding energy parameters of these two ad-hoc energy terms took values of $cs = 30.0$ and $ci = 15.0$, respectively.

To explain why the greedy local search and the proposed method behave differently, we included, in Fig. 7, a graphic with the percentage of the TAN node shifts that implied a maintenance or improvement (decrement) in terms of energy, and for each step in the segmentation of the optic disc of Fig. 6. In the graphic, the main difference between the proposed method and the greedy local search is clear. Using the greedy method, all the movements of the TAN nodes imply a new position with an energy at least the same as the previous one, and better if possible (100 % in the graph). That is why, in this particular segmentation, the greedy method falls in local minima, because the nodes cannot find a better position in the neighborhood and in few steps. However, with the proposed method, the ANN learned to produce "bad" movements (an average of 50 % at the final steps), that implied worse energies in the short term, but they were suitable to find a correct segmentation in terms of the entire segmentation process.

3.3 Segmentation of Real Images

Moreover, as in the case with artificial images, we trained the ANNs with a given set of medical CT images, and after that, we tested the method with a different dataset. We selected a set of images that included objects with different shapes and with different levels of complexity. The CT images correspond to a CT image of the head, the feet, the knee and a CT image at the level of the shoulders. The images used in the testing correspond to CT images of the same close areas, but with a slightly different shape and with deeper concavities.

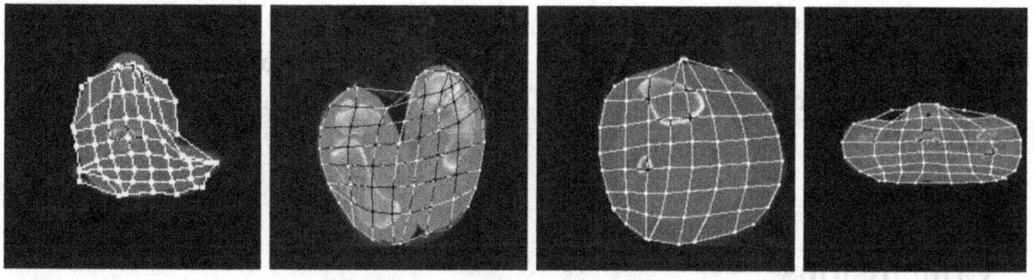

Fig. 8. Results obtained with the best evolved ANN and the training set of real CT images.

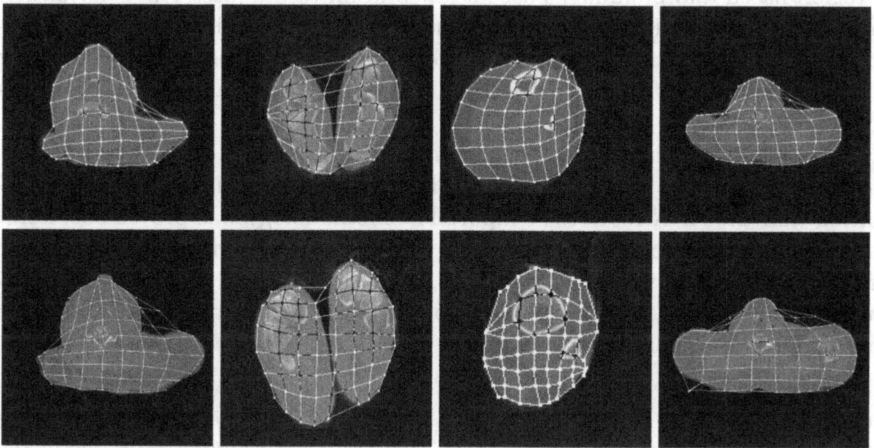

Fig. 9. Results obtained with the best evolved ANN and the test dataset of real CT images.

All these CT images presented some noise surrounding the object, noise that was introduced by the capture machines when obtaining the medical CT images.

Figure 8 includes the final segmentations with the training dataset, whereas Fig. 9 details the final segmentations obtained with the best trained ANN and the test set of images. In both cases, the evolved ANN was capable to provide acceptable results, including a correct boundary detection and overcoming the presence of noise in the images.

Again, in the difficult parts of the images, like the concavities, some external nodes fall incorrectly in the background. This can be improved changing the energy parameters, increasing the TAN energy *GD* (Gradient Distance), but it deteriorates other objectives like smoothness. So, the energy parameters are always a compromise to obtain acceptable results in different kind of images.

For example, in the second row of testing images, that are sections farther from the corresponding images in the training set, some external nodes tend to finally fall outside the image boundaries in the areas with deep concavities.

This is because the training images included few situations with deep concavities, which can be improved, as indicated previously, increasing parameter values like δ, which weights Gradient Distance (GD), and τ, which weights distance In-Out (IOD). However, in doing so we can worse the homogeneous distribution of the nodes.

4 Conclusions

We proposed a new methodology for image segmentation using deformable models. We used Topological Active Nets as extended model which integrates features of region-based and boundary-based segmentation techniques. The deformation through time was defined by an evolutionary trained ANN, since the ANN determined the movements of each one of the nodes. The process was repeated for all the nodes and in different temporal steps until the final segmentation was obtained.

Thus, the ANN provides an "emergent" segmentation, as a result of the local movements provided by the ANN and the local and surrounding energy information that the ANN receives as input. The methodology was proved successful in the segmentation of different artificial and real images, and overcoming noise problems. Moreover, we tested the ANN, trained with a set of images, with different testing images, obtaining acceptable results. So, our trained ANNs can be considered as "segmentation operators".

Acknowledgments. This paper has been partly funded by the Ministry of Science and Innovation through grant contracts TIN2011-25476 and TIN2011-27294 and by the Consellería de Industria, Xunta de Galicia through grant contract 10/CSA918054PR.

References

1. Tsumiyama, K., Yamamoto, K.: Active net: active net model for region extraction. IPSJ SIG Notes **89**(96), 1–8 (1989)
2. Kass, M., Witkin, A., Terzopoulos, D.: Snakes: active contour models. Int. J. Comput. Vis. **1**(2), 321–323 (1988)
3. Ansia, F., Penedo, M., Mariño, C., Mosquera, A.: A new approach to active nets. Pattern Recog. Image Anal. **2**, 76–77 (1999)
4. Williams, D.J., Shah, M.: A fast algorithm for active contours and curvature estimation. CVGIP: Image Underst. **55**(1), 14–26 (1992)
5. Ibáñez, O., Barreira, N., Santos, J., Penedo, M.: Genetic approaches for topological active nets optimization. Pattern Recogn. **42**, 907–917 (2009)
6. Buján, J.N., Santos, J., Penedo, M.G.: Optimization of topological active nets with differential evolution. In: Dobnikar, A., Lotrič, U., Šter, B. (eds.) ICANNGA 2011, Part I. LNCS, vol. 6593, pp. 350–360. Springer, Heidelberg (2011)
7. McInerney, T., Hamarneh, G., Shenton, M., Terzopoulos, D.: Deformable organisms for automatic medical image analysis. Med. Image Anal. **6**, 251–266 (2002)
8. Price, K., Storn, R.: Differential evolution - a simple and efficient heuristic for global optimization over continuous spaces. J. Glob. Optim. **11**(4), 341–359 (1997)

9. Price, K., Storn, R., Lampinen, J.: Differential Evolution: A Practical Approach to Global Optimization. Natural Computing Series. Springer, Heidelberg (2005)
10. Feoktistov, V.: Differential Evolution: In Search of Solutions. Springer, New York (2006)
11. Novo, J., Penedo, M.G., Santos, J.: Localisation of the optic disc by means of GA-optimised topological active nets. Image Vis. Comput. **27**, 1572–1584 (2009)

Hand Gesture Recognition for Human Computer Interaction: A Comparative Study of Different Image Features

Paulo Trigueiros[1(✉)], Fernando Ribeiro[1], and Luís Paulo Reis[2]

[1] Departamento de Electrónica Industrial da Universidade do Minho, Campus de Azurém, 4800-058 Guimarães, Portugal
ptrigueiros@gmail.com, fernando@dei.uminho.pt
[2] EEUM – Escola de Engenharia da Universidade do Minho – DSI, Campus de Azurém, 4800-058 Guimarães, Portugal
lpreis@dsi.uminho.pt

Abstract. Hand gesture recognition for human computer interaction, being a natural way of human computer interaction, is an area of active research in computer vision and machine learning. This is an area with many different possible applications, giving users a simpler and more natural way to communicate with robots/systems interfaces, without the need for extra devices. So, the primary goal of gesture recognition research is to create systems, which can identify specific human gestures and use them to convey information or for device control. For that, vision-based hand gesture interfaces require fast and extremely robust hand detection, and gesture recognition in real time. In this study we try to identify hand features that, isolated, respond better in various situations in human-computer interaction. The extracted features are used to train a set of classifiers with the help of RapidMiner in order to find the best learner. A dataset with our own gesture vocabulary consisted of 10 gestures, recorded from 20 users was created for later processing. Experimental results show that the radial signature and the centroid distance are the features that when used separately obtain better results, with an accuracy of 91 % and 90,1 % respectively obtained with a Neural Network classifier. These to methods have also the advantage of being simple in terms of computational complexity, which make them good candidates for real-time hand gesture recognition.

Keywords: Hand gesture recognition · Machine vision · Hand features · Hog (Histogram of oriented Gradients) · Fourier descriptors · Centroid distance · Radial signature · Shi-Tomasi corner detection

1 Introduction

Hand gesture recognition, being a natural way of human computer interaction, is an area of active current research, with many different possible applications, in order to create simpler and more natural forms of interaction, without using extra devices [1, 2]. To achieve natural human-computer interaction, the human hand could be considered as an input device. Hand gestures are a powerful way of human communication, with

J. Filipe and A. Fred (Eds.): ICAART 2013, CCIS 449, pp. 162–178, 2014.
DOI: 10.1007/978-3-662-44440-5_10

lots of potential applications, and vision-based hand gesture recognition techniques have many proven advantages compared with traditional devices. Compared with traditional HCI (Human Computer Interaction) devices, hand gestures are less intrusive and more convenient to explore, for example, three-dimensional (3D) virtual worlds. However, the expressiveness of hand gestures has not been fully explored for HCI applications. So, hand gesture recognition has become a challenging topic of research. However, recognizing the shape (posture) and the movement (gesture) of the hand in images or videos is a complex task [3].

The approach normally used for the problem of vision-based hand gesture recognition consists of identifying the pixels on the image that constitute the hand, extract features from those identified pixels in order to classify the hand, and use those features to train classifiers that can be used to recognize the occurrence of specific pose or sequence of poses as gestures.

In this paper we present a comparative study of seven different algorithms for hand feature extraction, for static hand gesture classification. The features were analysed with RapidMiner (http://rapid-i.com) in order to find the best learner, among the following four: *k-NN*, *Naïve Bayes*, *ANN* and *SVM*. We defined our own gesture vocabulary, with 10 gestures as shown in Fig. 1, and we have recorded videos from 20 users performing the gestures, without any previous training, for later processing. Our goal in the present study is to learn features that, isolated, respond better in various situations in human-computer interaction. The results show that the radial signature and the centroid distance are the features that when used separately obtain better results, being at the same time simple in terms of computational complexity. The features were selected due to their computational simplicity and efficiency in terms of computation time, and also because of the good recognition rates shown in other areas of study, like human detection [4]. The rest of the paper is as follows. First we review related work in Sect. 2. Section 3 introduces the actual data pre-processing stage and feature extraction. Machine learning for the purpose of gesture classification is introduced in Sect. 4. Datasets and experimental methodology are explained in Sect. 5. Section 6 presents and discusses the results. Conclusions and future work are drawn in Sect. 7.

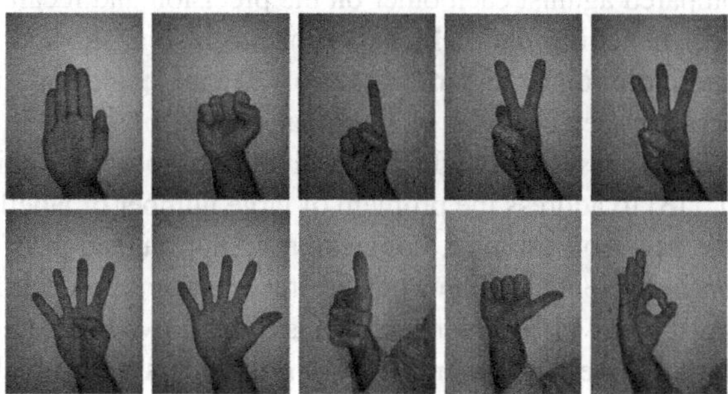

Fig. 1. The defined gesture vocabulary.

2 Related Work

Hand gesture recognition is a challenging task in which two main approaches can be distinguished: hand model based and appearance-based methods [5, 6]. Although appearance-based methods are view-dependent, they are more efficient in computation time. They aim at recognizing a gesture among a vocabulary, with template gestures learned from training data, whereas hand model-based methods are used to recover the exact 3D hand pose. Appearance-based models extract features that are used to represent the object under study. These methods must have, in the majority of cases, invariance properties to translation, rotation and scale changes. There are many studies on gesture recognition and methodologies well presented in [7, 8]. Wang et al. [9] used the discrete Adaboost learning algorithm integrated with SIFT features for accomplishing in-plane rotation invariant, scale invariant and multi-view hand detection. Conceil et al. [6] compared two different shape descriptors, Fourier descriptors and Hu moments, for the recognition of 11 hand postures in a vision based approach. They concluded that Fourier descriptors gives good recognition rates in comparison with Hu moments. Barczak et al. [10] performed a performance comparison of Fourier descriptors and geometric moment invariants on an American Sign Language database. The results showed that both descriptors are unable to differentiate some classes in the database. Bourennane et al. [3] presented a shape descriptor comparison for hand posture recognition from video, with the objective of finding a good compromise between accuracy of recognition and computational load for a real-time application. They run experiments on two families of contour-based Fourier descriptors and two sets of region based moments, all of them invariant to translation, rotation and scale-changes of hands. They performed systematic tests on the Triesch benchmark database [11] and on their own with more realistic conditions, as they claim. The overall result of the research showed that the common set Fourier descriptors when combined with the k-nearest neighbour classifier had the highest recognition rate, reaching 100 % in the learning set and 88 % in the test set. Huynh [12] presents an evaluation of the SIFT (scale invariant feature transform), Colour SIFT, and SURF (speeded up robust features) descriptors on very low resolution images. The performance of the three descriptors are compared against each other on the precision and recall measures using ground truth correct matching data. His experimental results showed that both SIFT and colour SIFT are more robust under changes of viewing angle and viewing distance but SURF is superior under changes of illumination and blurring. In terms of computation time, the SURF descriptors offer themselves as a good alternative to SIFT and CSIFT. Fang et al. [13] to address the problem of large number of labelled samples, the usually costly time spent on training, conversion or normalization of features into a unified feature space, presented a hand posture recognition approach with what they called a co-training strategy [14]. The main idea is to train two different classifiers with each other and improve the performance of both classifiers with unlabelled samples. They claim that their method improves the recognition performance with less labelled data in a semi-supervised way. Rayi et al. [15] used the centroid distance Fourier descriptors as hand shape descriptors in sign language recognition. Their test results showed that the Fourier descriptors and the Manhattan distance-based classifier achieved recognition rates of 95 % with small computational latency. Classification involves a learning procedure, for which the number of training images and the number of gestures are important facts. Machine learning algorithms have been applied successfully to many fields of research like, face recognition [16], automatic recognition of a musical gesture by a computer [17], classification of robotic soccer formations [18], classifying human physical activity from on-body accelerometers [19], automatic road-sign detection [20, 21], and static hand gesture classification [2]. K-Nearest Neighbour (k-NN) was used in [16, 18]. This classifier represents each example as a data in d–dimensional space, where d is the number of attributes. Given a test sample, the proximity to the rest of the data points in the training set is computed using a measure of similarity or dissimilarity. In the distance calculation, the standard Euclidean distance is normally used, however other metrics can be used [22]. An artificial neural network is a mathematical /computational model that attempts to simulate the structure of biological neural systems. They accept features as inputs and produce decisions as outputs [23]. Maung et al. [1, 18, 21, 24] used it in a gesture recognition system, Faria et al. [18] used it for the classification of robotic soccer formations, Vicen-Buéno [21] used it applied to the problem of traffic sign recognition and Stephan et al. used it for static hand gesture recognition for human-computer interaction. Support Vector Machines (SVM's) is a technique based on statistical learning theory, which works very well with high-dimensional data. The objective of this algorithm is to find the optimal separating hyper plane between two classes by maximizing the margin between them [25]. Faria et al. [16, 18] used it to classify robotic soccer formations and the classification of facial expressions, Ke et al. [26] used it in the implementation of a real-time hand gesture recognition system for human robot interaction, Maldonado-Báscon [20] used it for the recognition of road-signs and Masaki et al. used it in conjunction with SOM (Self-Organizing Map) for the automatic learning of a gesture recognition mode. Trigueiros et al. [2] have made a comparative study of four machine learning algorithms applied to two hand features datasets. In their study the datasets had a mixture of hand features. In this paper all the features extracted are analysed individually with machine learning algorithms to understand their performance and robustness in terms of scale, translation and rotation invariant static hand gesture recognition.

3 Pre-processing and Feature Extraction

Hand segmentation and feature extraction is a crucial step in computer vision applications for hand gesture recognition. The pre-processing stage prepares the input image and extracts features used later with the classification algorithms. In the present study, we used seven data sets with different features extracted from the segmented hand. The hand features used for the training datasets are: the *Radial Signature* (RS), the *Radial Signature Fourier Descriptors* (RSFDs), the *Centroid Distance* (CD), the *Centroid Distance Fourier descriptors* (CDFDs), the *Histogram of Oriented Gradients* (HoG), the *Shi-Tomasi Corner Detector* and the *Uniform Local Binary Patterns* (ULBP).

For the problem at hand, two types of images obtained with a Kinect camera were used in the feature extraction phase. The first one, the hand grey scale image was used in the HoG operator, the LBP (local binary pattern) operator and the Shi-Tomasi corner detector. The second one, the segmented hand blob, was used in the radial signature and the centroid distance signature after contour extraction.

3.1 Radial Signature

Shape signature is used to represent the shape contour of an object. The shape signature itself is a one-dimensional function that is constructed from the contour coordinates. The radial signature is one of several types of shape signatures.

A simple method to assess the gesture would be to measure the number of pixels from the hand centroid to the edges of the hand along a number of equally spaced radials [27]. For the present feature extraction problem, 100 equally spaced radials were used. To count the number of pixels along a given radial we only take into account the ones that are part of the hand, eliminating those that fall inside gaps, like the ones that appear between fingers or between the palm and a finger (Fig. 2). All the radial measurements can be scaled so that the longest radial has a constant length. With this measure, we can have a radial length signature that is invariant to hand distance from the camera.

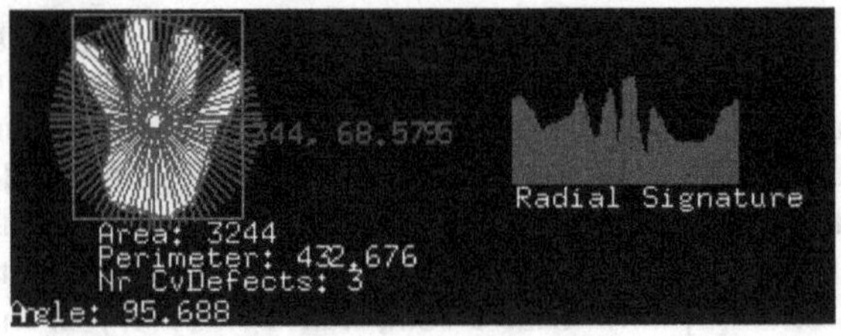

Fig. 2. Hand radial signature: hand with drawn radials (left); obtained radial signature (right).

3.2 Histogram of Gradients (HoG)

Pixel intensities can be sensitive to lighting variations, which lead to classification problems within the same gesture under different light conditions. The use of local orientation measures avoids this kind of problem, and the histogram gives us translation invariance. Orientation histograms summarize how much of each shape is oriented in each possible direction, independent of the position of the hand inside the camera frame [28]. This statistical technique is most appropriate for close-ups of the hand. In our work, the hand is extracted and separated from the background, which provides a uniform black background, which makes this statistical technique a good method for the identification of different static hand poses, as it can be seen in Fig. 3.

This method is insensitive to small changes in the size of the hand, but it is sensitive to changes in hand orientation.

We have calculated the local orientation using image gradients, represented by horizontal and vertical image pixel differences. If d_x and d_y are the outputs of the derivative operators, then the gradient direction is $\arctan(d_x, d_y)$, and the contrast is

$\sqrt{d_x^2 + d_y^2}$. A contrast threshold is set as some amount k times the mean image contrast, below which we assume the orientation measurement is inaccurate. A value of k = 1.2 was used in the experiments. We then blur the histogram in the angular domain as in [29], with a (1 4 6 4 1) filter, which gives a gradual fall-off in the distance between orientation histograms.

This feature descriptor was extensively used in many other areas like human detection [4, 30], in conjunction with other operators like the Scale Invariant Feature Transformation (SIFT) [31], the Kanade-Lucas-Tomasi (KLT) feature tracker [32] and local binary patterns for static hand-gesture recognition [33]. Lu et al. [34] and Kaniche et al. [32] used temporal HOGs for action categorization and gesture recognition.

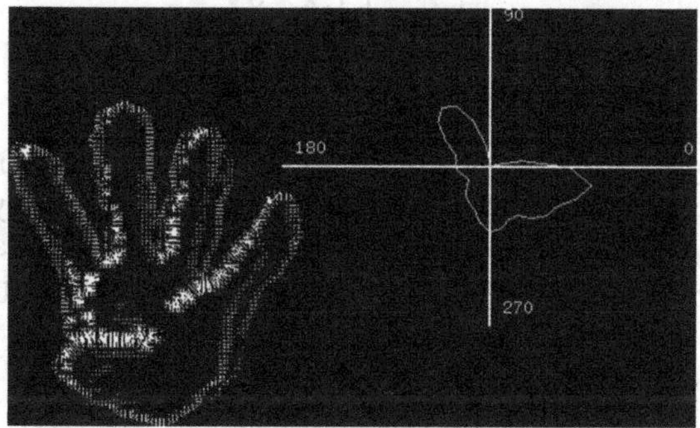

Fig. 3. Hand gradients (left), Histogram of gradients (right).

3.3 Centroid Distance Signature

The centroid distance signature is another type of shape signature. The centroid distance function is expressed by the distance of the hand contour boundary points, from the centroid (x_c, y_c) of the shape. In our study we used N = 128 as the number of equally sampled points on the contour.

$$d(i) = \sqrt{[x_i - x_c]^2 + [y_i - y_c]^2}, i = 0, \ldots, N - 1 \quad (1)$$

where $d(i)$, is the calculated distance, and x_i and y_i are the coordinates of contour points. This way, we obtain a one-dimensional function that represents the hand shape. Due to the subtraction of centroid, which represents the hand position, from boundary coordinates, the centroid distance representation is invariant to translation. Rayi Yanu Tara et al. [15] demonstrated that this function is translation invariant and that a rotation of that hand results in a circularly shift version of the original image.

3.4 Local Binary Patterns

LBP (local binary pattern) is a grey scale invariant local texture operator with powerful discrimination and low computational complexity [35–38]. This operator labels the pixels of the image by thresholding the neighbourhood of each pixel $g_0(p = 0 \ldots P-1)$, being P the values of equally spaced pixels on a circle of radius R (R > 0), by the grey value of its center (g_c) and considers the result as a binary code that describes the local texture [35, 37, 38].

The code is derived as follows:

$$LBP_{P,R} = \sum_{p=0}^{P-1} s\left(g_p - g_c\right) 2^p \tag{2}$$

where

$$s(x) = \begin{cases} 1, x \geq 0 \\ 0, x < 0 \end{cases} \tag{3}$$

Figure 4 illustrates the computation of $LBP_{8,1}$ for a single pixel in a rectangular 3×3 neighbourhood. g_0 is always assigned to be the grey value of neighbour to the right of g_c. In the general definition, LBP is defined in a circular symmetric neighbourhood, which requires interpolation of the intensity values for exact computation. The coordinates of g_0 are given by $(-R\sin(2\pi p/P), R\cos(2\pi p/P))$ [35].

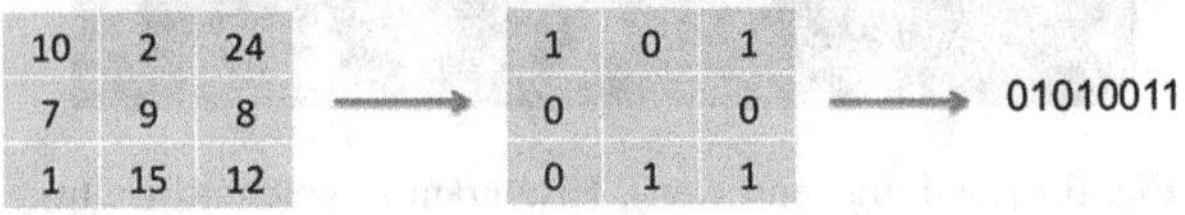

10	2	24
7	9	8
1	15	12

→

1	0	1
0		0
0	1	1

→ 01010011

Fig. 4. Example of computing ***LBP***$_{8,1}$ pixel neighbourhood (left); threshold version (middle); resulting binary code (right).

The $LBP_{P,R}$ operator produces 2^P different output values, corresponding to the 2^P different binary patterns that can be formed by the P pixels in the neighbourhood set. As a rotation of a textured input image causes the LBP patterns to translate into a different location and to rotate about their origin, if rotation invariance is needed, it can be achieved by rotation invariance mapping. In this mapping, each LBP binary code is circularly rotated into its minimum value

$$LBP^{ri}_{P,R} = \min_i ROR(LBP_{P,R}, i) \tag{4}$$

where $ROR(x, i)$ denotes the circular bitwise right shift on the P-bit number x, i steps. For example, 8-bit LBP codes 00111100b, 11110000b, and 00001111b all map to the minimum code 00001111b. For P = 8 a total of 36 unique different values is achieved. This operator was designated as LBPROT in [39]. Ojala et al. [35] had shown however, that LBPROT as such does not provide very good discrimination. They have observed that certain local binary patterns are fundamental properties of texture, providing the vast majority of all 3×3 patterns presented in observed textures. They called this fundamental patterns "uniform" as they have one thing in common – uniform circular structure that contains very few spatial transitions. They introduced a uniformity measure U(pattern), which corresponds to the number of spatial transitions (bitwise 0/1 changes) in the "pattern". Patterns that have a U value of at most 2 are designated uniform and the following operator for grey-scale and rotation invariant texture description was proposed:

$$LBP_{P,R}^{riu2} = \begin{cases} \sum_{p=0}^{P-1} s\left(g_p - g_p\right), \text{if } U\left(LBP_{P,R}\right) \leq 2 \\ P + 1, \text{ otherwise} \end{cases} \tag{5}$$

Equation (5) assigns a unique label corresponding to the number of "1" bits in the uniform pattern, while the non-uniform are grouped under the "miscellaneous" label $(P+1)$. In practice the mapping from $LBP_{P,R}$ to $LBP_{P,R}^{riu2}$ is best implemented with a lookup table of 2^P elements. The final texture feature employed in texture analysis is the histogram of the operator output (i.e., pattern labels).

In the present work, we used the histogram of the uniform local binary pattern operator, with R (radius) equal to 1 and P (number of pixels in the neighbourhood) equal to 8, as a feature vector for the hand pose classification.

3.5 Fourier Descriptors

Instead of using the original image representation in the spatial domain, feature values can also be derived after applying a Fourier transformation. The feature vector calculated from a data representation in the transform domain, is called Fourier descriptor [40]. The Fourier descriptor is another feature describing the boundary of a region [23, 41], and is considered to be more robust with respect to noise and minor boundary modifications. In the present study Fourier descriptors were obtained for the histograms calculated from the radial signature and the centroid distance. For computational efficiency of the FFT, the number of points is chosen to be a power of two [6]. The normalized length is generally chosen to be equal to the calculated histogram signature length (N). Hence the Fourier Transform leads to N Fourier coefficients C_k:

$$C_k = \sum_{i=0}^{N-1} z_i \exp\left(\frac{2\pi jik}{N}\right), \quad k = 0, \ldots, N-1 \tag{6}$$

Table 1 shows the relation between motions in the image and transform domains, which can be used in some types of invariance.

Table 1. Equivalence between motions in the image and transform domains.

In the image	In the transform
A change in size	Multiplication by a constant
A rotation of Ø about the origin	Phase shift
A translation	A change in the DC term

The first coefficient C_0 is discarded since it only contains the hand position. Hand rotation affects only the phase information, thus if rotation invariance is necessary, it can be achieved by taking the magnitude of the coefficients. Division of the coefficients by the magnitude of the second coefficient, C_1, on the other hand, achieves scale invariance. This way we obtain N-1 Fourier descriptors I_k:

$$I_k = \frac{|C_k|}{|C_1|}, k = 2, \ldots, N - 1 \tag{7}$$

Conceil et al. [6], showed that with 20 coefficients the hand shape is well reconstructed, so we used this in our experiments. Centroid Distance Fourier descriptors, obtained by applying Fourier transform on a centroid distance signature, were empirically proven to have higher performance than other Fourier descriptors [41, 42].

3.6 The Shi-Tomasi Corner Detector

The Shi-Tomasi corner detector algorithm [43] is an improved version of the Harris corner detector [44]. The improvement is in how a certain region within the image is scored (and thus treated as a corner or not). Where the Harris corner detector determines the score R with the eigenvalues λ_1 and λ_2 of two regions (the second region is a shifted version of the first one to see if the difference between the two is big enough to say if there is a corner or not) in the following way:

$$R = \det(\lambda_1 \lambda_2) - k(\lambda_1 + \lambda_2)^2 \tag{8}$$

Shi and Tomasi just use the minimum of both eigenvalues

$$R = \min(\lambda_1, \lambda_2) \tag{9}$$

and if R is greater than a certain predefined value, it can be marked as a corner. They demonstrated experimentally in their paper, that this score criterion is much better.

4 Machine Learning

The study and computer modelling of learning processes in their multiple manifestations constitutes the topic of machine learning [45]. Machine learning is the task of programming computers to optimize a performance criterion using example data or past experience [46]. For that, machine learning uses statistic theory in building mathematical models, since the core task is to make inference from sample data. In machine learning two entities, the teacher and the learner, play a crucial role. The teacher is the entity that has the required knowledge to perform a given task. The learner is the entity that has to learn the knowledge to perform the task. We can distinguish learning strategies by the amount of inference the learner performs on the information provided by the teacher. The learning problem can be stated as follows: given an example set of limited size, find a concise data description [45]. In our study, supervised learning was used, where the classification classes are known in advance. In supervised learning, given a sample of input-output pairs, called the training sample, the task is to find a deterministic function or model that maps any input to an output that can predict future observations, minimizing the error as much as possible. The models were learned from the extracted hand features with the help of the RapidMiner tool. The best learners identified for the produced datasets were the k-NN (k-nearest neighbour), the ANN (artificial neural network) and the SVM (support vector machines).

5 Datasets and Experimental Methodology

For data analysis, careful feature selection, dataset preparation and data transformation are important phases. In order to construct the right model it is necessary to understand the data under study. Successful data mining involves far more than selecting a learning algorithm and running it over your data [22]. In order to process the recorded videos, a C++ application, using openFrameworks and the OpenCV [47] and OpenNI [48] libraries, was developed. The application runs through all the recorded video files, and extracts for each algorithm the respective features. The features thus obtained are saved in text files, and converted later to Excel files so that they can be imported into Rapid Miner for data analysis, and find the best learner for each one. The experiments were performed in an Intel Core i7 (2,8 GHz) Mac OSX computer with 4 GB DDR3. The experiments were performed under the assumption of the k-fold method. The k-fold cross validation is used to determine how accurately a learning algorithm will be able to predict data that it was not trained with [16, 45]. A value of k = 10 (10-fold cross validation) was used, giving a good rule of approximation, although the best value depends on the used algorithm and the dataset [22, 46]. The algorithms performance, based on the counts of test records correctly and incorrectly predicted by the model, was analysed. Table 2 summarizes the best learners for each dataset with the corresponding parameters.

6 Results and Discussion

After analysing the different datasets, the obtained results were in most of the cases encouraging, although in other cases weaker than one could expect. In order to analyse how classification errors are distributed among classes, a confusion matrix was computed for each learner with the help of RapidMiner. Following we present the different results obtained with each dataset, in terms of best learner, the respective confusion matrix and the average accuracy recognition rate.

For the Radial Signature dataset, the best learner was the Neural Network with an accuracy of 91,0 %. Table 3 shows the respective confusion matrix. For the Centroid Distance dataset, the best learner was the neural network, with an accuracy of 90,1 %. Table 4 shows the respective confusion matrix. The k-NN classifier, with a value of k = 1, was the one that obtained the best values for the Radial Signature Fourier Descriptors and the Centroid Distance Fourier Descriptors with an accuracy of 82,28 %

and 79,53 % respectively. Tables 5 and 6 show their respective confusion matrixes. For the LBP operator and the HoG operator, the best learner was the SVM with a RBF (radial basis function) kernel type and soft margins with C = 6 and C = 2 and a bias (offset) of 0.032 and 0.149 respectively. The achieved accuracy was 89,3 % for the LBP operator and 61,46 % for the HoG operator. The SVM library used was the libSVM [49], since it supports multi-class classification. The obtained confusion matrixes are shown in Tables 7 and 8. For the Shi-Tomasi corner detector the best learner was the neural network with a learning rate of 0.1, but with very poor results. As it can be seen from the HoG confusion matrix and the Shi-Tomasi corner detector confusion matrix, a lot of misclassification occurred, resulting from similar results for different gestures (Tables 8 and 9).

Table 2. ML algorithms identified as best learners for each dataset and used parameters.

Dataset	Best learn. Algor.	Parameters	Accuracy
Radial Signature	Neural Net		**91,0 %**
Centroid Distance	Neural Net		**90,1 %**
Radial Sign. Fourier Descriptors	k-NN	k = 1	**82,3 %**
Centroid dist. Fourier Descriptors	k-NN	k = 1	**79.5 %**
Uniform Local Binary Patterns	SVM (libSVM)	Kernel = RBF; C = 6; Bias = 0.032	**89,3 %**
Histogram of Gradients	SVM (libSVM)	Kernel = RBF; C = 2; Bias = 0.149	**61,46 %**
Shi-Tomasi corners	Neural Net	Learning rate = 0.1	**21,90 %**

Table 3. Radial signature dataset confusion matrix.

Predicted class \ Actual class	1	2	3	4	5	6	7	8	9	10
1	234	1	2	2	3	4	2	6	4	6
2	2	290	8	2	2	3	1	3	0	6
3	2	1	273	2	4	5	5	2	2	8
4	1	1	4	252	6	3	2	4	1	0
5	5	1	4	2	291	7	1	5	0	0
6	2	1	2	5	1	281	8	6	2	0
7	2	1	2	4	1	3	290	3	0	6
8	2	3	5	3	2	4	0	250	1	5
9	7	3	9	0	2	3	2	1	276	4
10	0	8	3	4	4	2	2	2	1	258

Table 4. Centroid distance dataset confusion matrix.

Predicted class \ Actual class	1	2	3	4	5	6	7	8	9	10
1	343	7	2	2	5	1	2	2	6	12
2	9	335	4	4	8	4	12	3	1	1
3	1	2	314	5	43	0	1	3	0	5
4	1	0	2	287	7	3	1	12	1	8
5	2	1	1	2	309	3	8	7	0	9
6	2	1	0	7	4	345	3	5	9	4
7	5	4	4	4	0	4	321	1	2	2
8	3	3	9	3	5	2	1	299	3	3
9	2	4	6	0	7	3	3	5	308	1
10	2	4	3	8	11	5	5	9	1	271

Table 5. Radial signature Fourier confusion matrix.

Predicted class \ Actual class	**1**	**2**	**3**	**4**	**5**	**6**	**7**	**8**	**9**	**10**
1	250	1	4	2	9	12	3	3	2	2
2	2	275	10	6	8	3	17	8	1	17
3	3	5	249	9	7	5	6	17	0	16
4	7	12	11	248	8	6	7	10	1	0
5	6	2	4	20	241	16	10	14	2	8
6	12	3	3	2	21	245	9	4	2	2
7	3	8	3	5	4	7	228	2	0	10
8	3	2	13	6	7	9	12	220	1	9
9	9	1	1	0	2	4	0	6	287	1
10	1	3	6	0	2	1	6	5	1	232

Table 6. Centroid distance Fourier confusion matrix.

Predicted class \ Actual class	1	2	3	4	5	6	7	8	9	10
1	261	17	4	3	13	9	8	5	12	5
2	8	258	7	8	9	4	8	10	5	6
3	9	12	295	11	8	2	6	5	6	7
4	6	6	8	234	7	11	6	7	7	11
5	2	3	5	6	273	3	12	4	17	17
6	2	5	4	6	8	290	15	1	6	17
7	1	6	6	8	3	10	284	12	9	11
8	9	11	6	5	6	4	3	260	4	14
9	9	6	7	11	5	7	6	6	242	8
10	2	6	7	4	7	15	10	15	8	237

Table 7. Local binary patterns dataset confusion matrix.

	Actual class									
Predicted class	1	2	3	4	5	6	7	8	9	10
1	460	7	4	4	2	2	6	5	10	15
2	12	499	7	7	8	9	7	3	11	7
3	2	4	457	24	11	1	2	1	5	9
4	9	9	12	486	30	6	0	0	8	17
5	3	15	18	35	522	8	3	0	5	17
6	10	14	2	4	11	531	4	2	7	15
7	3	2	1	0	0	1	517	1	2	4
8	10	1	1	0	0	5	3	554	1	0
9	5	7	7	8	1	9	4	0	525	4
10	15	5	31	13	9	4	2	0	1	457

Table 8. Histogram of gradients dataset confusion matrix.

	Actual class									
Predicted class	1	2	3	4	5	6	7	8	9	10
1	174	15	14	11	5	0	1	17	19	17
2	24	207	8	11	10	13	8	9	25	12
3	18	10	199	25	12	4	2	6	20	13
4	7	5	22	168	24	15	3	4	10	24
5	8	7	11	18	181	19	15	4	6	19
6	0	7	2	9	24	195	19	5	7	15
7	16	39	16	21	34	62	259	39	20	38
8	10	4	3	5	6	2	1	189	5	3
9	30	19	17	9	8	3	1	12	176	14
10	10	15	16	23	13	11	11	3	19	161

Table 9. Shi-Tomasi corner detector confusion matrix.

	Actual class									
Predicted class	**1**	**2**	**3**	**4**	**5**	**6**	**7**	**8**	**9**	**10**
1	45	26	36	22	23	19	15	17	30	25
2	22	77	34	16	10	18	16	5	15	59
3	46	40	49	52	49	40	27	33	25	42
4	28	30	41	43	48	35	27	23	22	27
5	23	16	36	36	30	42	22	23	14	11
6	29	21	39	42	46	56	53	26	29	27
7	16	23	15	30	34	35	75	16	31	28
8	27	5	37	23	32	37	16	139	14	9
9	27	22	12	13	20	26	38	7	104	24
10	24	58	21	26	23	17	27	7	30	63

7 Conclusions and Future Work

This paper presented a comparative study of seven different algorithms for hand feature extraction, aimed at static hand gesture classification and recognition, for human computer interaction. We defined our own gesture vocabulary, with 10 gestures (Fig. 1), and we have recorded videos from 20 persons performing the gestures for hand feature extraction. The study main goal was to test the robustness of all the algorithms, applied individually to scale, translation and rotation invariance. After analysing the data and the obtained results we conclude that further pre-processing on the video frames is necessary in order to minimize the number of different feature values obtained for the same hand posture. The depth video images obtained with the Kinect have low resolution and some noise, so it was concluded that some imprecision on data recordings results from those problems, leading to more difficult class learning. There are several interpretations of noise as explained in [46]. Due to this situation, it was decided that a temporal filtering and/or a spatial filtering should be used and will be tested and analysed to see if better results are achieved. It has been found that the radial signature and the centroid distance are the best shape descriptors discussed in this paper in terms of robustness and computation complexity. Sometimes we have to apply the principle known as Occam's razor, which states that "simpler explanations are more plausible and any unnecessary complexity should be shaved off". The Shi-Tomasi corner detector implemented in OpenCV was the one that achieved the weaker results, and we will try it with the bag-of-features approach [50, 51]. Better results were expected from the Fourier descriptors, after having analysed related work on the area, so we will evaluate them further after having implemented the video streaming temporal filtering. In the local binary pattern operator, different radius and number of neighbours will be tested to analyse if better results are obtained.

Recent studies and implementations for image noise minimization, without degrading the performance in terms of frame rate was a cumulative average of hand position. We were able to prove in the recent implementations, that this method was able to improve feature extraction accuracy with implications in the final gesture classification.

References

1. Maung, T.H.H.: Real-time hand tracking and gesture recognition system using neural networks. Proc. World Acad. Sci. Eng. Technol. **50**, 466–470 (2009)
2. Trigueiros, P., Ribeiro, F., Reis, L.P.: A comparison of machine learning algorithms applied to hand gesture recognition. In: 7ª Conferência Ibérica de Sistemas e Tecnologias de Informação, Madrid, Spain (2012)
3. Bourennane, S., Fossati, C.: Comparison of shape descriptors for hand posture recognition in video. Signal Image Video Process. **6**(1), 147–157 (2010)
4. Dalal, N., Triggs, B.: Histograms of oriented gradients for human detection. In: International Conference on Computer Vision and Pattern Recognition, Grenoble, France (2005)
5. Ong, S., Ranganath, S.: Automatic sign language analysis: a survey and the future beyond lexical meaning. IEEE Trans. Pattern Anal. Mach. Intell. **27**(6), 873–891 (2005)

6. Conseil, S., Bourenname, S., Martin, L.: Comparison of Fourier descriptors and Hu moments for hand posture recognition. In: 15th European Signal Processing Conference (EUSIPCO), Poznan, Poland, pp. 1960–1964 (2007)
7. Mitra, S., Acharya, T.: Gesture recognition: a survey. IEEE Trans. Syst. Man Cybern. **37**, 311–324 (2007)
8. Murthy, G.R.S., Jadon, R.S.: A review of vision based hand gestures recognition. Int. J. Inf. Technol. Knowl. Manag. **2**(2), 405–410 (2009)
9. Wang, C.-C., Wang, K.-C.: Hand posture recognition using Adaboost with SIFT for human robot interaction. In: Proceedings of the International Conference on Advanced Robotics (ICAR'07), Jeju, Korea (2008)
10. Barczak, A.L.C., et al.: Analysis of feature invariance and discrimination for hand images: Fourier descriptors versus moment invariants. In: International Conference Image and Vision Computing, New Zealand (2011)
11. Triesch, J., von der Malsburg, C.: Robust classification of hand postures against complex backgrounds. In: International Conference on Automatic Face and Gesture Recognition, Killington, Vermont, USA (1996)
12. Huynh, D.Q.: Evaluation of Three local descriptors on low resolution images for robot navigation. In: Image and Vision Computing (IVCNZ '09), Wellington, pp. 113–118 (2009)
13. Fang, Y., et al.: Hand posture recognition with co-training. In: 19th International Conference on Pattern Recognition (ICPR '08), Tampa, FL (2008)
14. Blum, A., Mitchell, T.: Combining labeled and unlabeled data with co-training. In: Proceedings of the Eleventh Annual Conference on Computational Learning Theory, ACM, Madison, Wisconsin, USA, pp. 92–100 (1998)
15. Tara, R.Y., Santosa, P.I., Adji, T.B.: Sign language recognition in robot teleoperation using centroid distance Fourier descriptors. Int. J. Comput. Appl. **48**(2), 8–12 (2012)
16. Faria, B.M., Lau, N., Reis, L.P.: Classification of facial expressions using data mining and machine learning algorithms. In: 4ª Conferência Ibérica de Sistemas e Tecnologias de Informação, Póvoa de Varim, Portugal (2009)
17. Gillian, N.E.: Gesture recognition for musician computer interaction, in Music Department 2011, Faculty of Arts, Humanities and Social Sciences, Belfast, p. 206 (2011)
18. Faria, B.M., et al.: Machine learning algorithms applied to the classification of robotic soccer formations ans opponent teams. In: IEEE Conference on Cybernetics and Intelligent Systems (CIS), Singapore, pp. 344–349 (2010)
19. Mannini, A., Sabatini, A.M.: Machine learning methods for classifying human physical activity from on-body accelerometers. Sensors **10**(2), 1154–1175 (2010)
20. Maldonado-Báscon, S., et al.: Road-Sign detection and recognition based on support vector machines. IEEE Trans. Intell. Transp. Syst. **8**, 264–278 (2007)
21. Vicen-Bueno, R., et al.: Complexity Reduction in Neural Networks Applied to Traffic Sign Recognition Tasks (2004)
22. Witten, I.H., Frank, E., Hall, M.A.: Data Mining - Pratical Machine Learning Tools and Techniques, 3rd edn. Elsevier, Amsterdam (2011)
23. Snyder, W.E., Qi, H.: Machine Vision. Cambridge University Press, New York (2004)
24. Stephan, J.J., Khudayer, S.: Gesture recognition for human-computer interaction (HCI). Int. J. Adv. Comput. Technol. **2**(4), 30–35 (2010)
25. Ben-Hur, A., Weston, J.: A user's guide to support vector machines. In: Carugo, O., Eisenhaber, F. (eds.) Data Mining Techniques for the Life Sciences, pp. 223–239. Humana Press, Totowa (2008)
26. Ke, W., et al.: Real-Time Hand Gesture Recognition for Service Robot, pp. 976–979 (2010)

27. Lockton, R.: Hand Gesture Recognition Using Computer Vision. Oxford University, Oxford (2002)
28. Roth, M., et al.: Computer vision for interactive computer graphics. IEEE Comput. Graph. Appl. **18**, 42–53 (1998)
29. Freeman, W.T., Roth, M.: Orientation Histograms for Hand Gesture Recognition. Mitsubishi Electric Research Laboratories, Cambridge Research Center (1994)
30. Dalal, Navneet, Triggs, Bill, Schmid, Cordelia: Human detection using oriented histograms of flow and appearance. In: Leonardis, Aleš, Bischof, Horst, Pinz, Axel (eds.) ECCV 2006. LNCS, vol. 3952, pp. 428–441. Springer, Heidelberg (2006)
31. Lowe, D.G.: Distinctive image features from scale-invariant keypoints. Int. J. Comput. Vis. **60**(2), 91–110 (2004)
32. Kaaniche, M.-B., Bremond, F.: Tracking HOG descriptors for gesture recognition. In: IEEE International Conference on Advanced Video and Signal-Based Surveillance. IEEE Computer Society Press (2009)
33. Ding, Y., Pang, H., Wu, X.: Static hand-gesture recognition using HOG and improved LBP features. Int. J. Digit. Content Technol. Appl. **5**(11), 236–243 (2011)
34. Lu, W.-L., Little, J.J.: Simultaneous tracking and action recognition using the PCA-HOG descriptor. In: Proceedings of the 3rd Canadian Conference on Computer and Robot Vision, p. 6. IEEE Computer Society (2006)
35. Ojala, T., PeitiKainen, M., Maenpã, T.: Multiresolution gray-scale and rotation invariant texture classification with local binary patterns. IEEE Trans. Pattern Anal. Mach. Intell. **24** (7), 971–987 (2002)
36. Hruz, M., Trojanova, J., Zelezny, M.: Local binary pattern based features for sign language recognition. Pattern Recogn. Image Anal. **21**(3), 398–401 (2011)
37. Unay, D., et al.: Robustness of local binary patterns in brain MR image analysis. In: 29th Annual Conference of the IEEE EMBS, Lyon, France. IEEE (2007)
38. PietiKäinen, M., et al.: Computer Vision Using Local Binary Patterns, vol. 40. Springer, London (2011)
39. Pietikainen, M., Ojala, T., Xu, Z.: Rotation-Invariant Texture Classification using Feature Distributions. Pattern Recogn. **33**, 43–52 (2000)
40. Treiber, M.: An Introduction to Object Recognition. Springer, London (2010)
41. Zhang, D., Lu, G.: A comparative study of Fourier descriptors for shape representation and retrieval. In: Proceedings of 5th Asian Conference on Computer Vision (ACCV). Springer, Melbourne, Australia (2002)
42. Shih, F.Y.: Image Processing and Pattern Recognition: Fundamentals and Techniques. Wiley, New York (2008)
43. Shi, J., Tomasi, C.: Good features to track. In: International Conference on Computer Vision and Pattern Recognition, pp. 593–600. Springer, Seattle (1994)
44. Harris, C., Stephens, M.: A combined corner and edge detector. In: The Fourth Alvey Vision Conference (1988)
45. Camastra, F., Vinciarelli, A.: Machine Learning for Audio, Image and Video Analysis. Springer, London (2008)
46. Alpaydin, E.: Introduction to Machine Learning. MIT Press, Cambridge (2004)
47. Bradski, G., Kaehler, A., (eds.): Learning OpenCV: Computer Vision with the OpenCV library. O'Reilly Media (2008)
48. OpenNI: The standard framework for 3D sensing (2013). http://www.openni.org/
49. Chang, C.-C., Lin, C.-J.: LIBSVM: A library for support vector machines. ACM Trans. Intell. Syst. Technol. **2**(3), 27 (2011)

50. Jiang, Y.-G., Ngo, C.-W., Yang, J.: Towards optimal bag-of-features for object categorization and semantic video retrieval. In: Proceedings of the 6th ACM International Conference on Image and Video Retrieval, pp. 494–501. ACM, Amsterdam (2007)
51. Lazebnik, S., Schmid, C., Ponce, J.: Beyond bags of features: spatial pyramid matching for recognizing natural scene categories. In: Proceedings of the 2006 IEEE Computer Society Conference on Computer Vision and Pattern Recognition, vol. 2, pp. 2169–2178. IEEE Computer Society (2006)

Evaluation of Class Binarization and Feature Selection in Tear Film Classification using TOPSIS

Rebeca Méndez, Beatriz Remeseiro(✉), Diego Peteiro-Barral, and Manuel G. Penedo

Departamento de Computación, Universidade da Coruña, Campus de Elviña S/n, 15071 A Coruña, Spain
{rebeca.mendez,bremeseiro,dpeteiro,mgpenedo}@udc.es

Abstract. Dry eye syndrome is a prevalent disease which affects a wide range of the population and can be diagnosed through an automatic technique for tear film lipid layer classification. In this setting, class binarization techniques and feature selection are powerful methods to reduce the size of the output and input spaces, respectively. These approaches are expected to reduce the complexity of the multi-class problem of tear film classification. In previous researches, several machine learning algorithms have been tried and only evaluated in terms of accuracy. Up to now, the evaluation of artificial neural networks (ANNs) has not been done in depth. This paper presents a methodology to evaluate the classification performance of ANNs using several measures. For this purpose, the multiple-criteria decision-making method called TOPSIS has been used. The results obtained demonstrate that class binarization and feature selection improves the performance of ANNs on tear film classification.

Keywords: Tear film lipid layer · Class binarization techniques · Feature selection · Filters · Multiple-criteria decision-making · Multilayer perceptron

1 Introduction

The tear film is a complex layer of liquid covering the anterior surface of the eye. It was classically defined by Wolff [1] as a three-layered structure which consists of an anterior lipid layer, an intermediate aqueous layer and a deep mucin layer. The tear film is a essential component of the eye which plays some important functions [2], such as visual and cleaning functions. Also, it plays an essential role in the maintenance of ocular integrity by removing foreign bodies from the front surface of the eye.

The lipid layer is the outermost and thinnest layer of the tear film and it is mainly secreted by the meibomian glands [3]. It is a crucial component of the tear film because it provides a smooth optical surface for the cornea and retards

J. Filipe and A. Fred (Eds.): ICAART 2013, CCIS 449, pp. 179–193, 2014.
DOI: 10.1007/978-3-662-44440-5_11

evaporation of the eye during the inter-blink period [4]. Other functions of the lipid layer are establishing the tear film or sealing the lid margins during sleep.

Quantitative or qualitative changes in the normal lipid layer have a negative effect on the evaporation of tears from the ocular surface and on the quality of vision [5]. In fact, these changes are associated with the *evaporative dry eye* (EDE), since it refers to disorders of the tear film caused by poor tear quality, reduced tear production or excessive evaporation [6]. The international committee of Dry Eye Workshop (DEWS) defined the EDE as follows [7]:

> Dry Eye is a multifactorial disease of the tears and the ocular surface that results in symptoms of discomfort, visual disturbance, and tear film instability with potential damage to the ocular surface. It is accompanied by increases osmolarity of the tear film inflammation of the ocular surface

This disease affects a wide sector of the population, specially among contact lens users, and worsens with age. The proportion of people with EDE has increased due to the current work conditions [7], such as computer use.

EDE diagnosis is very difficult to accomplish, basically because of its multifactorial nature. There are several clinical tests which measures the tear quality and the quantity of tears. One of these test is called *lipid layer pattern assessment* and consists on evaluating tear film quality and lipid layer thickness by non-invasively imaging the superficial lipid layer by interferometry. This test is based on a standard classification defined by Guillon [8], who established various categories of lipid layer patterns: open meshwork, closed meshwork, wave and color fringe. Note that EDE is associated with the lipid layer thickness since a thinner lipid layer speeds up water evaporation, which means a reduction in tear film stability. Many eye care professionals have abandoned this test because it is very difficult to interpret the lipid layer patterns, specially the thinner ones which lack color and/or morphological features. Nevertheless, there is no doubt that this technique is a valuable test which provides relevant information by using noninvasive techniques. For this reason, the tear film lipid layer automatic classification could become a key step to diagnose EDE.

Some techniques have been designed to objectively calculate the lipid layer thickness by analyzing the interference color with an interference camera [9] or by using a sophisticated optic system [10]. However, first attempts to automatize the *lipid layer pattern assessment* test can be found in [11–13] which demonstrate how the interference phenomena can be characterized as a color texture pattern. Therefore, the automatic test can save time for experts and eliminate the subjectivity of the process. Further investigation was carried out in [14] where a set of color texture analysis techniques was applied to tear film lipid layer classification and the previous results were improved. Regarding machine learning techniques, the behavior of five different algorithms was studied over this set of color texture analysis methods in [15]. A statistical comparison of them was performed using only the accuracy of the classifiers.

To the best knowledge of the authors, there are no attempts in the literature to study this multi-class problem using class binarization techniques.

Class binarization techniques may improve performance on multi-class problems of learners which could directly handle multi-class classification [16,17]. Furthermore, all previous researches analyses the color texture characterization based on the accuracy of the classifiers, no other performance measures were studied. In relation to machine learning techniques, there is no deep study about the performance of *artificial neural networks* (ANNs). Finally, the number of features which define the color texture pattern used to characterize the interference phenomena is large enough to consider the use of feature selection techniques.

In this sense, there are a lot of unexplored areas of study in tear film lipid layer automatic classification. Thus, a research methodology is proposed in this work to analyze the performance of class binarization techniques and feature selection methods applied to tear film classification using ANNs. For this purpose, the obtained results will be analyzed in terms of a wide set of performance measures and a multiple criteria decision making method will be used in order to validate the different approaches.

This paper is organized as follows: Sect. 2 describes the steps of the research methodology, Sect. 3 explains the experimental study performed, Sect. 4 shows the results and discussion, and Sect. 5 includes the conclusions and future lines of research.

2 Research Methodology

The methodology proposed in this search aims to evaluate tear film lipid layer classification in terms of several criteria when using class binarization techniques and feature selection methods.

2.1 Class Binarization Techniques

Methods can be roughly divided between two different approaches—the "single machine" approaches, which construct a multi-class classifier by solving a single optimization problem, and the "error correcting" approaches, which use the ideas from error correcting coding theory to combine a set of binary classifiers [17]. There exist several techniques for turning multi-class problems into a set of binary problems [18–21]. A class binarization is a mapping of a multi-class learning problem to several two-class learning problems in a way that allows a sensible decoding of the prediction [20].

- The "*one-vs-all*" strategy consists in constructing one classifier per class, which is trained to distinguish the samples of one class from the samples of all remaining classes. These two-class problems are constructed by using the examples of class i as the positive examples and the examples of the rest of the classes as the negative examples.
- The "*one-vs-one*" strategy consists in training one classifier for each pair of classes. Thus, for a problem with c classes, $\frac{c(c-1)}{2}$ subproblems are constructed to distinguish the samples of one class from the samples of another class. The binary classifier for a problem is trained with examples of its corresponding classes i, j, whereas examples of the rest of classes are ignored for this problem.

Decoding Methods. If the classifiers are soft, as is the case of ANNs, they compute the "likelihood" of classes for a given input, that is they obtain a confidence p for the *positive* class and a confidence of $1 - p$ for the *negative* class. The decoding method in the *one-vs-all* technique, if we assume the *one*-part as the positive class and the *all*-part as the negative class, is simply done according to the maximum probability p among classes. However, this method is not appropriate for *one-vs-one* binarization techniques. Therefore, several decoding methods for *one-vs-one* binarization techniques are described as follows,

- *Hamming Decoding.* Dietterich and Bakiri [18] suggested the use of a matrix $M \in \{-1,1\}^{N\times F}$, where N is the number of classes and F is the number of binary classifiers. The i-th row of the matrix induces a partition of the classes into two "metaclasses", where a sample x_i is placed in the positive metaclass for the j-th classifier if and only if $M_{y_i j} = 1$ [17], where y_i stands for the desired class of sample x_i. If a new sample appears for classification, the Hamming distance between the sign of the output of every binary classifier $f_1(x), \ldots, f_F(x)$ and each row of the matrix M is then compared as follows, choosing the minimizer,

$$f(x) = arg \min_{r=1\ldots N} \sum_{i=1}^{F} \left(\frac{1 - sign(M_{ri} f_i(x))}{2} \right)$$

  where $sign(z) = +1$ if $z > 0$, $sign(z) = -1$ if $z < 0$, and $sign(z) = 0$ if $z = 0$. In [22], Allwein, Schapire and Singer extended the earlier work of Dietterich and Bakiri. They chose the matrix $M \in \{-1,0,1\}^{N\times F}$, rather than only allowing -1 and 1 as entries in the matrix. If $M_{y_i j} = 0$, then example x_i is not used when the j-th classifier is trained.
- *Loss-based Decoding.* The major disadvantage of Hamming decoding is that it ignores the significance of the predictions, which can be interpreted as a measure of confidence. If the classifiers are soft, in [22] the authors suggest using the loss function L instead of the Hamming distance. They proposed that the prediction for a sample x should be the class n that minimizes the total loss under the assumptions that the label for sample x in the f-th binary classifier is M_{nf}:

$$f(x) = arg \min_{r=1\ldots N} \sum_{i=1}^{F} L(M_{ri} f_i(x))$$

  The loss function depends on the learning algorithm. In this research, the most appropriate loss function is the logistic regression $L(z) = log(1 + e^{-2z})$ [22].
- *Accumulative Probability with Threshold.* If the classifiers obtain a confidence p for the *positive* class and a confidence of $1 - p$ for the *negative* class, the accumulative probability for every class is computed as the sum of their corresponding probabilities p. The prediction for a sample should be the class that maximizes the accumulative sum. The accumulative probability with threshold takes into consideration binary classifiers that will be ignored if the difference between p and $1-p$ is under a threshold ϵ. It is assumed that ignored

classifiers will correspond with class samples not used for their training procedure. In other words, only *significant* positive or negative probabilities will be considered.

2.2 Feature Selection

Feature selection is a dimensionality reduction technique aimed at detecting relevant features and discarding irrelevant ones, with the goal of obtaining a subset of features that describes properly the given problem with minimum degradation of performance [23]. Thus, feature selection is helpful in reducing the computational effort, allocated memory and training time.

There exists three different models for feature selection: filter, wrapper and embedded methods. Wrappers use a prediction method to score subsets of features. Filters rely on the general characteristics of the training data to select features with independence of the classifier. Halfway these two models, embedded methods perform feature selection as part of the training process of the classifier. It is well-known that wrappers and embedded methods have the risk of overfitting when having more features than samples [24], as it is the case in this research. Therefore, filters were chosen because they prevent the risk of overfitting and also allow for reducing the dimensionality of the data without compromising time and memory requirements of learning algorithms.

The three filters used in this work will be described as follows. They were selected based on previous researches [25,26].

- *Correlation-based Feature selection* (CFS) is a simple filter algorithm that ranks feature subsets according to a correlation based heuristic evaluation function [27]. The bias of the evaluation function is toward subsets that contain features that are highly correlated with the class and uncorrelated with each other. Irrelevant features should be ignored because they will have low correlation with the class. Redundant features should be screened out as they will be highly correlated with one or more of the remaining features. The acceptance of a feature will depend on the extent to which it predicts classes in areas of the instance space not already predicted by other features. CFS's feature subset evaluation function is defined as,

$$M_s = \frac{k\overline{r_{cf}}}{\sqrt{k + k(k-1)\overline{r_{ff}}}}$$

  where M_S is the heuristic "merit" of a feature subset S containing k features, $\overline{r_{cf}}$ is the mean feature-class correlation ($f \in S$) and $\overline{r_{ff}}$ is the average feature-feature intercorrelation. The numerator of this equation can be thought of as providing an indication of how predictive of the class a set of features is; and the denominator of how much redundancy there is among the features.
- *Consistency-based filter* [28] evaluates the worth of a subset of features by the level of consistency in the class values when the training instances are projected onto the subset of attributes. The algorithm generates a random

subset S from the number of features in every round. If the number of features of S is less than the current best, the data with the features prescribed in S is checked against the inconsistency criterion. If its inconsistency rate is below a pre-specified one, S becomes the new current best. The inconsistency criterion, which is the key to the success of this algorithm, specifies to what extent the dimensionally reduced data can be accepted. If the inconsistency rate of the data described by the selected features is smaller than a pre-specified rate, it means the dimensionally reduced data is acceptable.

- *INTERACT* [29] is a subset filter based on symmetrical uncertainty (SU) [30], which is defined as the ratio between the information gain (IG) and the entropy (H) of two features, x and y:

$$SU(x,y) = \frac{2IG(x|y)}{H(x)+H(y)}$$

where the information gain is defined as:

$$IG(x|y) = H(y) + H(x) - H(x,y)$$

being $H(x)$ the entropy and $H(x,y)$ the joint entropy. Besides SU, INTERACT also includes the consistency contribution (c-contribution). C-contribution of a feature is an indicator about how significantly the elimination of that feature will affect consistency. The algorithm consists of two major parts. In the first part, the features are ranked in descending order based on their SU values. In the second part, features are evaluated one by one starting from the end of the ranked feature list. If c-contribution of a feature is less than an established threshold, the feature is removed, otherwise it is selected. The authors stated in [29] that INTERACT can thus handle feature interaction, and efficiently selects relevant features.

2.3 Multiple-criteria Decision-making

Classification algorithms are normally evaluated in terms of multiple criteria such as accuracy, precision or training time. Thus, algorithm selection can be modeled as a multiple-criteria decision-making (MCDM) problem. MCDM methods evaluate classifiers from different aspects and produce rankings of classifiers [31]. Among many MCDM methods that have been developed up to now, *technique for order of preference by similarity to ideal solution* (TOPSIS) [32] is a well-known method that will be used in this research.

TOPSIS. TOPSIS is a MCDM method proposed by Hwang and Yoon in 1981 [32]. It finds the best algorithms by minimizing the distance to the ideal solution whilst maximizing the distance to the anti-ideal one. The extension of TOPSIS proposed by Opricovic and Tzeng [33] and Olson [34] is used in this research,

1. Compute the decision matrix consisting of m alternatives and n criteria. For alternative A_i, $i = 1, \ldots, m$, the performance measure of the j-th criterion C_j, $j = 1, \ldots, n$, is represented by x_{ij}.
2. Compute the normalized decision matrix. The normalized value r_{ij} is calculated as,

$$r_{ij} = \frac{x_{ij}}{\sqrt{\sum_{i=1}^{m} x_{ij}^2}}$$

3. Develop a set of weights w, where w_j is the weight of the j-th criterion and $\sum_{j=1}^{n} w_j = 1$, and compute the weighted normalized decision matrix. The weighted normalized value v_{ij} is computed as,

$$v_{ij} = x_{ij} w_j$$

4. Find the ideal alternative solution S^+ and the anti-ideal alternative solution S^-, which are computed as,

$$\begin{aligned} S^+ &= \{v_1^+, \ldots, v_n^+\} \\ &= \left\{ \left(\max_i v_{ij} | i \in I' \right), \left(\min_i v_{ij} | i \in I'' \right) \right\} \end{aligned}$$

and

$$\begin{aligned} S^- &= \{v_1^-, \ldots, v_n^-\} \\ &= \left\{ \left(\min_i v_{ij} | i \in I' \right), \left(\max_i v_{ij} | i \in I'' \right) \right\} \end{aligned}$$

respectively, where I' is associated with benefit criteria and I'' is associated with cost criteria.

5. Compute the distance of each alternative from the ideal solution and from the anti-ideal solution, using the Euclidean distance,

$$D_i^+ = \sqrt{\sum_{j=1}^{n} (v_{ij} - v_j^+)^2}$$

and

$$D_i^- = \sqrt{\sum_{j=1}^{n} (v_{ij} - v_j^-)^2}$$

respectively.

6. Compute the ratio R_i^+ equal to the relative closeness to the ideal solution,

$$R_i^+ = \frac{D_i^-}{D_i^+ + D_i^-}$$

7. Rank alternatives by maximizing the ratio R_i^+.

3 Experimental Study

The aim of this research is to evaluate the influence of binarization and feature selection in tear film lipid layer classification. The multilayer perceptron (MLP) was selected as base learning algorithm.

3.1 Data Source

The methodology proposed in this research has been tested on the VOPTICAL-I1 dataset [35]. This set includes 105 images categorized by optometrists from the Faculty of Optics and Optometry of the University of Santiago de Compostela (Spain). All these images were acquired from healthy subjects aged from 19 to 33 years. The dataset includes 29 open meshwork, 29 closed meshwork, 25 wave and 22 color fringe images. Table 1 shows one representative image for each Guillon category obtained from this dataset.

Table 1. Lipid layer interference patterns.

Open meshwork	Closed meshwork	Wave	Color fringe

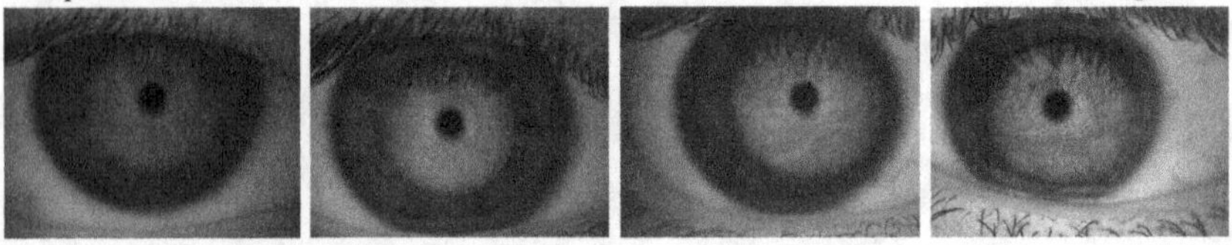

In [14], it was demonstrated that the interference phenomena can be characterized as a color texture pattern and the automatic classification into Guillon categories is feasible. The results presented by Remeseiro et al. [14] show how co-occurrence features [36], as a texture extraction method, and the Lab color space [37] provide the highest discriminative power from a wide range of methods analyzed. From a single image, a quantitative vector composed of 588 features is obtained to categorize it. Notice that the time to extract some of the textural features is too long which could prevent the practical clinical use of the automatic classification. Therein lies the importance of using feature selection in order to reduce the input space and, for this reason, the time to process the input images will be considered as a performance measure to evaluate the classification.

3.2 Performance Measures

Most performance measures in machine learning are defined to be used in two-class problems. Since a multi-class problem is studied in this research, all these measures will be calculated for each class individually. As tear film lipid layer classification is a 4-class problem, the total number of measures would be four times the number of binary measures. In order to reduce the total amount of measures, each multi-class measure will be obtained as the minimum of its four binary measures according to [38]. Thus, the performance of the learning algorithms are computed as a lower bound, or pessimistic, estimation.

The binary performance measures considered are:

- *Accuracy:* the proportion of true results, both true positives and negatives,

$$Accuracy = \frac{TN + TP}{TP + FP + FN + TN}$$

- *True Positive Rate* (TPR): the proportion of positives which are correctly classified (also called sensitivity or recall),

$$TPR = \frac{TP}{TP + FN}$$

- *True Negative Rate* (TNR): the proportion of negatives which are correctly classified (also called specificity),

$$TNR = \frac{TN}{TN + FP}$$

- *Precision:* the proportion of the true positives against all the positive results,

$$Precision = \frac{TP}{TP + FP}$$

- *F-measure:* the harmonic mean of precision and recall (also known as TPR),

$$F - measure = \frac{2 * Precision * Recall}{Precision + Recall}$$

- *Area Under the Curve* (AUC): the area under the receiver operating characteristic (ROC) curve, which is created by plotting the TPR versus the false positive rate ($FPR = \frac{FP}{TP+TN}$).

Finally, the image processing and the training times are also considered,

- *Image Processing Time* (IPT): the time elapsed for processing the input image and obtaining its quantitative vector. Note that this time is different for each class binarization technique, since the features selected are also different.
- *Training Time* (TT): the time elapsed for training a learning model. Note that this comprises training a set a classifiers when class binarization techniques are used.

Notice also that the testing time, that is the time elapsed for outputting a new classification, is negligible thus it will not be considered as a selection criterion.

3.3 Experimental Procedure

A leave-one-out cross-validation was used, which consists in using a single sample from the dataset as the test set and the remaining samples are retained as the training set. This process is repeated such that each sample is used once as the test set. The experimental research was carried out as follows,

1. Apply the three feature selection methods (CFS, consistency-based and INTERACT) to the VOPTICAL-I1 dataset, to provide the subset of features that properly describes the given problem. Note that the binarization techniques modify the output of the dataset thus the feature selection methods have to be applied on *each* "dataset", that is,
   - In the *one-vs-all* technique, four subsets of features are obtained corresponding with *1-vs-all*, *2-vs-all*, *3-vs-all* and *4-vs-all* datasets.
   - In the *one-vs-one* technique, six subsets of features are obtained corresponding with *1-vs-2*, *1-vs-3*, *1-vs-4*, *2-vs-3*, *2-vs-4* and *3-vs-4* datasets.
2. Train a MLP for each combination of binarization technique, feature selection method, and number of hidden units. In [39], it was demonstrated that a MLP that contains a single hidden layer with sufficient number of hidden units is able to approximate any function. Thus, only the number of hidden units will vary in this research ranging from 2 to 64. In particular, 2, 4, 8, 16, 32, and 64 hidden units were tested. Empirical results showed risk of overfitting for a larger number of hidden units. Finally, the mean square error was used as error function and the hyperbolic tangent sigmoid was used as transfer function in the processing units.
3. Compute the performance measures, that is, accuracy, TPR, TNR, precision, F-measure, AUC, image processing time and training time.
4. Apply TOPSIS in order to evaluate the different binarization techniques, feature selection methods and number of hidden units proposed in this research. The values of the weights (see Sect. 2.3) are assigned equally, except for the training time that is reduced to 0.01. Notice that the training step is executed off-line, making its value not as relevant as the other performance measures. Note also that the image processing and training times are cost criteria while the other measures are benefit criteria.

Experimentation was performed on an Intel© Core™ i5-650 CPU @ 4M Cache, 3.20 GHz with RAM 6 GB DDR3. Matlab was the software used to train the MLP networks.

4 Results

Table 2 shows the number of features selected by the three feature selection filters (CFS, consistency-based, and INTERACT) in single machine, one-vs-all, and one-vs-one approaches. The median percentage of features selected (out of 588 features) is in parenthesis.

Table 2. Number of features selected by the three filters in single machine, one-vs-all, and one-vs-one approaches (median percentage in parentheses).

Technique		Feature selection		
		CFS	Cons	INT
Single		27	6	21
	Median(%)	(4.59 %)	(1.02 %)	(3.57 %)
One-vs-all	1-vs-all	17	2	14
	2-vs-all	27	6	17
	3-vs-all	11	3	14
	4-vs-all	33	4	14
	Median(%)	(3.74 %)	(0.59 %)	(2.38 %)
One-vs-one	1-vs-2	20	2	12
	1-vs-3	53	1	53
	1-vs-4	23	1	23
	2-vs-3	27	3	14
	2-vs-4	24	3	14
	3-vs-4	27	4	13
	Median(%)	(4.34 %)	(0.43 %)	(2.38 %)

Broadly speaking, consistency-based filter performed the most aggressive selection retaining only the 1.02 %, 0.59 %, and 0.43 % of the features in single machine, one-vs-all, and one-vs-one approaches, respectively. CFS retained from four to ten times more features (4.59 %, 3.74 %, and 4.34 %) than the former. Halfway, INTERACT selected in average 3.57 %, 2.38 %, and 2.38 % of the features, respectively. As expected, in average the percentage of features selected in the single machine approach is larger than the percentage in binarization. Notice that binarization may reduce the complexity of the problem.

The set of techniques, methods and topologies used in this research lead to 120 alternatives in total. Thus, for purposes of simplicity only the most significant results are shown. Table 3 shows the top 20 results ranked by TOPSIS in terms of the binarization method, feature selection filter, number of hidden units (H), ratio R^+ (see TOPSIS, Sect. 2.3), accuracy, TPR, TNR, precision, F-measure, AUC, image processing time (in seconds) and training time (in seconds). Note that *single* stands for the single machine, multi-class, approach.

In general, the techniques and methods proposed in this research outperform the single machine approach (see Table 3). In the top 20, 14 out of 20 classifiers use binarization, and every classifier applies feature selection. Moreover, binarization leads to smaller topologies in the MLP. In the top 20, the average number of hidden units is 25.86 in binarization against 37.33 in the single machine approach. These are logical results because binarization techniques reduce the size of the output space. Notice that the low number of samples in the dataset, which is composed of 105 images, does not favor the use of the *one-vs-one* technique

Table 3. Top 20 measure results obtained by TOPSIS.

#	Method	Filter	H	R^+	Acc.	TPR	TNR	Prec.	F	AUC	TT(s)	IPT(s)
1	Single	CFS	64	0.9957	0.95	0.91	0.96	0.90	0.91	0.94	4.36	116.18
2	Single	CFS	32	0.9920	0.95	0.88	0.96	0.89	0.90	0.93	4.36	95.65
3	1-vs-1[b]	CFS	64	0.9894	0.95	0.90	0.97	0.91	0.90	0.93	9.75	223.71
4	Single	INT	64	0.9884	0.94	0.88	0.95	0.88	0.90	0.93	1.65	130.61
5	1-vs-1[b]	INT	64	0.9861	0.94	0.87	0.96	0.89	0.88	0.92	4.41	223.07
6	1-vs-1[a]	CFS	16	0.9854	0.95	0.89	0.96	0.88	0.90	0.93	9.75	187.08
7	Single	INT	16	0.9852	0.93	0.88	0.96	0.88	0.88	0.92	1.65	106.77
8	1-vs-1[a]	CFS	64	0.9841	0.95	0.89	0.96	0.87	0.89	0.94	9.75	221.06
9	1-vs-1[b]	CFS	8	0.9833	0.94	0.89	0.96	0.90	0.89	0.92	9.75	185.72
10	1-vs-1[a]	CFS	8	0.9830	0.94	0.88	0.96	0.88	0.90	0.93	9.75	183.44
11	1-vs-1[b]	INT	32	0.9817	0.94	0.86	0.96	0.88	0.88	0.91	4.41	198.80
12	1-vs-1[b]	CFS	2	0.9816	0.94	0.88	0.96	0.89	0.89	0.92	9.75	205.10
13	1-vs-1[b]	CFS	32	0.9792	0.94	0.87	0.96	0.89	0.88	0.92	9.75	203.15
14	1-vs-1[a]	CFS	32	0.9792	0.94	0.88	0.96	0.87	0.89	0.92	9.75	198.09
15	Single	INT	32	0.9763	0.93	0.87	0.95	0.87	0.87	0.91	1.65	112.00
16	Single	CFS	16	0.9758	0.94	0.86	0.95	0.87	0.87	0.91	4.36	89.49
17	1-vs-1[b]	INT	16	0.9746	0.93	0.85	0.96	0.87	0.87	0.91	4.41	196.30
18	1-vs-1[a]	CFS	4	0.9734	0.94	0.87	0.95	0.86	0.89	0.92	9.75	189.14
19	1-vs-1[b]	CFS	16	0.9719	0.93	0.86	0.96	0.88	0.88	0.91	9.75	188.79
20	1-vs-1[b]	CFS	4	0.9716	0.93	0.87	0.96	0.88	0.87	0.91	9.75	191.37

Decoding methods in 1-vs-1 binarization: [a]Hamming decoding, [b]Loss-based decoding.

since the training datasets are reduced to the samples of two classes. Thus, it is expected that in larger datasets *one-vs-one* approaches improve their results.

5 Conclusions and Future Research

Three binarization techniques and three feature selection methods have been used in this research for tear film lipid layer classification. The evaluation of the techniques and methods was based on several criteria: accuracy, TPR, TNR, precision, F-measure, AUC, image processing time and training time. TOPSIS method was used as a tool for selecting classification algorithm when algorithm selection involves more than one criterion. In general terms, binarization and feature selection outperform the single machine, multi-class, approach. To the best knowledge of the authors, the use of binarization techniques, features selection filters, and MCDM methods was not attempt so far in the literature for improving classification performance in the assessment of the tear film lipid layer. These results demonstrate the soundness of the methods presented in this research.

For future work, the authors plan to extend this research to different learning algorithms (e.g. naive Bayes classifier or decision trees) and different MCDM methods. Since different MCDM methods will evaluate different learning classifiers from different criteria, they may produce divergent rankings. Thus, the authors plan to implement an approach to resolve disagreeing rankings.

Acknowledgements. This research has been partially funded by the Secretaría de Estado de Investigación of the Spanish Government and FEDER funds of the European Union through the research projects PI10/00578, TIN2009-10748 and TIN2011-25476; and by the Consellería de Industria of the Xunta de Galicia through the research project CN2011/007. Beatriz Remeseiro and Diego Peteiro-Barral acknowledge the support of Xunta de Galicia under *Plan I2C* Grant Program.

We would also like to thank the Escuela de Óptica y Optometría of the Universidade de Santiago de Compostela for providing us with the annotated image dataset.

References

1. Wolff, E.: Anatomy of the Eye and Orbit, 4th edn. H. K. Lewis and Co., London (1954)
2. Korb, D.: The Tear Film: Structure, Function and Clinical Examination. Butterworth-Heinemann, Oxford (2002)
3. Nichols, K., Nichols, J., Mitchell, G.: The lack of association between signs and symptons in patients with dry eye disease. Cornea **23**, 762–770 (2004)
4. Bron, A., Tiffany, J., Gouveia, S., Yokoi, N., Voon, L.: Functional aspects of the tear film lipid layer. Exp. Eye Res. **78**, 347–360 (2004)
5. Rolando, M., Iester, M., Marcrí, A., Calabria, G.: Low spatial-contrast sensitivity in dry eyes. Cornea **17**, 376–379 (1998)
6. Rolando, M., Refojo, M., Kenyon, K.: Increased tear evaporation in eyes with keratoconjunctivitis sicca. Arch. Ophthalmol. **101**, 557–558 (1983)
7. Lemp, M., Baudouin, C., Baum, J., Dogru, M., Foulks, G., Kinoshita, S., Laibson, P., McCulley, J., Murube, J., Pfugfelder, S., Rolando, M., Toda, I.: The definition and classification of dry eye disease: report of the definition and classification subcommittee of the internation dry eye workshop (2007). Ocul. Surf. **5**, 75–92 (2007)
8. Guillon, J.: Non-invasive tearscope plus routine for contact lens fitting. Cont. Lens Ant. Eye **21**(Suppl 1), 31–40 (1998)
9. Goto, E., Yagi, Y., Kaido, M., Matsumoto, Y., Konomi, K., Tsubota, K.: Improved functional visual acuity after punctual occlusion in dry eye patients. Am. J. Ophthalmol. **135**, 704–705 (2003)
10. King-Smith, P., Fink, B., Fogt, N.: Three interferometric methods for measuring the thickness of layers of the tear film. Optom. Vis. Sci. **76**, 19–32 (1999)
11. Calvo, D., Mosquera, A., Penas, M., García-Resúa, C., Remeseiro, B.: Color texture analysis for tear film classification: a preliminary study. In: Campilho, A., Kamel, M. (eds.) ICIAR 2010, Part II. LNCS, vol. 6112, pp. 388–397. Springer, Heidelberg (2010)
12. Ramos, L., Penas, M., Remeseiro, B., Mosquera, A., Barreira, N., Yebra-Pimentel, E.: Texture and color analysis for the automatic classification of the eye lipid layer. In: Cabestany, J., Rojas, I., Joya, G. (eds.) IWANN 2011, Part II. LNCS, vol. 6692, pp. 66–73. Springer, Heidelberg (2011)

13. García-Resúa, C., Giráldez-Fernández, M., Penedo, M., Calvo, D., Penas, M., Yebra-Pimentel, E.: New software application for clarifying tear film lipid layer patterns. Cornea **32**, 538–546 (2012)
14. Remeseiro, B., Ramos, L., Penas, M., Martínez, E., Penedo, M., Mosquera, A.: Colour texture analysis for classifying the tear film lipid layer: a comparative study. In: International Conference on Digital Image Computing: Techniques and Applications (DICTA), Noosa, Australia, pp. 268–273 (2011)
15. Remeseiro, B., Penas, M., Mosquera, A., Novo, J., Penedo, M., Yebra-Pimentel, E.: Statistical comparison of classifiers applied to the interferential tear film lipid layer automatic classification. Comput. Math. Methods Med. 2012 (2012)
16. Fürnkranz, J.: Pairwise classification as an ensemble technique. In: Elomaa, T., Mannila, H., Toivonen, H. (eds.) ECML 2002. LNCS (LNAI), vol. 2430, pp. 97–110. Springer, Heidelberg (2002)
17. Rifkin, R., Klautau, A.: In defense of one-vs-all classification. The Journal of Machine Learning Research **5**, 101–141 (2004)
18. Dietterich, T., Bakiri, G.: Solving multiclass learning problems via error-correcting output codes. J. Artif. Intell. Res. **2**, 263–286 (1995)
19. Crammer, K., Singer, Y.: On the learnability and design of output codes for multiclass problems. Mach. Learn. **47**, 201–233 (2002)
20. Furnkranz, J.: Round robin classification. J. Mach. Learn. Res. **2**, 721–747 (2002)
21. Hsu, C., Lin, C.: A comparison of methods for multiclass support vector machines. IEEE Trans. Neural Netw. **13**, 415–425 (2002)
22. Allwein, E., Schapire, R., Singer, Y.: Reducing multiclass to binary: a unifying approach for margin classifiers. J. Mach. Learn. Res. **1**, 113–141 (2001)
23. Guyon, I., Gunn, S., Nikravesh, M., Zadeh, L.: Feature Extraction: Foundations and Applications. Springer, Heidelberg (2006)
24. Loughrey, J., Cunningham, P.: Overfitting in wrapper-based feature subset selection: the harder you try the worse it gets. In: Bramer, M., Coenen, F., Allen, T. (eds.) Research and Development in Intelligent Systems XXI, pp. 33–43. Springer, London (2005)
25. Bolón-Canedo, V., Sánchez-Maroño, N., Alonso-Betanzos, A.: On the behavior of feature selection methods dealing with noise and relevance over synthetic scenarios. In: The 2011 International Joint Conference on Neural Networks (IJCNN), pp. 1530–1537. IEEE (2011)
26. Bolón-Canedo, V., Peteiro-Barral, D., Alonso-Betanzos, A., Guijarro-Berdiñas, B., Sánchez-Maroño, N.: Scalability analysis of ANN training algorithms with feature selection. In: Lozano, J.A., Gámez, J.A., Moreno, J.A. (eds.) CAEPIA 2011. LNCS, vol. 7023, pp. 84–93. Springer, Heidelberg (2011)
27. Hall, M.: Correlation-based feature selection for machine learning. Ph.D. thesis, The University of Waikato (1999)
28. Dash, M., Liu, H.: Consistency-based search in feature selection. Artif. Intell. **151**, 155–176 (2003)
29. Zhao, Z., Liu, H.: Searching for interacting features. In: Proceedings of the 20th International Joint Conference on Artifical Intelligence, pp. 1156–1161. Morgan Kaufmann Publishers Inc. (2007)
30. Press, W., Flannery, B., Teukolsky, S., Vetterling, W., et al.: Numerical Recipes, vol. 547. Cambridge University Press, Cambridge (1986)
31. Kou, G., Lu, Y., Peng, Y., Shi, Y.: Evaluation of Classification Algorithms using MCDM and Rank Correlation. Int. J. Inf. Technol. Decis. Making (IJITDM) **11**, 197–225 (2012)

32. Hwang, C., Yoon, K.: Multiple Attribute Decision Making: Methods and Applications: A State-of-the-Art Survey, vol. 13. Springer, New York (1981)
33. Opricovic, S., Tzeng, G.: Compromise solution by MCDM methods: a comparative analysis of VIKOR and TOPSIS. Eur. J. Oper. Res. **156**, 445–455 (2004)
34. Olson, D.: Comparison of weights in TOPSIS models. Math. Comput. Modell. **40**, 721–727 (2004)
35. Remeseiro, B.: VOPTICAL_I1, VARPA optical dataset annotated by optometrists from the Faculty of Optics and Optometry, University of Santiago de Compostela (Spain) (2012). http://www.varpa.es/voptical_I1.html. Accessed May 2013
36. Haralick, R.M., Shanmugam, K., Dinstein, I.: Textural features for image classification. IEEE Trans. Syst. Man, Cybern. **3**, 610–621 (1973)
37. McLaren, K.: The development of the CIE 1976 (L*a*b) uniform colour-space and colour-difference formula. J. Soc. Dyers Colour. **92**(9), 338–341 (1976)
38. Fernandez Caballero, J., Martínez, F., Hervás, C., Gutiérrez, P.: Sensitivity versus accuracy in multiclass problems using memetic pareto evolutionary neural networks. IEEE Trans. Neural Netw. **21**, 750–770 (2010)
39. Hecht-Nielsen, R.: Neurocomputing. Addison-Wesley, Reading (1990)

SMACH: Agent-Based Simulation Investigation on Human Activities and Household Electrical Consumption

Édouard Amouroux[1(✉)], Thomas Huraux[1,2], François Sempé[3], Nicolas Sabouret[1], and Yvon Haradji[2]

[1] LIP6 - Université Pierre and Marie Curie, Paris, France
edamouroux@gmail.com, nicolas.sabouret@upmc.fr
[2] EDF Research and Development, Clamart, France
{thomas.huraux,yvon.haradji}@edf.fr
[3] Franois Sempé AE, Paris, France
sempe.francois@gmail.com

Abstract. This paper proposes the SMACH multi-agent simulation framework that allows energy experts to run scenario-based experiments to investigate the link between residential electricity consumption and inhabitants behaviour. We first present the proposed meta-model and the associated simulator. We illustrate their use by specialist on concrete examples featuring classical household activities. We also put an emphasis on the systems adaptation mechanism that permits to outline emergent habits and other behavioural patterns.

Keywords: Agent-based modelling · Social simulation · Energy control · Inhabitants' dynamic behaviour

1 Introduction

Energy efficiency and consumption reduction is a major challenge for our society due to awareness raising to the greenhouse effect and growing tensions on the energy market. European Union (EU) set the ambitious objective to divide by four greenhouse gas emissions by 2050. Yet, a large part of the final energy consumed in Europe, 26.6 %, is used within residential sector, according to the EEA [2]. For this reason, several programmes in the residential sector have been proposed such as building renovation, definition of low energy building (LEB) and smart energy controller [4], consumer awareness to cost and carbon emissions thanks to real-time feedback [13]. At a larger scale, smart grid have been proposed [9] in order to optimise the production and the distribution of electricity depending on consumption.

Nevertheless, individuals' behaviour also strongly influences energy consumption. In France, according to [12], despite a moderate increase of household electricity consumption (8 % from 1973 to 2003), a strong increase of the specific

J. Filipe and A. Fred (Eds.): ICAART 2013, CCIS 449, pp. 194–210, 2014.
DOI: 10.1007/978-3-662-44440-5_12

uses of electricity (*i.e.* electricity used except for heating) occurred (85 % for the same period). In this context, the study of propositions to diminish specific uses of electricity becomes a crucial issue.

One aspect of the problem is to study the consumption of electrical appliances in real-life situations. That aspect is at the core of the REMODECE[1] european project, that provides knowledge on electricity waste due to inefficient appliances and standby consumption. A complementary approach is to study household activities. Several works have been proposed in this direction such as [1,7,8], but they usually focus on electricity demand prediction, so as to optimise energy control systems. Nevertheless, one might want to consider influencing people's consumption behaviour through incentives such as variable electricity pricing, awareness campaigns, etc. For instance, [10] suggests that a critical peak price program might reduce by 30 % the peak load.

Several models allows to take into account human activities and their resulting electricity demands. Many of them rely on statistical approaches such as [18,20] that use hidden Markov chains to generate human activities related to electricity demands. Despite their statistical validity, they focus on representing an "average" familly and scenario and, thus, do not allow to investigate on the activity dynamics related, for instance, to specific events. Actually, agent-based models are best fitted for such analysis, as recently exhibited by the model proposed in [7]. This model relies on the Brahms language [16] to allow explicit representation and organisation of human activities. Nevertheless, the parametrization of this model appears to be very complex. They are hardly accessible to field experts and do not allow simulation of complex and long situations.

In this paper, we present a meta-model and a simulator, called SMACH, that allows experts to model, simulate and study the household activities and their relation with electrical consumption depending on specific pricing policies or appliance use. This system can be used to evaluate possible incentives to diminish peak hours electricity demand.

In numerous modelling efforts, expertise collection is combined with definition of the technical architecture which often limits the scalability of the model. In contrary, our approach, incremental and situated modelling [15], clearly separated the two processes: (1) we propose a meta-model generic enough to (2) let field experts integrate their knowledge and evaluate their hypotheses by defining scenarios (for instance, in the present application: a household of two adults, two kids, one infant, their activities their habits, house environment and specific events). Once a new question emerges or an incoherence is pointed out by domain experts, the cycle starts again by making amendment to the previous meta-model. In practice, our meta-model and the dedicated simulator (SMACH) allow experts to define fine-grain activities (ranging from few minutes to hours) and to study their evolution over long period of time (one year). Using an advanced and intuitive user interface, the simulator allows experts to understand the respective influence of activities and energy consumption, and the co-influence of activities.

[1] http://remodece.isr.uc.pt

In this paper, we focus on the presentation of the meta-model of human activities within the household (presented in Sect. 2) and the dynamics of this model which includes communication, beliefs, action selection and behaviour adaptation (detailed in Sect. 3). Section 4, introduces the simulator GUI and provides two distinctive examples of household emergent adaptation forced by action competition and variable electricity pricing. Section 5 concludes the paper and presents the ongoing work.

2 Meta-Model of Human Activity

Our meta-model of human activity follows two purposes that are tightly connected. First, it aims at describing human behaviours in the context of household electricity consumption. This description must remain easy to manipulate, even for non-computer specialists. To this purpose, we followed an individual-centered agent-based approach in which human activity is decomposed into tasks. Second, it serves as agent description model for our multi-agent simulator (Sect. 3). This simulator allows to study the evolution of human behaviour depending on the characteristic*i.e.*s of energy pricing and household appliances, that are defined in the *environment*.

2.1 Environment

Let $[d_s, d_e]$ be the considered time period. Energy prices can be specified to different time periods $\{[d_i; d_{i+1}], price_i\}$ with $d_0 = d_s$ and $price_i \in \mathbb{R}^+$, the kilowatt hour price (kWh) for the ith sub-period.

The house is composed of several *rooms* where electrical appliances are spread. Let $\mathcal{R}$ be the set of rooms and $\mathcal{E}$ the set of appliances. For each room r ($r \in R$), we note $E_r \subset \mathcal{E}$ the set of electrical appliances in this room. In our model, each appliance can only be in one room, fixed for the duration of the simulation.

Appliances. Each appliance $e \in E$ is characterised by its electrical consumption θ_i. We note *power* : $\mathcal{E} \to \mathbb{R}^+$ the function that returns the current electrical consumption of an appliance. In our model, we consider two different kinds of appliances:

State-based appliances are defined as a tuple $\{\theta_o, \theta_s, st\}$ where θ_o and θ_s are the electrical consumptions (in $\mathbb{R}^+$) when e is running or in standby mode, and $st \in \{\text{off}, \text{standby}, \text{on}\}$ is the state of the appliance, modified by *individuals* in the house during their activities. Heaters, TVs, fridges... can be represented by state-based appliances.

Program-based appliances are defined as a tuple $< P_e, st >$ where P_e is a set of operating programs characterised by load curves. Each program p is a couple (τ_p, ϕ_p) where τ_p is the program duration and $\phi_p : [0, \tau_p] \to \mathbb{R}^+$ gives the appliance consumption at each time of the program. The status st of the appliance is then defined by a couple $st = (p_c, t_c)$ where p_c is the currently selected program and t_c is the time since the beginning of this program. Thus, $power(e) = \phi_{p_c}(t_c)$. Ovens can be represented by this kind of appliances. Note that state-based appliances can be seen as specific cases of program based appliances (with three programs and constant load curves).

All energy consumption profiles comes in our model from real data from the REMODECE project.

2.2 Household Members and Their Behaviours

Individuals represent the household members. Each individual $i \in \mathcal{I}$ is characterised by its responsibility level res_i and the set of *actions* it can perform A_i (see below).

The responsibility level allows us to distinguish between *children*, *youngsters*, *adults* and *elderlies* in the simulation (see Sect. 3). Moreover, at each time of the simulation, we note:

- $room(i) \in \mathcal{R}$ the room in which the individual is located;
- $action(i) \in A_i$ the individual's current activity;
- B_i the individual's beliefs set (see Sect. 3.1);
- C_i the individual's communications set (see Sect. 3.1);

Tasks. A task $t \in \mathcal{T}$ represents a generic activity in the house, from which individual actions are derived. A task is a tuple $< \tau_{min}, \tau_{max}, bene, visi, coll, E_t, T_{pre} >$ where:

- τ_{min}, τ_{max} the minimum and the maximum task duration;
- $bene \in \{alone, collective\}$ describes whether this task, once achieved, can be used by other individuals or not (see *preconditions* below);
- $visi \in \{none, individual, room, house\}$ describes the visibility (by other individuals) during and after the task realisation (see *visibility of actions* in the following subsection);
- $coll \in \{none, allowed, mandatory\}$ describes whether this task cannot, can or must be performed alone or with other individuals.;
- $E_t = \{< e, p >\} \mid e \in E \,\&\, p \in \{e.Pe\}$ the set of appliances used during this task realisation and the associated programs (for program-based appliances);
- $T_{pre} \subset \mathcal{T}$ is the set of pre-conditional tasks of t. An individual can perform a given task if and only it has the information that all pre-conditional tasks have been achieved by himself (if *bene* = *alone*) or by others (if *bene* = *collective*). The precondition relation maps into a graph of tasks;

Actions, Rythms and Events. An action $a \in \mathcal{A}$ represents the instanciation of a task by an individual. We denote $actor(a)$ the unique $i \in \mathcal{I}$ such that $a \in \mathcal{A}_i$.[2]

[2] When different individuals can perform the same task, each one is associated with a different instance.

An action is defined by a tuple $a = \langle t, w, R_a, st \rangle$ where $t \in \mathcal{T}$ is the associated task, $w \in \mathcal{W}$ is the action rhythm (see below), $R_a \in \mathcal{R}$ is the set of rooms in which this action can be performed and $st \in undone, done$ is the action status, whose dynamics is described in Sect. 3.2. When an action has been achieved ($st = done$), we note $rooms(a)$ the set of rooms in which it has been done.

Rhythms. In order to express habits of humans, the concept of *rhythm* has been introduced in the meta-model. A rhythm w ($w \in W$) allows to define, for each action, a frequency and preferred periods. The preferred period allows to specify the month, day of the week and the time slots in which an agent may perform a task. To each of these specifications is associated a force indicating if the system should more or less take into account these periods. More formally, a rhythm is a tuple $\langle per_w, freq_w, var_w, Pp_w \rangle$ where:

- $per \in \{day, week, month, year\}$ is the period considered;
- $freq \in \mathbb{N}^+$ is the frequency for this period;
  For instance, $per = day$ and $freq = 2$ means "twice a day".
- $var \in \{weak, medium, strong\}$ is the frequency variability;
- PP is a set of preferred sub-periods in the considered period. Each preferred period pp_i is a tuple with $\langle [d_1, d_2], strength \rangle$ where d_1 and d_2 define the sub-period, $strength \in \{weak, medium, imperative\}$ the strength of the preferred period;

For instance, let us consider the task "eating". We might want to define the default rhythm for this task as being performed three times a day in most situations ($per = day$, $freq = 3$, $var = weak$) with preferred periods $pp_1 =< [7:00, 9:00], imperative >$, $pp_2 =< [12:00, 14:00], weak >$ and $pp_3 =< [19:00, 22:00], strong >$, which means that our individual will eventually eat in the morning, possibly at lunch and very probably at dinner. Note that the number of preferred periods does not need to be equal to $freq$ (in which case some executions of the task will remain completely free over the period).

Events. Events represents exceptional situations (such as holidays, sickness, etc.) during which usual actions cannot be performed. An event $q \in \mathcal{Q}$ can be defined as a couple $([d_{s_q}, d_{e_q}], W_q$ with W_q a set of couples (a, w). Concretely, an event associates new rhythms w to some actions a for a given time period $[d_{s_q}, d_{e_q}]$. For instance, during holidays, the rhythm associated with actions "work" is null.

Collective Aspects. Our meta model was designed so as to integrate the collective aspects in family organisation, such as helping the children, sharing domestic tasks or spending time together during certain activities. The *coll* and *bene* parameters in tasks play a key role in leading to a cooperation mechanism among individuals, following the simulation model that is presented in the next section. As an illustration, there is a synchronisation mechanism between agents when $coll = mandatory$ so that individuals wait for each other to begin the task. Similarly, the fact that some tasks with collective benefits can be used by other agents allows to really describe complex cooperation in the house.

3 Simulation of Human Activities

Based on the meta-model presented in the previous section, human activity is simulated in a multi-agent simulator called SMACH. In this simulator, agents correspond to the human individuals in the model and their procedural loop is presented in the next two subsections. The adaptation of this loop over time to the scenario constraints is presented in Subsect. 3.3.

3.1 Multi-agent Model

To each individual $i \in \mathcal{I}$ corresponds an agent in SMACH. All agents run synchronously in the platform and each step consists into selecting the best current action based on the agent's beliefs. In this subsection, we present the agent beliefs and the communication model. Next subsection presents the agent's dynamics.

Beliefs. A belief b of an individual is a tuple $b = \langle d, a, s \rangle$ such that d is the creation date, $a \in \mathcal{A}$ an action and $s \in \{\text{undone}, \text{running}, \text{done}\}$ is the believed status of this action. $< d, a, s > \in B_i$ means that, at time d, individual i had an information about action a being in status s (with $s = running$ when $\exists i \in \mathcal{I}$ such that $action(i) = a$). This belief is kept in i's beliefs base as long as no observation or deduction contradicts it.

The initial beliefs set B_i of an agent i is that all actions have the status: *undone*. We also consider individuals know from the start which one can perform which task. The dynamics of the beliefs set is presented in Sect. 3.2.

Communications. In addition to individual actions, people in the household must communicate to exchange information or request the participation of others in tasks. This is represented using a multi-agent communication approach such as FIPA-ACL [3], based on speech-act theory by Searle [14].

A conversation $c \in C_i$ is an ordered set of n messages, $msg_1, ..., msg_n$ with $msg_i =< d, to, from, perf \in Perf, c >$ where d is the date of the message, *to* and $from$ are the sender and the receiver of the message, $perf$ is the message performative and c its content.

In our model, the main considered performatives are: *I do ...*, *Are you ready to ... ?*, *What are you doing?*, *Did you ... ?*, *Can you ... ?* and their following replies *No*, *Yes*, *Later*. The content of the message, when required, is always a single task $t \in \mathcal{T}$.

The selection of messages, based on the agents beliefs, is presented in the next subsection.

3.2 Agents' Dynamics

This section first presents how beliefs are maintained in the agents base. Then, we present how actions are selected, based on individual's preferences, beliefs and communications.

Beliefs Update. Beliefs in the agent's base B_i are added or removed at each turn, based on the agent's perception (either direct perception in the visibility zone of an action, or via a message) and on automatic inferences on actions status and individual's possible rooms.

More formally, let d_0 be the current time stamp and let us note $+_ib$ and $-_ib$ the addition and removal of belief b in B_i.

We first define the visibility zone of an action $a \in \mathcal{A}$, depending on its status and task's visibility, as follows (all cases are exclusive):

- if $a.t.visi = none$, then it is not visible: $visi(a) = \emptyset$;
- if a is active (*i.e.* $\exists i \in \mathcal{I}$ such that $action(i) = a$) and has visibility $a.t.visi \in \{individual, room\}$, then $visi(a) = \{room(i)\}_{\forall i | action(i)=a}$;
- if a is active and $a.t.visi = home$, then $visi(a) = \mathcal{R}$
- if a is finished (*i.e.* $a.st = done$) and a is visible on individuals ($a.t.visi = individual$), then $visi(a) = room(actor(a))$;
- if a is finished and $a.st.visi \in \{room, home\}$, then $visi(a) = rooms(a)$;

The agent belief base B_i is updated when observing actions from their visibility zone:

$\forall a | room(i) \in visi(a), \nexists \langle d', a, status(a) \rangle \in B_i \Rightarrow +_i\langle d_0, a, status(a) \rangle$

Similarly, when receiving a message with performative *I do* or an answer to a message *Did you* in a conversation, a new belief is added: $+_i\langle d_0, a, status(a) \rangle$, with a the action corresponding to the sender and the task (content) of the message.

Moreover, a coherence mechanism removes all previous incompatible belief:

- An action can only have one status: $+_i\langle d_0, a, status(a) \rangle \Rightarrow \forall d' < d_0, -_i\langle d', a, s' \neq status(a) \rangle$;
- An agent can only do one action at a time: $+_i\langle d_0, a, status(a) \rangle \Rightarrow \forall a' | actor(a) = actor(a'), -_i\langle d', a', s' \rangle$ and $+_i \langle d_0, a', done \rangle$;
- A task "must" be over after its maximum duration: if $\exists b \in B_i$ such that $b.d + b.a.t.\tau_{max} > d_0$, then $-_ib$ and $+_i\langle d_0, b.a, done \rangle$;
- Two actions associated with one single "exclusive" task ($a_1.t = a_2.t = t$ and $t.coll = none$) cannot be active simultaneously: $-_i\langle d', a_2, running \rangle$ and $+_i\langle d_0, a_2, done \rangle$.

Note that when a previous belief is updated, its status is moved to *done* (actions that can no longer be performed are considered as achieved by default).

Action Dynamic. The status of an action *st* (from undone to done) is actually more complex than a simple *done/undone* boolean. It is controlled by four internal variables:

- $real_{number} \in \mathbb{N}^+$ is the number of realisation already conducted within the current day. The value of $a.st \in \{done, undone\}$ used in beliefs is directly derived from $a.real_{number} \geq 1$;
- $real_{max} \in \mathbb{N}^+$ is the planned maximum number of realisation for the current day (which directly depends on w);

Table 1. Action availability conditions.

(a) $\forall t' \in a.t.T_{pre}, \exists a' \in \mathcal{A} | a'.t = t' \wedge a'.st = done \wedge (actor(a') = actor(a) \vee t'.bene = i.e.collective)$
(b) $\forall e \in a.t.E_t, \nexists a'/a'.running \wedge e \in a'.t'.E_{t'}$

- $\tau \leq a.t.\tau_{max}$ is the elapsed duration when a is running;
- $pr \in [-1;1]$ is the action priority.

The priority *a.pr* evolves in time (see below, Sect. 3.2) and the agent selects the action with the highest priority amongst all *possible* actions. An action is possible if and only if all the following criteria are met (see also Table 1):

- Every precondition tasks have been conducted;
- All needed appliances are available;

Note that $a.st$ cannot be computed directly by the agent. On the contrary, the agent will use its belief base to decide whether actions are done or undone and whether they can be performed. In the algorithm in Table 1, $a.st = x$ means $\exists < d, a, done > \in B_i$. However, when starting an action, the simulator will check all the actual preconditions and an agent will not be able to perform an action that it believed possible if Table 1 is not checked. In this case, all inconsistent beliefs are removed from the agent base.

Interruption and Realisation. The running action of an individual ($a = action(i)$), can be interrupted for two reasons: (1) another (possible) action, a', has a higher priority or (2) a became impossible. When this occurs, another action will be selected and the status of a is modified depending on its duration time:

- If a has been executed for a duration $\tau \geq \tau_{min}$, its number of realisation $a.real_{number}$ is incremented and $a.\tau$ is reset to 0. The action status $a.st$ switches do *done*.
- If $a.\tau < \tau_{min}$ The action is put in a "standby mode": $a.\tau$ is blocked at its current value, its number of realisation is not increased. For instance, a child is interrupted during homework, (s)he does not loose the benefit of having started working.

Daily Reset. The action's state evolves over time depending on the individual behaviour and his/her environment. It is reset at midnight except for the sleep action which is reset at noon. In practice, $a.st$ is reset to *undone*, $a.real_{number}$, $a.\tau$ and $a.pr$ are reset to 0, and the maximum number of realisation is recomputed depending on the action rhythm if the new day contains a preferential period, *ppi*, and if some realisation are to be done ($w.real < w.real_{max}$).

Table 2. Raw priority external factors.

(a) $pref \in [-0,01;+0,01]$ is the individual preference for the action;
(b) $inf_{real} \in \{-0,2;0\}$ is the penalty if the action already reached its maximum number of realisation ($a.real_{max}$);
(c) $inf_{pp} \in \{penalty, 0, bonus\}$ is the action's rhythm influence, with *penalty* and *bonus* computed as described below in section 3.3. $inf_{pp} = 0$ if $a.pp = \emptyset$ and is negative (penalty) when the current date is outside a preferred period and positive (bonus) otherwise.
(d) $inf_{eng} \in [-0.1;+0,1]$ is the commitment or lassitude influence. Its value is set to 0 for all non running actions. Otherwise, it is defined by a linear interpolation from 0.1 when the action just began, to 0 when it reaches τ_{min} and -0.1 when at τ_{max}.
(e) inf_{ener} is the electricity price influence, defined by:
- $inf_{ener} = 0$ if $a.t.cons = 0$ or $price = medium$;
- $inf_{ener} = -0.1$ if $price = high$;
- $inf_{ener} = +0.02$ if $price = low$.

Tasks that consume energy are strongly penalised when the energy price is high, but only marginally favored when it is low.
(f) $inf_{inci} \in [0;+0,1]$ computes the influence of other individuals, through messages with performative *Are you ready to* and *Can you*, also called *invitations*. When $a.t.coll = none$, $inf_{inci} = 0$. Otherwise, it is increased by $+0,02$ per invitation (with a maximum of 0.1).
(g) $inf_{eve} \in [-0,1;+0,1]$ is the events' influence. For each $q \in \mathcal{Q}$ such that $d_{current} \in [d_{s_q}, d_{e_q}]$ and $\exists(a,w) \in W_q$, inf_{eve} is modified by ± 0.05, depending on the new rythm w's properties compared to the action's initial rythm $a.w$.

Action Priority. An action priority takes into account the individual's internal state: preference[3], commitment to the current action (see Table 2 for details) and the influence of the associated rhythm ($a.w$, see also Sect. 3.3). In addition to the individual's internal state, the priority of an action may be influenced by external factors: energy price level (variability of the energy price is summarised as 3 levels), other individuals invitations (through messages) and events influence. Table 2 describes the computation of this raw priority, called pr_{raw}:

$$pr_{raw} = pref + inf\_real + inf\_pp + inf\_eng + inf\_ener + inf\_inci + inf\_eve$$

All the coefficient values have been determined empirically, only their relative order is significant. For instance, the individual preference is much less important than its commitment/lassitude to his/her current action.

In order to allow the representation of sequential behaviour (e.g. *leave for work* requires to be *suit up* which requires to have taken a *shower*), the action priority must also consider the priority of the most urgent depending action, *i.e.* the maximum of priorities of all actions for which a is in precondition:

$$pr_{dep} = max_{a.t \in a'.T_{pre}}\{a'.pr\}$$

[3] Minimal factor enabling complete differentiation between actions with similar priorities.

Thus, the action priority $a.pr$ is the maximum of these two values:

$$a.pr = max\{a.pr_{raw}, pr_{dep}\}$$

3.3 Behaviour Adaptation

Adaptation is essential in our model as we want to study the possible reactions of a household to variable energy pricing, habits emergence and other single events (*e.g.* holidays, sickness, etc.). Adaptation is conducted trough re-organisation of the household, *i.e.* when tasks are made and who does which collective task.

We implemented two adaptation mechanisms during a simulation: (1) everyday life obligations or strong habits are represented through rhythms with imperative frequencies and/or preferred period (PP) and (2) habits may emerge thanks to the controlled mobility of actions.

Everyday Life Strong Constraints. Some everyday life actions may require to be conducted at specific time. Such constraint is controlled through the PP influence (see Table 2): positive during a PP and negative outside of any PP, in order to favour within PP and penalise outside PP realisation respectively. Unfortunately, as in the everyday life, *i.e.* several actions may compete for a realisation during an overlapping timeslot (*e.g. have breakfast* and *take shower* both should be done between 7 to 8am). To lessen such competition between imperative rhythms, each action at the end of the day reevaluates its *bonus* and *penalty* values according to the following policy:

bonus must remain between 0 and 0.15;
penalty must remain between −0.15 and 0;
When the action could not be executed during its PP this day, *bonus* is increased 0.02;
When the action was achieved during its PP for this day, the *bonus* is decreased by 0.01. This ensures a slow re-organisation capacity.
When the action was executed outside a PP, *bonus* is increased by 0.01;
When the system could not reach the target realisation number for this action (*i.e.*, $real_{number} < real_{max}$), *penalty* is decreased by 0.02, since we want to give priority to action achievement over PP constraints.

In other words, actions that could be done during their PP during day n will be less favoured on their PP in day $n+1$ and vice-versa. Moreover, actions that missed some executions will be encouraged. Although this policy cannot guarantee the satisfaction of all realisation constraints (which may not be possible at all), it provides modeller more freedom regarding rhythms definition.

Everyday Life Habits. Outside the competitive timeslot, habits may emerge as in everyday life. This is achieved in SMACH via the automatic creation of non-imperative rhythms during simulation. In practice, if an action has been triggered at a given period, this period will be favoured the following days (using a limited memory window)[4]. As a consequence, all actions with no specified PP are allowed to find the most suitable periods for their realisations and to keep them as long they are suitable.

The maximum values for bonus and penalty are lesser than those of imperative PP, so this kind of actions can change its PP more easily. The next section will give an example of such adaptation: in conjunction with the priority penalty during periods with expensive energy, the household organisation is altered.

4 Implementation and Evaluation

The SMACH simulator has been implemented in Java and several example scenarios have been proposed to validate our approach.

We developed our own agent-based simulation platform for the SMACH project because we required a GUI adapted to domain expert (*e.g.* use of a programming language was out of the question) with an intuitive way to define the model. Such experts also demanded a specific simulation analysis GUI to correlate activities and electricity consumption. This GUI is detailed in the following subsection. We will also discuss two examples that illustrate the ability of the model to express rhythm constraints and, at the same time, and the actions reorganisation process. The first example focuses on action competition whereas the second one demonstrates how is handled household adaptation in the situation of a change in electricity pricing policy.

4.1 Simulation Analysis GUI

The SMACH simulation analysis GUI shown in Fig. 1 can be detailed as follows. The overall electricity consumption is shown in panel (1). Each color represents a different appliance's consumption (the central gap correspond to holidays). Panel (1') presents some global variable (total electricity consumption, associated price and social indicators). Below, panel (2), details individuals activities over the week selected in panel 1 (S45) whereas panels (3 and 3') presents a zoom for even more details (one rectangle representing one minute). Finally, panel (4) allows to investigates actions actual rhythms (only some actions are selected). Concretely, the horizontal axe represent the passing of days whereas the vertical axe represen the time of the day. For instance, we can see that the *work* actions (blocks centered horizontally) occurs only during week days.[5]

[4] The implementation detail of this mechanism is not detailed in this paper but it is very similar to the one presented in the previous subsection.

[5] In addition, another simulation analysis GUI mode is also available in order to compare several simulations: overall evolution and specific period of time can be compared with side by side diagrams.

4.2 Dealing with Competing Actions

Our first example considers a family of 3 with a conflict situation: they have to *make diner*, *have diner* and *have shower* within the 7–9 pm time slot. This time slot imposes a constraint due to the actions durations and the exclusiveness of the *have shower* action (one at a time). The adaptation process will organise progressively the actions to ease their execution.

In the simulation first week, individuals usually fails to *have shower* as shown in Fig. 2(a). This diagram represents the individuals' acitvities as colored bar over time. In particular, the *sleep* action (strawberry pink) and the *work* action (brown) can serve as reference points. These actions have regular schedule since the beginning (no adaptation needed) as they have no strong competitors and large preferred periods (around 8 hours). In the conflict timeslot, diner-related actions are occuring whereas *have shower* is not (only the mother do it on monday). The advantage of diner-related actions is due to two factors: (1) *make dinner* is a collective benefit task (one individual can cook for 3) and (2) *have dinner* is a coordinated one which imply strongly incentive invitations.

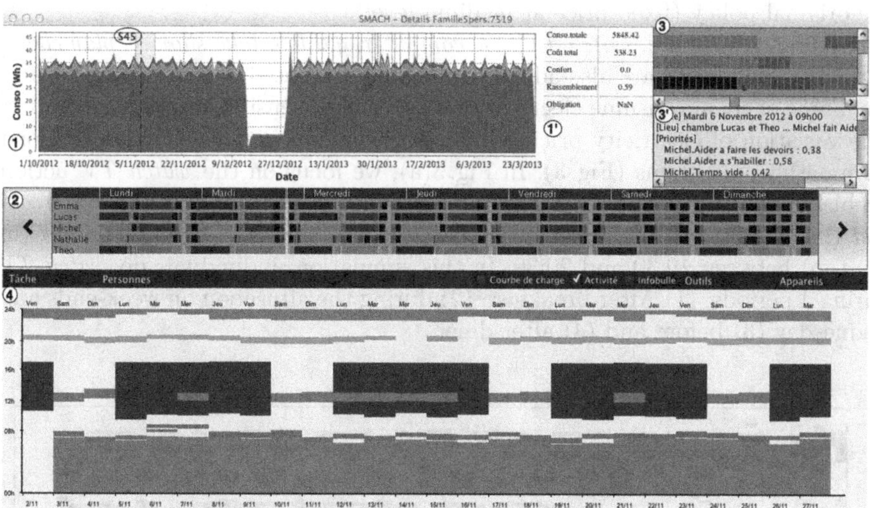

Fig. 1. SMACH GUI (analysis mode).

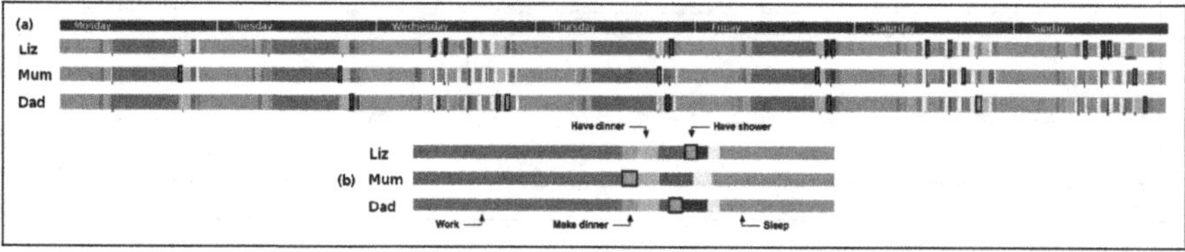

Fig. 2. Activity diagram: (a) first week and (b) working day pattern.

The conflict is resolved through adaptation of the preferred periods (PP) and results in the following *working-day pattern* showed in Fig. 2(b). After work, the mother takes her shower while the father and Liz make diner. Once diner is ready, the father or Liz invite the others to have diner. After diner, the father takes a shower followed by Liz.

This example demonstrates how the adaptation process can organize the actions in relation with PP constraints. Although, this organization is not fully stable, due to the continuous adaptations of the PP, it can last several weeks.

4.3 Adaptation of Habits in Relation with a New Pricing

The second example is based on similar parameters but shows how PP modifications work with agents sensitivity to the electricity price. In this example, the simulation spans over 10 weeks from January to March. In order to evaluate the capabilities of adaptation to variable electricity price we make the following hypotheses. In January, the electricity price is fixed to a medium level. The following month, we introduce a variable price policy: high from 6 to 8 pm and low for the rest of day (everyday). Finally, in March, the price is switched back to the original policy (fixed price at medium level).

Several actions, *i.e. watch TV*, *use computer*, *garden*, *take shower*, *play chess*, without specified PP are also added to the ones presented in the previous example. Some of them consume electricity and are, thus, sensible to electricity price. The variation of electricity pricing induce actions mobility as show on the long term activity diagrams (Fig. 3). In Fig. 3(a), we focus on the *watch TV* action (in black). Although, two actions have been added as time landmark: *have breakfast* (in the bottom) that takes place between 6:30 and 8:15 and *have diner* (in the top) between 19:30 and 20:30. In this simulation, individuals do *watch TV* during 4 periods: (1) After breakfast, (2) during the afternoon on week-ends and wednesday (3) before and (4) after diner.

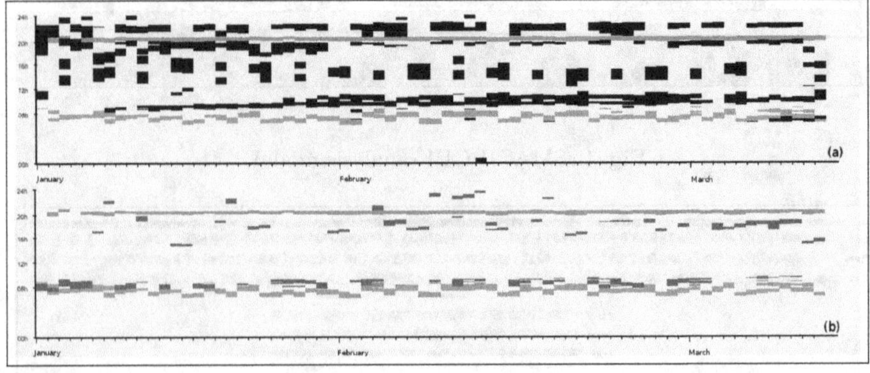

Fig. 3. Long term activity diagram: (a) watch Tv and (b) homework (Color figure online).

In January, individuals mostly *watch TV* before the diner though a slow change from after diner to after breakfast habit is appearing all along this month. When February comes, with its special pricing, the before diner period is abandoned to the benefit of the after breakfast and after-diner periods due to the energy price penalty. One may notice that a slim black line remains before diner in February. Indeed only 2 agents have completely quit watching TV before diner. The third one continues to do it but for a shorter duration. It means that the other influences, mainly the strength of the before-diner PP, have balanced the energy-price penalty. It is interesting to notice that the effect of the penalty is progressive (it may completely stop or just shorten an action) and vary from one agent to another. In March, when the special pricing is stopped, we can observe a motion from after-breakfast and after-diner periods to the before-diner period as there is no electricity price penalty. Nevertheless, the last two weeks of simulation still bear this penalty influence (as adaptations are a progressive process): the before-diner period happens later and lasts shorter. This evolution demonstrates the capacity both to create and to modify habits thanks to the adaptation of the PP.

Note that, the movement of the *watch TV* action implies that other action have moved too. On the second long-term diagram (Fig. 3(b)), we track the evolution of the *do homework* action (red). As the time slot occupied by the *watch TV* action in January is free in February, the action *do homework* happens more often during the before-diner period. We observe that the return of an uniform pricing does not push back the *do homework* action: Energy special pricing effects persists even after its end.

4.4 Adaptation to Unforeseen Event

Our third example is a similar simulation, lasting 10 weeks, considering a family of three (John and Mary and their children Bill). In contrary to the previous examples, we have here a change of schedule. Concretely, Mary starts as unemployed but gets a job on the 5*th* week (full time from monday to friday).

Once Mary starts to work, she has more activities to conduct but the same amount of time. As our agents have a tendency to stability, she tries to conduct all her previous activities plus the work one. The result of such contradiction is a drop of the completion rate (from 97 to 93 %): Mary starts some action but does not have time to finish them. Such phenomenon may not be realistic we do not study it. The one phenomenon to consider here is the evolution of the household chore reputation before and after the employment of Mary. During the first 4 weeks, Mary perform more than 70 % of them because she has more spare time than John as shown on the Fig. 4(b). Later on, her workload rises thus, a significant part of the housework migrates toward John: Mary having less time to deal with them, those tasks are more likely to be made by John. As we set her working hours longer than his, John then takes the bigger part of the housework, around 60 %. Bill, on his side, can participate a bit to the collective tasks making breakfast and lunch, the only housework tasks possible for him.

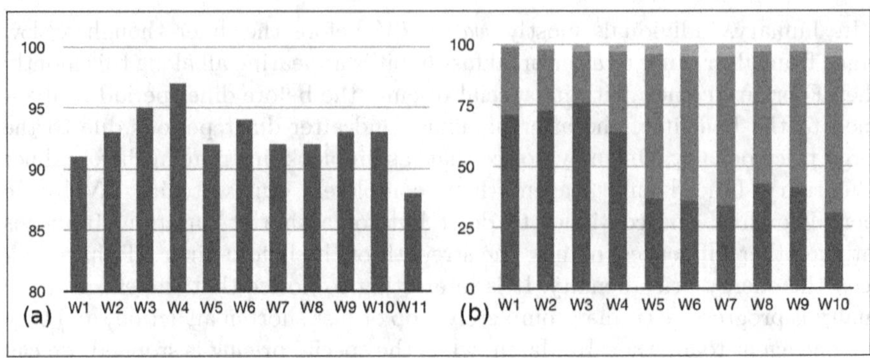

Fig. 4. (a) Completion rate in % by week and (b) Housework tasks sharing in % (Mary in blue, John in green and Bill in yellow) (Color figure online).

Even though a balanced housework sharing is not a general feature of a "real world household", we believe that the workload allocation ability of our model to be useful as a general trend. Although, when necessary, several possibilities to constrain the sharing are offered to the modeller.

4.5 Discussion on Evaluation

These three examples illustrate the ability of the model to express rhythm constraints and, at the same time, and the actions reorganisation process due to various. In particular, any individuals can have too many activities to conduct in a given time period. Some of these activities are strongly constrained, in terms of frequency and time (*e.g.* work), of synchronisation with other individuals (*e.g.* dinner together, homework help) whereas others are much less constrained (*e.g.* various household chore) or even almost not constrained (leisure mostly). These challenges are tackled thanks to the adaptive priority computation and the emergence of habits. Once, the household organisation is in place, our model also provide dynamic organisation mechanisms that allows the household to cope with unforeseen events (*e.g.* energy tariff change or new activities in our examples).

5 Conclusions and Current Work

In this paper, we presented the model and implementation of SMACH, a multiagent simulator of human activity. This simulator supports the investigation of activity adaptation and energy consumption evolution in response to different appliances or pricing policies. We could not present all the details of this simulator that results from a 5-years collaboration between the French EDF energy company and AI researchers, but we outlined its main features: accessibility of the model to non-computer specialists and intelligent interface for activity analysis and explanation. SMACH also comprises a machine learning algorithm for automated management of temperature in the house [5] and an interactive modelling system that helps refining the agent's behaviour [15].

This model has been evaluated in several example scenarios. The three examples presented in this paper illustrated the ability of our model to represent both the constraints and some of the "degrees of freedom" of everyday life. Furthermore, with the help of the two adaptation processes (actions competition and habits emergence), agents are able to explore new organisation and to discover pattern of actions in relation with time constraints and energy price for saving purpose and other unforeseen events. In addition to this evaluation, our simulator is provided with a participatory-simulation user interface (introduced in [6]) that allow to give control of one or several agents to users. Students in our lab "played their own role" in our test scenarios, which allowed us to validate the believability of the model. In most situations, students could not distinguish between artificial agents and human-controlled ones.

We are currently extending the SMACH model to study the activity of groups of families in different environments, over long period of time (one year) and taking into account external temperature and building's thermodynamical properties. This lead us to reconsider the action rhythm model and to use multi-level agent systems for individuals, families and activities. Our long-term goal is to allow energy companies to be able to investigate incentive to reduce or to have a better prediction of consumption peaks using simulation of human activity.

References

1. Ha, D.L., Ploix, S., Zamaï, E., Jacomino, M.: A home automation system to improve household energy control. In: Proceedings of The 12th IFAC Symposium INCOM2006 (2006)
2. European Environment Agency. Energy and environment report. Technical report 6 (2008)
3. FIPA consortium. FIPA Communicative Act Library Specification and FIPA ACL Message Structure Specification. Technical report (2003)
4. Freire, R.Z., Oliveira, G.H., Mendes, N.: Predictive controllers for thermal comfort optimization and energy savings. Energ. Build. **40**(7), 1353–1365 (2008)
5. Gil-Quijano, J., Sabouret, N.: Prediction of humans' activity for learning the behaviors of electrical appliances in an intelligent ambiant environment. In: Proceedings of the IEEE/WIC/ACM IAT'10 International Conference, pp. 283–286 (2010)
6. Haradji, Y., Poizat, G., Sempé, F.: Human activity and social simulation. In: Duffy, V.G. (ed.) Advances in Applied Human Modeling and Simulation, pp. 416–425. CRC Press, Boca Raton (2012)
7. Kashif, A., Ploix, S., Dugdale, J., Le, X.H.B.: Simulating the dynamics of occupant behaviour for power management in residential buildings. Energ. Build. (2012, to appear)
8. Mahdavi, A., Pröglhöf, C.: Toward empirically-based models of people's presence and actions in buildings. In: Proceedings of Building Simulation 09, pp. 537–544 (2009)
9. Massoud, A.S., Wollenberg, B.: Toward a smart grid: power delivery for the 21st century. IEEE Power Energ. Mag. **3**(5), 34–41 (2005)

10. Newsham, G.R., Bowker, B.G.: The effect of utility time-varying pricing and load control strategies on residential summer peak electricity use: a review. Energ. Policy **38**(7), 3289–3296 (2010)
11. North, M., Howe, T., Collier, N., Vos, J.: A declarative model assembly infrastructure for verification and validation. In: Takahashi, S., Sallach, D., Rouchier, J. (eds.) Advancing Social Simulation: The First World Congress, pp. 129–140. Springer, Kanazawa (2007)
12. Poquet, G., Dujin, A.: Pour les ménages, la recherche du confort prime encore sur les économies d'énergie. Consommation & Modes de Vie (CREDOC), 210 (2008)
13. Rogers, A., Maleki, S., Ghosh, S., Nicholas, R.J: Adaptive home heating control through Gaussian process prediction and mathematical programming. In: ATES'10, pp. 71–78 (2011)
14. Searle, J.: Speech Acts. Cambridge University Press, Cambridge (1969)
15. Sempé, F., Gil-Quijano, J.: Incremental and situated modeling for multi-agent based simulations. In Proceedings of the IEEE RIVF'10 International Conference, pp. 1–6 (2010)
16. Sierhuis, M., Clancey, W.J., van Hoof, R., de Hoog, R.: Modeling and simulating human activity. In: Intelligent Agents for Computer Supported Co-operative Work Workshop (2000)
17. Taillandier, P., Vo, D.-A., Amouroux, E., Drogoul, A.: GAMA: a simulation platform that integrates geographical information data, agent-based modeling and multi-scale control. In: Desai, N., Liu, A., Winikoff, M. (eds.) PRIMA 2010. LNCS, vol. 7057, pp. 242–258. Springer, Heidelberg (2012)
18. Widén, J., Wäckelgard, E.: A high-resolution stochastic model of domestic activity patterns and electricity demand. Appl. Energ. **87**(6), 1880–1892 (2010)
19. Wilensky, U., Evanston, I.: Netlogo center for connected learning and computer based modeling. Technical report, Northwestern University (1999)
20. Yamaguchi, Y., Fujimoto, T., Shimoda, Y.: Occupant behavior model for households to estimate high-temporal resolution residential electricity demand profile. In: Proceedings of BS2011, pp. 1548–1555, Australia, Sydney (2011)

Mapping Multichannel Documents to Attentive Tasks: Ensuring Information Gain and Detecting Failure

Kristin Stamm(✉) and Andreas Dengel

German Research Center for Artificial Intelligence, Trippstadter Str. 122, 67663 Kaiserslautern, Germany
{kristin.stamm,andreas.dengel}@dfki.de
http://www.dfki.de

Abstract. Our approach of process-driven document analysis (DA) aims at supporting enterprises in managing the complexity of multiple input channels. Within this approach, we proposed earlier to map each incoming document to its corresponding task context - denominated as Attentive Task (AT) - by applying search with Dempster-Shafer theory. In this paper, we extend the search algorithm with methods from machine learning for addressing the challenges in real enterprise domains: (1) information gain trees for optimizing initial evidence selection and (2) five strategies for detecting search failures. We evaluate all proposed methods on a corpus from a financial institution and give an overview on how the approach enables automation services in multichannel management.

Keywords: Evidence based search · Information gain tree · Search failure detection · Dempster-Shafer theory · Multichannel document analysis

1 Introduction

Today, enterprises are truly challenged by the management of new communication channels, such as email, having to deal with information overload. According to Bellotti et al., the quantity and the complexity of incoming requests can explain this overload [1]. Enterprises strive toward managing the multichannel complexity, but fail when relying on existing IT solutions. The systems often suffer from the fragmentation between communication channels and also from the lack of connection to internal processes leading to information gaps. Mostly, their functionality is limited to legal requirements only. Instead, users need a system that helps them understanding the request, finding the related process instance, and extracting relevant information.

We proposed the approach of process-driven document analysis (DA) [2]. A document arriving through an input channel is mapped to the corresponding

J. Filipe and A. Fred (Eds.): ICAART 2013, CCIS 449, pp. 211–227, 2014.
DOI: 10.1007/978-3-662-44440-5_13

task. The information expectations of the task are then used for conducting an analysis of the document and for extracting all relevant information. We applied two concepts: (1) *Attentive Tasks (ATs)* formally describing information expectations toward incoming documents and (2) the *Specialist Board (SB)*, first introduced by [3], describing all available DA methods. First, we generate a DA plan. Second, we extract information about the document according to the DA plan. Finally, we search the corresponding AT based on this information. If necessary, the DA plan is adopted according to the AT. All steps are repeated until the matching AT is found and no more information can be extracted.

In this paper, we focus on improving the novel AT search algorithm that enables mapping on a task instance level. In [4], we use DA results as evidences for prioritizing the available AT set by calculating a degree of belief (DoB) for each AT and evidence before combining them with Dempster-Shafer theory [5]. First evaluations demonstrated promising search results and good robustness, but also that the selection of initial evidences is crucial to search performance. Applying our approach to enterprises raises two challenges: (1) The introduced two step evidence structure remains insufficient for domains with more evidence types. Learning a sophisticated structure is necessary. (2) The approach fails when no AT fits the document which is either the case when a new process is triggered by an incoming document, or when the mechanism of generating ATs failed due to processing errors. A failure detection method is needed.

Our goal is to address these enterprise requirements by enhancing AT search with methods from machine learning: (I) Learning evidence type trees by maximizing the average information gain, (II) using strategies for detecting search failure: (i) identifying evidences that appear only in documents leading to a new AT, (ii) comparing the maximum DoB to an expected DoB, (iii) and introducing general AT templates, (iv) as well as hybrid combinations from the previous strategies. We evaluate all approaches on a corpus from a financial institution.

Next, we review related work. We give a brief overview on our approach of process-driven DA focusing on the concept of ATs and the search algorithm. We then introduce our two approaches and present the results of their evaluations. Finally, we present an outlook on automation services, draw conclusions, and discuss future work.

2 Related Work

There exist many approaches for mapping documents to processes or tasks - especially in the email environment, but they all have numerous drawbacks regarding our problem. They consider usually a few processes and ignore important process context information instead of numerous task instances. They are often costly to transfer to new domains, and they do not respect the importance of search criteria or search failure.

Some approaches rely on heuristics for mapping documents to tasks, e.g., *thrasks* that are a combination of conversation threads and tasks [1] or other context information for aggregation [6]. They assume a direct connection between heuristic and task. Other approaches use established classification methods, like Naïve Bayes or Support Vector Machines. For example, Cohen et al. classify emails into sender intentions based on verb-noun pairs called *speech acts* [7] as well as Scerri et al. who apply rule based task classification with speech acts [8]. Dredze et al. combine classification methods that rely on involved people or topics [9]. Faulring et al. propose a regular logistic regression algorithm for task type classification [10], whereas Granitzer et al. pursue to aggregate tasks from user interaction behavior [11]. Unfortunately, all these approaches do not involve a dynamic task set and are, therefore, not applicable to Attentive Tasks (ATs). Krämer recognizes the importance of tasks instances but uses manual task assignment [12]. Only Kushmerick and Lau use unsupervised learning for deriving process structures from emails. Their approach is applicable to personal email management with unstructured and implicit processes [13]. However, their approach has a limited applicability for well-defined processes as they appear in enterprises. Overall, none of the existing approaches consider search criteria, as for example, results from DA, or provide handling of search failure.

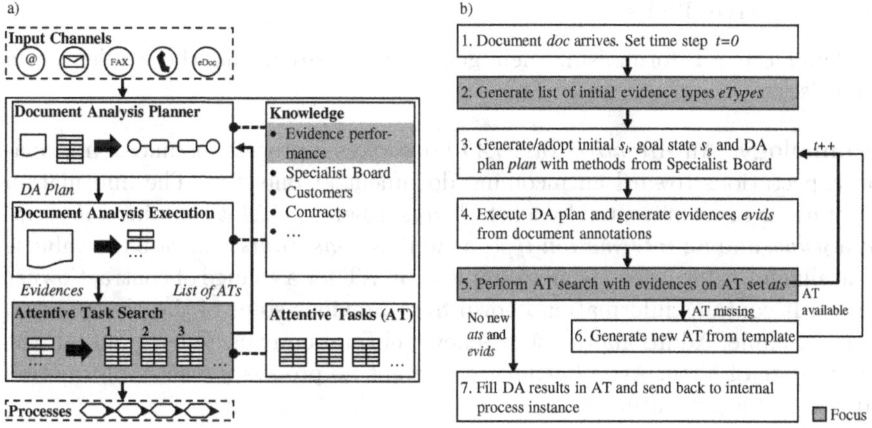

Fig. 1. (a) Process-driven document analysis system. (b) Main steps of the process-driven document analysis algorithm.

3 Overall Approach

This section presents the process-driven document analysis (DA) approach focusing on Attentive Task (AT) search [2,4]. We detail concept, AT terminology and generation. We conclude with the main challenges from enterprise application.

3.1 Process-driven Document Analysis

The basic elements of the process-driven DA system are depicted in Fig. 1(a). The system deals with documents coming from the main input channels in enterprises: email, mail, fax, call center, and eDocs. The system's core consists of the

DA planner, the DA executor, and an AT search module. The system iteratively analyzes the document according to a plan and searches for the corresponding AT in the available AT set. The modules use knowledge about evidence types, available DA methods described in the Specialist Board (SB), and enterprise knowledge. This work focuses on AT search and the use of initial evidences.

The main steps of the algorithm are outlined in Fig. 1(b). When a document arrives, the system decides which evidences have to be extracted initially. Based on these evidence types, it generates the initial state, the current goal state, and a DA plan. This plan is then executed and DA results are created in form of annotations. An annotation contains at least a type, value, and reference to the text sequence. Annotations are used as evidences for performing priority search on the set of available ATs. If there is a fitting AT and more information needs to be extracted, the system adopts the goal state, the initial state, and the DA plan before proceeding. If the AT is detected as missing, the corresponding AT template is identified for generating a new AT and adopting the goal. The algorithm stops when no more information is necessary or available.

3.2 Attentive Tasks

We detail the AT formalism, their generation, search, and the challenges in enterprises.

Terminology. An *Attentive Task (AT)* describes a process instance's information expectations toward an incoming document at one step. The information expectations are represented by a list of *slots*, where each slot contains a *descriptor*, a *value*, and an *information type*, as well as *constraints* – in case the value is not available. Table 1 depicts an example of an AT for a change of contract owner request. It contains information known from previous steps of the process, e.g., customer name. Additionally, there is new information expected, e.g., about the owner's date of birth. An *AT template* contains no process instance information and is used for generating ATs.

Generating Attentive Tasks. Since ATs formalize the information expectations of internal processes, they need to be generated by them. For example,

Table 1. Example of an Attentive Task.

Descriptor	Value	Type	Constraints
SenderEmail	anna@blue.org	EmailAddress	in(customer.email)
SenderName	Anna Blue	Person	in(customer.name)
RequestClass	ChangeOfOwner	Class	in(requestClasses)
NewOwnerName	Klaus Mustermann	Person	-
NewOwnerDoB	?	Date	DD.MM.YYYY
AdmissionOffice	?	Organization	in(organizations)

?: New value expected

a service employee processes a customer request, sends out a request, asking for missing information, and waits for reply. At this point, an AT is generated, i.e., the correct AT template is filled with known and expected information of the process instance. Depending on the enterprise's IT infrastructure, there are several options for triggering AT generation:

1. *Manual Generation.* The user manually selects the template, fills in all information, and stores the AT on the server. This option requires high manual effort and might result in a high error rate.
2. *Full Automatic Generation.* The ideal generation of an AT is driven by an underlying system. This can be a workflow, an ERP[1], or any other system. Depending on the size and type of the system (e.g., standard software or self-tailored solutions) this option requires expensive customization. It is recommended to use existing APIs[2] of these systems for keeping adaptation effort low.
3. *Supported Generation.* An AT generation software supports the user in generating new ATs. It operates on the user's computer and communicates with a central system. Whenever the user needs to generate a new AT, he uses the system with a few selections. Due to system independence, this option is less cost intense but also less convenient than the full automatic generation.

Depending on each process and its underlying systems, the generation method can be a mixture of them. A complete set of ATs requires full process knowledge and perfect generation of ATs either by employees or by the systems. Each of these factors can fail resulting in an incomplete set of ATs.

Attentive Task Search. In our previous work, we proposed a search algorithm that performs prioritization of a set of ATs using DA results as evidences.

It calculated for each evidence and AT a degree of belief (DoB) by assigning a mass value and normalizing over the search whole set. All normalized mass functions were combined with the Dempster-Shafer rule [5] (see details in [2]). Evaluations showed that the AT search is robust in terms of parameterization. We also examined that selected evidence types influence search performance and that an evidence structure is needed for optimizing search performance. A two level structure was sufficient for our simple evaluation corpus. We believe that for larger evidence type sets, as appearing in enterprises, we need a more sophisticated structure.

Enterprise Requirements. The application of AT search faces two main challenges in the enterprise environment:

1. *Initial Evidence Structure.* We need a structure for the initial evidence-based search for prioritizing the AT set with a minimum number of search steps, i.e., number of evidences used for search.

[1] ERP = Enterprise Resource Planning.
[2] API = Application Interface.

2. *Identification of documents without Attentive Tasks.* We need a failure detection strategy for identifying documents without a corresponding AT - either documents that trigger a new process or cases where AT generation failed. So we can avoid processing errors.

4 Information Gain Trees

In this section, we present a structure for deciding initial evidence extraction for search. This structure is build with supervised learning and applied automatically to Attentive Task (AT) search. We propose to generate evidence trees labeled with the average information gain at this level. In the following, we introduce the tree structure, the supervised learning algorithm and the integration into the AT search.

4.1 Learning

Figure 2 displays an exemplary information gain tree. Apart from the root node, it contains nodes, each labeled with an evidence type and the average information gain value of this evidence type at the current level. Leaves are reached when no evidence type generates an information gain above a defined threshold. The tree span is limited by the number of evidence branches at each level.

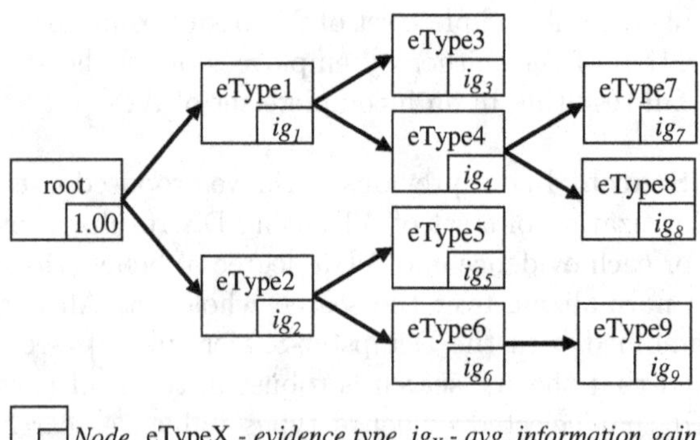

Fig. 2. Information gain tree.

We rely on the concept of information gain IG introduced by Kullback and Leibler, because it measures the difference between the current entropy H and the expected entropy H_e after applying one more attribute (=evidence) e to the current search set [14]. The information gain for an evidence e on a set of ATs A is defined as follows:

$$\begin{aligned} IG(A,e) &= H(A) - H_e(A|e) \\ &= \sum_{v \in val(e)} \frac{|\{a|a_e = v\}|}{|A|} H_e(\{a|a_e = v\}) \end{aligned} \quad (1)$$

where $a \in A$ and a_e is the slot in a with evidence type of e. Since the information gain depends on the current AT set, we learn average information gains for random AT sets repeatedly for each tree level.

The tree learning algorithm is outlined in Algorithm 1. It consists of two functions, *generateTree* and *avgInfoGains*. The first one is a recursive function that learns a tree *tree* for a given test set *set* consisting of documents and their related ATs, based on average information gain values. First, we calculate for all evidence types *ets* the average information gains and return a list of nodes *nodeList*. From this list, we select the top items limited by a branching factor *branch* and a fixed minimum threshold *thresh* for the information gain value. If the *topList* does not contain any more evidence types, we have reached a leaf and return. Otherwise, we add each node from *topList* to the tree and perform *generateTree* on the next level from the current node $n2$.

The function *avgInfoGains* calculates repeatedly information gains for the remaining evidence types *ets* on a random AT *set*. First, we get a list of all used evidence types *usedEts* from the tree and reduce the list to the available evidence

Algorithm 1. Generate information gain tree.

```
function GENERATETREE(set,ets,tree,n)
    nodeList ← avgInfoGains(set, ets, tree, n)
    topList ← getTopItems(nodeList, thresh, branch)
    if isEmpty(topList) then return tree
    end if
    for all n2 in topList do
        tree ← addNode(tree, n, n2)
        tree ← generateTree(docs, ats, ets, tree, n2)
    end for
    return tree
end function
function AVGINFOGAINS(set, ets, tree, n)
    usedEts ← getPath(tree, n)
    leftEts ← reduceList(ets, usedEts)
    for i ← 0 : i ≤ iterations; i + + do
        ats ← createRandomATSet(set)
        doc ← selectRandomDoc(ats, set)
        doc.evids ← analyseDoc(usedEts)
        prioAts ← atSearch(ats, doc.evids)
        subAts ← createSubgroup(prioAts)
        for all e in lefEts do
            g ← calcInfoGain(subAts, doc, e)
            infoGains(e).add(g)
        end for
    end for
    avgIGs ← calcAvgInfoGains(infoGains)
    nodes ← createNodes(leftEts, avgIGs)
return sort(nodes)
end function
```

Algorithm 2. Extract evidences from document *doc* according to evidence decision tree *tree*.

```
function APPLYEVIDENCETREE(doc, ats, tree)
    while tree.hasNext() do
        node ← tree.getNextWithMaxInfoGain()
        e ← analyse(doc, node.eType)
        if e! = null then
            evidList.add(e)
        else
            tree.stepBack()
            tree.prunePaths(node.eType)
        end if
    end while
    prioList ← ATsearch(ats, evidList)
return prioList
end function
```

types *leftEts*. We repeat information gain calculation *iterations* times. For each iteration, we select a random AT search set *ats* and a corresponding document *doc*. Then, we extract all evidences *doc.evids* according to the used evidence types. AT search is performed. Based on the priority list of ATs, we select the remaining AT subgroup *subAts*. For this subgroup, we calculate the information gain g for each evidence type. Finally, we calculate the average information gain for each evidence type and return a sorted node list.

4.2 Application to Search

Algorithm 2 outlines, how we apply the learned information gain tree to AT search.

The function *applyEvidenceTree* generates one path of evidences *evidList* within the tree *tree* that can be extracted from the document *doc*. The DA results are applied as evidences to AT search. For generating the evidence list *evidList*, the next node *node* in the tree is selected by the maximum information gain assigned to the descendants of the current node. If this evidence type can be extracted from the document, the evidence e is added to the list of evidences. If not, we move one level up in the tree and prune all paths in the tree that include this evidence type. The resulting evidence list is used for AT search and the function finally returns a sorted AT list.

5 Failure Detection Strategies

Sometimes, when a document arrives, there does not exist a matching Attentive Task (AT). This is either the case if the document invokes a new process instance in the enterprise or if the generation of the AT failed (see Sect. 3.2). During AT search, we need to decide fast if there is an AT or not for avoiding processing errors. These search failures can be handled by creating a new AT from the corresponding AT template. In the following, we present three strategies and combinations of them for identifying such documents during or in advance to AT search.

5.1 Specific Evidence Types

Documents triggering a new process instance often contain evidence types that are not contained in other documents and vice-versa. These are most likely basic information that is not mentioned again during a conversation. We propose learning of evidence types specific for new requests and extracting them before AT search. Equation 2 formalizes the rule for determining AT failure for a document d depending on evidence types E_{new} specific for *new* documents:

$$fail_{spec}(d, E_{new}) = \begin{cases} 1.0 & \text{if } \exists e \in d.E | e.t \in E_{new} \\ 0.0 & \text{else} \end{cases} \tag{2}$$

where failure is true (1.0) if there exists at least one evidence e extractable from the document $d.E$, whose evidence type $e.t$ is contained in E_{new}. This approach is not costly in terms of search steps, because it does only require extraction steps. It cannot detect AT generation failures.

5.2 Expected Degree of Belief

The degree of belief (DoB) measures to which extent each AT matches the evidences from a document in comparison to all other ATs. Therefore, we propose to use the DoB value for detecting documents, where we believe that no AT matches. We compare an expected DoB dob_e for a set of evidence types E to the actual DoB of the first AT in the prioritized list dob_{top}. If the difference is beyond a threshold t, a failure is detected. Equation 3 formalizes failure detection for a document d, the AT set A, and an expected DoB function dob_e, as well as a threshold function t:

$$fail_{DoB}(d, A, dob_e, t) = \begin{cases} 1.0 & \text{if } dob_e(d.E, |A|) - dob_{top}(d.E, A) > t \\ 0.0 & \text{else} \end{cases} \tag{3}$$

where failure is detected if the difference between the expected DoB dob_e and the actual top DoB after search dob_{top} is greater than the defined threshold. This strategy postulates that the DoB of documents with existing AT differs significantly from documents without AT. We conduct evaluations to confirm this assumption. Since the detection strategy includes information about the current AT set, it addresses both failure cases.

5.3 Attentive Task Templates

For failure handling we generate new ATs from AT templates. We, therefore, propose to add all AT templates to the AT search set. Equation 4 formalizes template failure detection for a document d, the current ATs A, and all templates T:

$$fail_{tem}(d, A, T) = \begin{cases} 1.0 & \text{if } a_{top}(d, (A \cup T)) \in T \\ 0.0 & \text{else} \end{cases} \tag{4}$$

where failure is detected if the top AT a_{top} after search on the combined AT set A and T is a template. This strategy addresses both failure cases and is simple to implement, since it does not require learning.

5.4 Hybrid Strategies

We consider combining the different strategies for achieving better and faster detection results. The *Expected Degree of Belief* and *AT Templates* strategies exclude each other, because inserting templates in the search set prevents using the DoB of a non-matching AT on top of the list. Thus, we combine the *Specific Evidence Types* strategy with the others. First, we detect if a document contains an evidence type specific for new documents. If the document passes, we apply the second or third strategy. In this way, we expect to reduce search steps for new documents and to improve overall detection.

6 Evaluation of Information Gain Trees

We conduct evaluations with the information gain tree structure. First, we learn the tree and apply it then to Attentive Task (AT) search.

6.1 Evaluation Setup

We perform the evaluations on a corpus generated from two business processes of a financial institution. The corpus includes 49 emails from probands that conducted requests toward a bank. Each document in the corpus has been annotated with document analysis (DA) results and we have generated an AT for each document. Our approach is general to all input channels, but we focus on email here for reducing complexity not relevant to search performance. It is possible to extend the approach to the other channels. The evaluations of the information gain tree have been conducted in two steps:

1. *Tree Learning.* The proposed tree learning algorithm depends on the information gain threshold and the number of branches per node. We varied both parameters for analyzing resulting trees in terms of number of nodes and average tree depth.
2. *Tree Search.* The goal of using information gain trees is to provide a structure that reaches good search results in a minimal number of search steps. We compare the tree setups generated during learning and compare them to simpler structures as random selection from all evidences (*All*), a set of best performing structures (*Top7*), and the two level structure (*Top7 2-Level*).

Table 2. Information gain tree properties for alternating branches and thresholds.

Branches	Number of nodes					Average depth				
	Threshold									
	0.4	0.3	0.2	0.15	0.1	0.4	0.3	0.2	0.15	0.1
1	0	2	5	3	3	0.0	2.0	5.0	3	3
2	0	6	69	104	87	0.0	2.0	5.8	7	7,1
3	0	12	365	1,898	5 K	0.0	2.0	5.9	7.8	8.9
4	0	15	792	9 K	83 K	0.0	2.0	5.8	7.9	10.1
5	0	18	1,392	23 K	>1,000 K	0.0	2.0	5.7	7.9	11.7

Table 3. Information gain tree search results.

Branches	AvgRank				Search steps (extraction)			
	Threshold							
	0.3	0.2	0.15	0.1	0.3	0.2	0.15	0.1
1	0.74	0.75	0.74	0.74	1.1 (2.0)	1.3 (2.2)	1.4 (2.2)	1.3 (2.2)
2	0.75	0.74	0.75	0.75	1.1 (2.9)	1.3 (3.1)	1.3 (3.1)	1.3 (3.1)
3	0.75	0.74	0.75	0.74	1.1 (3.7)	1.3 (4.0)	1.3 (4.0)	1.3 (4.0)
4	0.75	0.74	0.74	0.74	1.2 (4.6)	1.4 (5.0)	1.4 (5.0)	1.4 (5.0)

Table 4. Performance of previous methods.

Method	Evidences	AvgRank	Search steps (extraction)
All	E = 6	1.04	6.0 (6.0)
	E = 7	0.77	7.0 (7.0)
Top7	E = 3	1.17	3.0 (3.0)
	E = 4	0.54	4.0 (4.0)
Top7 2-level	E = 2	0.81	2.0 (2.0)
	E = 3	0.59	3.0 (3.0)

6.2 Tree Learning

The overall goals of implementing information gain trees are the minimization of search and extraction steps, while keeping good search results, creating a structure that is robust to non-extractable evidences, and minimizing learning time.

During learning evaluation, we, alternated the two main parameters - branch factor and threshold - to terminate branch extension. For each tree, we counted the number of nodes that directly correlates to learning time, and the average tree depth that influences number of search steps. We derive the main findings depicted in Table 2 as follows:

1. *Learning Time.* The lower the threshold and higher the branch factor is, the larger the tree becomes – growing exponentially. In terms of learning time, the threshold should be limited to 0.2, whereas branches to 4. A threshold of 0.4 or higher does not generate any node (except the root node).
2. *Search Steps.* Average tree depth depends on the threshold and increases when decreasing the threshold. Experienced in simple search, good search results derive from 3 or more search steps. A threshold between 0.3 and 0.4 is corresponding.
3. *Branches.* The more branches, the more robustness to not extractable evidences we achieve. Therefore, a high branching factor is preferable, but does also influence learning time tremendously. The results show, that a limitation of the number of branches, can help to limit overall tree size.

We conclude that the limitation of threshold and branches is necessary for limiting tree learning time.

6.3 Tree Search

For tree search, we compare search performance and runtime optimization for each tree configuration. Then, we compare tree search with the three previously used methods for determining initial evidences: *All*, *Top7*, and *Top7 2-level.* For search performance, we use the average ranks as main measure. Optimization is measured in search and extraction steps. We summarize the results in Table 3 as follows:

1. *Average Rank.* All trees perform similar with an average rank between 0.74 and 0.75. A small, simple tree structure is sufficient for achieving good search results for our corpus. The evidences in the first branch are most likely extractable.
2. *Search steps.* Average number of search steps is low (from 1.1 to 1.4) and increases slightly with decreasing threshold. This supports that in most cases the first branches are used for search.
3. *Extraction Steps.* Average number of extraction steps increases from 2.0 up to 5.0 with decreasing threshold and increasing branching factor. When an evidence in the first branches cannot be used, several extraction steps are necessary.

Comparing the tree search results to the previous methods (see Table 4) reveals that tree search reaches similar search performance as *All* between 6 and 7 evidences, as *Top7* between 3 and 4, and as *Top7 2-level* between 2 and 3. We infer that tree search optimizes search and extraction steps in comparison to simpler methods.

In conclusion, we found a structure that optimizes search and extraction steps and delivers good search results with relatively low effort in training time and calibration of the method. We believe, the information gain trees will enable our system to deal with more complex setups.

7 Evaluation of Failure Detection

In this section, we evaluate the different failure detection strategies regarding detection performance. We pre-evaluate the degree of belief (DoB) in dependence on the search set size and the evidence type to prepare the second strategy (expected DoB).

7.1 Evaluation Setup

We evaluate on the same corpus in two steps:

1. *Degree of Belief Values.* We conduct Attentive Task (AT) search on random search setups for evaluating the dependency of the degree of belief (DoB) value on search set size and evidence type. Further, we repeat the experiment for understanding, how DoB develops in case of a search failure, and for generating a threshold. We repeat each search setup 20,000 times.

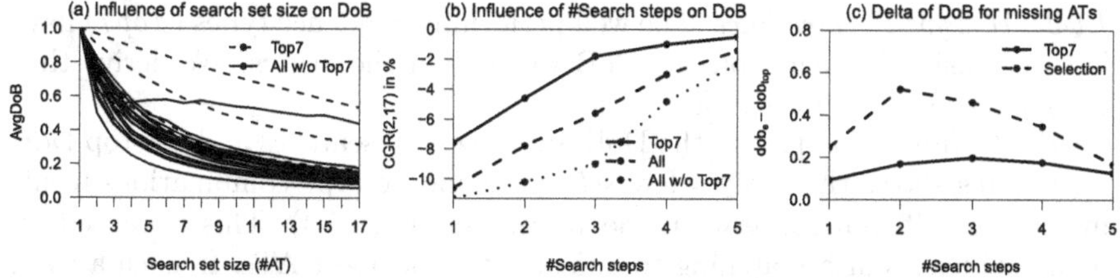

Fig. 3. Influencing factors on Degree of Belief (DoB) values: (a) Influence of search set size for all evidence types on DoB, (b) Influence of search steps (=no. of evidences) on average compound growth rate of DoB, (c) and influence of search steps and selection of evidence types on distance between expected DoB and top DoB when the Attentive Task is missing.

2. *Failure Detection Strategies.* We evaluate each of the proposed strategies: (1) specific evidence types, (2) expected DoB, (3) inclusion of AT templates, as well as hybrid strategies, (1) & (2) and (1) & (3). We compare them with established classification measures: precision $Pr = tp/(tp + fp)$, recall $Re = tp/(tp + fp)$, and accuracy $Acc = (tp + fp)/(tp + fp + tn + fn)$. True positives tp are correctly detected failures, false positives fp non-failures classified as failures, true negatives tn correctly detected non-failures, and false negatives fn not detected failures. We also conduct a separate evaluation of the two failure cases. Additionally, we aim at minimizing the costly search steps. Experiments were repeated 80,000 times for each setup including varying number of search steps from 1 to 6, which are the number of evidences used for search.

7.2 Degree of Belief Evaluation

We repeated DoB experiments for different ATs search sets and varied the search set size, number of evidences as input for search, and the type of evidence group. For evidence groups, we differentiate between the best performing evidence types from our previous work (*Top7*), all evidence types (*All*), and all possible evidence types without the *Top7* (*All w/o Top7*). For each search experiment, we generate a random AT set of random size, select one corresponding document, extract evidences according to the evidence type group, and execute search. The findings depicted in Fig. 3(a)–(c) are summarized as follows:

1. *Search Set Size.* The larger the search set is, the smaller the DoB value of the corresponding AT. Figure 3(a) displays the DoB development for all evidence types when one evidence is used. This effect is diminished with increasing number of evidences (see Fig. 3(b)). To measure the development over search set size we calculate the compound growth rate (CGR)[3] between search set size 2 and 17 for different evidence numbers.

[3] $CGR(s_0, s_n) = (\frac{avgDoB(s_n)}{avgDoB(s_0)})^{\frac{1}{s_n - s_0}} - 1$, s_i is the search set size and $avgDoB(s_i)$ the average DoB for search set size s_i.

2. *Evidence Type Performance.* The well performing evidence types (*Top7*) have less decreasing influence on the DoB value than the others. We derive that DoB is more stable for calibrated searches.
3. *Search Failures.* Comparing the DoB for successful searches and the top DoB for failures shows that only a few *selected* evidence type combinations result in relevant differences between the values (see Fig. 3(c)). This is caused by many evidences also matching to one or more incorrect ATs. In such a case, the ATs get a higher matching value and after normalization they get a value similar to the correct AT. For the expected DoB strategy, we use only the selected evidence types and half of the average difference as threshold.

We conclude that in our setup the DoB value is highly sensitive to search set size and evidence type. There are only a few evidence type combinations that allow to use the DoB distance to an expected DoB for identifying if the corresponding AT is not included in the search set. We will further evaluate the related strategy, but these results indicate that the expected DoB strategy could become fragile in other domains.

Table 5. Classification performance of the failure detection strategies.

#Search steps	(1) Evidence types			(2) Expected DoB			(3) Templates			(1) & (2)			(1) & (3)		
	Pr	Re	Acc	Pr	Re	Acc	Pr	Re	Acc	Pr	Re	Acc	bf Pr	Re	Acc
0	1.00	0.23	0.47	-	-	-	-	-	-	1.00	0.23	0.47	1.00	0.23	0.47
1	-	-	-	0.77	0.54	0.57	1.00	0.23	0.34	0.82	0.71	0.69	1.00	0.52	0.59
2	-	-	-	0.93	0.80	0.82	0.99	0.53	0.60	0.94	0.87	0.87	0.99	0.73	0.77
3	-	-	-	0.93	0.77	0.80	0.99	0.73	0.76	0.94	0.86	0.86	0.99	0.86	0.87
4	-	-	-	0.93	0.59	0.69	0.98	0.85	0.86	0.94	0.75	0.80	0.98	0.93	0.93
5	-	-	-	0.92	0.51	0.63	0.98	0.88	0.88	0.94	0.70	0.76	0.98	0.94	0.94
6	-	-	-	0.92	0.39	0.55	0.98	0.91	0.90	0.95	0.62	0.71	0.98	0.96	0.95

7.3 Failure Detection Strategies

We evaluate the five proposed detection strategies on a randomly generated AT set for a randomly selected document. We alternate the number of evidences used for search, because this is the most expensive calculation step ($O(n^2)$). We repeat all experiments for search failure and for non-failure. For documents triggering a new process compared to documents related to one process instance, we use the ratio from the corpus (new: 38 %, instance: 62 %). For the case of AT generation failure, we assume a 50 % ratio. We expect a much lower ratio in enterprise application. Due to the dependency on the AT generation approach, it is difficult to predict this ratio. We apply the same ratios for all strategies, so the results remain comparable. The main findings are depicted in Table 5 and a separate overview of the two cases of search failure is displayed in Fig. 4(a) and (b). We summarize the results for each strategy as follows:

(1) *Selected Evidences.* This strategy does not involve any search steps. Precision is optimal (1.0) whereas recall (0.23) and accuracy (0.47) are very low. The reason for the discrepancy is that the strategy only detects documents triggering a new process (see Fig. 4(a) and (b)).

(2) *Expected DoB.* This strategy performs optimal when using two evidences. It reaches precision of 0.93, recall of 0.80, and accuracy of 0.82. According to the DoB pre-evaluations, the difference between expected DoB and DoB in case of failure is best differentiating and leads to good results. Both failure cases develop similar.

(3) *Templates.* When including AT templates, precision decreases slightly (from 1.00 to 0.98) with increasing search steps, whereas recall and accuracy increase tremendously (from 0.23 to 0.91, from 0.34 to 0.90). This correlates to the general AT search development, where increasing number of evidences improve search results. The strategy performs better for generation failures than new documents. A similar performance to strategy (2) at search step two is reached with four.

(1) & (2). The combination leads to better failure detection performance overall. There is again an optimum for two search steps. Precision reaches 0.94, recall 0.87, and accuracy 0.87. This is caused by the improvements in new document detection (see Fig. 4(a)).

(1) & (3). This hybrid strategy also improves detection performance. Accuracy (from 0.47 to 0.98) and recall (from 0.23 to 0.96) increase with number of search steps. Precision decreases again from 1.0 to 0.98. The improvements are caused by improvements in new email detection (see Fig. 4(a)). A similar performance to strategy (1) & (2) at search step two is reached with three.

We conclude that it is recommendable using a hybrid strategy. The combination with the expected DoB strategy results in best detection performance with only two search steps. Nevertheless, this strategy also has drawbacks. The learning of evidence combinations is intricate, the results seem fragile and depend on the application domain. Additionally, the required evidences for a good detection performance might not perfectly fit with the optimal evidences for initial search. Hence, we hesitate recommending this strategy in general for any domain.

The combination with templates appears more reliable, even if it produces similar results as (1) & (2) with three search steps. The selection of evidences for search is compatible with initial evidence selection and the method does not

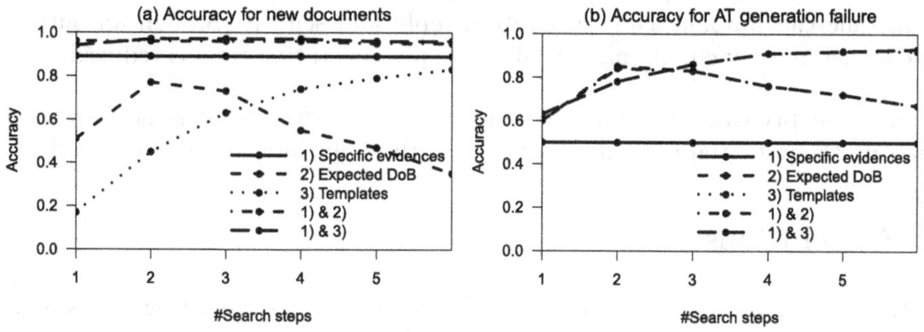

Fig. 4. Accuracy of the failure detection strategies separated by the case of absent AT: (a) New document without related AT, (b) AT of the document is missing.

require pre-learning. We, therefore, recommend implementing template search in the first place and evaluating the performance of expected DoB in the particular domain.

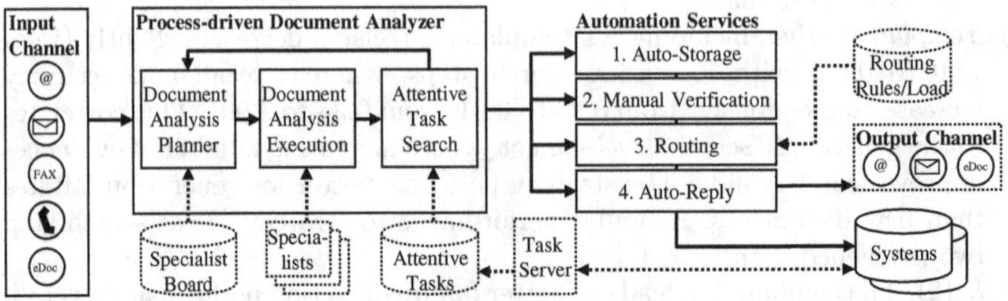

Fig. 5. System architecture including selected automation services.

8 Automation Services

The presented process-driven DA approach enables many *automation services* in enterprise communication. Figure 5 depicts an exemplary architecture of the overall system including four major automation services.

1. *Auto-storage.* This module stores the extracted information in databases of the internal enterprise systems. Hence, no manual processing is necessary.
2. *Manual Verification.* This module enhances the user's view on the current document with the extracted and the additional AT information. Since the user only needs to verify the data, the manual document processing time is expected to decrease.
3. *Routing.* This module can use the information from the AT and the internal routing rules and load information for routing the document to a service employee with an appropriate skill-profile. Manual routing is avoided.
4. *Auto-Reply.* For simple requests or requests with incomplete information, a module can automatically generate a reply and send it through an output channel, mainly email, mail, or eDoc. Reply generation time is reduced.

In order to prioritize the implementation of such services, it is necessary to quantify the potential time and cost savings through these automation services.

9 Conclusions

In this paper, we propose two approaches enhancing our existing AT search algorithm and making it more robust to real world requirements: (i) information evidence gain trees and (ii) missing Attentive Task (AT) detection strategies. First evaluations already show that the application of trees significantly minimizes search steps and we expect it to support even more complex search domains. For search failure detection strategies, we found that combining the specific evidence type decisions with the two strategies integrating the search set performs best. For simplification, we recommend applying first the insertion of AT templates and then investigating whether the expected degree of belief (DoB) comparison is applicable to the corresponding domain or not. Further, we present four initial automation services based on our approach.

For future work, we plan transferring the results to more complex domains and increasing the search set size. Further, we aim at evaluating DA planning and the presented automation services.

References

1. Bellotti, V., et al.: Quality vs. quantity: email-centric task-management and its relationship with overload. Hum.-Comput. Interact. **20**, 1–2 (2005)
2. Stamm, K., Dengel, A.: Attentive tasks: process-driven document analysis for multichannel documents. In: Proceedings of DAS (2012)
3. Dengel, A., Hinkelmann, K.: The SPECIALIST BOARD - a technology workbench for document analysis and understanding. In: IDPT (1996)
4. Stamm, K., Dengel, A.: Searching attentive tasks with document analysis evidences and dempster-shafer theory. In: Proceedings of ICPR (2012)
5. Shafer, G.: A Mathematical Theory of Evidence, vol. 1. Princeton University Press, Princeton (1976)
6. Katz, A., Berman, I.: Designing an e-mail prototype to enhance effective communication and task management: a case study. Serdica J. Comput. **5**, 39–64 (2011)
7. Cohen, W., Carvalho, V., Mitchell, T.: Learning to classify email into "speech acts". In: Proceedings of EMNLP (2004)
8. Scerri, S., Gossen, G., Davis, B., Handschuh, S.: Classifying action items for semantic email. In: Proceedings of LREC (2010)
9. Dredze, M., Lau, T., Kushmerick, N.: Automatically classifying emails into activities. In: Proceedings of IUI (2006)
10. Faulring, A., et al.: Agent-assisted task management that reduces email overload. In: Proceedings of IUI (2010)
11. Granitzer, M., et al.: Machine learning based work task classification. J. Digit. Inf. Manag. **7**, 306–314 (2009)
12. Krämer, J.: PIM-Mail: consolidating task and email management. In: Proceedings of CHI (2010)
13. Kushmerick, N., Lau, T. A.: Automated email activity management: an unsupervised learning approach. In: Proceedings of IUI (2005)
14. Kullback, S., Leibler, R.: On information and sufficiency. Ann. Math. Stat. **22**, 79–86 (1951)

Constraint-Handling with Support Vector Decoders

Jörg Bremer(✉) and Michael Sonnenschein

University of Oldenburg, 26129 Oldenburg, Germany
{joerg.bremer,michael.sonnenschein}@uni-oldenburg.de

Abstract. A comparably new application for support vector machines is their use for meta-modeling the feasible region in constrained optimization problems. Applications have already been developed to optimization problems from the smart grid domain. Still, the problem of a standardized integration of such models into (evolutionary) optimization algorithms was as yet unsolved. We present a new decoder approach that constructs a mapping from the unit hyper cube to the feasible region from the learned support vector model. Thus, constrained problems are transferred into unconstrained ones by space mapping for easier search. We present result from artificial test cases as well as simulation results from smart grid use cases for real power planning scenarios.

Keywords: Smart grid · Constraint-handling · Decoder · Constraint modeling · SVDD

1 Introduction

A popular class of commonly used heuristics for solving hard optimization problems is known as evolutionary search methods. These methods usually work with candidate solutions that encode each parameter within an allowed interval between a lower and an upper limit and try to improve them within these bounds. Thus, all solutions are defined in a d-dimensional hypercube. Nevertheless, due to additional constraints, not all of these solutions are usually feasible. Effectively solving real world optimization problems often suffers from the additional presence of constraints that have to be obeyed when exploring alternative solutions. Evolutionary algorithms have been widely noticed due to their potential for solving complex (discontinuous or non differentiable) numerical functions. However, a full success in the field of nonlinear programming problems is still missing, because constraints have not been addressed for integration in a systematic way [1,2]. For constraint handling, the general constrained continuous nonlinear programming (NLP) problem is often used as problem formulation:

Find $x \in \mathbb{R}^d$ that optimizes $f(x)$ subject to a set of constraints:

$$\begin{aligned} \text{equalities:} \quad & g_i(x) = 0; \quad 1 \leq i \leq m \\ \text{inequalities:} \quad & g_j(x) \leq 0; \quad 1 \leq j \leq n. \end{aligned} \tag{1}$$

J. Filipe and A. Fred (Eds.): ICAART 2013, CCIS 449, pp. 228–244, 2014.
DOI: 10.1007/978-3-662-44440-5_14

Real world problems often additionally face nonlinear constraints or such constraints that are not given as explicit formulation. One example for a not explicitly given constraint is a simulation model that devalues given solutions as not feasible judged by simulation runs. We are going to focus on (but not restrict ourselves to) the latter type.

In general, the set of constraints defines a region within a search space (the hypercube defined by parameter bounds) that contains all feasible solutions. Taking into account non-linear constraints, the NLP is generally intractable [1]. Evolutionary Algorithms approximately solve non linear optimization very efficiently. Nevertheless, surprisingly low effort has been put in the integration of constraint handling and evolutionary optimization (cf. [2]). Standard constraint-handling techniques are for example the introduction of a penalty for infeasible solutions, the separation of objectives and constraints to transform a given optimization problem into an unconstrained many-objective one, or decoder approaches to give an algorithm hints on how to construct feasible solutions by imposing a relationship between feasibility and decoder solution.

At the same time, support vector machines and related approaches have been shown to have excellent performance when trained as classifiers for multiple purposes, especially real world problems. In [3] a support vector model has been developed for the feasible region of an optimization problem specific to the smart grid domain. This model only allows for afterwards checking the feasibility of an already given solution.

We integrate these two approaches to a new decoder approach for constraint handling [4]. Such a decoder is a constraint-handling technique that maps the constrained problem space to some other not-restricted space where the search operates. The basic idea is to construct a mapping from the original, unconstrained domain of the problem (the hypercube) to the feasible space. The mapping will be derived from the support vector model. After a brief review of constraint handling techniques and black-box modelling with support vector approaches, we introduce the underlying model and describe the construction of our mapping approach in detail. We present results from several test scenarios with artificial optimization problems and conclude with results from applying our method to the load balancing problem in smart grid scenarios.

2 Related Work

Several techniques for handling constraints are known. Nevertheless, many are concerned with special cases of NLP or require priori knowledge of the problem structure for proper adaption [1]. We will briefly discuss some prominent representatives of such techniques. A good overview can for instance be found in [5] or, more recently, in [2].

Penalty. A widely and long since used approach for constraint handling is the introduction of a penalty into the objective function that devalues all solutions that violate some constraint. In this way, the problem is transformed into an unconstrained one. Most commonly used are exterior penalties that draw outside solutions towards the feasible region in contrast to interior ones that keep solutions inside, but require to start with a feasible solution [5].

Separation of Objectives and Constraints. Constraints or aggregations of constraints may be treated as separate objectives. This leads to a transformation into a (unconstrained) many objective problem. Such approaches have some computational disadvantages from determining Pareto optimality or may lack the ability (in the case of a disjoint region) to escape a sub-region [5]. Moreover, a functional description of constraints must be known here in advance, what is not the case when using surrogate models that hide original relations and only model the original behaviour.

Solution Repair. Some combinatorial optimization problem allow for an easy repair of infeasible solutions. In this case, it has been shown that repairing infeasible solutions often outperforms other approaches [6]. This approach is closely related to the decoder based approaches.

Decoder. In order to give hints for solution construction, so called decoders impose a relationship between feasibility and decoder solutions. For example, [7] proposed a homomorphous mapping between an n-dimensional hyper cube and the feasible region in order to transform the problem into an topological equivalent one that is easier to handle, although with a need for extra parameters that have to be found empirically and with some extra computational efforts. In contrast, we will see later how a similar approach can be automatically derived from a given support vector description. Earlier approaches e.g. used Riemannien mapping [8].

A relatively new constraint handling technique is the use of meta-models for black-box optimization scenarios with no explicitly given constraint boundaries. Such a model allows for efficiently checking feasibility and thus eases the search for the constraint boundary between a feasible and an infeasible solution in case a repair of a mutation is needed. Various classification or regression methods might be harnessed for creating such models for the boundary [2].

An example from the smart grid for the latter case that has been realized by an SVDD approach can be found in [9] and is also an example for scenarios with (at least partly) unknown functional relationships of the constraints. When lacking full knowledge on hidden variables or intrinsic relations that determine the operability of a electric device, the feasible region can only be derived by sampling a simulation model [3]. The model is learned by SVDD from a set of operable (feasible) examples; in another example, [10] used a two-class SVM for learning operation point and bias (regarding allowed voltage and current bands) of a line in a power grid for easier classifying a grid state as feasible or not. In both cases, at the time of searching for the optimum, the only available information is the model, i.e. a set of support vectors and associated weights. Every information about the original constraints is no longer available in such scenarios.

For our real world use case we will briefly review load balancing. Within the framework of today's (centralized) operation planning for power stations, different heuristics are harnessed. Short-term scheduling of different generators assigns (in its classical interpretation) discrete-time-varying production levels to energy generators for a given planning horizon [11]. It is known to be an NP-hard problem [12]. Determining an exact global optimum is not possible in practice until ex post due to uncertainties and forecast errors. Additionally, it is hard to exchange operational constraints in case of a changed setting (e.g. a new composition of energy resources) of the generation system.

Coordinating a pool of distributed generators and consumers with the intent to provide a certain aggregated load schedule for active power has some objective similarities to controlling a virtual power plant. Within the smart grid domain the volatile character of such a coalition has additionally to be taken into account. On an abstract level, approaches for controlling groups of distributed devices can be roughly divided into centralized and distributed scheduling algorithms.

Centralized approaches have long time dominated the discussion [13] and are discussed in the context of static pools of energy unit with drawbacks and restrictions regarding scalability and particularly flexibility. Recently, distributed approaches gained more and more importance. Different works proposed hierarchical and decentralized architectures based on multi-agent systems and market based computing [14]. Newer approaches try to establish self-organization between actors within the grid [15,16].

In load balancing scenarios, a scheduling algorithm (centralized or distributed) must know for each participating energy resource which load schedules are actually operable (satisfy all constraints) and which are not. Each energy resource has to restrict its possible operations due to several constraints. These can be distinguished into hard constraints (usually technically rooted, e.g. minimum and/or maximum power input or output) and soft constraints (often economically or ecologically rooted, e.g. personal preferences like noise pollution in the evening). When determining an optimal partition of the schedule for power production distribution, an alternative schedule is sought from each unit's search space of individual operable schedules (individual feasible region) in order to assemble a desired aggregate load schedule.

3 Mapping Algorithm

We now describe the integration of a SVDD based black-box for feasible regions into an arbitrary evolutionary optimization algorithm with proper and effective constraint handling and propose handling constraints in a different way: by learning a mapping that transforms the original parameter hypercube to resemble the feasible region.

3.1 SVDD-Model for Feasible Regions

As a prerequisite for our mapping, we assume that the feasible region of an optimization problem has been encoded by SVDD as e.g. described in [9]. We will briefly describe this approach before deriving our new utilization method. Given a set of data samples $x_i \in \mathcal{X}$, the inherent structure of the region where the data resides in is derived as follows: After mapping the data to a high dimensional feature space, the smallest images enclosing sphere is determined. When mapping back the sphere to data space, its pre-image forms a contour (not necessarily connected) enclosing the data sample.

This task is achieved by determining a mapping $\Phi : \mathcal{X} \subset \mathbb{R}^d \to \mathcal{H}, x \mapsto \Phi(x)$ such that all data from a sample from a region $\mathcal{X}$ is mapped to a minimal hypersphere in some high-dimensional space $\mathcal{H}$. The minimal sphere with radius $R_\mathcal{S}$ and center a in $\mathcal{H}$ that encloses $\{\Phi(x_i)\}_N$ can be derived from minimizing $\|\Phi(x_i) - a\|^2 \leq R^2 + \xi_i$ with $\|\cdot\|$ as the Euclidean norm and slack variables $\xi_i \geq 0$ for soft constraints.

After introducing Lagrangian multipliers and further relaxing to the Wolfe dual form, the well known Mercer's theorem (cf. e.g. [17]) may be used for calculating dot products in $\mathcal{H}$ by means of a kernel in data space: $\Phi(x_i) \cdot \Phi(x_j) = k(x_i, x_j)$. In order to gain a more smooth adaption, it is known to be advantageous to use a Gaussian kernel: $k_G(x_i, x_j) = e^{-\frac{1}{2\sigma^2}\|x_i - x_j\|^2}$ [18]. SVDD delivers two main results: the center $a = \sum_i \beta_i \Phi(x_i)$ of the sphere in terms of an expansion into $\mathcal{H}$ and a function $R : \mathbb{R}^d \to \mathbb{R}$ that allows to determine the distance of the image of an arbitrary point from $a \in \mathcal{H}$, calculated in $\mathbb{R}^d$ by:

$$R^2(x) = 1 - 2\sum_i \beta_i k_G(x_i, x) + \sum_{i,j} \beta_i \beta_j k_G(x_i, x_j). \tag{2}$$

Because all support vectors are mapped right onto the surface of the sphere, the radius $R_\mathcal{S}$ can be determined by the distance of an arbitrary support vector to the center a. Thus the feasible region is modeled as $\mathcal{F} = \{x \in \mathbb{R}^d | R(x) \leq R_\mathcal{S}\} \approx \mathcal{X}$.

This model might be used as a black-box that abstracts from any explicitly given form of constraints and allows for an easy and efficient decision on whether a given solution is feasible or not. Moreover, as the radius function Eq. 2 maps to $\mathbb{R}$, it allows for a conclusion about how far away a solution is from feasibility. Nevertheless, a systematic constraint-handling during optimization is not induced in this way. In the following, we present a way of integrating such SVDD surrogate models into optimization.

3.2 The Decoder

Let $\mathcal{F}$ denote the feasible region within the parameter domain of some given optimization problem bounded by an associated set of constraints. It is known, that pre-processing the data by scaling it to $[0,1]^d$ leads to better adaption [19]. For this reason, we consider optimization problems with scaled domains and denote with $\mathcal{F}_{[0,1]}$ the likewise scaled region of feasible solutions. We construct a mapping

$$\gamma : [0,1]^d \to \mathcal{F}_{[0,1]} \subseteq [0,1]^d; \; x \mapsto \gamma(x) \tag{3}$$

that maps the unit hypercube $[0,1]^d$ onto the d-dimensional region of feasible solutions. We achieve this mapping as a composition of three functions: $\gamma = \Phi_\ell^{-1} \circ \Gamma_a \circ \hat{\Phi}_\ell$. Instead of trying to find a direct mapping to $\mathcal{F}_{[0,1]}$ we go through kernel space. The commutative diagram (Eq. 4) sketches the idea. We start with an arbitrary point $x \in [0,1]^d$ from the unconstrained d-dimensional hypercube and map it to an ℓ-dimensional manifold that is spanned by the images of the ℓ support vectors. After drawing the mapped point to the sphere in order to pull it into the image of the feasible region, we search the pre-image of the modified image to get a point from $\mathcal{F}_{[0,1]}$.

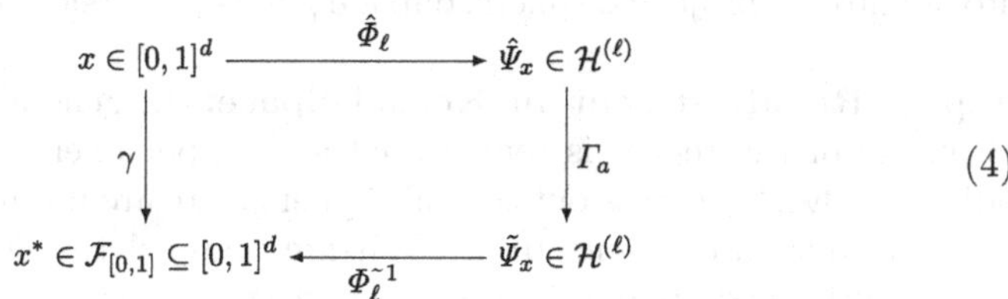

$x \in [0,1]^d$
$\hat{\Phi}_\ell$
$\hat{\Psi}_x \in \mathcal{H}^{(\ell)}$
γ
Γ_a
$x^* \in \mathcal{F}_{[0,1]} \subseteq [0,1]^d$
Φ_ℓ^{-1}
$\tilde{\Psi}_x \in \mathcal{H}^{(\ell)}$

(4)

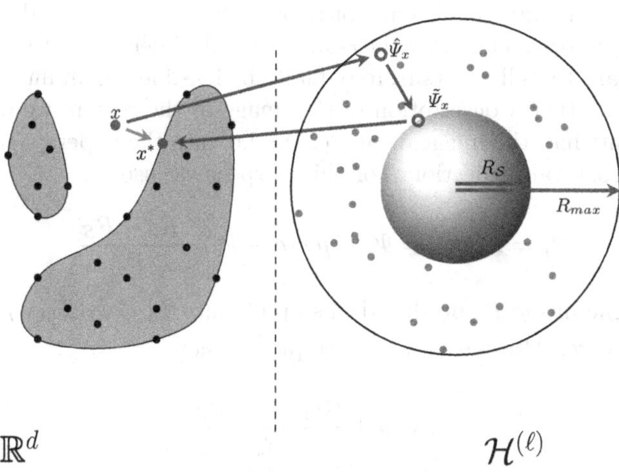

Fig. 1. Deriving the decoder from the support vector model.

Step 1: Mapping to the SV Induced Subspace $\mathcal{H}^{(\ell)}$ with an Empirical Kernel Map. We will now have a closer look onto the respective steps of this procedure. Let

$$\begin{aligned} \Phi_\ell : \mathbb{R}^d &\to \mathbb{R}^\ell, \\ x &\mapsto k(.,x)|_{\{s1,\ldots,s_\ell\}} \\ &= (k(s_1,x),\ldots,k(s_\ell,x)) \end{aligned} \tag{5}$$

be the empirical kernel map w.r.t. the set of support vectors $\{s_1, \ldots, s_\ell\}$. Then

$$\hat{\Phi}_\ell : \mathbb{R}^d \to \mathcal{H}^{(\ell)}, \qquad (6)$$
$$x \mapsto K^{-\frac{1}{2}}(k(s_1, x), \ldots, k(s_\ell, x))$$

with $K_{ij} = k(s_i, s_j)$: the kernel Gram Matrix, maps points x, y from input space to $\mathbb{R}^\ell$, such that $k(x, y) = \hat{\Phi}_\ell(x) \cdot \hat{\Phi}_\ell(y)$ (cf. [17]). With $\hat{\Phi}_\ell$ we are able to map arbitrary points from $[0,1]^d$ to some ℓ-dimensional space $\mathcal{H}^{(\ell)}$ that contains a lower dimensional projection of the sphere. Again, points from $\mathcal{F}_{[0,1]}$ are mapped into or onto the projected sphere, outside points go outside the sphere (cf. Fig. 1).

Step 2: Re-adjustment in Kernel Space. In general, in kernel space $\mathcal{H}$ the image of the region is represented as a hypersphere $\mathcal{S}$ with center a and radius $R_\mathcal{S}$ (Eq. 2). Points outside this hypersphere are not images of points from $\mathcal{X}$, i.e. in our case, points from $\mathcal{F}_{[0,1]}$ are mapped (by Φ) into the sphere or onto its surface (support vectors), points from outside $\mathcal{F}_{[0,1]}$ are mapped outside the sphere. Actually, using a Gaussian kernel, Φ maps each point into a n-dimensional manifold (with sample size n) embedded into infinite dimensional $\mathcal{H}$. In principle, the same holds true for a lower dimensional embedding spanned by ℓ mapped support vectors and the ℓ-dimensional projection of the hypersphere therein. We want to pull points from outside the feasible region into that region. As we do have rather a description of the image of the region, we draw images of outside points into the image of the region, i.e. into the hypersphere; precisely into its ℓ-dimensional projection. For this purpose we use

$$\tilde{\Psi}_x = \Gamma_a(\hat{\Psi}_x) = \hat{\Psi}_x + \mu \cdot (a - \hat{\Psi}_x) \cdot \frac{R_x - R_\mathcal{S}}{R_x} \qquad (7)$$

to transform the image $\hat{\Psi}_x$ produced in step (1) into $\tilde{\Psi}_x \in \hat{\Phi}_\ell(\mathcal{F}_{[0,1]})$ by drawing $\hat{\Psi}_x$ into the sphere. Alternatively, the simpler version

$$\tilde{\Psi}_x = a + \frac{(\hat{\Psi}_x - a) \cdot R_\mathcal{S}}{R_x} \qquad (8)$$

may be used for drawing $\hat{\Psi}_x$ just onto the sphere but then without having to estimate parameter $\mu \in [1, R_x]$. Parameter μ allows us to control how far a point is drawn into the sphere ($\mu = 1$ is equivalent to Eq. 8, $\mu = R_x$ draws each point onto the center). If μ is set to $\frac{R_\mathcal{S}}{R_{max}}$ (compare Fig. 1), a larger sphere containing all images (including infeasible) is rescaled onto the smaller one. In this way, each image is re-adjusted proportional to the original distance from the sphere and drawn into the direction of the center.

Points from the interior are also moved under mapping γ in order to compensate for additional points coming from the exterior. In this way, the whole unit hypercube is literally squeezed to the form of the feasible region without a too large increasing of the density at the boundary. Though, if the feasible region is very small compared with the hypercube, density at the boundary increases (depending on the choice of μ). On the other hand, the likelihood of an optimum being at the boundary increases likewise. So, this might be a desired effect.

After this procedure we have $\tilde{\Psi}_x$ which is the image of a point from $\mathcal{F}_{[0,1]}$ in terms of a modified weight vector $\tilde{w}^{\Gamma_a}$.

Step 3: Finding an Approximate Pre-image. As a last step, we have to find the pre-image of $\tilde{\Psi}_x$ in order to finally get the wanted mapping to $\mathcal{F}_{[0,1]}$. A major problem in determining the pre-image of a point from kernel space is that not every point from the span of Φ is the image of a mapped data point [17]. As we use a Gaussian kernel, none of our points from kernel space can be related to an exact pre-image except for trivial expansions with only one term [20]. For this reason, we will look for an approximate pre-image whose image lies closest to the given image using an iterative procedure after [21]. In our case (Gaussian kernel), we iterate x^* to find the point closest to the pre-image and define approximation $\tilde{\Phi_\ell^{-1}}$ by equation

$$x^*_{n+1} = \frac{\sum_{i=1}^{\ell}(\tilde{w}_i^{\Gamma_a} e^{-\|s_i - x^*_n\|^2/2\sigma^2} s_i)}{\sum_{i=1}^{\ell}(\tilde{w}_i^{\Gamma_a} e^{-\|s_i - x^*_n\|^2/2\sigma^2})}. \tag{9}$$

As an initial guess for x^*_0 we take the original point x and iterate it towards $\mathcal{F}_{[0,1]}$. As this procedure is sensitive to the choice of the starting point, it is important to have some fixed starting point in order to ensure determinism of the mapping. Empirically, x has showed up to be a useful guess.

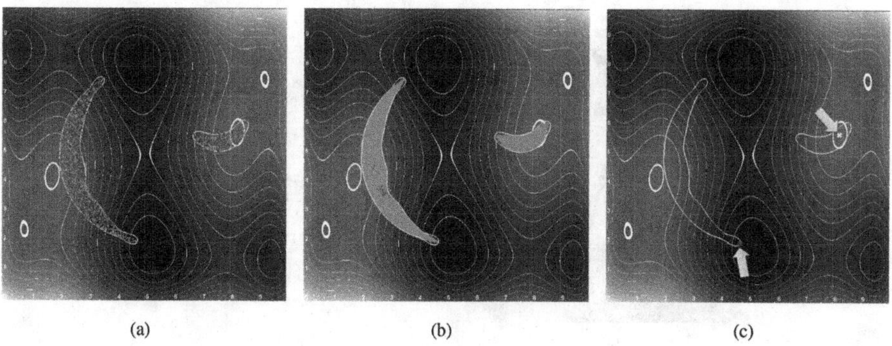

Fig. 2. 2(a): Sample from a artificial double banana shaped region. 2(b): Re-sampling the feasible region by mapping random points from $[0, 1]^2$. 2(c): marked optima of the Six-hump camel back objective function withing the used domain (depicted as heat map in the background).

Finally, we have achieved our goal to map an arbitrary point from $[0, 1]^d$ into the region of feasible solutions described merely by a given set of support vectors and associated weights: x^*_n is the sought after image under mapping γ of x that lies in $\mathcal{F}_{[0,1]}$. We may use this decoder approach to transform constrained optimization problems into unconstrained ones by automatically constructing mapping γ from a SVDD model of the feasible region that has been learned from a set of feasible example solutions.

4 Experiments

We present evaluation results of our decoder method with several theoretical test cases as well as results from the smart grid power planning problem.

4.1 General Test Cases

We started with several artificially constrained optimization problems and test functions. We consider optimization problems as described in Sect. 1 and use the above described procedure as constraint handling technique, i.e. we transform problem Eq. 1 into an unconstrained optimization problem by applying mapping γ:

$$\text{optimize} \quad f(\gamma(x)), \text{ s.t.} \quad x \in [0,1]^d. \tag{10}$$

Of course, the restriction to the unit hypercube still entails a box constraint, but as these are easily handled by almost all algorithm implementations, this is not a serious obstacle. If $x^\circ \in [0,1]^d$ is the found position of the optimum in the unconstrained space then $\tilde{x} = \gamma(x^\circ) \in \mathcal{F}_{[0,1]}$ is the solution to the original, constrained problem.

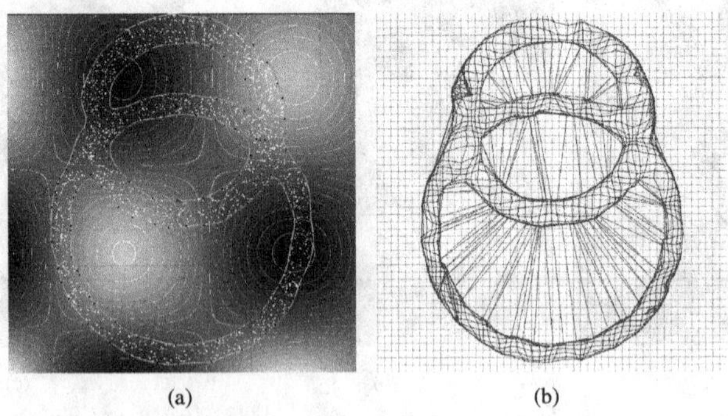

Fig. 3. 3(a): Randomly generated double ring data set as representation of a second toy region. Again, the orange line denotes the learned boundary that encloses the feasible space. 3(b): Mapping a mesh with grid size 0.02 into the learned region of a double ring data set.

In the case of evolutionary algorithms, the method can be easily applied by defining the neighborhood in $[0,1]^d$ and search the whole unit hypercube, but evaluate a solution x at the position $\gamma(x)$. Note that mapping $\gamma(x)$ generates a feasible solution regardless of the choice of x. Therefore optimization might

Table 1. PSO and ABC and their absolute fitnesses (lower is better) after n iterations for the Shubert function as test function and double banana as constraint region.

ALGORITHM	n	PENALTY	MAPPING
PSO	5	70.912 ± 89.714	-13.360 ± 0.256
	10	24.734 ± 68.949	-13.435 ± 0.278
	25	5.923 ± 47.904	-13.446 ± 0.28
	50	0.013 ± 41.368	-13.477 ± 0.286
ABC	5	67.189 ± 89.783	-13.310 ± 0.17
	10	22.128 ± 64.272	-13.367 ± 0.137
	25	-2.897 ± 35.965	-13.496 ± 0.175
	50	-10.236 ± 15.765	-13.596 ± 0.153

always start with an arbitrary (randomly chosen) $x \in [0,1]^d$ without having to find a feasible start solution first.

For some first tests, we generated random samples from toy regions and used them as training sets. The retrieved support vectors and weights are taken as a model for feasible region $\mathcal{F}_{[0,1]}$. Figure 2(a) shows an example with a 2-dimensional double banana set. With these models, we constructed our mapping γ. As a first test, a set of 1 million equally distributed points has been randomly picked from $[0,1]^2$ and mapped. Figure 2(b) shows the result with mapped points.

Next, we applied standard particle swarm optimization (PSO) [22] and standard artificial bee colony (ABC) optimization [23] in order to find optima of several standard test objective functions. For this purpose, both algorithms have been equipped with mapping γ, while the topology of the neighbourhood that both algorithms operate on is defined as the whole unit hypercube. Figure 2(c) shows an example of found optima for the above sketched setting (both succeeded equally good). In this case, the well known Six-hump camel back function [24] has been used with the domain $-1.9 \leq x_1 \leq 1.9,\ -1.1 \leq x_2 \leq 1.1$ scaled to $[0,1]^2$.

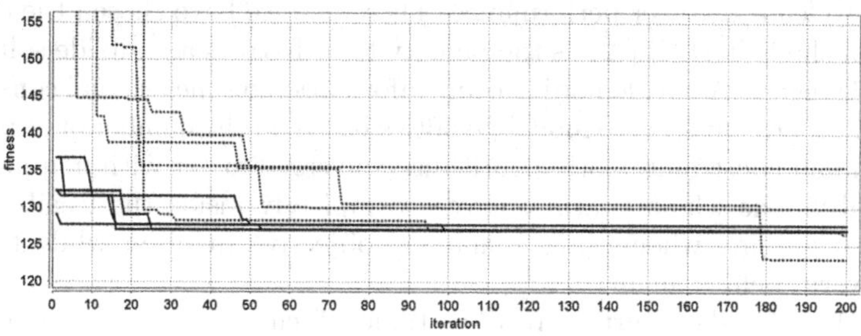

Fig. 4. A typical result for the speed of convergence in a higher dimensional test case; dashed: penalty approach.

Table 2. Results for different objective functions and algorithms. A double banana set has been used for all objectives. ABC: 87.98 and PSO: 83.22 % were valid solutions for the penalty case; mapping: 100 %.

BANANA				RINGS	
OBJECTIVE	ALG.	PENALTY	MAPPING	PENALTY	MAPPING
Shubert	PSO 5	-1.63 ± 38.95	-13.3 ± 0.41	-13.61 ± 9.02	-14.07 ± 0.75
Shubert	ABC 5	-11.59 ± 8.35	-13.6 ± 0.35	-14.14 ± 0.49	-14.25 ± 0.22
Shubert	PSO 50	-13.99 ± 0.06	-13.87 ± 0.13	-14.43 ± 0.0	-14.43 ± 0.01
Shubert	ABC 50	-13.93 ± 0.08	-13.89 ± 0.01	-14.43 ± 0.0	-14.42 ± 0.01
Branin	PSO 5	135.39 ± 80.35	36.36 ± 0.91	43.61 ± 40.24	33.14 ± 0.17
Branin	ABC 5	46.91 ± 33.78	36.15 ± 0.19	33.56 ± 1.73	33.12 ± 0.02
Zakharov	PSO 5	1.54 ± 14.9	0.39 ± 0.08	0.18 ± 0.15	0.14 ± 0.01
Zakharov	ABC 5	0.51 ± 3.9	0.38 ± 0.0	0.18 ± 0.08	0.14 ± 0.0
Bohachevsky 2	PSO 5	0.93 ± 11.21	0.26 ± 0.1	0.43 ± 0.22	0.32 ± 0.05
Bohachevsky 2	ABC 5	0.4 ± 2.76	0.24 ± 0.01	0.38 ± 0.11	0.28 ± 0.02
Bohachevsky 2	PSO 50	0.24 ± 0.0	0.24 ± 0.0	0.27 ± 0.0	0.27 ± 0.0
Bohachevsky 2	ABC 50	0.24 ± 0.01	0.24 ± 0.0	0.28 ± 0.01	0.27 ± 0.0
Himmelblau	PSO 5	179.84 ± 30.05	137.6 ± 1.96	127.11 ± 19.04	121.84 ± 0.31
Himmelblau	ABC 5	145.08 ± 14.38	136.03 ± 1.1	123.1 ± 1.69	121.74 ± 0.06

As a second test case, double ring data sets (Fig. 3(a)) have been generated. The contour plot in the background shows as objective Shubert's function [25]. For the depicted configuration, different almost equally good local optima are situated near different distant positions at the boundary of the feasible region. Nevertheless, all algorithms equipped with mapping γ succeeded in finding optima inside (or at the boundary of) the feasible region.

As a next step, we compared how fast a solution converges with a mapped objective function. We compared the performance, i.e. the speed of convergence, with exterior penalty approaches. Such a constraint handling approach entails additional penalty values to solutions outside the feasible region. According to [26], a penalty function that reflects the distances from the feasible region, is supposed to lead to better performance. Therefore, we have chosen the distance function of the SVDD (Eq. 2) as the penalty that attracts an outside solution to the feasible region. As we do not have any information on the original constraints, it is not in general possible to model penalties based on the number of or based on any individual constraint. Both algorithms converged faster with mapping than with penalty. The whole swarm operates completely inside the feasible region from the beginning when using a mapped objective function while retaining normal swarm behaviour in $[0,1]^d$.

Tables 1 and 2 show further results. Table 1 focusses on the population size of swarm based approaches. Table 2 shows further results (the lower the better) on various combinations of algorithms and further objective functions for the case of the double banana dataset. Stated are respectively absolute achieved fitnesses, thus the ratio between mapping and penalty is to be compared. A major drawback of the penalty approach is the fact that it not always converges to a feasible solution. Whereas the mapping method always served feasible solutions, the penalty approach failed in up to 17 % of the test runs.

Nevertheless, the inaccuracy inherent in the model from learning the region still remains an inaccuracy for mapping. But, the same holds true for all approaches that are based on such a surrogate model, including the penalty approach. Although, we made the observation that γ performs better at sharp edges than the decision boundary Eq. 2 (cf. Fig. 2(b)).

Figure 3(b) shows the result of mapping a regular mesh from $[0, 1]^2$ onto the double rings. The mapped mesh shows how points from different parts of the feasible region become neighbours under the γ by bypassing the infeasible region inside the rings. Figure 4 shows some results for test runs on an 8-dimensional problem with a stretched ellipse as feasible region and Himmelblau [27] as objective function. We compared artificial bee algorithms with 5 individuals for the mapping case and 200 individuals for the penalty case. Nevertheless, the mapping approach performs better and some penalty runs still converged to a infeasible solution, showing the superiority of the mapping approach.

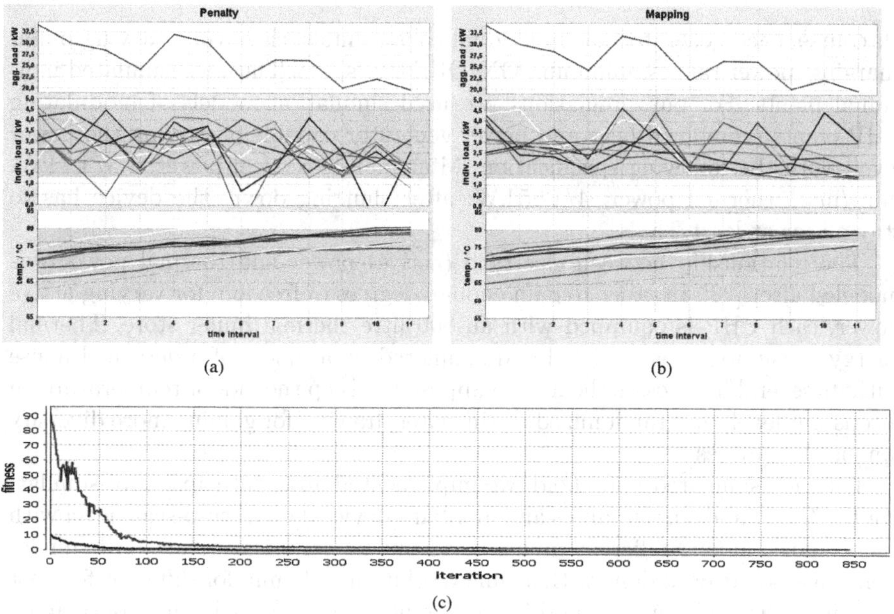

Fig. 5. Results from a smart grid load balancing scenario with a standard penalty constraint-handling technique on the left (5(a)) and the mapping based approach on the right (5(b)); 5(c) compares the speed of convergence.

4.2 The Smart Grid Use Case

Finally, we applied our method to the following real world problem from the smart grid domain: An individual schedule has to be determined for each member of a pool of micro-co-generation (CHP) plants such that the aggregated electric load schedule of all plants resembles a given (probably demanded by market) target schedule in an optimal way. For the sake of simplicity, we will consider optimality as a close as possible adaption of the aggregated (sum of individual loads) schedule to the requested on. Optimality usually refers to additional local (individual cost) as well as to global (e.g. environmental impact) objectives. When determining an optimal partition of the schedule for load distribution, exactly one alternative schedule is taken from each generators search space of individual operable schedules in order to assemble the desired aggregate schedule.

Therefore, the optimization problem is: finding any combination of schedules (one from each energy unit with $\mathcal{X}_i$ as the set of possible choices) that resembles the target schedule l_T as close as possible, i.e. minimize some distance between aggregated and target schedule:

$$\|\sum_i x_i - l_T\| \rightarrow \min, \text{ s.t. } x_i \in \mathcal{X}_i. \quad (11)$$

Of course, each generator has individual constraints such as time varying buffer charging, power ranges, minimum ON/OFF times, etc. Thus, we simulated individual plants. For our simulations, we used simulation models of modulating CHP-plants (combined heat and power generator capable of varying the power level) with the following specification: Min./max. electrical power: 1.3/4.7 kW, min./max. thermal power: 4/12.5 kW; after shutting down, the device has to stay off for at least 2 h.

The relationship between electrical (active) power and thermal power was modeled after [28]. In order to gain enough degrees of freedom for varying active power, each CHP is equipped with an 800 litre thermal buffer store. Thermal energy consumption is modeled and simulated by a model of a detached house with its several heat losses (heater is supposed to keep the indoor temperature on a constant level) and randomized warm water drawing for gaining more diversity among the devices.

For each simulated household, we implemented an agent capable of simulating the CHP (and surroundings and auxiliary devices) on a meso-scale level with energy flows among different model parts but no technical details. All simulations have so far been done with a time resolution of 15 min for different forecast horizons. Although, our method is indifferent about any such time constraints. We have run several test series with each CHP randomly initialized with different buffer charging levels, temperatures and water drawing profiles.The feasible spaces of individual CHP had been encoded with the SVDD approach. These support vector models have then been used for the search for optimal schedules: with a penalty approach on the one hand and with the proposed mapping on the other. Figure 5 shows a typical result. We used a co-variance matrix adaption

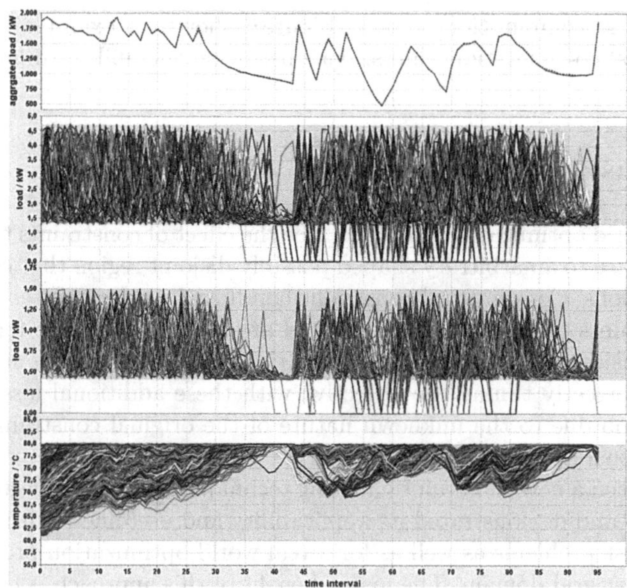

Fig. 6. Power planning result with 750 micro co-generation plants. The top chart shows the target (dotted) as well as the achieved schedule. The load charts in the middle show the individual schedules of two types of chp in the group, the bottom chart shows resulting buffer temperatures. The grey bands denote allowed ranges of values.

evolution strategy (CMA-ES) approach [29] for finding combinations of schedules that best resemble the dashed target schedule in the top chart (Fig. 5(a) and (b)). Both seem to have equally good results, but, looking at individual loads (in middle) and the temperatures (bottom) reveals that the penalty approach gets easily stuck at an (at least partly) infeasible solution whereas the mapping approach succeeds with feasible solutions. This effect amplifies with the number of plants and therefore with the number of used penalties. Moreover, the mapping approach most times converges faster as Fig. 5(c) shows for this specific example.

Considering the complexity, additional computational costs are entailed on solution evaluation. Step 1 of the mapping growing quadratically with the number of support vectors ℓ is decisive together with the number of iterations necessary for finding the pre-image in step 3. Empirically, during our experiments, we observed for instance a mean number of iterations of 6.75 ± 0.3 for the case of the 2-dimensional double banana and 36.3 ± 26.4 for the case of a stretched 8-dimensional ellipse in order to reach convergence with 10^{-8} accuracy. Additionally, this number reduces in the course of optimization as soon as the evolution approaches feasible space. Otherwise, fewer function evaluations are necessary with our decoder approach, because we never evaluate infeasible solutions and we do not have to check feasibility during optimization. Both effects put into perspective the computational costs. Figure 6 shows an example from a scenario with 750 co-generation plants, demonstrating the ability to handle larger problems.

5 Conclusions

Many real world optimization problems face the effect of constraints that restrict the search space to an arbitrary shaped possibly disjoint region that contains the feasible solutions. Conventional constraint handling techniques often require the set of constraints to be a priori known and are hardly applicable for black-box models of feasible regions. Although penalties may be used with such models, the task of correctly tuning the objective with these additional losses stays an error prone job due to the unknown nature of the original constraints that are no longer known at optimization time.

We proposed a new constraint handling technique for support vector modeled search spaces and demonstrated its applicability and usefulness with the help of theoretical test problems as well as for a real world optimization problem taken from the smart grid domain. The major benefit of this approach is the universal applicability for problem transformation, solution repair and standardized integration in arbitrary evolutionary algorithms by constructing a modified objective function and treating the whole unconstrained domain as valid for search. So far, we have restricted ourselves to problems scaled to $[0, 1]^d$. Further tests will show whether this limitation should be kept or whether arbitrary domains perform equally good.

Acknowledgements. The Lower Saxony research network 'Smart Nord' acknowledges the support of the Lower Saxony Ministry of Science and Culture through the Niedersächsisches Vorab grant programme (grant ZN 2764).

References

1. Michalewicz, Z., Schoenauer, M.: Evolutionary algorithms for constrained parameter optimization problems. Evol. Comput. **4**, 1–32 (1996)
2. Kramer, O.: A review of constraint-handling techniques for evolution strategies. Appl. Comp. Intell. Soft Comput. **2010**, 3:1–3:19 (2010)
3. Bremer, J., Rapp, B., Sonnenschein, M.: Support vector based encoding of distributed energy resources' feasible load spaces. In: IEEE PES Conference on Innovative Smart Grid Technologies Europe, Chalmers Lindholmen, Gothenburg, Sweden (2010)
4. Bremer, J., Sonnenschein, M.: Constraint-handling for optimization with support vector surrogate models - a novel decoder approach. In: Filipe, J., Fred, A. (eds.) ICAART 2013 - Proceedings of the 5th International Conference on Agents and Artificial Intelligence. Barcelona, vol. 2, pp. 91–105. SciTePress, Spain (2013)
5. Coello Coello, C.A.: Theoretical and numerical constraint-handling techniques used with evolutionary algorithms: a survey of the state of the art. Comput. Methods Appl. Mech. Eng. **191**, 1245–1287 (2002)

6. Liepins, G.E., Vose, M.D.: Representational issues in genetic optimization. J. Exp. Theor. Artif. Intell. **2**, 101–115 (1990)
7. Koziel, S., Michalewicz, Z.: Evolutionary algorithms, homomorphous mappings, and constrained parameter optimization. Evol. Comput. **7**, 19–44 (1999)
8. Kim, D.G.: Riemann mapping based constraint handling for evolutionary search. In: SAC, pp. 379–385 (1998)
9. Bremer, J., Rapp, B., Sonnenschein, M.: Encoding distributed search spaces for virtual power plants. In: IEEE Symposium Series in Computational Intelligence 2011 (SSCI 2011), Paris, France (2011)
10. Blank, M., Gerwinn, S., Krause, O., Lehnhoff, S.: Support vector machines for an efficient representation of voltage band constraints. In: Innovative Smart Grid Technologies, IEEE PES (2011)
11. Pereira, J., Viana, A., Lucus, B., Matos, M.: A meta-heuristic approach to the unit commitment problem under network constraints. Int. J. Energ. Sect. Manage. **2**, 449–467 (2008)
12. Guan, X., Zhai, Q., Papalexopoulos, A.: Optimization based methods for unit commitment: Lagrangian relaxation versus general mixed integer programming. In: IEEE Power Engineering Society General Meeting, vol. 2, p. 1100 (2003)
13. Tröschel, M., Appelrath, H.-J.: Towards reactive scheduling for large-scale virtual power plants. In: Braubach, L., van der Hoek, W., Petta, P., Pokahr, A. (eds.) MATES 2009. LNCS, vol. 5774, pp. 141–152. Springer, Heidelberg (2009)
14. Kok, K., Derzsi, Z., Gordijn, J., Hommelberg, M., Warmer, C., Kamphuis, R., Akkermans, H.: Agent-based electricity balancing with distributed energy resources, a multiperspective case study. In: Hawaii International Conference on System Sciences, p. 173 (2008)
15. Mihailescu, R.-C., Vasirani, M., Ossowski, S.: Dynamic coalition adaptation for efficient agent-based virtual power plants. In: Klügl, F., Ossowski, S. (eds.) MATES 2011. LNCS, vol. 6973, pp. 101–112. Springer, Heidelberg (2011)
16. Ramchurn, S.D., Vytelingum, P., Rogers, A., Jennings, N.R.: Agent-based control for decentralised demand side management in the smart grid. In: Sonenberg, L., Stone, P., Tumer, K., Yolum, P. (eds.) AAMAS, IFAAMAS, pp. 5–12 (2011)
17. Schölkopf, B., Mika, S., Burges, C., Knirsch, P., Müller, K.R., Rätsch, G., Smola, A.: Input space vs. feature space in kernel-based methods. IEEE Trans. Neural Netw. **10**(5), 1000–1017 (1999)
18. Ben-Hur, A., Siegelmann, H.T., Horn, D., Vapnik, V.: Support vector clustering. J. Mach. Learn. Res. **2**, 125–137 (2001)
19. Juszczak, P., Tax, D., Duin, R.P.W.: Feature scaling in support vector data description. In: Deprettere, E., Belloum, A., Heijnsdijk, J., van der Stappen, F. (eds.) Proceedings of the ASCI 2002, 8th Annual Conference of the Advanced School for Computing and Imaging, pp. 95–102 (2002)
20. Kwok, J., Tsang, I.: The pre-image problem in kernel methods. IEEE Trans. Neural Netw. **15**, 1517–1525 (2004)
21. Mika, S., Schölkopf, B., Smola, A., Müller, K.R., Scholz, M., Rätsch, G.: Kernel PCA and de-noising in feature spaces. In: Proceedings of the 1998 Conference on Advances in Neural Information Processing Systems II. MIT Press, Cambridge, pp. 536–542 (1999)
22. Kennedy, J., Eberhart, R.: Particle swarm optimization. In: Proceedings of the 1995 IEEE International Conference on Neural Networks, vol. 4, IEEE, pp. 1942–1948 (1995)

23. Karaboga, D., Basturk, B.: A powerful and efficient algorithm for numerical function optimization: artificial bee colony (ABC) algorithm. J. Glob. Optim. **39**, 459–471 (2007)
24. Molga, M., Smutnicki, C.: Test functions for optimization needs. Technical report (2005). http://www.zsd.ict.pwr.wroc.pl/files/docs/functions.pdf
25. Michalewicz, Z.: Genetic algorithms + data structures = evolution programs, 3rd edn. Springer, London (1996)
26. Richardson, J.T., Palmer, M.R., Liepins, G.E., Hilliard, M.R.: Some guidelines for genetic algorithms with penalty functions. In: Proceedings of the 3rd International Conference on Genetic Algorithms. Morgan Kaufmann Publishers Inc., San Francisco, pp. 191–197 (1989)
27. Himmelblau, D.: Applied Nonlinear Programming. McGraw-Hill, New York (1972)
28. Thomas, B.: Mini-Blockheizkraftwerke: Grundlagen, Gerätetechnik, Betriebsdaten. Vogel Buchverlag (2007)
29. Hansen, N.: The CMA evolution strategy: a comparing review. In: Lozano, J., Larranaga, P., Inza, I., Bengoetxea, E. (eds.) Towards a new evolutionary computation. Advances in the Estimation of Distribution Algorithms, vol. 192, pp. 75–102. Springer, Heidelberg (2006)

Generation of Learning Situations According to the Learner's Profile Within a Virtual Environment

Kevin Carpentier(✉) and Domitile Lourdeaux

Heudiasyc - UMR CNRS 7253, Université de Technologie de Compiègne, 60200 Compiègne, France
{kevin.carpentier,domitile.lourdeaux}@hds.utc.fr
http://www.hds.utc.fr

Abstract. Some working contexts have such a complexity that initial training cannot prepare the workers to handle every kind of situation they migh encounter. This lack of training comes at a high price and leads to productivity loss or low quality manufacturing in industry. Above all, it may be the cause of major accident in high-risk domains. To prevent this risks, virtual environments for training should provide a wide range of learning situations, especially the hard ones, to train the learner how to cope with them. Our purpose is to generate such situations according to the user's capacities. Drawing on the Zone of Proximal Development, we designed a learner's profile based on a multidimensional space of classes of situations. Each point of the space depicts a belief on the learner's ability to handle a kind of situation.

Keywords: Virtual environment for training · Adaptative · Knowledge model

1 Introduction

Nowadays' working contexts are getting more and more complex, they are composed of a wide range of situations. Training is a major issue in industry for different reasons. It prevents accident in domain where security is critical (high-risk industry, nannies training), it fosters productivity in high-performance industry (aeronautic assembly, submarine maintenance), it also prevents manufacturing defects where customer satisfaction is a key point. Most commonly, in a professional environment, operative attends a short training before getting on the site. They lack of experience and each new situation is difficult to handle because it is a whole new one. It is widely accepted that experience is the most important way to develop professional skills in these domains. By encountering various situations, apprentices may consolidate their knowledge and build their own effective mental representations of the task processing. Moreover, it is accepted that situated learning can offer an efficient learning framework.

J. Filipe and A. Fred (Eds.): ICAART 2013, CCIS 449, pp. 245–260, 2014.
DOI: 10.1007/978-3-662-44440-5_15

As such training is expensive and requires the material to be requistionned, virtual environment for training have been proven to be a good solution to provide learning in complex situations [1].

By simulating the work context, these environments deliver a wide range of real situations. However, providing content is not enough to ensure an efficient learning. The content must be adapted to the learner's profile and historic: what has been learned? What needs to be learned next? Which errors are most commonly made? Besides, the content answering these questions must be provided in an engaging way. Our goal is to generate pedagogical content adapted to the learner level and presented through a story in which the learner will feel involved. The content proposed must enable learners to meet many and varied kinds of situations and keep their motivation at a high level. To fulfill this requirement, we propose to dynamically generate relevant learning situations with regard of the learner's trace and learning objectives. A relevant learning situation is a set of states of the world that will test a subset of skills and knowledge in a efficient and engaging way. As our works fits in the situated learning theory, we considered that each learner builds his own mental representation in disregard of an elicitation of knowledge and skills. Thus, it makes it difficult to control knowledge acquisition. Another issue is to ensure that the generated content is relevant, which means it fulfills both pedagogical and narrative requirements. This also raised the underlying question about the balance between narrative and motivational factors and pedagogical needs.

SELDON, standing for ScEnario and Learning situations adaptation through Dynamic OrchestratioN, aim to generate and control scenario within a virtual environment. As part of the SELDON model, we propose the TAILOR model to generate a *canvas* which is a sequence of constraints on the state of the world, called situations, that should be met or prevented to facilitate knowledge learning and skills acquisition. The canvas is then used by the other part of SELDON, a scenario planner, DIRECTOR [2] to constrain the simulation. This paper presents our contribution on activities selection based on belief about learner's aptitudes and pedagogical needs. In Sect. 2 we present how our contribution positions in relation to different approaches on adaptive scenarisation. Then, we introduce the overall process of situation constraints generation and present a detailled method of selection of the constraints depending on pedagogical needs in Sect. 3. Section 4 shows an illustration of this selection through the case of nannies training. Then we will present the perspectives we foresee to extend this work and conclude over the whole contribution.

2 Related Works

Adaptive scenarisation is the process of reacting to user's actions to provide content fitted to their need. In videogames, it might be used to adjust difficulty according to player's level without using typical discrete mode such as "Easy", "Hard", etc. With adaptive features, players are always in the *flow* [3]: the difficulty remains high enough to propose a suitable challenge, yet, players can overcome it so that they do not get bored or frustrated. Such a concept might be used to adapt difficulty in a training session so that learners keep a high level of motivation. The system can propose activities that are always difficult enough to challenge the learner but always manageable to prevent frustration and loss of motivation. Our objective is twofold: providing adapted content (1) and presenting this content in such a manner it does not cut the user from the flow and, moreover, motivate him (2).

The adaptation can be made at different levels of granularity. A first approach is to have a *global adaptation*: a whole scenario has been written [4] or generated [5] and the outcomes of the events were scripted beforehand. This approach allows the building of a scaffolding scenario which present many advantages:

- *Pedagogical Coherence:* the scenario ensures a progressive learning through the session, assistance can be given easily at relevant key points;
- *Narrative Involvement:* it is therefore possible to unfold the event as a story which will involve the learner.

A main drawback is the lack of reactivity of the system. As the whole session has been planned, the system cannot reorient the scenario to adapt to the very current learner's state. The only way to cope with it is to foresee each possible path which can represent a huge amount of work. An opposite approach is to provide *reactive adaptation* by controlling the outcomes of learner's actions. It enables:

- *Dynamic Adaptation:* the system triggers outcomes of learner's actions and provides assistances depending on pedagogical needs.

For example, in the application V3S [6], the triggering of a hasardous matter leak is computed in real-time by HERA [7], an intelligent tutoring system, according to a learner's model.

The simulation where the adaptation takes place can be run with opposite approaches: the *controlled approaches* versus the *emergent approaches.*

The *controlled approach* aims to provide a very efficient learning by orchestrating each part of the simulation: state of the objects, virtual character's behaviours, possibilities of action the learner, etc. It permits:

- *Pedagogical Control:* each element of the simulation serves the scenario and pedagogical needs.

This approach which is used in the Generic Virtual Training [8] helps building pedagogically efficient scenarios but disables the possibility to encounter unintended - though relevant - situations. Moreover, such an approach demands an exhaustive modeling of the world functionment which handicaps the evolutivity of the system. The whole modeling has to be reconsidered to avoid incoherence each time an author adds new contents. Any attempt to interfere with the simulation can cause incoherence for the learner: virtual characters become unpredictible, states of objects changes with no coherent reason. As a result, there is no way to explain *a posteriori* the unfolding of events. These explanations are critical for the learner to understand causes and consequences of events and actions and they can be provided at the end of the session or reviewed by a teacher.

By a clever modelling of small behaviors of the world, *emergent approaches* allow new situations to arise [9]. It also enables:

- *Freedom of Action:* learners are not framed by the task they are supposed to do, they can experiment and discover the outcomes of their actions;
- *Autonomous Virtual Characters:* as they are not being controlled by a supervisor, virtual characters maintain their autonomy and their behaviours remain coherent throughout the simulation run.

The issue with emergent approaches is the lack of pedagogical control. The simulation runs itself according to initial parameters and there is no way to orchestrate the events to adapt the simulation to the current learner's state. Each of these approaches has attractive features but none of them fulfills our requirements as explained below.

3 Proposition

3.1 Approach

Our work aims to provide a relevant adaptation at different level of granularity. At the lowest level, adaptation should modulate the consequences of the actions of the learner, this means an even set of events might have different outcomes depending of the expertise of the learner. Then, the adaptation must work on a middle level basis by producing complex sequences of events leading to a specific learning in a session. Finally, skills development requires a learner to follow a path of different learning situations during different learning sessions, the adaptation should also provide information about the path to follow between different sessions. For this purpose, we will try to adopt a balanced approach which is both *global* and *local.*

Besides, learners should have a total freedom and the system must react as it would in reality to help them to develop skills from their mistakes. Technical, organisational and human systems are getting more and more complex in working context. An exhaustive explicitation of each possible scenarios beforehand would result in a combinatorial explosion. To address the growing complexity of such systems, we chose to model them through an emergent approach. However, as our purpose is to provide an efficient situated learning, we must ensure that relevant assistances are provided to learners as they would be provided in a working context. Moreover, we need to orchestrate dynamically the course of the training to adapt to current learner state. This can only be achieved by controlling the flow of events to some extent. We need to adopt an *emergent* approach to model the world but we want to provide pedagogical *control* over it.

To be able to have both global and local adaptation with pedagogical control over an emergent simulation, we propose to orient dynamically the simulation towards specific situations which are consistant with the current state of the world, without breaking the coherence of neither object states nor the behaviour of virtual characters. This is the purpose of SELDON, standing for ScEnario and Learning situation adaptation through Dynamic OrchestratioN, which is a part of the HUMANS platform described below.

3.2 HUMANS Framework

The HUman Models-based Artificial eNvironments Software platform is dedicated to the simulation of virtual environments within complex domains where human factors are critical. HUMANS platform allows high cognitive virtual characters and learners to coexist in a simulation.

HUMANS uses three models which were designed to be informed by domain experts (ergonomists, didacticians, etc.):

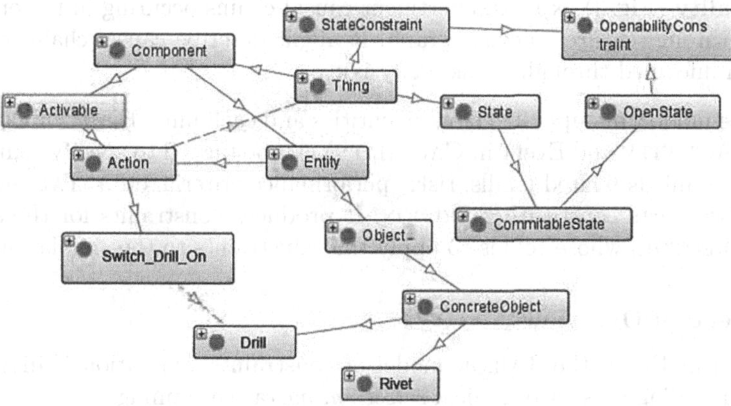

Fig. 1. Part of an ontological representation of DOMAIN.

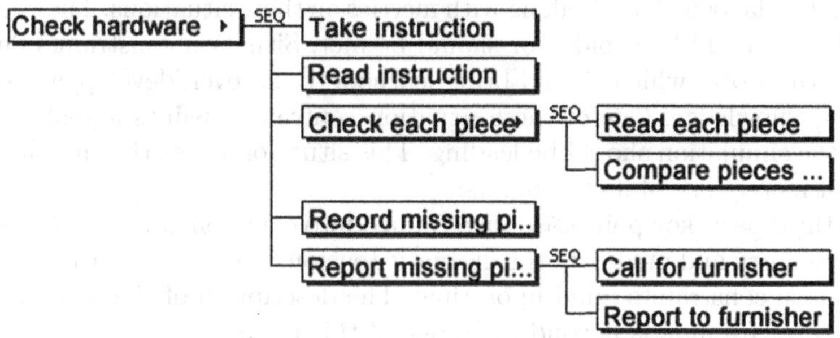

Fig. 2. Hierarchical representation of ACTIVITY.

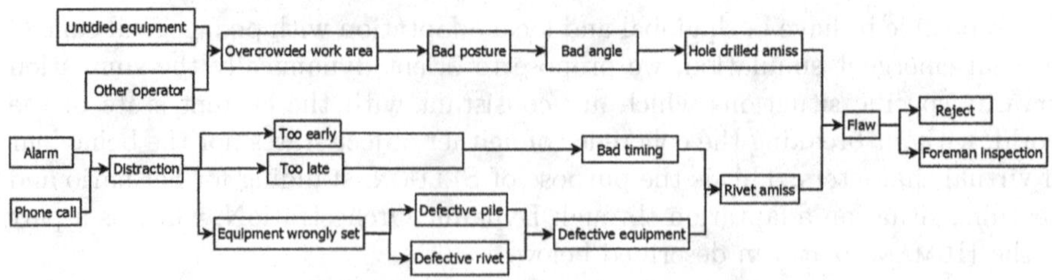

Fig. 3. Graph representation of CAUSALITY.

- **Domain** (Fig. 1) describes the world in a static way, the object, physical or abstract, that exists in the world and the relations between them through an ontology. It also includes a dynamic description: possible actions, the behaviours these actions trigger and events that might occur through rules;
- **Activity** (Fig. 2) uses a hierarchical representation of the task to describe the activity as observed on a real site and not as depicted in procedures and protocols. The basic tasks are the actions referenced in DOMAIN;
- **Causality** (Fig. 3) expresses pertinent causal chains occuring in the environment through a direct acyclic graph. It might describe causal chains of risks (when informed through a risk analysis);

These models manipulate common entities and each unit (Entity in DOMAIN, Task in ACTIVITY and Event in CAUSALITY) can be tagged to specify something to which a unit is related (skills, risks, performance criteria, etc.). TAILOR is the first of two parts constituting SELDON. It produces constraints for the second part, DIRECTOR, whose role is to apply this constraints to the simulation.

3.3 General Overview

As shown in Fig. 4, the TAILOR model of constraints generation is divided in three parts: diagnosis, pedagogical selection, narrative framing.

The first part updates a dynamic model based on the Zone Of Proximal Development to establish a diagnosis of learner's capacities.

Second part computes this model to determine a set of situation constraints that fulfill pedagogical needs along with metrics on these situations. They describe if situations should be avoided or should be met. Situation constraints describe states of the world which should bring learners to discover/develop/use specific skills and knowledge. One of these situation contraints defines a goal situation toward the simulation should be leading. This situation is not the end of the scenario but merely one of its key points.

In a third part, key points are then framed into common narrative patterns to generate a story and modulate the dramatic tension. The canvas is the succession of situations constraints build upon time. The description of the metrics and of the narrative framing is beyond the scope of this paper.

We present in the following subsection a model for selecting a goal situation according to a uncertain learner's model.

3.4 Description of the Pedagogical Process

Input Data. The dynamic mechanism of selection of activities underlying TAILOR lies on both inputs from the learner and the teacher.

- *Learner's inputs:* each session of training the learner follows is recorded through a trace based on HERA model [7]. As the model is based on activity analysis, traces identify *previous situations encountered*, *errors*, *causes and consequences*, *risk produced.* Traces are also enriched with activity traces of virtual characters as well as the tracking of causal chains within the environment;
- *Teacher's inputs:* the teacher can influence the simulation beforehand at different levels: he can select *situations* which should be encounter during the session in the CAUSALITY model, *task* to be performed in ACTIVITY model and *performance criteria* to favour.

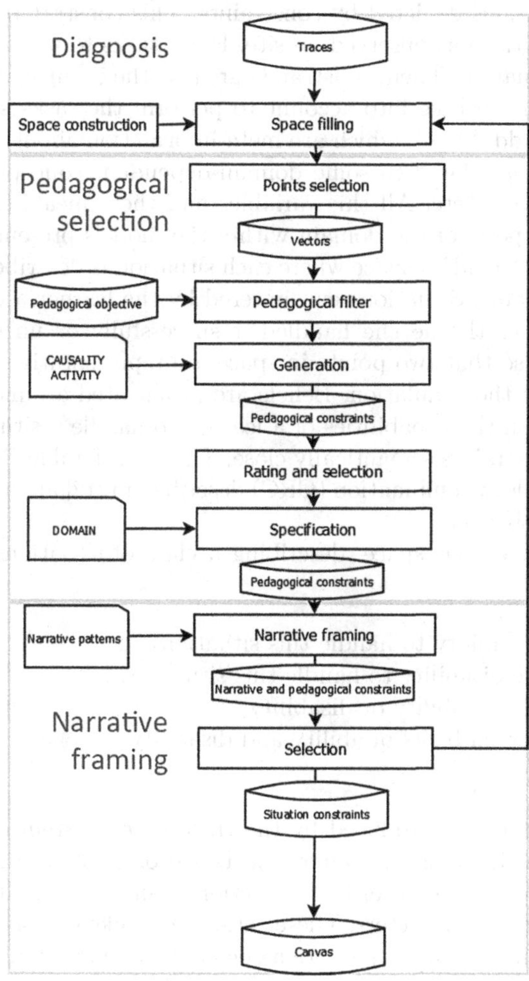

Fig. 4. General overview.

Diagnosis. On this purpose, the first matter is to establish and maintain a diagnosis of learner's current level of knowledge. As seen in [10], most systems use an elicitation of knowledge, of the influences they have between each other and of the events which are clues of learning.

Actually, we fit our work in the paradigm of situated learning, it would be paradoxal to build a model of skills and knowledge acquisition. Moreover, we want to produce a progressive learning individualized to each learner. Vygotsky proposes the model of Zone Proximal of Development (ZPD) [11] for the context of education in which a student can develop skills inside its confort zone and enlarge it by the help of the teacher. We think the ZPD can be used in a more general learning context than education and that the teacher, which is responsible of the scaffolding, might be played by virtual scaffolding and by an dynamic scenarisation of events. To operationnalize this approach, we choose to deal with a belief the system has in the capabilities of a learner to handle a certain class of situations depicted by constraints. This constraints include all the variable of a situations as observed on site. First, tasks to perform are an obvious variable of situation. Then, constraints are also the cognitive variables which are the parameters to take into account to perform the tasks successfully. We finally choose to add "tags", which are meta-information about task. They help defining if a task is related to some domain-dependant concept such as *Quality*, *Safety*, *Cleanness*, etc. All this variables and there meanings are informed by pedagogical experts of the domain within the models presented in Sect. 3.2. These constraints "mold" a space where each situation is described by is component for each variable. Situations encountered by the learner are reported with a belief on whether the he/she handled it successfully or unsucessfully. This space is designed so that two points in space are representative of semantically close situations in the simulation. Beliefs are propagated around each point to estimate a belief on the capabilities of a learner to handle a situation matching another set of constraints semantically close. The Transferable Belief Model and the conjunctive rule of combination (CRC) described in [12] are used to represent and udpate these beliefs.

For each point of this space, describing a class of situations, we have four values:

- a - Belief on the ability to handle this situation,
- d - Belief on the disability to handle this situation,
- i - Ignorance, either ability or disability
- c - Conflict between belief of ability and disability

With $a + d + i + c = 1$

TAILOR parses traces produced by the trace-based system called MONITOR that exists within the HUMANS framework. Based on ACTIVITY and CAUSALITY models, MONITOR aims to record every action agents makes whether they are real learners or virtual characters. These actions are linked to task and high-level tasks in the activity hierarchy and are associated to a potentiality to trigger an error, a risk or affecting a performance criteria. Each trace is used as a source of information to update the beliefs about a class of situations. New values are compute according to the application of the conjunctive rule of combination as shown in Eqs. (1, 2, 3 and 4).

$$a_{new} = a_{cur} * a_{source} + i_{cur} * a_{source} + i_{source} * a_{cur} \tag{1}$$

$$d_{new} = d_{cur} * d_{source} + i_{cur}r * d_{source} + i_{source} * d_{cur} \tag{2}$$

$$i_{new} = i_{cur} * i_{source} \tag{3}$$

$$c_{new} = 1 - h_{new} - d_{new} - i_{new} \tag{4}$$

Where $h_{cur}, d_{cur}, i_{cur}$ are the current values, $h_{source}, d_{source}, i_{source}$ are values provided by the trace and $h_{new}, d_{new}, i_{new}, c_{new}$ are the updated values.

The association between beliefs and the multidimensionnal space described above draws our ZPD we call *zpd-space.*

3.5 Pedagogical Selection of Activities

As the learner progresses throughout activities and sessions, the space is filled with points and associated beliefs are updated thanks to the monitoring module.

TAILOR will then select a set of points in this space to generate a new situation. The difficulty lies in determining which points will produce an efficient learning. The selection is made based on the 4 values aforementionned using pedagogical rules.

- Points where belief has a high ignorance-value are not likely to be interesting;
- Points where belief has a high ability-value are not interesting to produce new learning, but they can be used in the beginning of the session to make the learner at ease;
- Points where belief has a high disability-value are interesting, because they are the proof of an error, a violation and more generally a misconception. Depending on specific pedagogical rules, the situation will be avoided or, on the contrary, a learning situation will be generate to break the misconception through an assistance;
- Points where belief has a high conflict-value are interesting. Mathematically, it means the different sources of information are contradictory. In our case, it means the learner is able to handle a situation in a specific context but a misconception prevent him from using the same skills in another context.

A set of pedagogical rules helps selecting relevant points according to these values and pedagogical objectives. After this filtering, TAILOR compute DOMAIN, ACTIVITY and CAUSALITY model to determine which events and which activities responds to these constraints.

Output Data. At each iteration, TAILOR generates a set of *situation constraints* associated to a desirability which represent how desired this state of the world is (see Table 1). A negative value describe a situation that should be avoid. One situation is tagged as the goal situation. A situation is depicted by a subset of triple describing a specific state of the world using the formalism of DOMAIN.

Table 1. Situations and desirability.

Situation constraints	Desirability
Sit_1	$D_1 \in [-1, 1]$
...	...
Sit_n	$D_n \in [-1, 1]$
Sit_{Goal}	1

4 Example: Training in Aeronautics Assembly

For the purpose of the NIKITA (Natural Interaction, Knowledge and Immersion in Training for Aeronautics) we applied the model generation to a scenario of airplane assembly operative training. The LATI lab of Paris-Descartes University made a torough study of the work environment in Méaulte (Picardy, France) facility of the AEROLIA group. Their analyses, video and comments made possible the authoring of the DOMAIN model and the ACTIVITY tree of the operatives. The Méaulte facility capabilities are mainly the assembly of the

Fig. 5. A screenshot of NIKITA - Aeronautics training simulator.

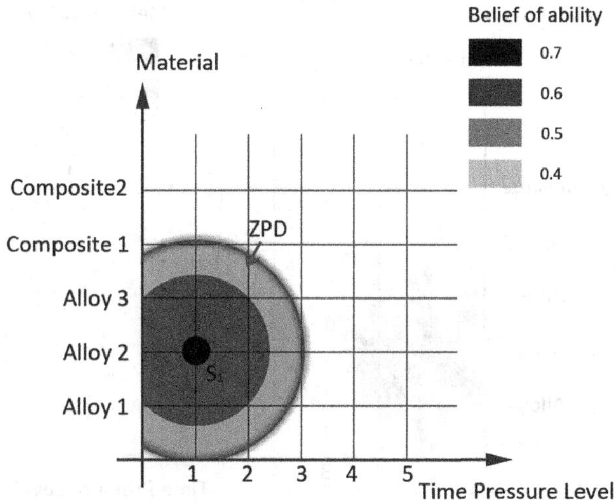

Fig. 6. ZPD-space initialisation in aeronautics training simulator.

nose fuselage and of the lower shell fuselage. Those fuselage has been made of composite panel since 2010. The NIKITA application aims to train the operative to perform riveting task on various material (Fig. 5). The LATI Lab runs an analysis based on conceptual structure for the representation [13]. We use this information to design a zpd-space. For the sake of the example, we will only focus on two dimensions of the zpd-space. The first dimension we consider, named *Material*, depicts the different materials on which the learner has to work. These include common alloy but also composite material which requires special care. The second dimension, named *Time Pressure*, depicts the level of time which is set upon the operative to perform his work. The pedagogical objective has arbitrarily been set to *Material* = *Composite*. In the following example M stand for the Material axis and TPL for the Time Pressure Level axis.

Step 1: Initialisation. In this example we consider there is no conflict, and that the learner has successfully handled situation S_1 (Fig. 6). The darker the color the surer the system knows that the learner will be able to handle a situation generated from this point. Blank areas express the lack ok knowledge about the learners habilities. The ZPD is where the belief on the ability of the learner is beyond a threshold (0.4 in this case).

Step 2. In regard of the pedagogical objectives, which here emphasize on $M = Composite$, the system selects points to privilege this kind of situation. The point $(M = Composite1, TPL = 1)$ is selected (Fig. 7). By computing the ACTIVITY model, TAILOR determines tasks requiring a $(M = Composite1, TPL = 1)$ set of skills. The task "Drilling the front bark on the A3YY" is an activity that

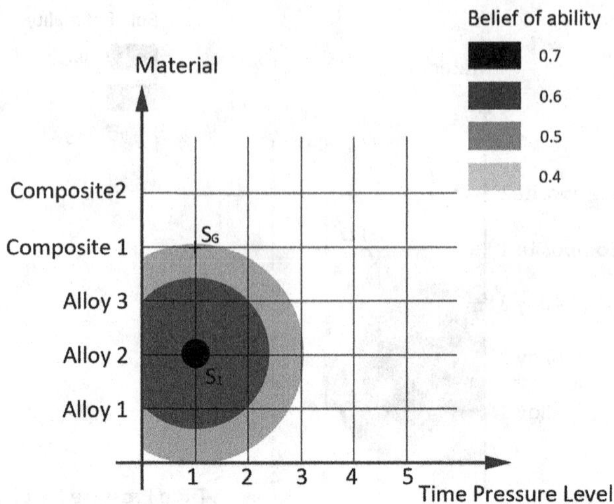

Fig. 7. Situations generation.

fulfills this requirement. In regard with this, the scene is initialized with a bark of an A3YY where the learner would be asked to fix a support on the bark.

```
Situations
  Goal
      Desirability:1
      States:
              (?prescription :has-task ?Fix_piece)
 (?Fix_piece :has-support Support01)
              (?Fix_piece :has-bark ?Bark01)
              (Bark01 :has-type :composite)
              (?prescription :has-delivering-delay ?time)
              (?time :has-hour"24")
```

Step 3. The learner reacted well to the previously generated situation by making good quality drilling and taking into account specificities of composite material, the ZPD-space is updated. The point $SG(M = Composite1, TPL = 3)$ is now selected (Fig. 8), the system has a belief of 0.4 for the learner to handle this class of situations. This class of situations will allow the evaluation of the capacities of the learner to work with composite material with a time pressure. By computing the ACTIVITY model, TAILOR determines that time pressure is induced when the delivering delay is reduces and the foreman ask for a quicker delivering (which is an action called *AskForHaste*). But, a "rush" in work may cause an overcrowded workspace by virtual agent which will react to the new state of the world, yet this is not the kind of situation that has to be encountered. TAILOR generate another constraints to keep the crowd level in workspace low.

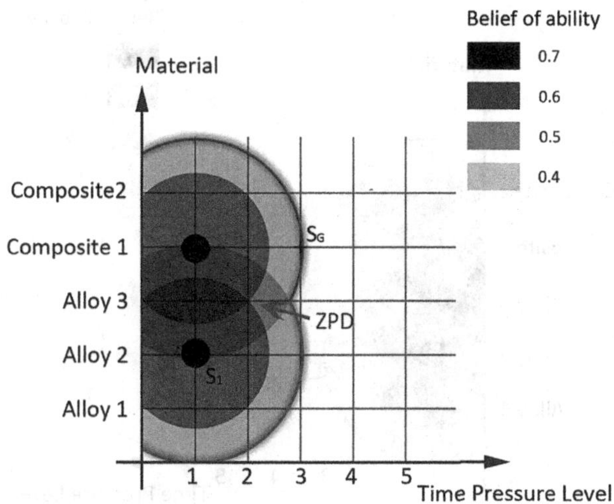

Fig. 8. ZPD-space udpate and new activities selection.

```
Situations
   Goal
       Desirability:1
       States:
              (?prescrition rdf:type :Prescription)
              (?prescription :has-task ?Fix_piece)
 (?Fix_piece :has-support :Support01)
              (?Fix_piece :has-bark ?Bark01)
              (Bark01 :has-type :composite)
              (?prescription :has-delivering-delay ?time)
              (?time :has-hour "18")
   Situation1
Desirability:-1
       States:
(:Learner00 :has-workspace ?w)
             (?w :has-crowd ?number)
             greater(?number,4)
Events
      (?evt rdf:type :AskForHaste)
      (?evt :agent :Foreman01)
      (?evt :cible :Learner00)
```

Final Step. In order to deal with the time pressure, the learner choose not to do some specific tasks. These task are allowed not to be done when handling common material. But, these task are mandatory when handling composite material. This shows a lack in the knowledge of the learner. The ZPD-space

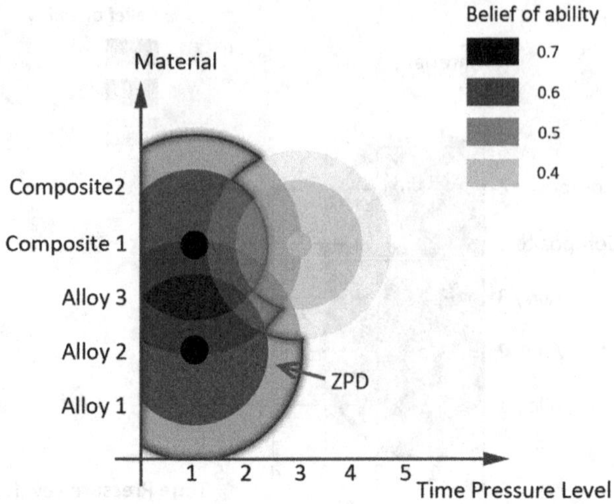

Fig. 9. End of training session.

is updated accordingly (Fig. 9). In order to prevent future mistake, TAILOR propose to trigger crack in the panel. Thus, the learner will likely understand that more care were needed. In the ZPD-Space, the information of a remediation has been recorded for this class of situations ($M = Composite1, TPL = 3$). The effectiveness of the remediation will be tested in a further training session.

5 Perspectives and Future Works

The ZPD-space we are currently using are designed by-hand according to the knowledge models informed by didacticians and ergonomists, i.e., we choose the axis, their scale and their meaning. Future works will explore how to generate those axis automatically by parsing our knowledge models. The issue is that some variables migh correlated which may add a flow on our process. We may use data analysis method such as principal component analysis [14] to build a new space with uncorrelated variables.

Selection of activities is the first part of our work. To provide adapted content is essential but to involve the learner, we need to use motivational factors. Modulating the dramatic tension is a possible solution. To create tension, a story must be built upon the events and the world depicted within the simulation. The aim is to provide an interest for the learner by showing the virtual characters as story characters who can be helpers or opponents, the events as plot points that will increase or decrease the tension. We plan to use narrative pattern, as described by [15,16] or [17] to extends current pedagogicial situations. The element described by the situations will be fitted with element from a pattern such as *location*, *helpers*, *opponents*, *goal*,etc. For one pedagogical situation, many narrative configurations are possible. We will use a measure of the narrative utility based on earlier events in the simulation. The utility will maximize if it furthers the development of the story depicted in past events without disrupting the whole coherence.

6 Conclusions

We proposed in this paper a model to dynamically generate scenarios in a virtual environment regarding learner's capacities. The process uses a phase of diagnosis which compute traces at the initialisation and in real time. It operationnalizes the theory of zone of proximal development through a multidimensionnal space of beliefs, updated at each task performed by the learner within the virtual environment. Then the system computes current world state to determine which situation can take place to answer ZPD and pedagogical objectives requirements. We build a first prototype within the HUMANS platform working on the example of aeronautics assembly. Our future works will focus in the narratives consideration by framing the successive situations in a narrative pattern to relate a story. Besides, we are exploring new method to build the zpd-space.

Acknowledgements. This work is part of the ANR project: NIKITA (Natural Interaction, Knowledge and Immersive systems for Training in Aeronautic). Partners are: Heudiasyc, Paris Descartes University, CEA-LIST, Emissive, EADS, AEROLIA and the technical school Henry Potez. We want to thank Catherine Delgoulet and Vincent Boccara from the LATI for their torough analysis which enable us to build our use-case.

References

1. Amokrane, K., Lourdeaux, D.: Virtual reality contribution to training and risk prevention. In: Proceedings of the 2009 International Conference on Artificial Intelligence (2009)
2. Barot, C., Lourdeaux, D., Lenne, D.: Dynamic scenario adaptation balancing control, coherence and emergence. In: Proceedings of the 5th International Conference on Agents and Artificial Intelligence (2013)
3. Csikszentmihalyi, M.: Flow: The Psychology of Optimal Experience. Harper Perennial, New York (1991)
4. Marion, N.: Modélisation de Scénarios Pédagogiques pour les Environnements de Réalité Virtuelle d'Apprentissage Humain, Ph.D. thesis, Université de Bretagne Occidentale (2010)
5. Niehaus, J.M., Li, B., Riedl, M.O.: Automated scenario adaptation in support of intelligent tutoring systems. In: Proceedings of the 24th Conference of the Florida Artificial Intelligence Research Society, Palm Beach, Florida (2011)
6. Barot, C., Burkhardt, J.-M., Lourdeaux, D., Lenne, D.: V3S, a virtual environment for risk management training. In: JVRC11: Joint Virtual Reality Conference of EGVE - EuroVR, Nottingham (2011)
7. Amokrane, K., Lourdeaux, D.: Pedagogical system in virtual environment for high-risk sites. In: Proceedings of the 2nd International Conference on Agents and Artificial Intelligence (2010)

8. Gerbaud, S., Mollet, N., Ganier, F., Arnaldi, B., Tisseau, J.: GVT: a platform to create virtual environments for procedural training. In: IEEE Virtual Reality, pp. 225–232. IEEE Press, New York (2008)
9. Shawver, D.: Virtual actors and avatars in a flexible user-determined-scenario environment. In: Virtual Reality Annual International Symposium (1997)
10. Brusilovsky, P., Millán, E.: User models for adaptive hypermedia and adaptive educational systems. In: Brusilovsky, P., Kobsa, A., Nejdl, W. (eds.) Adaptive Web 2007. LNCS, vol. 4321, pp. 3–53. Springer, Heidelberg (2007)
11. Vygotsky, L.S.: Mind in Society. Harvard University Press, Cambridge (1978)
12. Smets, P., Kennes, R.: The transferable belief model. Artif. Intell. **66**, 191–234 (1994)
13. Pastré, P.: La Conceptualisation dans l'Action: Bilan et Nouvelles Perspectives. Éducation Permanente **139**, 13–35 (1999)
14. Pearson, K.: On lines and planes of closest fit to systems of points in space. Phil. Mag. **2**(11), 559–572 (1901)
15. Campbell, J.: The Hero With a Thousand Faces. New World Library, Novato (2008)
16. Propp, V.I.: Morphology of the Folktale. University of Texas Press, Austin (1968)
17. Greimas, A.J.: Sémantique structurale: recherche et méthode, Larousse edition (1966)

Sentence Reduction Algorithms to Improve Multi-document Summarization

Sara Botelho Silveira[1,2(✉)] and António Branco[1,2]

[1] University of Lisbon, Lisbon, Portugal
[2] Edifício C6, Departamento de Informática, Faculdade de Ciências, Universidade de Lisboa, Campo Grande, 1749-016 Lisbon, Portugal
{sara.silveira,antonio.branco}@di.fc.ul.pt
http://nlx.di.fc.ul.pt/

Abstract. Multi-document summarization aims to create a single summary based on the information conveyed by a collection of texts. After the candidate sentences have been identified and ordered, it is time to select which will be included in the summary. In this paper, we describe an approach that uses sentence reduction, both lexical and syntactic, to help improve the compression step in the summarization process. Three different algorithms are proposed and discussed. Sentence reduction is performed by removing specific sentential constructions conveying information that can be considered to be less relevant to the general message of the summary. Thus, the rationale is that sentence reduction not only removes expendable information, but also makes room for further relevant data in a summary.

Keywords: Sentence reduction · Compression · Multi-document summarization

1 Introduction

The increased use of mobile devices brought concerns about text compression, by providing less space for the same amount of text. Compression must be accurate and all the information displayed should be essential. Multi-document text summarization seeks to identify the most relevant information in a collection of texts, complying with a compression rate that determines the length of the summary.

Ensuring at the same time the compression rate and the informativeness of the summary is not an easy task. The most common solution allows the last sentence to be cut in two in the number of words, where the exact compression rate has been reached, compromising the fluency and grammaticality of the summary, and thus the quality of the final text. An alternative is the one where the last candidate sentence is kept in full, surpassing the compression rate. None of these solutions is optimal. Compromising the compression rate by enhancing the quality of the text may not introduce relevant information. Still, compromising

J. Filipe and A. Fred (Eds.): ICAART 2013, CCIS 449, pp. 261–276, 2014.
DOI: 10.1007/978-3-662-44440-5_16

the quality of the text can be troublesome for a user wanting to make use of the summary.

Given this, our proposal is to use sentence reduction to compress the extracted sentences down to their main content only, so that more information can fit into the summary, producing a more informative text. After the summarization process has determined the most significant sentences, sentential structures, that are less essential to figure in the summary's short space, can be removed.

The rationale behind using sentence reduction in a summarization context is twofold. On the one hand, it removes expendable information, generating a simpler and easier to read text. On the other hand, it allows the addition of more individual (reduced) sentences to the summary, that otherwise have not been included. Experiments made with human users [1] have shown that reduction indeed helps to improve the summaries produced.

Note that, sentence reduction is also referred in the literature as sentence compression. In this work, the expression "sentence reduction" is used to define "sentence compression", in order to distinguish it from "compression" itself. We name "compression" as the step that follows reduction in the summarization process, where the sentences identified as the most relevant ones are selected, based on a predefined compression rate, thus compressing the initial set of sentences contained in the collection of texts submitted as input.

At this point, consider the following list of sentences that can be part of the summary:

1. EU leaders signed a new treaty to control budgets on Friday.
2. Only Britain and the Czech Republic opted out of the pact, signed in Brussels at a summit of EU leaders.
3. UK Prime Minister David Cameron, who with the Czechs refused to sign it, said his proposals for cutting red tape and promoting business had been ignored.
4. The countries signed up to a promise to anchor in their constitutions – if possible – rules to stop their public deficits and debt spiralling out of control in the way that led to the eurozone crisis.
5. The treaty must now be ratified by the parliaments of the signatory countries.

This list contains 105 words. However, a compression rate of 80 % of the original text states that the summary must only contain 84 words. As the sum of the words of the three first sentences (57 words) does not meet the desired total number of words for the summary, the fourth sentence is also added. Yet, by adding the fourth sentence, the summary makes up 92 words, so the total number of words defined by the compression rate has been surpassed in 9 words. The first option would be to cut the last nine words of the last sentence. That would produce an incorrect sentence.

There are particular constructions that can be removed from these sentences making room for the inclusion of more relevant information. Appositions, parenthetical phrases and relative clauses are examples of those constructions. Consider, for instance, the following expressions candidates for removal:

- The parenthetical phrase: *signed in Brussels at a summit of EU leaders.*
- The relative clause: *who with the Czechs refused to sign.*
- The parenthetical phrase: *if possible.*

These expressions sum a total of 18 words. The last sentence that has not been added to the summary sums a total of 13 words. So, if all these expressions were removed from the sentences, we would have been able to include in the summary the last sentence. Otherwise that sentence would not be included in the final text, despite being relevant to the overall informativeness of the summary.

The summary, in which sentences have been simplified, contains 84 words and is shown below:

EU leaders signed a new treaty to control budgets on Friday. Only Britain and the Czech Republic opted out of the pact. UK Prime Minister David Cameron said his proposals for cutting red tape and promoting business had been ignored. The countries signed up to a promise to anchor in their constitutions rules to stop their public deficits and debt spiraling out of control in the way that led to the eurozone crisis. The treaty must now be ratified by the signatory countries' parliaments.

In a pilot study [2], Lin showed the potential of sentence reduction to improve a multi-document summarization system, using a noisy-channel model approach. Also, [3] used a machine learning approach to perform sentence extraction and compression for multi-document summarization, which proved to be effective in improving the quality of the summaries produced.

In a different perspective, [4] demonstrated that "a hybrid approach to sentence compression – explicitly modeling linguistic knowledge – rather than a fully data-driven approach" is the better way to perform sentence reduction.

As shown in the summary, it is possible to produce a summary containing the maximum relevant information conveyed by the original collection of texts. Hence, this summary can be a comprehensible and fluent one.

Thus, this work uses an hybrid approach by combining a statistical parser, that was trained on a specific corpus, with linguistic rules designed based on the output of the parser, defining the structure of the phenomena taken into account in this procedure.

Sentence reduction condenses, then, the initial summary, in order to produce a new text containing simpler, more precise and more concise sentences, and conveying only the essential information.

This paper is organized as follows: Sect. 2 reports the related work; Sect. 3 overviews the summarization process; Sect. 4 details the algorithms experimented in the context of sentence reduction; Sect. 5 describes a pilot study involving the three algorithms; Sect. 6 argues about the pros and cons of each algorithm; and, finally, in Sect. 7, some final conclusions are drawn.

2 Related Work

Text simplification is an Natural Language Processing (NLP) task that aims at making a text shorter and more readable by simplifying its sentences structurally, while preserving as much as possible the meaning of the original sentence. This task is commonly addressed in two ways: lexical and syntactic simplification. Lexical simplification involves replacing infrequent words by their simpler more common and accessible synonyms. Syntactic simplification, in turn, includes a linguistic analysis of the input texts, that produces detailed tree-structure representations, over which transformations can be made [5]. Syntactic simplification can also be named after sentence reduction.

Previous works ([6,7]) have focused on syntactic simplification, targeting specific types of structures identified using rules induced through an annotated aligned corpus of complex and simplified texts.

Jing and McKeown [8] used simplification in a single-document summarizer, by performing operations, based on the analysis of human abstracts, that remove inessential phrases from the sentences. Blair-Goldensohn et al. [9] remove appositives and relative clauses in a preprocessing phase of a multi-document summarization process. Another proposal is the one of [10], that combine a simplification method, that uses shallow parsing to detect lexical cues that trigger phrase eliminations, with an HMM sentence selection approach, to create multi-document summaries.

Closer to our work is the work of [11], in which sentence simplification is applied together with summarization. However, they used simplification to improve content selection, that is, before extracting sentences to be summarized. Their simplification system is based on syntactic simplification performed using hand-crafted rules that specify relations between simplified sentences.

Zajic et al. [12] applied sentence compression techniques to multi-document summarization, using a parse-and-trim approach to generate headlines for news stories. Constituents are removed iteratively from the sentence parse tree, using rules that perform lexical simplification – by replacing temporal expressions, preposed adjuncts, determiners, conjunctions, modal verbs –, and syntactic simplification – by selecting specific phenomena in the parse tree.

A different approach was used by [13], that experimented a tree-to-tree transduction method for sentence compression. They trained a model that uses a synchronous tree substitution grammar, which allows local distortions of a tree topology, used to capture structural mismatches between trees.

A word graph method, to create a single simplified sentence of a cluster of similar or related sentences, was used by [14]. Considering all the words in these related sentences, a directed word graph is built by linking word A to word B through an adjacency relation, in order to avoid redundancy. This method was used to avoid redundancy in the summaries produced.

Lloret [15] proposed a text summarization system that combines textual entailment techniques, to detect and remove information, with term frequency metrics used to identify the main topics in the collection of texts. In addition, a word graph method is used to compress and fuse information, in order to produce abstract summaries.

More recently, [16] investigated the usage of a machine translation technique to perform sentence simplification. They created a method for simplifying sentences by using Phrase Based Machine Translation, along with a re-ranking heuristic based on dissimilarity. Then, they trained it on a monolingual parallel corpus, and achieved state-of-the-art results.

Finally, [17] proposed new semantic constraints, to perform sentence compression. These constraints are based on semantic roles, in order to directly capture the relations between a predicate and its arguments.

3 Summarization Process

The system used is an extractive multi-document summarizer that receives a collection of texts in Portuguese and produces highly informative summaries.

Summarization is performed by means of two main phases executed in sequence: clustering by similarity and clustering by keywords. Aiming to avoid redundancy, sentences are clustered by similarity, and only one sentence from each cluster is selected. Yet, the keyword clustering phase seeks to identify the most relevant content within the input texts. The keywords of the input texts are retrieved and the sentences that are successfully grouped to a keyword cluster are selected to be used in the next step of the process. Furthermore, each sentence has a score, which is computed using the *tf-idf* (term frequency – inverse document frequency) of each sentence word, smoothed by the number of words in the sentence. This score defines the relevance of each sentence and it is thus used to order all the sentences. Afterwards, the reduction process detailed in Sect. 4 is performed, producing the final summary. A detailed description of this extractive summarization process can be found in [18].

4 Sentence Reduction

In this work, reduction is performed together with compression.

Firstly, from the original input list of sentences, a new list is created, by selecting one sentence at the time, until the total number of words in the list surpasses the maximum number of words determined by the compression rate.

Afterwards, sentences are reduced by removing the expendable information in view of the general summarization purpose. There are a number of structures that can be seen as containing "elaborative" information about the content already expressed.

Due to the fact that reduction removes words from the sentence, once sentences have been reduced, new sentences are added to the list of sentences to achieve the maximum number of words of the summary once again. Those newly added sentences are then reduced. This process is repeated while the list is changed or if the compression rate has not been meet.

Sentence reduction algorithms can consider many structures. These structures are described in Sect. 4.1. Afterwards, the algorithms that perform sentence reduction are discussed in Sect. 4.2.

4.1 Targeted Structures

Different structures for different algorithms are targeted. At most six types of structures can be targeted:

- Appositions;
- Adjectives;
- Adverbs or adverb phrases;
- Parentheticals;
- Relative clauses;
- Prepositional phrases.

Appositions are noun phrases that describe, detail or modify its antecedent (also a noun phrase). The following sentence contains a an apposition (in bold).

ORIGINAL SENTENCE:
*José Sócrates, **primeiro-ministro**, e Jaime Gama querem cortar os salários dos seus gabinetes.*
José Sócrates, **the Prime Minister**, and Jaime Gama want to cut the salaries of their offices.
SIMPLIFIED SENTENCE:
José Sócrates e Jaime Gama querem cortar os salários dos seus gabinetes.
José Sócrates and Jaime Gama want to cut the salaries of their offices.

Adjectives qualify nouns or noun phrases, thus being structures prone to be removed. The following sentence contains an adjective (in bold).

ORIGINAL SENTENCE:
*O palco tem um pilar **central**, com 50 metros de altura.*
The stage has a **central** pillar, 50 meters high.
SIMPLIFIED SENTENCE:
O palco tem um pilar, com 50 metros de altura.
The stage has a pillar, 50 meters high.

Adverbs or adverb phrases are considered differently whether they appear in a noun or in a verb phrase, due to the usage of the adverbs of negation, which typically precede the verb. The adverbs appearing in a verb phrase are handled differently, to avoid removing negative adverbs and modifying the meaning of the sentence. The following sentence contains an adverb phrase (in bold).

ORIGINAL SENTENCE:
José Sócrates chegou ***um pouco*** *atrasado ao debate.*
José Sócrates arrived **a little late** to the debate.
SIMPLIFIED SENTENCE:
José Sócrates chegou atrasado ao debate.
José Sócrates arrived late to the debate.

Parenthetical phrases are phrases that explain or qualify other information being expressed. The following sentence contains a parenthetical phrase (in bold).

ORIGINAL SENTENCE:
O Parlamento aprovou, ***por ampla maioria****, a proposta.*
The Parliament approved **by large majority** the proposal.
SIMPLIFIED SENTENCE:
O Parlamento aprovou a proposta.
The Parliament approved the proposal.

Relative clauses are clauses that modify a noun phrase. They have the same structure as appositions, differing in the top node. The following sentence contains a relative clause (in bold).

ORIGINAL SENTENCE:
O Parlamento aprovou a proposta, ***que reduz os vencimentos dos deputados****.*
The Parliament approved the proposal, **which reduces the salaries of deputies**.
SIMPLIFIED SENTENCE:
O Parlamento aprovou a proposta.
The Parliament approved the proposal.

Prepositional phrases are phrases that modify nouns and verbs, indicating various relationships between subjects and verbs. They are used to include additional information within sentences. The following sentence contains a prepositional phrase (in bold).

ORIGINAL SENTENCE:
No Médio Oriente*, apenas Israel saudou a operação.*
In the Middle East, only Israel welcomed the operation.
SIMPLIFIED SENTENCE:
Apenas Israel saudou a operação.
Only Israel welcomed the operation.

In order to perform sentence reduction, a parse tree is created for each sentence, using a constituency parser for Portuguese [19]. The structures prone to be removed are identified in the tree using Tregex [20], a utility for matching patterns in trees. Tregex takes a parse tree and a regular expression pattern. It, then, returns a subtree of the initial tree which top node meets the pattern.

After identifying the subtrees representing each structure, these subtrees are replaced by null trees in the original sentence parse tree, removing its content and generating a new tree without the identified structure.

4.2 Algorithms

There were several algorithms that were experimented for sentence reduction. This section describes three of them: `main clause`, `blind removal`, and `best removal`. These algorithms differ not only in the structures that are removed, but also on the way those are removed. All these algorithms take a collection of sentences and return them reduced. The targeted structures are identified. Afterwards, reduced sentences are created by applying the algorithm that combines the removal of those structures.

The final step of the algorithm determines if the new reduced sentence can replace the former sentence, based on a specific criteria that takes into account the sentence score. In the summarization context, the sentence score defines the sentence relevance in the complete collection of sentences found in the input texts. This score is then a measure of informativeness. It states whether a sentence is important in the context of all the sentences in the texts to be summarized. Likewise, the score of a reduced sentence determines its informativeness.

The algorithms proposed in this work are described below. Thereafter, their pros and cons are discussed.

Main Clause. This is a two step algorithm. First, the main clause of the sentence is identified. In this phase, other than the next, the desired subtree is selected, ignoring the other subtrees of the main tree. Consider the following sentence:

No Médio Oriente, apenas Israel saudou a operação.
In the Middle East, only Israel welcomed the operation.

The main clause of this sentence is:

Apenas Israel saudou a operação.
Only Israel welcomed the operation.

The expression "*No Médio Oriente*" is ignored, since it is not part of the main clause (in bold). The original sentence is replaced by the reduced one, in which further reduction rules are applied. In this step, clauses in a SVO structure are considered. If the sentence is not in this format, the whole original sentence is used.

After the main clause has been obtained, it is used to identify the structures to be removed. The subtrees of the structures are identified in the sentence parse tree. Five types of structures are targeted: appositions, adjectives, adverbs, parenthetical phrase, and relative clauses. In fact, this first step removes the previously mentioned prepositional phrases, since those are typically the structures used in a sentence before its main clause. So that, prepositional phrases are not taken into account in the next step. After the targeted passages have been identified, a reduced sentence is build by removing all the structures found in the main clause of the original sentence.

In this example, the main clause of this sentence contains just one removable passage:

- Adverb phrase – *Apenas* (only).

So that, the reduced sentence produced by this algorithm would be the following.

> *Israel saudou a operação.*
> Israel welcomed the operation.

A detailed description of this algorithm can be found in [21].

Blind Removal. This algorithm takes four types of structures and removes them all from the original sentence. The structures considered in this algorithm are: appositions, parenthetical phrases, relative clauses, and prepositional phrases.

Consider the following sentence:

> *Também hoje, na conferência de líderes, o ministro dos Assuntos Parlamentares, Jorge Lacão, afirmou ter-se descoberto que o gabinete do primeiro-ministro tinha ficado de fora.*
> Today also, at the leadership conference, the Minister for Parliamentary Affairs, Jorge Lacão, said to have discovered that the office of the prime minister had been excluded.

Removable passages:

- Apposition – *Jorge Lacão.*
- Prepositional phrase – *na conferência de líderes* (at the leadership conference).

In this algorithm, all these passages are removed from the original sentence, building the following reduced sentence.

> *Também hoje, o ministro dos Assuntos Parlamentares afirmou ter-se descoberto que o gabinete do primeiro-ministro tinha ficado de fora.*
> Today also, the Minister for Parliamentary Affairs said to have discovered that the office of the prime minister had been excluded.

This reduced sentence is the one used to be compared to the original sentence.

Best Removal. This is an algorithm that uses the concept of power set, the set of all subsets of a given set. In the context of this work, the power set of a given sentence is composed by all the sentences obtained by combining the removal of the structures that have been identified as removable. Four types of structures are considered in this algorithm: appositions, parenthetical phrases, relative clauses, and prepositional phrases. Recall the sentence illustrated in the previous algorithm and its removable passages.

Também hoje, na conferência de líderes, o ministro dos Assuntos Parlamentares, Jorge Lacão, afirmou ter-se descoberto que o gabinete do primeiro-ministro tinha ficado de fora.
Today also, at the leadership conference, the Minister for Parliamentary Affairs, Jorge Lacão, said to have discovered that the office of the prime minister had been excluded.

This sentence contains two removable passages (underlined): the apposition – *Jorge Lacão* –, and the prepositional phrase – *na conferência de líderes.* The following example shows the original sentence and its score.

Também hoje, na conferência de líderes, o ministro dos Assuntos Parlamentares, Jorge Lacão, afirmou ter-se descoberto que o gabinete do primeiro-ministro tinha ficado de fora Today also, at the leadership conference, the Minister for Parliamentary Affairs, Jorge Lacão, said to have discovered that the office of the prime minister had been excluded	1.7200

The following table describes the sentences in the power set and their respective scores. These sentences were created by combining the removal of the identified structures. Their scores were obtained by summing the score (obtained in the summarization process) of each word composing the reduced sentence divided by the total number of words defining the new sentence. From the first sentence was removed the apposition phrase *Jorge Lacão.* The second sentence does not contain both removable passages *Jorge Lacão* and *na conferência de líderes.* Finally, the third one does not include the parenthetical phrase *na conferência de líderes.*

After the power set has been defined, all the sentences are ordered by their score. As shown in the table, depending on the passage that has been removed or the combination of passages removed, the score of the reduced sentence keeps changing. This means that there are some expressions that contain more information than others, as the sentence score is a measure of informativeness. The reduced sentence will then be the sentence in the power set that has the maximum score.

Também hoje, na conferência de líderes, o ministro dos Assuntos Parlamentares afirmou ter-se descoberto que o gabinete do primeiro-ministro tinha ficado de fora Today also, at the leadership conference, the Minister for Parliamentary Affairs said to have discovered that the office of the prime minister had been excluded	1.8175
Também hoje o ministro dos Assuntos Parlamentares afirmou ter-se descoberto que o gabinete do primeiro-ministro tinha ficado de fora Today also the Minister for Parliamentary Affairs said to have discovered that the office of the prime minister had been excluded	1.7053
Também hoje o ministro dos Assuntos Parlamentares, Jorge Lacão, afirmou ter-se descoberto que o gabinete do primeiro-ministro tinha ficado de fora Today also the Minister for Parliamentary Affairs, Jorge Lacão, said to have discovered that the office of the prime minister had been excluded	1.6000

4.3 Sentence Selection

After the structures have been removed from the sentence, it is time to determine if this new reduced sentence should replace the original one.

Hence, the sentence score is considered. As mentioned above, in the summarization algorithm, the sentence score defines the sentence relevance to the complete collection of sentences obtained from the input texts. This score is computed using the *tf-idf* metric, which states that the relevance of a term not only depends on its frequency over the collection of texts, but also it depends on the number of documents in which the term occurs. Equation 1 describes the computation of the sentence score.

$$score_S = \frac{\sum_w tf - idf_w}{totalWords_S} \tag{1}$$

Hence, $score_S$ of the sentence S measures the relevance of this sentence considering the collection of sentences obtained from the input texts.

As words or expressions were removed from the original sentence to create the new reduced sentence, the score of this reduced sentence must be computed, considering only the words that it now contains. After having both sentence scores, the original sentence score is compared to the one of its reduced version. If the reduced sentence score is higher than the one of the original sentence, the reduced sentence replaces the former one in the summary.

This procedure ensures that sentence reduction indeed helps to improve the content of the summary, by including only the reduced sentences that contribute to maximize the informativeness of the final summary.

5 Pilot Study

In order to illustrate the previous algorithms, a pilot study including a summary composed by two sentences has been conducted. Note that, in this study, after sentence reduction is applied to the summary, no more information is being added to it, despite that the summarization process completes the summary until the number of words defined by the compression rate is met.

Consider the following summary:

Esta foi a primeira pesquisa da série CNI/Ibope feita já com a lista oficial de candidatos à Presidência registrados no TSE (Tribunal Superior Eleitoral). Se a eleição fosse hoje, o presidente Luiz Inácio Lula da Silva, candidato à reeleição, teria 44 % das intenções de voto, contra 25 % de Geraldo Alckmin, de acordo com a pesquisa CNI/Ibope divulgada nesta sexta-feira.

This was the first survey in the series CNI/IBOPE, done already with the official list of presidential candidates registered in the TSE (Supreme Electoral Tribunal). If the election were today, President Luiz Inacio Lula da Silva, candidate for re-election, would have 44 % of the vote, against 25 % of Geraldo Alckmin, according to CNI/Ibope released on Friday.

This summary contains the following structures (underlined in the example) that can be targeted to be removed:

- Adverb#1 – *já.*
- Adjective – *oficial.*
- Parenthetical phrase – *Tribunal Superior Eleitoral.*
- Adverb#2 – *hoje.*
- Apposition phrase – *candidato à reeleição.*
- Prepositional phrase – *de acordo com a pesquisa CNI/Ibope divulgada nesta sexta-feira.*

Also, the main clauses of each have been identified:

Main clause#1. *Esta foi a primeira pesquisa da série CNI/Ibope.*

Main clause#2. *O presidente Luiz Inácio Lula da Silva, candidato à reeleição, teria 44 % das intenções de voto, contra 25 % de Geraldo Alckmin, de acordo com a pesquisa CNI/Ibope divulgada nesta sexta-feira.*

Table 1 describes which structures were removed using each algorithm.

As illustrated in the previous Table, `main clause` does not take into account the first four structures, since its first step is to obtain the main clause, and those structures are not part of the main clause. Yet, both `blind removal` and `best removal` do not consider adjectives and adverbs.

Table 2 describes the number of words removed by all these algorithms.

In this very small example, there are some issues to be noticed. Despite that by applying `best removal` there is no more space in the summary for another sentence, it is possible to be sure that, with this algorithm, the best reduced sentence is created, maximizing the information of the current summary. Yet,

Table 1. Structures removed using each algorithm.

	Main clause	Blind removal	Best removal
Adverb#1	N/A	-	-
Adjective	N/A	-	-
Parenthetical phrase	N/A	Yes	Yes
Adverb#2	N/A	-	-
Apposition phrase	Yes	Yes	Yes
Prepositional phrase	-	Yes	No
Main clause#1	Yes	-	-
Main clause#2	Yes	-	-

Table 2. Algorithm statistics (number of words removed).

	Main clause	Blind removal	Best removal
Sentence#1	16	3	3
Sentence#2	8	12	3
Total	24	15	6

`blind removal` removes all the structures allowing for more room to include new information, whether this information is relevant or not. Otherwise, when using `main clause`, two much information is lost, and there are no guarantees that the sentences added afterwards would include this information.

6 Discussion

The main assumption of a reduction process is that the identified structures are considered prone to be removed because they express additional information in the context of the sentence that can be avoided without jeopardizing the key content of the sentence they belong to. In addition, a well-defined sentence is easier to understand. Based on these two assumptions was created the very first approach to sentence reduction: the `main clause` algorithm. Firstly, the sentence is reduced to its main content, by identifying its SVO structure, and afterwards, the additional information is removed considering five types of passages.

However, this algorithm has some drawbacks. In fact, the SVO structure was difficult to retrieve, since there are many sentences that do not follow this structure. Furthermore, there were too many passages identified to be removed and sometimes the meaning of the sentence was not expressed, specially when adjectives and adverbs were removed.

These observations brought new decisions concerning the type of structures targeted. As not all these structures should be considered dispensable, a subset of them was selected. Considering their specific nature, appositions, parenthetical phrases, prepositional phrases and relative clauses are phrases that contain additional information to the content already expressed.

Thus, the next two algorithms, `blind removal` and `best removal`, considered only these types of passages. The next approach to the current reduction process, `blind removal`, defines that all the information expressed in those structures is dispensable. Thus, all the candidate passages are blindly removed from all the sentences that go through this process. Considering the parenthetical nature of these passages, their simple removal would make room for more information to be included in the summary. In fact, the verification of the score, made after the sentence has been reduced, accounts for the informativeness of the sentence, and thus of the summary. However, after applying this algorithm, we concluded that there were some passages that by being removed would compromise the comprehensiveness of the text.

This conclusion drove the decision of applying the third algorithm, `best removal`. This algorithm aims to both maximize the information in the sentence and improve the comprehension of that sentence. By removing the structures carefully, taking into account the ones that improve the sentence informativeness, it is expected that consequently the informativeness of the summary also improves. Despite that by definition these structures constitute additional information, this information might not have been expressed yet in the summary. As stated above, the simple removal of all these structures can create incomprehensible sentences with too few information. The sentence score, by being the measure of the sentence informativeness, determines which of the reduced sentences created is the best, that is, the one that contains more information and, at the same time, discards the additional information.

In conclusion, `best removal` was then the final algorithm selected, since it verifies three important conditions: (1) it considers only the structures that indeed make up additional information; (2) it produces the best combination of a reduced sentence, and (3) in itself it takes into account the informativeness of the reduced sentences within the whole collection of sentences by considering their score.

7 Final Remarks

This paper presents three possible algorithms to perform sentence reduction. The idea behind all these algorithms is detailed. Also, pros and cons of each one are commented and some final conclusions about their differences are drawn.

The approach that combines summarization with sentence reduction is an effective procedure that seeks to maximize the relevant information within a summary. In fact, by reducing the sentences from the initial set of sentences into their main content, sentence reduction allows for the inclusion of further sentences containing novel and relevant information. Moreover, the type of structures that are removed is also a matter of concern. As was discussed above, there are some structures that should not be removed, in order to ensure that the meaning of a sentence is kept. The algorithms presented also take this issue into account.

In the context of summarization, such a combination – summarization followed by sentence reduction – aims to produce highly informative summaries, containing the maximum amount of significant information.

References

1. Silveira, S.B., Branco, A.: Enhancing multi-document summaries with sentence simplification. In: ICAI 2012: International Conference on Artificial Intelligence, Las Vegas, USA, July 2012, pp. 742–748 (2012)
2. Lin, C.Y.: Improving summarization performance by sentence compression: a pilot study. In: Proceedings of the Sixth International Workshop on Information Retrieval with Asian Languages, AsianIR '03, Stroudsburg, PA, USA, vol. 11, 1–8. Association for Computational Linguistics (2003)
3. Berg-Kirkpatrick, T., Gillick, D., Klein, D.: Jointly learning to extract and compress. In: Proceedings of the 49th Annual Meeting of the Association for Computational Linguistics: Human Language Technologies, HLT '11, Stroudsburg, PA, USA, vol. 1, pp. 481–490. Association for Computational Linguistics (2011)
4. Marsi, E., Krahmer, E., Hendrickx, I., Daelemans, W.: Empirical Methods in Natural Language Generation. Springer, Heidelberg (2010)
5. Feng, L.: Text simplification: a survey. Technical report, The City University of New York (2008)
6. Chandrasekar, R., Doran, C., Srinivas, B.: Motivations and methods for text simplification. In: Proceedings of the Sixteenth International Conference on Computational Linguistics (COLING '96), pp. 1041–1044 (1996)
7. Jing, H.: Sentence reduction for automatic text summarization. In: Proceedings of the Sixth Conference on Applied Natural Language Processing, Morristown, NJ, USA, pp. 310–315. Association for Computational Linguistics (2000)
8. Jing, H., McKeown, K.R.: Cut and paste based text summarization. In: Proceedings of the 1st North American Chapter of the Association for Computational Linguistics Conference, NAACL 2000, Stroudsburg, PA, USA, pp. 178–185. ACL (2000)
9. Blair-Goldensohn, S., Evans, D., Hatzivassiloglou, V., Mckeown, K., Nenkova, A., Passonneau, R., Schiffman, B., Schlaikjer, A., Advaith, Siddharthan, A., Siegelman, S.: Columbia university at duc. In: Proceedings of the 2004 Document Understanding Conference (DUC 2004), HLT/NAACL 2004, Boston, Massachusetts, pp. 23–30 (2004)
10. Conroy, J., Schlesinger, J., Stewart, J.: Classy query-based multidocument summarization. In: Proceedings of 2005 Document Understanding Conference, Vancouver, BC (2005)
11. Siddharthan, A., Nenkova, A., McKeown, K.: Syntactic simplification for improving content selection in multi-document summarization. In: COLING '04: Proceedings of the 20th International Conference on Computational Linguistics, Morristown, NJ, USA, p. 896. ACL (2004)
12. Zajic, D., Dorr, B.J., Lin, J., Schwartz, R.: Multi-candidate reduction: sentence compression as a tool for document summarization tasks. Inf. Process. Manag. **43**(6), 1549–1570 (2007)
13. Cohn, T., Lapata, M.: Sentence compression as tree transduction. J. Artif. Intell. Res. (JAIR) **34**, 637–674 (2009)

14. Filippova, K.: Multi-sentence compression: finding shortest paths in word graphs. In: Proceedings of the 23rd International Conference on Computational Linguistics, COLING '10, Stroudsburg, PA, USA, pp. 322–330. ACL (2010)
15. Lloret, E.: Text summarisation based on human language technologies and its applications. Ph.D. thesis, Universidad de Alicante (2011)
16. Wubben, S., van den Bosch, A., Krahmer, E.: Sentence simplification by monolingual machine translation. In: ACL - The 50th Annual Meeting of the Association for Computational Linguistics, Proceedings of the Conference, Jeju Island, Korea, 8–14 July 2012, vol. 1: Long Papers, pp.1015–1024 The Association for Computer Linguistics (2012)
17. Yoshikawa, K., Iida, R., Hirao, T., Okumura, M.: Sentence compression with semantic role constraints. In: ACL - The 50th Annual Meeting of the Association for Computational Linguistics, Proceedings of the Conference, Jeju Island, Korea, 8–14 July 2012, vol. 2: Short Papers, pp. 349–353. The Association for Computer Linguistics (2012)
18. Silveira, S.B., Branco, A.: Combining a double clustering approach with sentence simplification to produce highly informative multi-document summaries. In: IRI 2012: 14th International Conference on Artificial Intelligence, Las Vegas, USA, August 2012, pp. 482–489 (2012)
19. Silva, J., Branco, A., Castro, S., Reis, R.: Out-of-the-box robust parsing of Portuguese. In: Pardo, T.A.S., Branco, A., Klautau, A., Vieira, R., de Lima, V.L.S. (eds.) PROPOR 2010. LNCS, vol. 6001, pp. 75–85. Springer, Heidelberg (2010)
20. Levy, R., Andrew, G.: Tregex and Tsurgeon: tools for querying and manipulating tree data structures. In: Proceedings of the 5th Language Resources and Evaluation Conference (LREC) (2006)
21. Silveira, S.B., Branco, A.: Compressing multi-document summaries through sentence simplification. In: ICAART 2013: 5th International Conference on Agents and Artificial Intelligence, Barcelona, Spain, February 2013

Diverse Planning for UAV Trajectories

Jan Tožička(✉), David Šišlák, and Michal Pěchouček

Agent Technology Center, Department of Computer Science,
Czech Technical University in Prague, Prague, Czech Republic
{jan.tozicka,david.sislak,michal.pechoucek}@agents.fel.cvut.cz
http://agents.fel.cvut.cz

Abstract. Nowadays, unmanned aerial vehicles (UAVs) are more and more often used to solve various tasks in both the private and the public sector. Some of these tasks can often be performed completely autonomously while others are still dependent on remote pilots. They control an UAV using a command display where they can control it manually using joysticks or give it a simple task. The command displays allow to plan the UAV trajectory through waypoints while avoiding no-fly zones. Nevertheless, the operator can be aware of other preferences or soft restrictions for which it's not feasible to be inserted into the system especially during time critical tasks. We propose to provide the operator with several different *alternative* trajectories, so he can choose the best one for the current situation. In this contribution we propose several metrics to measure the diversity of the trajectories. Then we explore several algorithms for the alternative trajectories creation. Finally, we experimentally evaluate them in a benchmark 8-grid domain and we also present the evaluation by human operators.

Keywords: Trajectory planning · UAV · Human-machine interface

1 Introduction

Unmanned aerial vehicles (UAVs) are more and more often used in military operations, in humanitarian and rescue missions, and in private sector tasks. Some of the tasks, e.g. the photo-mapping, can often be performed completely autonomously, while others are still dependent on remote pilots. They control an UAV using a command display where they can control it manually using joysticks or give it a simple task, e.g. to fly through a sequence of points on the map.

A human operator (pilot) seems to be a bottleneck of the system when several UAVs collaborate on a single mission. Each operator or a team of operators is responsible for one UAV and controls its actions. The human operators communicate among themselves and coordinate their actions in order to achieve a common goal. The whole system containing UAVs and all HMI machines used to control the UAVs is called Unmanned Aerial System (UAS). One of the main goals of research tackling UAVs is to improve the UAS so that a controller or a group of controllers can control larger groups of UAVs easily. This can be achieved by two means:

J. Filipe and A. Fred (Eds.): ICAART 2013, CCIS 449, pp. 277–292, 2014.
DOI: 10.1007/978-3-662-44440-5_17

- increase UAV autonomy,
- improve human–machine interface (HMI).

In this article we explore a solution which is overlapping both of these approaches. It increases the autonomy of UAS as a whole by extension of UAV planning capability (still not increasing its own autonomy) and changes the HMI. We will focus on the problem of the trajectory planning. Usually, all UAVs are controlled directly by remote operators (pilots) or they can fly following predefined trajectories. In the latter case, once the operator realizes that a trajectory needs to be changed, it can define a new trajectory, e.g. by means of waypoints and no-fly zones. When the waypoints are updated, the new trajectory is planned (on UAV or within ground control station). If the operator agrees with the trajectory it is applied. If the operator does not want to use the planned trajectory he can reject it and specify a new set of waypoints or introduce a new no-fly zone to get the trajectory matching his preferences better.

Even thought the planned trajectory is the optimal solution with respect to the fuel consumption, needed time, or other user specified criteria, the operator can be aware of other preferences, where the plane should fly, or soft restrictions on areas which would be nice to avoid. These can contain, for example, possible future colliding traffic, weather conditions, flights over inhabited areas, etc. It is not feasible to insert all these preferences into the system, especially during time critical tasks. The operator typically does not accept proposed trajectory in the cases when he sees other which is suboptimal but more preferable one. Then he has to change input values to force the system to give the desired solution. This can be repeated several times before the trajectory meets all the operator's criteria and preferences.

This iterative process can be improved by a system giving several possible trajectories out of which the operator selects one based on his preferences which is then applied. These proposed trajectories should be *different* by means of operator perception and preferences. For example, imagine an UAV flying directly through a no-fly zone. Shorter way to go around this no-fly zone is the southern way but the operator sees that the northern way is just a bit longer and he knows (based on his experience) that the southern trajectory can later collide with some other currently unknown traffic for the planner. Currently used trajectory planners, e.g. A* [1], or Θ* [2], would propose the optimal trajectory, i.e. the southern one. It can be quite difficult for the operator to make the UAV to pass around the no-fly zone by north – he can add an extra way-point or block the southern direction by new a no-fly zone. At this moment, it would be very helpful for the operator to have a possibility to select between the optimal southern way and an alternative northern way as it's illustrated in Fig. 1.

It is very difficult to create several plans which are different enough and understandable from the human operator's perspective. Currently there are several algorithms allowing to give k-best solutions but in our domain all these solution would be usually very similar to the best one and can be even indistinguishable for the human operator. They would typically differ in a small speed

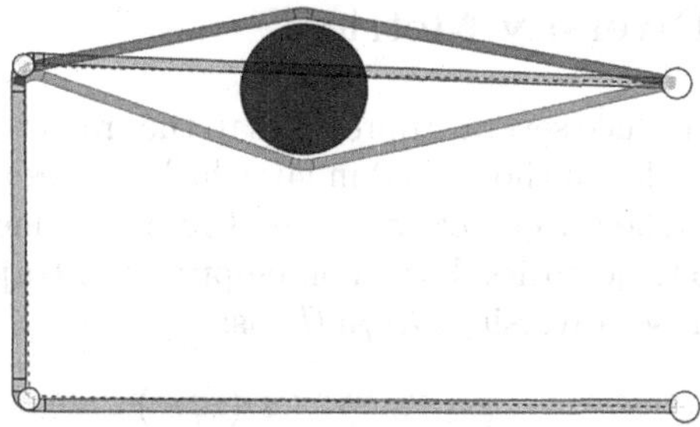

Fig. 1. New generation of HMI displays will allow a user to select from several proposed trajectories when the current trajectory needs to be replanned. This figure illustrate a situation when a new no-fly zone (orange circle) has been inserted. Since the current UAV trajectory (black colored stripe) is crossing this new no-fly zone, the trajectory has to be replanned. Along with the optimal trajectory (cyan trajectory) several alternatives (green trajectory) will be proposed to the user. He can then easily choose new trajectory based on his own preferences, stay with the current one, or change the definition of the trajectory by changing its waypoints or by adding new no-fly zone or removing an existing one (Color figure online).

change or in an unobservable deviation from the optimal trajectory. What we really need are the *alternatives* which are different from the operator's perspective.

The goal of our work is to extend a common trajectory planner so it allows us to create distinguishably different trajectories. Firstly, we need to define what *different* actually means. The notion of difference is connected to the human perception and thus can be individual. However, it's necessary to formally define it.

In this contribution we propose several metrics measuring how much the trajectories differ and several approaches to generate *different* trajectories. We start with the definition of several trajectory diversity metrics in Sect. 2. In Sect. 3, we describe a trajectory metric based approach which penalizes the trajectories similar to the previously generated ones. Section 4 describes an approach which systematically extends obstacles and then uses any traditional optimal trajectory planner to find individual alternative trajectories. The last approach, described in Sect. 5, extends this idea by using the Voronoi and the Delaunay graphs. All the proposed approaches are evaluated using the presented metrics in benchmark experimental domain and they are also evaluated by human operators. All the results are examined in Sect. 6.

Our benchmark experiments are based on a 8-grid domain [3] and in Sect. 7 we show how the diverse planning is implemented in a real mission control display. Some of the proposed diverse planning algorithms do not change the planners and thus any planner (e.g. maneuver planner) can be used.

Obviously, similar approach can be used in other real world domains where a system proposes a solution to a human operator. The operator typically has broader knowledge about the task and the related environment. Thus, giving the operator several possibilities can help him to choose the best overall solution.

2 Trajectory Diversity Metrics

In this section, we introduce several approaches to the trajectory comparison. We will use definitions similar to those used in [4], which defines the diversity metric for a general plan as follows. Let $D : \pi \times \pi \to [0, \infty)$ be a metric describing the distance between two trajectories. For a non-empty set of trajectories Π, Coman in [4] defines the plan-set diversity $Div_D(\Pi)$ as:

$$Div_D(\Pi) = \frac{\sum_{\pi,\pi' \in \Pi} D(\pi, \pi')}{\frac{|\Pi| \times (|\Pi|-1)}{2}},$$

and the relative diversity $RelDiv_D(\pi, \Pi)$ of plan π relative to plan-set Π:

$$RelDiv_D(\pi, \Pi) = \frac{\sum_{\pi' \in \Pi} D(\pi, \pi')}{|\Pi|}$$

where $|\Pi|$ stands for the number of plans in the plan-set.

We will use the plan-set diversity to aggregate trajectory distances over the whole set of trajectories.

2.1 Metric: Different States

The *different states* metric D_{States} takes into consideration states of the plans only. In the case of trajectory, the plan state is the robot location together with some other attributes, e.g. direction, battery level, etc. In our experimental domains, the state represents a 2D location only. Metric D_{States} then counts the number of states of one plan which are also in the other plan and transforms it into a distance metric:

$$D_{States}(\pi, \pi') = 1 - \frac{\sum_{s \in \pi} \begin{cases} 1 & \text{for } s \in \pi' \\ 0 & \text{for } s \notin \pi' \end{cases}}{|\pi|}$$

where the $|\pi|$ stands for the number of states in the path.

This metric is very general and can be used to any planning problem, not necessarily to the trajectory planning. In the continuous domain, it would be useful to add a threshold determining which plane states are considered to be the same, e.g. based on the position and heading of the planes.

2.2 Metric: Trajectory Distance

The *trajectory distance* metric $D_{Distance}$ is a generalization of the *different states* metric. It requires some knowledge about the domain – the distance metric between the states $\delta(s_1, s_2)$. For each state in the first plan it counts it's distance to the second plan, i.e. the distance to the closest state of the other plan.

$$D_{Distance}(\pi, \pi') = \sum_{s \in \pi} \min_{s' \in \pi'} \delta(s, s')$$

2.3 Metric: Obstacle Avoidance

The *obstacle avoidance* metric $D_{Obstacles}$ takes also into consideration how obstacles are avoided by each trajectory. This idea is based on the human perception of what are different trajectories. Most of the trajectories well evaluated by the metrics described in the previous sections are perceived to be very similar and quite unreasonable – just worsening the optimal trajectory without changing anything significantly. Human preferred alternatives are often described by means of *how the obstacles are avoided.* Therefore we need a metric that captures that the obstacles have been avoided from some side. For that we need to specify what the 'same side' exactly means. We say that a robot passes obstacle o by direction d when a ray going from o in direction d crosses the trajectory. Metric $D_{Obstacles}$ is then defined as follows:

$$D_{Obst.}(\pi, \pi') = 1 - \frac{\sum_{o \in \mathcal{O}} \sum_{d \in \mathcal{D}} \begin{cases} 1 & \text{if } \pi \text{ passes } o \text{ by } d \\ & \quad \Leftrightarrow \pi' \text{ passes } o \text{ by } d \\ 0 & \text{otherwise} \end{cases}}{|\mathcal{O}||\mathcal{D}|}$$

where the $\mathcal{O}$ is the set of all obstacles and $\mathcal{D}$ is a set of all directions we are testing. In our experiments, we use the set of four directions: north, east, south and west.

3 Metrics Based Planners

In this section, we introduce a most general approaches to the trajectory comparison. They are solely based on the metrics described in Sect. 2. This is the most general case which can be easily generalized to be applied in a general STRIPS planning problem [5].

Firstly this planner, listed as Algorithm 1, finds the optimal trajectory π^* using provided trajectory *planner*. Then it iteratively looks for other diverse trajectories. It updates the goal function to use the trajectory distance metric D together with the current set of found trajectories Π. The goal function for every trajectory π is then calculated as the relative diversity $RelDiv_D(\pi, \Pi)$.

Let's have a metric $D : \pi \times \pi \rightarrow [0, \infty)$ evaluating the distance of two trajectories and the relative diversity metric $RelDiv(\pi, \Pi)$ as described in Sect. 2. We can use it in a planning algorithm to get the next optimized trajectory which is different enough with respect to Π trajectories already calculated. This can easily be done by defining the new evaluating function

$$g^D(\pi) = g(\pi) + \alpha(MaxDiv - RelDiv_D(\pi, \Pi)),$$

Algorithm 1. Trajectory distance metric based diverse trajectory planner.

Data: G – state graph
Data: $\mathcal{O}$ – set of obstacles
Data: $start, target$ – start and target states
Data: $planner$ – any trajectory planner
Data: n – required number of trajectories
Data: D – trajectory distance metric
Result: Π – set of trajectories
$\pi^* \leftarrow planner$.findPath$(G, \mathcal{O}, start, target)$;
$\Pi = \{\pi^*\}$;
while $|\Pi| < n$ **do**
  $planner$.updateGoalFunction(D, Π) ;
  $\pi \leftarrow planner$.findPath$(G, \mathcal{O}, start, target)$;
  $\Pi \leftarrow \Pi \cup \{\pi\}$;
end
return Π ;

where $g(\pi)$ is the original price of the trajectory (e.g. it's length) and α is the weight of the *RelDiv* relative diversity metric value which is transformed into the penalty by being subtracted from $MaxDiv$, the maximal value of the D metric, which is 1 for most of our cases.

The pro of trajectory based metrics is that, unlike the other metrics described in the following sections, they can create different trajectories also for domains without any obstacles.

3.1 Trajectory Distance Metric Planner

Trajectory distance metric planner uses $D_{Distance}$ trajectory distance metric. Trajectories created when using this metric are very sensitive to the α value. They can be very suboptimal when the value of α is large. We can avoid this problem if we omit the trajectories much worse than the optimal one, e.g. trajectories more than 20 % longer than the optimal trajectory. Note that we know the quality of the optimal trajectory because it's found as the first trajectory, before any metric is used. See Fig. 2 for illustration how the planner with this metric would work.

In our experiments we limit the maximal diversity value to 2 ($MaxDiv$ in the updated goal function g^D). All the Div_D values bigger than 2 are considered to be 2 and thus result in 0 penalty.

Trajectory Distance Metric MaxMin Planner. The trajectory distance metric planner tries to minimize the penalty derived from the $Div_{D_{Distance}}$ diversity function. That means that it tries to find a trajectory, which is in average the most different to the previously found trajectories. Another possibility is to look for a

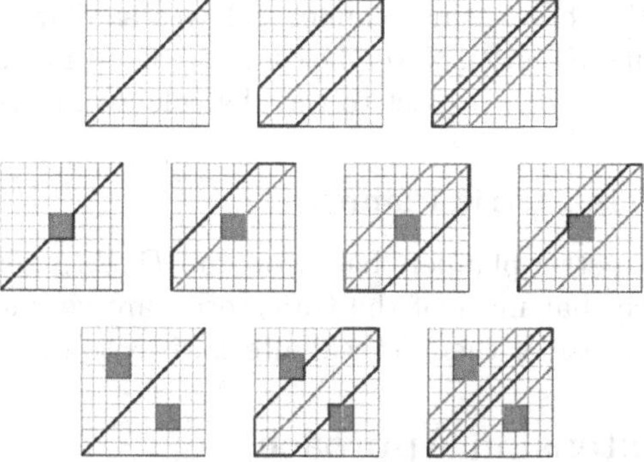

Fig. 2. Trajectory distance metric. Blue lines show the trajectories created during the subsequent runs of the trajectory planner. Dark gray lines show the trajectories forming the set Π, i.e. the trajectories created during previous iterations. We can see that this method is very sensitive to the threshold specifying how much created trajectory can differ from the optimal one. In the 2-obstacles case the allowed deviation from the optimal price is not large enough to cover the cases where the obstacles are passed around. Note, that even if the algorithm would run more iterations, such a solution would not be found (Color figure online).

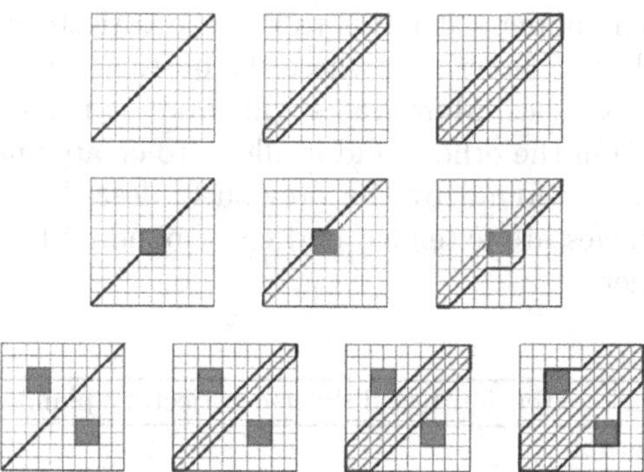

Fig. 3. Different state metric. Blue and dark gray lines have the same meaning as in Fig. 2. It needs several iterations to find a solution avoiding the 2-obstacles case by going around – which is better behavior than we observed in the trajectory distance metric described in Sect. 3.1 (Color figure online).

trajectory which is the most different to the most similar trajectory, i.e. to compute the $RelDiv_D$ function as the minimal distance instead of their average:

$$RelDiv_D^{Min}(\pi, \Pi) = \min_{\pi' \in \Pi} D(\pi, \pi')$$

On our illustrative cases, this planner behaves similarly to the trajectory distance metric planner (Fig. 2). Nevertheless in our experiments it showed better performance, especially with respect to the obstacle avoidance metric.

3.2 Different State Metric Planner

The different state metric planner, based on the D_{States} metric, is illustrated in Fig. 3. We can see that most of the trajectories are very similar and human operator would not consider them as real alternatives to the optimal trajectory.

4 Obstacle Extension Approach

This approach works differently than the previous ones. It transforms the planning task into several new tasks and then runs a traditional trajectory planner to find the optimal trajectory in each transformed task as illustrated by Algorithm 2.

The transformed task contains obstacles extended in different directions. Having that each obstacle can be extended to one of 4, or 8, possible directions, the algorithm tries all possible combinations of extensions (generated by function *allObstacleExtensions($\mathcal{O}$, directions)*) and for each combination it takes the shortest trajectory found by the trajectory planner. This approach is very computational power demanding – it needs to run the trajectory planner d^k-times, where d is the number of directions, where the obstacles can be expanded, and k is the number of obstacles. Many cases will result in the same trajectories or in no solution at all. On the other hand it allows to create many *different* alternatives which cannot be found by the previously described planners. Figure 4 shows how the obstacles are extended and corresponding trajectories found by the trajectory planner.

Algorithm 2. Obstacle extension based diverse trajectory planner.

Data: G – state graph
Data: $\mathcal{O}$ – set of obstacles
Data: $start, target$ – start and target states
Data: *planner* – any trajectory planner
Data: *directions* – possible extension directions
Result: Π – set of trajectories
$\mathcal{O}^* \leftarrow$ allObstacleExtensions($\mathcal{O}, directions$) ;
$\Pi = \{\}$;
forall the $\mathcal{O}' \in \mathcal{O}^*$ **do**
  $\pi \leftarrow$ *planner*.findPath($G, \mathcal{O}', start, target$) ;
  $\Pi \leftarrow \Pi \cup \{\pi\}$;
end
return Π ;

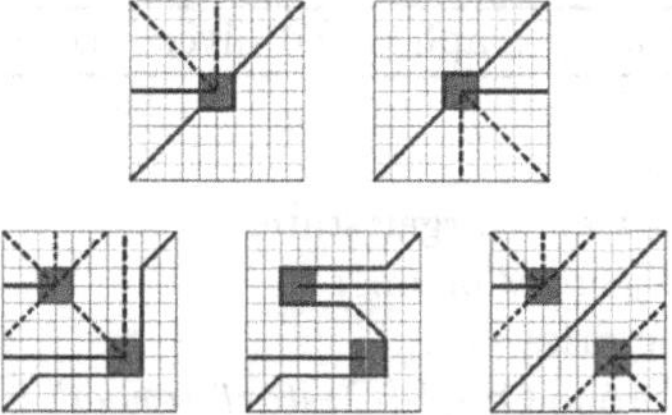

Fig. 4. Obstacle extension approach. The blue line is a trajectory found by the trajectory planner for a task, where the obstacles are extended in the direction of continuous red lines. Dashed red lines show other possible obstacle extensions producing the same trajectory. In the 2-obstacles case, we can see that this approach proposed also a S-shaped trajectory which has not been proposed by any other approach yet. Even though this trajectory is much longer than the shortest one and thus would not be probably chosen by the operator, it well demonstrates that this approach is more general than the previous ones (Color figure online).

5 Voronoi–Delaunay Graph Based Trajectories

For each point in the space we can find the closest obstacle to that point. Voronoi diagram [6] is a decomposition of the space into disjunctive Voronoi areas containing points with the same closest obstacle. The Voronoi graph is composed of the borders between the Voronoi areas. The edges represent an abstraction of each passage between the obstacles. Since this graph is discreet even for 2D space, it is often used for the trajectory planning [7,8]. The Delaunay graph [9] is an inverted graph to the Voronoi graph. The vertexes represent the centers of Voronoi areas, i.e. the obstacles in our case, and the edges show which two Voronoi areas have a common border. For planning alternative trajectories, the algorithm works with the extended Voronoi graph, where start and target points are connected to the graph. The Delaunay graph is extended to contain edges connecting centers of outermost Voronoi areas (those which are crossing the planning area border) towards the borders[1].

We propose to use the extended Voronoi and the Delaunay graphs in the problem of finding diverse trajectories as described in Algorithm 3.

In principal, this algorithm generates all the paths connecting the start and the target states in extended Voronoi graph G^{π}. Although these paths represent nice set of different paths, they are not locally optimal (they pass half way between two obstacles) and they do not fulfill all the requirements on the trajectory (e.g. the UAV aerodynamics). To overcome these shortcomings, for each path we convert unused edges of the Voronoi graph into new obstacles using their dual representation in the Delaunay graph. Then, similarly to the Obstacle Extansion approach, we just add these new obstacles to the original task and using any state of the art trajectory planner we find a trajectory fulfilling all the requirements.

[1] Additional nodes are placed on the intersection of the border and the added edge into the Delaunay graph.

Algorithm 3. Voronoi-Delaunay graph based diverse trajectory planner.

Data: G – state graph
Data: $\mathcal{O}$ – set of obstacles
Data: $start, target$ – start and target states
Data: $planner$ – any trajectory planner
Result: Π – set of trajectories
$G^V \leftarrow$ createExtendedVoronoiGraph($\mathcal{O}, start, target$) ;
$P^V \leftarrow$ findAllPaths($G^V, start, target$) ;
$\Pi = \{\}$;
forall the $\pi^V \in P^V$ **do**
    $G^D \leftarrow$ createDelaunayGraph(G^V) ;
    $G^\pi \leftarrow$ removeDualEdges(G^D, π^V) ;
    $\mathcal{O}^\pi \leftarrow$ convertEdgesToObsacles(G^π) ;
    $\pi \leftarrow planner$.findPath($G, \mathcal{O} \cup \mathcal{O}^\pi, start, target$) ;
    $\Pi \leftarrow \Pi \cup \{\pi\}$;
end
return Π ;

The extended Voronoi and Delaunay graphs with G^π from one iteration of the planning algorithm is shown in Fig. 5. Multiple iterations of the algorithm in the 8-grid domain [3] with few obstacles are shown in Fig. 6. This approach is more efficient than the Obstacle Extension Approach because every call of the trajectory planner on defined sub-planning problem will result in a new, original, alternative trajectory.

6 Experiments

We have evaluated all proposed diverse trajectory planners in two domains with different number of obstacles. Here, we present results of the 10×10 *8-grid* domain. The *start* location is placed to the upper-left corner [0, 0] and the *target* to the bottom-right corner [10, 10]. A certain number, ranging from 2 to 16, of randomly generated obstacles are added to each scenario. These obstacles represent restricted nodes in the grid graph. During the generation of the obstacles the following rules had to be fulfilled:

1. no two obstacles can be adjacent, and
2. no obstacle can be on the border line, and
3. there exists a path from *start* to *target* (implied by the previous conditions).

These conditions assure that every obstacle can be avoided by every side and also that there can be a path between each pair of obstacles. Each run with a given number of randomly generated obstacles has been repeated 10 times and the average value are presented.

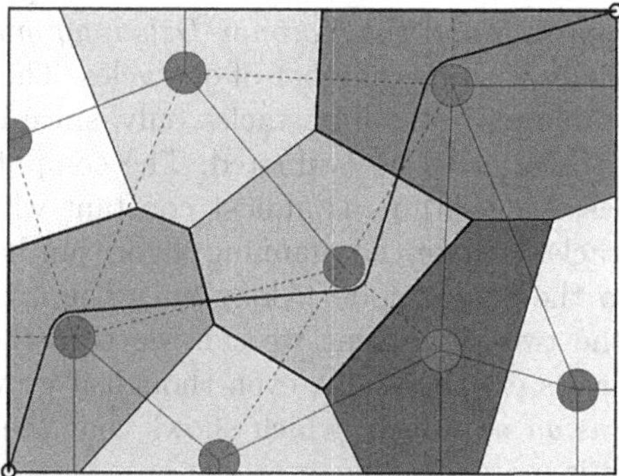

Fig. 5. The no-fly zones, represented by the red circles, define the Voronoi diagram (gray areas). Its dual graph, the extended Delaunay graph, is shown by the red lines. When a path (thicker black line) in the Voronoi graph is found, all the edges of the extended Delaunay graph, that do not cross that path, are considered to be the obstacles (continuous red lines) and the shortest path (blue line) is found using any optimal trajectory planner (Color figure online).

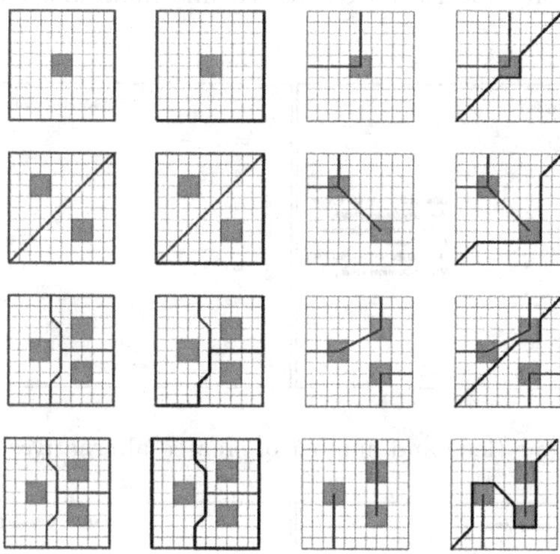

Fig. 6. Voronoi–Delaunay graph based trajectories. Each row demonstrates subsequent steps of the algorithm. The first column shows the extended Voronoi graph (red lines) derived from the obstacles. Then all the paths from the start to the target are found – an example trajectory (blue line) is shown in the second column. The third column consists of extended Delaunay graphs (red lines) without the edges which have been crossed by the current path from the second column. Red lines are considered to be obstacles in the last column, where the alternative trajectory (blue line) is found by an optimal trajectory planner (Color figure online).

First two graphs (Fig. 7) show how many alternatives have been found for a different number of obstacles and how long it took. As expected, values for the *Obstacle extension* approach and the *Voronoi–Delaunay graph* based approach are growing exponentially with the number of obstacles. The *Obstacle extension* approach has been evaluated up to 6 obstacles only, since it took too long for the cases with more obstacles to be evaluated. The computational complexity of diversity metric based algorithms is almost constant with a small grow for small number of obstacles, where the planning algorithm has to explore larger area before it gets to the target node. Along with the exponentially growing time complexity of the two algorithms we can see that the number of found different paths also grows exponentially, even though it grows only a bit faster for the *Obstacle extension* approach, which shows that the *Voronoi–Delaunay graph* based approach is more effective.

Since the *Voronoi–Delaunay graph* based planner has found too many possible trajectories for even few obstacles and it would be inappropriate to present all these trajectories to the user, we decided to limit the number of evaluated trajectories. Since the main criteria for the trajectory planning is the trajectory length, we decided to select 5 or 100 shortest paths respectively.

The left graph of Fig. 8 shows the average length of trajectories given by each planner. And the following graphs (right graph of Fig. 8 and graphs in Fig. 9) show the plan-set diversity metric values defined in Sect. 2. As expected, the trajectory diversity metric based algorithms maximized the corresponding

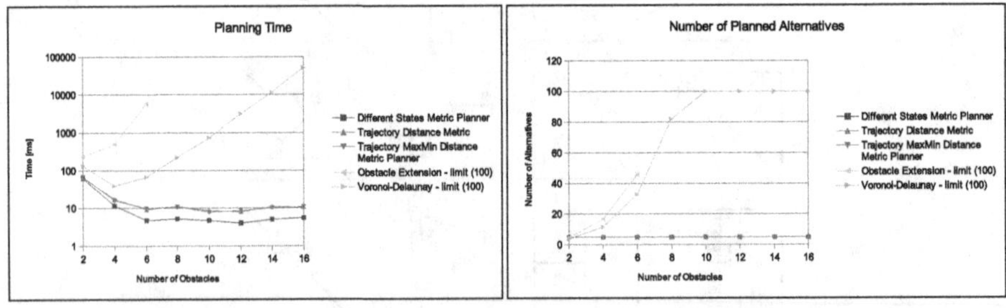

Fig. 7. Time (left) and number of created alternatives (right).

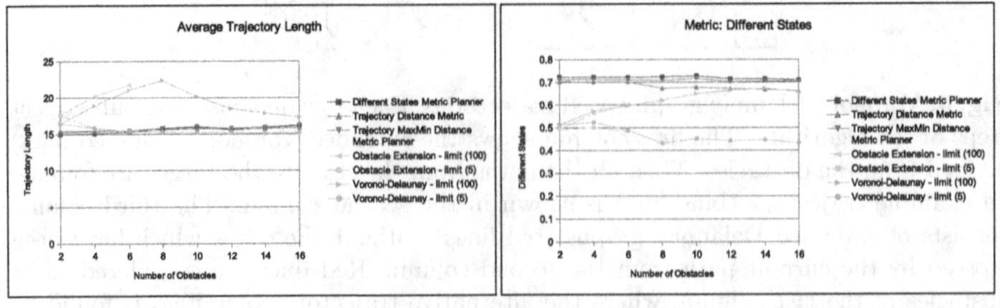

Fig. 8. Trajectory Length (left) and Different States metric (right).

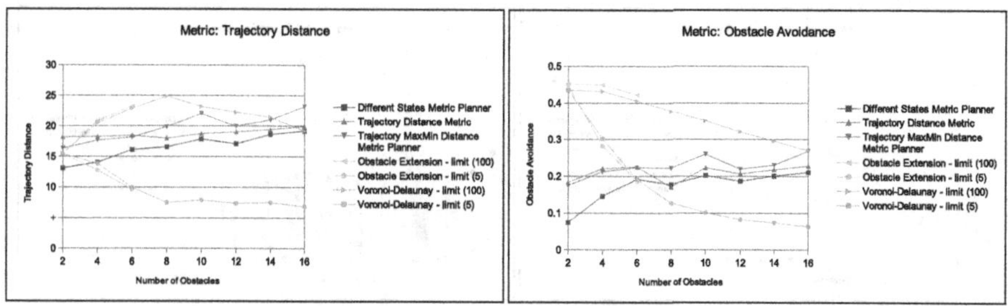

Fig. 9. Trajectory Distance (left) and Obstacle Avoidance (right) metrics.

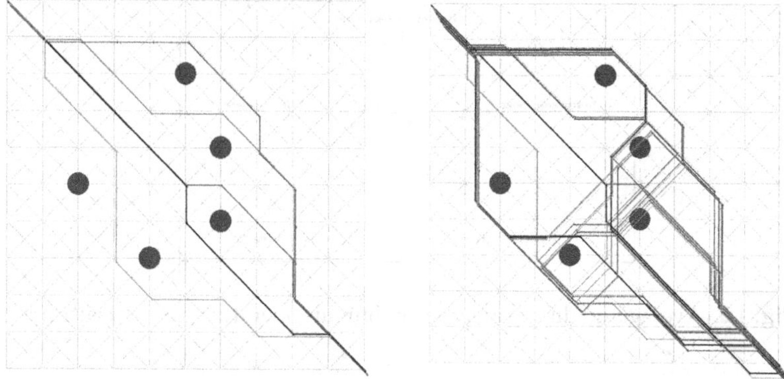

Fig. 10. Example of trajectories generated by the Voronoi-Delaunay graph based diverse trajectory planner. In the left figure we can see the shortest 5 trajectories and all 21 found trajectories are depicted in the right one.

metric. There is one exception in the graph of *trajectory distance* metric where, in most cases, the Voronoi-Delaunay graph based planner had higher score. This is caused by the limitation of the maximal distance of trajectories (introduced by the $MaxDiv$ parameter in the updated goal function) which prevents creation of trajectories too far from each other.

The last Fig. 10 shows examples of trajectories created by the Voronoi-Delaunay graph based diverse trajectory planner in the scenario with 5 obstacles. We can see that the 5 shortest trajectories give user a good selection of different possibilities how to pass the obstacles even though these trajectories were not evaluated very well by the presented trajectory diversity metrics. The reason for that is that even though the human perception of diversity of trajectories is based on the trajectory–obstacle relation it is mostly just binary. Thus if two trajectories avoid any obstacle from different direction than they are considered to be different. We are now about to proceed with the experiments with human users to verify this hypothesis and, hopefully, to create a metric which will better reflect human perception.

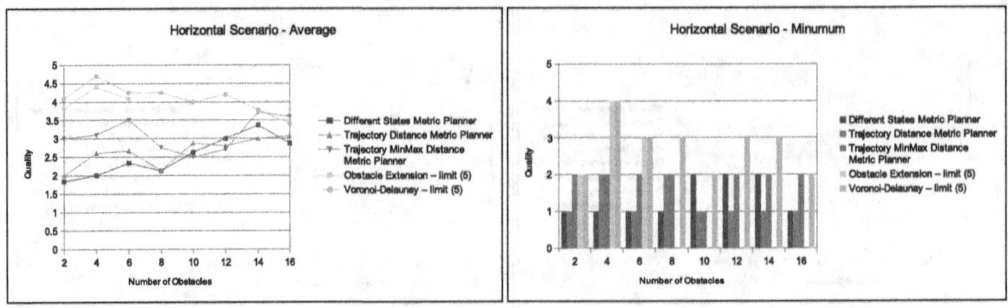

Fig. 11. Average (left) and the worst (right) quality marks given by human operators.

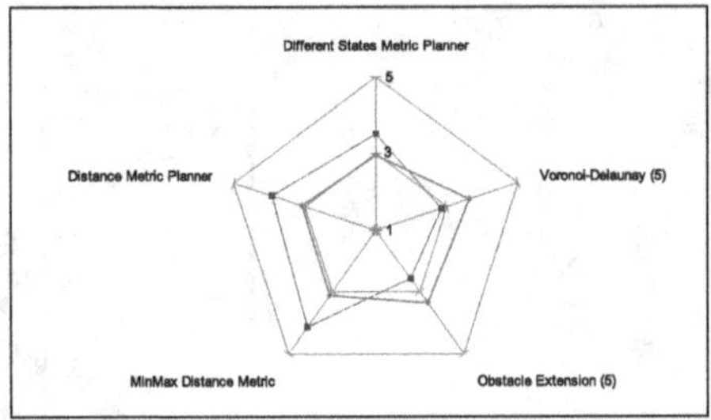

Fig. 12. Average quality evaluated by human operator: cluster centroids.

6.1 Human Operator Test

It can be very difficult to measure the usefulness of created diverse trajectories using the metrics described above only. Thus, we have also performed a user test where a group of 12 people, familiar with the trajectory planning and the UAV control problem, have manually evaluated results of each method. Each user has evaluated 15 problem instances of the 8-grid scenario with randomly placed obstacles and a set of 5 trajectories proposed by each method. User graded each solution with 1 to 5 points (more points means better solution).

Average and the worst quality evaluation of each method for different number of obstacles are shown in Fig. 11. We can see that the best score was achieved by the Trajectory Distance Metric MaxMin planner and the Voronoi-Delaunay graphs based planner. The Voronoi-Delaunay graphs based planner outperformed other methods mainly in the horizontal scenario with up to 12 obstacles. Based on our experience, one segment of the UAV trajectory typically does not avoid more obstacles which makes this method very suitable for use in operators' control panels.

Closer evaluation shows that the users can be divided into two groups. Some have preferred trajectories whose length is closer the to optimum while the others preferred more diverse trajectories. First group of users, graded higher the Voronoi-Delaunay graphs based planner while the latter one preferred the Trajectory Distance Metric MaxMin planner. We used k-means clustering to find centroids of both groups. These centroids of evaluations both groups are shown

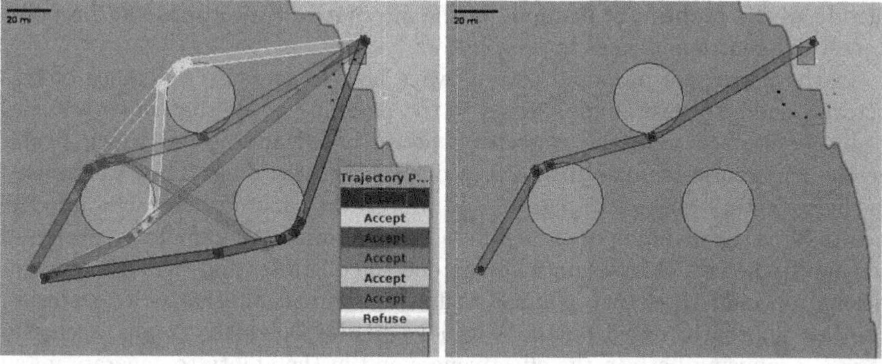

Fig. 13. Upper screenshot shows several trajectories, which are proposed to the user after he set up two new waypoints for the UAV (whose last radar positions are shown by gray scaled dots). We can see that all the trajectories avoid the obstacles in different ways and thus the user can select the one which the best fits his preferences. When the user selects green trajectory, it is applied by the UAV as shown in the lower screenshot.

in the Fig. 12. This observation will direct our future research to create a method which will satisfy both groups.

7 Voronoi-Delaunay Graphs Based Planner Deployment

We have implemented the Voronoi-Delaunay graphs based planner together with RRT* (optimal rapid-random trees) planner into a prototype of UAV control display. RRT* allows to find a non-optimal trajectory in high dimensional non-graph based search space. It randomly samples the space and constructs a tree of states reachable from the start position. Whenever new sample is taken, RRT* connects it to the existing tree if there is a direct connection. The algorithm can reorganize the tree to assure the convergence to the optimal path, see [10,11] for details.

When user specifies new waypoints, several diverse trajectories are created and proposed to the user, as shown in Fig. 13. User can choose one trajectory or refuse all of them. When a trajectory is accepted, the green one in our example, it is sent to the UAV and it starts to follow it.

8 Conclusions and Future Work

A human-UAV interaction is a bottleneck of today's unmanned aerial systems. The interface during the trajectory planning can be certainly improved by providing a user with several alternative trajectories from which the user can choose the most suitable one. This problem has not been targeted by the scientific community yet even though it has a significant practical impact. This contribution introduces the problem of planning of the alternative trajectories and proposes several different approaches to its solution.

In the paper, we proposed several ways how to measure difference of trajectories and also several approaches to the planning of alternative trajectories itself. We started with the trajectory metric based approaches which penalize the trajectories similar to the previously generated ones. Then we focused on the trajectory-obstacles relations and proposed to add new obstacles into the area to force the planning of more different trajectories. And finally we proposed two approaches which systematically extend the obstacles and then use any traditional optimal trajectory planner to find individual alternative trajectories. The last approach, based on the Voronoi and the Delaunay graphs, seems to be very promising both in the effectiveness and in the ability to generate many alternative trajectories. In the time critical scenarios a trajectory metric based algorithm can be used. All the approaches have been evaluated in a benchmark scenario by both the designed metrics and by the human users. We also have implemented the Voronoi-Delaunay graphs based planner together with RRT* planner into a prototype of UAV control display.

References

1. Hart, P., Nilsson, N., Raphael, B.: A formal basis for the heuristic determination of minimum cost paths. IEEE Trans. Syst. Sci. Cybern. **4**(2), 100–107 (1968)
2. Nash, A., Daniel, K., Koenig, S., Felner, A.: Theta*: Any-angle path planning on grids. In: Proceedings of the AAAI Conference on Artificial Intelligence (AAAI), pp. 1177–1183 (2007)
3. Yap, P.: Grid-based path-finding. In: Proceedings of the Canadian Conference on Aritificial Intelligence, pp. 44–55 (2002)
4. Coman, A., Muñoz-Avila, H.: Generating diverse plans using quantitative and qualitative plan distance metrics. In: AAAI. AAAI Press (2011)
5. Fikes, R.E., Nilsson, N.J.: Strips: A new approach to the application of theorem proving to problem solving. Artif. Intell. **2**, 189–208 (1971)
6. Aurenhammer, F.: Voronoi diagrams - A survey of a fundamental geometric data structure. ACM Comput. Surv. **23**, 345–405 (1991)
7. Garrido, S., Moreno, L., Blanco, D.: Voronoi diagram and fast marching applied to path planning. In: Proceedings of the 2006 IEEE International Conference on Robotics and Automation, ICRA 2006, pp. 3049–3054. IEEE (2006)
8. Hui-ying, D., Shuo, D., Yu, Z.: Delaunay graph based path planning method for mobile robot. In: 2010 International Conference on Communications and Mobile Computing (CMC), vol. 3, pp. 528–531 (2010)
9. Fortune, S.: Voronoi diagrams and Delaunay triangulations. In: Goodman, J.E., O'Rourke, J. (eds.) Handbook of Discrete and Computational Geometry, pp. 377–388. CRC Press LLC, Boca Raton (1997)
10. Karaman, F.: Sampling-based algorithms for optimal motion planning. Int. J. Robot. Res. **30**, 846–894 (2011)
11. LaValle, S.M.: Planning Algorithms. Cambridge University Press, Cambridge (2006). http://planning.cs.uiuc.edu/

Behavioral Reasoning on Semantic Business Processes in a Rule-Based Framework

Fabrizio Smith(✉) and Maurizio Proietti

National Research Council, IASI "Antonio Ruberti",
Via dei Taurini 19, 00185 Roma, Italy
{fabrizio.smith,maurizio.proietti}@iasi.cnr.it

Abstract. We propose a representation method for semantically enriched business processes by combining in a uniform logical framework both the procedural and the domain dependent knowledge. First, we define a rule-based procedural semantics for a relevant fragment of BPMN, a very popular graphical notation for specifying business processes. Our semantics defines a state transition system by following an approach similar to the Fluent Calculus, and allows us to specify state change in terms of preconditions and effects of the enactment of activities. Then, we show how the procedural process knowledge can be seamlessly integrated with the domain knowledge specified by using the OWL-RL rule-based ontology language. As a result, our framework provides a wide range of reasoning services by using standard logic programming inference engines.

Keywords: Business processes · Ontologies · Rule-based reasoning · Verification

1 Introduction

The adoption of structured and systematic approaches for the management of the Business Processes (BPs) operating within an organization is constantly gaining popularity in various industrial sectors, especially in medium to large enterprises, and in the public administration. The core of such approaches is the development of BP models that represent the knowledge about processes in machine accessible form. However, standard BP modeling languages are not fully adequate to capture process knowledge in all its aspects. While their focus is on the procedural representation of a BP as a workflow graph that specifies the planned order of operations, the domain knowledge regarding the entities involved in such a process, i.e., the business environment in which processes are carried out, is often left implicit. This kind of knowledge is typically expressed through natural language comments and labels attached to the models, which constitute very limited, informal and ambiguous pieces of information.

This work has been partly funded by the European Commission through the ICT Project BIVEE: Business Innovation and Virtual Enterprise Environment (FoF-ICT-2011.7.3-285746).

J. Filipe and A. Fred (Eds.): ICAART 2013, CCIS 449, pp. 293–313, 2014.
DOI: 10.1007/978-3-662-44440-5_18

The above issues are widely recognized as an obstacle for the further automation of BP Management (BPM) tools and methodologies [8]. Process modeling, in particular, is still mainly a manual activity, where a very limited support is given in terms of reuse and retrieval functionalities, or automated analysis facilities, i.e., for verifying whether the requirements specified over the models are enforced. The latter aspect is addressed in the BPM community mainly from a control flow perspective, with the aim of verifying whether the behavior of the modeled system presents logical errors (see, for instance, the notion of soundness [24]).

However, in order to verify that a BP actually behaves as expected, additional domain knowledge is required. In this respect, the application of well-established techniques stemming from the area of Knowledge Representation in the domains of BP modeling [8,11,26] and Web Services [2,6] has been shown as a promising approach. In particular, the use of computational ontologies is the most established approach for representing in a machine processable way the knowledge about the domain where business processes operate, providing formal definitions for the basic entities involved in a process, such as activities, actors, data items, and the relations between them. However, there are still several open issues regarding the combination of BP modeling languages (with their execution semantics) and ontologies, and the accomplishment of behavioral reasoning tasks involving both these components.

The main objective of this paper is to design a framework for representing and reasoning about business process knowledge from both the procedural and ontological point of views. To achieve this goal, we do *not* propose yet another business process modeling language, but we provide a rule-based framework for reasoning about process-related knowledge expressed by using de-facto standards for BP modeling, like BPMN [17], and ontology definition, like OWL [9]. To this end we define a rule-based procedural semantics for a relevant fragment of BPMN, and we extend it in order to take into account OWL annotations that describe preconditions and effects of activities and events occurring within a BP. Our procedural BP semantics seamlessly integrates with OWL-RL [9], a fragment of the OWL ontology language which has a suitable rule-based presentation, and is achieving increasing success because it constitutes an excellent compromise between expressivity and efficiency.

In essence, the contributions of this paper can be summarized as follows. In Sect. 2 we introduce a set of rules, expressed in the logic programming formalism [13], for modeling the procedural semantics of a BP regarded as a workflow. The proposed rule set can cope with a relevant fragment of the BPMN 2.0 pecification, allowing us to deal with a large class of process models. We then propose in Sect. 3 an approach for the semantic annotation of BP models, where preconditions and effects of BP elements are described by using an OWL-RL ontology. In Sect. 4 we provide a general verification mechanism by encoding the temporal logic CTL [4] as a set of rules which allow us to analyze properties of BPs depending on both the control flow and semantic annotations. Finally, in Sect. 5 we show how we can perform some very sophisticated reasoning tasks, such as verification, querying and trace compliance checking, that combine both the procedural and domain knowledge relative to a BP.

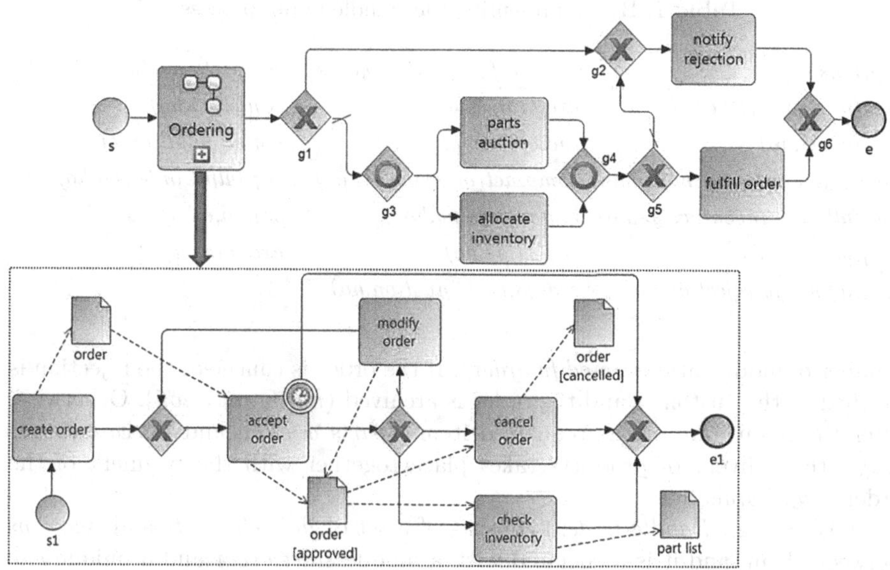

Fig. 1. Handle Order BP.

2 Behavioral Semantics of BP Schemas

In this section we introduce a formal representation of business processes by means of the notion of *Business Process Schema* (BPS). A BPS, its meta-model, and its procedural (or *behavioral*) semantics will all be specified by sets of rules, for which we adopt the standard notation and semantics of logic programming (see, for instance, [13]). In particular, a rule is of the form $A \leftarrow L_1 \wedge \ldots \wedge L_n$, where A is an *atom* (i.e., a formula of the form $p(t_1, \ldots, t_m)$) and $L_1, \ldots, L_n$ are *literals* (i.e., atoms or negated atoms). If $n = 0$ we call the rule a *fact*. A rule (atom, literal) is *ground* if no variables occur in it. A *logic program* is a finite set of rules. Throughout the paper we will consider the class of (*locally*) *stratified* logic programs, i.e., programs that can be layered into strata such that negated atoms in higher strata are defined by rules in lower strata. Every program P in this class has a unique *perfect model*, denoted *Perf*(P), constructed as shown in [18].

2.1 Business Process Schemas

We show how a BPS is specified by means of an example. The full definition can be found in [21]. Let us consider the BP depicted in Fig. 1, where the handling of a purchase order is represented using the BPMN notation. The process starts with the *ordering* activity, which is a *compound* activity where, upon receiving a customer request, a purchase order is created (*create order*), approved (*accept order*) or canceled (*cancel order*). An approved order can also be subjected to a

Table 1. BPS representing the Handle Order process.

bp(ho,s,e)	*seq(notify_rejection, g6, ho)*	*seq(parts_auction, g4, ho)*
seq(ordering,g1,ho)	*exc_branch(g1)*	*seq(g4,g5,ho)*
seq(g1,g3,ho)	*inc_branch(g3)*	*seq(g5,fulfill_order,ho)*
seq(g3,allocate_inventory,ho)	*comp_act(ordering,*s_1*,* e_1*)*	*seq(fulfill_order,g6,ho)*
seq(allocate_inventory,g4,ho)	*seq(s,ordering,ho)*	*seq(g6,e,ho)*
seq(g5,g2,ho)	*seq(g1,g2,ho)*	*exc_merge(g2)*
seq(g2,notify_rejection,ho)	*seq(g3,parts_auction,ho)*	...

number of modifications (*modify order*). If the order is canceled, the rejection is notified to the customer and the order is archived (*notify rejection*). Otherwise, after the requisition of the requested items (*parts auction* and *allocate inventory*), the delivery of products takes place together with the payment of the order (*fulfill order*).

A BPS (e.g., *Handle Order*) consists of a set of *flow elements* and *relations* between them, and it is associated with a unique *start event* and a unique *end event*, which are flow elements that represent the entry point and the exit point, respectively, of the process. An *activity* is a flow element that represents a unit of work performed within the process. A *task* represents an atomic activity (e.g., *accept order*), i.e., no further decomposable, while a *compound activity* is associated with a process that provides the definition of its internal structure (e.g., *ordering*). An *intermediate event* represents "something that occurs during the process execution" (e.g., the *time-out exception* attached to the *accept order* activity). The sequencing of flow elements is specified by the *sequence flow* relation (corresponding to solid arrows), and the *branching/merging* of the control flow is specified by using three types of *gateways*: *exclusive* (XOR, e.g., *g1*), *inclusive* (OR, e.g., *g3*), and *parallel* (AND, not exemplified in Fig. 1). The *item flow* relation (corresponding to dotted arrows) specifies that a flow element uses as *input* (e.g., *accept order* and *order*) or produces as *output* (e.g., *create order* and *order*) a particular *item*, i.e., a physical or information object.

A BPS can also represent other entities usually employed to model processes, such as *participants* and *messages*, not presented here for lack of space. Indeed, by following our approach we can represent the constructs common to the most used BP modeling languages and, in particular, the ones based on the BPMN specification [17].

Formally, a BPS is specified by a set of ground facts of the form $p(c_1, \ldots, c_n)$, where $c_1, \ldots, c_n$ are constants denoting flow elements (e.g., activities, events, and gateways) and p is a predicate symbol. An excerpt of the translation of the Handle Order process (referred to as *ho*) as a BPS is shown in Table 1.

Our formalization also includes a set of rules that represent the *meta-model*, defining a number of structural properties which regard a BPS as a directed graph, where edges correspond to sequence and item flow relations. Two categories of structural properties should be verified by a *well-formed* (i.e., syntactically correct) BPS: *(i) local* properties related to its elementary components (e.g., every activity must have at most one ingoing and at most one outgoing sequence flow), and *(ii) global* properties related to the overall structure of the BPS (e.g., every flow element must lie on a path from the *start* to the *end* event). Furthermore, other meta-model properties are related to the notions of path and reachability between flow elements, such as the following ones, which will be used in the sequel: $seq^+(E_1, E_2, P)$, representing the transitive closure of the *sequence flow* relation, and $n\_reachable(E_1, E_2, E_3, P)$, which holds if there is a path in P between E_1 and E_2 not including E_3.

2.2 Behavioral Semantics

Now we present a formal definition of the behavioral semantics, or *enactment*, of a BPS, by following an approach inspired to the *Fluent Calculus*, a well-known calculus for action and change (see [23] for an introduction). In the Fluent Calculus, the state of the world is represented as a collection of *fluents*, i.e., terms representing atomic properties that hold at a given instant of time.

An action, also represented as a term, may cause a change of state, i.e., an update of the collection of fluents associated with it. Finally, a *plan* is a sequence of actions that leads from the initial to the final state.

For states we use set notation (here we depart from [23], where an associative-commutative operator is used for representing collections of fluents). A fluent is an expression of the form $f(a_1, \ldots, a_n)$, where f is a fluent symbol and $a_1, \ldots, a_n$ are constants or variables. In order to model the behavior of a BPS, we represent states as *finite sets* of ground fluents. We take a closed-world interpretation of states, that is, we assume that a fluent F holds in a state S iff $F \in S$. This set-based representation of states relies on the assumption that the BPS is *safe*, i.e., during its enactment there are no concurrent executions of the same flow element [24]. This assumption enforces that the set of states reachable by a given BPS is finite.

A *fluent expression* is built inductively from fluents, the binary function symbol *and*, and the unary function symbol *not*. The satisfaction relation assigns a truth value to a fluent expression with respect to a state. This relation is encoded by a predicate $holds(F, S)$, which holds if the fluent expression F is true in the state S. We also introduce a constant symbol *true*, such that $holds(true, S)$ holds for every state S. Accordingly to the closed-world interpretation given to states, the satisfaction relation is defined by the following rules:

$$holds(F, S) \leftarrow F = true$$
$$holds(F, S) \leftarrow F \in S$$
$$holds(not(F), S) \leftarrow \neg holds(F, S)$$
$$holds(and(F_1, F_2), S) \leftarrow holds(F_1, S) \wedge holds(F_2, S)$$

We will consider the following two kinds of fluents: $cf(E_1, E_2, P)$, which means that the flow element E_1 has been executed and the flow element E_2 is waiting for execution, during the enactment of the process P (*cf* stands for *control flow*); $en(A, P)$, which means that the activity A is being executed during the enactment of the process P (*en* stands for *enacting*). To clarify our terminology note that, when a flow element E_2 is waiting for execution, E_2 might not be enabled to execute, because other conditions need to be fulfilled, such as those depending on the synchronization with other flow elements (see, in particular, the semantics of merging behaviors below).

We assume that the execution of an activity has a beginning and a completion (although we do not associate a *duration* with activity execution), while the other flow elements execute instantaneously. Thus, we will consider two kinds of actions: *begin*(A) which starts the execution of an activity A, and *complete*(E), which represents the completion of the execution of a flow element E (possibly, an activity). The change of state determined by the execution of an action will be formalized by a relation *result*(S_1, A, S_2), which holds if the action A can be executed in the state S_1 leading to the state S_2. For defining the relation *result*(S_1, A, S_2) the following auxiliary predicates will be used: (i) *update*(S_1, T, U, S_2), which holds if $S_2 = (S_1 - T) \cup U$, where S_1, T, U, and S_2 are sets of fluents, and (ii) *setof*(F, C, S), which holds if S is the set of ground instances of fluent F such that condition C holds.

The relation $r(S_1, S_2)$ holds if a state S_2 is *immediately reachable* from a state S_1, that is, some action A can be executed in state S_1 leading to state S_2: $r(S_1, S_2) \leftarrow result(S_1, A, S_2)$.

We say that a state S_2 is *reachable* from a state S_1 if there is a finite sequence of actions (of length ≥ 0) from S_1 to S_2, that is, *reachable_state*(S_1, S_2) holds, where the relation *reachable_state* is the reflexive-transitive closure of r.

In the rest of this section we present a fluent-based formalization of the behavioral semantics of a BPS by focusing on a core of the BPMN language. The proposed formal semantics, reported in Table 2, mainly refers to the BPMN semantics, as described (informally) in the most recent specification of the language [17]. Most of the constructs considered here (e.g., parallel or exclusive branching/merging) have the same interpretation in most workflow languages. However, when different interpretations are given, e.g., in the case of inclusive merge, we stick to the BPMN one.

Activity and Event Execution. The enactment of a process P begins with the execution of the associated start event E in a state where the fluent *cf*(*start*, E, P) holds, being *start* a reserved constant. After the execution of the start event, its unique successor waits for execution (rule E1). The execution of an end event leads to the final state of a process execution, in which the fluent *cf*(E, *end*, P) holds, where E is the end event associated with the process P and *end* is a reserved constant (rule E2).

The execution of an activity is enabled to begin after the completion of its unique predecessor flow element. The effects of the execution of an activity vary depending on its type (i.e., atomic task or compound activity). The beginning of an atomic task A is modeled by adding the *en*(A, P) fluent to the state (rule A1). At the completion of A, the *en*(A, P) fluent is removed and the control flow moves on to the unique successor of A (rule A2). The execution of a compound activity, whose internal structure is defined as a process itself, begins by enabling the execution of the associated *start event* (rule A3), and completes after the execution of the associated *end event* (rule A4).

Table 2. Fragment of the behavioral semantics of the BPAL language.

(E1) $result(S_1, complete(E), S_2) \leftarrow start\_event(E) \land holds(cf(start, E, P), S_1) \land seq(E, X, P) \land update(S_1, \{cf(start, E, P)\}, \{cf(E, X, P)\}, S_2)$
(E2) $result(S_1, complete(E), S_2) \leftarrow end\_event(E) \land holds(cf(X, E, P), S_1) \land update(S_1, \{cf(X, E, P)\}, \{cf(E, end, P)\}, S_2)$
(E3) $result(S_1, complete(E), S_2) \leftarrow int\_event(E) \land holds(cf(X, E, P), S_1) \land seq(E, Y, P) \land update(S_1, \{cf(X, E, P)\}, \{cf(E, Y, P)\}, S_2)$
(E4) $result(S_1, complete(E), S_2) \leftarrow exception(E, A, P) \land int\_event(E) \land holds(en(A, P), S_1) \land seq(E, Y, P) \land update(S_1, \{en(A, P)\}, \{cf(E, Y, P)\}, S_2)$

(A1) $result(S_1, begin(A), S_2) \leftarrow task(A) \land holds(cf(X, A, P), S_1) \land update(S_1, \{cf(X, A, P)\}, \{en(A, P)\}, S_2)$
(A2) $result(S_1, complete(A), S_2) \leftarrow task(A) \land holds(en(A, P), S_1) \land seq(A, Y, P) \land update(S_1, \{en(A, P)\}, \{cf(A, Y, P)\}, S_2)$
(A3) $result(S_1, begin(A), S_2) \leftarrow comp\_act(A, S, E) \land holds(and(cf(X, A, P), not(en(A, P))), S_1) \land update(S_1, \{cf(X, A, P)\}, \{cf(start, S, A), en(A, P)\}, S_2)$
(A4) $result(S_1, complete(A), S_2) \leftarrow comp\_act(A, S, E) \land holds(and(cf(E, end, A), en(A, P)), S_1) \land seq(A, Y, P) \land update(S_1, \{en(A, P), cf(E, end, A)\}, \{cf(A, Y, P)\}, S_2)$

(B1) $result(S_1, complete(B), S_2) \leftarrow inc\_branch(B) \land holds(cf(X, B, P), S_1) \land setof(cf(B, Y, P), (c\_seq(G, B, Y, P) \land holds(G, S_1)), Succ) \land update(I, \{cf(X, B, P)\}, Succ, S_2)$
(B2) $result(S_1, complete(B), S_2) \leftarrow par\_branch(B) \land holds(cf(X, B, P), S_1) \land setof(cf(B, Y, P), seq(B, Y, P), Succ) \land update(S_1, \{cf(X, B, P)\}, Succ, S_2)$

(O1) $result(S_1, complete(M), S_2) \leftarrow inc\_merge(M) \land enabled\_im(M, S_1, P) \land seq(M, Y, P) \land setof(cf(X, M, P), holds(cf(X, M, P), S_1), PredM) \land update(S_1, PredM, \{cf(M, Y, P)\}, S_2)$
(O2) $enabled\_im(M, S_1, P) \leftarrow holds(cf(X, M, P), S_1) \land \neg exists\_upstream(M, S_1, P)$
(O3) $exists\_upstream(M, S_1, P) \leftarrow seq(X, M, P) \land holds(not(cf(X, M, P)), S_1) \land holds(cf(Y, U, P), S_1) \land upstream(U, X, M, S_1, P)$
(O4) $upstream(U, X, M, S_1, P) \leftarrow n\_reachable(U, X, M, P) \land \neg exists\_path(U, M, S_1, P)$
(O5) $exists\_path(U, M, S_1, P) \leftarrow holds(cf(K, M, P), S_1) \land n\_reachable(U, K, M, P)$
(P1) $result(S_1, complete(M), S_2) \leftarrow par\_merge(M) \land \neg exists\_non\_executed\_pred(M, P, S_1) \land seq(M, Y, P) \land setof(cf(X, M, P), seq(X, M, P), PredM) \land update(S_1, PredM, \{cf(M, Y, P)\}, S_2)$
(P2) $exists\_non\_executed\_pred(M, P, S_1) \leftarrow seq(X, M, P) \land holds(not(cf(X, M, P)), S_1)$

According to the informal semantics of BPMN, *intermediate events* are intended as instantaneous patterns of behavior that are registered at a given time point. Thus, we formally model the execution of an intermediate event as a single state transition, as defined in rule E3. Intermediate events in BPMN can also be attached to activity boundaries to model exceptional flows. Upon occurrence of an *exception*, the execution of the activity is interrupted, and the control flow moves along the sequence flow that leaves the event (rule E4).

Branching Behaviors. When a branch gateway is executed, a subset of its successors is selected for execution. We consider here exclusive, inclusive, and parallel branch gateways. An exclusive branch leads to the execution of exactly one successor, while an inclusive branch leads to the concurrent execution of a non-empty subset of its successors. The set of successors of exclusive or inclusive decision points is selected by using *guards*, i.e., fluent expressions whose truth value is tested with respect to the current state. The value of guards may depend on fluents different from $cf(E_1, E_2, P)$ and $en(A, P)$. Indeed, extra fluents can be introduced for modeling the effects of the execution of flow elements (e.g., operations on items) as shown in Sect. 3.2. A guard is associated with a gateway by the predicate $c\_seq(G, B, Y, P)$ modeling a *conditional sequence flow*, where G is a fluent expression denoting a guard, B is an exclusive or inclusive branch gateway and Y is a successor flow element of B in the process P. We also have the rule $seq(B, Y, P) \leftarrow c\_seq(G, B, Y, P)$. The semantics of inclusive branches is defined in rule B1. The semantics of exclusive branches can be defined in a similar way and is omitted. Finally, a parallel branch leads to the concurrent execution of all its successors (rule B2).

Merging Behaviors. An exclusive merge can be executed whenever at least one of its predecessors has been executed. Here we omit the straightforward formal definition.

For the inclusive merge several operational semantics have been proposed, due to the complexity of its non-local semantics, see e.g., [10]. An inclusive merge is supposed to be able to synchronize a varying number of threads, i.e., it is executed only when $n(\geq 1)$ predecessors have been executed and no other will be eventually executed. Here we refer to the semantics described in [25] adopted by BPMN, stating that (rule O1) an inclusive merge M can be executed if the following two conditions hold (rules O2, O3):

(1) at least one of its predecessors has been executed,
(2) for each non-executed predecessor X, there is no flow element U which is waiting for execution and is *upstream* X. The notion of being upstream captures the fact that U may lead to the execution of X, and is defined as follows. A flow element U is upstream X if (rules O4, O5): *(a)* there is a path from U to X not including M, and *(b)* there is no path from U to an executed predecessor of M not including M.

Finally, a parallel merge can be executed if all its predecessors have been executed as defined in rule P1, where $exists\_non\_executed\_pred(M, P, S_1)$ holds if there exists no predecessor of M which has not been executed in state S_1 (rule P2).

3 Semantic Annotation

In the previous section we have shown how the behavioral semantics of the workflow specified by a BPS can be modeled in our rule-based framework. However, not all the relevant knowledge regarding process enactment is captured by a workflow model, which defines the planned order of operations but does not provide an explicit representation of the domain knowledge regarding the entities involved in such a process, i.e., the business environment in which processes are carried out.

Similarly to proposals like *Semantic BPM* [8] and *Semantic Web Services* [6], we will make use of *semantic annotations* to enrich the procedural knowledge specified by a BPS with domain knowledge expressed in terms of a given business reference ontology. Annotations provide two kinds of ontology-based information: *(i)* formal definitions of the basic entities involved in a process (e.g., activities, actors, items) to specify their meaning in an unambiguous way (*terminological* annotations), and *(ii)* specifications of preconditions and effects of the enactment of flow elements (*functional* annotations). In this work we focus on functional annotations and on their interaction with the control flow to define the behavior of a BPS, thus extending the framework presented in [21] where terminological annotations only were considered.

3.1 Rule-Based Ontologies

A business reference ontology is intended to capture the semantics of a business scenario in terms of the relevant vocabulary plus a set of axioms (TBox) which define the intended meaning of the vocabulary terms. In order to represent the semantic annotations and the behavioral semantics of a BPS in a uniform way, we will represent ontologies by sets of rules. To this end, we consider a fragment of OWL falling within the OWL 2 RL [9] profile, which is an upward-compatible extension of RDF and RDFS whose semantics is defined via a set of Horn rules, called OWL 2 RL/RDF rules. OWL 2 RL ontologies are modeled by means of the ternary predicate $t(s,p,o)$ representing an OWL statement with subject s, predicate p and object o. For instance, the assertion $t(a, \mathit{rdfs{:}subClassOf}, b)$ represents the inclusion axiom $a \sqsubseteq b$. Reasoning on triples is supported by OWL 2 RL/RDF rules of the form $t(s,p,o) \leftarrow t(s_1,p_1,o_1) \land \cdots \land t(s_n,p_n,o_n)$. For instance, the rule $t(A, \mathit{rdfs{:}subClassOf}, B) \leftarrow t(A, \mathit{rdfs{:}subClassOf}, C) \land t(C, \mathit{rdfs{:}subClassOf}, B)$ defines the transitive closure of the subsumption relation.

Table 3. Business Reference Ontology excerpt.

$\mathit{ClosedPO} \sqsubseteq \mathit{Order}$	$\mathit{ApprovedPO} \sqsubseteq \mathit{Order}$
$\mathit{CancelledPO} \sqsubseteq \mathit{ClosedPO}$	$\mathit{FulfilledPO} \sqsubseteq \mathit{ClosedPO}$
$\mathit{UnavailablePL} \sqsubseteq \mathit{PartList}$	$\mathit{AvailablePL} \sqsubseteq \mathit{PartList}$
$\mathit{payment} \sqsubseteq \mathit{related}$	$\exists\, \mathit{payment}^{-} \sqsubseteq \mathit{Invoice}$
$\mathit{CancelledPO} \sqcap \mathit{ApprovedPO} \sqsubseteq \bot$	$\mathit{UnavailablePL} \sqcap \mathit{AvailablePL} \sqsubseteq \bot$
$\mathit{ApprovedPO} \sqcap \exists \mathit{related}.\mathit{Invoice} \sqsubseteq \mathit{FulfilledPO}$	$\mathit{Order} \sqcap \exists \mathit{related}.\mathit{UnavailablePL} \sqsubseteq \mathit{CancelledPO}$

An OWL 2 RL ontology is represented as a set $\mathcal{O}$ of rules, consisting of a set of facts of the form $t(s,p,o)$, called *triples*, encoding the OWL TBox and the set of Horn rules encoding the OWL 2 RL/RDF rules. This kind of representation allows us to take advantage of the efficient resolution strategies developed for logic programs, in order to perform the reasoning tasks typically supported by Description Logics reasoning systems, such as concept subsumption and ontology consistency.

3.2 Functional Annotation

By using the ontology vocabulary and axioms, we define semantic annotations for modeling the behavior of individual process elements in terms of *preconditions* under which a flow element can be executed and *effects* on the state of the world after its execution. Preconditions and effects, collectively called *functional annotations*, can be used, for instance, to model input/output relations of activities with data items, which are the standard way of representing information storage in BPMN diagrams. Fluents can represent the *status* of a data item affected by the execution of an activity at a given time during the execution of the process. A precondition specifies the status a data item must posses when an activity is enabled to start, and an effect specifies the status of a data item after having completed an activity. In order to provide concrete examples to illustrate the main ideas, in the rest of the paper we refer to the excerpt of reference ontology reported in Table 3, describing the items involved in the BPS depicted in Fig. 1.

Functional annotations are formulated by means of the following two relations:

- *pre*(A, C, P), which specifies the fluent expression C, called *enabling condition*, which must hold to execute an element A in the process P;
- *eff*(A, E^-, E^+, P), which specifies the set E^- of fluents, called *negative effects*, which do not hold after the execution of A and the set of fluents E^+, called *positive effects*, which hold after the execution of A in the process P. We assume that E^- and E^+ are disjoint sets.

In the presence of functional annotations, the enactment of a BPS is modeled as follows. Given a state S_1, a flow element A can be enacted if A is waiting for execution according to the control flow semantics, and its enabling condition C is satisfied, i.e., *holds*(C, S_1) is true. Moreover, given an annotation *eff*(A, E^-, E^+, P), when A is completed in a given state S_1, then a new state S_2 is obtained by taking out from S_1 the set E^- of fluents and then adding the set E^+ of fluents. We will assume that effects satisfy a *consistency condition* which guarantees that: (i) no contradiction can be derived from the fluents of S_2 by using the state independent axioms of the reference ontology, and (ii) no fluent belonging to E^- holds in S_2. This consistency condition will be formally defined later in this section, and can be regarded as a way of tackling the *Ramification Problem* due to indirect effects of actions (see e.g., [19,23]). The state update is formalized by extending the *result* relation so as to take into account the *pre* and *eff* relations. We only consider the case of task execution. The other cases are similar and will be omitted.

Table 4. Functional annotations for the Handle Order process.

Flow Element	Enabling Condition	Effects
create order		$t_f(o, rdf{:}type, bro{:}Order)$
accept order	$t_f(o, rdf{:}type, bro{:}Order)$	$t_f(o, rdf{:}type, bro{:}ApprovedPO)$
cancel order	$t_f(o, rdf{:}type, bro{:}ApprovedPO)$	$\neg t_f(o, rdf{:}type, bro{:}ApprovedPO)$, $t_f(o, rdf{:}type, bro{:}CancelledPO)$
check inventory	$t_f(o, rdf{:}type, bro{:}ApprovedPO)$	$t_f(o, bro{:}related, pl), t_f(pl, rdf{:}type, bro{:}PartList)$
check inventory	$t_f(o, rdf{:}type, bro{:}ApprovedPO)$	
parts auction	$t_f(pl, rdf{:}type, bro{:}PartList)$	$t_f(pl, rdf{:}type, bro{:}AvailablePL)$
parts auction	$t_f(pl, rdf{:}type, bro{:}PartList)$	$\neg t f(o, rdf{:}type, bro{:}ApprovedPO)$, $t_f(pl, rdf{:}type, bro{:}UnavailablePL)$
fulfill order	$t_f(o, rdf{:}type, bro{:}ApprovedPO)$	$t_f(o, bro{:}payment, i)$

Gateway	Target	Guard
g1	g3	$t_f(o, rdf{:}type, bro{:}ApprovedPO)$
g1	g2	$not(t_f(o, rdf{:}type, bro{:}ApprovedPO))$
g3	parts auction	$and(t_f(o, related, pl), t_f(pl, rdf{:}type, bro{:}PartList))$
g5	g2	$t_f(o, rdf{:}type, bro{:}CancelledPO)$
g5	fulfill order	$not(t_f(o, rdf{:}type, bro{:}CancelledPO))$

$$result(S_1, begin(A), S_2) \leftarrow task(A) \wedge holds(cf(X,A,P), S_1) \wedge pre(A,C,P) \wedge holds(C, S_1) \wedge update(S_1, \{cf(X,A,P)\}, \{en(A,P)\}, S_2)$$

$$result(S_1, complete(A), S_2) \leftarrow task(A) \wedge holds(en(A,P), S_1) \wedge eff(A, E^-, E^+, P) \wedge seq(A,Y,P) \wedge update(S_1, \{en(A,P)\} \cup E^-, \{cf(A,Y,P)\} \cup E^+, S_2)$$

The enabling conditions and the negative and positive effects occurring in functional annotations are fluent expressions built from fluents of the form $t_f(s,p,o)$, corresponding to the OWL statement $t(s,p,o)$, where we adopt the usual *rdf*, *rdfs*, and *owl* prefixes for names in the OWL vocabulary, and the *bro* prefix for names relative to our specific examples. We assume that the fluents appearing in functional annotations are either of the form $t_f(a, rdf{:}type, c)$, corresponding to the unary atom $c(a)$, or of the form $t_f(a,p,b)$, corresponding to the binary atom $p(a,b)$, where a and c are *individuals*, while c and p are concepts and properties, respectively, defined in the reference ontology $\mathcal{O}$. Thus, fluents correspond to assertions about individuals, i.e., the ABox of the ontology, and hence the ABox may change during process enactment due to the effects specified by the functional annotations, while $\mathcal{O}$, providing the ontology definitions and axioms, i.e., the TBox of the ontology, does not change.

Let us now present an example of specification of functional annotations. In particular, our example shows nondeterministic effects, that is, a case where a flow element A is associated with more than one pair (E^-, E^+) of negative and positive effects.

Example 1. *Consider again the* Handle Order *process in Fig. 1. After the execution of* create order, *a purchase order is issued. This order can be approved or canceled upon execution of the activities* accept order *and* cancel order, *respectively. Depending on the inventory capacity checked during the* check inventory *task, the requisition of parts performed by an external supplier is performed* (parts auction)*. Once that all the order parts are available, the order can be fulfilled and an invoice is associated with the order. This behavior is specified by the functional annotations reported in Table 4.*

In order to evaluate a statement of the form *holds*$(t_f(s,p,o),X)$, where $t_f(s,p,o)$ is a fluent and X is a state, the definition of the *holds* predicate given previously must be extended to take into account the axioms belonging to the reference ontology $\mathcal{O}$. Indeed, we want that a fluent of the form $t_f(s,p,o)$ be true in state X not only if it belongs to X, but also if it can be inferred from the fluents in X and the axioms of the ontology. For instance, let us consider the fluent $F = t_f(o, \mathit{rdf{:}type}, \mathit{bro{:}CancelledPO})$. We can easily infer that F holds in a state which contains $\{t_f(o, \mathit{rdf{:}type}, \mathit{bro{:}CancelledPO})\}$ (e.g., reachable after the execution of *cancel order*) by using the rule $\mathit{holds}(F,X) \leftarrow F \in X$. However, by taking into account the ontology excerpt given in Table 3, we also want to be able to infer that F holds in a state which contains $\{t_f(o, \mathit{rdf{:}type}, \mathit{bro{:}Order}), t_f(o, \mathit{bro{:}related}, \mathit{pl}), t_f(\mathit{pl}, \mathit{rdf{:}type}, \mathit{bro{:}UnavailablePL})\}$ (e.g., reachable after the execution of *parts auction*).

In our framework the inference of new fluents from fluents belonging to states is performed by including extra rules derived by translating the OWL 2 RL/RDF entailment rules as follows: every triple of the form $t(s,p,o)$, where s refers to an individual, is replaced by the atom $\mathit{holds}(t_f(s,p,o),X)$. Below we show the rules for concept subsumption (1), role subsumption (2), domain restriction (3), transitive property (4), and concept disjointness (5).

1. $\mathit{holds}(t_f(S, \mathit{rdf{:}type}, C), X) \leftarrow \mathit{holds}(t_f(S, \mathit{rdf{:}type}, B), X) \wedge t(B, \mathit{rdfs{:}subClassOf}, C)$
2. $\mathit{holds}(t_f(S,P,O),X) \leftarrow \mathit{holds}(t_f(S,P1,O),X) \wedge t(P1, \mathit{rdfs{:}subPropertyOf}, P)$
3. $\mathit{holds}(t_f(S, \mathit{rdf{:}type}, C), X) \leftarrow \mathit{holds}(t_f(S,P,O),X) \wedge t(P, \mathit{rdfs{:}domain}, C)$
4. $\mathit{holds}(t_f(S,P,O),X) \leftarrow \mathit{holds}(t_f(S,P,O_1),X) \wedge \mathit{holds}(t_f(O_1,P,O),X) \wedge t(P, \mathit{rdf{:}type}, \mathit{owl{:}TransitiveProperty})$
5. $\mathit{holds}(\mathit{false},X) \leftarrow \mathit{holds}(t_f(I_1, \mathit{rdf{:}type}, A), X) \wedge \mathit{holds}(t_f(I_2, \mathit{rdf{:}type}, B), X) \wedge t(A, \mathit{owl{:}disjointWith}, B)$

We denote by $\mathcal{F}$ the set of rules that encode the functional annotations, that is, the facts defining the relations $\mathit{pre}(A,C,P)$ and $\mathit{eff}(A,E^-,E^+,P)$, along with the rules for evaluating $\mathit{holds}(t_f(s,p,o),X)$ atoms (such as rules 1–5 above). The rules in $\mathcal{O} \cup \mathcal{F}$ may also be needed to evaluate atoms of the form $\mathit{holds}(G,X)$ in the case where G is a guard expression associated with inclusive or exclusive branch points via the relation $\mathit{c\_seq}(G,B,Y,P)$. Indeed, G may depend on fluents introduced by functional annotations.

We are now able to define the consistency condition for effects in a rigorous way. We say that *eff* is *consistent* with process P if, for every flow element A and states S_1, S_2, the following implication is true:

If the state S_1 is reachable from the initial state of P, the relation *result* $(S_1, \mathit{complete}(A), S_2)$ holds, and the relation $\mathit{eff}(A,E^-,E^+,P)$ holds,

Then $\mathcal{O} \cup \mathcal{F} \cup \{\neg holds(false, S_2)\}$ is consistent *And* for all $F \in E^-$, $\mathcal{O} \cup \mathcal{F} \cup \{\neg holds(F, S_2)\}$ is consistent.

We will show in Sect. 5 how the consistency of effects can be checked by using the rule-based temporal logic we will present in the next section.

4 Temporal Reasoning

In order to provide a general verification mechanism for behavioral properties, in this section we propose a model checking methodology based on a formalization of the temporal logic CTL (*Computation Tree Logic*, see [4] for a comprehensive overview) as a set of rules. Model checking is a widely accepted technique for the formal verification of BP schemas, as their execution semantics is usually defined in terms of states and state transitions, and hence the use of temporal logics for the specification and verification of properties is a very natural choice [7,12]. The abstract syntax of a CTL formula F is defined as follows:

$$F ::= e \mid true \mid false \mid \neg F \mid F_1 \wedge F_2 \mid \mathbf{EX}(F) \mid \mathbf{EU}(F_1, F_2) \mid \mathbf{EG}(F)$$

where e is a fluent expression. Other operators can be defined in terms of the ones given above, e.g., $\mathbf{EF}(F) \equiv \mathbf{EU}(true, F)$ and $\mathbf{AG}(F) \equiv \neg\mathbf{EF}(\neg F)$ [4].

The semantics of CTL formulas is defined by taking into account the immediate reachability relation r between states (i.e., finite sets of ground fluents) introduced in Sect. 2.2, which here is also called the *transition relation*.

In the definition of the semantics of CTL given in [4], the transition relation r is assumed to be *total*, that is, every state S_1 has at least one *successor state* S_2 for which $r(S_1, S_2)$ holds. This assumption is justified by the fact that the reactive systems considered in [4] can be thought as ever running processes. However, this assumption is not realistic in the case of business processes, for which there is always at least one state with no successors, namely one where the *end* event of a BPS has been completed. For this reason the semantics of the temporal operators given in [4], which refers to *infinite* sequences of states, is suitably changed here by taking into consideration *maximal paths*, i.e., sequences of states that are either infinite or end with a state that has no successors, called a *sink*.

Now we give a rule-based formalization of the semantics of CTL by extending the definition of the predicate *holds*. (A similar formalization based on constraint logic programming is proposed in [16], where however the semantics refers to infinite paths).

$\mathbf{EX}(F)$ holds in state S_0 if F holds in a successor state of S_0:

$holds(ex(F), S_0) \leftarrow r(S_0, S_1) \wedge holds(F, S_1)$

$\mathbf{EU}(F_1, F_2)$ holds in state S_0 if there exists a maximal path π: $S_0\ S_1 \ldots$ such that for some S_n occurring in π we have that F_2 holds in S_n and, for $j = 0, \ldots, n-1$, F_1 holds in S_j:

$holds(eu(F_1, F_2), S_0) \leftarrow holds(F_2, S_0)$
$holds(eu(F_1, F_2), S_0) \leftarrow holds(F_1, S_0) \wedge r(S_0, S_1) \wedge holds(eu(F_1, F_2), S_1)$

EG(F) holds in a state S_0 if there exists a maximal path π starting from S_0 such that F holds in each state of π. Since the set of states is finite, **EG**(F) holds in S_0 if there exists a finite path $S_0 \ldots S_k$ such that, for $i = 0, \ldots, k$, F holds in S_i, and either (1) $S_j = S_k$, for some $0 \leq j < k$, or (2) S_k is a sink state. Thus, the semantics of the operator **EG** is encoded by the following rules:

$holds(eg(F), S_0) \leftarrow fpath(F, S_0, S_0)$
$holds(eg(F), S_0) \leftarrow holds(F, S_0) \wedge r(S_0, S_1) \wedge holds(eg(F), S_1)$
$holds(eg(F), S_0) \leftarrow sink(S_0) \wedge holds(F, S_0)$

where: (i) the predicate $fpath(F, X, X)$ holds if there exists a path from X to X itself, consisting of at least one r arc, such that F holds in every state on the path and (ii) the predicate $sink(X)$ holds if X is a sink state.

Finally, we define a special fluent expression $final(P)$ the *final* state of a process P, whose semantics is given by the following rule:

$holds(final(P), Z) \leftarrow bp(P, S, E) \wedge holds(cf(E, end, P), Z)$

Note that our definition of the semantics of **EG** avoids the introduction of greatest fixed points of operators on sets of states which are required by the approach described in [4]. Indeed, the rules defining $holds(eg(F), S_0)$ are interpreted according to the usual least fixpoint semantics (i.e., the least Herbrand model [13]). Note also that in some special cases the assumption that paths are maximal, but not necessarily infinite, matters. For instance, if S_0 is a sink state, then $holds(ag(F), S_0)$ is true iff $holds(F, S_0)$ is true, since the only maximal path starting from S_0 is the one constituted by S_0 only.

5 Reasoning Services

Our rule-based framework supports several reasoning services which can combine complex knowledge about business processes from different perspectives, such as the workflow structure, the ontological description, and the behavioral semantics. In this section we will illustrate three such services: verification, querying, and trace compliance.

Let us consider the following sets of rules: (1) $\mathcal{B}$, representing a set of BP schemas and the BP meta-model defined in Sect. 2.1, (2) $\mathcal{T}$, defining the behavioral semantics presented in Sect. 2.2, (3) $\mathcal{O}$, collecting the OWL triples and rules which represent the business reference ontology defined in Sect. 3.1, (4) $\mathcal{F}$, encoding the functional annotations defined in Sect. 3.2, and (5) $\mathcal{CTL}$, defining the semantics of CTL presented in Sect. 4. Let $\mathcal{KB}$ be the set of rules $\mathcal{B} \cup \mathcal{T} \cup \mathcal{O} \cup \mathcal{F} \cup \mathcal{CTL}$. $\mathcal{KB}$ is called a *Business Process Knowledge Base* (BPKB). We have that $\mathcal{KB}$ is a locally stratified logic program and its semantics is unambiguously defined by its unique perfect model, denoted by $Perf(\mathcal{KB})$ [18].

Verification. In the following we present some examples of properties that can be specified and verified in our framework. A property is specified by a predicate *prop* defined by a rule C in terms of the predicates defined in $\mathcal{KB}$. The verification task is performed by checking whether or not $prop \in Perf(\mathcal{KB} \cup \{C\})$.

(1) A very relevant behavioral property of a BP p is that from any reachable state, it is possible to complete the process, i.e., reach the final state. This property, also known as *option to complete* [24], can be specified by the following rule, stating that the property *opt_com* holds if the CTL property $\mathbf{AG}(\mathbf{EF}(\mathit{final}(p)))$ holds in the initial state s_0 of p:

$opt\_com \leftarrow holds(ag(ef(final(p))), s_0)$

where $s_0 = \{cf(start, st\_ev, p)\}$ and st_ev is the start event associated with p.

(2) Temporal queries allow us to verify the consistency conditions for effects introduced in Sect. 3.2. In particular, given a BPS p, inconsistencies due to the violation of some integrity constraint defined in the ontology by rules of the form $false \leftarrow G$ (e.g., concept disjointness) can be verified by defining the *inconsistency* property as follows:

$inconsistency \leftarrow holds(ef(false), s_0)$

(3) Temporal queries can also be used for the verification of *compliance rules*, i.e., directives expressing internal policies and regulations aimed at specifying the way an enterprise operates. In our Handle Order example, one such compliance rule may be that every *order* is eventually *closed.* In order to verify whether this property holds or not, we can define a *noncompliance* property which holds if it is possible to reach the final state of the process where, for some O, it can be inferred that O is an *order* which is not *closed.* In our example *noncompliance* is satisfied, and thus the compliance rule is not enforced. In particular, if the exception attached to the *accept order* task is triggered, the enactment continues with the *notify rejection* task (due to the guards associated to $g1$), and the order is never *canceled* nor *fulfilled.*

$$\begin{aligned}&noncompliance \leftarrow holds(ef(and(t_f(O, rdf{:}type, bro{:}Order),\\&\quad and(not(t_f(O, rdf{:}type, bro{:}ClosedPO)), final(p)))), s_0)\end{aligned}$$

The verification of a property *prop* is performed by evaluating the query $\leftarrow prop$ in $\mathcal{KB} \cup \{C\}$ using *SLG-resolution*, that is, resolution for general logic programs augmented with the *tabling* mechanism [3]. The following definition is needed for presenting the termination, soundness, and completeness of query evaluation.

Definition 1. Let f be a term representing a CTL formula. A subterm e of f is *grounding* if one of the following conditions hold: (i) f is an atomic fluent and e is f, (ii) f is $and(f_1, f_2)$ and e is a grounding subterm of either f_1 or f_2, (iii) f is $ex(f_1)$ and e is a grounding subterm of f_1, (iv) f is $eu(f_1, f_2)$ and e is a grounding subterm of f_2, (v) f is $eg(f_1)$ and e is a grounding subterm of f_1.

Theorem 1. Let C be a rule of the form $prop \leftarrow L_1 \wedge \ldots \wedge L_n$, where, for $i = 1, \ldots, n$, the predicate of L_i is defined in $\mathcal{KB}$. Suppose that: (i) if L_i is of the form $holds(f, S)$, all free variables of f occur in atomic fluents, and (ii) each variable X of C has its leftmost occurrence in a positive literal L_i such that either (ii.1) L_i has not predicate *holds* or (ii.2) $L_i = holds(f, S)$ and the occurrence of X is in a grounding subterm of f.

Then: (1) the evaluation of the query $\leftarrow$ *prop* in $\mathcal{KB} \cup \{C\}$ terminates by using SLG-resolution with left-to-right computation rule, and (2) the query succeeds iff $prop \in Perf(\mathcal{KB} \cup \{C\})$.

Hypothesis (i) guarantees that no variable ranges over an infinite domain, such as the set of all CTL formulas. Hypothesis (ii) guarantees that the query *does not flounder*, that is, non-ground negative literals are never selected during SLG resolution. The termination property (1) can be proved by showing that $\mathcal{KB} \cup \{C\}$ satisfies the *bounded-term-size property* [3]. The soundness and completeness property (2) follows from the soundness and completeness of SLG resolution with respect to the perfect model semantics [3].

Querying. The inference mechanism based on SLG-resolution can be used for computing boolean answers to ground queries, but also for computing, via unification, substitutions for variables occurring in non-ground queries. By exploiting this query answering mechanism we can easily provide, besides the verification service described in the previous section, also reasoning services for the retrieval of process fragments.

The following queries show how process fragments can be retrieved according to different criteria: q_1 computes every activity A (and the process P where it occurs) which operates on an *order* as an effect (e.g., *create order* and *cancel order*); q_2 computes every exclusive branch G occurring along a path delimited by two activities A and B which operate on *orders* (e.g., *create order*) and *invoices* (e.g., *fulfill order*), respectively; finally, q_3 is a refinement of q_2, where it is also required that the enactment of B is always preceded by the enactment of A.

$$
\begin{aligned}
&q_1(A,P) \leftarrow \mathit{eff}(A,E^-,E^+,P) \land \mathit{holds}(t_f(O,\mathit{rdf{:}type},\mathit{bro{:}Order}),E^+)\\
&q_2(A,G,B,P) \leftarrow \mathit{eff}(A,E_A^-,E_A^+,P) \land \mathit{seq}^+(A,G,P) \land\\
&\quad \mathit{holds}(t_f(O,\mathit{rdf{:}type},\mathit{bro{:}Order}),E_A^+) \land \mathit{exc\_branch}(G) \land \mathit{seq}^+(G,B,P) \land\\
&\quad \mathit{eff}(B,E_B^-,E_B^+,P) \land \mathit{holds}(t_f(I,\mathit{rdf{:}type},\mathit{bro{:}Invoice}),E_B^+)\\
&q_3(A,G,B,P) \leftarrow q_2(A,G,B,P) \land \mathit{holds}(\mathit{not}(\mathit{eu}(\mathit{not}(\mathit{en}(A,P)),\mathit{en}(B,P))),s_0)
\end{aligned}
$$

Trace Compliance. The execution of a process is modeled as an *execution trace* (corresponding to a plan in the Fluent Calculus), i.e., a sequence of actions of the form $[act(a_1),\ldots,act(a_n)]$ where *act* is either *begin* or *complete*. The predicate $trace(S_1,T,S_2)$ defined below holds if T is a sequence of actions that lead from state S_1 to state S_2:

$$
\begin{aligned}
&\mathit{trace}(S_1,[\,],S_2) \leftarrow S_1 = S_2\\
&\mathit{trace}(S_1,[A|T],S_2) \leftarrow \mathit{result}(S_1,A,U) \land \mathit{trace}(U,T,S_2)
\end{aligned}
$$

A *correct trace* T of a BPS P is a trace leading from the initial to the final state of P:

$$
\mathit{ctrace}(T,P) \leftarrow \mathit{trace}(s_0,T,Z) \land \mathit{holds}(\mathit{final}(P),Z)
$$

The correctness of a trace t with respect to a given BPS p can be verified by evaluating a query of the type $\leftarrow ctrace(t,p)$, where t is a ground list and p

is a process name. The rules defining the predicate *ctrace* can also be used to *generate* the correct traces of a process p that satisfy some given property. This task is performed by evaluating a query of the type $\leftarrow ctrace(T,p) \wedge cond(T)$, where T is a free variable and $cond(T)$ is a property that T must enforce. For instance, we may want to generate traces where the execution of a flow element a is followed by the execution of a flow element b:

$$cond(T) \leftarrow concat(T_1, T_2, T) \wedge complete(a) \in T_1 \wedge complete(b) \in T_2$$

The termination of querying and trace correctness checking can be proved under assumptions similar to the ones of Theorem 1. However, stronger assumptions are needed for the termination of trace generation if we want to compute the set of *all* correct traces satisfying a given condition, as this set may be infinite in the presence of cycles.

6 Related Work

Among several mathematical formalisms proposed for defining a formal semantics of BP models, Petri nets [24] are the most used paradigm to capture the execution semantics of the control flow aspects of graph-based procedural languages. (The BPMN case is discussed in [5].) Petri net models enable a large number of analysis techniques, but they do not provide a suitable basis to represent and reason about additional domain knowledge. In our framework we are able to capture the token game semantics underlying workflow models, and we can also declaratively represent constructs, such as exception handling behavior or synchronization of active branches only (inclusive merge), which, due to their non-local semantics, are cumbersome to capture in standard Petri nets. In addition, the logical grounding of our framework makes it easy to deal with the modeling of domain knowledge and the integration of reasoning services.

Program analysis and verification techniques have been largely applied to the analysis of process behavior, e.g., [7,12]. These works are based on the analysis of finite state models through model checking techniques [4] where temporal logics queries specify properties of process executions. However, these approaches are restricted to properties regarding the control flow only (e.g., properties of the ordering, presence, or absence of tasks in process executions), and severe limitations arise when taking into consideration ontology-related properties representing specific domain knowledge.

There is a growing body of contributions beyond pure control flow verification. In [26] the authors introduce the notion of Semantic Business Process Validation, which aims at verifying properties related to the absence of logical errors which extend the notion of workflow soundness [24]. Validation is based on an execution semantics where token passing control flow is combined with the AI notion of state change induced by domain related logical preconditions/effects. The main result is constituted by a validation algorithms which runs in polynomial time under some restrictions on the workflow structure and on the expressivity of the logic underlying the domain axiomatization, i.e., binary Horn clauses.

This approach is focused on providing efficient techniques for the verification of specific properties, while the verification of arbitrary behavioral properties, such as the CTL formulae allowed in our framework, is not addressed. Moreover, our language for annotations is more expressive than binary Horn clauses.

Several works propose the extension to business process management of techniques developed in the context of the semantic web [8]. Meta-model process ontologies, e.g., [11], are derived from BP modeling languages and notations with the aim of specifying in a declarative, formal, and explicit way concepts and constraints of a particular language. Semantic Web Services approaches, such as OWL-S [2] and WSMO [6], make an essential use of ontologies in order to facilitate the automation of discovering, combining and invoking electronic services over the Web. To this end they describe services from two perspectives: from a *functional* perspective a service is described in terms of its functionality, preconditions and effects, input and output; from a process *perspective*, the service behavior is modeled as an orchestration of other services. However, in the above approaches the behavioral aspects are abstracted away, since the semantics of the provided constructs is not axiomatized within their respective languages, hampering the availability of reasoning services related to the execution of BPs.

To overcome such limitations, several solutions for the representation of service compositions propose to translate the relevant aspects of the aforementioned service ontologies into a more expressive language, such as first-order logic, and to add a set of axioms to this theory that constrains the models of the theory to all and only the intended interpretations. Among them, [22] adopts the high-level agent programming language Golog [1,15,19] rely on Situation Calculus variants. However, such approaches are mainly tailored to automatic service composition (i.e., finding a sequence of service invocations such that a given goal is satisfied). Thus, the support provided for process definition, in terms of workflow constructs, is very limited and they lack a clear mapping from standard modeling notations. In contrast, our framework allows a much richer procedural description of processes, directly corresponding to BPMN diagrams. Moreover, a reference ontology can be used to "enrich" process descriptions by means of OWL-RL annotations, a widespread language for ontology representation.

Other approaches based on Logic Programming which are worth to mention are [14,20]. These approaches mainly focus on the verification and on the enactment of BPs, while we are not aware of specific extensions that deal with the semantic annotation of procedural process models with respect to domain ontologies.

Finally, with respect to our previous works [21], we have proposed several extensions: (1) we have increased the expressivity from a workflow perspective, by modeling arbitrary cycles, unstructured diagrams and exceptions; (2) we have introduced functional annotations and we have provided a semantics for their integration with the control flow; (3) we have introduced a general verification mechanism based on CTL.

7 Conclusions

The rule-based approach for representing and reasoning about business processes presented in this paper offers several advantages. First of all, it enables the combination of the procedural and ontological perspectives in a very smooth and natural way, thus providing a uniform framework for reasoning on properties that depend on the sequence of operations that occur during process enactment and also on the domain where the process operates. Another advantage is the generality of the approach, which is open to further extensions, since other knowledge representation applications can easily be integrated, by providing a suitable translation to logic programming rules. Our approach does not introduce a new business process modeling language, but provides a framework where one can map and integrate knowledge represented by means of existing formalisms. This is very important from a pragmatic point of view, as one can express process-related knowledge by using standard modeling languages such as BPMN for business processes and OWL for ontologies, while adding extra reasoning services. Finally, since our rule-based representation can be directly mapped to a class of logic programs, we can use standard logic programming systems to perform reasoning tasks such as verification and querying.

We have implemented in the XSB logic programming system[1] the various sets of rules representing a Business Process Knowledge Base, and on top of the latter, the verification, querying, and trace compliance services. The resolution mechanism based on tabling [3] provided by XSB guarantees a sound and complete evaluation of a large class of queries. We have also integrated the aforementioned services in the tool described in [21], which implements an interface between the BPMN and OWL representations of business processes and reference ontology specifications on one hand, and our rule-based representation on the other hand, so that, as already mentioned, we can use the reasoning facilities offered by our framework as add ons to standard tools. First experiments are encouraging and show that very sophisticated reasoning tasks can be performed on business process of small-to-medium size in an acceptable amount of time and memory resources. Currently, we are investigating various program optimization techniques for improving the performance of our tool and enabling our approach to scale to large BP repositories.

References

1. Battle, S., et al.: Semantic Web Services Ontology (2005). http://www.w3.org/Submission/SWSF-SWSO
2. Burstein, M., et al.: OWL-S: Semantic markup for web services. W3C Member Submission (2004). http://www.w3.org/Submission/OWL-S/
3. Chen, W., Warren, D.S.: Tabled evaluation with delaying for general logic programs. JACM **43**, 20–74 (1996)
4. Clarke, E.M., Grumberg, O., Peled, D.A.: Model Checking. The MIT Press, Cambridge (1999)

[1] The XSB Logic Programming System. Version 3.2: http://xsb.sourceforge.net.

5. Dijkman, R.M., Dumas, M., Ouyang, C.: Semantics and analysis of business process models in BPMN. Inf. Softw. Technol. **50**, 1281–1294 (2008)
6. Fensel, D., et al.: Enabling Semantic Web Services: The Web Service Modeling Ontology. Springer, Berlin (2006)
7. Fu, X., Bultan, T., Su, J.: Analysis of interacting BPEL web services. In: International Conference on World Wide Web, pp. 621–630. ACM Press, New York (2004)
8. Hepp, M., et al.: Semantic business process management: a vision towards using semantic web services for business process management. In: International Conference on e-Business Engineering, IEEE Computer Society (2005)
9. Hitzler, P., Krötzsch, M., Parsia, B., Patel-Schneider, P.F., Rudolph, S.: OWL 2 Web Ontology Language. W3C Recommendation (2009). http://www.w3.org/TR/owl2-primer/
10. Kindler, E.: On the semantics of EPCs: Resolving the vicious circle. Data Knowl. Eng. **56**(1), 23–40 (2006)
11. Lin, Y.: Semantic annotation for process models: Facilitating process knowledge management via semantic interoperability. Ph.D. Thesis, Norwegian University of Science and Technology (2008)
12. Liu, Y., Müller, S., Xu, K.: A static compliance-checking framework for business process models. IBM Syst. J. **46**, 335–361 (2007)
13. Lloyd, J.W.: Foundations of Logic Programming. Springer-Verlag New York Inc., New York (1987)
14. Montali, M., Pesic, M., van der Aalst, W.M.P., Chesani, F., Mello, P., Storari, S.: Declarative specification and verification of service choreographies. ACM Trans. Web **4**(1), 3:1–3:61 (2010)
15. Narayanan, S., McIlraith, S.: Analysis and simulation of web services. Comp. Netw. **42**, 675–693 (2003)
16. Nilsson, U., Lübcke, J.: Constraint logic programming for local and symbolic model-checking. In: Palamidessi, C., Moniz Pereira, L., Lloyd, J.W., Dahl, V., Furbach, U., Kerber, M., Lau, K.-K., Sagiv, Y., Stuckey, P.J. (eds.) CL 2000. LNCS (LNAI), vol. 1861, pp. 384–398. Springer, Heidelberg (2000)
17. OMG: Business Process Model and Notation (2011). http://www.omg.org/spec/BPMN/2.0
18. Przymusinski, T.C.: On the declarative semantics of deductive databases and logic programs. In: Minker, J. (ed.) Foundations of Deductive Databases and Logic Programming. Morgan Kaufmann Publishers Inc, San Francisco (1988)
19. Reiter, R.: Knowledge in Action: Logical Foundations for Specifying and Implementing Dynamical Systems. The MIT Press, Cambridge (2001)
20. Roman, D., Kifer, M.: Semantic web service choreography: contracting and enactment. In: Sheth, A.P., Staab, S., Dean, M., Paolucci, M., Maynard, D., Finin, T., Thirunarayan, K. (eds.) ISWC 2008. LNCS, vol. 5318, pp. 550–566. Springer, Heidelberg (2008)
21. Smith, F., Missikoff, M., Proietti, M.: Ontology-based querying of composite services. In: Ardagna, C.A., Damiani, E., Maciaszek, L.A., Missikoff, M., Parkin, M. (eds.) BSME 2010. LNCS, vol. 7350, pp. 159–180. Springer, Heidelberg (2012)
22. Sohrabi, S., Prokoshyna, N., McIlraith, S.A.: Web service composition via the customization of golog programs with user preferences. In: Borgida, A.T., Chaudhri, V.K., Giorgini, P., Yu, E.S. (eds.) Conceptual Modeling: Foundations and Applications. LNCS, vol. 5600, pp. 319–334. Springer, Heidelberg (2009)
23. Thielscher, M.: Introduction to the fluent calculus. Electron. Trans. Artif. Intell. **2**, 179–192 (1998)

24. van der Aalst, W.M.P.: The application of Petri nets to workflow management. J. Circ. Syst. Comput. **8**(1), 21–66 (1998)
25. Völzer, H.: A new semantics for the inclusive converging gateway in safe processes. In: Hull, R., Mendling, J., Tai, S. (eds.) BPM 2010. LNCS, vol. 6336, pp. 294–309. Springer, Heidelberg (2010)
26. Weber, I., Hoffmann, J., Mendling, J.: Beyond soundness: on the verification of semantic business process models. Distrib. Parallel Dat. **27**, 271–343 (2010)

An Algorithm for Checking the Dynamic Controllability of a Conditional Simple Temporal Network with Uncertainty - Revisited

Carlo Combi[1], Luke Hunsberger[2], and Roberto Posenato[1](✉)

[1] Computer Science Department, University of Verona, Verona, Italy
roberto.posenato@univr.it
[2] Computer Science Department, Vassar College, Poughkeepsie, NY, USA

Abstract. A Simple Temporal Network with Uncertainty (STNU) is a framework for representing and reasoning about temporal problems involving actions whose durations are bounded but uncontrollable. A dynamically controllable STNU is one for which there exists a strategy for executing its time-points that guarantees that all of the temporal constraints in the network will be satisfied no matter how the uncontrollable durations turn out. A Conditional Simple Temporal Network with Uncertainty (CSTNU) augments an STNU to include observation nodes, the execution of which incrementally and dynamically determines the set of constraints that must be satisfied. Previously, we generalized the notion of dynamic controllability to cover CSTNUs and presented a sound algorithm for determining whether arbitrary CSTNUs are dynamically controllable. That algorithm extends edge-generation/constraint-propagation rules from an existing DC-checking algorithm for STNUs with new rules required to deal with the observation nodes. This paper revisits that algorithm, modifying some of its rules to cover more cases, while preserving the soundness of the algorithm.

Keywords: Temporal Network · Temporal Controllability · Temporal Uncertainty · Temporal Workflow

1 Introduction

Workflow systems have been used to model business, manufacturing and medical-treatment processes. To meet the needs of such domains, Combi and Posenato [1] presented a new workflow model that accommodates tasks with uncertain/uncontrollable durations; temporal constraints among tasks; and branching paths, where the branch taken is not known in advance. Subsequently, Hunsberger et al. [2] introduced a *Conditional Simple Temporal Network with Uncertainty (CSTNU)* to represent the key features of that workflow model. The important property of *dynamic controllability (DC)* for CSTNUs was also defined.

L. Hunsberger: Funded in part by the Phoebe H. Beadle Science Fund.

J. Filipe and A. Fred (Eds.): ICAART 2013, CCIS 449, pp. 314–331, 2014.
DOI: 10.1007/978-3-662-44440-5_19

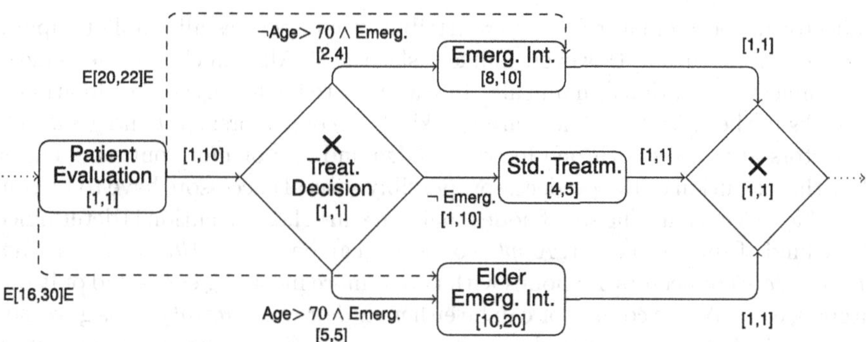

Fig. 1. An excerpt of a healthcare workflow schema.

A CSTNU is dynamically controllable if there exists a strategy for executing the tasks in the associated workflow in a way that ensures that all temporal constraints will be satisfied no matter how the uncontrollable durations or branching events turn out.

A previous version of this paper [3] presented an algorithm for determining whether arbitrary CSTNUs are dynamically controllable. That algorithm, which is proven to be sound, extends the DC-checking algorithm for a simpler class of networks, called STNUs, developed by Morris and Muscettola [4]. Our algorithm propagates *labeled values* on graph edges in a way that draws from prior work by Conrad and Williams [5]. This paper revisits the DC-checking algorithm for CSTNUs, modifying some of its rules to cover additional cases, while preserving the soundness of the algorithm. Finding a *complete* DC-checking algorithm for CSTNUs is the goal of ongoing research.

2 Motivating Example

In the following, we will consider, as a motivating example, a process taken from the healthcare domain. More precisely, consider the excerpt from a workflow schema depicted in Fig. 1, which follows the model proposed by Combi and Posenato [1].

The *workflow schema* is a directed graph where nodes correspond to *activities* and edges represent *control flows* that define dependencies on the order of execution. There are two types of activity: *tasks* and *connectors*. *Tasks* represent elementary work units that will be executed by external agents. Each task is represented graphically by a rounded box and has a mandatory *duration* attribute that specifies the allowed temporal spans for its execution. Typically, the duration of a task is not controlled by the system responsible for managing the overall execution of the workflow (i.e., the Workflow Management System, WfMS). Unlike a task, a *connector* represents an internal activity whose execution *is* controlled by the WfMS. In particular, the WfMS uses connectors to coordinate the execution of the tasks. Connectors are represented graphically by diamonds. Like tasks, each connector has a mandatory *duration* attribute that specifies allowable temporal spans for its execution. However, unlike tasks, the WfMS can choose the value of each connector duration dynamically, in real time, to facilitate the coordination of the tasks in the workflow. There are two kinds of connectors: *split* and *join*. *Split* connectors are nodes with one incoming edge and two or more outgoing edges. After the execution of the predecessor, possibly several successors have to be considered for execution. The set of nodes that can start their execution is determined by the kind of split connector. A *split* connector can be: *Total*, *Alternative* or *Conditional*. *Join* connectors are nodes with two or more incoming edges and only one outgoing edge. A *join* connector can be either *And* or *Or*. *Control flow* is governed by oriented edges. Each oriented edge connects two activities, where the execution of the first activity (the *predecessor*) must be finished before starting the execution of the second one. Every edge has a *delay* attribute that specifies the allowed times that can be spent by the WfMS for possibly delaying the execution of the second activity.

Besides the temporal constraints associated with the duration and delay attributes of tasks, connectors and edges, a workflow schema can also include *relative constraints*. A relative constraint constrains the temporal interval between (the starting or ending time-points of) two non-consecutive workflow activities. Graphically, a relative constraint is represented by a directed edge from one activity to another, labeled by an expression of the form, $\mathsf{t_1[MinD, MaxD]t_2}$, where $t_1 \in \{S, E\}$ specifies whether the constraint applies to the starting or ending time-point of the first activity; $t_2 \in \{S, E\}$ specifies whether the constraint applies to the starting or ending time-point of the second activity; and $\mathsf{[MinD, MaxD]}$ specifies the allowed range for the temporal interval between the specified time-points.

The graph instance in Fig. 1 is a small excerpt from a process in a clinical domain. After the initial task, *Patient Evaluation,* whereby a physician determines whether the patient is in need of immediate medical attention (emergency state), there is an *alternative* connector, labeled *Treatment Decision*, from which three different treatment paths are possible, depending upon the age and emergency status of the patient. The three different treatments involve the following tasks: (1) *Elder Emergency Intervention*, (2) *Standard Treatment*, and (3) *Emergency Intervention*. The times at which the *Elder Emergency Intervention* and *Emergency Intervention* tasks must be completed, relative to the initial *Patient Evaluation* task, are restricted by the relative temporal constraints emanating from the *Patient Evaluation* node. These constraints are labeled $\mathsf{E[16, 30]E}$ and $\mathsf{E[20, 22]E}$, respectively, in the figure.

Given a particular workflow schema, it is important to determine in advance whether the WfMS is able to successfully execute the tasks in the schema, while observing all relevant temporal constraints, no matter how the durations of the tasks turn out. (Task durations are typically not controllable by the WfMS.) It is interesting to observe that the overall workflow schema in Fig. 1 may not be successfully executed by the WfMS for some possible task durations, even though each possible workflow subschema (or workflow path) is controllable when age and emergency status are known before execution begins.

A CSTNU is a more general formalism that allows the representation of all kinds of temporal constraints for workflow execution. In the following, after some background on related kinds of temporal networks, we will discuss CSTNUs and a new algorithm for determining the dynamic controllability of CSTNUs.

3 Background

Dechter et al. [6] introduced Simple Temporal Networks (STNs). An STN is a set of time-point variables (or time-points) together with a set of simple temporal constraints, where each constraint has the form $Y - X \leq \delta$, where X and Y are time-points and δ is a real number. The *all-pairs, shortest-paths* matrix for the associated graph is called the *distance matrix* for the STN. Any STN has a *solution* (i.e., a set of values for the time-points that satisfy all of the constraints) if and only if the associated graph has no negative loops (i.e., the distance matrix has zeros on its main diagonal).

Morris et al. [7] presented Simple Temporal Networks with Uncertainty (STNUs) that augment STNs to include *contingent links* that represent uncontrollable-but-bounded temporal intervals. They gave a formal semantics for the important property of *dynamic controllability,* which holds if there exists a strategy for executing the time-points in the network that guarantees that all of the constraints will be satisfied no matter how the contingent durations turn out.[1] Crucially, the durations of contingent links are observed in real time, as they complete; execution decisions can only depend on past observations.

Morris et al. [7] also presented a *pseudo-polynomial-time* algorithm—called a *DC-checking algorithm*—for determining whether any given STNU is *dynamically controllable (DC).* Later, Morris and Muscettola [4] presented the first polynomial DC-checking algorithm, which operates in $O(N^5)$ time. Because this algorithm plays an important role in this paper, it will henceforth be called the MM5 algorithm. Morris [9] subsequently presented an $O(N^4)$-time DC-checking algorithm for STNUs, but it will not be discussed further in this paper.

Tsamardinos et al. [10] introduced the Conditional Temporal Problem (CTP) which augments an STN to include *observation nodes.* When an observation node is executed, the truth value of its associated proposition becomes known. Each node in a CTP has a propositional label that is a conjunction of zero or more (positive or negative) literals. A node is executable only in scenarios where its propositional label is true. Tsamardinos et al. presented a formal semantics for the important property of *dynamic consistency,* which holds if there exists a strategy for executing the time-points in the network that guarantees that all of the constraints will be satisfied no matter how the observations turn out. Crucially, the truth values of propositions associated with observation nodes only become known in real time, as the observation nodes are executed. They showed how to convert the semantic constraints inherent in the definition of dynamic consistency into a Disjunctive Temporal Problem (DTP). They then

[1] Hunsberger [8] subsequently corrected a minor flaw in the semantics of dynamic controllability.

Table 1. Edge-generation rules for the MM5 algorithm. (Generated edges are dashed.)

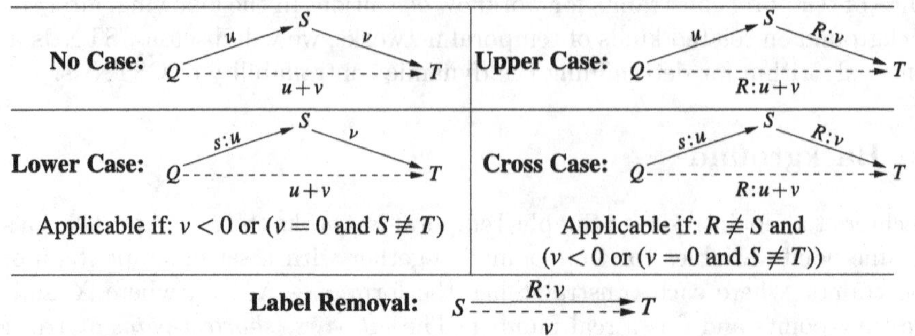

used an off-the-shelf DTP solver to determine the dynamic consistency of the original network in exponential time.

Hunsberger et al. [2] combined the features of STNUs and CTPs to produce a Conditional Simple Temporal Network with Uncertainty (CSTNU). They proved that their definition of a CSTNU generalizes both STNUs and CTPs. In addition, they introduced a definition of dynamic controllability for CSTNUs that they proved generalizes the corresponding notions for STNUs and CTPs. They noted that because the existing DC-checking algorithms for STNUs and CTPs work so differently, they could not be easily combined to yield a DC-checking algorithm for CSTNUs. Instead, they suggested that a new kind of algorithm be defined that incorporates new edge generation rules that take into account the propositional truth values generated by the observation nodes. In preparation for this kind of algorithm, they presented a preliminary *Label-Modification* rule for edges in a CSTNU.

This paper discusses a DC-checking algorithm for CSTNUs that follows the proposal mentioned above.[2] It extends the edge-generation/constraint-propagation rules used by the MM5 algorithm for STNUs to accommodate observation nodes. The algorithm, called the CSTNU DC-checking algorithm, generates edges that are labeled by conjunctions of propositional literals, where the truth values of individual literals are determined in real time as the corresponding observation nodes are executed. Because there can be multiple such labeled edges between any pair of time-points, the algorithm carefully manages the potentially-exponential explosion of labels using techniques inspired by the work of Conrad and Williams [5].

3.1 DC-Checking for STNUs

Following Morris et al. [7], an STNU is a set of time-points and temporal constraints, like those in an STN, together with a set of contingent links. Each contingent link has the form, (A, x, y, C), where A and C are time-point

[2] A preliminary version of this algorithm was presented previously [3].

variables (or time-points) and $0 < x < y < \infty$. A is called the *activation time-point*; C is the *contingent time-point.* Once A is executed, C is guaranteed to execute such that $C - A \in [x, y]$. However, the particular time at which C executes is uncontrollable. Instead, it is only observed as it happens.

Let $\mathcal{S} = (\mathcal{T}, \mathcal{C}, \mathcal{L})$ be an STNU, where $\mathcal{T}$ is a set of time-points, $\mathcal{C}$ is a set of constraints, and $\mathcal{L}$ is a set of contingent links. The graph for $\mathcal{S}$ has the form, $(\mathcal{T}, \mathcal{E}, \mathcal{E}_\ell, \mathcal{E}_u)$, where each time-point in $\mathcal{T}$ serves as a node in the graph; $\mathcal{E}$ is a set of *ordinary* edges; $\mathcal{E}_\ell$ is a set of *lower-case* edges; and $\mathcal{E}_u$ is a set of *upper-case* edges [4]:

- Each ordinary edge has the form, $X \xrightarrow{v} Y$, representing the constraint, $Y - X \leq v$.
- Each lower-case edge has the form, $A \xrightarrow{c:x} C$, representing the *possibility* that the contingent duration, $C - A$, might take on its minimum value, x.
- Each upper-case edge, $C \xrightarrow{C:-y} A$, represents the *possibility* that the contingent duration, $C - A$, might take on its maximum value, y.

The MM5 algorithm works by recursively generating new edges in the STNU graph using the rules shown in Table 1. For each rule, pre-existing edges are denoted by solid arrows and newly generated edges are denoted by dashed arrows. Note that each of the first four rules takes two pre-existing edges as input and generates a single edge as its output. The Label-Removal rule takes only one edge as input. Finally, applicability conditions of the form, $R \not\equiv S$, should be construed as stipulating that R and S must be distinct time-point variables, not as constraints on the *values* of those variables.

Procedure 1. MM5-DC-Check(G).

```
Input: G: STNU graph instance to analyze.
Output: the controllability of G.
for 1 to Cutoff_Bound do
    if (AllMax matrix inconsistent) then return false;
    generate new edges using rules from Table 1;
    if (no edges generated) then return true;
return false
```

Note that the edge-generation rules only generate new ordinary or upper-case edges. Unlike the upper-case edges in the original graph, the upper-case edges generated by these rules represent conditional constraints, called *waits* [7]. In particular, an upper-case edge, $Y \xrightarrow{C:-w} A$, represents a constraint that as long as the contingent time-point, C, remains unexecuted, then the time-point, Y, must wait at least w units after the execution of A, the activation time-point for C.

Procedure 1 gives pseudocode for the MM5 DC-checking algorithm. It has been shown that its time complexity is $O(N^5)$ [4].

3.2 Conditional Simple Temporal Networks with Uncertainty

A Conditional Simple Temporal Network with Uncertainty (CSTNU) is a network that combines the observation nodes and branching from a CTP with the contingent links of an STNU [2]. There is a one-to-one correspondence between observation nodes and propositional letters: the execution of an observation node generates a truth value for the corresponding proposition. However, nodes and edges in a CSTNU graph may be labeled by conjunctions of propositional literals. The time-point corresponding to a node with label, ℓ, need only be executed in scenarios where ℓ is true. Similarly, the constraint corresponding to an edge with label, ℓ, is only applicable in scenarios where ℓ is true. The *label universe*, defined below, is the set of all possible labels.

Definition 1 (Label, Label Universe). *Given a set P of propositional letters, a* label *is any (possibly empty) conjunction of (positive or negative) literals from P. For convenience, the empty label is denoted by $\boxdot$. The* label universe *of P, denoted by P^*, is the set of all labels whose literals are drawn from P.*

In the following, when not specified, lower-case Latin letters will denote propositions of P, while Greek lower-case letters will denote labels of P^*.

Definition 2 (Consistent Labels, Label Subsumption). *Labels, ℓ_1 and ℓ_2, are called* consistent, *denoted by $Con(\ell_1, \ell_2)$, if and only if $\ell_1 \wedge \ell_2$ is satisfiable. A label ℓ_1* subsumes *a label ℓ_2, denoted by $Sub(\ell_1, \ell_2)$, if and only if $\models (\ell_1 \Rightarrow \ell_2)$.*

The following definition of a CSTNU is extracted from Hunsberger et al. [2]. The most important ingredients of a CSTNU are: $\mathscr{T}$, a set of time-points; $\mathscr{C}$, a set of *labeled* constraints; $\mathscr{O}\mathscr{T}$, a set of observation time-points; and $\mathscr{L}$ a set of contingent links.

Definition 3 (CSTNU). *A Conditional STN with Uncertainty (CSTNU) is a tuple, $\langle \mathscr{T}, \mathscr{C}, L, \mathscr{O}\mathscr{T}, \mathscr{O}, P, \mathscr{L} \rangle$, where:*

- *$\mathscr{T}$ is a finite set of real-valued time-points;*
- *P is a finite set of propositional letters;*
- *$L : \mathscr{T} \to P^*$ is a function that assigns a label to each time-point in $\mathscr{T}$;*
- *$\mathscr{O}\mathscr{T} \subseteq \mathscr{T}$ is a set of observation time-points;*
- *$\mathscr{O} : P \rightarrowtail \mathscr{O}\mathscr{T}$ is a bijection that associates a unique observation time-point to each propositional letter;*
- *$\mathscr{L}$ is a set of contingent links;*
- *$\mathscr{C}$ is a set of* labeled *simple temporal constraints, each of the form, $(Y - X \leq \delta,\ \ell)$, where $X, Y \in \mathscr{T}$, δ is a real number, and $\ell \in P^*$;*
- *for any $(Y - X \leq \delta,\ \ell) \in \mathscr{C}$, ℓ is satisfiable and subsumes both $L(X)$ and $L(Y)$;*
- *for any $p \in P$ and $T \in \mathscr{T}$, if p or $\neg p$ appears in T's label, then*
  - *$Sub(L(T), L(\mathscr{O}(p)))$, and*
  - *$(\mathscr{O}(p) - T \leq -\epsilon,\ L(T)) \in \mathscr{C}$, for some $\epsilon > 0$;*
- *for each $(Y - X \leq \delta,\ \ell) \in \mathscr{C}$ and each $p \in P$, if p or $\neg p$ appears in ℓ, then $Sub(\ell, L(\mathscr{O}(p)))$; and*

– $(\mathcal{T}, \lfloor\mathcal{C}\rfloor, \mathcal{L})$ *is an STNU, where* $\lfloor\mathcal{C}\rfloor$ *is the following set of unlabeled constraints:* $\{(Y - X \leq \delta) \mid (Y - X \leq \delta, \ell) \in \mathcal{C}$ *for some* $\ell\}$.

The graph for a CSTNU is similar to that for an STNU except that some nodes may be observation nodes; and there may be propositional labels on nodes and edges. If p is a proposition, then the observation node whose execution generates a truth value for p shall be denoted by $P?$ The propositional label of a node is usually represented near the node name, enclosed in square brackets. For example, a node labeled by $[cd]$ is only applicable to scenarios where propositions c and d are both true. Since edges in a CSTNU graph can have both propositional labels (associated with observation nodes) and alphabetic labels (associated with lower-case and upper-case edges in an STNU), these different kinds of labels are clearly distinguished in the *labeled values* for an edge, as follows.

Definition 4 (Labeled Values). *A* labeled value *is a triple,* $\langle$*PLabel*, *ALabel*, *Num*$\rangle$, *where:*

- *PLabel* $\in P^*$ *is a propositional label,*
- *ALabel, an alphabetic label, is one of the following:*
  - *an upper-case letter, C, as on an upper-case edge in an STNU;*
  - *a lower-case letter, c, as on a lower-case edge in an STNU; or*
  - $\diamond$, *representing no alphabetic label, as for an ordinary STN edge.*
- *Num is a real number.*

For example, $\langle p\neg q,\ c,\ 3\rangle$ is a labeled value for a lower-case edge; $\langle pq\neg r,\ C,\ -8\rangle$ is a labeled value for an upper-case edge; $\langle\neg p,\ \diamond,\ 2\rangle$ is a labeled value for an ordinary edge.

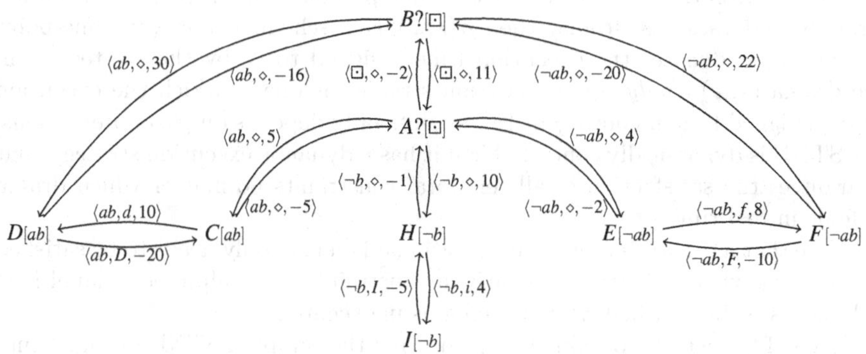

Fig. 2. A possible CSTNU graph mapping the main part of the workflow schema of Fig. 1.

Figure 2 shows a sample CSTNU that represents a possible mapping of the main part of the workflow schema of Fig. 1. Initially, each ordinary edge in the network has only one labeled value, while each edge associated with a contingent link has two labeled values: one representing an ordinary STN constraint and the other representing an upper-case or lower-case STNU constraint. However, the new edge-generation rules given below will typically result in situations where a single edge may have numerous labeled values associated with it. The graph in the figure includes two observation nodes and three contingent links. Observation node $A?$ generates a truth value for the proposition, a, which represents that the patient in question is over age 70. Observation node $B?$ generates a truth value for the proposition, b, which represents that the patient is in need of immediate medical attention. The contingent link, $(C, 10, 20, D)$, represents an *Elder Emergency Intervention* task that takes between 10 and 20 min; the contingent link, $(H, 4, 5, I)$, represents a *Standard Treatment* task that takes between 4 and 5 min; and the contingent link, $(E, 8, 10, F)$, represents an *Emergency Intervention* task that takes between 8 and 10 min. To simplify the graph, only the lower-case and upper-case edges for each contingent link are explicitly represented.[3] All other edges in the sample CSTNU represent ordinary temporal constraints. For example, the edges between $B?$ and $A?$ represent that the observation of proposition a must occur between 2 and 11 min after the observation of proposition b.

As defined previously [2], a *scenario* s is a label that specifies a truth value for every propositional letter. The STNU formed by the nodes and edges (i.e., time-points and constraints) whose labels are true in a given scenario is called a *projection* of the CSTNU onto that scenario. A *situation* ω for an STNU specifies fixed durations for all of the contingent links. A *drama* (s, ω) is a scenario/situation pair that specifies fixed truth values for all propositional letters and fixed durations for all of the contingent links.

An *execution strategy* is a mapping from dramas to *schedules*. A schedule assigns an execution time to all of the time-points. Thus, if σ is an execution strategy and (s, ω) is drama, then $\sigma(s, \omega)$ is a schedule. For any time-point X, $[\sigma(s, \omega)]_X$ denotes the execution time assigned to X by the strategy σ in the drama (s, ω). A *dynamic* execution strategy is one in which the execution times assigned to non-contingent time-points only depends on *past* observations. A CSTNU is dynamically controllable if it has a dynamic execution strategy that guarantees the satisfaction of all temporal constraints no matter which drama unfolds in real time.

Note that a constraint whose propositional label is ℓ only needs to be satisfied in scenarios where ℓ is true. Similarly, a constraint whose alphabetic label is C only needs to be satisfied while C remains unexecuted.

Each of the STNUs obtained by projecting the sample CSTNU of Fig. 2 onto the scenarios, ab, $\neg ab$ and $\neg b$, is dynamically controllable—as an STNU. However, as will be shown below, the sample CSTNU is not dynamically controllable—as a CSTNU. This conforms to the observation by Combi and Posenato [12] that the independent controllability of each *path* through a workflow is a necessary,

[3] As proven elsewhere [11], the ordinary edges associated with contingent links are not needed for the purposes of DC checking.

but insufficient condition for the controllability of the entire workflow. For the workflow in Fig. 1, it turns out that there is no execution time for the observation node, $A?$, that will enable the rest of the network to be safely executed no matter how subsequent observations turn out.

4 DC-Checking for CSTNUs

This section presents a DC-checking algorithm for CSTNUs. A preliminary version of this algorithm was presented previously [3]. This paper modifies some of the edge-generation rules used by the algorithm. The basic approach is to extend the MM5 algorithm for STNUs to accommodate propositional labels. The presence of observation nodes also requires some new *label-modification* rules. In addition, since the propagation of labeled values involves conjoining labels, which can lead to an exponential number of labeled values, it is important to carefully manage the sets of labeled values, an issue that we address elsewhere [3].

A *partial scenario* is a scenario that assigns truth values to some subset of propositional letters. Partial scenarios represent the outcomes of past observations. A label ℓ (on a node or edge) is said to be *enabled* in a (possibly partial) scenario s if none of the propositional literals in ℓ is false in s. For example, the label $a\neg c$ is enabled in the partial scenario $b\neg c$, but not in the partial scenario bcd. Note that the truth value of a is not determined in either of these partial scenarios.

During the execution of a CSTNU instance, the WfMS keeps track of all past observations, which together determine a partial scenario. For any as-yet-unexecuted non-contingent time-point, the WfMS must consider *all* enabled labeled constraints involving that time-point/node and verify that those constraints are satisfiable. For any pair of time-points, X and Y, it is possible that more than one labeled constraint from X to Y is enabled because they are compatible with the current partial scenario and, therefore, all of them have to be satisfiable. Thus, it is necessary to generate all possible constraints/edges for all possible (partial) scenarios in order to evaluate if a CSTNU is dynamically controllable. Hereinafter, we indifferently refer to the set of labeled constraints/edges for a given pair of time-points as a set of different labeled constraints/edges or as different labeled values of the same constraint/edge.

4.1 Edge Generation for CSTNUs

The edge generation rules for CSTNUs fall into two main groups. The first group extends the edge-generation rules of the MM5 algorithm to accommodate labeled edges; the second group consists of label-modification rules that address interactions involving observation nodes.

Labeled Constraint Generation. We begin by modifying the edge-generation rules for STNUs (cf. Table 1) to accommodate labeled edges. The new rules are shown in Table 2. Note that each of the first four rules generates an edge whose PLabel is the conjunction of the PLabels of its parent edges. If the resulting

Table 2. New edge-generation rules for CSTNUs. (Only new edges with satisfiable labels are kept.)

Labeled No Case: $Q \xrightarrow{\langle\alpha,\diamond,u\rangle} S \xrightarrow{\langle\beta,\diamond,v\rangle} T$; generated: $Q \dashrightarrow T$ $\langle\alpha\beta,\diamond,u+v\rangle$	**Labeled Upper Case:** $Q \xrightarrow{\langle\alpha,\diamond,u\rangle} S \xrightarrow{\langle\beta,R,v\rangle} T$; generated: $Q \dashrightarrow T$ $\langle\alpha\beta,R,u+v\rangle$
Labeled Lower Case: $Q \xrightarrow{\langle\alpha,s,u\rangle} S \xrightarrow{\langle\beta,\diamond,v\rangle} T$; generated: $Q \dashrightarrow T$ $\langle\alpha\beta,\diamond,u+v\rangle$ Applicable if: $v<0$ or ($v=0$ and $S \not\equiv T$)	**Labeled Cross Case:** $Q \xrightarrow{\langle\alpha,s,u\rangle} S \xrightarrow{\langle\beta,R,v\rangle} T$; generated: $Q \dashrightarrow T$ $\langle\alpha\beta,R,u+v\rangle$ Applicable if: $R \not\equiv S$ and ($v<0$ or ($v=0$ and $S \not\equiv T$))
Labeled Label Removal: $S \xrightarrow{\langle\alpha,R,v\rangle} T$; generated: $S \dashrightarrow T$ $\langle\alpha,\diamond,v\rangle$ Applicable if: $v \geq -x$, where x is the lower bound for the contingent link from T to R	**Observation Case:** $Y \xrightarrow{\langle\alpha\beta p,\diamond,u\rangle} X$, $X \xrightarrow{\langle\beta\gamma\neg p,\diamond,-v\rangle} Y$; generated: $P? \dashleftarrow Y$ $\langle\alpha\beta\gamma,\diamond,0\rangle$ Applicable if: $0 \leq u < v$, and α,β and γ are labels that do not share any literals; and $p,\neg p$ are literals that do not appear in α, β or γ.

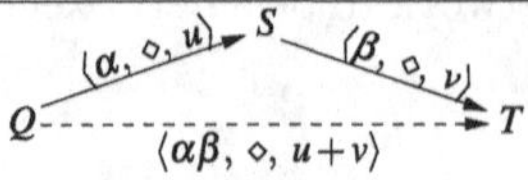

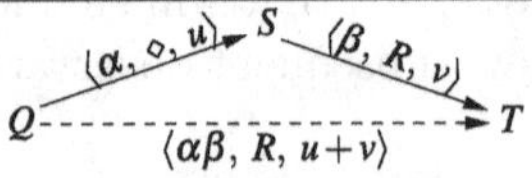

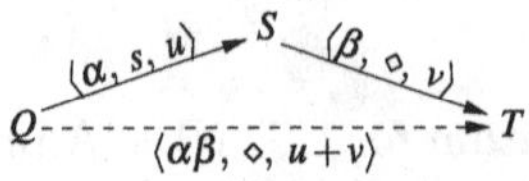

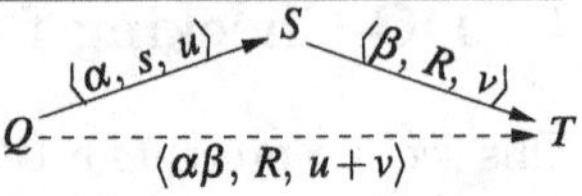

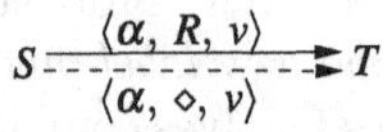

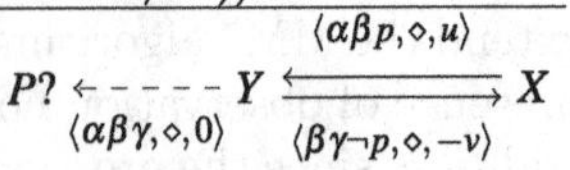

$P?$ $Y \xrightarrow{\langle\alpha\beta p,\diamond,u\rangle} X$, $X \xrightarrow{\langle\beta\gamma\neg p,\diamond,-v\rangle} Y$

(a) Pre-existing edges, where $0 \leq u < v$, and α,β and γ are labels that do not share any literals; and $p,\neg p$ are literals that do not appear in α,β or γ.

$P? \dashleftarrow Y$ $\langle\alpha\beta\gamma,\diamond,0\rangle$; $Y \xrightarrow{\langle\alpha\beta p,\diamond,u\rangle} X$, $X \xrightarrow{\langle\beta\gamma\neg p,\diamond,-v\rangle} Y$

(b) Generated edge (dashed).

Fig. 3. The Observation Case rule (cf. Lemma 1).

PLabel is unsatisfiable (e.g., $p\neg p$), then the new edge is not generated (or kept). The fifth rule effectively removes the upper-case (alphabetic) label, resulting in a labeled ordinary edge.

The sixth rule, the *Observation Case* rule, does not extend any of the MM5 rules; however, it is included here for convenience. This new rule addresses circumstances where an existing labeled edge from X to Y is inconsistent with an existing labeled edge from Y to X. To avoid having to satisfy both of these constraints—which would be impossible—this rule adds a new edge that ensures that the value of the proposition p, which appears in both labels, will be known before having to decide which constraint to satisfy. The soundness of this rule is ensured by the following lemma.

Lemma 1 (Observation Case). *Let σ be a dynamic execution strategy that satisfies the labeled constraints in Fig. 3-(a). Then σ must also satisfy the labeled constraint, $(P? - Y \leq 0, \alpha\beta\gamma)$, shown in Fig. 3-(b).*[4]

[4] Recall that an execution strategy need only satisfy labeled constraints in scenarios where their labels are true.

Proof. Let σ be as in the statement of the lemma. Suppose there is a drama, (s, ω), such that:

- the label $\alpha\beta\gamma$ is true in scenario s; but
- the schedule $\sigma(s, \omega)$ does *not* satisfy the constraint, $(P? - Y \leq 0, \alpha\beta\gamma)$.

Then, in that schedule, $P? - Y > 0$ and, hence, $Y < P?$ Next, since $X - Y \leq -v < 0$, it follows that $X < Y$. Thus, $X < Y < P?$ (i.e., both X and Y precede $P?$).

Next, let $\tilde{s}$ be the same scenario as s except that the truth value of p is flipped. Let t be the first time at which the schedules, $\sigma(s, \omega)$ and $\sigma(\tilde{s}, \omega)$, differ. Thus, there must be some time-point T that is executed in one of the schedules at time t, and in the other at some time later than t. In that case, the corresponding histories (of past observations) at time t must be different. However, since all other propositions and contingent durations are identical in the dramas, (s, ω) and $(\tilde{s}, \omega)$, the only possible difference must involve the value of the proposition p, whence $P?$ must be executed in both schedules before the time of first difference, t.

Now, in the schedule $\sigma(s, \omega)$, we have seen that both X and Y are executed before $P?$, and hence before t. Thus, $[\sigma(s, \omega)]_X = [\sigma(\tilde{s}, \omega)]_X$ and $[\sigma(s, \omega)]_Y = [\sigma(\tilde{s}, \omega)]_Y$. But this is not possible because in one scenario $Y - X \leq u < v$, while in the other $Y - X \geq v$. Both constraints cannot be satisfied using the same values of X and Y. □

Label Modification. This section introduces a variety of *label-modification* rules that share some resemblance to the Label-Removal rule in Table 2. Thus, we begin with a short description of the Label-Removal rule.

Suppose a CSTNU contains a contingent link, $(A, 5, 12, C)$. In other words, the contingent duration, $C - A$, is uncontrollable, but guaranteed to be within the interval, $[5, 12]$. Suppose further that the network also contains an upper-case edge, $Y \xrightarrow{C:-2} A$, which represents the following *wait* constraint: "As long as the contingent time-point C remains unexecuted, Y must wait at least 2 units after the execution of the activation time-point, A." Given that the minimum duration of this contingent link is 5, it follows that the contingent time-point C must remain unexecuted until after the wait time of 2 has expired. As a result, the decision to execute Y must, in *every* situation, wait at least 2 units after A. For this reason, the Label-Removal rule generates the ordinary edge, $Y \xrightarrow{-2} A$, which represents the *unconditional* constraint, $A - Y \leq -2$ (i.e., $Y \geq A + 2$). This example illustrates that in certain circumstances, a constraint conditioned on an uncontrollable event—in this case, the execution of the contingent time-point C—might have the force of an unconditional constraint because the uncertainty associated with the uncontrollable event will definitely not be resolved at the time a particular execution decision—in this case, the decision to execute Y—must be made.

The label-modification rules in Table 3 have the same general flavor, except that they deal with the uncertainty associated with observation nodes, rather

Table 3. Label-modification rules for CSTNUs. Labeled values in shaded boxes replace those in dashed boxes.

$\mathrm{R_0}$ Case: $P? \xrightarrow[\langle\alpha,\hbar,-w\rangle]{\langle\alpha p,\hbar,-w\rangle} X$ Applicable if: $0 \le w$, p is a literal not in α, and $\hbar$ is either $\diamond$ or an upper-case letter.	**$\mathrm{R_1}$ Case:** $P? \xrightarrow{\langle\alpha\beta,\diamond,-w\rangle} X \xrightarrow[\langle\alpha\beta\gamma,\hbar,v\rangle,\ \langle\neg\alpha\beta\gamma p,\hbar,v\rangle]{\langle\beta\gamma p,\hbar,v\rangle} Y$ Applicable if: $0 \le w$; $v \le w$; α,β and γ are labels that do not share any literals; p is a literal that does not appear in α,β or γ; and $\hbar$ is $\diamond$ or an upper-case letter.
$\mathrm{R_2}$ Case: $P? \xleftarrow[\langle\alpha,\hbar,w\rangle]{\langle\alpha p,\hbar,w\rangle} X$ Applicable if: $0 \le w$; p is a literal not in α, and $\hbar$ is either $\diamond$ or an upper-case letter.	**$\mathrm{R_3}$ Case:** $P? \xrightarrow{\langle\alpha\beta,\diamond,-w\rangle} X \xleftarrow[\langle\alpha\beta\gamma,\hbar,-v\rangle,\ \langle\neg\alpha\beta\gamma p,\hbar,-v\rangle]{\langle\beta\gamma p,\hbar,-v\rangle} Y$ Applicable if: $0 \le w$; $v \le w$; α,β and γ are labels that do not share any literals; p is a literal that does not appear in α,β or γ; and $\hbar$ is $\diamond$ or an upper-case letter.

$$P? \xrightarrow{\langle\alpha p,\hbar,-w\rangle} X \qquad\qquad P? \xrightarrow{\langle\alpha,\hbar,-w\rangle} X$$

(a) Pre-existing edge, where $0 \le w$, p is a literal that does not appear in α, and $\hbar$ can be either $\diamond$ or an upper-case letter.

(b) Modified label.

Fig. 4. The Label-Modification rule, $\mathrm{R_0}$ (cf. Lemma 2).

than contingent links. For example, consider the edge, $P? \xrightarrow{\langle\alpha p,\ \diamond,\ -w\rangle} X$, where neither p nor $\neg p$ appears in α, and $w \ge 0$. This edge represents the conditional constraint that "in scenarios where αp is true, $X - P? \le -w$ (i.e., $X + w \le P?$) must hold." Given that $w \ge 0$, it follows that in scenarios where αp is true, X must be executed before the observation node $P?$ But that, in turn, implies that the truth value of p cannot be known at the time X is executed. And, of course, the truth value of p cannot be known when the decision to execute $P?$ is made either. As a result, decisions about when to execute X and $P?$ cannot depend on the truth value of p. Thus, the PLabel on the edge from $P?$ to X should be modified to remove the occurrence of p, yielding the new edge, $P? \xrightarrow{\langle\alpha,\ \diamond,\ -w\rangle} X$, which represents the constraint that in scenarios where α holds, $X - P? \le -w$ (i.e., $X + w \le P?$) must hold. This is the idea behind the label-modification rule, $\mathrm{R_0}$, shown in Table 3. For each rule in the table, pre-existing labeled values are represented as usual, those to be modified (or replaced by new ones) are shown within a dashed box, and newly generated labeled values are shown within a shaded box. The following lemma shows that Rule $\mathrm{R_0}$ is sound.

Lemma 2 (Label-Modification Rule, $\mathrm{R_0}$). *Suppose that $w \ge 0$ and α is a label that does not contain the literal p. If σ is a dynamic execution strategy that satisfies the labeled constraint, $(X - P? \le -w, \alpha p)$, as shown in Fig. 4-(a), then σ must also satisfy the labeled constraint, $(X - P? \le -w, \alpha)$, as shown in*

$$P? \xrightarrow{\langle\alpha\beta,\diamond,-w\rangle} X \xrightarrow{\langle\beta\gamma p,\hbar,v\rangle} Y$$

(a) Pre-existing edges, where $0 \leq w; v \leq w; \alpha,\beta$ and γ are labels that do not share any literals; p is a literal that does not appear in α,β or γ; and $\hbar$ is either $\diamond$ or an upper-case letter.

$$P? \xrightarrow{\langle\alpha\beta,\diamond,-w\rangle} X \xrightarrow[\langle\neg\alpha\beta\gamma p,\hbar,v\rangle]{\langle\alpha\beta\gamma,\hbar,v\rangle} Y$$

(b) New labels on the edge from X to Y.

Fig. 5. The Label-Modification rule, R_1 (cf. Lemma 3).

Fig. 4-(b). The rule also applies to upper-case edges (i.e., edges with an upper-case alphabetic label, $\hbar$).

Proof. Let (s,ω) be a drama such that:

- the label $\alpha\neg p$ is true in scenario s; but
- the schedule $\sigma(s,\omega)$ does *not* satisfy the constraint, $(X - P? \leq -w)$.

In that case, $X + w > P?$ Next, let s' be the same scenario as s except that p is true in s'. Then αp is true in s', which implies that $(X - P? \leq -w)$ holds in $\sigma(s',\omega)$. Thus, $X + w \leq P?$ holds in $\sigma(s',\omega)$.

Next, let t be the first time at which the schedules, $\sigma(s,\omega)$ and $\sigma(s',\omega)$, differ. Then there must be some time-point T that is executed in one of the schedules at time t, and in the other at some time after t. But in that case, the corresponding histories at time t must be different. Since the dramas, (s,ω) and (s',ω), are identical except for the truth value of p, it follows that the observation node, $P?$, must be executed before time t. Now, in the drama (s',ω), the constraint, $X + w \leq P?$, is satisfied; thus, both X and $P?$ must be executed before time t in that drama. Since the schedules, $\sigma(s,\omega)$ and $\sigma(s',\omega)$, are identical prior to time t, it follows that the same constraint is satisfied by $\sigma(s',\omega)$, contradicting the choice of (s',ω). □

Rule R_1 in Table 3 first appeared in [2]. The corresponding lemma, given below, shows that it is sound. Its proof is not repeated here.

Lemma 3 (Label-Modification Rule, R_1). *Let σ be a dynamic execution strategy that satisfies the labeled constraints in Fig. 5-(a). Then σ must also satisfy the labeled constraint $(Y - X \leq v, \alpha\beta\gamma)$. The original constraint, $(Y - X \leq v, \beta\gamma p)$, is replaced by the pair of labeled constraints, $(Y - X \leq v, \alpha\beta\gamma)$ and $(Y - X \leq v, \neg\alpha\beta\gamma p)$, as depicted in Fig. 5-(b).*

We remark that when $v > w$ the rule is not needed because, in that case, the execution of Y could be postponed until after the execution of $P?$, in which case the truth value of p would become known.

Now, let us consider the case of an edge between X and $P?$ with a labeled positive value containing literal p.

Lemma 4 (Label-Removal Rule, R_2). *Suppose that $w \geq 0$ and α is a label that does not contain the literal p. If σ is a dynamic execution strategy that satisfies the labeled constraint, $(P? - X \leq w, \alpha p)$, as shown in Fig. 6-(a), then σ must also satisfy the labeled constraint, $(P? - X \leq w, \alpha)$, as shown in Fig. 6-(b). The rule also applies to upper-case edges (i.e., edges with an upper-case alphabetic label, $\hbar$).*

Proof. It is straightforward to prove the soundness of this rule, since it is similar to the proof for Lemma 2. □

In the previous work [3], Rule R_2 was less general because it was applicable only when $P?$ was for sure after X. It is straightforward to show that if $P?$ occurs before X, then the constraint is not considered; on the other way, when $P?$ is after X, the value of literal p cannot be known and, thus, we have to consider the stronger constraint without p to be sure that any possible execution will satisfy the given constraints.

When there is a negative value on a constraint from Y to X, we have another case of label modification as shown in the following lemma.

Lemma 5 (Label-Modification Rule, R_3). *Let σ be a dynamic execution strategy that satisfies the labeled constraints shown in Fig. 7-(a). Then σ must also satisfy the labeled constraint, $(X - Y \leq -v, \alpha\beta\gamma)$. The original constraint, $(X - Y \leq -v, \beta\gamma p)$, is replaced by the pair of labeled constraints, $(X - Y \leq -v, \alpha\beta\gamma)$ and $(X - Y \leq -v, \neg\alpha\beta\gamma p)$, as shown in Fig. 7-(b).*

Proof. Let σ be as in the statement of the lemma. Suppose that there is some drama, (s, ω), such that:

- the label $\alpha\beta\gamma$ is true in scenario s; but
- the schedule $\sigma(s, \omega)$, does *not* satisfy the constraint, $(X - Y \leq -v)$.

In that case, $X - Y > -v$, which implies that $Y < X + v \leq X + w \leq P?$ (Recall that $v \leq w$ and, given that $\alpha\beta$ is true, the constraint, $(X - P? \leq -w)$, must be satisfied by σ.) Note also that $X \leq P?$

Next, let $\tilde{s}$ be the same scenario as s except that the truth value of p is flipped. Let t be the first time at which the schedules, $\sigma(s, \omega)$ and $\sigma(\tilde{s}, \omega)$, differ. Thus, there must be some time-point T that is executed in one of the schedules at time t, and in the other at some time later than t. But in that case, the corresponding histories at time t must be different. But the only possible difference must involve the value of the proposition $P?$, since all other propositions and contingent durations are identical in the dramas, (s, ω) and $(\tilde{s}, \omega)$. Thus, $P?$ must be executed before time t. Now, in the schedule $\sigma(s, \omega)$, we have seen that both Y and X are executed before $P?$, and hence before t. Thus, $[\sigma(s, \omega)]_X = [\sigma(\tilde{s}, \omega)]_X$ and $[\sigma(s, \omega)]_Y = [\sigma(\tilde{s}, \omega)]_Y$. But then the value of $Y - X$ must be the same in both schedules. Thus, the constraint $X - Y \leq -v$ must be violated in both schedules. But this contradicts that the constraint $X - Y \leq -v$ is satisfied in scenarios where $\beta\gamma p$ is true.

$P? \xleftarrow{\langle \alpha p, \hbar, w \rangle} X$ $\qquad$ $P? \xleftarrow{\langle \alpha, \hbar, w \rangle} X$

(a) Pre-existing edges, where $0 \le w$; p is a literal not in α; and $\hbar$ is either $\diamond$ or an upper-case letter.

(b) New label on the edge from X to $P?$.

Fig. 6. The Label-Modification rule, R_2 (cf. Lemma 4).

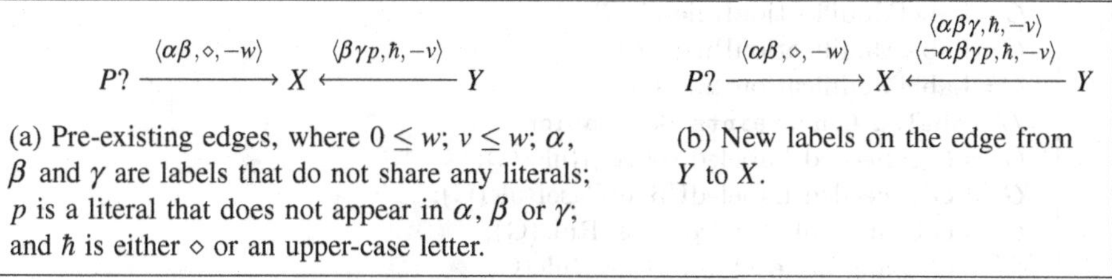

$P? \xrightarrow{\langle \alpha\beta, \diamond, -w \rangle} X \xleftarrow{\langle \beta\gamma p, \hbar, -v \rangle} Y$
$P? \xrightarrow{\langle \alpha\beta, \diamond, -w \rangle} X \xleftarrow{\langle \alpha\beta\gamma, \hbar, -v \rangle, \langle \neg\alpha\beta\gamma p, \hbar, -v \rangle} Y$
(a) Pre-existing edges, where $0 \le w$; $v \le w$; α, β and γ are labels that do not share any literals; p is a literal that does not appear in α, β or γ; and $\hbar$ is either $\diamond$ or an upper-case letter.
(b) New labels on the edge from Y to X.

Fig. 7. The Label-Modification rule, R_3 (cf. Lemma 5).

Regarding the constraint $(X - Y \le -v, \neg\alpha\beta\gamma p)$, it is straightforward to show that it is necessary to introduce it to maintain equivalence with the original constraint from Y to X. Indeed, when α is false, the relation between $P?$ and X is not known. □

The application of rules R_0, R_1, R_2 and R_3 has to be considered for all pairs of time-points with respect to all suitable observation points.

4.2 A CSTNU DC-Checking Algorithm

Our CSTNU DC-checking algorithm works by applying the labeled constraint-generation rules of Table 2 and the label-modification rules of Table 3 to all relevant combinations of edges until:

- the associated AllMax matrix is found to be inconsistent; or
- the rules cannot generate any more new (stronger) edges; or
- a maximum number of rounds of rule applications has been reached.

The pseudocode for the algorithm is shown in Procedure 2, below.

The algorithm performs $p(n^2+nk+k)$ rounds, where n is the number of time-points, k is the number of contingent links, and p is the number of propositional letters that appear in the network.

Given the lemmas presented in this paper, it is straightforward to verify that the algorithm is sound. Thus, whenever the algorithm is given a DC network, the algorithm invariably declares it to be DC.

Procedure 2. CSTNU-DC-Check(G).

```
Input: G = ⟨𝒯, 𝒞, L, 𝒪𝒯, 𝒪, P, ℒ⟩: a CSTNU instance
Output: the dynamic controllability of G.
G' = G;
for 1 to |P|(|𝒯|^2 + |𝒯||ℒ| + |ℒ|) do
    if (AllMax matrix of G is inconsistent) then return false;
    // Label Modification Rules
    G =LabelModificationRuleR0(G);
    G =LabelModificationRuleR1(G);
    G =LabelModificationRuleR2(G);
    G =LabelModificationRuleR3(G);
    // Labeled Constraints Generation
    G' = G'∪ needed LabeledNoCaseRule(G);
    G' = G'∪ needed LabeledUpperCaseRule(G);
    G' = G'∪ any LabeledCrossCaseRule(G);
    G' = G'∪ any LabeledLowerCaseRule(G);
    G' = G'∪ any LabeledLabelRemovalRule(G);
    G' = G'∪ any ObservationCaseRule(G);
    if (no rules were applied) then return true;
    G = G';
return false
```

5 Discussion and Conclusions

This paper presented a DC-checking algorithm for CSTNUs. It modifies rule R_2 with respect to the preliminary version of the algorithm presented previously [3]. Rule R_2 has been generalized and now it has a similar form as Rule R_0. Now, the pair R_0 and R_2 allows the simplification of all possible constraints involving observation nodes.

For future work, we aim to provide additional rules to make the algorithm complete.

References

1. Combi, C., Posenato, R.: Controllability in temporal conceptual workflow schemata. In: Dayal, U., Eder, J., Koehler, J., Reijers, H.A. (eds.) BPM 2009. LNCS, vol. 5701, pp. 64–79. Springer, Heidelberg (2009)
2. Hunsberger, L., Posenato, R., Combi, C.: The dynamic controllability of conditional STNs with uncertainty. In: Workshop on Planning and Plan Execution for Real-World Systems: Principles and Practices (PlanEx) @ ICAPS-2012, Atibaia, pp. 1–8 (2012)
3. Combi, C., Hunsberger, L., Posenato, R.: An algorithm for checking the dynamic controllability of a conditional simple temporal network with uncertainty. In: 5th International Conference on Agents and Artificial Intelligence (ICAART-2013). SciTePress (2013)

4. Morris, P.H., Muscettola, N.: Temporal dynamic controllability revisited. In: Veloso, M.M., Kambhampati, S. (eds.) The 20th National Conference on Artificial Intelligence (AAAI-05), pp. 1193–1198. AAAI Press, Menlo Park (2005)
5. Conrad, P.R., Williams, B.C.: Drake: an efficient executive for temporal plans with choice. J. Artif. Intell. Res. (JAIR) **42**, 607–659 (2011)
6. Dechter, R., Meiri, I., Pearl, J.: Temporal constraint networks. Artif. Intell. **49**, 61–95 (1991)
7. Morris, P.H., Muscettola, N., Vidal, T.: Dynamic control of plans with temporal uncertainty. In: Nebel, B. (ed.) The 17th International Joint Conference on Artificial Intelligence (IJCAI-01), pp. 494–502. Kaufmann, San Francisco (2001)
8. Hunsberger, L.: Fixing the semantics for dynamic controllability and providing a more practical characterization of dynamic execution strategies. In: Lutz, C., Raskin, J.F. (eds.) TIME, pp. 155–162. IEEE Computer Society, New York (2009)
9. Morris, P.: A structural characterization of temporal dynamic controllability. In: Benhamou, F. (ed.) CP 2006. LNCS, vol. 4204, pp. 375–389. Springer, Heidelberg (2006)
10. Tsamardinos, I., Vidal, T., Pollack, M.E.: CTP: a new constraint-based formalism for conditional, temporal planning. Constraints **8**, 365–388 (2003)
11. Hunsberger, L.: Magic loops in simple temporal networks with uncertainty. In: 5th International Conference on Agents and Artificial Intelligence (ICAART-2013). SciTePress (2013)
12. Combi, C., Posenato, R.: Towards temporal controllabilities for workflow schemata. In: Markey, N., Wijsen, J. (eds.) TIME, pp. 129–136. IEEE Computer Society, New York (2010)

Magic Loops and the Dynamic Controllability of Simple Temporal Networks with Uncertainty

Luke Hunsberger(✉)

Computer Science Department, Vassar College, Poughkeepsie, NY 12604, USA
hunsberg@cs.vassar.edu

Abstract. A Simple Temporal Network with Uncertainty (STNU) is a structure for representing and reasoning about temporal constraints and uncontrollable-but-bounded temporal intervals called contingent links. An STNU is dynamically controllable (DC) if there exists a strategy for executing its time-points that guarantees that all of the constraints will be satisfied no matter how the durations of the contingent links turn out. The fastest algorithm for checking the dynamic controllability of STNUs is based on an analysis of the graphical structure of STNUs. This paper (1) presents a new method for analyzing the graphical structure of STNUs, (2) determines an upper bound on the complexity of certain structures—the indivisible semi-reducible negative loops; (3) presents an algorithm for generating loops—the *magic loops*—whose complexity attains this upper bound; and (4) shows how the upper bound can be exploited to speed up the process of DC-checking for certain networks.

Keywords: Temporal networks · Dynamic controllability

1 Background

Agent-based applications invariably involve actions and temporal constraints. Dechter et al. [1] introduced Simple Temporal Networks (STNs) to facilitate the management of temporal constraints. Vidal and Ghallab [14] were the first to incorporate actions with uncertain durations into an STN-like framework, and to define a notion of dynamic controllability. Morris et al. [6] developed the most widely accepted formalization of Simple Temporal Networks with Uncertainty (STNUs) and dynamic controllability. Morris and Muscettola [7] developed an $O(N^5)$-time algorithm for checking the dynamic controllability of STNUs. Morris [5] presented an $O(N^4)$-time DC-checking algorithm based on an analysis of the structure of STNU graphs; it is the fastest DC-checking algorithm to date. This paper presents a new way of analyzing the structure of STNU graphs, and shows how it can be used to speed up DC checking for some networks.

The rest of this section summarizes the definitions and results for STNs, STNUs and dynamic controllability that will be used in the rest of the paper.

J. Filipe and A. Fred (Eds.): ICAART 2013, CCIS 449, pp. 332–350, 2014.
DOI: 10.1007/978-3-662-44440-5_20

1.1 Simple Temporal Networks

Dechter et al. [1] introduced *Simple Temporal Networks (STNs)* and presented the basic theoretical results for them. An STN is a pair, $(\mathcal{T}, \mathcal{C})$, where $\mathcal{T}$ is a set of time-point variables (or time-points) and $\mathcal{C}$ is a set of constraints, each having the form, $Y - X \leq \delta$, for some $X, Y \in \mathcal{T}$, and real number δ. Typically, the time-points in $\mathcal{T}$ represent starting or ending times of actions, or abstract coordination times. The constraints in $\mathcal{C}$ can accommodate release, deadline, duration and inter-action constraints. An STN is *consistent* if there exists a set of values for its time-points that together satisfy all of its constraints.

For any STN, $\mathcal{S} = (\mathcal{T}, \mathcal{C})$, there is a corresponding graph, $\mathcal{G}$, where the nodes in $\mathcal{G}$ correspond to the time-points in $\mathcal{T}$, and for each constraint, $Y - X \leq \delta$, in $\mathcal{C}$, there is an edge in $\mathcal{G}$ of the form, $X \xrightarrow{\delta} Y$. For convenience, this paper calls the constraints and edges in an STN *ordinary* constraints and edges.

The *all-pairs, shortest-paths* (APSP) matrix for $\mathcal{G}$ is called the *distance matrix* for $\mathcal{S}$ (or $\mathcal{G}$) and is denoted by $\mathcal{D}$. Thus, for any X and Y in $\mathcal{T}$, $\mathcal{D}(X, Y)$ equals the length of the shortest path from X to Y in the graph $\mathcal{G}$. If $\mathcal{D}$ has nothing but zeros down its main diagonal, then $\mathcal{D}$ is said to be consistent.

Theorem 1 (Fundamental Theorem of STNs). *For any STN $\mathcal{S}$, with graph $\mathcal{G}$, and distance matrix $\mathcal{D}$, the following are equivalent: (1) $\mathcal{S}$ is consistent; (2) $\mathcal{G}$ has no negative loops; and (3) $\mathcal{D}$ is consistent.*

1.2 STNs with Uncertainty

Some applications involve actions whose durations are uncontrollable, but nonetheless guaranteed to fall within known bounds. For example, when I turn on my laptop, I do not control how long it will take to load its operating system; however, I know that it will take anywhere from one to four minutes. A *Simple Temporal Network with Uncertainty (STNU)* augments an STN to include *contingent links* that represent this kind of uncontrollable-but-bounded temporal interval [6]. A contingent link has the form, (A, x, y, C), where A and C are time-points and $0 < x < y < \infty$. A is called the *activation time-point;* C is called the *contingent time-point.* Intuitively, the duration of the interval from A to C is uncontrollable, but guaranteed to fall within the interval $[x, y]$. Typically, an agent controls the execution of the activation time-point A, but only *observes* the subsequent execution of the contingent time-point C in real time.[1]

Formally, an STNU is a triple, $(\mathcal{T}, \mathcal{C}, \mathcal{L})$, where $(\mathcal{T}, \mathcal{C})$ is an STN, and $\mathcal{L}$ is a set of contingent links. N is used to denote the number of time-points in an STNU, K the number of contingent links. The most important property of an STNU is whether it is *dynamically controllable* (DC)—that is, whether there exists a strategy for executing the non-contingent time-points that guarantees that all of the constraints in the network will be satisfied *no matter how the contingent durations turn out.* The strategy is *dynamic* in that its execution decisions are

[1] Agents are not part of the semantics of STNUs; they are used here for illustration.

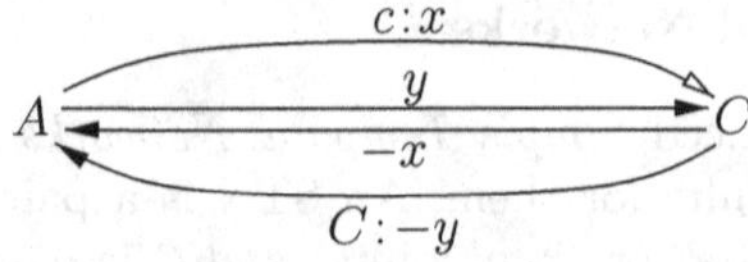

Fig. 1. The ordinary and labeled edges associated with a contingent link, (A, x, y, C).

allowed to react to past observations, but not present or future observations. The formal semantics for dynamic controllability is quite complicated, but it need not be presented here because a more convenient—and equivalent—graphical characterization is available, as follows.

Graph for an STNU. Let $\mathcal{S} = (\mathcal{T}, \mathcal{C}, \mathcal{L})$ be an STNU. The graph for $\mathcal{S}$ contains all edges from the STN, $(\mathcal{T}, \mathcal{C})$, as well as additional edges derived from the contingent links in $\mathcal{L}$. In particular, for each contingent link $(A, x, y, C) \in \mathcal{L}$, the graph contains the edges shown in Fig. 1. The ordinary edges, $A \xrightarrow{y} C$ and $C \xrightarrow{-x} A$, represent the constraints, $C - A \leq y$ and $A - C \leq -x$ (i.e., $C - A \in [x, y]$). The other edges are *labeled* edges representing uncontrollable *possibilities.* In particular, $A \xrightarrow{c:x} C$, which is called a *lower-case* (LC) edge, represents the possibility that the contingent duration might take on its minimum value, x; and $C \xrightarrow{C:-y} A$, which is called an *upper-case* (UC) edge, represents the possibility that the contingent duration might take on its maximum value, y.

Because the graph of an STNU contains ordinary, lower-case and upper-case edges, paths in an STNU graph can be quite complicated. However, as shall be seen, the so-called *semi-reducible* paths are particularly important. For expository convenience, the definition of a semi-reducible path is postponed; however, the *SR-distance matrix*, $\mathcal{D}^*$, can be defined now as the all-pairs, shortest-*semi-reducible*-paths matrix for an STNU graph (i.e., for any time-points X and Y, $\mathcal{D}^*(X, Y)$ equals the length of the shortest *semi-reducible* path from X to Y).

Theorem 2 (Fundamental Theorem of STNUs). *For any STNU $\mathcal{S}$, with graph $\mathcal{G}$, and SR-distance matrix $\mathcal{D}^*$, the following are equivalent: (1) $\mathcal{S}$ is dynamically controllable; (2) $\mathcal{G}$ has no* semi-reducible *negative loops; and (3) $\mathcal{D}^*$ is consistent.*[2]

1.3 DC-Checking Algorithms

In view of Theorem 2, the problem of determining whether an STNU is dynamically controllable can be answered by computing the SR-distance matrix $\mathcal{D}^*$. If, during the process, a negative entry along the main diagonal is ever discovered—which would correspond to a semi-reducible negative loop—then the network

[2] Morris and Muscettola [7] showed that an STNU is DC iff a certain matrix is consistent. Morris [5] highlighted semi-reducible paths and showed that an STNU is DC iff its graph has no semi-reducible negative loops. Hunsberger [3] showed that the matrix computed by Morris and Muscettola *is* the SR-distance matrix, $\mathcal{D}^*$.

cannot be dynamically controllable. Algorithms for determining whether an STNU is dynamically controllable are called *DC-checking algorithms.*

Two polynomial-time DC-checking algorithms have been presented so far in the literature: the $O(N^5)$-time algorithm of Morris and Muscettola [7], henceforth called the N^5 algorithm; and the $O(N^4)$-time algorithm of Morris [5], henceforth called the N^4 algorithm. The N^5 algorithm uses a set of rules to generate new edges in the graph, effectively a new kind of constraint propagation that accommodates labeled edges. After at most $O(N^2)$ rounds of edge generation, the algorithm is guaranteed to have computed the matrix $\mathcal{D}^*$ or determined that it is inconsistent. Since each round takes $O(N^3)$ time, the overall complexity is $O(N^5)$. The N^4 algorithm uses the same edge-generation rules but, as will be seen, restricts their application to "reducing away" LC edges. This restricted form of edge-generation is sufficient to compute the matrix $\mathcal{D}^*$ or determine that it is inconsistent. Based on an analysis of the structure of semi-reducible negative loops, the N^4 algorithm requires only $K \leq N$ rounds of edge-generation. Since each round can be done in $O(N^3)$ time, its overall time-complexity is $O(N^4)$.

Edge-generation Rules. Intuitively, the ordinary constraints in an STNU are constraints that the agent in charge of executing time-points wants to satisfy. In contrast, the lower-case and upper-case edges represent uncontrollable *possibilities* that could potentially threaten the satisfaction of the ordinary constraints. Typically, to eliminate such threats, the agent must satisfy additional constraints—or, in graphical terms, add new edges to the graph. Toward that end, Morris and Muscettola [7] presented the five edge-generation rules in Table 1, where pre-existing edges are denoted by solid arrows and newly generated edges are denoted by dashed arrows. Each rule takes two pre-existing edges as input and generates a single edge as output. Incidentally, applicability conditions of the form, $Y \not\equiv Z$, should be construed as stipulating that Y and Z must be distinct time-point variables, not as constraints on the *values* of those variables.

Table 1. The edge-generation rules from Morris and Muscettola [7].

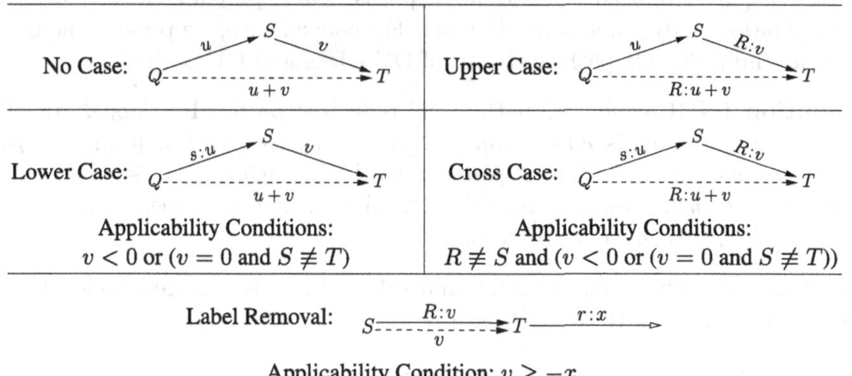

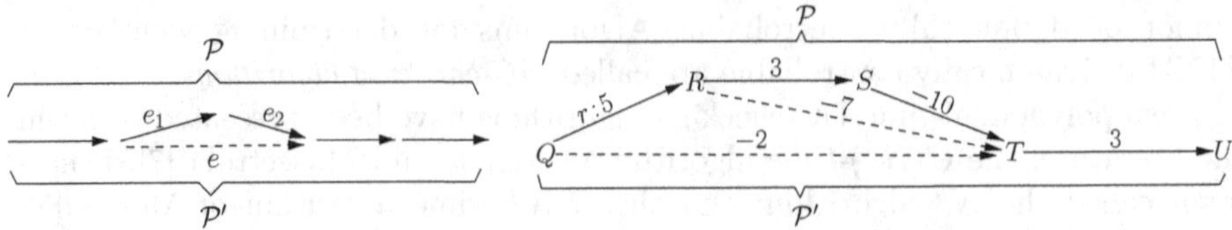

Fig. 2. Two examples of transforming a path $\mathcal{P}$ into a path $\mathcal{P}'$.

The rules only generate new ordinary or upper-case edges, never new lower-case edges. The generated ordinary edges represent additional constraints that must be satisfied to avoid threatening the satisfaction of the original constraints. The generated upper-case edges represent additional *conditional* constraints that the agent must satisfy. A generated UC edge of the form, $Y \xrightarrow{C:-w} A$, represents a conditional constraint that can be glossed as: "As long as the contingent duration $C - A$ might take on its maximum value, then $A - Y \leq -w$ (i.e., $Y \geq A + w$) must be satisfied (i.e., Y must *wait* at least w after A)."

Path Transformations. Morris [5] showed that the process of edge generation can also be viewed as one of *path transformation* or *path reduction.* For example, suppose a path $\mathcal{P}$ contains two adjacent edges, e_1 and e_2, to which one of the first four edge-generation rules can be applied to generate a new edge e, as illustrated in the lefthand side of Fig. 2. Let $\mathcal{P}'$ be the path obtained from $\mathcal{P}$ by replacing e_1 and e_2 by the new edge e. We say that $\mathcal{P}$ has been *transformed into* (or *reduced* to) $\mathcal{P}'$. Similarly, if $\mathcal{P}$ contains a UC edge E to which the Label-Removal rule can be applied to generate a new ordinary edge E^o, then $\mathcal{P}$ can be transformed by replacing E by E^o. Finally, any *sequence* of zero or more such transformations also counts as a path transformation. The righthand side of Fig. 2 illustrates a two-step transformation of a path $\mathcal{P}$, using the No-Case and Lower-Case rules.

Importantly, path transformations preserve *unlabeled length* (i.e., the length of the path ignoring any alphabetic labels on its edges). This follows directly from the fact that each edge-generation rule preserves unlabeled length.

Morris [5] introduced *semi-reducible* paths, which play a central role in the determination of dynamic controllability. For convenience, we present the definition of semi-reducible paths in terms of OU-edges and OU-paths.

Definition 1 (OU-edge, OU-path, Semi-reducible path, SRN loop)**.** *An* OU-edge *is an edge that is either ordinary or upper-case. An* OU-path *is a path consisting solely of OU-edges. A path in an STNU graph is called* semi-reducible *if it can be transformed into an OU-path. A semi-reducible loop with negative unlabeled length is called an* SRN loop.

Note that the path, $\mathcal{P}$, on the righthand side of Fig. 2 is semi-reducible, since it can be transformed into the OU-path, $\mathcal{P}'$.

The N^4 DC-checking Algorithm. The N^4 algorithm takes a two-step approach to determining whether an STNU has any SRN loops. In Step 1, it generates

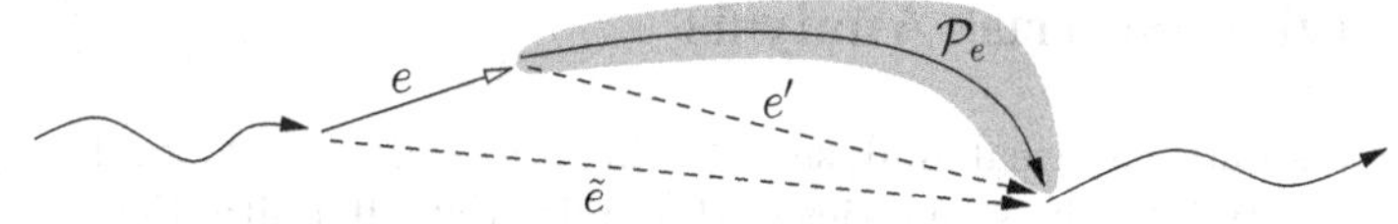

Fig. 3. Reducing away a lower-case edge, e.

the OU-edges that could arise from the transformation of semi-reducible paths into OU-paths. The dashed edges in Fig. 2 are examples of such edges. In Step 2, it gathers the OU-edges from Step 1—minus any alphabetic labels—into an STN, $\mathcal{S}^\dagger$. It then computes the corresponding distance matrix, $\mathcal{D}^\dagger$, which turns out to equal the SR-distance matrix, $\mathcal{D}^*$, for the original STNU.

To illustrate Step 1, suppose $\mathcal{P}$ is a semi-reducible path consisting of original STNU edges, including at least one LC edge e, as shown in Fig. 3. Since $\mathcal{P}$ is semi-reducible, there must be a sequence of reductions by which $\mathcal{P}$ is transformed into an OU-path. Thus, sometime during that transformation, the Lower-Case or Cross-Case rule must be applied to e and some other edge e' to yield a new OU-edge $\tilde{e}$, effectively removing e from the path. We say that e has been "reduced away". To enable this, the original path $\mathcal{P}$ must have a sub-path, $\mathcal{P}_e$, immediately following e, such that $\mathcal{P}_e$ reduces to the edge e', as shown in Fig. 3. The concatenation of the LC edge e with the sub-path $\mathcal{P}_e$ is called a *lower-case reducing sub-path* (LCR sub-path); edges such as $\tilde{e}$ that are generated by transforming an LCR sub-path into a single edge, are called *core edges* [3].

In view of the above, every occurrence of an LC edge, e, in any semi-reducible path, $\mathcal{P}$, must belong to an LCR sub-path in $\mathcal{P}$. Equivalently, the edges in any semi-reducible path, $\mathcal{P}$, that do *not* belong to an LCR sub-path must be OU-edges from the original STNU. Thus, Step 1 of the N^4 algorithm searches for LCR sub-paths and the core edges they generate. Crucially, this search does not require exhaustively applying the edge-generation rules from Table 1. Instead, as will be seen, the search can be limited to *extension sub-paths,* which have an important nesting property. After Step 1, the algorithm has a set, $\mathcal{E}$, of OU-edges.

For Step 2, note that there is a one-to-one correspondence between shortest semi-reducible paths in the original STNU and shortest paths consisting of edges in $\mathcal{E}$. In particular, if $\mathcal{P}$ is a shortest semi-reducible path, then it can be transformed into a path, $\mathcal{P}'$, whose edges are in $\mathcal{E}$; and since path transformations preserve unlabeled length, $|\mathcal{P}| = |\mathcal{P}'|$. Conversely, if $\mathcal{P}'$ is a shortest path with edges in $\mathcal{E}$, then, by "unwinding" the transformations that generated the edges in $\mathcal{E}$, $\mathcal{P}'$ can be "un-transformed" into a semi-reducible path $\mathcal{P}$, with $|\mathcal{P}'| = |\mathcal{P}|$.

Next, since alphabetic labels are irrelevant to the computation of unlabeled lengths, let $\mathcal{E}^\dagger$ be the set of ordinary edges obtained by stripping any alphabetic labels from the edges in $\mathcal{E}$; let $\mathcal{S}^\dagger$ be the corresponding STN; and let $\mathcal{D}^\dagger$ be the corresponding distance matrix. Then $\mathcal{D}^\dagger$ is equal to the all-pairs, shortest-paths matrix for paths with edges in $\mathcal{E}$, and hence $\mathcal{D}^\dagger = \mathcal{D}^*$. Thus, the N^4 algorithm concludes that the original STNU is DC iff $\mathcal{D}^\dagger$ is consistent.

2 Modifying Morris' Analysis

To simplify his mathematical analysis, Morris [5] introduces two kinds of instantaneous reactivity into the semantics of dynamic controllability. First, he allows contingent links of the form, $(A, 0, y, C)$, in which the lower bound on the contingent duration is zero. This effectively allows scenarios in which it is uncertain whether the temporal interval between a cause and its effect will be instantaneous. Second, he allows an agent to react instantaneously to an observation of a contingent execution. Although these sorts of instantaneous reactions may be applicable to some domains, this author prefers to stick with the more realistic assumptions of the original semantics—and the edge-generation rules in Table 1—in which both the lower bounds of contingent durations and agent reaction times must be positive. The rest of this section shows how Morris' approach can be modified to conform to the original semantics of dynamic controllability.

Given his assumptions, Morris changed the conditions for the Lower-Case rule to $v < 0$ (i.e., he eliminated the case, $v = 0$). The reason is that when $v = 0$, the edge, $S \xrightarrow{\ v\ } T$, represents the constraint, $T - S \leq 0$ (i.e., $T \leq S$), which expresses that T must execute no later than the contingent time-point S. If able to react instantaneously, an agent need only wait for S to execute and then instantaneously execute T. Thus, no additional constraint is required to guard against S executing early. If unable to react instantaneously, then the new edge from Q to T is needed. Similar remarks apply to the Cross-Case rule.

Extension Sub-paths. Let e be some LC edge in a path, $\mathcal{P}$; and let $e_1, e_2, \ldots$ be the sequence of edges immediately following e in $\mathcal{P}$. If e can be reduced away in $\mathcal{P}$, then it may be that there are many values of $m \geq 1$ for which the sub-path, $e_1, e_2, \ldots, e_m$, could be used to reduce away e. For example, the LC edge from Q to R in Fig. 2 can be reduced away not only by the two-edge sub-path from R to T, as shown in the figure, but also by the three-edge sub-path from R to U. In such cases, the *extension sub-path,* defined below, will turn out to be the sub-path that can reduce away e for which the value of m is the smallest.

Definition 2 (Extension sub-path; moat edge). *Let e be an LC edge in a path $\mathcal{P}$. Let $e_1, e_2, \ldots$ be the sequence of edges that immediately follow e in $\mathcal{P}$. For each $i \geq 1$, let $\mathcal{P}_e^i$ be the sub-path of $\mathcal{P}$ consisting of the edges, $e_1, \ldots, e_i$. If it exists, let m be the smallest integer such that either: (1) $|\mathcal{P}_e^m| < 0$; or (2) $|\mathcal{P}_e^m| = 0$ and $\mathcal{P}_e^m$ is* not *a loop. Then the* extension sub-path *(ESP) for e in $\mathcal{P}$, notated $\mathcal{P}_e$, is the sub-path $\mathcal{P}_e^m$; and its last edge, e_m, is called the* moat edge *for e in $\mathcal{P}$. If no such m exists, then e has no ESP or moat edge in $\mathcal{P}$.*[3]

For the LC edge from Q to R in Fig. 2, the extension sub-path is the two-edge path labeled $\mathcal{P}_e$; and the moat edge is the edge from S to T.

[3] For Morris [5], case (2) is not needed because he eliminated the case, $v = 0$, from the applicability conditions for the Lower-Case and Cross-Case rules.

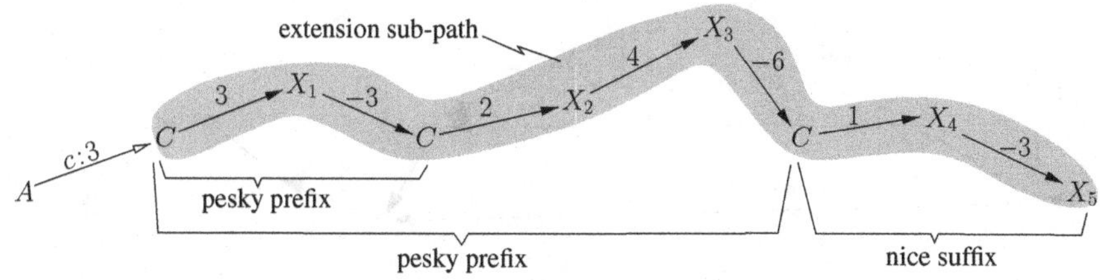

Fig. 4. An extension sub-path with two pesky prefixes.

Structure of ESPs. Given the setup in Definition 2, m is the smallest value for which $|\mathcal{P}_e^m| < 0$ or $\mathcal{P}_e^m$ is a zero-length non-loop. Conversely, for any $i < m$, either $|\mathcal{P}_e^i| > 0$ or $\mathcal{P}_e^i$ is a zero-length loop. This implies that any ESP must consist of *zero or more* loops of length zero, followed by a (non-empty) sub-path that has no prefixes that are zero-length loops. These observations motivate the following.

Definition 3 (Pesky prefix; nice path). *A* pesky prefix *of $\mathcal{P}$ is a non-empty prefix of $\mathcal{P}$ that is a loop of length* 0. *A* nice *path is one having no pesky prefixes.*

In general, an ESP may have zero or more pesky prefixes, followed by a non-empty nice path.[4] Figure 4 shows an ESP with two pesky prefixes, one nested inside the other, followed by a non-empty nice suffix.

Nesting Property for ESPs. The following lemma confirms that ESPs as defined in Definition 2 have the nesting property highlighted by Morris [5].[5]

Lemma 1 (Nesting Property for ESPs). *Let $\mathcal{P}_1$ and $\mathcal{P}_2$ be two ESPs within the same path $\mathcal{P}$. Then $\mathcal{P}_1$ and $\mathcal{P}_2$ are either disjoint (i.e., share no edges) or one is nested inside (i.e., is a sub-path of) the other.*

Breaches and Usable/Unusable Moat Edges. Suppose that $\mathcal{P}$ is a path that contains an occurrence of a lower-case edge, e, that derives from a contingent link, (A, x, y, C). Thus, e has the form, $A \xrightarrow{c:x} C$. Suppose further that e has an extension sub-path, $\mathcal{P}_e$, in $\mathcal{P}$. The existence of an ESP for e in $\mathcal{P}$ turns out to be a necessary, but insufficient condition for reducing away e in $\mathcal{P}$. For example, using Fig. 3 as a reference, if the edge, e', into which $\mathcal{P}_e$ is transformed, happens to be an upper-case edge with alphabetic label C (i.e., that matches the lower-case label on e), then the Cross-Case rule cannot be applied to e and e', blocking the reducing away of e. (Recall the condition, $R \not\equiv S$, for the Cross-Case rule.) Such moat edges are called *unusable.* (It could also be said that $\mathcal{P}_e$ is unusable.) The following definitions specify the characteristics of usable/unusable moat edges.

[4] Unlike Morris [5], for whom every ESP has negative length, this paper must carefully distinguish pesky prefixes from ESPs of length zero.

[5] Proofs for this lemma and all subsequent results are in a companion paper [4].

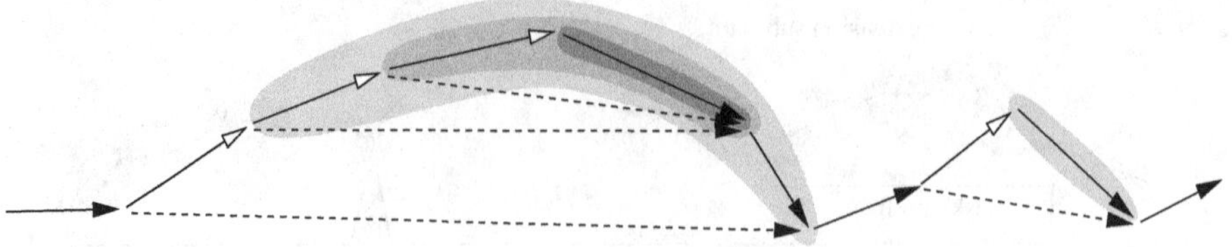

Fig. 5. A semi-reducible path with nested ESPs.

Definition 4 (Breach; usable/unusable moat edge). *Let e be an LC edge for a contingent link, (A, x, y, C); let $\mathcal{P}_e$ be the ESP for e in some path $\mathcal{P}$; and let e_m be the corresponding moat edge. Any occurrence in $\mathcal{P}_e$ of an upper-case edge labeled by C is called a* breach. *If $\mathcal{P}_e$ has no breaches, it is called* breach-free. *If e_m is a breach and $|\mathcal{P}_e| < -x$, then e_m is said to be* unusable; *else, it is* usable.

Theorem 3 shows the crucial role of usable moat edges for semi-reducible paths [5].

Theorem 3. *A path $\mathcal{P}$ is semi-reducible if and only if each of its lower-case edges has a usable moat edge in $\mathcal{P}$.*

Since a pesky prefix, by definition, has length zero, extracting a pesky prefix from an extension sub-path cannot affect its length. In addition, since a pesky prefix cannot constitute the entirety of an extension sub-path, extracting a pesky prefix cannot affect the moat edge. Therefore, the usability of a moat edge cannot be affected by extracting a pesky prefix from an ESP and, hence, the semi-reducibility of a path cannot be affected by extracting pesky prefixes.

Corollary 1. *Let $\mathcal{P}$ be any path. Let $\mathcal{P}'$ be the path obtained from $\mathcal{P}$ by extracting all pesky prefixes from any extension sub-paths within $\mathcal{P}$. Then $\mathcal{P}$ is semi-reducible if and only if $\mathcal{P}'$ is semi-reducible.*

Given this result, the rest of this paper presumes that all pesky prefixes are extracted from any path without affecting its semi-reducibility.

Corollary 2. *Any semi-reducible path, $\mathcal{P}$, can be transformed into an OU-path using a sequence of reductions whereby each LC edge e in $\mathcal{P}$ is reduced away by its corresponding extension sub-path $\mathcal{P}_e$.*

Figure 5 illustrates a semi-reducible path with nested extension sub-paths. In the figure, lower-case edges are shown with a distinctive arrow type, ESPs are shaded, and the core edges are dashed.

Morris [5] proved that an STNU with K contingent links has an SRN loop if and only if it has a breach-free SRN loop in which extension sub-paths are nested to a depth of at most K. Thus, his N^4 DC-checking algorithm performs K rounds of searching for breach-free extension sub-paths that could be used to reduce away lower-case edges, each round effectively increasing the nesting depth of the extension sub-paths it considers. The core edges generated in this way are then collected—minus any upper-case labels—into an STN, $\mathcal{S}^\dagger$, as previously described, to compute the distance matrix, $\mathcal{D}^\dagger$, which equals the all-pairs, shortest-*semi-reducible*-paths matrix for the original STNU.

3 Indivisible SRN Loops

This section introduces a new approach to analyzing the structure of semi-reducible negative loops. The key feature of the approach is its focus on the number of occurrences of lower-case edges in what it calls *indivisible* SRN loops (or iSRN loops). As will be seen, for the purposes of DC checking, it suffices to restrict attention to iSRN loops. However, the main result of this section is that the number of occurrences of LC edges in any iSRN loop in any STNU having K contingent links is at most $2^K - 1$.

Definition 5. *For any path, $\mathcal{P}$, the number of occurrences of lower-case edges in $\mathcal{P}$ is denoted by $\#\mathcal{P}$.*

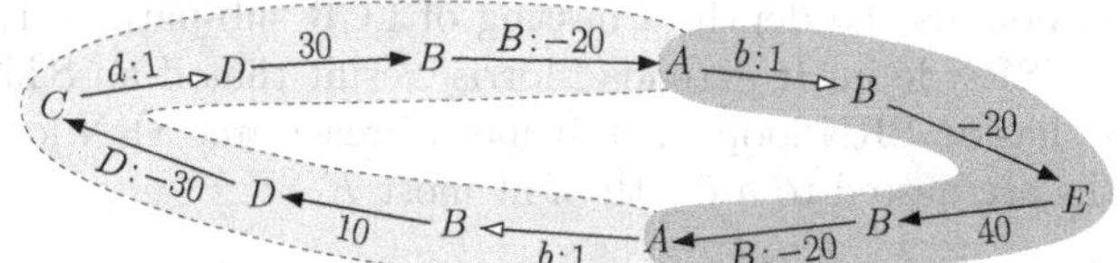

Fig. 6. An indivisible SRN loop, $\mathcal{P}$.

Suppose that $\mathcal{P}$ is an SRN loop and $\mathcal{Q}$ is a sub-loop of $\mathcal{P}$ that also happens to be an SRN loop (i.e., $\mathcal{Q}$ is an SRN sub-loop of $\mathcal{P}$). Since every LC edge in $\mathcal{Q}$ also belongs to $\mathcal{P}$, it follows that $\#\mathcal{Q} \leq \#\mathcal{P}$. However, if $\mathcal{P}$ is an *indivisible* SRN loop, then $\#\mathcal{Q}$ must equal $\#\mathcal{P}$. That is, no SRN sub-loop of an iSRN loop $\mathcal{P}$ can have *fewer* occurrences of LC edges than $\mathcal{P}$.

Definition 6 (iSRN loop)**.** *Let $\mathcal{P}$ be an SRN loop. $\mathcal{P}$ is called an* indivisible SRN loop *(or iSRN loop) if $\#\mathcal{Q} = \#\mathcal{P}$ for every SRN sub-loop $\mathcal{Q}$ of $\mathcal{P}$.*

Figure 6 shows an example of an SRN loop, $\mathcal{P}$, that has no SRN sub-loops and, thus, is indivisible. $\mathcal{P}$ contains three occurrences of LC edges (two from A to B, one from C to D); thus, $\#\mathcal{P} = 3$. $\mathcal{P}$ is semi-reducible because each LC edge has a corresponding breach-free extension sub-path that can be used to reduce it away. In addition, $|\mathcal{P}| = -7 < 0$. Finally, although $\mathcal{P}$ has many sub-loops, two of which are shaded in the figure, none of them are SRN sub-loops. For example, the lefthand shaded sub-loop is not semi-reducible and the righthand shaded sub-loop is non-negative. Thus, $\mathcal{P}$ is an iSRN loop.

Lemma 2, below, shows that for DC checking, it suffices to restrict attention to iSRN loops. The iSRN loop, $\mathcal{P}'$, is obtained by recursively extracting SRN sub-loops until, eventually, an iSRN loop is found.

Lemma 2. *If an STNU $\mathcal{S}$ has an SRN loop $\mathcal{P}$, then $\mathcal{S}$ also has an iSRN loop $\mathcal{P}'$. Furthermore, $\mathcal{P}'$ can be chosen such that $\#\mathcal{P}' \leq \#\mathcal{P}$.*

The search for an upper bound on the number of occurrences of LC edges in any iSRN loop begins by focusing on *root-level* LCR sub-paths (i.e., LCR sub-paths that are not contained within any other). This notion can be defined since, by Lemma 1, ESPs in any semi-reducible path must be disjoint or nested.

Definition 7 (Root-level). *Let e be an occurrence of an LC edge in a semi-reducible path $\mathcal{P}$; and let $\mathcal{P}_e$ be the extension sub-path for e in $\mathcal{P}$. If $\mathcal{P}_e$ is not contained within any other ESP in $\mathcal{P}$, then $\mathcal{P}_e$ is called a* root-level *ESP in $\mathcal{P}$; e is called a* root-level *LC edge in $\mathcal{P}$; and the LCR sub-path formed by concatenating e and $\mathcal{P}_e$ is called a* root-level *LCR sub-path.*

Theorem 4 bounds the number of root-level LCR sub-paths in any iSRN loop.

Theorem 4. *Any iSRN loop in any STNU with K contingent links has at most K root-level LCR sub-paths.*

Theorem 5, below, bounds the depth of nesting of LCR sub-paths (or, equivalently, ESPs) in an iSRN loop. It extends Morris' result that if an STNU with K contingent links has an SRN loop, then it has a breach-free SRN loop whose extension sub-paths are nested to a depth of at most K.

Theorem 5. *Let $\mathcal{P}$ be an iSRN loop in an STNU having K contingent links. Then $\mathcal{P}$ is breach-free and has LCR sub-paths nested to a depth of at most K.*

Although Theorem 5 bounds the nesting depth of LCR sub-paths in an iSRN loop, it does not limit the number of LC edges within any root-level LCR sub-path. Theorem 6, below, shows that any non-trivial iSRN loop must have an LC edge that occurs exactly once—and at the root level. Theorem 6 provides the key for the inductive proof of Theorem 7, below, the main result of this section.

Theorem 6. *If $\mathcal{P}$ is an iSRN loop that contains at least one lower-case edge, then $\mathcal{P}$ must have a root-level LC edge that occurs exactly once in $\mathcal{P}$.*

Theorem 7. *If $\mathcal{P}$ is an iSRN loop in an STNU with K contingent links, then $\#\mathcal{P} \leq 2^K - 1$.*

Finally, Theorem 8 shows that the *ordinary* edges associated with contingent links (cf. Fig. 1) can be ignored for the purposes of DC checking. Although this does not affect the worst-case complexity of DC checking, it has the potential to limit the branching factor of edge generation in practice.

Theorem 8. *Any STNU having an SRN loop has an iSRN loop that contains none of the ordinary edges associated with contingent links.*

4 Magic Loops

Section 3 showed that the number of LC edges in any iSRN loop is at most $2^K - 1$. This section defines a *magic loop* as any iSRN loop that has exactly $2^K - 1$ occurrences of LC edges. It then presents an algorithm for constructing such loops, thereby proving that the $2^K - 1$ bound is tight. Interestingly, the STNUs used to generate these magic loops have only $2K + 1$ time-points (two time-points for each contingent link, plus one extra time-point) and $4K$ edges.

Definition 8 (Magic Loop). *A* magic loop of order K *is any iSRN loop that (1) belongs to an STNU having K contingent links; and (2) contains exactly* $2^K - 1$ *occurrences of LC edges*

The algorithm for constructing magic loops is recursive. For each $K \geq 1$, it defines an STNU, $\mathcal{S}_K$, that contains a magic loop, $\mathcal{M}_K$, of order K. The STNUs and magic loops employ edges whose lengths are specified by numerical parameters, such as $x_i, y_i, \alpha_i, \beta_i, \gamma_i$, and δ_i, where $1 \leq i \leq K$. All of these parameters have positive integer values; thus, any negative values are specified with explicit negative signs, as in: $-y_i, -\alpha_i$ or $-\gamma_i$. Each magic loop, $\mathcal{M}_K$, also has several sub-paths, called ϕ_i, χ_i and ω_i. These sub-paths have important properties that are exploited in the proofs. Whereas all of the parameters are positive, the lengths of the sub-paths, ϕ_i, χ_i and ω_i, are invariably negative. For convenience, the rest of this section uses k instead of K, and $*$ instead of $k + 1$. Thus, for example, $\mathcal{S}_*$ is shorthand for $\mathcal{S}_{K+1}$.

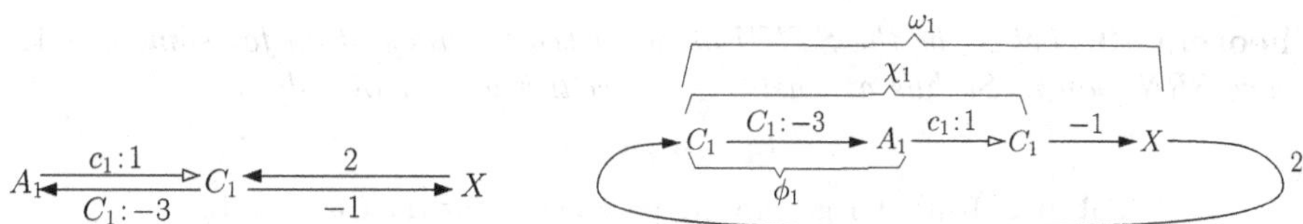

Fig. 7. The STNU $\mathcal{S}_1$ (left) and magic loop $\mathcal{M}_1$ (right).

For the base case, the STNU $\mathcal{S}_1$ and its magic loop $\mathcal{M}_1$ are shown in Fig. 7. $\mathcal{M}_1$ contains two sub-loops, neither of which is an SRN loop; thus, $\mathcal{M}_1$ is an iSRN loop. Also, $\mathcal{M}_1$ contains $2^1 - 1 = 1$ occurrence of an LC edge; thus, $\mathcal{M}_1$ is a magic loop of order 1.

For the recursive case, suppose $\mathcal{S}_k$ is an STNU with k contingent links with the form shown at the left of Fig. 8, and $\mathcal{M}_k$ is a magic loop of order k with the form shown at the right of Fig. 8. Note that $\mathcal{S}_1$ and $\mathcal{M}_1$ have the desired forms.

The values of γ_k, $|\phi_k|$ and $|\chi_k|$ suffice to generate the values of the parameters, $\alpha_*, \beta_*, \gamma_*, \delta_*, x_*$ and y_*, which are determined sequentially, as shown in Rules 1–6 of Table 2. (Recall that the asterisk is used as a shorthand for $k + 1$.) Once these values are in hand, the STNU, $\mathcal{S}_*$, is built out of $\mathcal{S}_k$ as shown in Fig. 9; and the magic loop, $\mathcal{M}_*$, is created with the structure shown in Fig. 10.

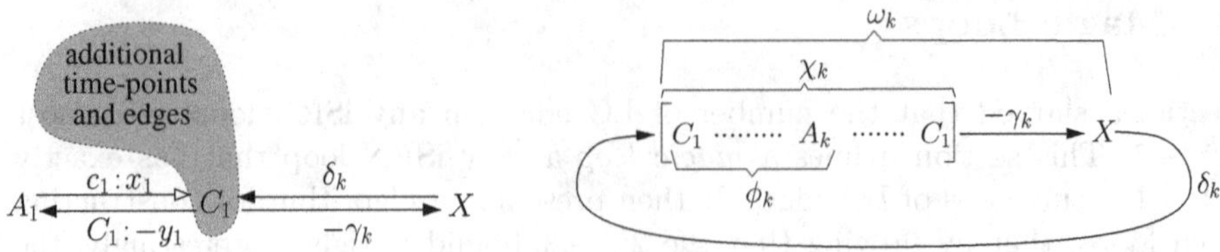

Fig. 8. The generic form of $\mathcal{S}_k$ (left) and $\mathcal{M}_k$ (right).

Notice, too, that $\mathcal{M}_*$ introduces a single, new lower-case edge associated with a contingent link, (A_*, x_*, y_*, C_*). Since each χ_k sub-path has $2^k - 1$ occurrences of LC edges, the total number of occurrences of LC edges in $\mathcal{M}_*$ is $1+2(2^k-1) = 2^{k+1}-1$, as desired. Figure 11 shows the STNU $\mathcal{S}_2$ and magic loop $\mathcal{M}_2$ generated using these parameters; the LCR sub-paths are shaded for convenience.

Finally, Theorem 9, below, shows that for each $k \geq 1$, the loop, $\mathcal{M}_k$, is indeed a magic loop; and Theorem 10 shows that for each $k \geq 1$, the only iSRN loops in $\mathcal{S}_k$ are necessarily magic loops; thus, there are no iSRN loops in $\mathcal{S}_k$ having fewer than 2^k-1 occurrences of lower-case edges. Taken together, these theorems show that magic loops are not only worst-case scenarios in terms of the number of occurrences of LC edges in an iSRN loop, but also that there are STNUs for which this worst-case scenario is the only case.

Theorem 9. *For each $k \geq 1$, the loop, $\mathcal{M}_k$, is a magic loop of order k (i.e., an iSRN loop having exactly $2^k - 1$ occurrences of lower-case edges).*

Theorem 10. *Let $\mathcal{S}_k$ be the STNU as described in this section for some $k \geq 1$. Every SRN loop in $\mathcal{S}_k$ has at least $2^k - 1$ occurrences of LC edges.*

Table 2. Rules for generating parameters for the case $k + 1$.

(1) $\alpha_* = \gamma_k$	(3) $\gamma_* = 2 - 2\lvert\phi_k\rvert + \lvert\chi_k\rvert + \gamma_k$	(5) $x_* = 1$
(2) $\beta_* = 1 - 2\lvert\phi_k\rvert + \gamma_k$	(4) $\delta_* = 2 - 3\lvert\phi_k\rvert + \gamma_k$	(6) $y_* = 3 - 3\lvert\phi_k\rvert + \lvert\chi_k\rvert$

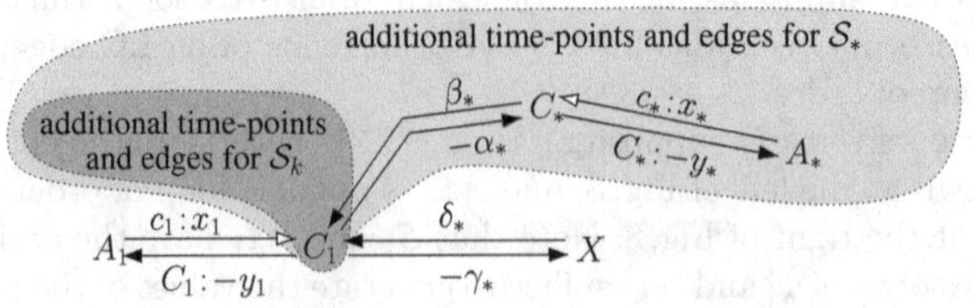

Fig. 9. Building the STNU, $\mathcal{S}_*$, from $\mathcal{S}_k$.

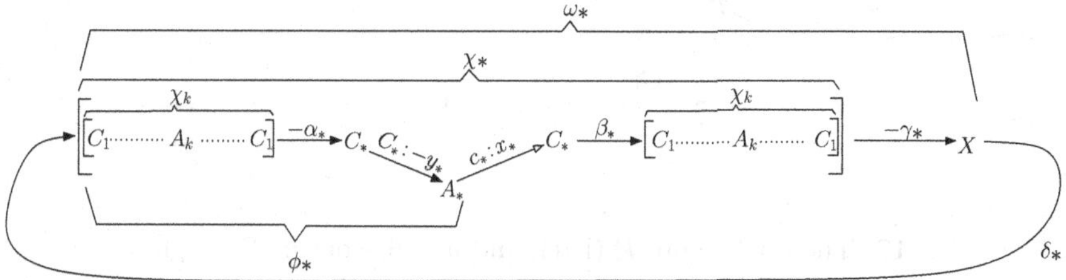

Fig. 10. The structure of $\mathcal{M}_*$, a magic loop of order $k+1$.

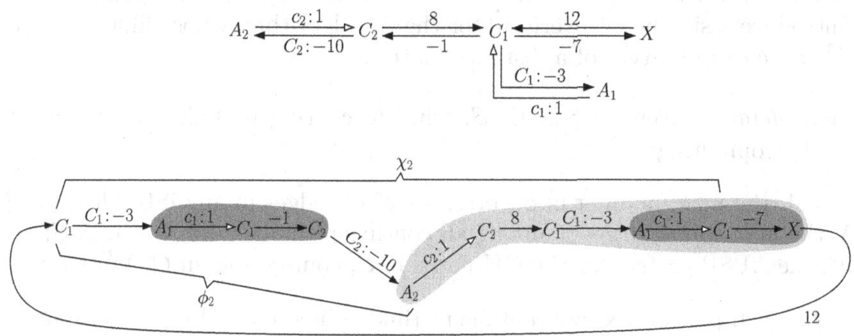

Fig. 11. STNU $\mathcal{S}_2$ (top) and magic loop $\mathcal{M}_2$ (bottom).

5 Speeding up DC Checking

This section presents a recursive $O(N^3)$-time pre-processing algorithm that exploits the $2^K - 1$ bound on the number of occurrences of LC edges in iSRN loops. For certain networks, this pre-processing algorithm decreases the computation time for the N^4 DC-checking algorithm from $O(N^4)$ to $O(N^3)$.

Let $\mathcal{S}$ be an STNU having K contingent links. The pre-processing algorithm computes, for each contingent time-point, C_j, an upper bound on the number of distinct contingent time-points that can co-occur in any iSRN loop in $\mathcal{S}$ that contains C_j. The largest of these upper bounds then serves as an upper bound, *UB*, on the number of distinct contingent time-points—and hence the number of distinct LC edges—that can co-occur in any single iSRN loop in $\mathcal{S}$. Since any iSRN loop having at most *UB* distinct lower-case edges can be viewed as an iSRN loop in an STNU having exactly *UB* contingent links, such a loop can have extension sub-paths nested to a depth of at most *UB* (cf. Theorem 5). Thus, *UB* also provides an upper bound on the number of rounds needed for the N^4 algorithm to check the dynamic controllability of $\mathcal{S}$.

In cases where $UB < K$, the pre-processing algorithm can provide significant savings. Indeed, for some STNUs, $UB = 1$, implying the need for only one $O(N^3)$-time round of the N^4 algorithm, even though the unaware N^4 algorithm might still perform K rounds at a cost of $O(N^4)$. At the other extreme, for

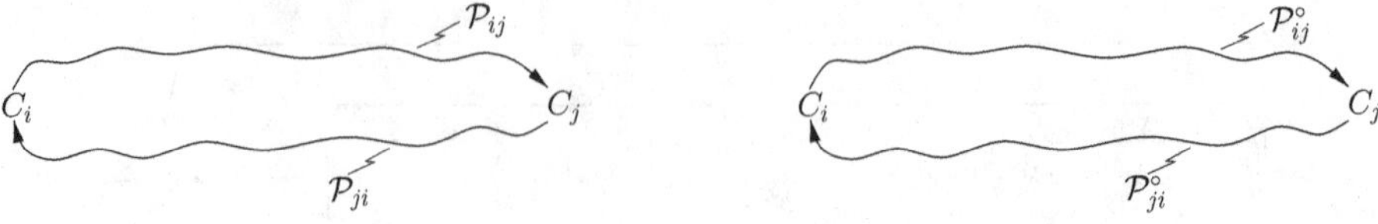

Fig. 12. The iSRN loop, $\mathcal{P}$ (left), and its OU-cousin, $\mathcal{P}^\circ$ (right).

some STNUs, $UB = K$, in which case, the pre-processing algorithm provides no benefit. However, since the pre-processing algorithm runs in $O(N^3)$ time, it does not introduce a significant overhead for the N^4 algorithm, whose first step is an $O(N^3)$-time computation of a distance matrix.

In more detail. Given an STNU, $\mathcal{S}$, with K contingent links, the algorithm begins by computing:

- $2^K - 1$, the max. number of occurrences of LC edges in any iSRN loop in $\mathcal{S}$;
- Δ, the max. value of $y - x$ among all contingent links, (A, x, y, C), in $\mathcal{S}$; and
- $\mathcal{D}^\circ$, the APSP matrix for the OU-paths in $\mathcal{S}$, computable in $O(N^3)$ time.

Next, for each pair of *distinct* contingent time-points, C_i and C_j, it computes:

$$LB_{ij} \;=\; \mathcal{D}^\circ(C_i, C_j) + \mathcal{D}^\circ(C_j, C_i) - (2^K - 1)\Delta.$$

As will be shown, if $\mathcal{P}$ is any iSRN loop in $\mathcal{S}$ that contains both C_i and C_j, then $|\mathcal{P}| \geq LB_{ij}$ (i.e., LB_{ij} is a *Lower Bound* for the lengths of iSRN loops that contain both C_i and C_j). Thus, if $LB_{ij} \geq 0$, it follows that C_i and C_j cannot co-occur in any iSRN loop in $\mathcal{S}$. But in that case, any iSRN loop—if such exists—can have at most $K - 1$ *distinct* LC edges and, thus, no more than $2^{(K-1)} - 1$ *occurrences* of LC edges.

If the upper bound on the number of occurrences of LC edges in iSRN loops in $\mathcal{S}$ can be lowered in this way, the algorithm recursively seeks to identify additional combinations of contingent time-points that cannot co-occur within any iSRN loop. It terminates when no further combinations can be found.

Consider the scenario in Fig. 12, where the lefthand loop is an iSRN loop, $\mathcal{P}$, that contains a pair of *distinct* contingent time-points, C_i and C_j. Note that the sub-path from C_i to C_j is called $\mathcal{P}_{ij}$, and the sub-path from C_j to C_i is called $\mathcal{P}_{ji}$. Next, define the *ordinary cousin* of an LC edge, $A \xrightarrow{c:x} C$, to be the corresponding ordinary edge, $A \xrightarrow{y} C$, for the contingent link (A, x, y, C) (cf. Fig. 1). The righthand loop, $\mathcal{P}^\circ$, in Fig. 12 is the same as $\mathcal{P}$, except that any occurrences of LC edges have been replaced by their *ordinary cousins*. Since $\mathcal{P}^\circ$ may yet contain upper-case edges, we call it the *OU-cousin* of $\mathcal{P}$. Notice that $\mathcal{P}^\circ$ is the concatenation of the OU-cousins of $\mathcal{P}_{ij}$ and $\mathcal{P}_{ji}$. Furthermore, since $\mathcal{P}^\circ_{ij}$ and $\mathcal{P}^\circ_{ji}$ are OU-paths, it follows that their lengths are bounded below by the corresponding OU-distance-matrix entries, whence:

$$\mathcal{D}^\circ(C_i, C_j) + \mathcal{D}^\circ(C_j, C_i) \;\leq\; |\mathcal{P}^\circ_{ij}| + |\mathcal{P}^\circ_{ji}| \;=\; |\mathcal{P}^\circ| \tag{1}$$

Now, by Theorem 7, since $\mathcal{P}$ is an iSRN loop, $\#\mathcal{P} \leq 2^K - 1$. Thus, the difference in the lengths of $\mathcal{P}$ and $\mathcal{P}^\circ$ is bounded as follows:

$$\Delta_\mathcal{P} \;=\; |\mathcal{P}^\circ| - |\mathcal{P}| \;\leq\; \#\mathcal{P}(2^K - 1)\Delta \;\leq\; (2^K - 1)\Delta \qquad (2)$$

where Δ is the maximum value of $y - x$ over all the contingent links in the STNU. Combining the inequalities (1) and (2) then yields:

$$|\mathcal{P}| \;\geq\; |\mathcal{P}^\circ| - (2^K - 1)\Delta \;\geq\; \mathcal{D}^\diamond(C_i, C_j) + \mathcal{D}^\diamond(C_j, C_i) - (2^K - 1)\Delta$$

Since this inequality must hold whenever $\mathcal{P}$ is an iSRN loop in which the distinct contingent time-points, C_i and C_j, both occur, it follows that if

$$\mathcal{D}^\diamond(C_i, C_j) + \mathcal{D}^\diamond(C_j, C_i) - (2^K - 1)\Delta \;\geq\; 0$$

then there cannot be any such loop. ($|\mathcal{P}|$ must be negative if $\mathcal{P}$ is an iSRN loop.)

Next, for each pair of contingent time-points, C_i and C_j, let $\mathcal{F}(i,j) = \mathcal{D}^\diamond(C_i, C_j) + \mathcal{D}^\diamond(C_j, C_i)$. Then the preceding rule, which is the main rule used by the pre-processing algorithm, can be re-stated as:

- If C_i and C_j are distinct contingent time-points such that $\mathcal{F}(i,j) \geq (2^K - 1)\Delta$, then C_i and C_j cannot both occur in the same iSRN loop.

Pseudo-code for the pre-processing algorithm is given in Table 3. For each contingent time-point, C_i, it defines the following variables:

- ctr_i, an upper bound (initially $\mathrm{ctr}_i = K$) on the number of distinct contingent time-points that can co-occur in any iSRN loop that contains C_i.
- L_i, a list of entries from row i of the $\mathcal{F}$ matrix, sorted into decreasing order.

As the algorithm runs, any entry, $(i, j, \mathcal{F}(i,j))$ from L_i, for which $\mathcal{F}(i,j) \geq (2^{\mathrm{ctr}_i} - 1)\Delta$, signals that C_j could not occur in the same iSRN loop with C_i. Such entries are popped off L_i and pushed onto the global queue. As each entry from the global queue is processed, the corresponding ctr_i value decreases, which may lead to further entries moving from L_i to the global queue. The algorithm terminates whenever the global queue is emptied, at which point no further reductions in ctr_i values can be made. The algorithm returns the maximum ctr_i value, which specifies the maximum number of distinct contingent time-points that can co-occur in any iSRN loop in the given STNU. The Appendix proves that the algorithm's worst-case running time is $O(N^3)$.

In best-case scenarios, the pre-processing algorithm results in all off-diagonal entries in $\mathcal{F}$ being crossed out, implying that there can be no nesting of LCR paths in any iSRN loop. In such cases, it is only necessary to do one $O(N^3)$-time round of the N^4 algorithm to ascertain whether the STNU is dynamically controllable. The benefit in such cases can be dramatic, for if the network contains even one semi-reducible path having K levels of nesting, then the unaided N^4 algorithm would needlessly perform K rounds of processing in $O(N^4)$ time.

Table 3. Pseudo-code for the pre-processing algorithm.

Given: An STNU $\mathcal{S}$ with K contingent links.

0. Initialization:
   - Let Δ and $\mathcal{F}$ be as defined in the text.
   - For each $i \in \{1, 2, \ldots, K\}$,
     - $\text{ctr}_i := K$.
     - $L_i :=$ a list of K entries, $(i, j, \mathcal{F}(i, j))$, sorted into decreasing order of the $\mathcal{F}(i, j)$ values.
   - $\mathcal{Q} :=$ the empty list.
1. Pop all entries off all L_i lists for which $\mathcal{F}(i, j) \geq (2^{\text{ctr}_i} - 1)\Delta$.
2. While $\mathcal{Q}$ not empty:
   a. Pop an entry, $(i, j, \mathcal{F}(i, j))$, off of $\mathcal{Q}$.
   b. If (i, j) entry in $\mathcal{F}$ not yet crossed out:
      i. Cross out the (i, j) entry in $\mathcal{F}$, and decrement the counter, ctr_i.
      ii. Pop all entries, $(i, j', \mathcal{F}(i, j'))$, from L_i for which $\mathcal{F}(i, j') \geq (2^{\text{ctr}_i} - 1)\Delta$, and push them onto $\mathcal{Q}$.
   c. Do Step b, above, for the entry, $(j, i, \mathcal{F}(j, i))$.
3. Let $UB = \max\{\text{ctr}_i\}$.

6 Conclusions

This paper presented a new way of analyzing the structure of STNU graphs with the aim of speeding up DC checking. It proved that the number of occurrences of lower-case edges in iSRN loops is bounded above by $2^K - 1$. It presented an algorithm for constructing STNUs that contain iSRN loops that attain this upper bound, thereby showing that the bound is tight. Given their highly convoluted structure, such loops are called *magic loops.* And it presented an $O(N^3)$-time pre-processing algorithm that exploits the $2^K - 1$ bound to speed up DC checking for some networks. Thus, the paper makes theoretical and practical contributions.

Other researchers have sought to speed up the process of DC checking using incremental algorithms. Stedl and Williams [11] developed *Fast-IDC,* an incremental algorithm that maintains the dispatchability of an STNU after the insertion of new constraints or the tightening of existing constraints. Shah et al. [10] extended *Fast-IDC* to accommodate the removal or weakening of constraints. Although intended to be applied incrementally, their algorithm showed orders of magnitude improvement over an earlier pseudo-polynomial DC-checking algorithm when evaluated empirically, checking dynamic controllability from scratch. It would be interesting to see if their work could be applied to generate an incremental version of the Morris' N^4 algorithm.

Others have extended the concept of dynamic controllability to accommodate various combinations of probability, preference and disjunction. Tsamardinos [12] augmented contingent durations with probability density functions and provided a method that, under certain restrictions, finds "the schedule that maximizes the probability of executing the plan in a way that respects the temporal constraints." Tsamardinos et al. [13] developed algorithms to compute lower and upper bounds for the probability of a legal plan execution. Morris et al. [8] used probability density functions to represent the uncertainties associated with contingent durations, but also incorporated preferences over event durations. Rossi et al. [9] augmented STNUs with preferences (but not probabilities) and defined the *Simple Temporal Problem with Preferences and Uncertainty* (STPPU) and notions of weak, strong and dynamic controllability.

Effinger et al. [2] defined dynamic controllability for *temporally-flexible reactive programs* that include the following constructs: "conditional execution, iteration, exception handling, non-deterministic choice, parallel and sequential composition, and simple temporal constraints". They presented a DC-checking algorithm for temporally-flexible reactive programs that frames the problem as an "AND/OR search tree over candidate program executions."

References

1. Dechter, R., Meiri, I., Pearl, J.: Temporal constraint networks. Artif. Intell. **49**, 61–95 (1991)
2. Effinger, R., Williams, B., Kelly, G., Sheehy, M.: Dynamic controllability of temporally-flexible reactive programs. In: Gerevini, A., Howe, A., Cesta, A., Refanidis, I. (eds.) Proceedings of the Nineteenth International Conference on Automated Planning and Scheduling (ICAPS 09). AAAI Press (2009)
3. Hunsberger, L.: A fast incremental algorithm for managing the execution of dynamically controllable temporal networks. In: Proceedings of the 17th International Symposium on Temporal Representation and Reasoning (TIME-2010), pp. 121–128. IEEE Computer Society, Los Alamitos (2010)
4. Hunsberger, L.: Magic loops in simple temporal networks with uncertainty. In: Proceedings of the Fifth International Conference on Agents and Artificial Intelligence (ICAART-2013) (2013)
5. Morris, P.: A structural characterization of temporal dynamic controllability. In: Benhamou, F. (ed.) CP 2006. LNCS, vol. 4204, pp. 375–389. Springer, Heidelberg (2006)
6. Morris, P., Muscettola, N., Vidal, T.: Dynamic control of plans with temporal uncertainty. In: Nebel, B. (ed.) 17th International Joint Conference on Artificial Intelligence (IJCAI-01), pp. 494–499. Morgan Kaufmann (2001)
7. Morris, P.H., Muscettola, N.: Temporal dynamic controllability revisited. In: Veloso, M.M., Kambhampati, S. (eds.) The 20th National Conference on Artificial Intelligence (AAAI-05), pp. 1193–1198. The MIT Press (2005)
8. Morris, R., Morris, P., Khatib, L., Yorke-Smith, N.: Temporal constraint reasoning with preferences and probabilities. In: Brafman, R., Junker, U. (eds.) Proceedings of the IJCAI-05 Multidisciplinary Workshop on Advances in Preference Handling, pp. 150–155 (2005)
9. Rossi, F., Venable, K.B., Yorke-Smith, N.: Uncertainty in soft temporal constraint problems: a general framework and controllability algorithms for the fuzzy case. J. Artif. Intell. Res. **27**, 617–674 (2006)
10. Shah, J., Stedl, J., Robertson, P., Williams, B.C.: A fast incremental algorithm for maintaining dispatchability of partially controllable plans. In: Boddy, M., et al. (ed.) Proceedings of the Seventeenth International Conference on Automated Planning and Scheduling (ICAPS 2007). AAAI Press (2007)

11. Stedl, J., Williams, B.C.: A fast incremental dynamic controllability algorithm. In: Proceedings of the ICAPS Workshop on Plan Execution: A Reality Check, pp. 69–75 (2005)
12. Tsamardinos, I.: A probabilistic approach to robust execution of temporal plans with uncertainty. In: Vlahavas, I.P., Spyropoulos, C.D. (eds.) SETN 2002. LNCS (LNAI), vol. 2308, pp. 97–108. Springer, Heidelberg (2002)
13. Tsamardinos, I., Pollack, M.E., Ramakrishnan, S.: Assessing the probability of legal execution of plans with temporal uncertainty. In: Proceedings of the ICAPS-03 Workshop on Planning under Uncertainty and Incomplete Information (2003)
14. Vidal, T., Ghallab, M.: Dealing with uncertain durations in temporal constraint networks dedicated to planning. In: Wahlster, W. (ed.) 12th European Conference on Artificial Intelligence (ECAI-96), pp. 48–54. Wiley, Chichester (1996)

Evolving Optimal Spatial Allocation Policies for Complex and Uncertain Environments

Marta Vallejo(✉), David W. Corne, and Verena Rieser

School of Mathematical and Computer Sciences,
Heriot-Watt University, Edinburgh, UK
mv59@hw.ac.uk

Abstract. Urban green spaces play a crucial role in the creation of healthy environments in densely populated areas. Agent-based systems are commonly used to model processes such as green-space allocation. In some cases, this systems delegate their spatial assignation to optimisation techniques to find optimal solutions. However, the computational time complexity and the uncertainty linked with long-term plans limit their use. In this paper we explore an approach that makes use of a statistical model which emulates the agent-based system's behaviour based on a limited number of prior simulations to inform a Genetic Algorithm.

The approach is tested on a urban growth simulation, in which the overall goal is to find policies that maximise the inhabitants' satisfaction. We find that the model-driven approximation is effective at leading the evolutionary algorithm towards optimal policies.

Keywords: Agent-based model · Genetic algorithm · Statistical model · Optimisation · Uncertainty · Green space planning

1 Introduction

The main purpose of urban planning is to improve the community's quality of life by creating a better social, economical and physical environment. One of the most urgent research issues within this broad field is the study of mechanisms that can mitigate the ecological degradation that is linked with modern urban expansion. One possible strategy is reserving a collection of selected areas to transform them into recreational parks.

However, this process is not as simple as choosing arbitrarily a random number of stands, the time planning and geographic distribution of these spaces needs careful consideration to ensure the quality and quantity of environmental services provided to the surrounding community [2].

This paper is a revised and extended version of a previous publication [1] reported in the Proceedings of the 5th International Conference on Agents and Artificial Intelligence. The key additions cover: Sects. 3 and 4 improvement of the complexity of non-urban cells prices and its inclusion as a new source of uncertainty. In Sect. 5, a new heuristic is studied to enrich the comparison phase. Finally in Sect. 6 more experimental results and comparative evaluations are performed.

J. Filipe and A. Fred (Eds.): ICAART 2013, CCIS 449, pp. 351–369, 2014.
DOI: 10.1007/978-3-662-44440-5_21

There is much active research in designing long-term feasible public open space plans, whereby researchers interested in urban planning and sustainability have investigated a range of agent-based systems and similar mechanisms to explore the consequences of different strategies [3–5].

One of the most common interests in such work is the study of the dynamics involved in urban growth, which is linked with the relative distribution of urbanised, industrial and green spaces along with their impact on quality-of-life issues, and how these factors depend on the broad strategies in place for land-use [6].

However, the computational time complexity of simulations and the many and varied sources of uncertainty can limit the use of these systems. The aim of this paper is to address this situation by wrapping optimisation over the agent-based simulation process, but use a statistical model of the agent-based simulation in place of the real knowledge. This requires a limited number of prior simulations of the agent-based urban growth system in order to allows the use of an evolutionary algorithm to optimise urban growth policies.

Note that similar simulation-based approximations for optimisation are also used in other fields, such as user simulations for spoken dialogue systems [7], emulators for managing uncertainty in complex models, such as climate models (MUCM) or to reduce the computational time required to run the optimisation procedure in combinatorial problems [8].

The approach is tested on a typical urban growth simulation, in which the overall goal is to find policies that maximise the 'satisfaction' of the residents by the protection of a optimal subset of green spaces. The computational results are compared and evaluated with those gathered from several simple heuristics.

The remainder of the paper is organised as follows. Section 2 focusses on various introductory and preliminary details, covering the urban planning problem, the role of agent based simulation, and evolutionary algorithms. Section 3 then provides a detailed account of the models, assumptions and processes we employ in our experiments. Section 4 is devoted to the sources of uncertainty that are handled by our new statistical genetic algorithm approach. Computational experiments are specified in Sect. 5, and the results are presented and discussed in Sect. 6. Section 7 then draws some conclusions and we discuss further research.

2 Problem Definition

Open green urban areas play an important role in maintaining a healthy urban environment. Among all their favourable effects, their crucial impact in the economy, quality of life and in the local climate of the cities [9, 10] can be highlighted. However their distribution and location should be carefully studied by developing an adequate, long-term planning strategy. The fact that makes this task particularly difficult is the fact that the urban expansion is a complex process where their effects can appear at many time-scales.

2.1 Urban Open Space Planning

There is a lack of agreement on how to implement and implant a given planning process and which measures should be selected. On this regard, the most remarkable points to discuss are:

- Goal settings: how to select adequate planning criteria.
- Deciding the most suitable size for the open space according to the current and expected necessities of the population.
- Accessibility & location.
- The design of the potential activities according to different age, cultures and ethnic groups.

The present work follows a *demand approach* where the planning process is based on attributes of the specific target population. These attributes are:

- Size of the urban population.
- Subjective personal preferences.
- Residential distribution.

2.2 Problem Formulation and Techniques

The problem domain of the present paper can be included within the field of stochastic control theory. The developed model represents a paradigm of allocation of resources within a sequential decision-making simulator.

Generally speaking, a sequential planning problem can be defined as follows: an environment which can be described as a state-space set S and an action set A where S and A are both finite. Each state $s \in S$ is dependent on the previous state of the system and the action $a \in A$ taken. The transition function δ controls how actions modify the state of its environment.

$$s_{t+1} = \delta(s_t, a) \tag{1}$$

We define a policy Π such that the mechanism in charge of selecting the next action is based on the current perception of the environment. This perception can be total or partial:

$$\begin{aligned} \Pi &: S \rightarrow A \\ \Pi(s_t) &= a_t \end{aligned} \tag{2}$$

In turn, the action a influences as well its environment provoking the change of the current state. The process starts in the state s_0 and by means of the sequential application of the policy Π, further actions are chosen.

2.3 Cellular Automata and Agent-Based Modelling

The present study is based on the results collected from a basic urban growth model where topological layout of the city is represented by a Cellular Automata (CA). CA was proposed in the late 1940 s by John von Neumann and Stanislaw

Ulam for discrete space-time representation of problems which obey their local physics [11]. It is based on the assumption that by means of local interactions, the model is capable of representing complex phenomena. The dynamics of the CA are generated by a set of transition functions which define how cells can evolve from one state to another.

The inhabitants who populate the city are modelled with the use of an Agent-Based Model (ABM) approach. ABM has been used to understand the interconnections, interdependences and feedbacks created among a set of heterogeneous individual entities in order to fulfil their goals.

ABM along with CA taking the role of representing land-use change dynamics have been applied broadly in the field of urban development. Mentionable is their use to simulate allocation decisions [12,13] or in residential selection within a non-stationary housing market [14,15]. Reference [16] applies these tools to analyse how prices affect urban agent behaviour. Finally, [17] studied the role of transportation in the evolution of an urban region.

2.4 Genetic Algorithm

Genetic Algorithm (GA) [18] can be defined as an heuristic that mimics the behaviour of natural selection postulated by the English naturalist Charles Darwin in the 19th Century [19]. This search strategy is based on the assumption that nature evolves by the course of new generations preserving the species more suited to their environment. The tools defined by a GA to improve the population over time are the use of mechanisms like reproduction, mutation, crossover and selection.

Here we use GA to optimise an allocation of resources problem, concretely the placement of green spaces over a urban area such that some objectives are met. GA has been successfully used to solve complex spatial problems [20,21]. However, its performance in uncertain environments has been questioned [22,23] due to the fact that a simple GA has insufficient data to deal directly with uncertainty. This weakness is the main reason why a GA, under this kind of scenarios, should be defined carefully and provided with the support of external tools in order to overcome these difficulties.

There exist different attempts and techniques that can be applied to GA to provide it with this extra functionality. In [24] a Genetic-Algorithm-Aided Stochastic Optimisation Model is applied to cope with the uncertainty related to the study of air quality in urban areas. In contrast to probabilistic approaches [25] resorts to anti-optimisation techniques (local search) to overcome the uncertainty generated by the ageing factor presented in many engineering problems. Following the same approach [26] successfully applies a variant constrained multi-objective GA in a simulated topology and shape optimisation problem under uncertainty.

3 Model Description

The selected ABM-CA framework is used to represent a basic urban growth model with a monocentric spatial structure based on the traditional Alonso's urban economic model [27]. The strategy of this model to explain the modern urbanisation process is based on the maximisation of a utility function. Urban pattern formation is the consequence of individual urban residence preferences which achieve an economic competitive equilibrium between housing and commuting costs.

The physical layout of the city is configured by a 2-dimensional lattice of 50×50 cells. Each cell corresponds to a physical portion of the city and it can be populated by more than one agent (a family unit). The evolution of the city is ruled by an internal schedule with a determined time-horizon of finite duration. The dynamics of agents and cells allow the model to evolve between a set of predefined one-directional states at each time step.

The types of the cell presented in the grid can be broadly divided into two main groups: urbanised and non-urbanised cells.

3.1 Urban Cells

Urban cells represent cells that have been transformed from native ecosystems into either impermeable surfaces or green areas formed normally by non-native species [28].

In the model, when cells receive the permission to be urbanised, which figuratively means that dwellings are constructed, they can allocate population that is represented by agents. Agents decide their residence location by searching a trade-off between their personal preferences and their economical restrictions. This search involves the interaction among different parameters of the model and assumes global knowledge of the current offer. The decision is represented by the maximisation of the following utility function:

$$\begin{aligned} \max U =& (w, z, x, p : w > 0, z > 0, x \geq 0, p > 0) \\ & \text{such that: } w - z - kx + p = 0 \end{aligned} \tag{3}$$

where x represents the distance from the household to the Central Business District (CBD) that is located in the centre of the lattice, w is the wage received monthly. This quantity is defined by a uniform random process and does not change throughout the life time of the agent, z is the price of the residential good and k is the constant marginal community cost. Finally, p represents the agent's preference for houses located close to green areas which implies his acceptance to pay more for this kind of houses. This parameter is an extension of the economic competitive equilibrium described by [27]. Following this utility function agents populate the urban cells of the grid.

Prices of the Urban Cells. They represent the amount of money that agents have to pay regularly as a rental cost. Its value varies with the time and is dependant on the following factors:

- **The Demand.** The demand is defined according to the number of agents living in a given cell.
  - The demand for certain preferred locations increases their price.
  - The drop in population of a cell decreases its price.
  - If one cell does not receive any new neighbour during a determined period of time, its value is reduced.
- **Proximity to Green Areas.** This factor affects positively the final price of the dwellings in 10 %.

3.2 Non-urban Cells

Non-urban cells are cells that have not undergone a urbanisation transformation.

Biological Value. At the beginning of the simulation the model assigns a stochastic value called *BioCellValue* to the set of non-urbanised cells. This parameter represents the ecological value of this parcel of land and is generated by a uniformly random process $\mathcal{U}(0,1)$. Apart from its initial value, the cells are influenced by its neighbourhood:

```
BioNeighbourValue(c)=0;
for each cell n in neighbourhood(c){
        if(BioCellValue(n)>= 0.7)
                BioNeighbourValue(c) += 0.01;
        if(BioCellValue(n)<= 0.3)
                  BioNeighbourValue(c) -= 0.01;
}
BioValue(c) = BioCellValue(c) + BioNeighbourValue(c);
```

The final *BioValue* is used to identify different land-types of the model. If it is bigger than 0.7 this cell is classified as a *forest* cell, otherwise it is considered *agricultural*. The belonging to each category is dynamic over the time. Furthermore the model experiences a continuous bio-degradation which provokes changes from *forest* to *agricultural* state due to the urban expansion.

Governments can adopt a wide range of interventionist mechanisms to restrict the ownership over the land and control its use, acting as a response to social requirements over gardens and parks to provide a set of services based on the proximity to potential users. Among these measures the local authority can assume the proper ownership of the land like in the case of Stockholm city [29] and assign them partially or totally the function of urban green spaces.

Based on that premise the model delegates the responsibility of selecting the best non-urbanised stands to a new special agent called *Municipality*. This agent does not interact with the rest of agents, but his main goal consists of managing the purchase and protection of green areas within the city by means of a monetary income received periodically called *budget*.

Purchase of Land. As it was stated previously, the location of green areas is a crucial factor in its future use because the kind of services that a park can provide is linked with the concept of proximity. Reference [30] states that the distance to a green area influences the frequency of use and the activities that can be undertaken. According to this criterion, green areas can be classified into the following groups:

- Access within a short walk (less than 300 m).
- Access within a long walk (from 300 to 600 m).
- Access with help of any means of transport (larger than 600 m).

The same study concludes that people do not generally use a green area if it is located beyond a threshold of 300–400 m. In the model the location selection is performed sequentially in each time-step and is limited by the *budget* and the configuration of the lattice in this precise moment. Once the purchase is concluded, the state of the cell is changed to *protected* and the future construction of urban facilities within it is forbidden.

This selection process can be formulated as follows: if C is defined as the finite set of cells included into the lattice, A the subset of rural cells that can be considered as a candidate cell to be purchased, P the subset of cells that are protected and U the urbanised cells such as $\{A, P, U\} \subset C$ and $A \cap P \cap U = \emptyset$, then the selection of a candidate cell in time t can be defined as:

$$\begin{aligned} &\forall \text{ cell } c \in C \\ &\text{if price}(c)_t < \text{budget}_t \wedge c_t \notin \{P, U\} \\ &\Longrightarrow c_t \in A \end{aligned} \tag{4}$$

Once the candidate set is defined, the purchasing and protection phase can be formalised as:

$$\begin{aligned} &\forall \text{ cell } a \in A \\ &\max_{satisfaction} \delta(a)_t \\ &\Longrightarrow a_t \in P \wedge a_t \notin A \wedge update(budget_t) \end{aligned} \tag{5}$$

The function δ represents the metric that measures the level of satisfaction of the population in terms of the distance to green areas. See formula 9. Every subset of selected cells has associated a level of satisfaction of the population allocated within the boundaries of the city. The model should select the configuration of green areas which achieves the highest possible level of satisfaction according to the restrictions of the system during the considered period of time.

Prices of Non-urban Cells. It is calculated based on a simplified version of the formula 9 developed in [31]. The price is defined in terms of the current urbanised prices and the distance of the cell to the boundary of the city as:

$$\begin{aligned} &\forall \text{ cell } c \in A \\ price(c) = &\text{priceBase(c)} * (1 - e^{-\alpha[Z - Z^*(t)]}) + \\ &\text{urbanPrice} * (e^{-\alpha[Z - Z^*(t)]}) \end{aligned} \tag{6}$$

Where *priceBase* corresponds to Table 1 based on prices of rural land in UK [32]. $\alpha = 0.2$ is the rate of change in price as the distance from CBC increases. Z is the current position of the cell and Z^* the boundary of the city. $Z - Z^*$ represents the distance from the cell to the limit of the city where $Z > Z^*$. Finally *urbanPrice* is the current price of the most recent developed cell multiplied by its population density.

Table 1. Prices per cell.

Type of cell	Area × price	Final price
1 cell forest	51.8 ha × £6,600 =	£854,700
1 cell agriculture	51.8 ha × £3,000 =	£388,500

The plot of the averaged values of the prices during the simulation is depicted in Fig. 1. It is noticeable the critical growth in prices that occurs at the end of the simulation. This is due to the fact that the number of available cells is scarce and their demand increment drastically its value.

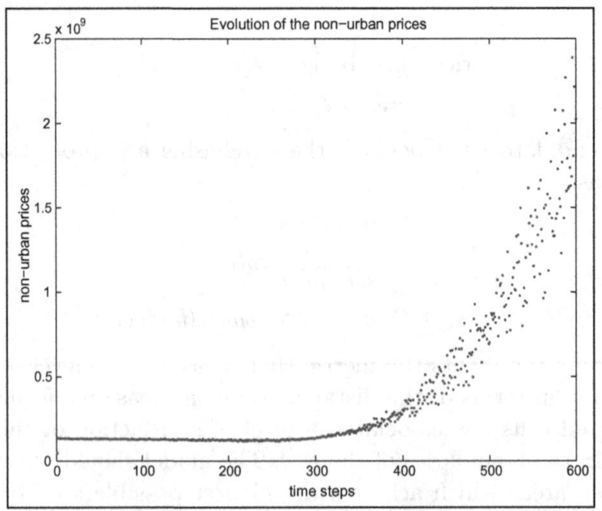

Fig. 1. Evolution of the prices of the non-urban cells throughout the simulation.

4 Sources of Uncertainty

In the present model uncertainty can emerge from a wide variety of sources. Apart from the fact that the implementation of long-term plans always implies to be able to cope with unpredicted future scenarios, the complexity resultant from the multiple interactions occurred between the elements represented in the model makes their management even more challenging.

Some factors which actively contribute to the increment of the level of uncertainty are mentioned in the list below:

4.1 Urban Property Prices and Green Areas

In the developed model, the selection of green spaces exerts a direct influence on the prices of the surrounding urban cells. [33, 34] analyse this tendency reporting a significant increment in the prices of residences located close to urban parks. This aspect is included in the model as the agents' desire to live close to these areas and is represented by the agent's acceptance to pay more for these specific locations. The inclusion of this personal desire provokes a significant growth in the demand of these areas and subsequently in the price and affects the urban spatial spread of the city.

4.2 Ecological Degradation Process and Non-urban Property Prices

From the point of view of the non-urbanised cells, one of the two main parameters which involves a high level of uncertainty is the relationship created between the non-urban price dynamics and the cells' ecological value. Due to the fact that this ecological value also influences its neighbourhood, a significant change in a specific area of the lattice spreads in all directions. The *bioValues* are steady until the distance to the city measured in Manhattan distance is less or equal to 3, otherwise it is applied the following update:

$$\forall \text{ non-urban cell } a \in A$$

$$bioValue(a) = \begin{cases} -0.1 & \text{if } \delta(a, city) = 1 \\ -0.05 & \text{if } \delta(a, city) = 2 \\ -0.01 & \text{if } \delta(a, city) = 3 \\ 0 & \text{otherwise} \end{cases} \tag{7}$$

Where δ is the distance from the cell to the boundaries of the city. The application of this formula produces an ecological degradation process with the growth of the city. This dynamic influences the *priceBase* of the non-urbanised cells that are closely located to the city and hence, the purchasing process of protected areas that it is restricted to our current *budget*.

4.3 Urbanisation Process

The underlying process of urbanisation is in nature partially random and mainly determined by two factors:

- **The rules of transition of the cells:** based on preselected probabilities.
- **The demand level:** controls the transformation of peri-urban into new urban cells.

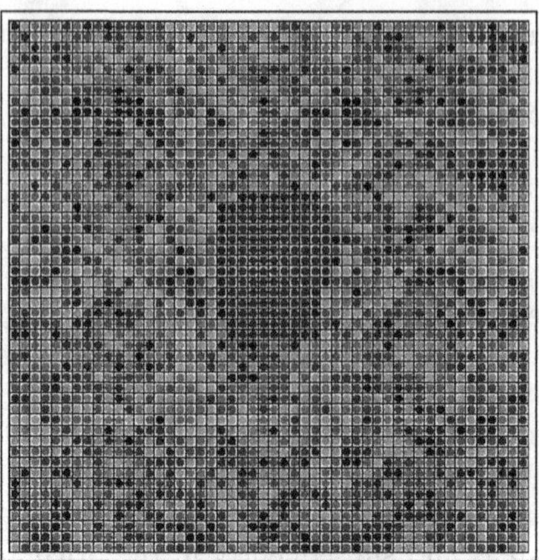

Fig. 2. Environmental values and the effect of the urbanisation process. The range of colours from green to black depicts the ecological values of the cell. Notice that in the centre where the city is located, the black eco-values represent the biological degradation or the metropolitan area (Color figure online).

The knowledge of the urbanisation process is crucial because the set of candidate cells to be protected are restricted to the non-urbanised ones and hence we need to be aware of the complete state of the cells in each time step in order to select and protect non-urban cells.

4.4 Flows of Population

Another significant characteristic of the model is that the city is a non-closed-system. This means that there is an external income flow of new population coming from migration as well as new offspring resulted from the current settled population. The dynamics of these flows are not fixed and predictable and they play a relevant role in the final population distribution within the city. However the density of each future neighbourhood cannot be totally predicted in advance even if there exists a general preference to live close to the city centre in line with the Alonso's model.

Consequently we are not able to know the percentage of population directly affected by a determined location of a new green area and hence, the final satisfaction achieved by a determined configuration of green spaces.

5 Case Study: Allocation of Green Areas

There are three parallel optimisation tasks which form the current case study. The more complex and main objective of the present paper is the GA flow, in contrast to the other two approaches, the random and the best non-optimised strategies that have been developed as a comparison tool.

5.1 Set-Up Phase

The point of departure of the following workflow consists of the definition of the initial model configuration. The model uses as a point of departure two common parameters which share with all the components of the optimisation framework. These parameters are:

- **The Budget.** A stochastic budget assigned to the *municipality* in each sequence of time is decided in advance and it is shared as well by the entire GA population.
- **The Ecological Scenario.** The initial ecological configuration of the lattice is defined by the initial random generation of ecological values. See Fig. 2.

5.2 Configuration of the GA

Chromosome Encoding. The GA evolves through time a population of individuals of size 20 which are chosen randomly from the set of candidate solutions. An individual is encoded as a sequential selections of cells grouped in a predefined number of time steps (Fig. 3). Each of these selections represents a gene and can contain $\{0, n\}$ protected cells chosen by the *Municipality* in one time-step. The superior limit n is bounded by the maximum *budget* available for this time step. Linked with each subset of cells, the remain budget is stored that can be calculated as:

$$remainBudget_t = budget_t - \sum_{i=0}^{n} price(c_t) + remainBudget_{t-1} \qquad (8)$$

Scheme Selection. There exist many selection schemes for GA, among them the present model uses tournament selection (TS) [35]. TS is a robust and simple to code selection mechanism for GA based on the idea of holding a tournament between a group of competitors randomly selected among the population.

Mutation Process. Mutation is a tool used to maintain the diversity among the population of individuals. The mutation process alters one or more values of the genes inherited from the parent. In the present case a mutation consists of changing the set of cells selected to be protected in a slot of time of the simulation. Additionally this implies the update of the associated budget. A successful mutation should meet some constraints:

- A cell cannot be selected twice or more for the same individual.
- The remain budget should be always positive. Debts are not permitted.
- Cells cannot have the state of urbanised when protecting them.

The *budget* can arise potential problems during the mutation process. Due to the fact that non-urbanised cells prices evolve with the time along with the aggregate nature of the budget, a single modification in the selected cells of a gene can influence substantially the amount of money that needs to be used in future purchases. The mutation process should not modify the rest of genes.

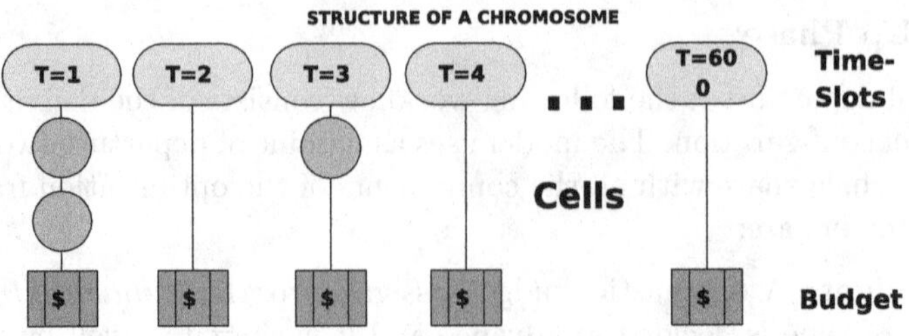

Fig. 3. Three-layers chromosome encoding.

Fitness Function. To measure the contribution of a determined green area to a solution, different kind of metrics can be used according to which aspects want to be emphasized. In the current model the quality of a solution or satisfaction represents the accumulative satisfaction achieved by each person settled on the city with respect to the topological distribution of green areas. Following this approach the fitness function can be defined as follows:

If A is the set of agents of the city, P is the subset of protected cells and C is the set of cells defined in the grid such as $P \subset C$, then for a given time t:

$$\forall \text{ agent } a \in \mathrm{A} \ \wedge \ \forall \text{ protected cell } c \in P$$

$$s(a) = \begin{cases} 3 \text{ if } \delta(a, green) = \underset{distance}{min}(a,c) = 1 \\ 2 \text{ if } \delta(a, green) = \underset{distance}{min}(a,c) = 2 \\ 1 \text{ if } \delta(a, green) = \underset{distance}{min}(a,c) = 3 \\ 0 \qquad\qquad\qquad\qquad \text{otherwise} \end{cases} \tag{9}$$

$$\Theta = \sum_{i=0}^{n} s(a_i)$$

δ is defined as the function that calculates the distance from the location of a given agent a to the closest green area in the grid using Manhattan distance. Besides we define s as the function which retrieves the individual satisfaction achieved by a given agent a. Finally, Θ represents the total satisfaction achieved by the population of size n in the lattice in time step t.

This fitness function is, in turn, linked directly with the spatial spread of the city and the population density of each stand. However, to be able to use a fitness function in the GA, it is necessary to know the location of the entire population in each time step.

5.3 GA Workflow

Collected Data. In this phase the knowledge that the GA cannot infer a priori is gathered from a urban growth version of the simulation. The collected data includes the following elements:

- **The Topological Development of the City.** Due to the fact that only non-urbanised cells can be candidate to be protected it should be gathered when each cell is more likely to be urbanised.
- **The Population Evolution (Number and Location).** The simulation collects statistical data about the amount of agents living in the city and their precise location in the grid in every time step. This density distribution is necessary to calculate the fitness function that is used to measure the quality of an individual solution.
- **The Non-urban Prices Dynamics.** Due to the fact that budget should be always positive and prices can change with the time, it is necessary to know which prices correspond with which non-urban cells throughout the simulation. In this case the mean of the prices in multiple simulations is annotated.

GA Optimisation. Once the data is gathered, the optimisation can be carried out. In this phase the GA population is generated and evolved using TS for 5000 iterations, assuring their convergence. For each new generation, the possible candidate cells should satisfy the constraints described in the mutation procedure to cope with the restrictions derived from the management of an uncertain future.

Test Component. Once the optimisation phase has been concluded and the final individual solution with the highest fitness is selected as the final solution, the test phase is carried out. The test component uses the output data from the GA phase to check the viability of the protected cells analysing how the statistical model compromises the model validity.

These simulations run in a modified version of the model where the green spaces are selected deterministically meanwhile the rest of factors and interactions maintain its complex and unpredictable behaviour. The main purpose of this test step consists of:

- Measuring the real satisfaction of the population.
- Detecting inconsistencies and incompatibilities of the cells selected by the GA. The inconsistencies are linked directly with the quality of the statistical data. With the appropriate data the GA can infer more accurately the situation of the lattice and better overcome the constraints, reducing the number of inconsistencies.

5.4 Other Heuristics

Random. Random approach is a heuristic that allows 10 attempts to randomly select a cell to be purchased in each time-step. The cell selected should have the state of non-urban and the current available budget should cover the price of the cell. The first cell that meets these conditions is protected.

Best Non-planning Option. This strategy is a heuristic which tries to give the best service in the current moment without performing any further plan. The approach buys the terrains located in any of the areas that are adjoining the new urban development. Concretely, the algorithm retrieves information about the last cell urbanised in the lattice and searches in the subset of cells which form its neighbourhood, the ones that are not urbanised yet. If its price is lower than the current budget, the cell is protected.

6 Computational Results

The results presented in the paper were calculated as averaged over 20 repeated optimisations, all of them in compliance with the assumptions and restrictions commented in previous sections.

Table 2. Satisfaction grouped in 50 time-steps over the three approaches analysed.

	Random	Best	GA
50	97.94	14.77	208.01
100	411.84	160.99	918.39
150	1407.58	729.74	3055.70
200	4651.23	2867.48	9716.36
250	15342.94	10623.94	29537.54
300	47089.13	35887.04	79909.52
350	89843.31	70444.26	130117.76
400	112007.76	91359.08	146638.63
450	119140.86	103118.51	148372.77
500	118023.17	109580.54	143162.94
550	113881.15	113274.05	135731.20
600	108935.25	114972.24	127935.58

Table 2 summarises the results achieved by the three analysed heuristics. The results measure the average of the satisfaction achieved by the population during the 600 ticks of the simulation grouped in 50 steps. The first column shows the random satisfaction, the second represents the best non-optimise heuristic and the third column includes the results for the GA-optimised satisfaction. Graphically, the same data is depicted in Fig. 4. From these results we can state that GA outperforms the random and the best non-optimised heuristic throughout the simulation.

6.1 Comments About the Random Approach

Due to its stochastic selecting mechanism, the random solution spreads more homogeneously and scattered their protected cells. It does not take advantage of the reduced prices at the beginning of the simulation but, in turns, when prices are too high to be able to purchase any new land (see peak in non-urban prices in Fig. 1), the random approach achieves to give service to the outskirts of the city in contrast to the other two approaches that are more sensitive to the significant increment in prices occurred at the end of the simulation. One limitation of the stochastic random approach is that the efficiency achieved depends strongly on the extension of the land analysed.

6.2 Comments About the Best Non-optimise Heuristic

This heuristic achieves acceptable results when the non-urban prices are low and the growth speed of the city is slow. However as the approach always tries to buy the most expensive non-urban cells that are the ones located closer to the boundaries of the city, when the city grows and the demand for land increases its price, the available budget is not enough to afford new purchases and the heuristic neglects to give proper services to the outskirs of the city. Due to that this heuristic shows the worst results at the end of the simulation. The total amount of cells protected are smaller and concentrated most of them around the city centre.

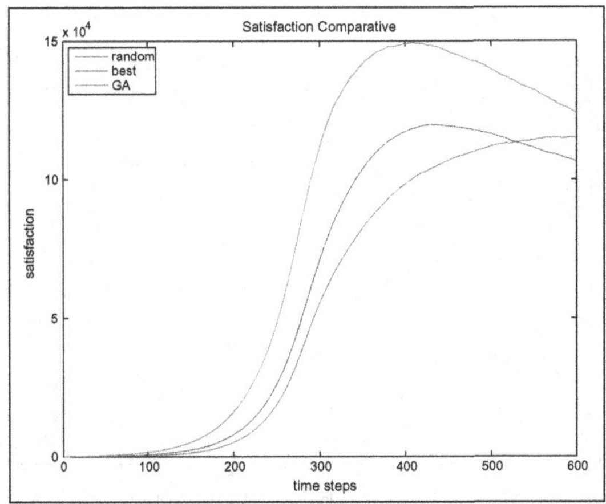

Fig. 4. Representation of the satisfaction achieved by the three heuristics developed.

6.3 Comments About the GA Approach

The GA overcomes both heuristics during the entire simulation. However, the results are closer to the best non-optimised heuristic at the beginning of the simulation and to the random approach at the end. The decline in the satisfaction at the end of the simulation is due to the fact that the algorithm is not able to buy new stands with the current budget and from the 400 time-steps the optimisation is poor. This negative effect could be avoided if the amount of budget assigned in the experiments would have been enough to buy homogeneously new green areas during the entire duration of the simulation.

6.4 Model Validity

The test component checks the validity of a given GA solution using an independent simulation. Moreover it gathers some data to provide information about the quality of the GA solution: the amount of urban inconsistencies and the satisfaction achieved by the solution. A urban inconsistency can be defined by the attempt to protect a cell that is already urbanised.

When an inconsistency occurs, the candidate cell to be protected is rejected and no reward is added to the final satisfaction. Its budget, in turns, is stored for future purchases. As a conclusion, for every inconsistency found in the GA solution, the algorithm reduces its final quality. The behaviour of the inconsistencies Fig. 5 shows that it is not necessary to gather a huge amount of data in order to achieve consistent results. It is noticeable that the model does not achieve a non-inconsistency state even if the number of simulations where the data is gathered increases. This is a consequence that the future cannot be completely predicted.

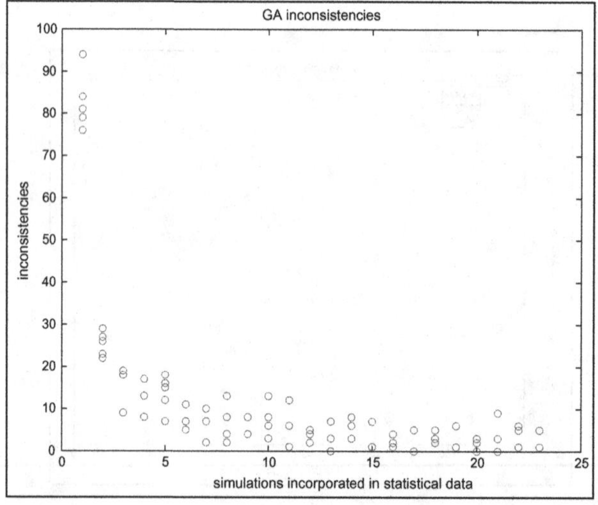

Fig. 5. Urban inconsistencies found in the test of the GA solutions.

7 Conclusions and Future Work

This paper reports results from a proof-of-concept study, which show that statistical model emulator can be used for policy optimisation. In particular, we show how we can capture and represent uncertainty in ABM using data from simulated runs and find optimal urban planning policies with the use of GA.

The strategy is tested in a monocentric urban model where the main objective of the experiment is to distribute a set of green protected areas throughout the lattice with the goal of achieving the maximum satisfaction from the inhabitants of the city. An individual is considered to be 'satisfied' if a green area is placed close enough to the location of his residence.

The main observation that we draw is that the appropriate prior use of non-optimised simulations was effective in guiding the GA to achieve successful outcomes. The specific approach we took is potentially applicable to a wide range of applications which concern sequential decision making and require time-consuming simulations to evaluate decisions. The results on our case study suggest there is considerable promise in our approach. The ability to successfully address a wider range of optimisation problems of this kind could lead to a new generation of tools for use in urban planning. However, in the meantime, various aspects of the approach need further investigation. Among them are three main directions:

Evaluation of Statistical Simulation-Based Approaches for ABM Optimisation. Related research fields, such as optimisation of natural conversational strategies in human-machine dialogue, make use of similar simulation techniques to approximate real-world behaviour. In the case of spoken dialogue systems, user simulations are build from small data set of real user interactions [7]. In future work, we want to explore how evaluation techniques for user simulations can be applied to estimate the quality and policy impacts of our ABM simulations.

Improving GA to Include Uncertainty for Sequential Decision Making Problems. In the previous experiments we have used a variant of genetic algorithms which does not explicitly encode uncertainty endured by the model environment. In future work, we plan to investigate advanced evolutionary algorithms, such as X Classifier Systems [36] for sequential decision tasks, which explore similarities between evolutionary approaches and Reinforcement Learning.

Improve the Complexity of the Urban Model. In particular, we plan to increment the complexity of our current metric including factors like size of the urban park and quality. We will also develop a new ecological metric based on preserving the ecosystems and conduct experiments to compare the trade-off between our current metric and the new one.

References

1. Vallejo, M., Corne, D.W., Rieser, V.: Evolving urbanisation policies - using a statistical model to accelerate optimisation over agent-based simulations. In: ICAART 2013–5th Conference on Agents and Artificial Intelligence, pp. 1–11 (2013)
2. Forsyth, A., Mussachio, L.: Designing Small Parks: A Manual for Addressing Social and Ecological Concerns. Wiley, New York (2005)
3. Parker, D.C., Hoffmann, M.J., Deadman, P., Parker, D.C., Manson, S.M., Manson, S.M., Janssen, M.A., Janssen, M.A.: Multi-agent systems for the simulation of land-use and land-cover change: a review. Ann. Assoc. Am. Geogr. **93**, 314–337 (2003)

4. Sasaki, Y., Box, P.: Agent-based verification of von thünen's location theory. J. Artif. Soc. Soc. Simul., **6** (2003)
5. Sanders, L., Pumain, D., Mathian, H., Gurin-Pace, F., Bura, S.: Simpop: a multiagent system for the study of urbanism. Environ. Plann. B Plann. Des. **24**, 287–305 (1997)
6. Robinson, D., Murray-Rust, D., Rieser, V., Milicic, V., Rounsevell, M.: Modelling the impacts of land system dynamics on human well-being: using an agent-based approach to cope with data limitations in koper, slovenia. Comput. Environ. Urban Syst. (Special Issue: Geoinformatics) **2010**(36), 164–176 (2012)
7. Rieser, V., Lemon, O.: Reinforcement Learning for Adaptive Dialogue Systems: A Data-driven Methodology for Dialogue Management and Natural Language Generation. Theory and Applications of Natural Language Processing. Springer, Heidelberg (2011)
8. Vallejo, M., Vargas, P., Corne, D.: A fast approximative approach for the vehicle routing problem. In: 2012 12th UK Workshop on Computational Intelligence (UKCI), pp. 1–8 (2012)
9. Costanza, R., d'Arge, R., de Groot, R., Farber, S., Grasso, M., Hannon, B., Limburg, K., Naeem, S., O'Neill, R., Paruelo, J., Raskin, R., Sutton, P., van den Belt, M.: The value of the world's ecosystem services and natural capital. Ecol. Econ. **25**, 3–15 (1998)
10. Nowak, D., McPherson, E.: Quantifying the impact of trees: the chicago urban forest climate project. Unasylva **44**, 39–44 (1993)
11. Newmann, J.V.: Theory of Self-Reproducing Automata. University of Illinois Press, Urbana (1966). (edited by Burks, A.W.)
12. Otter, H.S., van der Veen, A., de Vriend, H.J.: Abloom: location behaviour, spatial patterns, and agent-based modelling. J. Artif. Soc. Soc. Simul. **4**, 1147–1152 (2001)
13. Brown, D.G., Robinson, D.T.: Effects of heterogeneity in residential preferences on an agent-based model of urban sprawl. Ecol. Soc. **11**, 46 (2006)
14. Devisch, O., Timmermans, H., Arentze, T., Borgers, A.: An agent-based model of residential choice dynamics in nonstationary housing markets. Environ. Plann. A **41**, 1997–2013 (2009)
15. Parker, D.C., Filatova, T.: A conceptual design for a bilateral agent-based land market with heterogeneous economic agents. Comput. Environ. Urban Syst. **32**, 454–463 (2008). (GeoComputation: Modeling with spatial agents)
16. Filatova, T., Parker, D., van der Veen, A.: Agent-based urban land markets: agentś pricing behavior, land prices and urban land use change. J. Artif. Soc. Soc. Simul. **12**, 3 (2009)
17. Miller, E.J., Hunt, J.D., Abraham, J.E., Salvini, P.A.: Microsimulating urban systems. Comput. Environ. Urban Syst. **28**, 9–44 (2004)
18. Holland, J.: Adaptation in Natural and Artificial Systems. The University of Michigan Press, Ann Arbor (1975)
19. Darwin, C.: On the Origin of Species by Means of Natural Selections: or the Preservation of Favoured Races in the Struggle for Life. Murray, London (1861)
20. Pukkala, T., Kurttila, M.: Examining the performance of six heuristic optimisation techniques in different forest planning problems. Silva Fennica **39**, 67–80 (2005)
21. Lu, F., Eriksson, L.O.: Formation of harvest units with genetic algorithms. For. Ecol. Manag. **130**, 57–67 (2000)
22. Wu, J., Zheng, C., Chien, C.C., Zheng, L.: A comparative study of monte carlo simple genetic algorithm and noisy genetic algorithm for cost-effective sampling network design under uncertainty. Adv. Water Resour. **29**, 899–911 (2006)

23. Rieser, V., Robinson, D.T., Murray-Rust, D., Rounsevell, M.: A comparison of genetic algorithms and reinforcement learning for optimising sustainable forest management. In: GeoComputation (2011)
24. Qin, X., Huang, G., Liu, L.: A genetic-algorithm-aided stochastic optimization model for regional air quality management under uncertainty. J. Air Waste Manag. Assoc. **60**, 63–71 (2010)
25. Wang, N., Yang, Y.: Target geometry matching problem for hybrid genetic algorithm used to design structures subjected to uncertainty. In: IEEE Congress on Evolutionary Computation, CEC '09, pp. 1644–1651 (2009)
26. Wang, N., Zhang, X., Yang, Y.: A hybrid genetic algorithm for constrained multiobjective optimization under uncertainty and target matching problems. Appl. Soft Comput. **13**, 3636–3645 (2013)
27. Alonso, W.: Location and Land Use. Publications of the Joint Center for Urban Studies. Harvard University Press, Cambridge (1964)
28. Byomkesh, T., Nakagoshi, N., Dewan, A.: Urbanization and green space dynamics in greater dhaka, bangladesh. Landscape and Ecological Engineering, pp. 1–14 (2010). doi:10.1007/s11355-010-0147-7
29. Passow, S.S.: Land reserves and teamwork in planning stockholm. J. Am. Inst. Plan. **36**, 179–188 (1970)
30. Giles-Corti, B., Broomhall, M.H., Knuiman, M., Collins, C., Douglas, K., Ng, K., Lange, A., Donovan, R.J.: Increasing walking: how important is distance to, attractiveness, and size of public open space? Am. J. Prev. Med. **28**, 169–176 (2005). (Active Living Research)
31. Plantinga, A.J., Lubowski, R.N., Stavins, R.N.: The effects of potential land development on agricultural land prices. J. Urban Econ. **52**, 561–581 (2002)
32. Riley, C.: Comments on mills & evans. In: Proceedings of seminar on Land Use Regulation, Lincoln Institute for Land Policy, Cambridge Mass (2002)
33. Tyrväinen, L., Miettinen, A.: Property prices and urban forest amenities. J. Environ. Econ. Manage. **39**, 205–223 (2000)
34. Thorsnes, P.: The value of a suburban forest preserve: estimates from sales of vacant residential building lots. Land Econ. **78**, 426–441 (2002)
35. Goldberg, D.E.: A note on boltzmann tournament selection for genetic algorithms and population-oriented simulated annealing. Complex Syst. **4**, 445–460 (1990)
36. Wilson, S.W.: Classifier fitness based on accuracy. Evol. Comput. **3**, 149–175 (1995)

Author Index